THAILAND
9TH EDITION

Where to Stay and Eat
for All Budgets

Must-See Sights
and Local Secrets

Ratings You Can Trust

Fodor's Travel Publications   New York, Toronto, London, Sydney, Auckland
www.fodors.com

Fodor's Thailand

Editor: Carissa Bluestone

Editorial Production: David Downing

Editorial Contributors: David Allan, Mike Atkins, Collin Campbell, Karen Coates, Warwick Dixon, Mick Elmore, Reinhard Hohler, Wendy Kassel, Deb Kaufman, Natawee Kiatwerakul, Ivan New, Molly Petersen, Trevor Ranges, Howard Richardson, Mark Sullivan, Robert Tilley

Maps: David Lindroth, *cartographer;* Rebecca Baer and Robert Blake, *map editors;* additional cartography provided by Henry Colomb, Mark Stroud, and Ali Baird, Moon Street Cartography

Design: Fabrizio La Rocca, *creative director;* Guido Caroti, *art director;* Moon Sun Kim, *cover designer;* Melanie Marin, *senior picture editor*

Production/Manufacturing: Robert B. Shields

Cover Photo (Wat Pho Temple, Bangkok): Paul Chesley/Photographers/Aspen

COPYRIGHT

Ninth Edition

ISBN 1-4000-1478-6

ISSN 1064-0993

SPECIAL SALES

This book is available for special discounts for bulk purchases for sales promotions or premiums. Special editions, including personalized covers, excerpts of existing books, and corporate imprints, can be created in large quantities for special needs. For more information, write to Special Markets/Premium Sales, 1745 Broadway, MD 6-2, New York, New York 10019, or e-mail specialmarkets@randomhouse.com.

AN IMPORTANT TIP & AN INVITATION

Although all prices, opening times, and other details in this book are based on information supplied to us at press time, changes occur all the time in the travel world, and Fodor's cannot accept responsibility for facts that become outdated or for inadvertent errors or omissions. So **always confirm information when it matters,** especially if you're making a detour to visit a specific place. Your experiences—positive and negative—matter to us. If we have missed or misstated something, **please write to us.** We follow up on all suggestions. Contact the Thailand editor at editors@fodors.com or c/o Fodor's at 1745 Broadway, New York, New York 10019.

PRINTED IN THE UNITED STATES OF AMERICA

10 9 8 7 6 5 4 3 2 1

DESTINATION THAILAND

Within Thailand's borders are jungles, mountains, rain forests, rice fields, and two fabled shorelines. The ruins of ancient empires sit right outside the dynamic modern cities that replaced them. Faith and tradition are ever-present, from glittering temples to roadside shrines. The food in this country alone is worth the price of airfare.

This book was completely updated following the tragic tsunami that hit Thailand's western shore on December 26, 2004. Our writers visited all the affected areas to ensure accuracy at this writing. We've given estimates as to when some areas would be operating normally, but you should check on their progress before traveling. A good place to start your research is Fodors.com, where writers often post updates and where readers exchange information on forums.

Tim Jarrell, Publisher

CONTENTS

Maps

CloseUps

ABOUT THIS BOOK

The best source for travel advice is a like-minded friend who's just been where you're headed. But with or without that friend, you'll be in great shape to find your way around your destination once you learn to find your way around your Fodor's guide.

SELECTION | Our goal is to cover the best properties, sights, and activities in their categories, as well as the most interesting communities to visit. We make a point of including local food-lovers' hot spots as well as neighborhood options, and we avoid all that's touristy unless it's really worth your time. You can go on the assumption that everything in this book is recommended wholeheartedly by our writers and editors. Flip to On the Road with Fodor's to learn more about who they are. It goes without saying that no property pays to be included.

RATINGS | Orange stars ★ denote sights and properties that our editors and writers consider the very best in the area covered by the entire book. These, the best of the best, are listed in the Fodor's Choice section in the front of the book. Black stars ★ highlight the sights and properties we deem Highly Recommended, the don't-miss sights within any region. In cities, sights pinpointed with numbered map bullets ❶ in the margins tend to be more important than those without bullets.

SPECIAL SPOTS | Pleasures & Pastimes and text on chapter-title pages focus on experiences that reveal the spirit of the destination. Also watch for Off the Beaten Path sights. Some are out of the way, some are quirky, and all are worthwhile. When the munchies hit, look for Need a Break? suggestions.

TIME IT RIGHT | Check On the Calendar up front and chapters' **Timing** sections for weather and crowd overviews and best days and times to visit.

SEE IT ALL | Use Fodor's exclusive Great Itineraries as a model for your trip. Either follow those that begin the book, or mix regional itineraries from several chapters. In cities, Good Walks guide you to important sights in each neighborhood; ► indicates the starting points of walks and itineraries in the text and on the map.

BUDGET WELL | Hotel and restaurant price categories from $ to $$$$ are defined in the opening pages of each chapter—expect to find a balanced selection for every budget. For attractions, we always give standard adult admission fees; reductions are usually available for children, students, and senior citizens. Look in Discounts & Deals in Smart Travel Tips for information on destination-wide ticket schemes. Want to pay with plastic? AE, D, DC, MC, V following restaurant and hotel listings indicate whether American Express, Discover, Diner's Club, MasterCard, or Visa are accepted.

BASIC INFO | Smart Travel Tips lists travel essentials for the entire area covered by the book; city- and region-specific basics end each chapter. To find the best way to get around, see the transportation section; see individual modes of travel ("Car Travel," "Train Travel") for details.

ON THE MAPS | Maps throughout the book show you what's where and help you find your way around. Black and orange numbered bullets ❶ ❶ in the text correlate to bullets on maps.

BACKGROUND | We give background information within the chapters in the course of explaining sights as well as in CloseUp boxes and in Understanding Thailand at the end of the book. To get in the mood, review the Books & Movies section. The glossary can be invaluable.

FIND IT FAST | Within the book, chapters are arranged in a roughly clockwise direction starting with Bangkok. Chapters are divided into small regions, within which towns are covered in logical geographical order. Heads at the top of each page help you find what you need within a chapter.

DON'T FORGET | Restaurants are open for lunch and dinner daily unless we state otherwise; we mention dress only when there's a specific requirement and reservations only when they're essential or not accepted—it's always best to book ahead. Hotels have private baths, phone, TVs, and air-conditioning and operate on the European Plan (aka EP, meaning without meals). We always list facilities but not whether you'll be charged extra to use them, so when pricing accommodations, find out what's included.

SYMBOLS

Many Listings

★ Fodor's Choice
★ Highly recommended
⊠ Physical address
⊕ Directions
🗐 Mailing address
☎ Telephone
🖷 Fax
⊕ On the Web
✉ E-mail
🎫 Admission fee
☉ Open/closed times
► Start of walk/itinerary
Ⓜ Metro stations
▭ Credit cards

Outdoors

🏌 Golf
⛺ Camping

Hotels & Restaurants

🏨 Hotel
🛏 Number of rooms
⚶ Facilities
🍽 Meal plans
✕ Restaurant
🍸 Reservations
🍺 BYOB
✕🏨 Hotel with restaurant that warrants a visit

Other

👪 Family-friendly
🛈 Contact information
⇨ See also
⊠ Branch address
☞ Take note

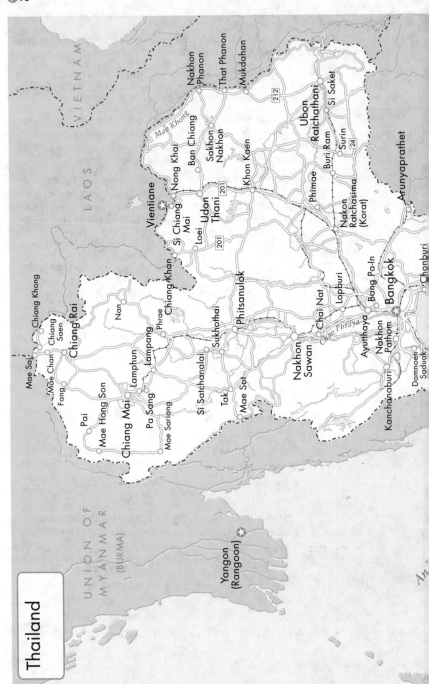

Thailand

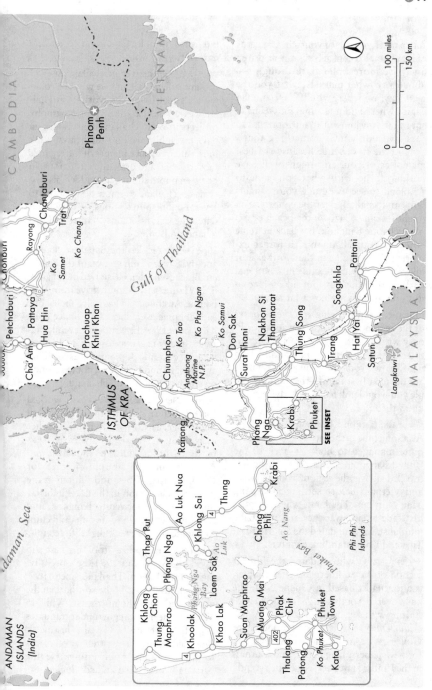

ON THE ROAD WITH FODOR'S

A trip takes you out of yourself. Concerns of life at home completely disappear, driven away by more immediate thoughts—about, say, what marvels await you the next day, or where you'll have dinner. That's where Fodor's comes in. We make sure that you know all your options, so that you don't miss something that's around the next bend. Because the best memories of your trip might well have nothing to do with what you came to Thailand to see, we guide you to sights large and small all over the country. You might set out to laze on the beach or explore chaotic Bangkok, but back at home you find yourself unable to forget exploring Khmer ruins in the Northeast or hiking up misty mountains in a national park. With Fodor's at your side, serendipitous discoveries are never far away.

Our success in showing you every corner of the region is a credit to our extraordinary writers. Although there's no substitute for travel advice from a good friend who knows your style, our contributors are the next best thing—the kind of people you would poll for travel advice if you knew them.

Mike Atkins found himself in Southeast Asia sometime in the late 1990s and never quite managed to make it back to the United Kingdom. Since arriving, he has traveled all over the region, living in Japan and Vietnam before settling in Chiang Mai, Northern Thailand, where he plies his trade as a newspaper and magazine journalist. Mike updated the Smart Travel Tips and Understanding chapters.

Karen Coates, who updated the Phuket section of the Southern Beaches chapter, is a journalist based in Chiang Mai. She has covered Southeast Asia since 1998, starting with a gig as an editor at the *Cambodia Daily*. She is a correspondent to *Gourmet Magazine* and writes regularly for newspapers, magazines, and journals in the United States and Asia. She recently published a book, *Cambodia Now: Life in the Wake of War.*

Warwick Dixon arrived in Thailand in 1995 and immediately fell in love with the country. He's been living and working in Thailand ever since. Extensive photography projects in both Thailand and Indonesia have taken him well off the beaten track in pursuit of illusive images of the region's most colorful and dramatic attractions. In between photo shoots, he's added his two cents on Thailand's remote destinations to several online publications. Warwick updated the Central Plains chapter and lent a hand on Isan, too.

Mick Elmore tackled the Bangkok chapter and the Eastern Gulf section of the Southern Beaches chapter. He arrived in Bangkok in 1991 after a five-month drive from Melbourne, Australia, and has called the chaotic capital home ever since. A freelance journalist since 1984, he writes for several magazines and wire services. Mick's a Fodor's veteran, covering destinations as far-flung as Indonesia and Colombia, not to mention several past editions of Thailand.

Former New Yorker Wendy Kassel worked for *Elle* before ditching the urban life to join the Peace Corps. After finishing her assignment in Nepal, Wendy traveled extensively throughout the Himalayas and Asia, writing the Bhutan chapter for Fodor's Nepal, Tibet, and Bhutan in the process. When a job in the hotel industry popped up, she moved to Bangkok, and she crawled through some pubs and clubs to update the chapter's nightlife section.

Isan updater Ivan New took his first trip to Southeast Asia in 1991; he's been living and working in Thailand since 1997, basing himself first in the south, then the north, and onto the northeast. While in Thailand he has taught undergraduates in the field of tourism, as well as instructed tour guides, and has written travel pieces for several online publications. Having personally organized and conducted several student tours across Thailand, he's no slouch when it comes to knowledge of the region and bringing the "Unseen" to light.

Settling in halfway around the world from her native Kansas City, Molly Petersen soaked up the sun in Phuket and braved tuk-tuks in Bangkok for nearly two years while working for a Thai publisher as a magazine editor. Her last act in Bangkok, before trading curry for fish and chips and moving to London, was updating the Shopping and A to Z sections of that chapter.

Trevor Ranges and Natawee Kiatwerakul updated the Western Gulf and Andaman Coast sections of the Southern Beaches chapter. In 2001, Trevor spent seven weeks in a hammock on Koh Tao as part of his transition from a Hawaiian lifestyle to a Thai one. Four years later he is still applying his hammock posturing skills on any and all Thai beaches and islands he and travel/writing partner Nat can find time to explore. In between these sojourns he writes for various magazines and a collaborative web-project, thailandroad.com. A native Thai, Natawee Kiatwerakul is a passionate traveler who made a life-changing decision to leave government service

and become a full-time travel enthusiast. Natawee feels fortunate to be able to explore her beautiful country and share her experiences with Fodor's readers, providing insight on Thailand's beaches and islands that she had previously reserved for select family and friends.

Howard Richardson, who updated the Around Bangkok chapter, is a magazine editor who has been based in Bangkok since 1996. Before moving to Thailand he worked as a journalist in North Africa. He writes freelance articles for numerous publications, mainly covering food and nightlife, and he initiated and managed the Bangkok Best Restaurant & Nightlife Awards. He was nominated for Best Travel feature for the 2003 Aseanta Awards.

Robert Tilley is a veteran Fodor's writer and researcher. He "masterminded" the first Gold Guide to Germany in 1988 and updated it regularly until 1999, when he left Europe for Asia. From his current base in Chiang Mai, Northern Thailand, he writes for several regional and international publications and is working on his third book. He updated the Northern Thailand, Cambodia, and Laos chapters.

The geographical organization of the following paragraphs mirrors the organization of the book. Beginning with Bangkok, coverage then moves to the city's outlying areas, up to the north, and then comes full circle with the beaches region. It's getting easier and easier to access Cambodia and Laos from Thailand and travelers are increasingly tacking on short or extended trips to these countries to their Thailand itinerary.

① Bangkok

Bangkok is a huge city that somehow manages to embrace the future without shunning its past. The famous canals that sprout from the Chao Phraya River and once gave the city its nickname of "Venice of the East" are still used to ferry the population of more than 6 million around this sprawling capital, but have been joined by superhighways, tuk-tuks, taxis, buses, a skytrain, and a subway. Treasured temples and bustling street markets now look out onto towering skyscrapers and ever grander shopping complexes, traditional puppet shows and classical dance performances compete with stadium rock shows and international film festivals, and the humble noodle stand has been complemented by some of the finest European cuisine in Asia.

Everything, though, comes back to the river, and along its banks lie some of Bangkok's most iconic locations: the Grand Palace and Temple of the Emerald Buddha; the legendary travelers' village of Banglamphu; the world-class National Museum and Theater; the towering Temple of Dawn; the wooden stilt houses of Thonburi and the maze of Chinatown. While some may find Bangkok too busy, noisy and confusing, others will never tire of exploring.

② Around Bangkok

If you need a break from the capital, but time is short, there are a number of good day or overnight trips to be had. And if you're really pushed for time, but desperate to see as much of the country as possible, a 20-km (12-mi) journey south of Bangkok to Muang Boran will provide the perfect answer: a miniature Thailand! More than 100 scale models of the country's major architectural sights are laid out as you would find them on a map, and a whole afternoon can be spent wandering around pretending you're Gulliver. A couple of hours north of Bangkok is the floating market at Damnoen Saduak—though nowadays you're more likely to find souvenir shops than a genuine market atmosphere, many people still enjoy coming here, as the floating market is iconic, even if it's being phased out.

Not content with being considered Thailand's oldest city, Nakhon Pathom is also home to Phra Pathom Chedi, the largest Buddhist structure in the world. Farther west, in Kanchanaburi, you can get a glimpse of the jungles and waterfalls for which Thailand is famous and immerse yourself in history. This is where the Japanese oversaw the construction of the Death Railway over the River Kwai. A scenic bus ride north of Kanchanaburi will bring you to the magnificent Erawan Waterfall. Set in a lush jungle, this seven-tier cascade affords either a grueling hike to the top or a refreshing swim at the bottom.

③ The Central Plains

The Central Plains are irresistible to those who want to delve deep into the region's fascinating history. A side trip from Bangkok to the former capital of Ayutthaya is a good start, but you must venture farther north to the even older cities at Sukhothai and Si Satchanalai to discover how these disparate communities finally became a country. Compared to some of the ancient cities found in Thailand, Sukhothai is a fairly recent addition to the landscape; the amazingly intact ruins you will find here are merely 800 years old. Beyond the temple tours, the Central Plains, which is often overlooked by tourists, has plenty to offer in terms of solitude and natural beauty. Sukhothai's sister city, Si Satchanalai, has hilltop temples where you can meditate for hours without seeing another soul. All around are the scenes of an age-old way of life, such as teams of water buffalo working the rice paddies. Tak Province, still off-the-beaten path, has vast teak forests, several noteworthy parks and wildlife sanctuaries, and river gorges that provide thrilling white-water rafting adventures.

④ Northern Thailand

In the country's northernmost reaches, you can find Thailand's most dramatic landscapes, most distinctive temples and palaces, most independent peoples, and most flavorful food. Make your first stop the walled city of Chiang Mai, where you can marvel at the spectacular ruins of Wat Chedi Luang, felled by an earthquake in 1545. Make sure to pay a visit to mountaintop Wat Phrathat Doi Suthep, one of four royal temple compounds. To the south there are the ancient cities of Lamphun, where you can sample a small, sweet fruit called the lamyai, and Lanpang, where one means of transportation, oddly enough, is horse-drawn carriage. Toward Myanmar is Mae Hong Son, which is surrounded by verdant countryside and villages populated by hill tribes. In the far north, more tribal villages surround the town of Chiang Rai, gateway to the so-called Golden Triangle. Once known for opium production and warlords, the region remains exhilarating, especially if you take an elephant trek into the bamboo-covered mountains.

(5) Isan

The country's heartland runs from the border of Myanmar to those of Cambodia and Laos. Mist-covered fields are interspersed with ancient ruins. The draws of Isan are threefold: outstanding Khmer ruins; national parks that take you away from the somewhat featureless plateau that makes up a good portion of the region and into misty mountain ranges; and a glimpse at traditional Thai life. As treks into Northern Thailand become more common, Isan is one of the last truly off-the-beaten-path regions of the country. You won't run into tour buses here . . . yet.

(6) The Southern Beaches

A long peninsula washed by the Gulf of Thailand on one side and the Andaman Sea on the other, Thailand's southern region is still paradise, however bittersweet that paradise may be in the wake of the tsunami. In truth, only a very small portion of the region was affected by disaster. The entire Gulf of Thailand was unaffected, and continues to cater to a wide variety of vacationers. Bangkok residents flee to the cities of Hua Hin and Cha'am for a relaxing, more "Thai" retreat, while Pattaya beckons those looking for a raucous (and at times raunchy) international nightlife scene. The islands on this side of the country run the gamut: mountainous Ko Chang is the most developed; Ko Samet, Ko Si Chang, and Ko Pha-ngan are much more laid-back, where luxury means a simple bungalow on the beach; and popular Ko Samui is somewhere in between—it's pretty built up, but there are still a few quiet beaches where you can escape the crowds.

The hub of the Andaman Coast is Phuket, the country's largest island. A few of its beaches were damaged in the tsunami, but efforts to rebuild are in full swing, and much of the island emerged from the disaster unscathed. You'll find more resorts here than budget bungalows. The nearby Phi Phi Islands, with their secret silver-sand coves, are more laid-back than Phuket though they sustained a lot of damage from the tsunami, and only a few resorts are fully operational at this writing. Phang Nga Bay is a true hideaway, where limestone outcroppings rise hundreds of feet above the sea and caves accessible only by boat wait to be explored.

(7) Cambodia

With its spectacular Angkor Temple Complex, colonial buildings, and Khmer cities, Cambodia is well worth a trip. The country is bordered by Vietnam to the east and south; Thailand and Laos share its northern border. It's not difficult to visit from Thailand, and exploring the ancient Khmer ruins of Phanom Rung National Park in Isan can easily be combined with a hop over the border and a trip to Siem Reap and the legendary temples of Angkor.

8 Laos

Landlocked Laos shares borders with Thailand, Myanmar, China, Vietnam, and Cambodia. Its western border, defined in many places by the Mekong River, abuts Thailand. Most of Laos's more accessible attractions—including its two major cities, Vientiane and Luang Prabang—are concentrated in the northern part of the country, close to Chiang Mai. Though it lacks a powerhouse attraction like Angkor to speed development along, the buzz surrounding Laos has been slow but steady.

Highlights of Thailand—Bangkok & Beaches
10 days

Almost every trip to Thailand begins in Bangkok. Don't be afraid to linger there a few days, because some of the country's most astounding sights can be found in and around the Old City. You'll probably be exhausted by the pace in a few days, so head down to explore the islands of Phuket and Ko Samui where you can swim in clear seas and sip cocktails on white sands.

AROUND BANGKOK 4 days. Start your first day with the most famous of all Bangkok sights, the Grand Palace. Make sure not to miss the gorgeously ornate Wat Phra Keo, home of the Emerald Buddha, and Thailand's oldest and biggest temple, Wat Po, where you can observe the Reclining Buddha and find one of the best traditional massages going. Take a ferry across the Chao Phraya to the western bank to visit Wat Arun, the Khmer-style Temple of the Dawn. Later, return to the eastern bank and spend the afternoon exploring the impressive National Museum and the National Gallery of Art.

On Day 2, head to one of the city's most beautiful temples, Wat Benjamabophit. The century-old structure is made of marble. Nearby is Dusit Park, a refuge from the heat and dust. Here you can find the Vimanmek Mansion, the largest teak structure in the world. A short tuk-tuk ride away is Sun Pakkard Palace, a series of five teak houses built on high columns. After lunch take in Jim Thompson's House. These upcountry buildings were brought to Bangkok by Thompson, an American entrepreneur who single-handedly revived the country's silk industry. The houses are filled with priceless pieces of Asian art.

On Day 3, take a train to see the towering temple at Nakhon Pathom, then continue to Kanchanaburi, site of the famous bridge over the River Kwai and some of the most beautiful jungle in Thailand. Return to Bangkok the next day and spend the afternoon wandering around the shops of Siam Square and the winding streets of Chinatown.

PHUKET 3 days. After all this sightseeing, you'll probably be in the mood for some rest and relaxation. Most people fly down to Phuket, one of the country's prettiest islands. If you want to take a day trip, a popular one is to Phang Nga Bay, where you can see the gravity-defying limestone formations that rise out of the sea.

SAMUI 3 days. For a change of scenery, jump on a plane and head over to Gulf of Thailand to see the country's second most popular island, Ko Samui. Although not as large or developed as Phuket, the island has plenty in the way of resorts and entertainment, while the eastern beaches are some of the best around. Samui is surrounded by smaller islands, including the quieter Ko Phangan, which comes alive for the world famous Full Moon Parties and Ko Tao, which many say has the best diving in the region. Both are worth excursions.

Highlights of Thailand—The North
10 days

The North of Thailand is an area of outstanding natural beauty. The ruins and temples of Sukhothai take you back hundreds of years, while Chiang Mai and Chiang Rai are ideal bases for exploring mountains, rivers, and hill tribe villages.

BANGKOK & SUKHOTHAI 2–3 days. After a day or two exploring Bangkok, fly up to Sukhothai, a dusty town in the Central Plains. Thailand's first capital, it deserves at least a day or two of exploration. The central temple of Wat Mahathat is splendid, with a frieze of walking monks surrounding a huge platform supporting several lotus-topped spires. Don't miss the outlying sights such as Wat Sri Chum, home to a huge Buddha almost totally enclosed in a towering building. Spend the night in town, making sure to explore the Night Market. The next morning take the hour's trip to Si Satchanalai, a nearby city with hilltop temples that impart a wonderful sense of calm.

CHIANG MAI 3 days. Fly north to Chiang Mai, an enchanting walled city. On the first day, rise early to explore the beautiful temples inside the walls, including Wat Phra Singh, Wat Chedi Luang, and Wat Chiang Man. In the afternoon check out the wonderful carvings in the crafts stores along Sankamphaeng Road. In the evening you'll want to walk through the city gates to the Night Market. On the second day go to Wat Phrathat Doi Suthep, the temple on a mountain overlooking the city. Ring the dozens of bells surrounding the main building for good luck. On the way back to Chiang Mai, visit the seven-spired temple called Wat Chedi Yot. On the third day, take a cookery class at one of the many schools that have sprung up in recent years and learn for yourself how to use all those strange herbs and vegetables you see in the markets.

CHIANG RAI 4 days. Either jump on a bus for a four-hour journey north on a beautiful mountain road, or take the plane to Chiang Rai. This is where you should arrange activities such as treks to hill tribe villages or rafting trips—a night or two camping out in the jungle or in a remote village is hard to beat. Chiang Rai is also known as the gateway to the Golden Triangle and it's easy to catch a bus or drive up to the Mekong River where you look out over Myanmar and Laos. Take a day to visit Mae Sai where you can cross a bridge over into Myanmar on a day pass. Then catch one of the daily flights back to Bangkok.

WHEN TO GO

Thailand has two climatic regions: tropical savanna in the northern regions and tropical rain forest in the south. Three seasons run from hot (March through May) to rainy (June through September) and cool (October through February). Humidity is high all year, especially during the hot season. The cool season is pleasantly warm in the south, but in the north, especially in the hills around Chiang Mai, it can become quite chilly. The cool season is the peak season. Prices are often twice as high then as in the low seasons, yet hotels are often fully booked.

Climate

The following are average daily maximum and minimum temperatures for Bangkok. The north will generally be a degree or two cooler.

🎞 Forecasts **Weather Channel Connection** ⊕ www.weather.com.

BANGKOK

Jan.	89F	32C	May	93F	34C	Sept.	89F	32C
	68	20		77	25		75	24
Feb.	91F	33C	June	91F	33C	Oct.	88F	31C
	72	22		75	24		75	24
Mar.	93F	34C	July	89F	32C	Nov.	88F	31C
	75	24		75	24		72	22
Apr.	95F	35C	Aug.	89F	32C	Dec.	88F	31C
	77	25		75	24		68	20

Every region of Thailand has its own packed calendar of festivals. Listed below are nationwide celebrations and a few of Bangkok's greatest hits. See individual chapters for information on regional festivals.

WINTER

December

On the 5th, the King's birthday, a trooping of the colors is performed in Bangkok by Thailand's elite Royal Guards.

January

New Year celebrations are usually at their best around temples. In Bangkok special ceremonies at Pramanae Ground include Thai dancing.

February

Magha Puja, held on the full moon of the third lunar month, commemorates the day when 1,250 disciples spontaneously heard Lord Buddha preach the cardinal Doctrine. The Flower Festival, held in Chiang Mai during the early part of the month when the province's flowers are in full bloom, features a parade with floral floats, flower displays, and beauty contests.

SPRING

April

Songkran marks the Thai New Year and is an occasion for setting caged birds and fish free, visiting family, dancing, and splashing everyone with water in good-natured merriment. The festival is at its best in Chiang Mai.

May

On the full moon of the sixth lunar month, the nation celebrates the holiest of Buddhist days, Visakha Puja, commemorating Lord Buddha's birth, enlightenment, and death. Monks lead the laity in candlelight processions around their temples.

SUMMER

August

On the 12th, Queen Sirikit's birthday is celebrated with religious ceremonies at Chitlada Palace, and the city is adorned with lights.

FALL

November

Held on the full moon of the 12th lunar month, Loi Krathong is the loveliest of Thai festivals. After sunset, people make their way to a body of water and launch small lotus-shape banana-leaf floats bearing lighted candles to honor the water spirits and wash away the sins of the past year. Of all Bangkok's fairs and festivals, the Golden Mount Festival is the most spectacular, with sideshows, food stalls, bazaars, and large crowds of celebrants.

PLEASURES & PASTIMES

Architecture

Successfully staving off occupation by European powers, Thailand has architecture that is refreshingly free of colonial touches. That isn't to say that other artistic styles aren't present. Throughout history, Thai architects borrowed ideas from Indian, Sri Lankan, and Cambodian structures, and Thai artists often used symbolic elements that began as Hindu concepts. Despite these antecedents, what emerged was uniquely Thai. The stolid stone temples built by the Khmers in the northeast, the lotus-topped spires of Sukhothai found in the Central Plains, and the gracefully curved roofs constructed by the Lannas in the north are unlike anything you'll find elsewhere.

Beaches

Thailand's two coasts, along the Gulf of Thailand and the Andaman Sea, lie slowly steaming below the Tropic of Cancer. This makes the beaches here a sun-worshipper's dream come true. They come in every flavor—lively shores lined with raucous bars and clubs, quiet coves sheltering exclusive hotels, isolated islands with thatched bungalows, and a few stretches of sand with no footprints at all. The two most popular islands, Phuket and Ko Samui, have domestic airports making the transition from Bangkok quick and hassle-free, while more remote destinations such as Ko Chang and Ko Pha Ngan are now easily accessible. Divers and snorkelers head straight to Ko Tao or Ko Phi Phi where the wonderful coral reefs and outstanding visibility are famous. Ko Samet is a few hours' drive south from the capital.

Food

Food is a consuming passion for the Thais. Nowhere is this more evident than on just about any street corner. Throughout the day, one food cart replaces another, each vendor stirring up a different tasty morsel. The range of Thai cuisine is vast; no restaurant worth its salt has fewer than 100 dishes on its menu. There are seasonal delights, and, of course, regional differences and specialties. You'll find a delicious spicy pork sausage in the north, where meals are usually eaten with sticky rice kneaded into balls and dipped in various sauces. In the northeast you can find barbecue chicken, minced beef, and a spicy papaya salad. Along the southern coast, seafood reigns supreme. Thousands of boats return each day filled with lobster, crabs, and shrimp. Because traders from neighboring lands often stopped here, you can find dishes that remind you of Malaysia, Indonesia, and even India. Added to this, most Thai towns also have a selection of good-quality foreign restaurants, so if you find you've had enough curries and noodles, steaks and pizzas are never far away.

Massage

Every visit to Thailand should include a massage or two. They came in a variety of styles, from gentle kneading of the muscles to joint-breaking pulls. Make sure to talk with your practitioner about what to expect. Traditional nuat boroan aims to release blocked channels of energy through methods similar to reflexology. Your aches and pains will melt away, and you'll find yourself invigorated as well. If you'd like to learn the techniques yourself, there are plenty of schools that teach massage.

Shopping

The first time you set foot in one of Thailand's ubiquitous night markets you'll find yourself hooked. You can find everything from hand-carved figurines and woven baskets to watches with recently affixed Rolex logos and polo shirts with the alligator slightly askew. The prices, after a little negotiating, are tantalizingly low. If you're in Bangkok or another larger city, you can also find a slew of department stores, shopping centers, and malls. The prices are significantly lower than in shopping meccas like Singapore or Hong Kong.

Trekking

The forests surrounding the northern cities of Chiang Mai and Chiang Rai would make good trekking just for their rugged beauty. But these misty hills are also home to villages belonging to various hill tribes, descendents of people who migrated here centuries ago from China. The various tribes—Karen, Hmong, Yao, and many others—have held onto ancient customs, making their communities a fascinating window into the past. Reaching the villages, however, is not always so easy. The easiest way to maneuver up the steep grades is often on the back of an elephant.

FODOR'S CHOICE

The sights, restaurants, hotels, and other travel experiences on these pages are our writers' and editors' top picks—our Fodor's Choices. They're the best of their type in the area covered by the book—not to be missed and always worth your time. In the destination chapters that follow, you will find all the details.

HOTELS

$$$$	**Four Seasons, Chiang Mai.** Location is everything here—views from this amazing resort include a lush valley, mountains, tropical gardens, and rice paddies.
$$$$	**J. W. Marriott Resort & Spa, Ko Phuket.** Finding a secluded resort on busy Phuket is getting harder, but the Marriott still stands alone on one of the island's prettiest streches of sand. And though it's not the cheapest option, it's still way more affordable than most of the other high-priced resorts.
$$$$	**The Oriental Hotel, Bangkok.** This opulent hotel on the Chao Phraya River is an institution in the city, still attracting celebs. It's such a landmark, that many people stop by at least once on their vacation to have a drink by the river.
$$$$	**Peninsula, Bangkok.** This is the ultimate in high-tech luxury hotels. However, all the various gadgets in the room will do little to distract you from the amazing view of the Bangkok skyline.
$$$$	**Sila Evason Hideaway & Spa, Ko Samui** The polar opposite of the beach bungalow, Sila offers private two-story villas (with private butlers), plunge tubs with panoramic ocean views, a clifftop infinity pool, and a full spa.
$$$$	**Sukhothai, Bangkok.** Sukhothai is the best of both worlds: its central location makes getting around the city easy, but its beautiful grounds and courtyards will make Bangkok seem very far away.
$$$$	**Tongsai Bay, Ko Samui.** The secluded oceanfront cottages here are simply stunning. You can lounge in air-conditioned luxury or sleep under the stars on your terrace's daybed. Be careful who you bring with you—this is the kind of place that makes you want to fall in love.
$$$–$$$$	**Anantara Golden Triangle, Northern Thailand.** You can see Myanmar and Laos from your balcony sofa, and the Mae Khong River from the infinity-edge pool at the Golden Triangle's top address. Indigenous woods and handmade fabrics mean the view inside is just as good.
$$$–$$$$	**Chakrabongse Villas, Bangkok.** Who says Bangkok is all high-rises? "Villa" is not a misnomer—you'll stay in a traditional Thai house right on the banks of the Chao Praya.

$$$–$$$$	**Koyao Island Resort, Andaman Coast.** Beautiful views are ubiquitous throughout the Southern Beaches region, but Koyao might just have the best view of any hotel here. So you don't miss an angle, bungalows are almost entirely open-air.
$$–$$$$	**Railei Beach Club, Andaman Coast.** Variety is the spice of this beach club, which is really a collection of privately owned homes. But don't worry about finding cookie-cutter condos here—you'll get dark woods and bright fabrics in place of pastel throwaway decor, and layouts vary from one-room huts to a lodge that sleeps six.
$$	**Belle Villa, Pai, Northern Thailand.** There's no better place to enjoy the beauty of Northern Thailand than from this resort. Teak chalets on stilts do their best to blend in with the land.
¢	**Mut Mee Guesthouse, Nong Kai, Isan.** Though the luxury resorts may tempt with all sorts of bells and whistles, staying at a friendly little guesthouse is a must. Mut Mee is not just a rest stop, but the heart of an artist's colony on the Mae Khong River.

RESTAURANTS

$$$$	**Bed Supperclub, Bangkok.** If you want to see the super-trendy side of Bangkok, you can't do better than Bed. No one will yell at you for getting crumbs on the sheets here.
$$$$	**Rang Mahal, Bangkok.** Bangkok does Indian food almost as well as it does Thai food. This is Indian gone upscale, and you'll get great views of the city with your meal.
$$$	**Zanotti, Bangkok.** This lively Italian restaurant won't disappoint—everything is top-notch from the excellent food to the extensive wine list to the attentive service.
$$–$$$$	**Baan Rim Pa, Ko Phuket.** Though the food is some of the best on Phuket, you really come here for the setting: on the edge of a cliff overlooking the ocean.
$	**Cook Kai, Koh Lanta.** You'll find Thailand's best dishes inside the most unpresupposing structures. Behind the doors of this simple wooden restaurant is amazing and authentic Thai cooking.
$	**Dream Café, Sukhothai, Central Plains.** You'll feel like you're eating in an antique shop, what with all the delightful odds and ends in this attractive restaurant. The food just happens to be outstanding, too.
¢–$	**Beachside barbecue, Koh Chang.** You can't leave the islands without having barbecue on the beach at least once. Mac Resort Hotel and Koh Chang Lagoon Resort, right next to each other on a pretty white sand beach, do the sunset barbecue better than anyone.
¢–$	**Polo Fried Chicken, Bangkok.** This is what fast food should be: garlicky fried chicken, sticky rice, and raw papaya salad for pocket change.

¢ Roti-Mataba, Bangkok. Whether you already love the Indian staple *roti* or don't have any idea what it is, you'll be a repeat customer at this tiny eatery on the Chao Praya.

TEMPLES AND SHRINES

Angkor Temple Complex, Cambodia. More than 300 monuments lie scattered throughout the jungle at the ruins of one of the largest capitals in Southeast Asia.

Prasat Hin Khao Phanom Rung, Buri Ram, Isan. This temple will set your pulse racing, literally and figuratively. You'll cross a bridge and climb several staircases to the top, where you'll be greeted by unparalleled Khmer art.

Prasat Hin Phimai, Phimai, Isan. This important Khmer structure has been carefully restored. The main tower, made of white sandstone, is exquisite.

Wat Arun, Bangkok. Wat Arun is the temple you see in so many Bangkok postcards and snaphots. Its name means "Temple of Dawn" and this is indeed the place to catch the sunrise over the river.

Wat Chedi Luang, Chiang Mai. An earthquake toppled the spire of this temple, making it one of Northern Thailand's most superb ruins.

Wat Chong Kham, Mae Hong Son, Northern Thailand. The golden spire of Wat Chong Kham rises over a placid lake. A Burmese-style Buddha image watches over this pretty temple.

Wat Phra Keo, Bangkok. Home of the revered Emerald Buddha, this sacred temple is among the most ornate in the country.

Wat Phra That Doi Suthep, Chiang Mai. Bring sunglasses to this beautiful temple complex, which has so much gold decoration, you'll do a lot of squinting as the sun bounces off the spires. This is every bit as fascinating as Wat Phra Keo, but far less crowded.

Wat Phra That Hariphunchai, Lamphun, Northern Thailand. The central chedi at this dazzling complex is covered in copper and topped with a nine-tier gold spire. A small sala houses four footprints of the Buddha.

Wat Phra That Lampang Luang, Lampang, Northern Thailand. Laterite walls, a gold-covered chedi, and intricately carved wooden facades make this one of the most striking temples in the north.

Wat Pumin, Nan, Northern Thailand. Wat Pumin makes the trek to this off-the-beaten-path part of the north worthwhile. The ascent to the temple is dramatic—up a flight of stairs past two nagas (statues of sea serpentlike creatures)—and the murals here are fascinating.

BEACHES

Ao Vong Duan, Ko Samet. Ko Samet's nickname is "Island with Sand Like Crushed Crystal," so it's no suprise that there are some amazing beaches here. Ao Vong Duan is in a lovely half-moon bay—if it's too crowded, head to one of its neighbors for more seclusion.

Ao Nang, Krabi. Towering pinnacles of limestone rising from the ocean grab your attention at this beach not far from Krabi.

Haad Tong Nai Pan, Ko Pha Ngan. You can shut out the world at this beach, one of the country's most idyllic retreats.

NATURAL WONDERS

Doi Inthanon National Park, Northern Thailand. Climb Thailand's highest mountain, hike through dense forest, or visit hill tribe villages within this park's boundaries.

Erawan National Park, Kanchanaburi Province. The main attraction of this spectacular park is Erawan Waterfall, which has seven tiers. You can hike to the top or just far enough to reach one of its pools for a swim.

Phu Kra Dueng National Park, Isan. The lone mountain that is the center of this park is often covered in mist. A hike to the top will give you an unforgettable view, but there's plenty to see even if you're not up to that particular challenge.

Phang Nga Bay, Southern Thailand. In one of Thailand's most photographed spots, you can kayak around pillars of limestone that rise majestically from the sea.

Thee Lo Su Waterfall, Umphang, Central Plains. Thee Lo Su is one of the most spectacular waterfalls in all of Southeast Asia.

QUINTESSENTIAL THAILAND

Elephant Conservation Center, Northern Thailand. If you want to see elephants, it's worth making the trip to this center outside of Chiang Mai. You'll be able to see some tricks (check out the elephant orchestra) and rest easy knowing that your dollars are going towards helping these amazing creatures.

Hall of Opium, Ban Sop Ruak. This would be a terrific space no matter what the subject matter, but the history of the opium trade in the Golden Triangle is certainly a scintillating topic. The musuem is extremely informative and fun—its simulation of an opium high is worth the price of admission alone.

Isan's Festivals. Every region has its calendar of annual festivals, but Isan really knows how to party. You won't find wilder or quirkier celebrations anywhere else in the country.

Jim Thompson's House, Bangkok. The former residence of Thailand's most famous expat provides a look at the history of the silk industry, examples of upcountry architecture, *and* a crash course in priceless Southeast Asian art.

Night Bazaar, Chiang Mai. One of Thailand's most exciting bazaars offers a little bit of everything, from hand-carved statues to knock-off Rolexes.

Sukhothai, Central Plains. Though Ayutthaya gets most of the attention, Sukhothai was also an important seat of power in Thailand's history. Its vast historical park is the place to go for an understanding of the importance of these ancient cities.

SMART TRAVEL TIPS

Finding out about your destination before you leave home means you'll be more streetwise when you hit the ground, better prepared to explore the aspects of Thailand that drew you here in the first place. The organizations in this section can provide information to supplement this guide; contact them for up-to-the-minute details, and consult the A to Z sections that end each chapter for facts on the various topics as they relate to the country's many regions. Happy landings!

AIR TRAVEL

BOOKING

On popular tourist routes during peak holiday times, domestic flights in Thailand are often fully booked. Make sure you have reservations, and make them well in advance of your travel date. Be sure to **reconfirm your flight** when you arrive in Thailand.

CARRIERS

About 70 airlines serve Bangkok, and more are seeking landing rights. Northwest Airlines and Japan Airlines (JAL) are both major carriers with daily flights from six U.S. cities. JAL is one of the best options around with a flight time of 17 hours from Dallas including a stopover at Narita airport, Tokyo. East coast travelers departing from New York or Washington D.C. could also consider using British Airways or Virgin Atlantic/Thai Airways via London or Singapore Airlines from Newark via Amsterdam. From the west coast, Thai Airways has good connections from Los Angeles, San Francisco, and Seattle. For those traveling on a budget there are also a number of East Asian airlines that fly from the western seaboard, including Asiana, China Airlines, and EVA Air.

➤ **Major Airlines Asiana Airlines** ☎ 800/227-4262. **British Airways** ☎ 800/247-9297. **Cathay Pacific** ☎ 800/233-2742. **China Airlines** ☎ 800/227-5118. **EVA Air** ☎ 800/695-1188. **Gulf Air** ☎ 800/433-7300. **Japan Airlines** ☎ 800/525-3663. **Korean Air** ☎ 800/438-5000. **Malaysia Airlines** ☎ 800/552-9264. **Northwest Airlines** ☎ 800/447-4747. **Singapore Airlines** ☎ 800/742-3333. **Thai Airways** ☎ 800/426-5204. **United Airlines** ☎ 800/864-8331.

🔲 From the U.K. **British Airways** ☎ 020/8897-4000, 0345/222111 outside London. **Gulf Air** ☎ 020/4081717. **Qantas** ☎ 0345/747767 or 0800/747767. **Thai Airways** ☎ 020/7499-9113.

CHECK-IN & BOARDING

Always **find out your carrier's check-in policy.** Plan to arrive at the airport about two hours before your scheduled departure time for domestic flights and 2½ to 3 hours before international flights. You may need to arrive earlier if you're flying from one of the busier airports or during peak air-traffic times. To avoid delays at airport-security checkpoints, try not to wear any metal. Jewelry, belt and other buckles, steel-toe shoes, barrettes, and underwire bras are among the items that can set off detectors.

Assuming that not everyone with a ticket will show up, airlines routinely overbook planes. When everyone does, airlines ask for volunteers to give up their seats. In return, these volunteers usually get a several-hundred-dollar flight voucher, which can be used toward the purchase of another ticket, and are rebooked on the next flight out. If there are not enough volunteers, the airline must choose who will be denied boarding. The first to get bumped are passengers who checked in late and those flying on discounted tickets, so get to the gate and check in as early as possible, especially during peak periods.

Always **bring a government-issued photo ID** to the airport; even when it's not required, a passport is best.

CUTTING COSTS

The least expensive airfares to Thailand are priced for round-trip travel and must usually be purchased in advance. Airlines generally allow you to change your return date for a fee; most low-fare tickets, however, are nonrefundable.

Consolidators are another good source. They buy tickets for scheduled international flights at reduced rates from the airlines, then sell them at prices that beat the best fare available directly from the airlines. Sometimes you can even get your money back if you need to return the ticket. Carefully read the fine print detailing penalties for changes and cancellations, purchase the ticket with a credit card, and **confirm your consolidator reservation with the airline.**

For independent travelers, check into "Circle Pacific" fares. The pricing and routing of these tickets depend on the arrangements that the airline has with the local carriers of the region. The tickets must be purchased at least 7 to 14 days in advance. You usually can add on extra stopovers, including Australian and South Pacific destinations, for a nominal charge. Several airlines work together to offer "Around the World" fares, but you must follow a specific routing itinerary and cannot backtrack. "Around the World" itineraries usually include a couple of Asian destinations before continuing through Africa and Europe.

Thai Airways has a pass that entitles you to fly to any three cities within Thailand for a discount. You also have the option of purchasing additional discount coupons if you need to add on a few more flights. Unfortunately, this deal is only available if you purchase your round-trip international ticket through Thai Airways.

🔲 Consolidators **Cheap Tickets** ☎ 800/377-1000 or 888/922-8849 ⊕ www.cheaptickets.com. **Discount Airline Ticket Service** ☎ 800/576-1600. **Unitravel** ☎ 800/325-2222 ⊕ www.unitravel.com. **Up & Away Travel** ☎ 212/889-2345 ⊕ www.upandaway.com. **World Travel Network** ☎ 800/409-6753.

🔲 Discount Passes **Cathay Pacific All Asia Pass** ☎ 800/233-2742 ⊕ www.cathay-usa.com.

ENJOYING THE FLIGHT

State your seat preference when purchasing your ticket, and then repeat it when you confirm and when you check in. For more legroom, you can request one of the few emergency-aisle seats at check-in, if you're capable of moving obstacles comparable in weight to an airplane exit door (usually between 35 pounds and 60 pounds)—a Federal Aviation Administration requirement of passengers in these seats. Seats behind a bulkhead also offer more legroom, but they don't have underseat storage. Don't sit in the row in front of the emergency aisle or in front of a bulkhead, where seats may not recline.

Ask the airline whether a snack or meal is served on the flight. If you have dietary concerns, request special meals when booking. These can be vegetarian, low-cholesterol, or kosher, for example. It's a good idea to pack some healthful snacks and a small (plastic) bottle of water in your carry-on bag. On long flights, try to maintain a normal routine, to help fight jet lag. At night, get some sleep. By day, eat light meals, drink water (not alcohol), and move around the cabin to stretch your legs. For additional jet-lag tips consult *Fodor's FYI: Travel Fit & Healthy* (available at bookstores everywhere).

FLYING TIMES

Bangkok is 17 hours from San Francisco, 18 hours from Seattle and Vancouver, 20 hours from Chicago, 22 hours from New York and Toronto, 11 hours from London, and 10 hours from Sydney. Add more time for stopovers and connections, especially if you're using more than one carrier.

TRAVEL WITHIN THAILAND

Thai Airways connects Bangkok with all major cities and tourist areas in Thailand, except Ko Samui. Bangkok Airways has numerous daily flights between Bangkok and Ko Samui, using 40-seat planes. It also flies daily between Ko Samui and Phuket, Ko Samui and Pattaya, and four times a week from Ko Samui to Krabi. Daily flights from Bangkok to cities in other Southeast Asian countries include Siem Reap and Phnom Penh in Cambodia, Luang Prabang in Laos, and Yangon, Myanmar. Bangkok Airways has domestic daily flights to Krabi, Trat, Phuket, Chiang Mai, and Sukhothai. Its fares are competitive with those of Thai Airways.

Thanks to a couple of new low-cost carriers servicing the region, domestic flights within Thailand have become much more affordable. Two new airlines offering no-frills service on flights within Thailand are Air Asia and Orient Thai Airlines. Air Asia has direct flights to Chiang Mai, Chiang Rai, Hat Yai, Khon Kaen, Ubon Ratchathani, and Udon Thani every day.

By booking online, you may find a ticket at a rock bottom price. Orient Thai Airlines flies to Chiang Rai, Chiang Mai, Phuket, Hat Yai, and Krabi, as well as on to Hong Kong and Singapore. Both of these airlines offer tickets at a lower rate than that of Thai and Bangkok Airways. You can find their ticketing offices in the domestic terminal at Don Muang International Airport and at all other Thai airports. Angel Airlines has cheap flights between Bangkok and Phuket.

🛪 Airlines **Air Asia** ☎ 02/515-9999 ⊕ www.airasia.com. **Angel Airlines** ☎ 02/535-6287 at Don Muang airport office. **Bangkok Airways** ✉ 60 Queen Sirikit National Convention Centre, New Ratchadaphisek Rd., Klongotey, Bangkok ☎ 02/229-3456 or 02/229-3434. **Orient Thai Airways** ☎ 02/535-6520 ⊕ www.orient-thai.com. **Thai Airways** ✉ 485 Silom Rd., Bangkok ☎ 02/232-8000.

AIRPORTS

The major gateway to Thailand was Bangkok's Don Muang International Airport, which is about 25 km (16 mi) north of Bangkok. But foreign arrivals will soon start landing at Bangkok's brand-new Suvarnabhumi Airport (pronounced Soo-wan-na-poom and also known as the Second Bangkok International Airport or SBIA). At this writing, the airport is scheduled to be operational in the fall of 2005, though a delay on such a major undertaking wouldn't be unheard of. Until SBIA opens, most international flights to Thailand will continue to land at Don Muang. Bangkok Airways built an airport outside Sukhothai, which was once slightly off the beaten track. Now a daily flight arrives from Chiang Mai and Bangkok. The airline has also initiated direct flights between Bangkok and Siem Reap and between Singapore and Ko Samui. (Because Bangkok Airways is the only carrier with rights on Samui, flights there are already very expensive and are likely to become truly exorbitant.) There's also a new airport at Krabi with flights to and from Bangkok.

🛪 Airport Information **Don Muang International Airport** ☎ 02/535-1111. **Suvarnabhumi Airport** ⊕ www.bangkokairport.org.

AIRPORT TRANSFERS

Bangkok has nonstop airport shuttles that serve the train stations as well as hotels. Shared hotel vans and taxis are also a popular mode of transport. It helps to **have a hotel brochure or an address in Thai for the driver.**

From the center of Bangkok to Don Muang, allow about 40 minutes in light traffic, 90 minutes at rush hour.

BUS TRAVEL

Long-distance buses are cheaper and faster than trains and reach every corner of the country. The level of comfort depends on the bus company, but luxury "super buses" with extra-wide reclining seats, air-conditioning, video, scheduled box or buffet meals, and restrooms are available. If you're setting out on a long bus journey, it's worth inquiring about on-board entertainment—14 hours on a bus with continuous karaoke VCDs blasting out old pop hits can be torturous. Be aware that air-conditioned buses are always so cold that you'll want to bring an extra sweater. On local buses, space at the back soon fills up with all kinds of oversized luggage that will take up your legroom, so it's best to sit toward the middle or front.

CUTTING COSTS

Travel agents on Khao San Road in Bangkok's Banglamphu neighborhood offer some of the cheapest deals for private buses, though these are often overbooked so make sure that there's a seat for you or you'll end up perching on somebody's lap.

FARES & SCHEDULES

Travel agents have bus schedules and can make reservations and issue tickets.

BUSINESS HOURS

BANKS & OFFICES

Thai and foreign banks are open weekdays 8:30–3:30, except for public holidays. Most commercial concerns in Bangkok operate on a five-day week and are open 8–5. Government offices are generally open 8:30–4:30 with a noon–1 lunch break.

GAS STATIONS

Gas stations in Thailand are usually open at least 8–8 daily; many, particularly those on the highways, are open 24 hours a day.

MUSEUMS & SIGHTS

Each museum keeps its own hours and may select a different day of the week to close (though it's usually Monday); it's best to call before visiting. Temples are generally open to visitors from 7 or 8 in the morning to 5 or 6 PM, but in truth they don't really have set hours. If a compound has gates, they open at dawn to allow the monks to do their rounds. Outside of major tourist sights like Wat Po in Bangkok, few temples appear to have fixed closing times.

SHOPS

Most small stores are open daily 8–8, whereas department and chain stores don't usually open until 10.

CAMERAS & PHOTOGRAPHY

Thailand, with its majestic landscapes and beautiful temples, is a photographer's dream. People here seem amenable to having picture-taking tourists in their midst, but you should always **ask permission before taking pictures of individuals.** The phrase *Tai roob dai mai?* means "Can I take a picture?

Make sure you have a few rolls of 400-speed film for shooting in shady places (Thais, rather sensibly, stay out of the sun as much as possible) and inside temples.

The *Kodak Guide to Shooting Great Travel Pictures* (available at bookstores everywhere) is loaded with tips.

🞄 Photo Help **Kodak Information Center** ☎ 800/242-2424 ⊕ www.kodak.com.

EQUIPMENT PRECAUTIONS

Don't pack film and equipment in checked luggage, where it's much more susceptible to damage. X-ray machines used to view checked luggage are becoming much more powerful and therefore are much more likely to ruin your film. Try to ask for hand inspection of film, which becomes clouded after repeated exposure to airport X-ray machines, and keep videotapes and computer disks away from metal detectors. Carry an extra supply of batteries, and be prepared to turn on your camera, camcorder, or laptop to prove to airport security personnel that the device is real.

Always **keep film, tape, and computer disks out of the sun.** Keep in mind that Thailand is very humid, so bring enough resealable bags to keep your equipment dry, and always keep film in its canister.

FILM & DEVELOPING

Expect to pay B100 to B125 for a roll of film with 36 exposures. Some resorts may charge a bit more. The most common brands are Kodak and Fuji.

The cost of developing film is usually about B40, plus B5 to B6 per exposure. Again, resorts are likely to be a bit more expensive. The quality is usually commensurate with that of a one-hour developing shop back home. If you're a serious photographer, it's worth hanging on to your film until you can hand it over to a professional lab in Bangkok—developers outside the capital don't always use gloves when handling film. While processing is generally pretty good nationwide, and certainly up to standard for snapshots, make sure important film goes to a top developer.

CAR RENTAL

Cars are available for rent in Bangkok and in major tourist destinations, however the additional cost of hiring a driver is small and the peace of mind great. If a foreigner is involved in an automobile accident, he or she—not the Thai—is likely to be judged at fault.

Rates in Thailand begin at $40 a day for an economy car with unlimited mileage. This includes neither tax, which is 7% on car rentals, nor the collision damage waiver. It's better to make your car-rental reservations when you arrive in Thailand, as you can usually secure a discount.

In Chiang Mai, Ko Samui, Pattaya, and Phuket, consider renting a jeep or motorcycle, popular and convenient ways to get around. Be aware that motorcycles skid easily on gravel roads. On Ko Samui, a sign posts the year's count of foreigners who never made it home from their vacations!

F **Major Agencies Alamo** ☎ 800/522-9696 ⊕ www.alamo.com. **Avis** ☎ 800/331-1084, 800/ 879-2847 in Canada, 0870/606-0100 in U.K., 02/ 9353-9000 in Australia, 09/526-2847 in New Zealand ⊕ www.avis.com. **Budget** ☎ 800/527-0700, 0870/156-5656 in U.K. ⊕ www.budget.com. **Dollar** ☎ 800/800-6000, 0800/085-4578 in U.K. ⊕ www.dollar.com. **Hertz** ☎ 800/654-3001, 800/ 263-0600 in Canada, 0870/844-8844 in U.K., 02/ 9669-2444 in Australia, 09/256-8690 in New Zealand ⊕ www.hertz.com. **National Car Rental** ☎ 800/227-7368, 0870/600-6666 in U.K. ⊕ www. nationalcar.com.

INSURANCE

When driving a rented car you are generally responsible for any damage to or loss of the vehicle. You may also be liable for any property damage or personal injury that you may cause while driving. Before you rent, see what coverage you already have under the terms of your personal auto-insurance policy and credit cards. Of course, it's important to ask the rental company to spell out exactly what you are covered for under their policies.

REQUIREMENTS & RESTRICTIONS

Technically, you're required to have an International Driver's License (IDL) to drive or rent a car in Thailand, though it's possible that your own driver's license, as long as it's written in English, will be acceptable if you are pulled over. However, IDL's are not difficult to obtain, and having one in your wallet may save you from unwanted headaches if you do have to deal with local authorities. IDL's are available from the American or Canadian Automobile Associations, and, in the United Kingdom, from the Automobile Association or Royal Automobile Club.

SURCHARGES

Before you pick up a car in one city and leave it in another, ask about drop-off charges or one-way service fees, which can be substantial. Note, too, that some rental agencies charge extra if you return the car before the time specified in your contract. To avoid a hefty refueling fee, fill the tank just before you turn in the car, but be aware that gas stations near the rental outlet may overcharge.

CAR TRAVEL

Driving in Thailand has its ups and downs. The major roads in Thailand tend to be congested, and street signs are often only in Thai. But the limited number of roads and the straightforward layout of cities combine to make navigation relatively easy. The exception, of course, is Bangkok. Don't even think about negotiating that tangled mass of traffic-clogged streets.

The main rule to remember is that traffic laws are routinely disregarded. Bigger vehicles have the unspoken right of way, motorcyclists seem to think they are invincible, and bicyclists often don't look around them. Drive carefully.

Always **avoid driving at night in rural areas,** especially north and west of Chiang Mai and in the south beyond Surat Thani, as highway robberies have been reported.

GASOLINE

A liter of gasoline costs approximately B18–B22. Many gas stations stay open 24 hours and have clean toilet facilities and minimarkets. As you get farther away from developed areas, roadside stalls sell gasoline from bottles or tanks.

PARKING

In cities, the larger hotels, restaurants, and department stores have garages or parking lots. Rates vary, but count on B10 an hour. If you purchase anything, parking is free, but you must have your ticket validated.

RULES OF THE ROAD

As in the United Kingdom, **drive on the left side** of the road. Speed limits are 60 kph (37 mph) in cities, 90 kph (56 mph) outside, and 130 kph (81 mph) on expressways. If you're renting a motorcycle, remember that it's the law to always wear a helmet and keep your headlight on day and night. Traffic police have really been cracking down on riders without helmets in recent years, though, somewhat strangely, only during daylight hours. If you're caught breaking traffic laws, you officially have to report to the police station to pay a large fine. In reality, an on-the-spot fine of B100 or B200 can usually be paid. Never presume to have the right of way in Thailand and always expect the other car to do exactly what you think they should not.

CHILDREN IN THAILAND

Youngsters are welcome in Thailand. You'll be amazed at how many people will want to hold and play with your kids, and at how their presence will actually open conversations and cut through cultural boundaries. Many activities, such as riding elephants and visiting the floating markets, will delight even the most finicky child. When traveling to the islands, boat rides can be long and the seas rough, so make sure to take some seasickness tablets. Also remember that tuk-tuks have no seatbelts and seats that are a little too easy to slide around on.

If you are renting a car, don't forget to arrange for a car seat when you reserve. For general advice about traveling with children, consult *Fodor's FYI: Travel with Your Baby* (available in bookstores everywhere).

Places that are especially appealing to children are indicated by a rubber-duckie icon (🦆) in the margin.

FLYING

If your children are two or older, ask about children's airfares. As a general rule, infants under two not occupying a seat fly at greatly reduced fares or even for free. But if you want to guarantee a seat for an infant, you have to pay full fare. Consider flying during off-peak days and times; most airlines will grant an infant a seat without a ticket if there are available seats. When booking, confirm carry-on allowances if you're traveling with infants. In general, for babies charged 10% to 50% of the adult fare you are allowed one carry-on bag and a collapsible stroller; if the flight is full, the stroller may have to be checked or you may be limited to less.

Experts agree that it's a good idea to use safety seats aloft for children weighing less than 40 pounds. Airlines set their own policies: if you use a safety seat, U.S. carriers usually require that the child be ticketed, even if he or she is young enough to ride free, because the seats must be strapped into regular seats. And even if you pay the full adult fare for the seat, it may be worth it, especially on longer trips. Do check your airline's policy about using safety seats during takeoff and landing. Safety seats are not allowed everywhere in the plane, so get your seat assignments as early as possible.

When reserving, request children's meals or a freestanding bassinet (not available at all airlines) if you need them. But note that bulkhead seats, where you must sit to use the bassinet, may lack an overhead bin or storage space on the floor.

FOOD

Although Thai food can often be too spicy for children, most restaurants are happy to make dishes that are milder. When all else fails, there are plenty of familiar fast-food restaurants in Bangkok and other large cities.

LODGING

Most hotels in Thailand allow children under a certain age to stay in their parents' room at no extra charge, but others charge for them as extra adults; be sure to find out the cutoff age for children's discounts.

SUPPLIES & EQUIPMENT

Supplies are easy to find in the major supermarkets in Thailand; you can get both Huggies and Pampers brand diapers in small to extra-large sizes. Baby wipes are not commonly used, so it's a good idea to bring some from home.

COMPUTERS ON THE ROAD

The business centers of many hotels in Thailand provide Internet access. In modern upscale hotels, you can often find in-room connections for your laptop. They use the same phone jacks you find in the United States.

Even the smallest towns have Internet shops, though speeds can be slow and connections temperamental. The standard price in a tourist area is B1 per minute, while shops aimed at locals can be as cheap as B20 per hour. Larger hotels and resorts can charge more—sometimes a lot more—so make sure to ask in advance.

Be forewarned that it's quite common to find Internet shops packed with schoolkids

playing linked-up computer games, so either check your e-mail when school's in session or have a back-up plan in case your location is too full or chaotic.

CRUISE TRAVEL

Some cruise lines, including Cunard and Royal Viking, call at major Southeast Asian ports as part of their around-the-world itineraries. Seabourn Cruises spends 14 days cruising the waters of Southeast Asia, including the Gulf of Thailand. Cunard's Sea Goddess provides a luxury trip in the Gulf of Thailand and through the Straits of Malacca into the Andaman Sea.

Plan to spend at least four weeks cruising from the West Coast of the United States to Southeast Asia, as these ships usually visit ports in the Pacific and Australia along the way.

🚢 **Cruise Lines Cunard's Sea Goddess** ✉ 555 5th Ave., New York, NY 10017 ☎ 212/880-7500 or 800/221-4770. **Royal Viking** ☎ 800/426-0821. **Seabourn Cruises** ✉ San Francisco St., San Francisco, CA 94133 ☎ 415/391-7444 or 800/929-9595.

CUSTOMS & DUTIES

When shopping abroad, keep receipts for all purchases. Upon reentering the country, **be ready to show customs officials what you've bought.** Pack purchases together in an easily accessible place. If you think a duty is incorrect, appeal the assessment. If you object to the way your clearance was handled, note the inspector's badge number. In either case, first ask to see a supervisor. If the problem isn't resolved, write to the appropriate authorities, beginning with the port director at your point of entry.

IN THAILAND

One liter of wine or liquor, 200 cigarettes or 250 grams of smoking tobacco, and all personal effects may be brought into Thailand duty-free. Visitors may bring in any amount of foreign currency; amounts taken out may not exceed those declared upon entry. Narcotics, pornographic materials, and firearms are strictly prohibited.

If you're bringing any foreign-made equipment from home, such as cameras, it's wise to carry the original receipt with you or register it with U.S. Customs before you leave (Form 4457). Otherwise, you may end up paying duty on your return.

IN AUSTRALIA

Australian residents who are 18 or older may bring home A$400 worth of souvenirs and gifts (including jewelry), 250 cigarettes or 250 grams of cigars or other tobacco products, and 1,125 ml of alcohol (including wine, beer, and spirits). Residents under 18 may bring back A$200 worth of goods. Members of the same family traveling together may pool their allowances. Prohibited items include meat products. Seeds, plants, and fruits need to be declared upon arrival.

🚩 **Australian Customs Service** ✑ Regional Director, Box 8, Sydney, NSW 2001 ☎ 02/9213-2000 or 1300/363263, 02/9364-7222 or 1800/020-504 quarantine-inquiry line 🖨 02/9213-4043 ⊕ www.customs.gov.au.

IN CANADA

Canadian residents who have been out of Canada for at least seven days may bring in C$750 worth of goods duty-free. If you've been away fewer than seven days but more than 48 hours, the duty-free allowance drops to C$200. If your trip lasts 24 to 48 hours, the allowance is C$50. You may not pool allowances with family members. Goods claimed under the C$750 exemption may follow you by mail; those claimed under the lesser exemptions must accompany you. Alcohol and tobacco products may be included in the seven-day and 48-hour exemptions but not in the 24-hour exemption. If you meet the age requirements of the province or territory through which you reenter Canada, you may bring in, duty-free, 1.5 liters of wine or 1.14 liters (40 imperial ounces) of liquor or 24 12-ounce cans or bottles of beer or ale. Also, if you meet the local age requirement for tobacco products, you may bring in, duty-free, 200 cigarettes and 50 cigars. Check ahead of time with the Canada Customs and Revenue Agency or the Department of Agriculture for policies regarding meat products, seeds, plants, and fruits.

You may send an unlimited number of gifts (only one gift per recipient, however) worth up to C$60 each duty-free to Canada. Label the package UNSOLICITED GIFT—VALUE UNDER $60. Alcohol and tobacco are excluded.

🚩 **Canada Customs and Revenue Agency** ✉ 2265 St. Laurent Blvd., Ottawa, Ontario K1G 4K3 🖨 800/461-9999 in Canada, 204/983-3500, or 506/636-5064 ⊕ www.ccra.gc.ca.

IN NEW ZEALAND

All homeward-bound residents may bring back NZ$700 worth of souvenirs and gifts; passengers may not pool their allowances, and children can claim only the concession on goods intended for their own use. For those 17 or older, the duty-free allowance also includes 4.5 liters of wine or beer; one 1,125-ml bottle of spirits; and either 200 cigarettes, 250 grams of tobacco, 50 cigars, or a combination of the three up to 250 grams. Meat products, seeds, plants, and fruits must be declared upon arrival to the Agricultural Services Department.

🚩 **New Zealand Customs** ✉ Head office: The Customhouse, 17–21 Whitmore St., Box 2218, Wellington ☎ 09/300-5399 or 0800/428-786 ⊕ www.customs.govt.nz.

IN THE U.K.

From countries outside the European Union, including Thailand, Laso, and Cambodia, you may bring home, duty-free, 200 cigarettes, 50 cigars, 100 cigarillos, or 250 grams of tobacco; 1 liter of spirits or 2 liters of fortified or sparkling wine or liqueurs; 2 liters of still table wine; 60 ml of perfume; 250 ml of toilet water; plus £145 worth of other goods, including gifts and souvenirs. Prohibited items include meat and dairy products, seeds, plants, and fruits.

🚩 **HM Customs and Excise** ✉ Portcullis House, 21 Cowbridge Rd. E, Cardiff CF11 9SS ☎ 0845/010-9000, 0208/929-0152 advice service, 0208/929-6731, 0208/910-3602 complaints ⊕ www.hmce.gov.uk.

IN THE U.S.

U.S. residents who have been out of the country for at least 48 hours may bring home, for personal use, $800 worth of foreign goods duty-free, as long as they haven't used the $800 allowance or any part of it in the past 30 days. This exemption may include 1 liter of alcohol (for travelers 21 and older), 200 cigarettes, and 100 non-Cuban cigars. Family members from the same household who are traveling together may pool their $800 personal exemptions. For fewer than 48 hours, the duty-free allowance drops to $200, which may include 50 cigarettes, 10 non-Cuban cigars, and 150 ml of alcohol (or 150 ml of perfume containing alcohol). The $200 allowance cannot be combined with other individuals' exemptions, and if you exceed it, the full value of all the goods will be taxed. Antiques, which U.S. Customs and Border Protection defines as objects more than 100 years old, enter duty-free, as do original works of art done entirely by hand, including paintings, drawings, and sculptures. This doesn't apply to folk art or handicrafts, which are in general dutiable.

You may also send packages home duty-free, with a limit of one parcel per addressee per day (except alcohol or tobacco products or perfume worth more than $5). You can mail up to $200 worth of goods for personal use; label the package PERSONAL USE and attach a list of its contents and their retail value. If the package contains your used personal belongings, mark it AMERICAN GOODS RETURNED to avoid paying duties. You may send up to $100 worth of goods as a gift; mark the package UNSOLICITED GIFT. Mailed items do not affect your duty-free allowance on your return.

To avoid paying duty on foreign-made high-ticket items you already own and will take on your trip, register them with Customs before you leave the country. Consider filing a Certificate of Registration for laptops, cameras, watches, and other digital devices identified with serial numbers or other permanent markings; you can keep the certificate for other trips. Otherwise, bring a sales receipt or insurance form to show that you owned the item before you left the United States.

For more about duties, restricted items, and other information about international travel, check out U.S. Customs and Border Protection's online brochure, *Know Before You Go.*

U.S. Customs and Border Protection ⊠ For inquiries and equipment registration, 1300 Pennsylvania Ave. NW, Washington, DC 20229 ⊕ www.cbp.gov ☎ 877/287-8667or 202/354-1000 ⊠ For complaints, Customer Satisfaction Unit, 1300 Pennsylvania Ave. NW, Room 5.2C, Washington, DC 20229.

DISCOUNTS & DEALS
Be a smart shopper and compare all your options before making decisions. A plane ticket bought with a promotional coupon from travel clubs, coupon books, and direct-mail offers or purchased on the Internet may not be cheaper than the least expensive fare from a discount ticket agency. And always keep in mind that what you get is just as important as what you save.

DISCOUNT RESERVATIONS
To save money, look into discount reservations services with Web sites and toll-free numbers, which use their buying power to get a better price on hotels, airline tickets (⇨ Air Travel), even car rentals. When booking a room, always **call the hotel's local toll-free number** (if one is available) rather than the central reservations number—you'll often get a better price. Always ask about special packages or corporate rates.

When shopping for the best deal on hotels and car rentals, look for guaranteed exchange rates, which protect you against a falling dollar. With your rate locked in, you won't pay more, even if the price goes up in the local currency.

Airline Tickets Air 4 Less ☎ 800/AIR4LESS; low-fare specialist.
Hotel Rooms Accommodations Express ☎ 800/444-7666 or 800/277-1064 ⊕ www.acex.net. **Hotels.com** ☎ 800/246-8357 ⊕ www.hotels.com. **Steigenberger Reservation Service** ☎ 800/223-5652 ⊕ www.srs-worldhotels.com. **Turbotrip.com** ☎ 800/473-7829 ⊕ www.turbotrip.com. **VacationLand** ☎ 800/245-0050 ⊕ www.vacation-land.com.

PACKAGE DEALS
Don't confuse packages and guided tours. When you buy a package, you travel on your own, just as though you had planned the trip yourself. Fly/drive packages, which combine airfare and car rental, are often a good deal. In cities, ask the local visitor's

bureau about hotel and local transportation packages that include tickets to major museum exhibits or other special events.

EATING & DRINKING

Thais know that eating out can be cheaper than eating in, and that inexpensive restaurants often serve food that's as good as, and sometimes better than, the fare at fancy places. That's why you see so many Thai families gathered around vendor carts or crowded around tables at a town's night market. As tempting as it might be to jump straight in and feast on streetside goodies, it's worth remembering that your stomach may need some time to adapt. That creamy pork curry and bamboo shoot stir-fry may well be tempting after a long flight, but taking it easy for the first few days could mean the difference between a week lazing on the beach and a week sweating in the bathroom. When you do try the food stalls, try not to choose dishes that may have been sitting out for hours on end and always add extra spices in moderation. Water is usually provided free and most places will have some bottles of Fanta and Coke kicking around.

Thai food is eaten with a fork and spoon; the spoon held in the right hand and the fork is used like a plow to push food into the spoon. Chopsticks are used only for Chinese food, such as noodle dishes. After you have finished eating, place your fork and spoon on the plate at the 5:25 position; otherwise the server will assume you would like another helping.

The restaurants we list are the cream of the crop in each price category. Unless otherwise noted, the restaurants listed in this guide are open daily for lunch and dinner.

MEALS & SPECIALTIES

Thai cuisine's distinctive flavor comes particularly from the use of fresh Thai basil, lemongrass, tamarind, lime, and citrus leaves. And though some Thai food is fiery hot from garlic and chilies, an equal number of dishes serve the spices on the side so that you can adjust the incendiary level. Thais use *nam pla*, a fish sauce, instead of salt.

If you're not sure what to order, start with some staples such as tom yam kung, which is prawn and lemongrass soup with mushrooms, then move on to pad thai, which is fried noodles with tofu, vegetables, eggs, and peanuts. Wash it down with a Singha, a tasty Thai beer.

MEALTIMES

Restaurants tend to open in late morning and serve food until 9 or 10 in the evening. Street vendors can be found in most places 24 hours a day.

RESERVATIONS & DRESS

Reservations are always a good idea: we mention them only when they're essential or not accepted. Book as far ahead as you can, and reconfirm as soon as you arrive.

Because Thailand has a hot climate, jackets and ties are rarely worn at dinner except in expensive restaurants, usually in the big hotels. We mention dress only when men are required to wear a jacket or a jacket and tie.

WINE, BEER & SPIRITS

The beer market is really beginning to open up in Thailand, with brands like San Miguel and Tiger joining the race for their share of the action. Singha and Heineken still lead the way at the top end while Chang and Leo fight it out for the budget drinkers. It's also becoming more common to find imports such as Guinness, Corona, and Budweiser lining the shelves of cosmopolitan bars.

Of course, if you want to drink like the hip locals, you won't be bothering with beer. Grab a bottle of whisky (Chivas Regal, Johnnie Walker or the very affordable 100 Pipers) to mix with cola or soda and head to a club, where you can dance around your table, while the staff make sure your glass is never empty.

Rice whiskey, which tastes sweet and has a whopping 35% alcohol content, is another favorite throughout Thailand. Mekong and Sam Song are by far the most popular rice whiskeys, but you will also see labels such as Kwangthong, Hong Thong, Hong Ngoen, Hong Yok, and Hong Tho.

Wine is increasingly available, however, the locally produced wines are likely to leave you with a nasty headache the next day, and the imported ones may do damage to your wallet. Also, imported wines are likely to be in poor condition due to the tropical heat.

DISABILITIES & ACCESSIBILITY

Thailand is a challenge for people with disabilities. The pavements are totally unsuitable for wheelchairs, making getting around most places difficult. But traveling with a car and driver is relatively affordable here, and the Thais are so helpful that a person with disabilities can expect to have a great deal of friendly assistance.

RESERVATIONS

When discussing accessibility with an operator or reservations agent, ask hard questions. Are there any stairs, inside *or* out? Are there grab bars next to the toilet *and* in the shower/tub? How wide is the doorway to the room? To the bathroom? For the most extensive facilities meeting the latest legal specifications, **opt for newer accommodations.**

ECOTOURISM

Unfortunately, Thailand's tourism boom has had many negative effects on Thai culture and resources; problems range from the overwhelming presence of sex tourism to water pollution to the transformation of hill tribe villages into veritable theme parks. Though these problems are far-reaching and difficult to reign in, there are a few simple things you can do to ensure that, at the very least, you're not contributing to the morass.

Don't litter. Garbage is now a common sight on Thailand's once-pristine beaches and even the more remote corners of the Andaman Sea might be marred by bobbing Styrofoam or plastic containers. Many places lack the resources and infrastructure to continually clean up the beaches and the sea, so that water bottle you casually leave behind after a day of sunbathing may have a lasting legacy. Non-biodegradable materials are particularly problematic—pay the extra few baht to buy water in glass bottles that can be recycled. Some-

times water comes in reusable plastic containers, which are clearly marked as such.

Don't disturb animal and plant life. Whether you're trekking through a forest or snorkeling along a reef, be as unobtrusive to the environment as possible. Don't remove plant life or coral for souvenirs—what may look like it won't be missed might in fact be rare or sacred to a community. Don't randomly feed fish or animals whatever food you happen to have on hand; though they'll probably eat it, trying to digest inappropriate foods could harm or kill them. It's not an exaggeration to say that tourists have been seen feeding tropical fish all manner of things (including M&M's!) for a few seconds of amusement. Unfortunately, many boat operators in the south seem not only to tolerate this behavior, but encourage it. This comes from a lack of understanding of environmental issues—the same one that prompts them to anchor their boats to coral reefs—so just because your boat driver waves you on doesn't mean you're not doing something harmful.

Respect local customs. Though this may seem more an issue of etiquette than ecotourism, demonstrating basic respect for and interest in a culture is part and parcel of sustainable tourism. True, Thais seem to be exceedingly tolerant of Western behavior—which can reach near Spring Break-levels of debauchery, especially in Bangkok and in the Southern Beaches region—but tourists' ever-present ignorance of even the most basic Thai customs does have lasting negative effects on the communities they encounter. Take the time to learn about major cultural sticking points (especially those related to Buddhism) and be patient and respectful when misunderstandings occur.

Tour agencies increasingly try to be ecofriendly, particularly on jungle treks in Northern Thailand. This is especially true in Chiang Mai and Chiang Rai, where many people enjoy elephant rides into the mountains. However, ecotourism has not blossomed here as much as it has in other regions of the world, so it may be hard to find a company that is truly ecofriendly.

Before booking a tour, ask tough questions about what the company does to preserve the environment and help local villages. Responsible Ecological Social Tours Project (REST) arranges remote village tours (with possible homestays) and ensure that 70% of the profits of each trip go directly to the community. Their Web site (www.ecotour.in.th) is a good place to start for a different perspective on hill tribe village visits.

ANIMAL RIGHTS

The elephant, revered for its strength, courage, and intelligence, has a long history in Thailand. These gentle giants were used to haul timber, including the teak pillars used in royal palaces and temples. In recent years, however, mechanization has made the domesticated elephant obsolete, and elephant trainers have come to rely on the tourist industry as their only source of income. To make sure they are not mistreated, the group Friends of the Asian Elephant monitors the treatment of elephants used in shows and treks. If you are going on an elephant-back trek and have concerns, check out how various companies treat their animals. Find out, for example, how many hours the elephants are worked each day and whether you'll be riding in the afternoon heat.

Friends of the Asian Elephant ⊠ 350 Moo 8, Ram-Indra Rd., Soi 61, Tharaeng, Bangkhen, Bangkok 10230 ☎☎ 02/945-7124 ⊕ www.elephant.tnet.co.th.

ELECTRICITY

To use your U.S.-purchased electric-powered equipment, **bring a converter and adapter.** The electrical current in Thailand is 220 volts, 50 cycles alternating current (AC); wall outlets take either two flat prongs, like outlets in the United States, or continental-type plugs, with two round prongs.

If your appliances are dual-voltage, you need only an adapter. Don't use 110-volt outlets marked FOR SHAVERS ONLY for high-wattage appliances such as blow-dryers. Most laptops operate equally well on 110 and 220 volts and so require only an adapter.

EMBASSIES & CONSULATES

Most nations maintain diplomatic relations with Thailand and have embassies in Bangkok; a few have consulates also in Chiang Mai. Should you need to apply for a visa to another country, the consulate hours are usually 8–noon daily.

In Bangkok Australian Embassy ⊠ 37 Sathorn Tai Rd. ☎ 02/287-2680. **British Embassy** ⊠ 1031 Wittayu (Wireless Rd.) ☎ 02/253-0191. **Canadian Embassy** ⊠ 15th fl., Abdulrahim Bldg., 990 Rama IV ☎ 02/636-0540. **New Zealand Embassy** ⊠ 93 Wireless Rd. ☎ 02/254-2530. **U.S. Embassy** ⊠ 120-122 Wireless Rd. ☎ 02/205-4000.

In Chiang Mai Australian Consulate ⊠ 165 Sirman Khalajan ☎ 053/221083. **British Consulate** ⊠ 201 Airport Business Park, 90 Mahidon ☎ 053/203405. **U.S. Consulate** ⊠ 387 Wichayanom Rd. ☎ 053/252629.

EMERGENCIES

Thais are generally quite helpful, so you should get assistance from locals if you need it. The Tourist Police will help you in case of a robbery or rip-off.

Many hotels can refer you to an English-speaking doctor. Major cities in Thailand have some of Southeast Asia's best hospitals, and the country is quickly becoming a ìmedical holidayî destination (i.e. a cost-effective place to have plastic surgery, dental work, etc. done). However, if you are still wary about treating serious health problems in Thailand, you could consider flying to Singapore.

Police ☎ 191. **Tourist Police** ☎ 1699.

ENGLISH-LANGUAGE MEDIA

Thailand has by and large a free press, with only a modicum of self-censorship (particularly when referring to the monarchy) in evidence.

NEWSPAPERS & MAGAZINES

There are two English-language newspapers published daily in Thailand: the *Bangkok Post* (morning edition) and the *Nation* (afternoon edition). The former has more of an international news staff, which is evident in the more Western-style reporting.

Popular newspapers and magazines—from the *International Herald Tribune* to *Time* magazine—are widely available throughout Thailand.

RADIO & TELEVISION

Bangkok has five VHF-TV networks, with English shows aired periodically during the day, although mostly in the mornings. Satellite and cable TV are widely available; you can expect to see HBO, MTV Asia, CNN International, and BBC World Service Television.

There are literally hundreds of radio stations available in Thailand. Check out 107 FM for CNN hourly updates. Radio Bangkok, at 95.5 FM, also has English-speaking DJs.

ETIQUETTE & BEHAVIOR

Displays of anger, raised voices, and confrontations are considered very bad form. Thais disapprove of public nudity and of public shows of affection. Do not step over a seated person or someone's legs. Don't point your feet at anyone; keep them on the floor, and take care not to show the soles of your feet. Never touch a person's head, even a child's (the head is considered sacred), and avoid touching a monk if you're a woman.

When visiting temples, **dress modestly.** Don't wear shorts or tank tops. If you show up improperly attired, some temples have wraps you can borrow. Others will not let you enter. Remove your shoes before entering the temple and don't point your toes at any image of the Buddha, as it's considered sacrilegious.

It's worth dressing modestly even outside temple grounds. At the beach Thais will often go swimming wearing jeans and T-shirts, so walking around a city center with your midriff (or worse) hanging out is not really the way to endear yourself to the locals.

GAY & LESBIAN TRAVEL

Thailand has always shown tolerance toward homosexuality, though public affection between couples of any gender is frowned on. In Bangkok, Patpong III has many gay bars, and you can also find them in Chiang Mai, Pattaya, and Phuket.

One of the best Web sites for gay travelers is Dreaded Ned's (www.dreadedned.com), which has frequently updated listings for all major destinations in the country. There are also handy maps for finding your way around the confusing streets and sois.

⚑ Gay- & Lesbian-Friendly Travel Agencies **Different Roads Travel** ✉ 8383 Wilshire Blvd., Suite 902, Beverly Hills, CA 90211 ☎ 323/651-5557 or 800/429-8747 🖷 323/651-3678 ✉ lgernert@tzell.com. **Kennedy Travel** ✉ 314 Jericho Tpke., Floral Park, NY 11001 ☎ 516/352-4888 or 800/237-7433 🖷 516/354-8849 ⊕ www.kennedytravel.com. **Now, Voyager** ✉ 4406 18th St., San Francisco, CA 94114 ☎ 415/626-1169 or 800/255-6951 🖷 415/626-8626 ⊕ www.nowvoyager.com. **Skylink Travel and Tour** ✉ 1006 Mendocino Ave., Santa Rosa, CA 95401 ☎ 707/546-9888 or 800/225-5759 🖷 707/546-9891 ⊕ www.skylinktravel.com, serving lesbian travelers.

HEALTH

The avian flu crisis that ripped through Southeast Asia at the start of the 21st century had a devastating impact on Thailand. Poultry farmers and chicken restaurants went out of business, tourists stayed away, and each week brought news of a new species found to be infected (including isolated cases of humans contracting the virus). As science desperately tries to catch up with and control the problem, check the media for up-to-date information. Be assured that most cases have occurred in rural areas outside of the tourist track.

Be aware that a high percentage of sex workers in Thailand are HIV positive, and unprotected sex is extremely risky.

FOOD & DRINK

In Thailand the major health risk is traveler's diarrhea, caused by eating contaminated fruit or vegetables or drinking contaminated water. So watch what you eat. Avoid ice, uncooked food, and unpasteurized milk and milk products, and **drink only bottled water** or water that has been boiled for at least 20 minutes, even when brushing your teeth. Mild cases may respond to Imodium (known generically as loperamide) or Pepto-Bismol (not as strong), both of which can be purchased over the counter; paregoric, another antidiarrheal agent, does not require a doctor's prescription in Thailand. Drink plenty of purified water or tea—chamomile is a good folk remedy. In severe cases, rehydrate yourself with a salt-sugar solution (½ teaspoon salt and 4 tablespoons sugar per quart of water).

MEDICAL PLANS
No one plans to get sick while traveling, but it happens, so consider signing up with a medical-assistance company. Members get doctor referrals, emergency evacuation or repatriation, hotlines for medical consultation, cash for emergencies, and other assistance.

⛨ Medical-Assistance Companies International SOS Assistance ⊕ www.internationalsos.com ✉ 8 Neshaminy Interplex, Suite 207, Trevose, PA 19053 ☎ 215/245-4707 or 800/523-6586 🖷 215/244-9617 ✉ Landmark House, Hammersmith Bridge Rd., 6th fl., London, W6 9DP ☎ 20/8762-8008 🖷 20/8748-7744 ✉ 12 Chemin Riantbosson, 1217 Meyrin 1, Geneva, Switzerland ☎ 22/785-6464 🖷 22/785-6424 ✉ 331 N. Bridge Rd., 17-00, Odeon Towers, Singapore 188720 ☎ 6338-7800 🖷 6338-7611.

SHOTS & MEDICATIONS
Although Thailand does not require or suggest vaccinations before traveling, we make the following recommendations:

Tetanus and polio vaccinations should be up-to-date, and you should be immunized against (or immune to) measles, mumps, and rubella. If you plan to visit rural areas, where there's questionable sanitation, you need a vaccination against hepatitis A. Malaria and dengue fever are also possible risks as you move out of the main tourist areas, so make sure to get fevers and nausea checked out by a doctor as soon as possible.

According to the U.S. government's National Centers for Disease Control (CDC) there's also a limited risk of hepatitis B, rabies, and Japanese encephalitis in certain rural areas of Thailand. In most urban or easily accessible areas you need not worry. However, if you plan to visit remote regions or stay for more than six weeks, check with the CDC's International Travelers Hotline.

In areas where malaria and dengue, both of which are carried by mosquitoes, are prevalent, use mosquito nets, wear clothing that covers the body, apply repellent containing DEET, and use spray for flying insects in living and sleeping areas. Also **talk to your doctor about taking antimalarial pills.** There's no vaccine to combat dengue, so if it's in the area, travelers should use aerosol insecticides indoors as well as mosquito repellents outdoors. Both Ko Samet and northern Thailand are known to have malarial mosquitoes, so take extra precautions if you visit these areas.

⛨ Health Warnings National Centers for Disease Control and Prevention CDC; National Center for Infectious Diseases, Division of Quarantine, Traveler's Health Section ✉ 1600 Clifton Rd. NE, M/S E-03, Atlanta, GA 30333 ☎ 888/232-3228 general information, 877/394-8747 traveler's health line, 800/311-3435 public inquiries 🖷 888/232-3299 ⊕ www.cdc.gov.

HOLIDAYS
New Year's Day (January 1); Chinese New Year (January 29, 2006); Magha Puja (on the full moon of the third lunar month); Chakri Day (April 6); Songkran (April 13–15); Coronation Day (May 5); Visakha Puja, May (on the full moon of the sixth lunar month); Queen's Birthday (August 12); King's Birthday (December 5). Government offices, banks, commercial concerns, and department stores are usually closed on these days, but smaller shops stay open.

INSURANCE
The most useful travel-insurance plan is a comprehensive policy that includes coverage for trip cancellation and interruption, default, trip delay, and medical expenses (with a waiver for preexisting conditions).

Without insurance you'll lose all or most of your money if you cancel your trip, regardless of the reason. Default insurance covers you if your tour operator, airline, or cruise line goes out of business—the chances of which have been increasing. Trip-delay covers expenses that arise because of bad weather or mechanical delays. Study the fine print when comparing policies.

If you're traveling internationally, a key component of travel insurance is coverage for medical bills incurred if you get sick on the road. Such expenses aren't generally covered by Medicare or private policies. U.K. residents can buy a travel-insurance policy valid for most vacations taken during the year in which it's purchased (but check preexisting-condition coverage). British and Australian citizens need extra medical coverage when traveling overseas.

Always **buy travel policies directly from the insurance company**; if you buy them from a cruise line, airline, or tour operator that goes out of business you probably won't be covered for the agency or operator's default, a major risk. Before making any purchase, review your existing health and home-owner's policies to find what they cover away from home.

F Travel Insurers In the U.S.: **Access America** ✉ 2805 N. Parham Rd., Richmond, VA 23294 ☎ 800/284-8300 🖷 804/673-1491 or 800/346-9265 ⊕ www.accessamerica.com. **Travel Guard International** ✉ 1145 Clark St., Stevens Point, WI 54481 ☎ 715/345-0505 or 800/826-1300 🖷 800/955-8785 ⊕ www.travelguard.com.

F In the U.K.: **Association of British Insurers** ✉ 51 Gresham St., London EC2V 7HQ ☎ 020/7600-3333 🖷 020/7696-8999 ⊕ www.abi.org.uk. In Canada: **RBC Insurance** ✉ 6880 Financial Dr., Mississauga, Ontario L5N 7Y5 ☎ 800/668-4342 or 905/816-2400 🖷 905/813-4704 ⊕ www.rbcinsurance.com. In Australia: **Insurance Council of Australia** ✉ Insurance Enquiries and Complaints, Level 12, Box 561, Collins St. W, Melbourne, VIC 8007 ☎ 1300/780808 or 03/9629-4109 🖷 03/9621-2060 ⊕ www.iecltd.com.au. In New Zealand: **Insurance Council of New Zealand** ✉ Level 7, 111-115 Customhouse Quay, Box 474, Wellington ☎ 04/472-5230 🖷 04/473-3011 ⊕ www.icnz.org.nz.

LANGUAGE

Thai is the country's national language. King Ramkhamhaeng created the Thai alphabet in 1283, basing its written symbols on the Khmer script. Thai is a tonal language with five tones, making it confusing to most foreigners. In polite conversation, a male speaker will use the word "krup" to end a sentence or to acknowledge what someone has said. Female speakers use "ka." It's easy to speak a few words, such

as "sawahdee krup" or "sawahdee ka" (good day) and "khop khun krup" or "khop khun ka" (thank you). You can find that attempting even a few words of Thai will be appreciated and greeted with one of those famous smiles. Remember that though English is taught in schools from an early age, many Thais are far from comfortable using it in day-to-day situations. As with many things in Thailand, patience is key. With the exception of taxi drivers, Thais working with travelers in the resort and tourist areas of Thailand generally speak sufficient English to permit basic communication.

LODGING

Every town of reasonable size offers accommodations. In the smaller towns the hotels may be fairly simple, but they will usually be clean and certainly inexpensive. In major cities or resort areas there are hotels to fit all price categories. At the high end, the luxury hotels can compete with the best in the world. Service is generally superb—polite and efficient—and most of the staff usually speak English. At the other end of the scale, the lodging is simple and basic—a room with little more than a bed. The least expensive places may have Asian toilets (squat type with no seat) and a fan rather than air-conditioning.

All except the budget hotels have restaurants and offer room service throughout most of the day and night. Most will also be happy to make local travel arrangements for you—for which they receive commissions. All hotels advise that you use their safe-deposit boxes.

During the peak tourist season, October–March, hotels are often fully booked and charge peak rates. At special times, such as December 30–January 2 and Chinese New Year, rates climb even higher, and hotel reservations are difficult to obtain. Weekday rates at some resorts are often lower, and virtually all hotels will discount their rooms if they are not fully booked. Don't be reticent about asking for a special rate. Breakfast is rarely included in the room tariff. Hotel rates tend to be lower if you reserve through a travel agent (in Thailand). The agent receives a reduced room rate from the hotel and passes some of this discount on to you.

The lodgings we list are the cream of the crop in each price category. We always list the facilities that are available, but we don't specify whether they cost extra; when pricing accommodations, always ask what's included and what costs extra.

Assume that hotels operate on the **European Plan** (EP, with no meals) unless we specify that they use either the **Continental Plan** (CP, with a continental breakfast), **Breakfast Plan** (BP, with a full breakfast), or the **Modified American Plan** (MAP, with breakfast and dinner) or are **all-inclusive** (including all meals and most activities).

HOSTELS

Bangkok has plenty of hostels where you can grab a cheap dorm bed for less than B100, or if you're willing to pay a bit more, decent private rooms can be had for similar prices to regular guesthouses. You can also find hostels in most other destinations in Thailand such as Chiang Mai, Hua Hin, and Phuket. For more information, check out the official Thai Youth Hostels Association Web site ⊕ www. thya.org. Another site with good up-to-date information is the Thailand page of ⊕ www.hostels.com. There are also YMCAs in Bangkok, Chiang Mai, and Chiang Rai.

MAIL & SHIPPING

Thailand's mail service is reliable and efficient. Major hotels provide basic postal services. Bangkok's central general post office on Charoen Krung (New Road) is open weekdays 8–6, weekends and public holidays 9–1. Up-country post offices close at 4:30 PM.

OVERNIGHT SERVICES

You can ship packages via DHL Worldwide, Federal Express, or UPS.

🏢 **DHL Worldwide** ✉ 22nd fl., Grand Amarin Tower, Phetburi Tat Mai, Bangkok ☎ 02/207-0600. **Federal Express** ✉ 8th fl., Green Tower, Rama IV, Bangkok ☎ 02/367-3222. **UPS** ✉ 16/1 Soi 44/1, Sukhumvit, Bangkok ☎ 02/712-3300.

POSTAL RATES

Letter, packet, and parcel rates are low—B27 for a letter to the United States, B17 for a letter to Europe. Allow at least 10 days for your mail to arrive. For speedier delivery, major post offices offer overseas express mail service, while a sea, air, and land service (SAL) is available for less urgent mail at a much cheaper rate.

RECEIVING MAIL

You may have mail sent to you "poste restante" at the following address: Poste Restante, General Post Office, Bangkok, Thailand. There's a B1 charge for each piece collected. Thais write their last name first, so be sure to have your last name written in capital letters and underlined.

SHIPPING PARCELS

Parcels are easy to send from Thailand. Parcel rates vary by weight, country of destination, and shipping style (air or surface). Expect to pay between B700 and B1,100 for a kilo package and then an additional B300 to B350 per added kilo.

MONEY MATTERS

It's possible to live and travel quite inexpensively if you do as Thais do—eat in small, neighborhood restaurants, use buses, and stay at non-air-conditioned hotels. Once you start enjoying a little luxury, prices jump drastically. For example, crossing Bangkok by bus is less than 15¢, but by taxi the fare may run to $10. Prices are typically higher in resort areas catering to foreign tourists, and Bangkok is more expensive than other Thai cities. Imported items are heavily taxed.

Prices throughout this guide are given for adults. Substantially reduced fees are almost always available for children, students, and senior citizens. For information on taxes, *see* Taxes, *below*.

ATMS

Twenty-four-hour automatic teller machines are widely available throughout Thailand. Some Thai ATMs take Cirrus, some take Plus, some take both.

CREDIT CARDS

Credit cards are accepted in restaurants, hotels, and shops. You may be levied a 3%

to 5% charge despite the fact that this is technically against Thai law, but you will likely receive a favorable exchange rate from your home bank that could make up the difference. Most ATMs take Visa cards and cash advances are easily obtainable through banks.

Throughout this guide, the following abbreviations are used: **AE,** American Express; **DC,** Diner's Club; **MC,** Master Card; and **V,** Visa.

🄵 Reporting Lost Cards **American Express** ☎800/441-0519. **Diners Club** ☎800/234-6377. **MasterCard** ☎800/622-7747. **Visa** ☎800/847-2911.

CURRENCY

The basic unit of currency is the baht. There are 100 satang to one baht. There are six different bills, each a different color: B10, brown; B20, green; B50, blue; B100, red; B500, purple; and B1,000, beige. Coins in use are 25 satang, 50 satang, B1, B5, and B10. The B10 coin has a gold-color center surrounded by silver.

All hotels will convert traveler's checks and major currencies into baht, though exchange rates are better at banks and authorized money changers. The rate tends to be better in Bangkok than up-country and is better in Thailand than in the United States. Major international credit cards are accepted at most tourist shops and hotels.

At this writing, B41 = US$1, B75 = £1, B33 = C$1, B31 = A$1, B28 = NZ$1.

CURRENCY EXCHANGE

For the most favorable rates, **change money through banks.** Although ATM transaction fees may be higher abroad than at home, ATM rates are excellent because they are based on wholesale rates offered only by major banks. You won't do as well at exchange booths in airports or rail and bus stations, in hotels, in restaurants, or in stores. To avoid lines at airport exchange booths, get a bit of local currency before you leave home.

🄵 Exchange Services **International Currency Express** ☎888/278-6628 for orders ⊕ www.foreignmoney.com. **Thomas Cook Currency Services** ☎800/287-7362 for telephone orders and retail locations ⊕ www.us.thomascook.com.

TRAVELER'S CHECKS

Do you need traveler's checks? It depends on where you're headed. If you're going to rural areas and small towns, go with cash; traveler's checks are best used in cities. Lost or stolen checks can usually be replaced within 24 hours. To ensure a speedy refund, buy your own traveler's checks—don't let someone else pay for them: irregularities like this can cause delays. The person who bought the checks should make the call to request a refund.

Though they are quietly slipping out of fashion, banks and most exchange counters in Thailand will still cash traveler's checks. Have your passport handy.

PACKING

Light cotton or other natural-fiber clothing is appropriate for Thailand; drip-dry is an especially good idea, because the tropical sun and high humidity encourage frequent changes of clothing. Avoid delicate fabrics because you may have difficulty getting them laundered. A sweater is welcome on cool evenings or overly in air-conditioned restaurants, buses, and trains.

The paths leading to temples can be rough, so **bring a sturdy pair of walking shoes.** Slip-ons are preferable to lace-up shoes, as they must be removed before you enter shrines and temples.

In your carry-on luggage, pack an extra pair of eyeglasses or contact lenses and enough of any medication you take to last a few days longer than the entire trip. You may also ask your doctor to write a spare prescription using the drug's generic name, since brand names may vary from country to country. In luggage to be checked, **never pack prescription drugs or valuables.** And don't forget to carry with you the addresses of offices that handle refunds of lost traveler's checks. Check *Fodor's How to Pack* (available in bookstores everywhere) for more tips.

To avoid customs and security delays, carry medications in their original packaging. Don't pack any sharp objects in your carry-on luggage, including knives of any size or material, scissors, manicure tools, and corkscrews, or anything else that might arouse suspicion.

CHECKING LUGGAGE

You are allowed one carry-on bag and one personal article, such as a purse or a laptop computer. Make sure that everything you carry aboard will fit under your seat or in the overhead bin. Get to the gate early, so you can board as soon as possible, before the overhead bins fill up.

If you are flying internationally, note that baggage allowances may be determined not by piece but by weight—generally 88 pounds (40 kilograms) in first class, 66 pounds (30 kilograms) in business class, and 44 pounds (20 kilograms) in economy.

Before departure, itemize your bags' contents and their worth, and label the bags with your name, address, and phone number. (If you use your home address, cover it so potential thieves can't see it readily.) Inside each bag, pack a copy of your itinerary. At check-in, make sure that each bag is correctly tagged with the destination airport's three-letter code. If your bags arrive damaged or fail to arrive at all, file a written report with the airline before leaving the airport.

PASSPORTS & VISAS

When traveling internationally, **carry your passport** even if you don't need one (it's always the best form of ID) and **make two photocopies of the data page** (one for someone at home and another for you, carried separately from your passport). If you lose your passport, promptly call the nearest embassy or consulate and the local police. Although it's rarely enforced, it's Thai law that you carry your passport with you at all times.

ENTERING THAILAND

Australian, Canadian, U.S., and U.K. citizens—even infants—need only a valid passport and an onward ticket to enter Thailand for stays of up to 30 days. New Zealanders are permitted to stay up to 90 days with a valid passport and onward ticket. The onward ticket is hardly ever checked.

The Immigration Division in Bangkok issues Thai visa extensions, but if you overstay by a few days, don't worry; you'll simply pay a B200 per diem fine as you go through immigration on departure.

⚡ Visa Extensions Immigration Division ⊠ Soi Suan Phlu, Sathorn Rd., Bangkok ☎ 02/287-3101.

RESTROOMS

Western-style facilities are usually available, although you still may find squat toilets in older buildings. For the uninitiated, squat toilets can be something of a puzzle. You will doubtless find a method that works best for you, but here's a general guide: squat down with feet on either side of the basin and use one hand to keep your clothes out of the way and the other for balance or, if you're really good, holding your newspaper. The Thai version of a bidet is either a hose or a big tank of water with a bowl. If you've had the foresight to bring tissues with you, throw the used paper into the basket alongside the basin. Finally, pour bowls of water into the toilet to flush it—and give yourself a pat on the back. With the exception of the plusher hotels and restaurants, plumbing in most buildings can be a little archaic, so resist the temptation to flush your paper. Self-consciousness about having a wet patch on the seat of your pants will quickly fade as you realize that every other *farang* (foreigner) has one, too.

SAFETY

Thailand is a safe country, but normal precautions should be followed: be careful late at night, watch your valuables in crowded areas, and lock your hotel rooms securely. Credit-card scams—from stealing your card to swiping it several times when you use it at stores—are a frequent problem. Don't leave your wallet behind when you go trekking and make sure you keep an eye on the card when you give it to a salesperson.

While it's never wise to become involved in a brawl, it's particularly foolish to do this in Thailand: (a) many of the locals are accomplished martial artists and/or are carrying weapons; and (b) as a foreigner you will likely be deemed at fault, even if you weren't.

LOCAL SCAMS

If a tuk-tuk driver rolls up and offers to drive you to the other side of Bangkok for

B20, think twice before accepting, because you will definitely be getting more than you bargained for. By dragging you along to his friend's gem store, tailor's shop, or handicraft showroom, he'll usually get a petrol voucher as commission. He'll tell you that all you need to do to help him put rice on his family's table is take a five-minute look around. Sometimes that's accurate, but sometimes you'll find it difficult to leave without buying something. Sometimes it can be fun to go along with it all and watch everybody play out their little roles, but other times you really just want a ride to your chosen destination.

Guesthouses also offer commission for customers brought in by drivers, so be wary of anyone telling you that the place where you booked a room has burned down overnight or is suddenly full. Smile, be courteous—they're just making a living—but be firm about where you want to go.

Agree on a taxi fair before you get in, and make sure everybody is clear that the fee is for your whole party, not per person.

Two-tier pricing—one price for Thais, another for foreigners—is quite prevalent in Thailand, and although it's up to you to determine how to deal with this, getting angry rarely achieves results.

WOMEN IN THAILAND
Foreign women in Thailand get quite a few stares, and Thai women as often as Thai men will be eager to chat and become your friend.

While there's no doubt that attitudes are changing, traditional Thai women dress and act modestly, so loud or overly confident behavior from a foreign woman can be a shock to both men and women alike.

It's also worth noting that Thai men often see foreign women as something exotic. If you're being subjected to unwelcome attention, be firm, but try to stay calm—"losing face" is big concern among Thai men and causing them undue embarrassment (even if it's deserved) can have ugly repercussions.

STUDENTS IN THAILAND
Thailand is a top destination for students. You'll run into many fellow travelers who'll clue you in to the best places to visit. Finding inexpensive dining or lodging options is easy.

IDs & Services STA Travel ☎ 212/627-3111 or 800/781-4040 🖷 212/627-3387 ⊕ www.sta.com. **Travel Cuts** ✉ 187 College St., Toronto, Ontario M5T 1P7, Canada ☎ 416/979-2406 or 888/838-2887 🖷 416/979-8167 ⊕ www.travelcuts.com.

TAXES
A 10% Value Added Tax (V.A.T.) is built into the price of all goods and services, including restaurant meals. You can reclaim this tax on some souvenirs (items must have a minimum value of B2,000) at the airport upon leaving the country. Shops that offer this refund will have a sign displayed; be sure to ask shopkeepers to fill out the necessary forms and make sure you keep your receipts. You'll have to fill out additional forms at the airport.

TELEPHONES

AREA & COUNTRY CODES
The country code for Thailand is 66. When dialing a Thailand number from abroad, drop the initial 0 from the local area code. The country code is 1 for the United States and Canada, 61 for Australia, 64 for New Zealand, and 44 for the United Kingdom.

DIRECTORY & OPERATOR ASSISTANCE
If you wish to receive assistance for an overseas call, dial 100/233-2771. For local telephone inquiries, dial 100/183, but you will need to speak Thai. In Bangkok, you can dial 13 for an English-speaking operator.

INTERNATIONAL CALLS
To make overseas calls, you should use either your hotel switchboard—Chiang Mai and Bangkok have direct dialing—or the overseas telephone facilities at the central post office and telecommunications building. You'll find one in all towns. In Bangkok, the overseas telephone center, next to the general post office, is open 24 hours; up-country, the facilities' hours may vary, but they usually open at 8 AM and some stay open until 10 PM. Some locations in Bangkok have AT&T USADi-

rect phones, which connect you with an AT&T operator.

LONG-DISTANCE CALLS

Long-distance calls can only be made on phones that accept both B1 and B5 coins. For a long-distance call in Thailand, dial the area code and then the number.

LONG-DISTANCE SERVICES

AT&T, MCI, and Sprint access codes make calling long distance relatively convenient, but you may find the local access number blocked in many hotel rooms. First ask the hotel operator to connect you. If the hotel operator balks, ask for an international operator, or dial the international operator yourself. One way to improve your odds of getting connected to your long-distance carrier is to travel with more than one company's calling card (a hotel may block Sprint, for example, but not MCI). If all else fails, call from a pay phone.

🔊 **Access Codes AT&T USADirect** ☎ 0019–991–1111, 800/222–0300 for other areas. **MCI WorldPhone** ☎ 001-999-1-2001 not from pay phones, 800/444–3333 for other areas. **Sprint International Access** ☎ 001-999-13-877, 800/877-4646 for other areas.

PUBLIC PHONES

Public telephones are available in most towns and villages and take B1 coins or both B1 and B5 pieces. Long-distance calls can be made only on phones that accept both B1 and B5 coins. For a long-distance call in Thailand, dial the area code and then the number.

TIME

Thailand is 7 hours ahead of Greenwich Mean Time. It's 12 hours ahead of New York, 15 hours ahead of Los Angeles, 7 hours ahead of London, and 3 hours behind Sydney.

TIPPING

In Thailand, tips are generally given for good service, except when a price has been negotiated in advance. A taxi driver is not tipped unless hired as a private driver for an excursion. With metered taxis in Bangkok, however, the custom is to round the fare up to the nearest B5. Hotel porters expect at least a B20 tip, and hotel staff

who have given good personal service are usually tipped. A 10% tip is appreciated at a restaurant when no service charge has been added to the bill.

TOURS & PACKAGES

Because everything is prearranged on a prepackaged tour or independent vacation, you spend less time planning—and often get it all at a good price.

BOOKING WITH AN AGENT

Travel agents are excellent resources. But it's a good idea to collect brochures from several agencies, as some agents' suggestions may be influenced by relationships with tour and package firms that reward them for volume sales. If you have a special interest, find an agent with expertise in that area; the American Society of Travel Agents (ASTA; ⇨ Travel Agencies) has a database of specialists worldwide. You can log on to the group's Web site to find an ASTA travel agent in your neighborhood.

Make sure your travel agent knows the accommodations and other services of the place being recommended. Ask about the hotel's location, room size, beds, and whether it has a pool, room service, or programs for children, if you care about these. Has your agent been there in person or sent others whom you can contact?

Do some homework on your own, too: local tourism boards can provide information about lesser-known and small-niche operators, some of which may sell only direct.

BUYER BEWARE

Each year consumers are stranded or lose their money when tour operators—even large ones with excellent reputations—go out of business. So check out the operator. Ask several travel agents about its reputation, and try to **book with a company that has a consumer-protection program.** (Look for information in the company's brochure.) In the United States, members of the United States Tour Operators Association are required to set aside funds ($1 million) to help eligible customers cover payments and travel arrangements in the event that the company defaults. It's also a good idea to choose a company that participates in the American Society of Travel Agents' Tour Operator Program; ASTA will act as mediator in any disputes between you and your tour operator.

Remember that the more your package or tour includes, the better you can predict the ultimate cost of your vacation. Make sure you know exactly what is covered, and beware of hidden costs. Are taxes, tips, and transfers included? Entertainment and excursions? These can add up.

🚺 Tour-Operator Recommendations **American Society of Travel Agents** (⇨ Travel Agencies). **National Tour Association** (NTA) ✉ 546 E. Main St., Lexington, KY 40508 ☎ 859/226-4444 or 800/682-8886 🖷 859/226-4404 ⊕ www.ntaonline.com. **United States Tour Operators Association** (USTOA) ✉ 275 Madison Ave., Suite 2014, New York, NY 10016 ☎ 212/599-6599 🖷 212/599-6744 ⊕ www.ustoa.com.

TRAIN TRAVEL

The State Railway of Thailand has four lines, all of which have terminals in Bangkok. The Northern Line connects Bangkok with Chiang Mai, passing through Ayutthaya and Phitsanulok; the Northeastern Line travels up to Nong Khai, near the Laotian border, with a branch that goes east to Ubon Ratchathani; and the Southern Line goes all the way south through Surat Thani—the stop for Ko Samui—to the Malaysian border and on to Kuala Lumpur and Singapore, a journey that takes 37 hours. The Eastern line goes to Pattaya and beyond. (There's no train to Phuket, though you can go as far as Surat Thani and change to a scheduled bus service.)

To save money, look into rail passes. But be aware that if you don't plan to cover many miles, you may come out ahead by buying individual tickets.

Many travelers assume that rail passes guarantee them seats on the trains they wish to ride. Not so. You need to book seats ahead even if you're using a rail pass; seat reservations are required on some trains and are a good idea on trains that may be crowded—particularly in summer on popular routes. You'll also need a

reservation if you purchase overnight sleeping accommodations.

Local trains are generally pretty slow and can get crowded. For information on schedules and passes, call the Bangkok Railway Station.

🚆 Train Stations **Bangkok Railway Station** ☎ 02/223-3762 or 02/223-0341.

CLASSES

Most trains offer second- or third-class tickets, but the overnight trains to the north (Chiang Mai) and to the south offer first-class sleeping cabins. Couchettes, with sheets and curtains for privacy, are available in second class. Second-class tickets are about half the price of first-class, and since the couchettes are surprisingly comfortable, most Western travelers choose these. Do not leave valuables unguarded on these overnight trains.

DISCOUNT PASSES

The State Railway of Thailand offers two types of rail passes. Both are valid for 20 days of unlimited travel on all trains in either second or third class. The **Blue Pass** costs B1,100 (children B750) and does not include supplementary charges such as air-conditioning and berths; for B3,000 (children B1,500), the **Red Pass** does. Currently, a special discounted rate, available for nonresidents of Thailand, gives a reduction of B1,000 for the Red Pass and B400 for the Blue Pass.

FARES & SCHEDULES

Train schedules in English are available from travel agents and from major railway stations.

An air-conditioned, second-class couchette, for example, for the 14-hour journey from Bangkok to Chiang Mai is B625; first class is B1,190.

PAYING

Tickets may be bought at railway stations. Travel agencies can also sell tickets for overnight trains.

RESERVATIONS

Reservations are strongly advised for all long-distance trains especially if you want a sleeper.

TRANSPORTATION AROUND THAILAND

SAMLORS

For short trips, these bicycle rickshaws are a popular, inexpensive form of transport, but they become expensive for long trips. Fares are negotiable, so **be very clear about what price is agreed upon.** Drivers have a tendency to create misunderstandings leading to a nasty scene at the end of the trip.

SONGTHAEWS

With a name that literally means "two rows, " these pickup trucks have a couple of wooden benches in the back. They operate on routes outside of Bangkok. Drivers generally wait until they are at least half full before departing. If you jump in a songthaew that already has people in it, a short trip usually costs between B10 and B20. However, they will be dropping off other customers before getting to you, so, if you're in a hurry, ask if they can take you solo.

TAXIS

Most Bangkok taxis now have meters installed, and these are the ones tourists should take. In other cities, fares are still negotiated. Taxis waiting at hotels are more expensive than those flagged down on the street. **Never enter an unmetered taxi until the price has been established.** Most taxi drivers do not speak English, but all understand the finger count. One finger means B10, two is for B20 and so on. Ask at your hotel what the appropriate fare should be.

TUK-TUKS

So-called because of their spluttering sound, these three-wheel cabs are slightly less expensive than taxis and, because of their maneuverability, sometimes a more rapid form of travel through congested traffic. All tuk-tuk operators drive as if your ride will be their last. Tuk-tuks are not very comfortable, and they subject you to the polluted air, so they're best used for short journeys.

TRAVEL AGENCIES

A good travel agent puts your needs first. Look for an agency that has been in business at least five years, emphasizes customer service, and has someone on staff who specializes in your destination. In addition, **make sure the agency belongs to a professional trade organization.** The American Society of Travel Agents (ASTA)—the largest and most influential in the field with more than 20,000 members in some 140 countries—maintains and enforces a strict code of ethics and will step in to help mediate any agent-client disputes involving ASTA members if necessary. ASTA (whose motto is "Without a travel agent, you're on your own") also maintains a Web site that includes a directory of agents. (If a travel agency is also acting as your tour operator, *see* Buyer Beware *in* Tours & Packages.)

◪ Local Agent Referrals **American Society of Travel Agents (ASTA)** ⊠ 1101 King St., Suite 200, Alexandria, VA 22314 ☎ 703/739-2782, 800/965-2782 24-hr hotline 🖷 703/684-8319 ⊕ www.astanet.com. **Association of British Travel Agents** ⊠ 68-71 Newman St., London W1T 3AH ☎ 020/7637-2444 🖷 020/7637-0713 ⊕ www.abta.com. **Association of Canadian Travel Agencies** ⊠ 130 Albert St., Suite 1705, Ottawa, Ontario K1P 5G4 ☎ 613/237-3657 🖷 613/237-7052 ⊕ www.acta.ca. **Australian Federation of Travel Agents** ⊠ Level 3, 309 Pitt St., Sydney, NSW 2000 ☎ 02/9264-3299 or 1300/363-416 🖷 02/9264-1085 ⊕ www.afta.com.au. **Travel Agents' Association of New Zealand** ⊠ Level 5, Tourism and Travel House, 79 Boulcott St., Box 1888, Wellington 6001 ☎ 04/499-0104 🖷 04/499-0786 ⊕ www.taanz.org.nz.

VISITOR INFORMATION

◪ Tourist Information **Tourism Authority of Thailand** ⊠ C/o World Publications, 304 Park Ave. S, 8th fl., New York, NY 10010 U.S. ☎ 212/219-7447 🖷 212/219-4697 ⊠ 611 N. Larchmont Blvd., 1st fl., Los Angeles, CA 90004 U.S. ☎ 213/461-9814 🖷 213/461-9834. ◪ In the U.K. **Thailand Tourist Board** ⊠ 49 Albemarle St., London W1X 3FE ☎ 0207/499-7679. ◪ In Australia & New Zealand **Tourism Authority of Thailand** ⊠ 75 Pitt St., Sydney 20000, NSW ☎ 02/9247-75719. ◪ U.S. Government Advisories **U.S. Department of State** ⊠ Overseas Citizens Services Office, Room 4811 N.S., 2201 C St. NW, Washington, DC 20520 ☎ 202/647-5225 interactive hotline, 301/946-4400 computer bulletin board 🖷 202/647-3000 interactive hotline.

WEB SITES

Do check out the World Wide Web when planning your trip. You'll find everything from weather forecasts to virtual tours of famous cities. Be sure to **visit Fodors.com** ⊕ www.fodors.com, a complete travel-planning site. You can research prices and book plane tickets, hotel rooms, rental cars, vacation packages, and more. In addition, you can post your pressing questions in the Travel Talk section. Other planning tools include a currency converter and weather reports, and there are loads of links to travel resources.

Other sites worth checking out are: www.tat.or.th, www.amazingsiam.com, www.thailand-travelsearch.com, and www.nectec.or.th for more information on Thailand.

BANGKOK

1

MOST REWARDING MORNING RITUAL
Climbing up Wat Arun, the Temple of Dawn,
to watch the sun rise ⇨*p.15*

BEST PLACE TO SPOT SOME STARS
At the rooftop hotspot Moonbar ⇨*p.60*

BEST ALTERNATIVE TO THAI ICED TEA
Lemongrass restaurant's sweet *nam takrai*,
brewed from . . . lemongrass ⇨*p.41*

BEST ONE-STOP SHOPPING
Any of Sukhumvit's swanky malls ⇨*p.72*

STILL SETTING THE STANDARDS
The legendary Oriental Hotel ⇨*p.51*

Updated by
Mick Elmore,
Wendy Kassel,
and Molly
Petersen

THERE ARE TWO BANGKOKS, the ancient soul of Thailand with its long and fascinating history and the frantic modern metropolis that embraces the latest trends both Eastern and Western. The two blend together remarkably well—even the most jarring juxtapositions of old and new will start to make sense after a few days, and shrines in front of car dealerships or monks on all manner of public transportation will be sights soon taken for granted.

Bangkok is not only the biggest city in Thailand, but also the most mesmerizing, with some of the country's most beautiful temples and shrines. Sunset at Wat Arun on the river is downright humbling, and even people with no interest in history will be impressed with the Grand Palace. The city's energy is palpable, especially at night, when traffic opens up a bit, its famous markets get going, and everything seems lit up from its proudest monuments to its seediest streets.

While tourism is huge in Bangkok, the city's identity and its economy is not as dependent on it as some other places in the region. This can be a good thing for visitors because they get to experience a real city—with all its problems and advantages—not a theme park. The Grand Palace may be a world-class attraction, but it's not there for tourism; it's Bangkok's most revered and often-visited site, and Thais enter for free.

That's not to say Bangkok is perfect. There's much to criticize about this city of 12 million people (nearly one-fifth of Thailand's total population). It's hot and humid and the pollution is so bad, traffic cops often wear gas masks to protect themselves from the fumes. But other problems are improving, the canals *(klongs)* are slowly being cleaned, the number of trees has dramatically increased and more green areas have been set aside.

The biggest improvements to the city have been the Skytrain, which opened in 1999, and the subway, which opened in 2004. Coupled with the river express boats, moving around most parts of Bangkok has become relatively easy. While traffic continues to be nightmarish, the Skytrain breezes people along, high above that gridlock. The Skytrain and subway also help organize the city, which, with its multiple city centers, can be rather confusing.

Perhaps a bigger critical issue is that a disproportionate amount of Thailand's wealth is in Bangkok. It's the financial, business, and entertainment capital of the country, as well as its government center. It's like Washington D.C., New York, and Los Angeles wrapped into one. In many respects is has grown apart from the rest of the country. The national government often acts like a city administration dealing with city development issues while the country at large can appear neglected. The city's wealth speaks, and the city residents demand attention. As much of the country keeps its traditions, Bangkok seems more brash in abandoning them. Some social critics say in Thailand people revere the Buddha, but in Bangkok they worship the Baht.

Thais call their capital Krung Thep, which means "City of Angels." The full name actually means a bit more than that and has 280 letters or so, depending on the translation. The city went through several name

If the jet lag and heat don't slow you down too much, you can cover a good number of Bangkok's attractions in three days. In another two days you can see more of the city or take short trips outside it. Between the Skytrain, subway, and express boats on the Chao Phraya River, you should be able to get most places with relative ease. Planning around Bangkok's traffic is a must, so look for sights near public transportation or close enough to one another to visit on the same day.

Numbers in the text correspond to numbers in the margin and on the Old City, Thonburi & Banglamphu, Dusit, Chinatown, and Downtown Bangkok maps.

1

If you have 2 days

Start your first day with the most famous of all Bangkok sights, the **Grand Palace ❶**. In the same complex is the gorgeously ornate **Wat Phra Keo ❷**. Not far south of the Grand Palace is Bangkok's oldest and largest temple, **Wat Po ❸**, famous for its enormous Reclining Buddha and for being the home of the development of traditional Thai massage. Later head toward Banglamphu to take the river walk from Pinklao Bridge to Santichaiprakarn Park. That will put you on Phra Athit Road, where you can find many good restaurants and bars. If you feel up for more after that take a tuk-tuk the short distance to Khao San Road for some shopping and more strolling. Another option is to go from Wat Po to the **National Museum ❻**, and then head to Phra Athit for dinner.

The next day take a taxi to **Wat Benjamabophit ❿**, which contains Bangkok's much-photographed Marble Temple. From there take a taxi to **Wat Traimit ⓮** so you can pay respects to its perfectly harmonious and glittering image of the Buddha. Your next stop should be Chinatown. Work your way to the Chao Phraya River and catch an express boat to the Saphan Taksin Skytrain stop. If it's a weekend head to **Kukrit Pramoj Heritage House ⓱**; if it's a weekday, visit **Jim Thompson's House ⓴**. Take the Skytrain in the evening to Sukhumvit Road, where there are many good restaurants.

If you have 3–4 days

Start your first day at the **Grand Palace ❶**. Visit the Emerald Buddha at **Wat Phra Keo ❷**, then walk to **Wat Po ❸** to see the Reclining Buddha. Cross the river to **Wat Arun ❹**, the beautiful Temple of Dawn, and climb the large spire for views of the entire city. Take an express boat upstream to the **Royal Barge Museum ❺**; the barges displayed are used on ceremonial occasions. Return to the Bangkok side, and if there's time remaining spend the rest of the afternoon browsing around the **National Museum ❻**, or stroll the river walk from Pinklao Bridge to Santichaiprakarn Park. From there you can walk down to Phra Athit to one of its many restaurants.

Start Day 2 at **Wat Benjamabophit ❿**. South of the Marble Temple is the golden dome of **Wat Saket ❾**, and the metal temple of **Wat Rachanatdaram ❽**. Now head to Chinatown for a little shopping before finding harmony at **Wat Traimit ⓮**. From there it's a short walk to the Hua Lamphong subway station, were you can go two stops to Silom station. Walk down Silom Road for great restaurants and night markets. Patpong Road also has a fun night market.

On Day 3 buy a one-day Skytrain pass and start at **Jim Thompson's House** ㉟, then go to **Suan Pakkard Palace** ㉑. Get back on the Skytrain and go to the river for a klong tour in Thonburi, which your hotel can arrange. Head back to the Skytrain and go to Sukhumvit Road for dinner. A fourth day could easily be filled with shopping if you've seen enough sights. If it's the weekend, be sure to explore the madness of Chatuchak market. Another must-see weekend sight is **Kukrit Pramoj Heritage House** ⑰; you could start there and take the Skytrain to Chatuchak afterwards.

---

changes until 1972 when a new government administration named it the first two words of the original name, Krungthep Mahanakhon. King Rama I named the original city after founding the capital in 1782. Rama I also founded the Royal House of Chakri, under which the present monarch, King Bhumibol Adulyadej, is the ninth king. Rama I moved the capital across the Chao Phraya River from Thonburi because he felt "the village of the wild plum trees, " as he called Bangkok, would be easier to defend against possible Burmese attacks from here. Rama I set out to build a city as beautiful as the old capital of Ayutthaya was before it was sacked by the Burmese in 1767.

Though some may contend that Bangkok's beauty has faded in the face of so much concrete, there certainly is no shortage of things to marvel at—from the requisite temples to fierce Thai boxing matches to the labyrinthine streets of the older neighborhoods to the sudden shift of congested streets into a flower market. You may not fall in love with Bangkok, but you'll never forget it.

EXPLORING BANGKOK

Bangkok's endless maze of streets is part of its fascination, but the downside is that finding your way around the city is a challenge. The S curve of the Chao Phraya River can throw you off base at first, but it's actually a good landmark; most of the popular sights are close to the river and you can use it to get quickly from one place to another. There's no faster way to get from Thonburi to Chinatown, for example, than by boat.

The Old City is the most popular destination for travelers, as it's home to opulent temples like Wat Po and Wat Phra Keo. Across the river is Thonburi, a mostly residential neighborhood, where you can find Wat Arun. At the northern tip of the Old City is Banglamphu, one of Bangkok's older residential neighborhoods. It's mostly known now for Khao San Road, a world-renowned backpacker street, though the neighborhood has much more to offer, like artsy Phra Athit Road and walks along the Chao Phraya River. North of Banglamphu is Dusit, the royal district since the days of Rama V. Dusit Park, one of the city's most appealing green spaces, is a highlight of this neighborhood, where wide avenues are lined by elegant buildings.

East of the Old City is Chinatown, a labyrinth of streets with restaurants, shops, and warehouses. Head east along Rama IV Road and you reach the parallel commercial streets of Silom and Surawong roads. Between them lies Patpong, the city's most notorious of several red-light districts. Continue farther south and you reach the riverbank and some of the city's leading hotels: the Oriental, the Peninsula, the Royal Orchid Sheraton, and the Shangri-La.

To the north of Rama IV Road is Bangkok's largest green area, Lumphini Park, a patch of green in the midst of endless blocks of concrete buildings. Continue north and you reach Sukhumvit Road, once a residential area. Since the '80s it has developed into a bustling district filled with restaurants, hotels, and shops.

Knowing your exact destination, its direction, and its approximate distance are all important in planning your day and negotiating *tuk-tuk* (three-wheeled taxi) fares. Note, however, that many sights have no precise written address and the spelling of road names changes from map to map and even block to block, thus Ratchadamri is often spelled *Rajdamri,* Ratchadamnoen is sometimes seen as *Rajdamnern,* Charoen Krung can be *Charoenkrung* or even *New Road.*

Crossing and recrossing the city is time-consuming, and you can lose many hours stuck in traffic jams. Remember that Bangkok is enormous, and distances are great; it can take a half hour or more to walk between two seemingly adjacent sights. Relying on the Skytrain and subway will make a huge difference, and knowing their routes will help you understand the city's layout.

Timing
November to March is the best time to see Bangkok. The city is at its coolest—a mere 85°—and driest. In April the humidity and heat build up to create a sticky stew until the rains begin in late May.

The Old City, Thonburi & Banglamphu

The Old City, which also includes Banglamphu on the north and Thonburi across the Chao Phraya River on the west, is the historical heart of Bangkok, where you can find most of the ancient buildings and the major tourist attractions. Because of the city's decision to preserve this historic area, it's the biggest part of Bangkok to escape constant transformation. Plans to clean the klongs that mark the eastern border of the Old City have made little progress, and much of the residential sections look rundown, but the whole area is safe and it's one of the best in the city for a stroll.

The Grand Palace and other major sights are within a short distance of the river and close to where express boats, which are like buses on the river, stop. The Skytrain ends at a boat stop as well, making the Chao Phraya convenient no matter where you're staying.

Of course, the magnificence of the sights, and the ease in reaching them, make them rather crowded. During rain storms are about the only time you find few people at the sights. The palace and the temples are busy every day, but you might have better luck earlier in the morning, when it's also cooler, and before some of the tour buses arrive. But whenever you go, be prepared for crowds. You might get lucky, but there are usually many other people arriving at the same time as you, hoping for the same kind of luck. The other downside to the surge of tourism in this area is the presence of phony tour guides, who will most likely approach you by offering tips about undiscovered or off-the-beaten-path places. Some will even tell you that the place you're going to is closed, and that you should join them for a tour instead. Often their "tours" (offered at too-good-to-be true prices) include a "short" visit to a gem shop for a bit of arm-twisting. The situation got bad enough in the mid-1990s that the government stepped in and distributed fliers to passengers on inbound flights warning of these gem scams.

Thonburi is largely residential, including areas where people still live on the klongs, which are worth a day trip if you have the time. Most of Thonburi beyond the river bank is of little interest to visitors. Many locals claim it retains more "Thainess" than Bangkok, but you have to live there, or visit for a long time, to appreciate that.

Banglamphu in the north part of Old City offers pleasant walks, markets, and the famous Khao San Road, one of the world's best known backpacker hubs. The block-long Khao San has become a truly international street with visitors from dozens of countries populating the scene year-round. During the high season up to 10,000 people a day call the Khao San Road area home, for better or for worse. There's a more serene river walk by the Pinklao Bridge and a few other sights; the rest of Banglamphu is mostly residential.

a good tour

Start at the **Grand Palace** ❶ ➤, Bangkok's most enduring landmark, then head to the adjoining **Wat Phra Keo** ❷ to see the Emerald Buddha. You can easily spend half a day here studying the detailed temples and grandeur of the place. But when you're finished, head south on Sanam-chai Road (take a taxi if the heat gets to you) to **Wat Po** ❸ for a glimpse of the enormous Reclining Buddha. From Wat Po, head west to the river and then north (toward the Grand Palace) about 250 yards to the Tha Thien jetty and take the ferry across the river to **Wat Arun** ❹. For a breathtaking view of the city, climb the steep staircase to the top. These four stops can easily take a day, especially if you take your time exploring each one.

If you're still on your feet, the **Royal Barge Museum** ❺ is also on the Thonburi side and can be easily reached by boat.

The next day start with the **National Museum** ❻, down the street from the Grand Palace. You can spend hours exploring this museum, and if you have more time the **National Gallery** ❼ is nearby. Then take a tuk-tuk to **Wat Rachanatdaram** ❽. Afterwards, walk east across Maha Chai Road to the towering **Wat Saket** ❾, one of the city's best-known landmarks. If you can handle the steep climb up Wat Saket, you'll be rewarded with a splendid view of the city and a temple to explore. In between the two wats on Ratchdamnoen Road is Mahakan Fortress, which is one of only two remaining watchtowers built to protect the city in the 1700s. The city government has tried to move residents out from behind the fortress walls and make a park there. If that happens,

Roaming the Waterways

Krung Thep used to be known as the Venice of the East, but many of the *klongs* (canals) that once distinguished this area have been paved over. Several klongs remain, though, and traveling along these waterways is one of the delights of Bangkok. They have been cleaned up in the last decade, and the water is no longer so black and smelly, especially on the Thonburi side. In the longtail boats and ferries that ply the Chao Phraya River, not only do you beat the stalled traffic, but you get to see houses on stilts, women washing clothing, and kids jumping in with a splash. A popular trip to the Royal Barge Museum, and the Khoo Wiang Floating Market, starts at the Chang Pier on the Chao Phraya River and travels along Klong Bangkok Noi and Klong Bangkok Yai.

A fun introduction to the river—and Bangkok for that matter—can be bought with a Chao Phraya Tourist Boat day pass. They are a bargain at B70 and good for the whole day. One advantage of the tourist boat is while traveling from place to place there's a running commentary in English about the historical sights along the river and how to visit them. Included with the tour is a map of the river with its piers marked, along with the Skytrain route. A small booklet of river-area tourist sights attached to the map is also very helpful. The tourist boat starts at the pier under Saphan Taksin Skytrain station, but you can pick it up at any of the piers where it stops, and you can get on and off as many times and places as you want.

Shopping

In the past, Hong Kong and Singapore were Asia's main shopping destinations, but now you would do well to hold off until you reach Bangkok, which is less expensive and offers much more in the way of traditional crafts and high-end brand names. Bangkok has ample malls to get lost in, and many more chaotic markets worth a look. Street vendors make a market out of much of Silom Road and Patpong in the evening; Khao San Road in Banglamphu closes off traffic and turns into a collection of vendor stalls. Shopping for gems and jewelry can also be a bargain, but stick with reputable dealers and not guys who "accidentally" meet you on the street.

There are endless shopping opportunities in Bangkok, but the one not to miss is the Chatuchak weekend market. The Skytrain stops nearby (Mor Chit station) and the subway stops right inside (Kamphaeng Phet station). You can get lost walking around this packed and extensive collection of open-air buildings. It's a hot and crowded experience, but little cafés and restaurants are plentiful for breaks. If you're looking for Thai crafts, Chatuchak is a must—the selection is big and the prices are good.

Temple-Gazing

Bangkok is, without doubt, the chief repository of the nation's most amazing art and artifacts. The wonderful *wats* (temples) contain some of the country's most beautiful buildings and images of Lord Buddha. At Wat Po you can find the golden statue of the Reclining Buddha, and at Wat Phra Keo is the much revered Emerald Buddha. The palaces, with traditional peaked roofs of green, orange, and red, call to mind the region's architectural history. The National Museum houses a fascinating collection of Southeast Asian masterpieces. The most venerable pieces are more than 5,000 years old. Then there are the little wats tucked away here and there that don't make it into guidebooks and are fun to discover.

Massage It All Away Massage has been part of Bangkok for centuries. The current techniques were developed at Wat Po, and traditional massage is also referred to as Wat Po–style massage. There are many options, from an hour-long foot massage to a 30-minute face treatment, but the traditional Thai massage is the best. Treat yourself to a two-hour massage to get the full benefit—they start on your feet and work up your legs to your back, and finish by massaging your head. The better hotels have in-house massage, or they can arrange them for you. Another option is trying one of the growing number of spa treatments in Bangkok—a blend of traditional Thai massage with spa water treatments that could be your best time spent in Bangkok. It's a good idea to have a hotel book a massage for you in order to avoid massage parlors that are fronts for illegal sex shops.

---

the park and remaining walls of the fortress could become a new attraction for visitors and residents alike, but for now there's not much more to do than gaze at the walls. Farther down Ratchdamnoen Road, toward the river, are Democracy Monument and the October 14 Monument, which is on the south side of the road that goes around the Democracy Monument.

Timing

It would be difficult to take in all those sights in one day, so break it up into at least two days, or decide which sights interest you most and plan your own route. It's best to begin early in the morning, take a break to escape the midday heat, and end late in the afternoon. You will want to spend a few hours wandering around the Grand Palace and Wat Phra Keo. Wat Po won't take as long unless you opt for a traditional massage. Allow at least two hours at the National Museum and an hour at the National Gallery. Both are closed on Monday, Tuesday, and public holidays.

What to See

OLD CITY   **Democracy Monument and October 14 Monument.** Democracy Monument is one of Bangkok's biggest and best-known landmarks. It was built after the military overthrew the absolute monarchy in 1932 and Thailand became a constitutional monarchy. Just to the south of the road that circles the Democracy Monument is the October 14 Monument, honoring the Thais killed during the student-led uprising against the military government that started on October 14, 1973, and left dozens dead. Tributes to those killed in October 1976 and May 1992, in other protests against military rule, are also part of the monument. Although mostly written in Thai, it's a sobering sight, especially so close to the Democracy Monument. Often there are painting exhibitions on display concerning the three uprisings. ☒ *Ratchdamnoen Rd., at Thanon Din So.*

★ ▶ ❶ **Grand Palace.** This is Thailand's most revered spot and one of its most visited. King Rama I built this walled city in 1782, when he moved the capital across the river from Thonburi. The palace and adjoining structures only got more opulent as subsequent monarchs added their own touches. The grounds are open to visitors, but none of the buildings are—they're used only for state occasions and royal ceremonies. On rare occasions, rooms in the Chakri Maha Prasat palace—considered the official residence of the king, even though he actually lives at Chitlada Palace in north Bangkok—are sometimes open to visitors. The Dusit Maha Prasat is a classic example of palace architecture, and Amarin Vinichai Hall, the original audience hall, is now used for the presentation of ambassadors' credentials. If the door to the hall is open, you might glimpse the glittering gold throne inside. Just east of the Grand Palace compound is the **City Pillar Shrine,** containing the foundation stone (Lak Muang) from which all distances in Thailand are measured. The stone is believed to be inhabited by a spirit that guards the well-being of Bangkok. Proper attire (no flip-flops, no shorts, shoulders and midriffs must be covered) is required, but if you forget they loan unflattering but more demure shirts and shoes at the entrance. ⊠ *Sana Chai Rd., Old City* ☎ *02/224–1833* 🖃 *B200, includes admission to Wat Phra Keo* ⊙ *Daily 8:30–3:30.*

---

need a break? | Taking in all the sights can be exhausting, especially on a hot-and-muggy Bangkok day. Fortunately two parks by the Grand Palace provide some respite from the heat. **Sanam Luang** is north of the palace and Wat Phra Keo and is a good spot for a rest. Trees offer shade around the border of the large field and benches offer a place to sit with a cold drink and a snack from one of the vendors. You can also buy bread if you want to feed the numerous pigeons. **Suan Saranrom,** across from the southeast corner of the palace, is smaller but just as pleasant. It's surrounded by well-kept old government buildings. In the late afternoon you can join the free community aerobics sessions. Thais really took to aerobics—including a world record-breaking biggest group session in 2003—and the popularity has continued.

❼ **National Gallery.** Though it doesn't get nearly as much attention as the National Museum, the gallery's permanent collection (modern and traditional Thai art) is worth taking the time to see; there are also frequent temporary shows from around the country and abroad. The easiest way to find out what's showing is to ask your hotel's concierge to call as you're not likely to get an English-speaker on the phone. To get to the gallery, walk down Na Phra That Road, past the National Theater and toward the river. Go under the bridge, then turn right and walk about 100 yards; it's on your left. The building used to house the royal mint. ⊠ *Chao Fa Rd., Old City* ☎ *02/281–2224* 🖃 *B30* ⊙ *Wed.–Sun. 9–4.*

★ ❻ **National Museum.** There's no better place to acquaint yourself with Thai history than the National Museum, which also holds one of the world's best collections of Southeast Asian art. Most of the masterpieces from the northern provinces have been transported here, leaving up-country museums looking a little bare. You have a good opportunity to trace

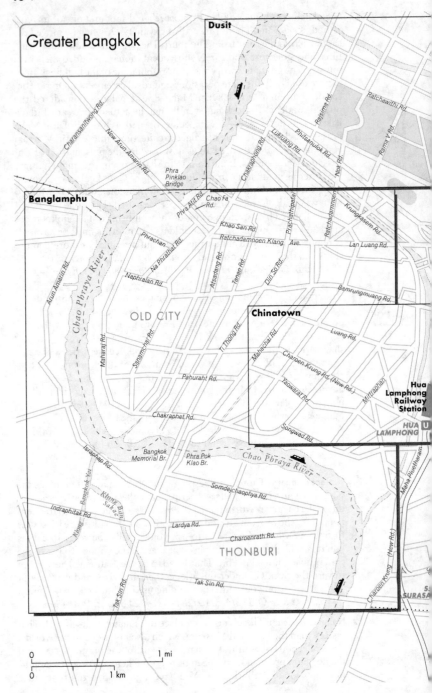

Greater Bangkok

Dusit

Rangsima Rd.
Ratchawithi Rd.
Rama V Rd.
Chakraphong Rd.
Lukluang Rd.
Phitsanulok Rd.
Nok Rd.

Phra Pinklao Bridge

Banglamphu

Chao Fa Rd.
Phra Atit Rd.
Khao San Rd.
Ratchadamnoen Klang Ave.
Prachathipatai
Ratchadamnoen
Krungkasem Rd.
Lan Luang Rd.

Phrachan
Na Phrathat Rd.
Atsadang Rd.
Tanao Rd.
Din So Rd.

Chao Phraya River

Naphralan Rd.

Bamrungmuang Rd.

Arun Amarin Rd.

OLD CITY

Maharaj Rd.
Sanamchai Rd.
Ti Thong Rd.

Chinatown

Luang Rd.
Mahachai Rd.
Charoen Krung Rd. (New Rd.)
Mitraphan

Pahurat Rd.

Yaowarat Rd.

Hua Lamphong Railway Station

Chakraphet Rd.

Songwad Rd.

HUA LAMPHONG

Isaraphap Rd.

Bangkok Memorial Br.
Phra Pok Klao Br.

Chao Phraya River

Somdejchaophya Rd.

Khlong Bang Sakae

Bangkok Yai

Indraphitak Rd.

Lardya Rd.

Charoenrath Rd.

THONBURI

Tak Sin Rd.

Tak Sin Rd.

Charoen Krung (New Rd.)

Maha Phuetharam

S. SURASA

0   1 mi
0   1 km

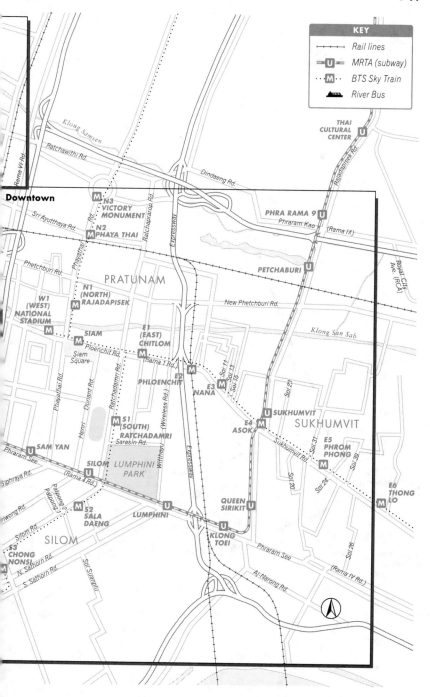

Skytrain &
Subway Stops

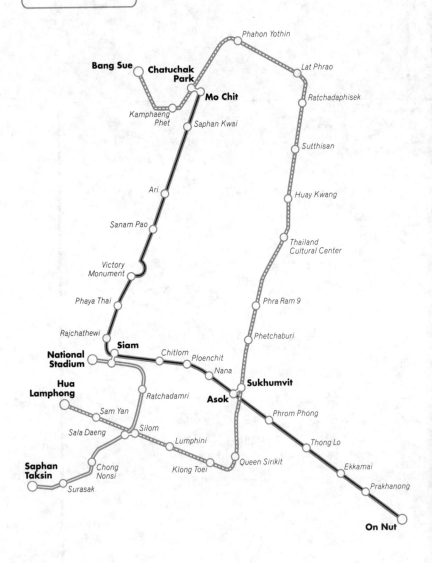

Bang Sue

Chatuchak
Park

Mo Chit

Phahon Yothin

Lat Phrao

Ratchadaphisek

Kamphaeng
Phet

Saphan Kwai

Sutthisan

Ari

Huay Kwang

Sanam Pao

Thailand
Cultural Center

Victory
Monument

Phaya Thai

Phra Ram 9

Rajchathewi

Phetchaburi

Siam

Chitlom

Ploenchit

National
Stadium

Nana

Sukhumvit

Hua
Lamphong

Ratchadamri

Asok

Sam Yan

Phrom Phong

Sala Daeng

Silom

Thong Lo

Saphan
Taksin

Lumphini

Chong
Nonsi

Klong Toei

Queen Sirikit

Ekkamai

Surasak

Prakhanong

On Nut

Thailand's long history, beginning with the ceramic utensils and bronze ware of the Ban Chiang people (3000–4000 BC). Head to the artifact gallery at the left of the ticket counter for a historical overview. Afterward explore the galleries that portray the Dvaravati and Khmer periods. This will prepare you for the different styles of Thai art, from the Sukhothai period (13th–14th centuries) to the Ayutthaya period (14th–18th centuries). There are free guided tours in English on Wednesday and Thursday; they're usually given at 9:30 AM, though sometimes the time changes. ⊠ *Na Phra That Rd., Old City* ☎ *02/224–1333* ⊕ *www.thailandmuseum.net* ✑ *B50* ⊙ *Wed.–Sun. 9:30–4.*

② **Wat Phra Keo** (Temple of the Emerald Buddha). No single structure within the Grand Palace elicits such awe as this, the most sacred temple in the kingdom. You may prefer the simplicity of some other wats, but you'll never quite get over Wat Phra Keo's opulence—no other wat in Thailand is so ornate or so embellished with glittering gold. As you enter the compound, take note of the 20-foot-tall statues of fearsome creatures in traditional battle attire standing guard. They set the scene—mystical, majestic, and awesome. Turn right as you enter the compound, because on the inner walls are lively murals depicting the whole epic tale of the Ramakien.

*Fodor's*Choice ★

Several *aponsis* (mythical half-woman, half-lion creatures) stand guard outside the main chapel, which has a gilded three-tier roof. Inside sits the Emerald Buddha. This most venerated image of Lord Buddha is carved from one piece of jade 31 inches high. No one knows its origin, but history places it in Chiang Rai in 1464. From there it traveled first to Chiang Mai, then to Lamphun, and finally back to Chiang Rai, where the Laotians stole it and took it home with them. The Thais sent an army to get it back; it reached its final resting place when King Rama I built this temple. The statue is high above the altar, so you can see it only from afar. Behind the altar and above the window frames are murals depicting the life and eventual enlightenment of the Buddha. At the back of the royal chapel you can find a scale model of Cambodia's Angkor Wat. ⊠ *Sana Chai Rd., Old City* ☎ *02/224–1833* ✑ *B200, includes admission to Grand Palace* ⊙ *Daily 8:30–3:30.*

★ **③** **Wat Po** (Temple of the Reclining Buddha). The city's largest wat has what is perhaps the most unusual representation of the Buddha in Bangkok. The 150-foot sculpture, covered with gold, is so large it fills an entire viharn. Especially noteworthy are the mammoth statue's 10-foot feet, with the 108 auspicious signs of the Buddha inlaid in mother-of-pearl. Many people ring the bells surrounding the image for good luck.

Behind the viharn holding the Reclining Buddha is Bangkok's oldest open university. A century before Bangkok was established as the capital, a monastery was founded here to teach traditional medicine. Around the walls are marble plaques inscribed with formulas for herbal cures, and stone sculptures squat in various postures demonstrating techniques for relieving pain. The monks still practice ancient cures, and the **massage school** is now famous. A massage lasts one hour and costs less than B200 (you should also tip B100), and grows increasingly enjoyable as you adjust to its somewhat rigorous style. Appointments aren't necessary—you

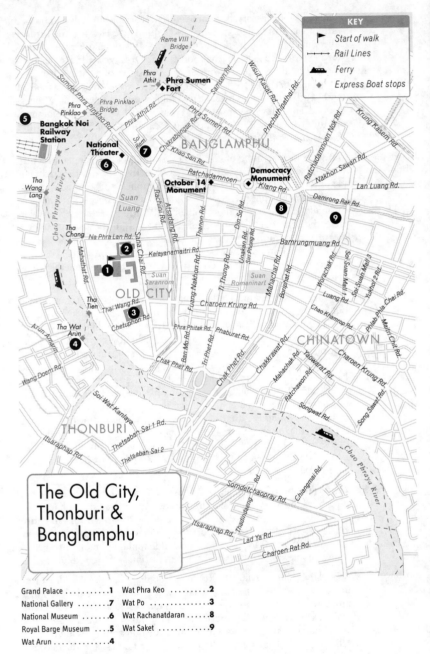

KEY

🏴 Start of walk
├┼┼┼ Rail Lines
⛴ Ferry
◆ Express Boat stops

The Old City, Thonburi & Banglamphu

usually won't have to wait long if you just show up. Massage courses of up to 10 days are also available.

At the northeastern quarter of the compound there's a pleasant three-tier temple containing 394 seated Buddhas. Usually a monk sits cross-legged at one side of the altar, making himself available to answer questions (in Thai, of course). On the walls, bas-relief plaques salvaged from Ayutthaya depict stories from the *Ramakien,* a traditional tale of the human incarnation of Vishnu. Around the temple area are four tall chedis decorated with brightly colored porcelain. Each chedi represents one of the first four kings of the Chakri Dynasty. Don't be perturbed by the statues that guard the compound's entrance and poke good-natured fun at *farangs* (foreigners). These towering figures, some of whom wear farcical top hats, are supposed to scare away evil spirits—they were modeled after the Europeans who plundered China during the Opium Wars. ⊠ *Chetuphon Rd., Old City* ⌸ *B20* ⊙ *Daily 8–5.*

❽ Wat Rachanatdaram (Temple of the Metal Castle). This wat was built to resemble a mythical castle of the gods. According to legend, a wealthy and pious man built a fabulous castle, Loha Prasat, from the design laid down in Hindu mythology for the disciples of the Buddha. Wat Rachanatdaram, meant to duplicate that castle, is the only one of its kind remaining. Outside there are stalls selling amulets that protect you from harm or increase your chances of finding love. These souvenirs tend to be expensive, but that's the price of good fortune. ⊠ *Mahachai Rd., near Ratchadamnoen Rd., Old City* ⌸ *Free* ⊙ *Daily 8–5.*

❾ Wat Saket. A well-known landmark, the towering gold chedi of Wat Saket, which is also known as the Golden Mount, was once the highest point in the city. King Rama III began construction of this temple, but it wasn't completed until the reign of Rama V. To reach the gilded chedi you must ascend an exhausting 318 steps, so don't attempt the climb on a hot afternoon. On a clear day the view from the top is magnificent. Every November, at the time of the Loi Krathong festival, the temple hosts a popular fair with food stalls and performances. ⊠ *Chakkaphatdi Phong Rd., Old City* ⌸ *B10* ⊙ *Daily 8–5.*

THONBURI **★ ❺ Royal Barge Museum.** These splendid ceremonial barges are berthed on the Thonburi side of the Chao Phraya River. The boats, carved in the early part of the 19th century, take the form of mythical creatures in the Ramakien. The most impressive is the red-and-gold royal vessel called *Suphannahongse* (Golden Swan), used by the king on special occasions. Carved from a single piece of teak, it measures about 150 feet and weighs more than 15 tons. Fifty oarsmen propel it along the river, accompanied by two coxswains, flag wavers, and a rhythm-keeper. ⊠ *Khlong Bangkok Noi, Thonburi* ☎ *02/424–0004* ⌸ *B30* ⊙ *Daily 9–5.*

Fodor'sChoice **★ ❹ Wat Arun** (Temple of Dawn). If this riverside spot is inspiring at sunrise, it's even more marvelous toward dusk when the setting sun throws amber tones over the entire area. The temple's design is symmetrical, with a square courtyard containing five Khmer-style prangs. The central prang, which reaches 282 feet, is surrounded by four attendant prangs at each of the corners. All five are covered in mosaics made from broken pieces

CloseUp

THE MONARCHY

THAILAND BECAME A CONSTITUTIONAL MONARCHY after a bloodless coup in 1932. The current king, His Majesty King Bhumibol Adulyadej, ascended to the throne 14 years later, following the death of his elder brother King Ananda Mahidol (Rama VIII). He is the world's longest reigning sovereign.

Thais display great devotion to their king, both in public and private. Any criticism of the monarchy will cause deep offense, and possibly worse, as it is forbidden by the law of lese majesty to speak ill of royalty, with a maximum penalty of seven years imprisonment (though deportation is a more likely sentence for foreigners).

Many families have photos of kings, past and present, displayed in their homes, and thousands of people gather in Sanam Luang park each December for the king's birthday celebrations. The king's birthday speech is eagerly anticipated—in recent years his criticism of government excesses has been especially pointed.

Official symbols of the monarchy's importance are seen in its representation by the blue bar on the Thai flag and photographs of royal figures in government buildings and public spaces. The national anthem is played daily throughout Thailand at 8 AM and 6 PM, broadcast by radio and TV stations and piped into railway and bus stations. People stand respectfully for the duration.

King Bhumibol is the ninth monarch of the Chakri dynasty, which has ruled Thailand since 1782. Two of his most illustrious ancestors, King Rama IV and his son King Rama V, are also particularly revered, and widely portrayed in photographs. They were largely responsible for the modernization of Thailand in the late 19th and early 20th centuries. Rama V's reforms included the first public hospitals, rail systems, and the abolishment of slavery. Both engaged in diplomacy with Western powers, and these efforts are recognized as sparing Thailand from colonial occupation.

Both kings placed great value on having foreign educators for their children. One of Rama IV's hired tutors was Anna Leonowens, who penned her memoirs The English Governess at the Siamese Court, on which several books and two films, including The King & I, are based. It's widely accepted that Leonowens exaggerated her position at the court, and Thais are extremely offended that she misrepresented the monarchy. The books and films are banned in Thailand.

During his 50-plus years on the throne, King Bhumibol has been a figure of stability for his people through some turbulent times, including coups d'etat, popular uprisings, and a bewildering number of civilian and military leaders. His public works—notably The King's Project, which supports small agricultural communities—further enhance the public's devotion. In a society rife with corruption at all levels of officialdom, the king is seen as an emblem of morality and the embodiment of the values that Thais hold dear. For those who feel engulfed by Western-style consumerism, he represents a gentler, possibly "more Thai" era. Even the younger generations, who are heavily into Western, Japanese, and Thai pop culture, and are less conservative than their parents, hold similar feelings towards the monarchy.

Another notable thing about King Bhumibol is that he's an accomplished jazz musician. As a saxophonist and clarinet player he has jammed with the likes of Benny Goodman and Stan Getz, and Thailand often holds jazz festivals in December to coincide with his birthday.

— Mag Ramsay

of Chinese porcelain. Energetic visitors climb the steep steps of the central prang for the view over the Chao Phraya; the less ambitious can linger in the small park by the river, a peaceful spot to gaze across at the city. Festivals are held here occasionally; check the Web site below for upcoming events. ✉ *Arun Amarin Rd., Thonburi* ☎ *02/466–3167* ⊕ *www.watarunfestival.com* ✉ *B20* ☼ *Daily 8:30–5:30.*

BANGLAMPHU   **Khao San Road.** Khao San, which means "Shining Rice, " has been the heart of the international backpacking scene for decades. In the past few years it's made an attempt at trendiness with new outdoor bars, restaurants, and hotels sharing the space with the ubiquitous low-budget guesthouses. The road is closed to traffic at night, making early evening the best time to stroll or sit back and people-watch. Nightfall also marks the start of a busy street market, where you can find clothing, Thai goods, bootleg CDs, fake IDs, used Western books, cheap street food, and more. The frenetic activity can, depending on your perspective, be infectious or overwhelming. During Songkran, the Thai New Year in mid-April, Khao San turns into one huge wet-and-wild water fight. Only join the fun if you don't mind being soaked to the bone.

Phra Athit Road. A more leisurely neighborhood stroll is the river walk off Phra Athit, which runs between Pinklao Bridge, near the National Museum, and Santichaiprakarn Park. The concrete walkway along the Chao Phraya is cooled by the river breeze and offers views of the life along the water. **Phra Sumen Fort,** one of the two remaining forts of the original 14 built under King Rama I, is in Santichaiprakarn Park. The park is a fine place to sit and watch the river. Phra Athit Road itself is an interesting street with buildings dating back more than 100 years. It has some good cafés, and at night the street comes alive with little bars and restaurants with live music. It's become a favorite for university students and Bangkok trendies since 2000.

Dusit

More than any other neighborhood in the city, Dusit—north of Banglamphu—seems calm and orderly. Its tree-shaded boulevards and elegant buildings truly befit the district that holds Chitlada Palace, the official residence of the king and queen. The neighborhood's layout was the work of King Rama V, the first of the country's monarchs to visit Europe. He returned with a grand plan to remake his capital after the great cities he had visited. Dusit is a rather big area, but luckily the major attractions, the Dusit Zoo and the numerous museums on the grounds of the Vimanmek Mansion, are close together.

a good tour   Begin by taking a taxi to the corner of Nakhon Pathom Road and Si Ayutthaya Road where you find not-to-be-missed **Wat Benjamabophit** ⑩, the elegant palace made of marble where the king spent his days as a monk. It's one of the most photographed sights in the city. From there enter Dusit Park, a square of green that sits like a postage stamp in this quiet corner of Bangkok. Walk through the park to **Vimanmek Mansion** ⑪, considered by many the largest teak structure in the world. An elegant pavilion on the water is a great place to gaze across the lake. From there,

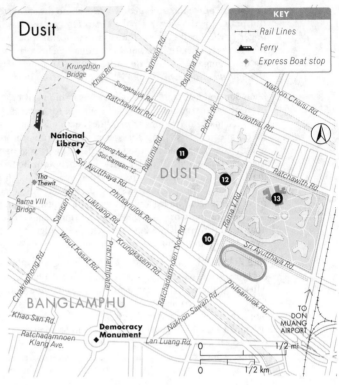

cross over Ratchadamnoen Nok Road for a chance to see eye to eye with white-handed gibbons and other rare creatures at the **Dusit Zoo** . Lovely **Chitlada Palace** , the king's private residence, is in a private compound just beyond.

TIMING   This tour can be done in a day, even after factoring in a few breaks, but it'll be a very full day.

What to See

13 Chitlada Palace. When in Bangkok, the king resides here, an area that takes up an entire block across from Dusit Park. Although the palace is closed to the public, the outside walls are a lovely sight, especially when lit up to celebrate the king's birthday on December 5. The extensive grounds are also home to a herd of royal white elephants, but it's difficult to arrange to see them. ⊠ *Ratchawith Rd. and Rama V Rd., Dusit* Ⓜ *Skytrain: Victory Monument (take a taxi from the station).*

12 Dusit Zoo. Komodo dragons and other rarely seen creatures, such as the Sumatran rhinoceros, are on display at this charming little zoo. There are also the usual suspects like giraffes and hippos from Africa. (If you've heard about the pandas China gave Thailand, they are in Chiang Mai, not Bangkok.) While adults sip coffee at the cafés, children can ride elephants. ⊠ *Ratchawith Rd. and Rama V Rd., Dusit* ☎ *02/*

281–0000 ✉ *B30* ⊙ *Daily 8–6* Ⓜ *Skytrain: Victory Monument (take a taxi from the station).*

★ ⓫ **Vimanmek Mansion.** The spacious grounds within Dusit Park include 20 buildings you can visit, but Vimanmek, considered the largest golden teak structure in the world, is truly the highlight. The mansion's original foundation remains on Koh Si Chang two hours south of Bangkok in the Gulf of Thailand, where it was built in 1868. In 1910 King Rama V had the rest of the structure moved to its present location and it served as his residence. The building itself is extensive with more than 80 rooms. The place fits its name, which means "Cloud Mansion, " as its extraordinary lightness is enhanced by a reflecting pond. The other 19 buildings include the **Royal Family Museum,** with portraits of the royal family, and the **Royal Carriage Museum,** with carriages and other vehicles used by the country's monarchs through the ages. There are several small air-conditioned restaurants offering a limited menu of Thai food. Admission includes everything on the grounds and the classical Thai dancing shows that take place mid-morning and mid-afternoon (10:30 AM and 2 PM at this writing, but these times are subject to change). English-language tours are available every half hour starting at 9:15. Admission is free if you have a ticket less than one week old from the Grand Palace. ✉ *Ratchawith Rd., Dusit* ☎ *02/281–1569* ✉ *B50* ⊙ *Daily 9:30–4* Ⓜ *Skytrain: Victory Monument (take a taxi from the station).*

★ ❿ **Wat Benjamabophit** (Marble Temple). This is a favorite with photographers because of its open spaces and light, shining marble. The wat was built in 1899; Thailand's present king spent his days as a monk here before his coronation. Statues of the Buddha line the courtyard, and the magnificent interior has cross beams of lacquer and gold. But Wat Benjamabophit is more than a splendid temple—the monastery is a seat of learning that appeals to Buddhist monks with intellectual yearnings. ✉ *Nakhon Pathom Rd., Dusit* ✉ *B20* ⊙ *Daily 8–5:30* Ⓜ *Skytrain: Victory Monument (take a taxi from the station).*

Chinatown

Even visitors from cities with large Chinatowns of their own are surprised at the size, liveliness, and density of Bangkok's most congested neighborhood, which is just east of the Old City. The neighborhood is an old and integral part of the city—almost as soon as Bangkok was founded, Chinatown started to form; it's the city's oldest residential area. Today it's a bustling area with many little markets (and a few big ones), teahouses, little restaurants tucked here and there, and endless traffic. Like much of the Old City, Chinatown is a great place to wander around in, too. Meandering through the maze of alleys, ducking into herb shops and temples along the way, can be a great way to pass an afternoon, though the constant crowd, especially on hot days, does wear on some people.

Yaowarat Road is the main thoroughfare and it's crowded with jewelry shops. Pahuraht Road, which is Bangkok's "Little India, " is full of textile shops; many of the Indian merchant families on this street have been here for generations.

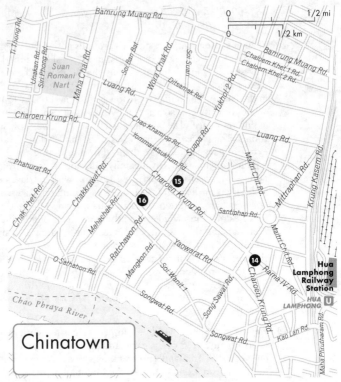

Chinatown

Getting to Chinatown is easiest by boat—simply get off at one of the nearby piers and walk into the morass. But you can also start at the Hua Lamphong subway station and head west to the river. The amount of traffic in this area cannot be overemphasized: avoid taking a taxi into the neighborhood if you can help it.

a good walk

Take the subway to Hua Lamphong and walk across Rama IV Road and the klong (which, unfortunately, is a rather polluted body of water at this point), and down Traimit Road to **Wat Traimit** ⓵, home of the Golden Buddha. When you leave the wat, turn right onto Traimit Road, walk to Charoen Krung (New Road) and turn right again. Go a short distance until Charoen Krung splits, and take the left-hand road, which is Yaowarat. Head north on Mangkorn Road to reach **Neng Noi Yee** ⓵, a beautiful Buddhist temple topped by dragons gazing heavenward. Go back to Yaowarat Road and continue west to experience the sights and sounds of the vibrant neighborhood, with its countless gold shops, and, in the evening, enough street food to satisfy the pickiest palates. At the northwest end of Yaowarat you can browse for treasures at the **Thieves Market** ⓵.

This itinerary can easily be reversed if you want to approach the neighborhood from the river instead.

TIMING   Allow a few hours at least to visit Chinatown, especially if you enjoy browsing at the many markets. You can also easily get lost in the labyrinth of small sois and lanes on your way from sight to sight. Keep in mind the horrendous traffic—the Skytrain doesn't come here and the subway ends at the eastern edge. Take a river boat or the subway to get here; you could lose hours in a taxi or tuk-tuk.

What to See

⑮ Neng Noi Yee. Unlike most temples in Bangkok, Neng Noi Yee has a glazed ceramic roof topped with fearsome dragons. Although it's a Buddhist shrine, its statues and paintings incorporate elements of Confucianism and Taoism as well. ⊠ *Mankon Rd., Chinatown* Ⓜ *Subway: Hua Lamphong.*

⑯ Thieves Market (Nakorn Kasem). The Thieves Market was once known for its reasonable prices for antiques, but stolen goods are no longer the order of the day. You won't find the same bargains either, but it's still fun to browse among the stalls, which carry mostly electronic goods. ⊠ *Yaowarat Rd. and Chakraphet Rd., Chinatown* Ⓜ *Subway: Hua Lamphong.*

★ **⑭ Wat Traimit** (Temple of the Golden Buddha). The actual temple has little architectural merit, but off to its side is a small chapel containing the world's largest solid-gold Buddha, cast about nine centuries ago in the Sukhothai style. Weighing 5½ tons and standing 10 feet high, the statue is a symbol of strength and power that can inspire even the most jaded person. It's believed that the statue was brought first to Ayutthaya. When the Burmese were about to sack the city, it was covered in plaster. Two centuries later, still in plaster, it was thought to be worth very little; when it was being moved to a new Bangkok temple in the 1950s it slipped from a crane and was simply left in the mud by the workmen. In the morning, a temple monk who had dreamed that the statue was divinely inspired went to see the Buddha image. Through a crack in the plaster he saw a glint of yellow, and soon discovered that the statue was pure gold. ⊠ *Tri Mit Rd., Chinatown* 🖻 *B20* ☉ *Daily 9–5* Ⓜ *Subway: Hua Lamphong.*

Downtown Bangkok

Bangkok has many downtowns that blend into each other—even residents have a hard time agreeing on a definitive city center—and so the large collective area considered "downtown" is actually seven neighborhoods. Most of the tourist attractions are in the adjacent neighborhoods of Silom and Pratunam. The Silom area, with a mix of tall buildings, residential streets, and entertainment areas, is the busiest business hub. Some of the city's finest hotels and restaurants are in this neighborhood, but it still retains some charm despite being so developed and so chock-full of concrete. Pratunam, north of Silom, is a large neighborhood that competes with Chinatown for the worst traffic in the city. There are numerous markets here, including those in the garment district (generally north of the Amari Watergate Hotel on Phetburi Road). Pratunam's Panthip Plaza is Thailand's biggest computer center with five floors of computer stores.

The other neighborhoods—Lumphini Park, Siam Square, Victory Monument, Sukhumvit, and Rajadapisek—are residential areas, business centers, shopping districts, or all the above. The Lumphini Park area, north of Silom, has many green spaces behind its numerous embassy compounds and is home to the Bangkok Royal Sports Club. East of Lumphini is Siam Square, home to Thailand's most prestigious university, Chulalongkorn. Former President Bill Clinton spoke at the campus in 1996 and flattered the university by saying Harvard was America's Chulalongkorn. Siam Square is also one of Bangkok's biggest shopping areas, with hundreds of stores north of the university and more in several shopping centers around the square. The central Skytrain station is here, making the action in this neighborhood even more frenetic.

North of Pratunam is Victory Monument, which remains predominately residential except for Phayathai Road, which is home to many businesses. Sukhumvit, east of Pratunam, is a mixed bag, with countless hotels and restaurants (many expat Westerners and Japanese live in the area, so restaurant pickings tend to be better than average), as well as many entertainment spots. Traffic is often gridlocked, but, fortunately, the neighborhood has good Skytrain service.

Lastly, north of Sukhumvit is Rajadapisek, an up-and-coming neighborhood little explored by tourists, though that may change thanks to the new subway. Numerous clubs, restaurants, and hotels are being built for the expected influx of foot traffic.

a good tour

The best way to see the sights is by Skytrain, which also offers a good view of the city as you travel. You can go everywhere in a day, but it's a very long one, with more time spent traveling than at the sights themselves. At the end of the day you might feel like you saw the Skytrain and little else. The top sights are Suan Pakkard Palace, Jim Thompson's House and Kukrit Pramoj Heritage House, although the Erawan Shrine shouldn't be missed either. It might be wise to pick what most interests you and map out your day from there, or better still, if you have two days, divide up your sightseeing. The fact that Kukrit Pramoj is only open on the weekend might make tough choices a little bit easier.

If you're doing this tour on the weekend, **Kukrit Pramoj Heritage House** ⑰ is a good place to start. To get there take the Skytrain to Chong Nonsi and walk down Narathiwat Road to the second lane on the left after Sathorn Road. After touring the house, return to the Skytrain station and go to Sala Daeng, which will let you out near **Lumphini Park** ⑱, a swath of green where Thais go to beat the heat; this is a great place to take a break. Across Ratchadamri Road is **Queen Saowapha Snake Farm** ⑲, where you can watch deadly snakes being milked for their venom. This is interesting, but if you have only one day to explore the area, it might be better to head back to the Skytrain, taking it to the National Stadium station and walking the short distance to **Jim Thompson's House** ⑳. From there continue on the Skytrain to Phaya Thai station and walk or take a tuk-tuk or taxi to **Suan Pakkard Palace** ㉑. The serene atmosphere makes the palace one of the most relaxing places to absorb the local culture.

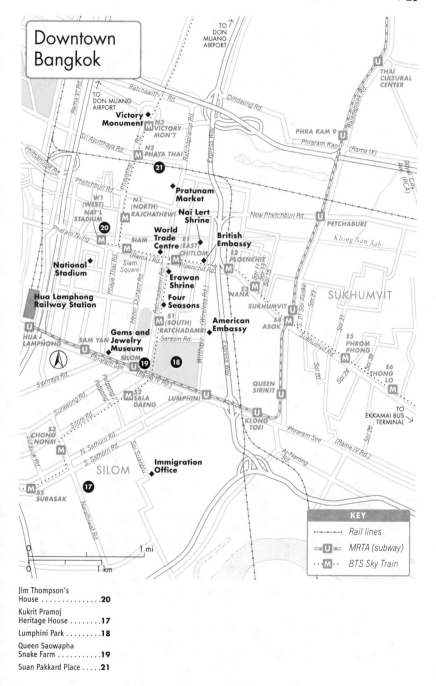

Downtown Bangkok

TO DON MUANG AIRPORT

TO DON MUANG AIRPORT

THAI CULTURAL CENTER

Ratchawithi Rd.

Rama VI Rd.

Dindaeng Rd.

Rajadapisek Rd.

Victory Monument

N3 VICTORY MON'T

PHRA RAM 9

Phraram Kao

(Rama 1X)

Royal City Ave. (RCA)

Sri Ayutthaya Rd.

N2 PHAYA THAI

Phitsanulok Rd.

21

Phetchburi Rd.

Pratunam Market

Ratchaprarop Rd.

Express Way

New Phetchburi Rd.

PETCHABURI

N1 (NORTH) RAJCHATHEWI

Nai Lert Shrine

Klong San Sab

W1 (WEST) NAT'L STADIUM

20

SIAM

World Trade Centre

E1 (EAST) CHITLOM

British Embassy

E2 PLOENCHIT

Phraram Nung

National Stadium

(Rama I Rd.)

Siam Square

Ploenchit Rd.

Sukhumvit Rd.

SUKHUMVIT

Henri Dunant Rd.

Ratchadamri Rd.

Erawan Shrine

E3 NANA

SUKHUMVIT

S. 21 Soi Asoke

Soi 23

Hua Lamphong Railway Station

Phaya Thai Rd.

Four Seasons

Soi 11

Soi 13

Soi 41

U HUA LAMPHONG

SAM YAN

Gems and Jewelry Museum

S1 (SOUTH) RATCHADAMRI

American Embassy

E4 ASOK

E5 PHROM PHONG

SILOM

19

18

Sarasin Rd.

Witthayu (Wireless Rd.)

Express Way

Soi 39

Soi 20

Soi 24

E6 THONG LO

Siphraya Rd.

Phraram See (Rama IV Rd.)

QUEEN SIRIKIT

U

TO EKKAMAI BUS TERMINAL

Surawong Rd.

Patpong 2

Patpong

SALA DAENG

S2

LUMPHINI

U

Phraram See (Rama IV Rd.)

Soi 26

Silom Rd.

Surasak Rd.

S3 CHONG NONSI

N. Sathorn Rd.

KLONG TOEI

U

Ai-Narong Rd.

SILOM

S. Sathorn Rd.

Soi Suanplu

Immigration Office

S5 SURASAK

17

Narathiwat Rd.

0 ——————— 1 mi
0 ——————— 1 km

KEY

+·+·+·+ Rail lines

⇒**U**⇐ MRTA (subway)

· · **M** · · BTS Sky Train

TIMING   The sights in this part of the city are spread out, but most are near Sky-train stations. Stations are generally a half-mile (and less than three minutes) from platform to platform, so Chong Nonsi to National Stadium, which is four stations, will take less than 12 minutes.

Though working your way through the sights in this area will keep you busy, keep in mind that the options here are many, with shopping in Siam Square and many good restaurants throughout Downtown.

What to See

PRATUNAM   **Erawan Shrine** (San Phra Phrom). Completed in 1956, this is not a particularly old shrine by Bangkok standards, but it's one of the more active ones, with many people stopping by on their way home to pray to Brahma. Thai dancers and a small traditional orchestra perform for a fee to increase the likelihood that your wish will be granted. It's at one of Bangkok's most congested intersections, next to the Grand Hyatt Erawan and near the Chitlom Skytrain station. It was built by the Thai Hotel and Tourism Co. when they built the Erawan Hotel, which was replaced by the Grand Hyatt Erawan in 1991. Originally, the hotel owners requested a spirit house, but after an astrologer recommended they build a Brahman shrine the hotel asked the Fine Arts Department to design and build it. Even with a traffic jam right outside the gates, the mix of burning incense, dancers in traditional dress, and many people praying can be quite an experience. Entry is free, but many people leave small donations. ⊠ *At Ratchadamri and Ploenchit Rds., Pratunam* Ⓜ *Skytrain: Chitlom.*

Fertility Shrine at Nai Lert Park. Hundreds of phalluses from small wooden carvings to big stone sculptures decorated with ribbons make this shrine quite the unique one. It honors Chao Mae Tuptim, a female fertility spirit. Women visit this shrine when they are trying to conceive, leaving offerings of lotus and jasmine, and if Bangkok gossip is worth anything, the shrine has a good success rate. To get there, go to the Nai Lert Park Hotel and walk to the end of the ground-level garage, where it's on your right. It's open every day until dusk. ⊠ *Nai Lert Park Hotel, 2 Wittayu (Wireless Rd.), Pratunam* Ⓜ *Skytrain: Chitlom.*

Gems and Jewelry Museum. The Gem and Jewelry Institute of Thailand (GIT) at Chulalongkorn University opened this museum in 2004 to illustrate Thailand's role as one of the world's largest centers for cutting and polishing colored stones. Thailand's mines have been dug almost dry, but rough stones from Myanmar, Cambodia, Sri Lanka, and other nations are brought here to be cut and polished. The institute offers a testing service if you want to know if your newly bought jewels are genuine. ⊠ *Southeast corner of Chulalongkorn University, Phaya Thai Rd., Pratunam* ☎ *02/218–5470* ☞ *Free* ⊙ *Weekdays 9–4* Ⓜ *Subway: Sam Yan.*

㉒   **Jim Thompson's House.** Formerly an architect in New York City, Jim
Fodor'sChoice   Thompson ended up in Thailand at the end of World War II, after a stint
★   as an officer of the OSS (an organization that preceded the CIA). After a couple of other business ventures, he moved into silk and is credited with revitalizing Thailand's moribund silk industry. The success of this

project alone would have made him a legend, but the house he left behind is also a national treasure. Thompson imported parts of several up-country buildings, some as old as 150 years, to construct his compound of six Thai houses (three are still exactly the same as their originals, including details of the interior layout). With true appreciation and a connoisseur's eye, Thompson then furnished them with what are now priceless pieces of Southeast Asian art. Adding to Thompson's notoriety is his disappearance: in 1967 he went to the Malaysian Cameron Highlands for a quiet holiday and was never heard from again. The entrance to the house is easy to miss—it's at the end of an unprepossessing lane, leading north off Rama I Road, west of Phayathai Road (the house is on your left). A good landmark is the National Stadium Skytrain station—the house is north of the station, just down the street from it. An informative 30-minute guided tour starts every 15 minutes and is included in the admission fee. ⊠ *Soi Kasemsong 2, Pratunam* ☎ *02/612–3668* 🖭 *B100* 🕑 *Daily 9–5:30* Ⓜ *Skytrain: National Stadium.*

⓲ **Lumphini Park.** Two lakes enhance this popular park, one of the few in the center of the city. You can watch children feed bread to the turtles or teenagers taking a rowboat to more secluded shores. During the dry season (November through February) keep an eye (and ear) out for Music in the Park, which starts around 5 PM each Sunday on the Singha stage; there are different bands each week playing classical and Thai oldies. ⊠ *Rama IV Rd., Pratunam* Ⓜ *Subway: Silom and Lumphini stations; Skytrain: Sala Daeng.*

★ ㉑ **Suan Pakkard Palace.** A collection of antique teak houses, built high on columns, complement undulating lawns and shimmering lotus pools at this compound. Inside the Lacquer Pavilion, which sits serenely at the back of the garden, there's gold-covered paneling with scenes from the life of the Buddha. Other houses display porcelain, stone heads, traditional paintings, and Buddha statues. ⊠ *352 Si Ayutthaya Rd., Pratunam* ☎ *02/245–4934* 🖭 *B100* 🕑 *Daily 9–4* Ⓜ *Skytrain: Phaya Thai (10-min walk from station).*

SILOM ► ★ ⓱ **Kukrit Pramoj Heritage House.** Former Prime Minister Kukrit Pramoj's house reflects his long influential life. After Thailand became a constitutional monarchy in 1932, he formed the country's first political party and was prime minister in 1974 and 1975. (Perhaps he practiced for that role 12 years earlier when he appeared with Marlon Brando as a Southeast Asian prime minister in *The Ugly American.*) He died in 1995 and much of his living quarters—five interconnected teak houses—has been preserved as he left it. Throughout his life, Kukrit was dedicated to preserving Thai culture, and his house and grounds are a monument to a bygone era; the place is full of Thai and Khmer art and furniture from different periods. The landscaped garden with its Khmer stonework is also a highlight. It took Pramoj 30 years to build the house, so it's no wonder that you can spend the better part of a day wandering around here. ⊠ *19 Soi Phra Pinit, South Sathorn Rd., Silom* ☎ *02/286–8185* 🖭 *B50* 🕑 *Weekends and official holidays 10–5:30* Ⓜ *Skytrain: Chong Nonsi (10-min walk from station).*

🏛 ⑲ **Queen Saowapha Snake Farm.** The Thai Red Cross established this unusual snake farm in 1923. Venom from cobras, pit vipers, and other deadly snakes is collected and used to make antidotes for snakebite victims. There are milking sessions at 11 AM on weekends and 2:30 PM weekdays, where you can watch the staff fearlessly handle these deadly creatures. There are a few displays that can be viewed any time, but the milking sessions are the big reason to come here. ✉ *1871 Rama IV Rd., Silom* ☎ *02/252-0161* 🎫 *B70* ⊙ *Weekdays 8:30–4, weekends 8:30–noon* Ⓜ *Subway: Silom; Skytrain: Sala Daeng.*

WHERE TO EAT

Food is reason enough to visit Bangkok. Thais are passionate about it: finding an out-of-the-way shop that prepares some specialty better than any other, then dragging a group of friends to share the discovery, is a national pastime. Thais always seem to be eating, so the tastes and smells of Thailand surround you day and night. At times it feels like half the people in the city are cooking for the other half. Food isn't confined to mealtimes and noodle stalls are never far away. If you want a midnight snack, it's likely that there's a night market nearby serving up delicious dishes into the wee hours.

When considering Thai restaurants, appearance is not the most important indicator of quality. In fact, some of the best Thai food is served in the most bare bones, even run-down restaurants. A good general rule: any place where you spot groups of office workers enjoying lunch or an after-work bite has to be good, as only a worthy restaurant would be chosen for such an important social outing.

If you want a break from Thai food, Bangkok has restaurants offering just about every cuisine out there, including fantastic Chinese, Indian, Italian, and Japanese options. And if you need something really familiar to appease grouchy kids or give a troubled stomach a rest from spicy food, most international chain restaurants have branches in Bangkok, including the usual suspects in the American fast-food world, as well as French, Australian, and Japanese chains.

As with anything in Bangkok, travel time is a major consideration when choosing a restaurant. Bangkok traffic continues to ruin the best-laid dinner plans. If you're short on time or patience, choose a place with Skytrain and subway access—many great restaurants are within easy walking distance from the stations. Note that often the easiest way to reach a riverside eatery is by taking the Skytrain to the Saphan Taksin station (where the line ends on the river next to the Shangri-La Hotel). From there you can take an express boat upriver to many restaurants, including a dozen or so reviewed below.

Dinner Cruises

Though they're definitely a very touristy endeavor, lunch or dinner cruises on the Chao Phraya River are worth considering. They're a great way to see the city while enjoying a good meal. Two-hour cruises on modern boats or refurbished rice barges include a buffet or set-menu dinner and often feature live music and sometimes a traditional dance show. Many companies also offer a less expensive lunch cruise. Reservations are a must for some of the more popular cruises; in general, it's wise to reserve a few days in advance for all dinner cruises.

The Horizon (✉ Shangri-La Hotel, 89 Soi Wat Suan Phu, New Rd., Silom ☎ 02/236–7777) departs each evening at 7:30 PM and costs B1,400 per person. There's also a daylong lunch cruise to Ayutthaya and back for B1,600. It departs at 8 AM and returns around 5 PM. **The Manohra Song** (✉ Marriott Royal Garden Riverside Hotel, 257/1–3 Charoen Krung Rd. (New Rd.), Thonburi ☎ 02/476–0021 ⊕ www.manohracruises.com) has both lunch and dinner cruises. This is the most beautiful dinner boat on the river, a refurbished old rice barge with wood so polished you can almost see your reflection. However, it's smaller than most of the others, with less space to walk around. Dinner is B1,400 per person. **Yok Yor** (✉ Wisutikasat Rd. at Yok Yor Pier, across from River City Shopping Center, Thonburi ☎ 02/863–0565) departs each evening at 8:30. The boat ticket costs B70; food is ordered à la carte.

Cooking Classes

Some of the best dining is done in a Thai cooking class. You won't be an expert even after a five-day course, but you can learn the fundamentals and some of the history of Thai cuisine. You can also find specialty classes that focus on things like fruit-carving (where the first lesson learned is that it's more difficult than it looks) or hot-and-spicy soups. All cooking schools concentrate on practical dishes that students will be able to make at home, and all revolve around having fun and the joy of eating. Most classes are small enough to allow individual attention and time for questions. Prices vary from B2,000 to more than B10,000.

The Oriental Cooking School (✉ 48 Oriental Ave., across from Oriental Hotel, Thonburi ☎ 02/236–0400) is the most established school, but far from being stuffy, it's fun and informative. Classes are taught in a beautiful century-old house. **The Landmark Cooking School** (☎ 02/254–0404 Ext. 4823) is also very good. Both daylong and week-long courses are offered. **The Manohra Song** (☎ 02/476–0021) offers half-day classes that include a "field trip" to the market.

WHAT IT COSTS In Baht				
$$$$	**$$$**	**$$**	**$**	**¢**
AT DINNER	over B400	B300–B400	B200–B300	B100–B200	under B100

Prices are per person for a main course, excluding tax and tip.

West Bangkok: Dusit to Chinatown

Dusit & Northern Bangkok

CHINESE   ✗ **Dynasty.** This restaurant has long been a favorite among government
$$$$ ministers and corporate executives for its outstanding Cantonese cuisine and 11 private areas that are good for business lunches or romantic dinners. The main dining room is elegant with crimson carpeting, carved screens, lacquer furniture, and porcelain objets d'art. The Peking duck is among the draws, but the seasonal specialties include everything

from hairy crabs (October and November) to Taiwanese eels (March). The service is efficient and friendly without being obtrusive. The restaurant is in Chatuchak, north of Pratunam on the way to Don Muang airport. ⊠ *Sofitel Central Plaza Bangkok, 1695 Phaholyothin Rd., Chatuchak, Northern Bangkok* ☎ *02/541–1234* ⌕ *Reservations essential* ⊟ *AE, DC, MC, V* Ⓜ *Subway: Phahon Yothin.*

THAI
$$

✕ **Kaloang Seafood.** An alley near the National Library leads to this off-the-beaten-track restaurant on the Chao Phraya. Kaloang might not look like much, with its plastic chairs and simple tables on a ramshackle pier, but it's a local favorite and worth the effort—and leap in imagination—for fantastic seafood on the river. Breezes coming off the water keep things comfortably cool most evenings. The generous grilled seafood platter is a bargain, as is the plate of grilled giant river prawns. Try the *yam pla duk foo*, a grilled fish salad that's rather spicy, but goes great with a cold beer. ⊠ *2 Sri Ayutthaya Rd., Dusit* ☎ *02/281–9228 or 02/282–7581* ⊟ *AE, DC, MC, V.*

The Old City & Banglamphu

INDIAN
¢
Fodor'sChoice
★

✕ **Roti-Mataba.** This little restaurant is the kind of place that earns Bangkok its reputation for excellent food. Roti (an unleavened, whole-wheat flatbread), filled with your choice of vegetables, chicken, beef, fish, seafood, or just sweetened with thick condensed milk, are cooked near the door of the restaurant; all versions are recommended. The curry chicken is another stand-out. Roti-Mataba is in a century-old building across from Santichaiprakarn Park on the Chao Phraya; the downstairs is narrow, hot, and usually crowded, but there's a more comfortable air-conditioned dining room upstairs. ⊠ *136 Pra Artit Rd., Banglamphu* ☎ *02/282–2119* ⊟ *No credit cards* ⊗ *Closed Mon.*

THAI
$–$$

✕ **Ton Pho.** This eatery doesn't look special—it resembles a small, open-air warehouse—but it's done a good trade since opening nearly two decades ago, well before Phra Athit area became trendy. A boardwalk along the river runs past the restaurant, and a pier where the express boats stop is off to one corner, so there's plenty of activity to watch as you eat. Try to secure a waterfront table where the breezes and views are better. The *tom khlong plaa salid bai makhaam awn,* a hot-and-sour soup made from local dried fish, chili, lime juice, lemongrass, young tamarind leaves, and mushrooms, is a full-frontal attack of seasonings, but delicious. Less potent, but equally good, are the *gai hor bai toey* (deep-fried chicken in pandanus leaves) and *haw moke plaa* (a curried fish custard thickened with coconut cream and steamed in banana leaves). ⊠ *43 Phra Athit Rd., Banglamphu* ☎ *02/280–0452* ⌕ *Reservations not accepted* ⊟ *AE, DC, MC, V.*

¢–$

✕ **Rub-ar-roon.** In the shadow of Wat Po, this is a nice place for a break when you're taking in the sights of the Old City. The Thai and Western dishes are good value—or you can just grab a beer or one of the best milk shakes in town. There are seats inside or on the shaded sidewalk. Next door is a store that has sold traditional medicine for nearly 100 years. ⊠ *310 Maharaj Rd., Old City* ☎ *02/262–2312* ⊟ *No credit cards.*

¢–$

✕ **Sunset Bar & Garden Restaurant.** Don't expect outstanding food here, just some decent Thai dishes and a few Western standards like sand-

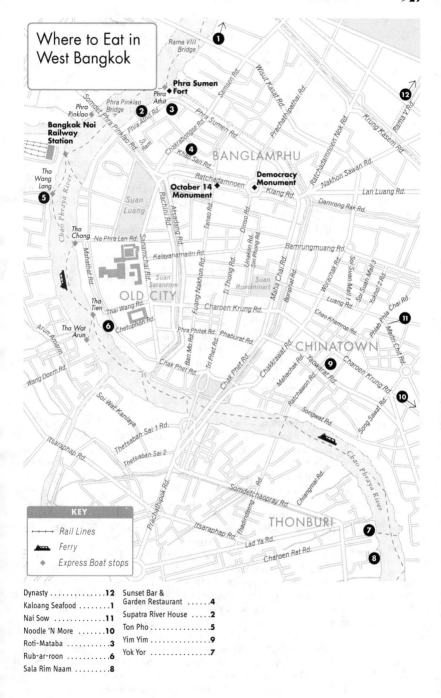

Where to Eat in West Bangkok

KEY

⊢—⊣ Rail Lines

🚢 Ferry

◆ Express Boat stops

wiches and french fries. There are tables inside and out, and a few more on a terrace. It's down a little lane off Khao San Road, next to a Starbucks and Kraichitti Gallery (which is also worth a look). ⊠ *201 Khao San Rd., Banglamphu* ☎ *02/282–5823* ▭ *No credit cards.*

Thonburi

THAI   ✕ **Sala Rim Naam.** To reach this elegant dining room you must take a
$$$$ boat across the Chao Phraya River from the Oriental Hotel. This is one of the best places to sample Royal Thai cuisine, elaborate dishes once served only to the king and his family. (You may feel bad about vandalizing the platters of fruits and vegetables carefully carved to resemble flowers.) Try some of the spicy salads, especially the shrimp version called *yam koong.* Make reservations for 7:30 PM and plan to stay on for the beautifully staged Thai dancing later in the evening. You can order à la carte or try the set menu for B1,700. The delicious lunch buffet (a reasonable B620) is always less crowded, and, during the hot season (generally from late March to mid-May), includes lighter recipes rarely found elsewhere in the city. ⊠ *48 Oriental Ave., across from Oriental Hotel, Thonburi* ☎ *02/437–6211* ⚞ *Reservations essential* ▭ *AE, DC, MC, V* Ⓜ *Skytrain: Saphan Taksin.*

$$$$ ✕ **Supatra River House.** Its location on the Chao Phraya River—and across from the Grand Palace—makes this restaurant worth a visit. A free ferry from Maharaj Pier shuttles diners back and forth. In the former home of Khunying Supatra, founder of the city's express boat business, the restaurant has a small museum dedicated to the art she collected. The food is good, and the set menus (B750–B1,200) make for easy ordering. There's dinner theater on Friday and Saturday evening. ⊠ *288 Soi Wat Rakhang, Arunamarin Rd., Thonburi* ☎ *02/411–0305* ⚞ *Reservations essential* ▭ *MC, V.*

Chinatown

CHINESE   ✕ **Yim Yim Restaurant.** This second-floor restaurant has been serving Chi-
$$ nese cuisine for more than 70 years. Though it lacks the elegance of the hotel restaurants in the area—the dining room is simple and you have to walk through the dishwashing room to reach the bathroom—it's a solid option in the heart of Chinatown. It's a favorite for family gatherings, but much smaller groups will still feel welcome. Try the sweet-and-sour fish, or if you're up for it, the chicken soup, which includes a whole bird in the bowl. ⊠ *89 Passai Rd., off Yaowarat Rd. near intersection with Ratchawong Rd., Chinatown* ☎ *02/224–2203* ▭ *No credit cards* Ⓜ *Subway: Hua Lamphong.*

¢–$ ✕ **Noodle 'N More.** This narrow restaurant would be at home in Tokyo or Hong Kong, with its three small floors, the top one a no-shoes-allowed tearoom with sofas and floor seating. The second floor has regular table-seating and a counter with benches along the window that offer great people-watching on the street below. It's a little more chic than your average noodle stand and its location near the Hua Lamphong train station makes it a good place to refuel before exploring the neighborhood or while waiting for your train. As the name implies, you can find plenty of noodle dishes here, but the rice dishes are equally good. ⊠ *513–514 Rong Muang Rd., at Rama IV, Chinatown* ☎ *02/254–8755* ▭ *No credit cards* Ⓜ *Subway: Hua Lamphong.*

EAT LIKE A LOCAL

THAILAND'S BORDERS HAVE AT TIMES included parts of Malaysia, Myanmar, and Laos, and all these peoples, along with Chinese, Indians, Indonesians, ethnic Mon and Khmer, Persians, Europeans, and the Thai themselves, have added ingredients to an extraordinarily diverse cuisine.

Thailand has four regional food styles—northern, northeastern, southern, and central—and in cosmopolitan Bangkok you get a chance to try them all. The city itself is in the central region (the country's fertile "Rice Bowl"), where many of the dishes most familiar to foreigners, such as tom yum goong (spicy shrimp soup), tom kha gai (coconut soup with chicken), and the red and green curries, originate. Central food owes much to the influence of the royal kitchens, where coconut was first added and a fondness for sweeter tones was developed.

The other famous dishes somtam (spicy green papaya salad) and laab (minced meat or fish with chilli and lime) are from the northeastern region of Isan, where viciously hot food is served with sticky rice and raw vegetables to cool the palate. Traditionally, you eat sticky rice by making a small flat disc of the rice, wrapping it around some food, and popping it in your mouth. Other Isan specialties found on Bangkok streets are insects gathered from the rice paddies. The black water beetles (maeng da or "pimps") are a particular favorite, with those-in-the-know choosing the females bearing tasty orange eggs.

Bangkok has a huge variety of both Western and Thai food in air-conditioned comfort, but many Thais still prefer to eat at food stalls, and not just because they're cheap (you're likely to see just as many Mercedes as mopeds parked nearby). Vendors specialize in one or two dishes, and poor ones quickly go out of business, so the food quality is astonishingly consistent. You'll find different specialities in each neighborhood: Chinatown has kway tio and ba mee (noodles), Dusit is known for Northern dishes, Phra Athit Road in Banglamphu has Southern-style curries as well as the Indian staple roti. Ubiquitous are gai yang (grilled chicken), yum (spicy salads), joke (rice porridge), and pad Thai (thin noodles with shrimp, bamboo shoots, and peanuts). Food-poisoning scares are hugely exaggerated—if you see a crowd of healthy diners, don't be afraid to join them, just make sure meat dishes are well-cooked. And remember: the super-sweet Thai iced tea should be avoided from vendors working off a block of ice—even frozen local water can make you sick.

Much of the famed local philosophy of sanuk (fun) revolves around the dinner table, with crowds of friends and family gathering to swap gossip and banter around piles of food. All dishes are shared by the entire group. Meals usually consist of at least one curry, a salad, a soup, and possibly a stir-fry or grilled fish dish, depending on the number of diners.

Utensils: Many Thais are baffled by foreigners' repeated requests for chopsticks. Thais only use chopsticks for Chinese or noodle dishes—everything else is eaten with a fork and spoon (the fork is used to push food onto the spoon).

Tipping: Outside of posh restaurants, there is no need to leave a tip, save for any loose change left over from your bill.

Mouth on fire?: First-timers might have some difficulty with the liberal use of chili in most Thai dishes. Water won't extinguish that fire; eat something sweet instead.

— Howard Richardson

THAI ✕ **Nai Sow.** Many regulars say this Chinese–Thai restaurant has the
¢–$ city's best *tom yam kung* (spicy shrimp soup). Chefs may come and go,
but the owner somehow manages to keep the recipe to this signature dish
a secret. The food here is consistently excellent; try the *naw mai thalay*
(sea asparagus in oyster sauce), the curried beef or the sweet-and-sour
mushrooms. The fried taro is an unusual and delicious dessert. Wat
Plaplachai is next door. ⊠ *3/1 Maitrichit Rd., Chinatown* ☎ *02/222–
1539* ⊜ *Reservations not accepted* ⊟ *MC, V* Ⓜ *Subway: Hua Lamphong.*

Downtown Bangkok

Pratunam & Siam Square

CHINESE ✕ **Tien Tien.** In 2004 Tien Tien moved from its rundown location on Pat-
$–$$ pong to the more up-market All Seasons Place. The dining room is now
roomy and comfortable, while the food remains just as good. The roast
pork is superb—order it any way you want, but it's so juicy and tender
that the most popular accompaniment is simple steamed rice. The Peking
duck is also a must; its skin is crisp and the pancakes accompanying it
are light and fluffy. There's a free shuttle bus between All Seasons Place
and the Skytrain station that runs about every 15 minutes. ⊠ *1st fl.,
All Seasons Pl., Wittayu (Wireless Rd.), Pratunam* ☎ *02/685–3918*
⊟ *AE, DC, MC, V* Ⓜ *Skytrain: Ploenchit.*

¢ ✕ **Coca Suki** (Siam Square). This branch of the popular Coca Suki chain
can be raucous on weekends and evenings, when Chinese families tuck
into a daunting variety of noodle dishes. Both wheat- and rice-based pastas are available in combination with a cornucopia of meats, fish, shell-
fish, and crunchy Chinese vegetables. Try some of the green wheat
noodles called *mee yoke*, topped with a chicken thigh, red pork, or crab-
meat. You can also try an intriguing Chinese variant of sukiyaki, which
you prepare yourself on a hot plate built into your table. This branch
was renovated recently and has more of a modern look with comfortable semi-private booths. ⊠ *461/3–8 Henri Dunant Rd., near Siam
Sq., Pathumwan* ☎ *02/251–6337 or 02/251–3538* ⊟ *MC, V* Ⓜ *Skytrain: Siam.*

ECLECTIC ✕ **Pickle Factory.** Though owner Jeff Fehr is a Chicago native, this un-
$ pretentious place looks straight out of South Florida—it's in an art
deco–style house and some tables are set beside a swimming pool. Fehr
started making pickles here in 1997 and the name stuck. But you can
find much more than pickles on the menu and most people come for
the ample plates of pasta and what's widely considered to be the best
pizza in town. Note that it's quite a hike (about 20 minutes) from the
Skytrain station. ⊠ *55 Soi Ratchawithi 2, Pratunam* ☎ *02/246–3036*
⊟ *No credit cards* Ⓜ *Skytrain: Victory Monument.*

ITALIAN ✕ **Pan Pan.** Despite the proliferation of Italian restaurants in Bangkok,
$ Pan Pan remains popular. The relaxed atmosphere, which is noticeably
lacking in the kitschy clutter of many of the city's Italian restaurants,
invites intimate conversations. The extensive menu includes such favorites
as linguine with a sauce of salmon, cream, and vodka that's a taste of
high-calorie heaven, and "chicken godfather, " served with a cream-and-
mushroom sauce. Save room for the traditional gelato. ⊠ *45 Soi Lang*

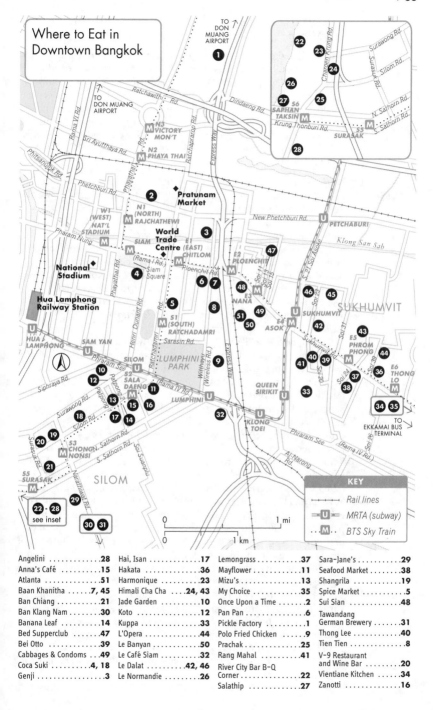

Where to Eat in Downtown Bangkok

Suan, off Ploenchit Rd., Pratunam ☎ *02/252–7104* ⊟ *AE, DC, MC, V* Ⓜ *Skytrain: Chitlom.*

JAPANESE
$$

✕ **Genji.** Bangkok has plenty of good Japanese restaurants, but many can be a bit chilly toward newcomers. Genji is the happy exception, and the staff is always pleasant. There's an excellent sushi bar here and several small private rooms where you can enjoy fine dishes like succulent grilled eel. Set menus for lunch and dinner are well conceived, and are a nice change from typical Thai fare. Lunch seats fill up quickly and dinner sometimes requires a wait. ⊠ *Nai Lert Park Bangkok, 2 Wittayu (Wireless Rd.), Pratunam* ☎ *02/253–0123* ⊟ *AE, DC, MC, V* Ⓜ *Skytrain: Ploenchit.*

THAI
$$–$$$$

✕ **Spice Market.** This popular place re-creates the interior of a well-stocked spice shop during a time when the only way to get to Bangkok was by steamer. Jars of spices line wooden shelves and sacks of garlic, piles of dried chilies, and heavy earthenware jars of fish sauce are lined up on the floor amid the tables. The dishes are tempered to suit the tender mouths of Westerners, but you may ask for your curry to be prepared Thai-style. From mid-January to late March you can try the *nam doc mai* (mango with sticky rice). Many people arrange trips to Bangkok at this time of year just for this dessert. If that doesn't satisfy your sweet tooth, there's also a comprehensive selection of old-fashioned Thai candies. ⊠ *Four Seasons Bangkok, 155 Ratchadamri Rd., Pratunam* ☎ *02/251–6127* ⌂ *Reservations essential* ⊟ *AE, DC, MC, V.*

★ $–$$

✕ **Once Upon a Time.** Period photos of the royal family, movie stars, and beauty queens cover the pink walls of this restaurant, which is really two old teak houses. The dining rooms are filled with delightful antiques; there are also tables in the garden between the houses. *Mieng khum,* a traditional snack of dried shrimp, dried coconut, peanuts, pineapple, chili pepper, and sweet tamarind sauce rolled together in a green leaf, makes an excellent appetizer. Afterward move on to the chopped pork with chili sauce or the beef fillet with pickled garlic. The music, often by local performers, is traditional Thai. The restaurant is about 100 yards down Soi 17, across the street from Panthip Plaza (a 15-minute walk from the Skytrain). ⊠ *Soi 17, Phetchburi Rd., Pratunam* ☎ *02/252–8629 or 02/653–7857* ⊟ *AE, DC, MC, V* Ⓜ *Skytrain: Rajchathewi.*

¢–$
Fodor'sChoice
★

✕ **Polo Fried Chicken.** After offering only a lunch menu for decades, Polo Fried Chicken finally responded to its unwaning popularity by expanding its hours until 10 PM. The addition of an air-conditioned dining room is also a recent concession to its loyal clientele. Here you'll get world-class fried chicken, flavored with black pepper and plenty of golden-brown garlic; the best way to sample it is with sticky rice and a plate of *som tam,* a hydrogen bomb of hot-and-sour raw papaya salad. The place is a bit hard to find—as you enter Soi Polo, it's about 50 yards in on your left. At lunchtime, you need to get here before noon to snag a table before the office workers descend. The restaurant will deliver to your hotel (if you're reasonably close to Lumphini Park) for B30. ⊠ *Soi Polo, off Wittayu (Wireless Rd.), Pratunam* ☎ *02/251–2772 or 02/252–0856* ⌂ *Reservations not accepted* ⊟ *No credit cards* Ⓜ *Subway: Lumphini.*

Silom

CHINESE
$$$$
✗ **Jade Garden.** You won't find a better dim sum brunch than the one at Jade Garden. The superb dishes are made without MSG, a rare practice in this part of the world. The decor is more understated than at many expensive Chinese restaurants, with a remarkable wood-beam ceiling and softly lighted Chinese-print screens. Private dining rooms are available with advance notice. Two good dinner specials are fried Hong Kong noodles and pressed duck with tea leaves. Look for the monthly "special promotion" dish featuring seasonal ingredients. ⊠ *Montien Hotel, 54 Surawong Rd., Silom* ☎ *02/233–7060* ⊟ *AE, DC, MC, V* Ⓜ *Skytrain: Sala Daeng.*

$$$$
✗ **Mayflower.** Regulars at this top Cantonese restaurant include members of the Thai royal family, heads of state, and business tycoons. They favor the five opulent private rooms (two- to three-day advance notice required), but the main dining room is equally stylish with carved wood screens and porcelain vases that lend an air of refinement that is perfectly in keeping with the outstanding Cantonese food. Two of the best items on the menu are the piquant abalone-and-jellyfish salad and the drunken chicken, which is made with steamed, skinned, and deboned chicken doused with Chinese liquor and served with two sauces, one sweet and one spicy. The excellent wine list assumes that price is no object. ⊠ *Dusit Thani Hotel, Rama IV Rd., Silom* ☎ *02/236–0450* ⌦ *Reservations essential* ⊟ *AE* Ⓜ *Subway: Silom; Skytrain: Sala Daeng.*

★ $$$–$$$$
✗ **Shangrila.** There's plenty to make your mouth water here, from Peking duck to thinly sliced pork with garlic, but at lunch it's hard to pass up the marvelous selection of dim sum. Attentive waiters will help you choose individual dishes, but at B45 each you can afford some reckless experimentation. The small restaurant's split levels, bright white tablecloths, and gleaming glassware make it more comfortable than most other options in the neighborhood. ⊠ *154/4–7 Silom Rd., Silom* ☎ *02/234–9147* ⊟ *MC, V* Ⓜ *Skytrain: Chong Nonsi.*

★ ¢–$
✗ **Prachak.** This little place with bare walls and tile floor serves superb *ped* (roast duck) and *moo daeng* (red pork) and is a favorite of many locals. Wealthy Thai families will send their maids here to bring dinner home; you may want to follow their lead as it can get crowded. Whether you eat in or take out, get here early—by 6 PM there's often no duck or pork left, and by 9 PM the place has closed for the night. Finding Prachak is a bit challenging. It's on busy Charoen Krung (New Road), across the street from the big Robinson shopping center near the Shangri-La Hotel. ⊠ *1415 Charoen Krung (New Rd.), Silom Bansak, Silom* ☎ *02/234–3755* ⊟ *No credit cards* Ⓜ *Skytrain: Saphan Taksin.*

¢
✗ **Coca Suki.** This is the original branch—opened in 1957—of the successful Coca Suki chain. The spacious ground-floor restaurant has big round tables for families and groups, which might leave a lone diner feeling very alone indeed. It's best visited with at least four diners. It's popular with locals, and the restaurant founder often eats lunch here. Try the sukiyaki: order from a vast selection of meats and vegetables and watch as the waitress cooks it on the communal hot plate built into the center of the table. ⊠ *8 Soi Anumarnratchathon, Surawong Rd., Silom* ☎ *02/238–1137 or 02/238–1138* ⊟ *MC, V* Ⓜ *Skytrain: Sala Daeng.*

ECLECTIC ✕ **Le Café Siam.** This quiet restaurant, in a pleasant old house far from
$$$$ traffic noise, offers a successful mix of spicy Thai and subtle French
cuisines. It's really like two restaurants in one, perfect for a group with
disparate tastes. Some might find the portions small, but the quality of
the food more than makes up for this, and, at any rate, it's worth sav-
ing room for the magnificent desserts. Many of the objects and artwork
that decorate the house are for sale, so do some browsing while you eat.
It's best to arrive by taxi as this place can be difficult to find on your
own; if you call the restaurant, they will help arrange transportation for
you. ⊠ *4 Soi Sri Akson, Silom* ☎ *02/671–0030* ⊕ *www.lecafesiam.com*
⊟ *AE, DC, MC, V* Ⓜ *Subway: Khlong Toei.*

★ $$$ ✕ **V-9 Restaurant and Wine Bar.** On the 37th floor of the Sofitel Silom
Bangkok, V-9 has great views through its ceiling-to-floor windows.
This is a great restaurant for the indecisive—the "entree tree, " a metal
tree holding a half-dozen different dishes, can be a meal in itself. There's
also a dessert tree and the wine bar offers three different wine varieties
served in a single set, with all three brought to your table at the begin-
ning of the meal. If you can settle on just one entrée, the Australian lamb
is a solid pick. If you want to pick just one wine, good luck to you—
long rows of crates with more than 60 vintages of French, Italian, Aus-
tralian, Californian, and South African wines line the entrance. ⊠ *Sofitel
Silom Bangkok, 188 Silom Rd., Silom* ☎ *02/238–2992* ⊟ *AE, DC, MC*
Ⓜ *Skytrain: Chong Nonsi.*

$ ✕ **Mizu's.** Opened by a Japanese man in the mid-1950s, Mizu's remains
an institution. Considered Japanese by many, the menu actually offers
an eclectic selection of dishes, including a range of spicy curries. Try the
sizzling charcoal-broiled steaks from cattle raised in the north. The
decor is a bit dated—some of the travel posters have been on the walls
since the '70s—but the food is good and it's a good place for a bite be-
fore exploring the Patpong night market. ⊠ *32 Patpong Rd., Silom* ☎ *02/
233–6447* ⊟ *AE, MC, V* Ⓜ *Subway: Silom; Skytrain: Sala Daeng.*

FRENCH ✕ **Le Normandie.** Perched atop the Oriental Hotel, this legendary restau-
★ $$$$ rant commands a peerless view of the Chao Phraya. France's most highly
esteemed chefs periodically take over the kitchen and often import in-
gredients from the old country to use in their creations. Even when no
superstar is on the scene, the food is remarkable; the pricey menu (it's
hard to get away with spending less than B3,000 on a meal) often in-
cludes classic dishes like slow-cooked shoulder of lamb. ⊠ *48 Oriental
Ave., Silom* ☎ *02/659–9000* ⌲ *Reservations essential* 🛈 *Jacket and tie*
⊟ *AE, DC, MC, V* ⊘ *No lunch Sun.* Ⓜ *Skytrain: Saphan Taksin.*

GERMAN ✕ **Tawandang German Brewery.** You can't miss Tawandang—it resem-
★ $–$$ bles a big barrel. Food may be an afterthought to the 40,000 liters of
lager and other beers brewed here each month, but the kitchen turns
out decent Thai food, with some German and Chinese fare thrown in
for good measure. The taproom is especially boisterous when Bruce Gas-
ton's Fong Nam Band is performing its fusion of Thai and Western music.
On nights that the band's not playing, local singers perform Thai and
Western favorites. You have to take a taxi from the Skytrain station.
⊠ *462/61 Rama III Rd., Yannawa, South of Silom* ☎ *02/678–1114*
⊟ *AE, DC, MC, V* Ⓜ *Skytrain: Chong Nonsi.*

INDIAN
$
✕ **Himali Cha Cha.** Cha Cha, who cooked for Indian Prime Minister Jawa-harlal Nehru, died in 1996, but his recipes live on and are prepared with equal ability by his son Kovit. The tandoori chicken is locally famous, but the daily specials, precisely explained by the staff, are usually too intriguing to pass up. The breads and the mango *lassis* (yogurt drinks) are delicious. The northern Indian cuisine is served in a pleasantly in-formal setting with the usual Mogul decor. A branch in Silom serves the same food in a more spacious dining area. ✉ *1229/11 Charoen Krung (New Rd.), Silom* ☎*02/235–1569* ▭*AE, DC, MC, V* Ⓜ*Skytrain: Saphan Taksin* ✉ *2 Sukhumvit, Soi 35, Silom* ☎ *02/258–8843* ▭ *AE, DC, MC, V* Ⓜ *Skytrain: Phrom Phong.*

ITALIAN
$$$$
✕ **Angelini.** The competition is stiff, but many consider this the best Ital-ian restaurant in Bangkok. It certainly sets out to impress with its high ceilings, balconies, and river views. The Italian dishes are consistently good, with the rack of lamb head and shoulders above the rest. The desserts alone are worth the visit. A duo plays soothing jazz in the evenings. ✉ *Shangri-La Hotel, 89 Soi Wat Suan Phu, Charoen Krung (New Rd.), Silom* ☎ *02/236–7777* ▭ *AE, DC, MC, V* Ⓜ *Skytrain: Saphan Taksin.*

$$$
Fodor'sChoice
★
✕ **Zanotti.** Everything about this place is top-notch, from the attentive service to the extensive menu focusing on the regional cuisines of Pied-mont and Tuscany. You can find everything from pizza and pasta to fish and steak, but the traditional osso buco served with vegetable gremo-lada and saffron risotto is recommended. There's an extensive wine list, all Italian, with selections by the bottle, glass, or carafe. The prix-fixe lunch is a bargain. The low ceilings and closely grouped tables give the place some intimacy, but the vibe is more lively than romantic, especially during the lunch and dinner rushes. ✉ *21/2 Soi Saladaeng, off Silom Rd., Silom* ☎ *02/626–0002, 02/626–0266* ▭ *AE, DC, MC, V* Ⓜ *Sky-train: Sala Daeng.*

JAPANESE
$
✕ **Koto.** This small—three tables, four booths, and a sushi bar for two—friendly eatery caters to a mostly Japanese clientele (it's close to Soi Thaniya, also known as Little Tokyo because the entire block is lined with bars that cater to Japanese). The menu has English translations and photos of dishes. Expect to pay twice as much for sushi as for entrées. ✉ *20 Surawong, Silom* ☎ *02/637–0755* ▭ *MC, V* Ⓜ *Subway: Silom; Skytrain: Sala Daeng.*

THAI
$$–$$$$
✕ **Salathip.** On a veranda facing the Chao Phraya, this restaurant's set-ting practically guarantees a romantic evening. Be sure to reserve an out-side table so you can enjoy the breeze. Although the food may not have as many chilies as some would like, it hasn't been adulterated to suit Western tastes, so it's also popular with Thais. The live traditional music makes everything taste even better. ✉ *Shangri-La Hotel, 89 Soi Wat Suan Phu, Charoen Krung (New Rd.), Silom* ☎ *02/236–7777* ☝ *Reservations essential* ▭ *AE, DC, MC, V* ☺ *No lunch* Ⓜ *Skytrain: Saphan Taksin.*

$$–$$$
✕ **Ban Klang Nam.** This restaurant is in a large house and terrace up-stream from the Hanging Bridge, so you'll need a taxi or perhaps a tuk-tuk (if traffic is manageable) to get here. Choose a table by the railing so you can gaze at the river and all the shipping activity; you can also

opt for a seat on the dock. The difficult-to-make *mee krob* (pan-fried rice noodles) shows off the skill of the kitchen. The fried sea bass in garlic and pepper and the snapper in oyster sauce are superb, as is the smooth *tom yam kung* (hot-and-sour shrimp soup). Ban Klang Nam has maintained enough popularity to justify a second branch a few miles down river, though that one is set back a bit, with no tables right over the water. ⊠ *288 Soi 14, Rama III Rd., Yannawa, South of Silom* ☎ *02/292–0175 or 02/292–2037* ⌂ *Reservations essential* ▭ *AE, DC, MC, V* ⊠ *762/ 7 Jatujak Market, Rama III Rd., Yannawa, South of Silom* ☎ *02/819– 3880* ⌂ *Reservations recommended* ▭ *AE, DC, MC, V.*

$–$$ ✕ **Anna's Café.** There are quite a few Anna's around town, but this is the original. With its sunny yellow walls, this restaurant exudes good cheer. Dining areas are separated by potted plants, affording you some privacy from other diners. There's a smattering of European dishes here, but most of the menu is modern Thai. The green curry with chicken and eggplant is mild and served with a salted boiled egg to counter its sweetness. The *tod mun kung* (fried prawn cakes) served with stir-fried vegetables and fried rice makes a full and tasty meal. A good appetizer to share is the extremely spicy grilled fish salad. ⊠ *118 Soi Sala Daeng, at top of Silom Rd., Silom* ☎ *02/632–0619* ▭ *AE, DC, MC, V* Ⓜ *Subway: Silom; Skytrain: Sala Daeng.*

$ ✕ **Ban Chiang.** An oasis in the concrete city, this wooden house was built around 1915; the decor is turn-of-the-20th-century Bangkok, with antique prints and old photographs adorning the walls. The food can be quite spicy, especially the roasted duck curry and the shrimp and vegetable soup. Other dishes, such as the fried fish cakes and grilled prawns, are much milder. Help for hapless farangs isn't in high supply here, so it's better if you know your way around a Thai menu before trying this spot. ⊠ *14 Srivieng Rd., Silom* ☎ *02/236–7045* ▭ *AE, MC, V* Ⓜ *Skytrain: Surasak.*

$ ✕ **Harmonique.** Choose between tables on the terrace or in the dining rooms of this small house near the river. Inside, Chinese antiques, chests scattered with bric-a-brac, and bouquets that seem to tumble out of their vases create the best kind of clutter—one that invites you to relax as if you're sitting down for a meal at a relative's house. The menu is small, but the entrées are carefully selected, and the staff is very good at assisting indecisive diners. Try the crisp fish sautéed in garlic, the mild crab curry, or the Chinese cabbage topped with salted fish—all are excellent. Over the years the crowd has become increasingly tourist-heavy, but there are still Thais and expats who eat here regularly. ⊠ *22 Charoen Krung (New Rd.), Soi 34, Silom* ☎ *02/237–8175* ▭ *AE, DC, MC, V* Ⓜ *Skytrain: Saphan Taksin.*

$ ✕ **River City Bar B-Q Corner.** This is a place where you can be the chef—a waiter brings you a hot plate and a mound of different meats and vegetables that you can grill to your own taste. Order some appetizers to nibble on while dinner is cooking; the northern Thai sausage is excellent. A live band entertains on Friday, Saturday, and Sunday evenings. There's an air-conditioned dining room, but you might prefer the tables on the roof of the River City Shopping Center, which have views of the Chao Phraya. ⊠ *River City Shopping Center, Captain Bush La., Silom* ☎ *02/237–0077* ▭ *AE, MC, V* Ⓜ *Skytrain: Saphan Taksin.*

¢-$ ✕ **Banana Leaf.** If you need a break from shopping on Silom Road, this is the place to try—the food is delicious and quite a bargain. Try the baked crab with glass noodles, grilled black band fish, or grilled pork with coconut milk dip. The menu also offers 11 equally scrumptious vegetarian selections. Note that there's a B400 minimum if you want to use a credit card. ⊠ *Silom Complex, Silom Rd., Silom* ☎ *02/231–3124* ▭ *AE, MC, V* Ⓜ *Skytrain: Sala Daeng.*

★ ¢-$ ✕ **Hai, Isan.** A sure sign of quality, Hai is packed with Thais sharing tables filled with northeast favorites like grilled chicken, spicy papaya salad, and spicy minced pork. The open-air dining area can be hot and is often crowded and noisy, but that's part of the fun. The staff doesn't speak English, so the best way to order is to point to things that look good on neighboring tables. ⊠ *2/4–5 Soi Covent, off Silom Rd., Silom* ☎ *02/631–0216* ▭ *No credit cards* Ⓜ *Subway: Silom; Skytrain: Sala Daeng.*

¢-$ ✕ **Sara-Jane's.** The owner, a Massachusetts native, moved to Bangkok more than 20 years ago when she married a Thai. Sara-Jane's has done so well that there are now three branches, but this big, comfortable restaurant is the best of them. The cuisine draws on the traditions of the northeastern part of the country, with salads served with *larb*, made from marinated minced pork, chicken, or tuna. A favorite is the grilled fish salad, always on the spicy side. There's also Italian food and wine. ⊠ *Narathiwat Rd., near Sathorn Rd., Silom* ☎ *02/679–3338* ▭ *No credit cards* Ⓜ *Skytrain: Chong Nonsi.*

Sukhumvit

CHINESE   ✕ **Sui Sian.** This longtime favorite serves delicious, if a bit inconsistent,
$$$$ Cantonese cuisine. Certainly the decor of both the main dining rooms and the adjoining private rooms make it a good spot for lunch or dinner meetings. The larger rooms with bamboo-tile eaves give the feeling of dining in an outdoor courtyard, an impression reinforced by the presence of jade trees. The Peking duck is particularly good and big enough for four. The barbecued suckling pig is equally good, either traditional or Hong Kong–style. A harp player entertains diners in the evening. ⊠ *Landmark Hotel, 138 Sukhumvit Rd., Sukhumvit* ☎ *02/254–0404* ▭ *AE, DC, MC, V* Ⓜ *Skytrain: Nana.*

ECLECTIC   ✕ **Bed Supperclub.** You have to be 20 years old to get in here, even for
$$$$ dinner. Make sure to bring a picture ID with you, no matter what your
Fodor'sChoice   age, because the place has experienced numerous police checks in re-
★   cent years. (Police raids are a rare occurrence and usually happen late at night after dinner hours, but be aware that if you're here when one happens, you may be required to participate in random drug testing.) But don't let any of that scare you away—this unique and trendy restaurant is worth the potential headache. The "tables" consist of a long beds with white sheets, lined up along the walls. The Mediterranean and Asian-fusion menu changes every two months, but the food is always good. The four-course set menu is a bit cheaper during the week. Note that men wearing sandals or shorts won't be allowed in. ⊠ *26 Sukhumvit Soi 11, Sukhumvit* ☎ *02/651–3537* ⊕ *www.bedsupperclub.com* ▭ *AE, DC, MC, V* Ⓜ *Skytrain: Nana.*

$$-$$$$ ✕ **Kuppa.** This light and airy space maintains the aura of its former life as a warehouse, but it's certainly more chic than shabby these days,

with polished metal and blond wood adding a hip counterpoint to cement floors. An advantage to a space like this is that, unlike many downtown eateries, each table has plenty of room around it. Kuppa offers traditional Thai fare as well as many international dishes, and it has a dedicated following because of its coffee (roasted on the premises) and its impressive desserts. The one drawback is that the portions are somewhat small for the price. ✉ *39 Sukhumvit Soi 16, Sukhumvit* ☎ *02/663–0450* ▭ *AE, DC, MC, V* Ⓜ *Subway: Sukhumvit; Skytrain: Asok.*

FRENCH   ✕ **Le Banyan.** You might never guess that inside this traditional Thai home
$$$$ you can find first-rate French cooking. The chef occasionally experiments with Asian influences, adding to his continental fare a note of lemongrass, ginger, or Thai basil. He changes the menu every four months, but duck and rabbit dishes are always a sure thing. Other delicious constants are the pan-fried foie gras and king lobster in mustard sauce. The steak tartar is tops, too. For a current menu check the Web site. ✉ *59 Sukhumvit Soi 8, Sukhumvit* ☎ *02/253–5556* ⊕ *www.le-banyan.com* ⌂ *Reservations essential* ▭ *AE, DC, MC, V* ☾ *Closed Sun.* Ⓜ *Skytrain: Nana.*

GERMAN   ✕ **Bei Otto.** Berlin comes to Bangkok in the form of Bei Otto, a restau-
$$$ rant with deliciously authentic cuisine. Otto Duffner came to Bangkok in 1980 to open the place and it's been popular ever since. The walls of the main dining room are covered with photos of the owner with people of note who've dropped by for lunch or dinner. The dining room is comfortable, if a tad cramped, and the food is tasty and the portions tremendous. There's also a bakery for takeout. ✉ *1 Sukhumvit Soi 20, Sukhumvit* ☎ *02/262–0892* ▭ *AE, DC, MC, V* Ⓜ *Subway: Sukhumvit; Skytrain: Asok or Phrom Phong.*

INDIAN   ✕ **Rang Mahal.** Savory food in a pleasant setting with great views of the
$$$$ city is the combination that brings people back to this upscale Indian
FodorsChoice   restaurant. It rates tops in a city that has no shortage of good Indian
★   restaurants; it also has some of the best vegetarian selections in town. The main dining room has Indian music, which can be loud to some ears, but there are smaller rooms for a quieter meal. Take a jacket—the air-conditioning can be overpowering—and ask for a window seat for a great view of the city. ✉ *Rembrandt Hotel, 19 Sukhumvit Soi 18, Sukhumvit* ☎ *02/261–7100* ⌂ *Reservations essential* ▭ *AE, DC, MC, V* Ⓜ *Subway: Sukhumvit; Skytrain: Asok.*

ITALIAN   ✕ **L'Opera.** For years now this family-run restaurant has drawn a loyal
$$ clientele. The staff takes pride in their work, and many of them have remained over the years despite overtures from the competition. The specialty of the house is homemade pastas; consider the large ravioli stuffed with spinach and cheese or the *spadella,* a combination of different types of seafood in a garlic-and-white-wine sauce. The table in the bay window is the nicest, but given its proximity to the air-conditioning, you might want to bring a sweater. It's a short taxi ride from the Skytrain station. ✉ *53 Sukhumvit Soi 39, Sukhumvit* ☎ *02/258–5606* ▭ *AE, DC, MC, V* Ⓜ *Skytrain: Phrom Phong.*

JAPANESE
$$–$$$$

✕ **Hakata.** Although there are many good Japanese restaurants in the Sukhumvit area near the Emporium shopping center, Hakata is a step above most. The main dining area and sushi bar are spacious and relaxing, and there are private rooms available. Expect to spend more to make a meal out of sushi, but the regular dishes like tempura and *katsu-don* (fried pork strips) are reasonably priced and tasty. ⊠ *4 Sukhumvit Soi 39, Sukhumvit* ☎ *02/258–8351* ☰ *AE, DC, MC, V* Ⓜ *Skytrain: Phrom Phong.*

LAOTIAN
★ ¢–$

✕ **Vientiane Kitchen.** This open-air restaurant named after the capital of Laos is set under thatched roofs; there's table seating or you can opt for traditional seating on floor mats. Laotian cuisine is similar to the Thai food found in the country's northeastern province of Isan. Among the Thai-style standards like grilled chicken, sticky rice, and *song tom* (spicy papaya salad) are a few riskier dishes. *Nam tok* (waterfall) is so called because it's so hot it makes your eyes run like a waterfall (however, it's actually toned down here, so don't think you can order it in Laos and still feel your tongue afterward). Other dishes like frog soup and grilled duck beak are actually quite good, despite the images they conjure up. It's best to go with a group so you can share several dishes. Live Laotian music and dance add to the experience. ⊠ *8 Sukhumvit Soi 36, Sukhumvit* ☎ *02/258–6171* ☰ *AE, DC, MC, V* Ⓜ *Skytrain: Thong Lo.*

THAI
$$$$

✕ **Seafood Market.** Although it's miles from the ocean, the fish here is so fresh it feels like the boats must be somewhere nearby. Like at a supermarket, you take a cart and choose from an array of seafood—crabs, prawns, lobsters, clams, oysters, and fish. The waiter takes it away and instructs the chef to cook it any way you like. Typically your eyes are bigger than your stomach, so select with prudence, not gusto. Unfortunately, the 1,500-seat setting and fluorescent lighting add to the supermarket feel, but it's a fun and unique dining experience. ⊠ *89 Sukhumvit Soi 24, Sukhumvit* ☎ *02/661–1252* ⌕ *Reservations not accepted* ☰ *AE, DC, MC, V* Ⓜ *Skytrain: Phrom Phong.*

$$$–$$$$

✕ **Lemongrass.** This is an elegant restaurant—Southeast Asian antiques are everywhere—where Thais and expats like to entertain visitors. Since it opened 20 years ago, the cuisine has gradually become geared to the milder palate of Westerners, which makes for a good introduction to Thai food. Be sure to try a glass of *nam takrai*, the cold, sweet drink brewed from lemongrass. ⊠ *5/1 Sukhumvit Soi 24, Sukhumvit* ☎ *02/ 258–8637* ☰ *AE, DC, MC, V* Ⓜ *Skytrain: Phrom Phong.*

$$–$$$

✕ **Baan Khanitha.** Half the pleasure of eating at Baan Khanitha is the attractive old house it's in; the dining room has wood paneling, traditional prints, and copper serving pieces. The food is strictly Thai, and the dishes are explained well by the English-speaking waiters. The recipes have been altered a bit to appeal more to tourists, which explains the absence of Thai diners. Ask for the complimentary appetizer *mieng khum* (spinach wraps). The fried soft-shell crabs in a hot-and-sour sauce and the *gaeng keow wan gai* (green curry with chicken and Thai eggplant) are two of the better entrees. A second branch in Pratunam doubles as an art gallery and is in the former Egyptian embassy. ⊠ *36/ 1 Sukhumvit 23 Soi Prasan, Sukhumvit* ☎ *02/258–4181* ⌕ *Reservations essential* ☰ *AE, DC, MC, V* Ⓜ *Subway: Sukhumvit; Skytrain: Asok*

✉ *49 Soi Ruam Rudee 2, Pratunam* ☎ *02/253–4638* ⌕ *Reservations essential* ▭ *AE, DC, MC, V* Ⓜ *Skytrain: Ploenchit.*

$ ✕ **Cabbages & Condoms.** Don't be misled by the restaurant's odd name or put off by the array of contraceptive devices for sale. This popular place raises funds for the Population & Community Development Association, the country's family planning program. You'll find the food here excellently prepared, the chicken wrapped in pandanus leaves, crisp fried fish with chili sauce, and shrimp in a mild curry sauce being the stand-outs. The eatery lost some of its charm when it expanded, but it's comfortable and still serves up good food for a good cause. ✉ *10 Sukhumvit Soi 12, Sukhumvit* ☎ *02/229–4610* ▭ *AE, DC, MC, V* Ⓜ *Subway: Sukhumvit; Skytrain: Asok.*

$ ✕ **My Choice.** Thais with a taste for their grandmothers' traditional recipes have flocked to this restaurant off Sukhumvit Road since the mid-'80s. The *ped aob*, a thick soup made from beef stock, is particularly popular. Foreigners may prefer the *tom kha tala*, a hot-and-sour soup with big pieces of shrimp. The interior is plain, so when the weather is cool most people prefer to sit outside. ✉ *Sukhumvit Soi 36, Sukhumvit* ☎ *02/258–6174 or 02/259–9470* ▭ *AE, DC, MC, V* Ⓜ *Skytrain: Thong Lo.*

★ **¢** ✕ **Atlanta.** Although it looks like a coffee shop in a budget hotel, the Atlanta serves surprisingly good Thai and vegetarian fare, thanks to innkeeper Charles Henn and longtime chef Khun Anong. The detailed menu, which explains the ingredients and their origin, makes for an interesting and amusing read. Don't pass up the *tom yam kung* (spicy shrimp soup)—it's especially smooth. For vegetarians, the Atlanta is a particular delight because the vegetarian dishes are purposely made so, not just Thai dishes that don't include meat. In the evening, classic jazz is usually piped in, and a movie of some repute is shown in the dining room, starting at 8 PM. Note that the hotel likes to keep the restaurant for hotel guests and well-mannered outsiders only—loud or rowdy groups will not be served. ✉ *78 Sukhumvit Soi 2, Sukhumvit* ☎ *02/252–1650 or 02/252–6069* ▭ *No credit cards* Ⓜ *Skytrain: Ploenchit.*

¢ ✕ **Thong Lee.** This small but attractive restaurant draws a devoted crowd to its air-conditioned dining room on the second floor. The menu is not very adventurous, but every dish has a distinct personality—evidence of the cook's vivid imagination. Almost everyone orders the *muu phad kapi* (pork fried with shrimp paste). The *yam hed sod* (hot-and-sour mushroom salad) is memorable, but might be too spicy for some people. This place is for lunch or early dinners only—it closes around 8 PM. ✉ *Sukhumvit Soi 20, Sukhumvit* ☎ *No phone* ⌕ *Reservations not accepted* ▭ *No credit cards* ⊘ *Closed Sun.* Ⓜ *Subway: Sukhumvit; Skytrain: Asok.*

VIETNAMESE ✕ **Le Dalat.** This classy restaurant, a favorite with Bangkok residents,
$$–$$$ consists of several intimate dining rooms in what was once a private home. Don't pass up the *naem neuang*, which requires you to place a garlicky grilled meatball on a piece of rice paper, then pile on bits of garlic, ginger, hot chili, star apple, and mango before you wrap the whole thing up in a lettuce leaf and pop it in your mouth. A nearby branch offers seafood—this one does not—and a pricier menu. ✉ *47/1 Sukhumvit Soi*

23, opposite Indian Embassy, Sukhumvit ☎02/260–1849 ⌚*Reservations essential* ☰*AE, DC, MC, V* Ⓜ *Subway: Sukhumvit; Skytrain: Asok* ✉ *14 Sukhumvit Soi 23, Sukhumvit* ☎ *02/661–7967* ⌚ *Reservations essential* ☰ *AE, DC, MC, V* Ⓜ *Subway: Sukhumvit; Skytrain: Asok.*

WHERE TO STAY

Bangkok offers a wide range of lodging, and some of the best rooms are affordable to travelers on a budget. The city has more than 450 hotels and guesthouses, and the number is growing. The most recent trend has been boutique hotels, some of which are truly world-class. Competition has brought the price down at many city hotels but service could suffer in the future as hotels cut corners to lower prices.

For first-class lodging, few cities in the world rival Bangkok. In recent years the Oriental, Peninsula, Four Seasons (formerly the Regent), and a handful of others have been repeatedly rated among the best in the world. These high-end hotels are surprisingly affordable, with rates comparable to standard hotels in New York or London. Even after the economic crisis of the '90s that saw businesses raising their prices to offset the beleaguered baht, hotels in Bangkok are still less expensive than those in Singapore and Hong Kong. Business hotels also have fine service, excellent restaurants, and amenities like health clubs. Even budget hotels have comfortable rooms and efficient staffs.

Wherever you stay, remember that prices fluctuate enormously and that huge discounts are the order of the day. Always ask for a better price, even if you have already booked a room (you can inquire about a discount upon check-in).

Hotels are concentrated in three neighborhoods: along Silom and Sathorn roads in Silom (where many of the river hotels are located); clustered in Siam Square and on Petchaburi Road in Pratunam; and along Sukhumvit Road, which has the greatest number of hotels and an abundance of restaurants. Backpackers often head to Khao San Road, with its mix of cheap cafés, secondhand bookstalls, trendy bars, and small guesthouses. It's still possible to get a room in that area for B150; even the newer, more up-market guesthouses only charge around B500.

WHAT IT COSTS In Baht				
$$$$	**$$$**	**$$**	**$**	**¢**
FOR 2 PEOPLE over B6,000	B4,000–B6,000	B2,000–B4,000	B1,000–B2,000	under B1,000

Price categories are assigned based on the range between the least and most expensive standard double rooms in high season based on the European Plan (EP, with no meals) unless otherwise noted. Tax (17%) is extra.

Northern Bangkok

$$$$ 🏨 **Amari Airport Hotel.** This is the only hotel within walking distance of Don Muang Airport. Rates are high but promotions are often available. A covered passageway leads from the international terminal to the lobby. Rooms are functional, but don't expect the opulence you'd

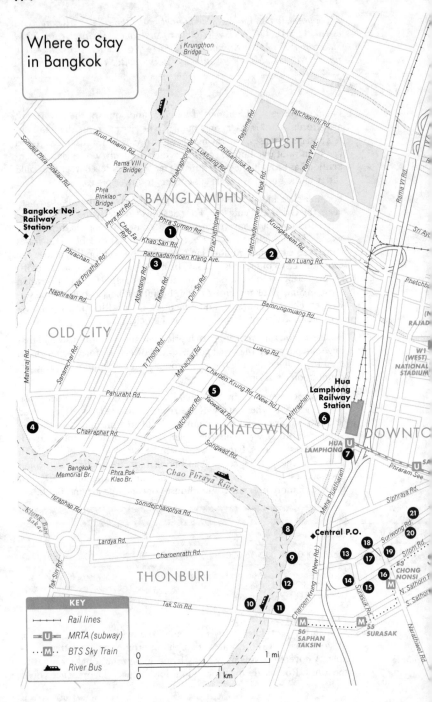

Where to Stay in Bangkok

TO DON
MUANG
AIRPORT

48 49

THAI
CULTURAL
CENTER

R. Samsen

Rd.

Dindaeng Rd.

N3
VICTORY
MONUMENT

PHRA RAMA 9

Phraram Kao (Rama IX)

N2
PHAYA THAI

PETCHABURI

52

51

PRATUNAM

New Phetchburi Rd.

Klong San Sab

World
Trade
Center

E1
(EAST)
CHITLOM

47

38

SIAM

Ploenchit Rd.

46

British
Embassy

36

45

44

(Rama I Rd.)

37

Sol 15

Sol 13

Sol 11

PHLOENCHIT

E2

40

39

Sol 3

Sol 5

Sol 7

NANA

E3

43

42

41

35

SUKHUMVIT

33

SUKHUMVIT

S1
(SOUTH)
RATCHADAMRI

Sarasin Rd.

American
Embassy

34

E4
ASOK

E5
PHROM
PHONG

SILOM

LUMPHINI
PARK

Witthayu (Wireless Rd.)

Sol 31

Sol 33

Sol 39

Rama 4 Rd.

24

32

Sol 24

Sol 26

25

LUMPHINI

QUEEN
SIRIKIT

29

30

31

SALA
DAENG

52

KLONG
TOEI

26

27

28

Phraram See

(Rama IV Rd.)

Ai-Narong Rd.

Sol Sianbun

Immigration
Office

find at similarly priced riverside hotels. For tired travelers waiting for connecting flights, there's a special daytime (8 AM–6 PM) rate of B1,400 ($35) for stays up to three hours; video screens in public areas display flight arrivals and departures. ⊠ *333 Chert Wudhakas Rd., Don Muang 10210* ☎ *02/566–1020* 🖷 *02/566–1941* ⊕ *www.amari.com* 🛏 *420 rooms* ⚥ *2 restaurants, coffee shop, pool, meeting rooms* 🚭 *AE, DC, MC, V.*

$$$–$$$$ 🏨 **Sofitel Central Plaza Bangkok.** Catering to corporate travelers, this huge hotel is north of much of the city, but it's close to the expressway to the airport and to subway and Skytrain stations. To the west is a view of the Railway Golf Course; the other side looks out onto the city's astounding vertical growth. The refreshingly cool lobby, with a cascading waterfall, is a welcome retreat from the city streets. Rooms are gracefully appointed—antique prints, bronze statues of mythological figures, and temple-dog lamp stands remind you that you're in Thailand. Among the hotel's numerous restaurants and bars is Dynasty, a popular spot for Chinese cuisine. ⊠ *1695 Phaholyothin Rd., Chatuchak, Northern Bangkok, 10210* ☎ *02/541–1234* 🖷 *02/541–1087* ⊕ *www. centralhotelsresorts.com* 🛏 *577 rooms, 7 suites* ⚥ *6 restaurants, pool, health club, bar, business services, meeting rooms* 🚭 *AE, DC, MC, V* Ⓜ *Subway: Phahon Yothin.*

The Old City, Banglamphu & Dusit

$$$–$$$$ 🏨 **Chakrabongse Villas.** Perhaps the best three rooms in Bangkok are here
Fodor'sChoice in the gardens of Chakrabongse House. The problem is there are only
★ three rooms, and the place is very popular, so you must book well in advance. Located on the banks of the Chao Phraya River in an old part of the city, the rooms are in traditional Thai houses, originally built up-country and brought to the grounds of the Chakrabongse House, which was built in 1908. The Riverside Villa and Garden Suite each offer more space and better views—the villa has a view of Wat Arun from the bedroom—but the Thai House is also unique and beautifully furnished. There's a sala next to the river for guests to enjoy, where Thai meals are served upon request. A minimum two-night stay is required. ⊠ *396 Maharay Rd., Old City, 10200* ☎ *02/622–3356* 🖷 *02/225–3861* ⊕ *www. thaivillas.com* 🛏 *3 rooms* ⚥ *Dining room, pool* 🚭 *AE, DC, MC, V.*

$$ 🏨 **Royal Princess.** This hotel is ideally located for exploring Dusit and the Old City, but it's far from Skytrain and subway stations, and the neighborhood is virtually deserted in the evening. Fortunately, it's a short taxi ride to riverside restaurants and the hotel offers Chinese, Italian, Japanese, and Thai cuisine. The tranquil lobby has gardens on two sides. The rooms are tastefully decorated in subdued colors that set off the dark-wood furnishings, but the bathrooms are on the small side. ⊠ *269 Larn Luang Rd., Old City, 10100* ☎ *02/281–3088* 🖷 *02/280–1314* ⊕ *www.royalprincess.com* 🛏 *160 rooms* ⚥ *3 restaurants, coffee shop, pool, business services, meeting rooms* 🚭 *AE, DC, MC, V* Ⓜ *Skytrain: National Stadium.*

$–$$ 🏨 **Buddy Lodge.** Buddy Lodge has contributed greatly to Khao San Road's new trendiness by offering Bangkok's backpacker center its first boutique hotel. Standard rooms are very comfortable, but paying the extra B500 for a deluxe room is worth it, considering the extra space and bigger balcony you get. You can really appreciate the rooftop pool after trekking around the Old City sights all day. The lodge is also close to the river and many attractions like the Grand Palace. ⊠ *265 Khao San Rd., Banglamphu, 10200* ☎ *02/629–4477* ⊟ *02/629–4744* ⊕ *www. buddylodge.com* ↘ *70 rooms* ↤ *Coffee shop, pool, spa, 2 bars, shops* ⊟ *AE, DC, MC, V.*

$ 🏨 **Royal Hotel.** Nearer to the Grand Palace and the Old City than any other of the city's lodgings, this hotel is a carefully kept secret of many frequent visitors. Its clean and comfortable rooms have homey touches like small writing tables. Several banquet rooms on the ground floor are popular with wedding parties. The lobby café is a good place to take a break from sightseeing. ⊠ *2 Rajdamnoen Ave., Old City, 10200* ☎ *02/ 222–9111* ⊟ *02/224–2083* ↘ *300 rooms* ↤ *3 restaurants, coffee shop, in-room VCRs, pool, bar, meeting rooms* ⊟ *AE, DC, MC, V.*

Chinatown

$$ 🏨 **Grand China Princess.** One good reason for staying in Chinatown is the chance to experience the sights and sounds of the city's oldest neighborhood. Another reason is this hotel, which occupies the top two-thirds of a 25-story tower. The rooms are plain, but have panoramic views of the city. The 10th-floor lobby has a bar, lounge, and coffee shop. Siang Ping Loh, serving Cantonese and Szechuan fare, is well worth a visit. ⊠ *215 Yaowarat Rd., at Ratchawongse Rd., Chinatown, 10100* ☎ *02/ 224–9977* ⊟ *02/224–7999* ⊕ *www.royalprincess.com* ↘ *139 rooms, 16 suites* ↤ *Restaurant, coffee shop, in-room safes, health club, business services* ⊟ *AE, DC, MC, V* Ⓜ *Subway: Hua Lamphong.*

$ 🏨 **Bangkok Centre.** This hotel on the edge of Chinatown is near Hua Lamphong Railway Station, convenient if you have to catch an early train. Note that the hotel caters to tour groups from Singapore, Japan, China, and Europe, so the lobby can be chaotic at times, but service is attentive to the individual, too. The rooms are small, but clean and comfortable. It has a 24-hour coffee shop. ⊠ *328 Rama 4, Chinatown, 10500* ☎ *02/ 238–4848* ⊟ *02/236–1862* ⊕ *www.bangkokcentrehotel.com* ↘ *145 rooms* ↤ *Restaurant, coffee shop, pool, meeting rooms* ⊟ *AE, DC, MC, V* Ⓜ *Subway: Hua Lamphong.*

¢ 🏨 **Krung Kasem Srikrung Hotel.** This hotel, across a canal from Hua Lamphong Train Station, is in its fifth decade and a bit worse for wear. But it's ideally located if you arrive on a late train or are departing early in the morning. Basically, the sparsely furnished rooms are air-conditioned, the baths are clean, and the price is right—and that's about all you can say about it. ⊠ *1860 Krung Kasem Rd., Chinatown, 10100* ☎ *02/225– 0132 or 02/225–8900* ⊟ *02/225–4705* ↘ *120 rooms* ↤ *Coffee shop* ⊟ *No credit cards* Ⓜ *Subway: Hua Lamphong.*

¢ 🏨 **River View Guest House.** This family-run hotel is one of the only budget accommodations that overlooks the river. The eighth-floor coffee shop has a great view. The accommodations may remind you of college dorm rooms (though they have far fewer amenities than the average dorm), but they're clean and comfortable. The staff will go out of its way for you, even staying up to accommodate late flights (someone sleeps downstairs during the night, in case you need something). One drawback is that tuk-tuk drivers sometimes have difficulty finding the place. The easiest way to find it is to head north from the Royal Orchid Sheraton; you can see the guesthouse's sign pointing down a side street. ✉ 768 Soi Panurangsri, Songvad Rd., Chinatown, 10100 ☎ 02/234–5429 🖷 02/237–5428 🛏 45 rooms ☖ Restaurant; no a/c in some rooms, no room TVs ▤ AE.

Thonburi

$$$$
Fodor's Choice
★
🏨 **Peninsula.** If you want to experience the latest in hotel technology, like bedside controls that dim the lights, turn on the sound system, and close the curtains, then the Peninsula is the place to stay. There's no end to the little marvels in each room—bathrooms have hands-free phones and a TV with a mist-free screen at the end of the tub. Because the hotel is in Thonburi, its spacious rooms get a crack view of the Bangkok skyline; a free shuttle across the river to the nearest Skytrain station is provided. The restaurants include Cantonese and Pacific Rim cuisine and barbecue buffets are often held in the evening by the river. The hotel has a long, attractive swimming pool with private gazebos where you can lounge about in sun or shade. ✉ 333 Charoen Krung (New Rd.), Klonsan, Thonburi, 10600 ☎ 02/861–2888 🖷 02/861–2351 or 02/861–1112 ⊕ www.peninsula.com 🛏 310 rooms, 60 suites ☖ 4 restaurants, coffee shop, health club, bar, business services, meeting rooms, helipad ▤ AE, DC, MC, V Ⓜ Skytrain: Saphan Taksin.

Pratunam

$$$$
🏨 **The Conrad.** After opening in 2002, this property quickly became one of Bangkok's top hotels. It's bigger than most, but service doesn't suffer—the staff is attentive and the rooms and other facilities are well-maintained. It's connected to All Seasons Place, which has dozens of restaurants and shops. A hotel shuttle bus is available to and from the Skytrain. ✉ All Seasons Place, 87 Wittayu (Wireless Rd.), Pratunam, 10330 ☎ 02/690–9999 🖷 02/690–9000 ⊕ www.conradhotels.com 🛏 383 rooms, 9 suites ☖ 4 restaurants, coffee shop, pool, spa, 2 bars, business services, meeting rooms ▤ AE, DC, MC, V Ⓜ Skytrain: Ploenchit.

$$$$
🏨 **Four Seasons Hotel Bangkok.** Formerly called the Regent, this hotel reigns over the embassy district and has long been one of Bangkok's leading hotels. Stride up the palatial steps and into the formal lobby where local society meets for morning coffee and afternoon tea. Off a delightful courtyard there are plenty of shops where you can browse. The large rooms are decorated with silk-upholstered furniture. The best rooms overlook the racetrack, but ask for a high floor so that the Skytrain doesn't block the view. A quartet of "cabana rooms, " whose private patios look onto a small garden with a lotus pond, are exquisite. Be sure to indulge yourself with the Four Season's fragrant-oil massage. ✉ 155 Ratchadamri Rd., Pratunam, 10330 ☎ 02/250–1000 🖷 02/253–9195 ⊕ www.fourseasons.com/bangkok 🛏 346 rooms, 10 suites ☖ 7 restaurants, pool, health club, massage, spa, shops, business services ▤ AE, DC, MC, V Ⓜ Skytrain: Ratchadamri.

$$$$
🏨 **Grand Hyatt Erawan.** This stylish hotel hovers over the auspicious Erawan Shrine. The impressive atrium, with an extensive modern art collection, soars four stories high to a glass roof. Rooms are spacious; the wood floors are strewn with tasteful rugs, the walls are hung with original art, and a desk and a couple of chairs are positioned directly in front

of bay windows. There are plenty of high-tech accoutrements, too. Baths have separate showers, oversize tubs, and private dressing areas. The Italian fare at Spasso, created by a Milanese chef, is especially creative; lunch here is a must whether or not you stay in the hotel. ⊠ *494 Ratchadamri Rd., Pratunam, 10330* ☏ *02/254–1234, 800/233–1234 in U.S.* 🖷 *02/254–6308* ⊕ *www.bangkok.grand.hyatt.com* ⮑ *364 rooms, 38 suites* ⚴ *8 restaurants, 2 tennis courts, pool, health club, squash, bar, business services, meeting rooms* ▭ *AE, DC, MC, V* Ⓜ *Skytrain: Ratchadamri.*

$$$$ ▦ **Inter-Continental Bangkok.** This fine hotel, formerly Le Royal Meridian, is in one of the city's prime business districts and does a good job of catering to its corporate clientele. Club Inter-Continental rooms have 24-hour butler service. The lounge on the 34th floor has great city views to gaze at while sipping evening cocktails (complimentary for Club floor guests). The rooftop pool is rather small, but feels cozy rather than cramped. The popular Summer Palace restaurant serves Cantonese cuisine. ⊠ *973 Ploenchit Rd., Pratunam, 10330* ☏ *02/656–0444* 🖷 *02/656–0555* ⊕ *www.intercontinental.com* ⮑ *318 rooms, 34 suites* ⚴ *3 restaurants, coffee shop, room service, in-room safes, pool, health club, spa, gift shop, babysitting, concierge, dry cleaning, laundry, business services, meeting rooms* ▭ *AE, DC, MC, V* Ⓜ *Skytrain: Chitlom.*

$$$–$$$$ ▦ **Nai Lert Park Bangkok.** The best thing about this hotel, part of the Swissotel chain, is the garden, so ask for a room that faces it. The rooms are large, and the baths have showers and bath tubs. The grounds and building were totally refurbished in 2003, but the excellent Japanese restaurant, Genji, was kept. This is a popular hotel for weddings, conferences, and parties. ⊠ *2 Wittayu (Wireless Rd.), Pratunam, 10330* ☏ *02/253–0123* 🖷 *02/254–8740* ⊕ *www.nailertpark.swissotel.com* ⮑ *303 rooms, 35 suites* ⚴ *3 restaurants, coffee shop, 2 tennis courts, pool, spa, squash, 2 bars, business services, meeting rooms* ▭ *AE, DC, MC, V* Ⓜ *Skytrain: Ploenchit.*

$$$ ▦ **Amari Watergate.** This huge flagship hotel has spacious and comfortable rooms, all decked out in silks and other rich fabrics. Baths are also quite large, although the separate showers are small. The executive floor has a lounge where complimentary cocktails are served in the afternoon. The restaurants serve up delicious Italian and Vietnamese fare, a Thai eatery specializes in fare from the country's four major regions, and the coffee shop serves a tasty buffet. The swimming pool is one of the largest in the city. ⊠ *847 Phetchburi Rd., Pratunam, 10400* ☏ *02/653–9000* 🖷 *02/653–9044* ⊕ *www.amari.com* ⮑ *549 rooms, 29 suites* ⚴ *4 restaurants, pool, health club, bar, business services, meeting rooms* ▭ *AE, DC, MC, V* Ⓜ *Skytrain: Chitlom.*

$$$ ▦ **Century Park Hotel.** The spacious lobby is a comfortable place to meet people; a pianist plays classical music here in the evenings. The rooms, though neat and clean, are a bit dark. The hotel is in the northern part of town where there are fewer hotels and the closest Skytrain station is a 10–15 minute walk. It's an easy 20-minute taxi ride to Don Muang International Airport, convenient for those with early flights. ⊠ *9 Ratchaprarop Rd., Pratunam, 10400* ☏ *02/246–7800* 🖷 *02/246–7197* ⊕ *www.centuryparkhotel.com* ⮑ *380 rooms* ⚴ *Restaurant, coffee shop, pool, bar* ▭ *AE, DC, MC, V* Ⓜ *Skytrain: Victory Monument.*

$$ ⌧ **The Novotel Bangkok on Siam Square.** This big hotel is convenient to shopping, dining, and entertainment. It's also a short walk from the Skytrain central station, which puts much of the city within reach. The rooms are comfortable and functional. Despite the size of the hotel, ample staff are always around to help you. One of Bangkok's top night clubs, CM2, is in the basement. ⌧ *Siam Sq. Soi 6, Pratunam, 10330* ☎ *02/ 255–6888* 🖷 *02/255–1824* ⊕ *www.accorhotels-asia.com* ⤴ *404 rooms, 25 suites* ♿ *3 restaurants, pool, 3 bars* ⊟ *AE, DC, MC, V* Ⓜ *Skytrain: Siam.*

$ ⌧ **First House.** Tucked behind the Pratunam Market in the bustling garment district, the First House is an excellent value for a hotel in this price range. The compact rooms are nicely furnished, but rather dark. In the small lobby you can catch up on the latest with the complimentary newspapers. The 24-hour coffee shop serves Thai dishes. ⌧ *14/20–29 Phetchburi Soi 19, Phaya Thai, Pratunam, 10400* ☎ *02/254–0300* 🖷 *02/ 254–3101* ⤴ *100 rooms* ♿ *Coffee shop, travel services* ⊟ *AE, MC, V* Ⓜ *Skytrain: Rajchathewi.*

Silom

$$$$ ⌧ **Banyan Tree Bangkok.** After checking in on the ground floor, you soar up to your room at this 60-story hotel. The light-filled suites in the slender tower all have sweeping views of the city. The generous use of native woods in everything from the large desks to the walk-in closets gives the rooms a warm glow. For those in need of pampering, a fully equipped spa offers the latest treatments, and a sun deck on the 53rd floor beckons with a relaxing whirlpool. For meals or a drink in the evening there's the rooftop Vertigo, a fair-weather restaurant that the hotel claims is the world's highest alfresco eatery. In September you can test your fitness in the annual "vertical marathon" up the hotel's stairs. ⌧ *21/ 100 S. Sathorn Rd., Silom, 10120* ☎ *02/679–1200* 🖷 *02/679–1199* ⊕ *www.banyantree.com* ⤴ *216 suites* ♿ *4 restaurants, pool, health club, spa, bar, business services, meeting rooms* ⊟ *AE, DC, MC, V* Ⓜ *Subway: Lumphini.*

$$$$ ⌧ **Dusit Thani.** This high-rise hotel has a distinctive pyramid shape that makes it immediately identifiable. The reception area, where a sunken lounge overlooks a small garden, is one floor up. Rooms here are spacious, especially the high-priced suites. Its proximity to Skytrain and subway stations make this hotel a convenient base for exploring the city. It's also across the street from Lumphini Park, Bangkok's best public park. The pool is in a central courtyard filled with trees, making it a peaceful oasis from the heat and humidity, and the Devarana Spa opened in 2003. A popular Chinese restaurant, an elegant Thai restaurant, and a shopping arcade occupy the street level. ⌧ *946 Rama IV Rd., Silom, 10500* ☎ *02/236–0450* 🖷 *02/236–6400* ⊕ *www.dusit.com* ⤴ *476 rooms, 24 suites* ♿ *8 restaurants, coffee shop, in-room VCRs, pool, health club, spa, bar, nightclub, shops, business services, meeting rooms* ⊟ *AE, DC, MC, V* Ⓜ *Subway: Silom; Skytrain: Sala Daeng.*

$$$$ ⌧ **Metropolitan Bangkok.** The Metropolitan has all the elements of hip: a crisp, modern esthetic; a pop-star clientele; a chic guests-and-members-only lounge; a sexy staff; and an ironic location in a refurbished YMCA. Some of the rooms are a bit small, but they're smartly turned out—dark woods and deep browns are offset by cream-color walls, pillows, and rugs. Though the rooms aren't dripping with high-tech gadgetry, they do have broadband Internet and 25-inch flatbed TVs with DVD players. ✉ 27 *South Sathorn, Silom, 10120* ☎ *02/625–3333* 🖷 *02/625–3300* ⊕ *www. metropolitan.como.bz* 🛏 *162 rooms, 9 suites* ♿ *2 restaurants, pool, spa, bar, business services, meeting rooms* ▭ *AE, DC, MC, V* Ⓜ *Subway: Lumphini; Skytrain: Sala Daeng or Chong Nonsi.*

$$$$
FodorsChoice
★

🏨 **The Oriental Hotel.** This opulent hotel on the Chao Phraya River still sets the standard that other hotels try to match. Part of its fame stems from the celebrities that stayed here in the past, but the recent guest book reveals no less impressive names. The four suites in the original building, now called the Author's Residence, offer a unique experience, with superlative service in big historical suites. In addition to its excellent restaurants, the hotel hosts a riverside barbecue every night. There are cooking classes that teach you the secrets of Thai cuisine, and a spa on the other side of the river that lets you indulge in all sorts of luxurious treatments from massage to facials to soothing herbal and milk baths in your own private suite. ✉ *48 Oriental Ave., Silom, 10500* ☎ *02/659–9000* 🖷 *02/659–0000* ⊕ *www.mandarinoriental.com* 🛏 *358 rooms, 35 suites* ♿ *6 restaurants, coffee shop, 2 tennis courts, 2 pools, health club, spa, squash, bar, business services, helipad* ▭ *AE, DC, MC, V* Ⓜ *Skytrain: Saphan Taksin.*

$$$$
🏨 **Royal Orchid Sheraton.** Of the luxury hotels along the riverfront, this 28-story palace is most popular with tour groups. All the well-appointed rooms face the river, but the color scheme of low-key peaches and creams is a little uninspired, and standard rooms tend to be long and narrow, making them feel cramped. The Thai Thara Thong restaurant is memorable, with subtle classical music accompanying your meal. You can also choose Japanese, Indian, or Italian cuisine. A glassed-in bridge leads to the adjacent River City Shopping Center. The hotel runs a free shuttle bus to the Skytrain every 30 minutes and free boat to Saphan Taksin station. ✉ *2 Captain Bush La., Silom, 10500* ☎ *02/266–0123* 🖷 *02/236–8320* ⊕ *www.sheraton.com* 🛏 *771 rooms* ♿ *8 restaurants, coffee shop, 2 tennis courts, 2 pools, health club, 2 bars, shops, business services, meeting rooms, helipad* ▭ *AE, DC, MC, V* Ⓜ *Skytrain: Chong Nonsi.*

★ **$$$$**
🏨 **Shangri-La Hotel.** Although it's one of Bangkok's best hotels, the Shangri-La has never managed to achieve the fame of the Oriental. That's a shame, because the marble lobby illuminated by crystal chandeliers is palatial, and the adjacent lounge, with its floor-to-ceiling windows, offers a marvelous view of the Chao Phraya River. The peace of the gardens is only interrupted by the puttering of passing boats. Many of the rooms, decorated in soothing pastels, are beginning to show their age, however. In the luxurious Krungthep Wing, a separate tower across the garden, the rooms are larger and quieter, with balconies overlooking the river, and cost a little more. Angelini's is considered one of city's finest Italian restaurants. ✉ *89 Soi Wat Suan Phu, New Rd., Silom, 10500* ☎ *02/236–7777* 🖷 *02/236–8579* ⊕ *www.shangrila.com* 🛏 *793 rooms, 6 suites* ♿ *9 restaurants, 2 tennis courts, 2 pools, health club, squash, 3 bars, shops, business services, helipad* ▭ *AE, DC, MC, V* Ⓜ *Skytrain: Saphan Taksin.*

$$$$ ⊡ **Sukhothai.** On six landscaped acres near Sathorn Road, the Sukhothai
Fodor'sChoice has numerous courtyards that make the hustle and bustle of Bangkok
★ seem worlds away. Standard rooms are spacious, but not exceptionally
well furnished. The one-bedroom suites, in contrast, have oversize baths
paneled in teak, with his and hers washbasins and mirrors. The hotel's
well-regarded restaurant is set in a pavilion on an artificial pond. The
dining room serving continental fare is comfortable, but the prices are
high. ⊠ *13/3 S. Sathorn Rd., Silom, 10120* ☎ *02/344–8888* 🖷 *02/344–
8899* ⊕ *www.sukhothai.com* 🛏 *140 rooms, 78 suites* ♨ *5 restaurants,
coffee shop, tennis court, pool, health club, massage, sauna, squash, bar*
▭ *AE, DC, MC, V* Ⓜ *Subway: Lumphini.*

$$$ ⊡ **Montien.** This hotel within stumbling distance of Patpong has been re-
markably well maintained since it was constructed in 1970. The rooms
are spacious, but the decor is not inspired. Prices are slightly higher than
you would expect for the area, but the hotel often gives discounts. Per-
haps a sign of the quirkiness that exists a few doors down in Patpong,
there are in-house fortune tellers who will read your palm for a small
fee. ⊠ *54 Surawong Rd., Silom, 10500* ☎ *02/233–7060 up to 9* 🖷 *02/
236–5218* ⊕ *www.montien.com* 🛏 *475 rooms* ♨ *2 restaurants, coffee
shop, in-room safes, pool, bar, nightclub, travel services, business services,
meeting rooms* ▭*AE, DC, MC, V* Ⓜ*Subway: Silom; Skytrain: Sala Daeng.*

★ **$$$**   ⊡ **The Siam Heritage.** Siam Heritage is a classy family-run boutique
hotel with a purpose, that being to preserve and promote Thai heritage.
Each room is individually furnished, mostly with pieces from Northern
Thailand. The bedrooms have wood floors and the bathrooms have
stonework in place of tiling. Much attention has been paid to small details from painted elevator doors to colorful weavings on the beds.
⊠ *115/1 Surawong Rd., Silom, 10500* ☎ *02/353–6101* 🖷 *02/353–
6123* ⊕ *www.thesiamheritage.com* 🛏 *55 rooms, 14 suites* ♨ *Restaurant, pool, bar, shops, business services* ▭ *AE, DC, MC, V* Ⓜ *Subway:
Silom; Skytrain: Sala Daeng.*

$$$ ⊡ **Swiss Lodge.** This small hotel not far from Silom Road offers a
friendly boutique option to the neighborhood. Nicely furnished rooms
still feel fresh. Single rooms are really the size of doubles; doubles are
large enough to hold king-size beds. There's a very small pool and sun-
deck on the fifth floor. A good restaurant has a daily breakfast buffet
and a lunch buffet on weekdays; in the evening it specializes in fondue.
⊠ *3 Convent Rd., Silom, 10500* ☎ *02/233–5345* 🖷 *02/236–9425*
⊕ *www.swisslodge.com* 🛏 *57 rooms* ♨ *Restaurant, in-room safes,
pool, business services, no-smoking floors* ▭ *AE, DC, MC, V* Ⓜ *Sky-
train: Sala Daeng.*

★ **$$$**   ⊡ **Triple Two Silom.** This trendy hotel is the sister property of the Narai
Hotel next door; guests here can use the Narai's pool and fitness cen-
ter. Spacious rooms have wood floors and modern fittings in what seem
to be the standard colors of hip these days: deep brown, cream, black,
and red. Unfortunately, the windows are small, so don't expect a lot of
natural light. There's a courtyard in the center of the hotel, and a restaurant and bar with indoor and outdoor sections is at street level. ⊠ *222
Silom Rd., Silom, 10500* ☎ *02/627–2222* 🖷 *02/627–2300* ⊕ *www.
tripletwosilom.com* 🛏 *75 rooms* ♨ *Restaurant, pool, bar* ▭ *AE, DC,
MC, V* Ⓜ *Skytrain: Chong Nonsi.*

$$–$$$ ⊞ **Holiday Inn Silom Bangkok.** With two towers of glass and steel, this former Crowne Plaza is impressive. It might be too big for some, however. The vast public areas make it seem like New York's Grand Central Station, especially with the clusters of airline employees and tour groups running to and fro. Less hectic are two executive floors with their own concierge and lounge. Rooms are generously proportioned, with lots of light streaming in. For meals, try the traditional fare at the Thai Pavilion, or the northern Indian cuisine at Tandoor. ⊠ *981 Silom Rd., Silom, 10500* ☎ *02/238–4300* 🖷 *02/238–5289* ⊕ *www.bangkok-silom. holiday-inn.com* 🗬 *671 rooms, 25 suites* ⌂ *2 restaurants, coffee shop, 1 tennis court, pool, health club, bar, business services, meeting rooms* ▭ *AE, DC, MC, V* Ⓜ *Skytrain: Surasak.*

$$ ⊞ **Narai Hotel.** Dating back to 1969, this is one of Bangkok's older hotels, but it's well-kept and conveniently located by the business district on Silom Road. It has basic but comfortable rooms and friendly service. This hotel's name refers to the god Vishnu (Narai is the Thai name for Vishnu), and an elegant bas-relief of the Hindu deity can be seen on the wall in front of the main staircase. Unfortunately, the hotel is a hike to the nearest Skytrain station. ⊠ *222 Silom Rd., Silom, 10500* ☎ *02/237– 0100* 🖷 *02/236–7161* ⊕ *www.narai.com* 🗬 *380 rooms, 16 suites* ⌂ *3 restaurants, coffee shop, pool, bar, nightclub, business services* ▭ *AE, DC, MC, V* Ⓜ *Skytrain: Chong Nonsi.*

$$ ⊞ **Tawana Ramada.** Rooms here have wood floors and tasteful furnishings with a few details that call to mind the region's history. A few rooms have balconies overlooking the very modest pool, but they are not worth the extra cost. The hotel's location, in the heart of the Silom-Surawong district, gives you easy access to Bangkok's sights. The Grill offers an international buffet and the coffee shop stays open until 2 AM. ⊠ *80 Surawong Rd., Silom, 10500* ☎ *02/236–0361* 🖷 *02/236–3738* ⊕ *www.tawanahotel.com* 🗬 *265 rooms* ⌂ *3 restaurants, in-room safes, pool, health club, bar, business services, meeting rooms* ▭ *AE, DC, MC, V* Ⓜ *Subway: Silom; Skytrain: Sala Daeng.*

$$ ⊞ **Tower Inn.** Head to the top of this slender tower on Silom Road where there's a fitness center, a rooftop swimming pool with views of the skyline, and a sauna (for an extra B200). The rooms are spacious, with plenty of light from picture windows, though the furnishings are a bit utilitarian. There's also a pleasant rooftop restaurant serving international and Thai dishes from 6 PM to midnight. The coffee shop on the second floor is open 24 hours. ⊠ *533 Silom Rd., Silom, 10500* ☎ *02/ 237–8300* 🖷 *02/237–8286* ⊕ *www.towerinnbangkok.com* 🗬 *147 rooms* ⌂ *Restaurant, coffee shop, pool, bar, travel services* ▭ *AE, DC, MC, V* Ⓜ *Skytrain: Chong Nonsi.*

$$ ⊞ **Wall Street Inn.** Most of the guests at this hotel on Surawong Road are from Japan, perhaps because of the many Japanese businesses in the immediate area. But its location near Lumphini Park, Patpong's night market, and Silom Road makes it an appealing option for anyone. Standard rooms are small and windowless, so make sure to ask for one of the deluxe rooms. There's not much of a view, however. The hotel offers traditional Thai massage, and there are also a row of traditional massage centers on the soi. Sarika Cafe, at the mouth of the soi, is a good little restaurant if the hotel's coffee shop doesn't do it for you. ⊠ *37/*

20–24 Soi Surawong Plaza, Surawong Rd., Silom, 10500 ☎ *02/233–4164* 🖷 *02/236-3619* 📞 *63 rooms* ♨ *Coffee shop, massage* 🚬 *AE, DC, MC, V* Ⓜ *Subway: Silom; Skytrain: Sala Daeng.*

★ $ 🖫 **La Residence.** You'd expect to find this charming little hotel on the Left Bank of Paris. It's one of the few low-key lodgings in this area dominated by office towers. The 16 rooms are small but comfortable and each is individually decorated in a variety of styles. Ask to look at a few rooms to decide which you like best. The seven suites are very big and include a kitchenette. A ground-floor restaurant serves Thai food and doubles as a sitting room for guests. The hotel entrance is just down Soi Anuman Rojdhon off Surawong. ✉ *173/8–9 Surawong Rd., Silom, 10500* ☎ *02/233–3301* 🖷 *02/237-9322* ⊕ *www.laresidencebangkok.com* 📞 *16 rooms, 7 suites* ♨ *Restaurant, laundry service* 🚬 *AE, MC, V* Ⓜ *Skytrain: Surasak.*

$ 🖫 **Manohra Hotel.** An expansive marble lobby is your first clue that this hotel is head and shoulders above others in its price range. Rooms have pleasant furnishings and spotless baths. There's a rooftop garden for sunbathing and a very small indoor pool next to the lobby. The best asset, though, may be the friendly staff. A lot of Asian tour groups stay here. The Skytrain is a 15-minute walk from the hotel. ✉ *412 Surawong Rd., Silom, 10500* ☎ *02/234–5070* 🖷 *02/237-7662* ⊕ *www.manohrahotel.com* 📞 *200 rooms, 6 suites* ♨ *Restaurant, pool, massage, meeting rooms* 🚬 *AE, DC, MC, V* Ⓜ *Skytrain: Surasak.*

$ 🖫 **Silom Village Inn.** Reasonable rates are just one of the draws at this small hotel. It's also well run, with rooms that are as neat as a pin. The king-size beds leave just enough space for a desk and a couple of chairs. Ask for a room at the back of the hotel to avoid the ruckus on Silom Road. The staff at the reception desk is helpful and reliable at taking messages. A small restaurant serves Italian food, but many other choices are just outside your door. ✉ *Silom Village Trade Centre, 286 Silom Rd., Silom, 10500* ☎ *02/635–6810* 🖷 *02/635-6817* 📞 *60 rooms* ♨ *Restaurant* 🚬 *AE, DC, MC, V* Ⓜ *Skytrain: Surasak.*

Sukhumvit

$$$$ 🖫 **Amari Boulevard.** This pyramid-shape tower certainly has a dashing profile. Rooms in the newer glass tower are modern and airy, with plenty of amenities. The use of dark wood in the older rooms lend them a more traditional ambience. Particularly attractive are those overlooking the pool in the older building. The ground-floor lobby is vast, with plenty of places to have a quiet conversation. The casual Peppermill restaurant serves a range of Thai and Japanese dishes. The hotel is on a one-way soi near Sukhumvit Road; it's convenient to shops and restaurants, but it can be noisy at night because there are also several bars on this street. ✉ *2 Sukhumvit Soi 5, Sukhumvit, 10110* ☎ *02/255–2930* 🖷 *02/255-2950* ⊕ *www.amari.com* 📞 *315 rooms* ♨ *Restaurant, pool, health club, bar, business services, meeting rooms* 🚬 *AE, DC, MC, V* Ⓜ *Skytrain: Nana.*

$$$$ 🖫 **The Davis Bangkok.** This fine medium-size boutique hotel opened in 2003, but it already has a new wing under construction. The showpiece of the place is two Thai villas—separate modern houses built in traditional Thai style—both top-of-the-line two- and three-bedroom struc-

tures with all the amenities, their own pool, and a price tag of B25,000 to B30,000 per day to go with them (there are big discounts for monthly stays). But there are comfortable and classy rooms to fit more humble budgets in the main building. Rooms are individually decorated, styles vary from Bali, Bombay, Thai, and even Florida. ⊠ *80 Sukhumvit Soi 24, Sukhumvit, 10110* ☎ *02/260–8000* ⊟ *02/260–8100* ⊕ *www. davisbangkok.net* ⤳ *174 rooms* ⟍ *Restaurant, pool, spa, bar, business services, meeting rooms* ⊟ *AE, DC, MC, V* Ⓜ *Skytrain: Phrom Phong.*

$$$$ 🏨 **Imperial Queen's Park.** Two gleaming white towers make up Bangkok's largest hotel. To keep its 1,300 rooms filled, the hotel makes special arrangements with guests staying a month or more. Standard rooms are spacious and have large desks, but the junior suites have separate work areas and plenty of natural light. Many rooms have whirlpool tubs (although not the latest models). The hotel is off busy Sukhumvit Road, next to a small park that is ideal for jogging. ⊠ *199 Sukhumvit Soi 22, Sukhumvit, 10110* ☎ *02/261–9000* ⊟ *02/261–9530* ⊕ *www. imperialhotels.com* ⤳ *1,145 rooms, 155 suites* ⟍ *8 restaurants, coffee shop, 2 pools, health club, bar, business services, convention center, meeting rooms* ⊟ *AE, DC, MC, V* Ⓜ *Skytrain: Phrom Phong.*

$$$$ 🏨 **Sheraton Grande Sukhumvit.** Soaring 33 floors above noisy city streets, the Sheraton Grande Sukhumvit is hard to miss. The suites on the upper floors get plenty of natural light and come with 24-hour butler service. Standard rooms are a bit formulaic—you won't find any Thai-influenced accoutrements—but they're pleasant enough. You never go hungry here: on street level is Riva's, a restaurant serving up a changing menu of international cuisine, while the Orchid Café on the second floor lays out an international buffet. In the afternoon you can enjoy tea in the lounge or cocktails in the rotunda. On the third floor, the health club and the serpentine swimming pool are laid out amid a lovely garden. Here you can also find a Thai restaurant and, during the dry months, a barbecue. Skytrain and subway stations are very close. ⊠ *250 Sukhumvit Rd., Sukhumvit, 10110* ☎ *02/649–8888* ⊟ *02/649–8000* ⊕ *www.starwood.com/bangkok* ⤳ *406 rooms, 23 suites* ⟍ *4 restaurants, pool, health club, bar, business services* ⊟ *AE, DC, MC, V* Ⓜ *Subway: Sukhumvit; Skytrain: Asok.*

$$$ 🏨 **Bel-Air Princess.** This well-managed hotel is steps from clamorous Sukhumvit Road, but it's on the quiet end of a bustling street, away from the bars. It gets its fair share of tour groups, but for the most part the lobby and lounge are peaceful retreats. The bowl of fruit on each floor is a thoughtful touch. Rooms at the back of the hotel look down on Soi 7, while those on the front have a view of the pool. ⊠ *16 Sukhumvit Soi 5, Sukhumvit, 10110* ☎ *02/253–4300* ⊟ *02/255–8850* ⊕ *www.dusit. com* ⤳ *160 rooms* ⟍ *2 restaurants, in-room safes, pool, health club, bar* ⊟ *AE, DC, MC, V* Ⓜ *Skytrain: Nana.*

$$$ 🏨 **Imperial Tara Hotel.** This hotel is on a side street near Sukhumvit Road, which means restaurants and clubs are practically at your doorstep. While you check in, enjoy a cup of tea in the spacious lobby lined with teak carvings. Rooms, all of which are on the small side, have cool marble floors and nice views. Many overlook the eighth-floor terrace with a swimming pool. The Tara is connected by a covered walkway to its sister property, the Imperial Impala Hotel on Soi 24. ⊠ *18/1 Sukhumvit*

Soi 26, Sukhumvit, 10110 ☎ *02/259–2900* 🖷 *02/259–2896* ⊕ *www.imperialhotels.com* ⤳ *195 rooms, 25 suites* ♿ *3 restaurants, coffee shop, pool, meeting rooms* ☰ *AE, DC, MC, V* Ⓜ *Skytrain: Phrom Phong.*

$$$ 🏨 **Landmark Hotel.** The hotel prides itself on being thoroughly modern, but the generous use of polished wood in its reception area suggests a grand European hotel. Rooms, elegant enough to satisfy the leisure traveler, are geared to corporate travelers, with good-size desks and business amenities. For a little extra, guests can stay in one of the Club Floors, which have more business services and complimentary breakfast and cocktails. There's a staff of 700, so it's no surprise that the service is attentive. There are shops and restaurants in the basement and first floors of the hotel building. ✉ *138 Sukhumvit Rd., Sukhumvit, 10110* ☎ *02/254–0404* 🖷 *02/253–4259* ⊕ *www.landmarkbangkok.com* ⤳ *372 rooms, 42 suites* ♿ *8 restaurants, coffee shop, snack bar, pool, health club, sauna, squash, shops, business services, meeting rooms* ☰ *AE, DC, MC, V* Ⓜ *Skytrain: Nana.*

$$ 🏨 **Imperial Impala Hotel.** Though it's connected to its pricier and classier sister property, the Imperial Tara Hotel, the Impala has smaller rooms with carpeted (not marble) floors. However, it shares all facilities and the staff of the Imperial Tara. There are entrances on Soi 24 and Soi 26. ✉ *9 Sukhumvit Soi 24, Sukhumvit, 10110* ☎ *02/259–0053* 🖷 *02/258–8747* ⊕ *www.imperialhotels.com* ⤳ *161 rooms, 4 suites* ♿ *3 restaurants, coffee shop, pool, meeting rooms* ☰ *AE, DC, MC, V* Ⓜ *Skytrain: Phrom Phong.*

$ 🏨 **Ambassador Hotel.** One of Bangkok's biggest hotels, the Ambassador has three wings, a dozen restaurants, and a shopping center with scores of stores. Its size makes it a bit impersonal, and rooms are compact and decorated in standard-issue pastels. The Tower Wing is more comfortable, but more expensive. The Sukhumvit Wing overlooks a busy street. Ask for a room above the sixth floor to avoid noise from the hotel's popular beer garden. ✉ *171 Sukhumvit Soi 11–13, Sukhumvit, 10110* ☎ *02/254–0444* 🖷 *02/253–4123* ⊕ *www.amtel.co.th* ⤳ *717 rooms, 42 suites* ♿ *12 restaurants, coffee shop, snack bar, 2 tennis courts, pool, health club, massage, bar, business services, meeting rooms* ☰ *AE, DC, MC, V* Ⓜ *Skytrain: Nana.*

$ 🏨 **City Lodge.** There are two City Lodges off Sukhumvit, but this is the better choice because of a better location and a good restaurant in its lobby. The compact rooms are functional, designed to fit a lot into a small space. Business services here are minimal, but you can use those, along with other facilities like the pool, at its nearby sister hotel, the Amari Boulevard. Subway and Skytrain stations are nearby. The hotel's restaurant, La Gritta, specializes in Italian food. ✉ *Sukhumvit Soi 19, Sukhumvit, 10110* ☎ *02/254–4783* 🖷 *02/255–7340* ⊕ *www.amari.com* ⤳ *34 rooms* ♿ *Restaurant* ☰ *AE, DC, MC, V* Ⓜ *Subway: Sukhumvit; Skytrain: Asok.*

$ 🏨 **Majestic Suites.** There are no actual suites here, but there are a wide selection of standard rooms. They range from studios barely big enough to fit a queen-size bed to larger deluxe rooms that have amenities like fluffy robes hanging in your closet. There's a bar and coffee shop in the small lobby. ✉ *110 Sukhumvit Rd., between Soi 4 and Soi 6, Sukhumvit, 10110* ☎ *02/656–8220* 🖷 *02/656–8201* ⊕ *www.majesticsuites.com*

➠ *55 rooms* ♿ *Coffee shop, in-room safes, minibars, bar, business services* ☰ *AE, DC, MC, V* Ⓜ *Skytrain: Nana.*

$ ⊡ **Stable Lodge.** On a residential street off Sukhumvit Road, this small hotel feels more like a guesthouse. The rooms are basic but clean and comfortable. Each has a private balcony where you can have your breakfast and most have private bathrooms. The rooms at the back are the quietest. The pool is a delightful place to relax in the afternoon. Make sure to return in the evening, when there's a barbecue in the garden. The lobby restaurant serves Thai and Danish food. ⊠ *39 Sukhumvit Soi 8, Sukhumvit, 10110* ☎ *02/653-0017* 🖷 *02/253-5125* ⊕ *www.stablelodge. com* ➠ *41 rooms* ♿ *Restaurant, pool, travel services* ☰ *AE, MC, V* Ⓜ *Skytrain: Nana.*

★ **¢–$** ⊡ **The Atlanta.** Writers in search of inspiration should head to this venerable hotel, which opened its doors in 1952, making it the oldest in Bangkok. It retains its original art deco lobby; the leatherette banquettes and circular sofas are often used for magazine fashion shoots. Just beyond the lobby is a swimming pool set next to a pleasant garden filled with tables and chairs. Owner Charles Henn, a part-time professor whose father Max opened the hotel more than a half century ago, caters to frugal travelers who return again and again. Simply decorated rooms come with fans or air-conditioning. The restaurant off the lobby serves excellent Thai and vegetarian food. Note that the Atlanta takes a strong stance against sex tourism and drug-and-alcohol abuse; rules of conduct are posted on their Web site and should be reviewed before booking. ⊠ *78 Sukhumvit Soi 2, Sukhumvit, 10110* ☎ *02/252-1650 or 02/252-6069* 🖷 *02/656-8123* ⊕ *www.theatlantahotel.bizland.com* ➠ *43 rooms, 6 suites* ♿ *Restaurant, pool, travel services; no a/c in some rooms, no room TVs* ☰ *No credit cards* Ⓜ *Skytrain: Ploenchit.*

NIGHTLIFE & THE ARTS

The English-language newspapers the *Bangkok Post* and the *Nation* have the latest information on current festivals, exhibitions, and nightlife. The Tourist Authority of Thailand's weekly *Where* also lists events. Monthly *Metro* magazine has an extensive listings section and offers reviews of new hot spots.

Nightlife

Although the law requires that bars and nightclubs close at 2 AM, Bangkok is a city that never sleeps. Many restaurants and other establishments stay open for late-night carousing. The city is awash with bars catering to all tastes, from classy watering holes to sleazy strip clubs. Off Sukhumvit Soi 55 (also called Soi Thonglor) there are several good bars and nightclubs. Soi Sarasin, across from Lumphini Park, is packed with friendly pubs and cafés that are popular with yuppie Thais and expats. Narathiwat Road, which starts at Surawong, intersects Silom, then runs all the way to Rama III, sees trendy bars and restaurants opening every month.

Many tourists, most out of curiosity more than anything else, take a stroll through the city's most infamous neighborhoods. Live sex shows, though

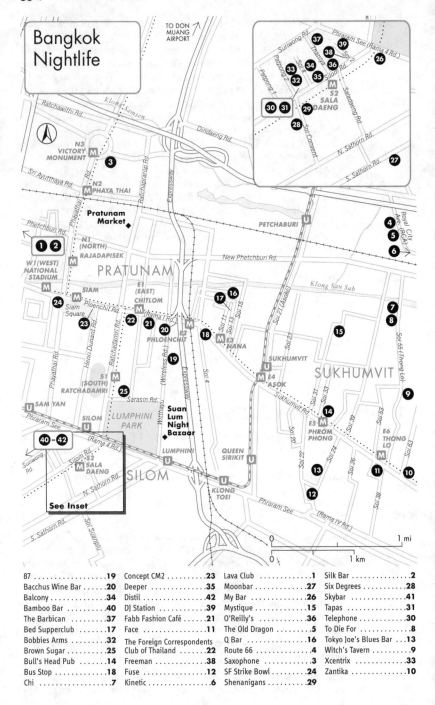

Bangkok Nightlife

87	**19**	Concept CM2	**23**	Lava Club	**1**	Silk Bar	**2**

officially banned, are still found in three areas. Patpong is the largest, and it includes three streets that run between Surawong and Silom roads. Lining Patpong 1 and 2 are go-go bars with hostesses by the dozen. Shows are generally found one flight up. The Patpong area is well patrolled by police, so it is quite safe. It even has a Night Market patronized by Thais.

Soi Cowboy, off Sukhumvit Road at Soi 21, is a less raunchy, more easygoing version of Patpong. Some bars have go-go dancers, while others are good for a quiet beer (with or without a temporary companion). Nana Plaza, at Soi 4, is popular with expats. The plaza is packed with three floors of hostess bars. The newest bars have spilled out along Soi 4.

Most gay bars and clubs happen to be located near Patpong on a pair of dead-end alleys off Silom Road. Soi 2 is filled with thumping discos, and Soi 4 is a bit more sedate. Other gay establishments are found near Sukhumvit Road.

Bars & Pubs

BANGLAMPHU Situated on one of the most famous roads in Bangkok, **Silk Bar** (⊠ 129-131 Khao San Rd., Banglamphu ☎02/281–9981) has commanding views of the sidewalk, where you can pass the time watching the droves of backpackers and travelers walk by.

PATPONG AREA The crowd of young Thais and expats at **The Barbican** (⊠ Soi Thaniya, off Silom Rd., Silom ☎ 02/234–3590 Ⓜ Subway: Silom; Skytrain: Sala Daeng), a split-level contemporary bar smack dab in the middle of the Japanese soi, is a bit more stylish and hip than at other pubs. It's a great place to hang out with friends. You can get a decent pint of beer at the **Bobbies Arms** (⊠ Patpong 2, Silom ☎ 02/233–6828 Ⓜ Subway: Silom; Skytrain: Sala Daeng), a rough approximation of an English pub. This longtime favorite remains popular even with the proliferation of new pubs. A good place to carouse is the smoky **Brown Sugar** (⊠ 231/20 Soi Sarasin, Silom ☎02/250–0103 Ⓜ Subway: Silom; Skytrain: Ratchadamri), which often has live blues and jazz.

The lively **O'Reillys** (⊠ 62/1–4 Silom Rd., Silom ☎ 02/632–7515 Ⓜ Subway: Silom; Skytrain: Sala Daeng) sometimes has live music. Due to its convenient location to the Skytrain and the gateway to Patpong, this place is always jumping. If you're a Beatles fan, check out the Betters, a great cover band dedicated to keeping the legend alive. Off Silom Road, **Shenanigans** (⊠ 1/5–6 Convent Rd., Silom ☎ 02/266–7160 Ⓜ Subway: Silom; Skytrain: Sala Daeng) is standing-room-only (with mostly British expats) from Tuesday to Friday. Beers on tap include Guinness.

SILOM Thai A-listers and entertainers have made **Distil** (⊠ State Tower, 1055 Silom Rd., Silom ☎ 02/624–9555 Ⓜ Skytrain: Surasak), on the 64th floor of one of Bangkok's tallest buildings, their stomping grounds. It's done out in black, coffee, and slate tones (the calling cards of upscale hip), and a full-time sommelier is on staff to take care of your wine desires. **My Bar** (⊠ 946 Rama IV, Silom ☎ 02/200–9000 Ⓜ Subway: Lumphini), a minimalist lounge-style bar, is in the Dusit Thani. It serves up signature drinks, hand-rolled Cuban cigars, and the finest single malt whisky in town.

Moonbar (⊠ Banyan Tree, 21/100 S. Sathorn Rd., Silom Ⓜ Subway: Lumphini; Skytrain: Sala Daeng) at Vertigo restaurant is an appropriate name for this open-air bar and restaurant sitting high atop the Banyan Tree hotel. If the weather is clear, do some stargazing with the bar's telescope. A few blocks down, off Sathorn, **Six Degrees** (⊠ Soi Convent, Silom ☎ 02/632–2995 Ⓜ Skytrain: Sala Daeng) restaurant and bar has a simple, minimalist style offering a variety of smooth cocktails. The bar crowd starts to filter in after 10 PM.

There's nothing else quite like **Skybar** (⊠ State Tower, 1055 Silom Rd., Silom ☎ 02/624–9555 Ⓜ Skytrain: Surasak), on the 65th floor of one of Bangkok's tallest buildings. Once you've made the trek up, head straight toward the eerie blue light at the extreme end of the restaurant. After you check out the head-spinning views, chill out with a drink while admiring the bustling city below.

SUKHUMVIT   Wine bars are slowly popping up around the city, and one worth mentioning is **Bacchus Wine Bar & Cafe Lounge** (⊠ 20/6–7 Ruam Rudee Village, Soi Ruam Rudee, Sukhumvit ☎ 02/650–8986 Ⓜ Skytrain: Ploenchit). This earth-tone establishment provides four floors of laidback ambience and, well, wine. The popular **Bull's Head Pub** (⊠ Sukhumvit Soi 33, Sukhumvit ☎ 02/259–4444 Ⓜ Subway: Sukhumvit; Skytrain: Phrom Phong) is very British—it even has a Quiz Night on the second Tuesday of each month. This is a good place for serious beer drinkers. Amid the swinging nightlife of Soi 4, **Bus Stop** (⊠ 14 Sukhumvit Soi 4, Sukhumvit ☎ 02/251–9222 Ⓜ Subway: Sukhumvit; Skytrain: Nana) is a pleasantly relaxed pub with outdoor seating. Gather around the two large-screen TVs to watch whatever sport happens to be on.

Chi (⊠ 998 Sukhumvit Soi 55, Sukhumvit ☎ 02/381–7587 Ⓜ Skytrain: Thong Lo), a Pan-Asian eatery with a bar and lounge, attracts a quirky mix of upscale diners and imbibers, including Thai designers, interior decorators, high-society folks, artists, and, of course, a few foreigners. Each room has a different theme—the living room has an eclectic range of chairs, cushions, and sofas to lounge about on. Tucked away in a Balinese-style house, **Face** (⊠ 29 Sukhumvit Soi 38, Sukhumvit ☎ 02/713–6048 Ⓜ Skytrain: Thong Lo) exudes peace with its unique blend of Asian crafts and furniture in a modern context. It brings in a mix of sophisticated Thais and foreigners. **Fuse** (⊠ Camp Davis, Sukhumvit Soi 24, Sukhumvit ☎ 02/204–0970 Ⓜ Skytrain: Phrom Phong) is a low-ceilinged, wood-paneled cocktail bar that draws in Thais, expats, and models.

Celebrating the famous American highway, **Route 66** (⊠ 29/37 Royal City Ave., Sukhumvit ☎ 02/203–0407) is often packed. **To Die For** (⊠ 998 Sukhumvit Soi 55, Sukhumvit ☎ 02/381–4714 Ⓜ Skytrain: Thong Lo) has an exquisitely manicured garden, perfect for sipping fancy drinks on brightly colored Moroccan seats. Situated in the midst of Japanese nightclubs, **Tokyo Joe's Blues Bar** (⊠ 9–11 Sivaporn Plaza, Sukhumvit Soi 24, Sukhumvit ☎ 02/661–0359 Ⓜ Skytrain: Phrom Phong) stands out with its rustic interior and live music that pours through the cracks in the walls. Littered with blues mementos, vintage guitars, and stereos, this cozy bar has live music every night; Sunday brings jazz and blues jam sessions.

ONE NIGHT IN BANGKOK . . .
WITH COCKTAILS & CURFEWS

BANGKOK IS RAPIDLY ESTABLISHING **ITSELF** as Asia's capital of cool, with excellent live music, jazz-and-blues clubs, hip bars, dance venues, and great restaurants. Nightlife across Bangkok has something for everyone, whether you want to sip a few beers at a pub on Khao San Road, dance at a trendy nightclub along Sukhumvit Road, or see seedy Patpong.

Due to a steady expat population, the city has a number of British and Irish pubs, most with live folk, pop, and rock music. Japanese newcomers have made karaoke bars a staple of Bangkok nightlife as well. And Thailand's own high society ("hi-so's") of the beautiful and young can be seen carousing at swish hotel bars and dancing in clubs so luxe, you have to line up behind black velvet ropes to get in. Thais most often hit the clubs in groups. It's common practice for a group to invest in a bottle of whisky to be shared among friends. The younger generation enjoy parties, and often host them in different venues around the city.

To keep up with the times, drinks have taken on an entirely new look. Bar owners pay big bucks to fly in "international mixologists" from pedigree nightclubs and bars to act as consultants. These mixologists create drinks using spices, flowers, herbs, and tropical fruit. As traditional drinks gather dust on the shelves, new drinks that caught on: Blood Orange Caipiroska; Mai Thai made with cucumber, coriander, and chili vodka; Mint Mule, which uses honey vodka as its base with ginger and mint leaves; and the infamous Tom Yumtini, made with chili and lemongrass, a martini you can only find in Bangkok.

In an effort to crack down on late-night clubs and the drug and sex tourism problems associated with them, the Thai government had posed a midnight curfew for all go-go bars, massage parlors, bars, pubs, and nightclubs in March 2004. The quest to rebrand the country as a land of beaches, temples, and sunshine immediately caused a huge outcry from club owners and workers, who warned that tourism would be hurt by the curfew and unemployment would skyrocket. Authorities compromised a few months later by dividing Bangkok into zones, allocating each area to have a different curfew, which moved back last call to 2 AM for some businesses. Nowadays, restaurants, pubs, and cafés close at midnight, bars and nightclubs close at 1, and massage parlors at 2. These curfews are still not 100% confirmed, as many owners have contested that certain establishments linked to the government are allowed to stay open later.

The old go-go bars of the infamous red light districts of Patpong and Soi Cowboy seem to be surviving the government's "Cinderella" scheme. There are still oodles of girly bars, pole-dancing escapades, sex clubs, and massage parlors. Of course, it's hard to ignore the ramifications of sex tourism—from the damage it does to Thai society to the part it plays in the spreading of AIDS. For many years, the Thai government had condom campaigns throughout the capital, and dispensed them freely amongst the sex workers. Nowadays, free condoms are not as widely available as they once were and so the famous red-light district is again a hot spot for the AIDS epidemic.

— Wendy Kassel

SIAM SQUARE If you're searching for something more than just a typical cocktail bar, look no further than **SF Strike Bowl** (✉ MBK Shopping Center, Phayathai Rd., Victory Monument ☎ 02/611–4555 Ⓜ Skytrain: National Stadium). One of the city's hottest night spots, this futuristic bowling alley, lounge, and bar has a sleek style that rivals most nightclubs in Asia. A DJ spins house tunes above the clatter of falling pins.

VICTORY MONUMENT **The Old Dragon** (✉ 29/78–81 Royal City Ave., Victory Monument ☎ 02/203–0972 Ⓜ Skytrain: Victory Monument) is filled with oddities, from wooden cinema seats to old mirrors etched with Chinese characters. The owner claims that little here besides the clientele is less than 50 years old. The snacks served here are a mix of Chinese and Thai. **Saxophone** (✉ 3/8 Victory Monument, Phayathai Rd., Victory Monument ☎ 02/246–5472 Ⓜ Skytrain: Victory Monument) is popular with locals and expats. Live blues, R&B, jazz, rock, reggae, and even ska house bands perform seven nights a week.

LUMPHINI PARK **Suan Lum Night Bazaar** (✉ At Rama IV and Wittayu Rds., Lumphini Park Ⓜ Subway: Lumphini) has grown into one of Bangkok's hippest and most happening night markets. It offers an all-in-one experience: shopping, eating, massage, and drinking. There are three beer gardens and free nightly concerts performed by various bands from 6:30 PM to midnight.

Clubs

Bed Supperclub (✉ 26 Sukhumvit Soi 11, Sukhumvit ☎ 02/651–3537 Ⓜ Skytrain: Nana) is Bangkok's answer to cool. The futuristic Jetsons-like bar and supper club has been the rage since its inception. You can take your drink and sprawl out on an enormous bed while listening to a mix of hip-hop, house, and a variety of other music.

Concept CM2 (✉ Novotel Siam, 392/44 Rama I, Soi 6, Siam Square ☎ 02/255–6888 Ⓜ Skytrain: Siam) is a flashy, energetic club with live pop bands every night. If you want to really cut loose, try **Deeper** (✉ 82 Silom Rd. Soi 4, Silom ☎ 02/233–2830 Ⓜ Subway: Silom; Skytrain: Sala Daeng), which tries hard for an underground vibe. Upstairs you can find people dancing hard to the latest trance and techno.

For something sleek and groovy try the Conrad's **87** (✉ All Seasons Pl., 87 Wittayu (Wireless Rd.), Sukhumvit ☎ 02/690–9999 Ⓜ Skytrain: Ploenchit), where the dance floor meanders throughout the bar, instead of concentrating in front of the DJ booth. The crowd is super trendy and very well-to-do. **Kinetic** (✉ Soi Soonvijai, Royal City Ave., Sukhumvit ☎ 02/260–7824) has a whopping five floors of clubs, bars, and lounge areas. Upstairs is a windowless warehouse space decorated only with hip-hop graffiti—in other words, a space for serious dancers to kick around in without breaking anything. **Lava Club** (✉ 249 Bayon Bldg., at Khao San Rd., Banglamphu ☎ 02/281–6565) also caters to serious dancers, with a DJ spinning house and some trance. It's in backpacker territory, so you'll see many T-shirts and flip-flops in the crowd, but the young, trendy Thai set is well-represented also.

New on the circuit, **Mystique** (✉ 71/8 Sukhumvit Soi 31, Sukhumvit ☎ 02/662–2374 Ⓜ Skytrain: Phrom Phong) pushes the limits of Bangkok nightlife with a constant flow of international performances and the best theme nights around town. Built from scratch, Mystique is a temple to extravagance and hedonism, offering superb drinks and beautiful bar staff in a Moulin Rouge–like setting. **Q Bar** (✉ 34 Sukhumvit Soi 11, Sukhumvit ☎ 02/252–3274 Ⓜ Skytrain: Nana) consistently plays quality music and regularly features international DJs. Upstairs there's a romantic lounge and a huge outdoor terrace perfect for any mood.

The funky and soulful **Tapas** (✉ 114/17 Silom Soi 4, Silom ☎ 02/234–4737 Ⓜ Subway: Silom; Skytrain: Sala Daeng) gets very crowded on weekends. There's a small, intimate, and sweaty dance floor upstairs with couches and live percussion in a Balearic style. Farther down the lane is **Xcentrix** (✉ 14/5 Silom Soi 4, Silom ☎ 02/632–9669 Ⓜ Subway: Silom; Skytrain: Sala Daeng), where the younger set comes to try their new moves in a warehouse-style club. Curvaceous lines, mock polished concrete walls, and a low ceiling in the back gives the space an intimate atmosphere. If hip-hop isn't your thing, head upstairs to the "Chill Out" room for lower volume and room to kick back. **Zantika** (✉ 235/11 Sukhumvit Soi 63, Sukhumvit ☎ 02/711–5886 Ⓜ Skytrain: Ekkamai) bedazzles both Thais and foreigners with two floors of trendiness. One level has a cozy lounge, another a stage and huge dance floor. DJs keep the crowd jumping by spinning the latest tunes.

Gay Bars

Balcony (✉ 86–88 Silom Soi 4, Silom ☎ 02/235–5891 Ⓜ Subway: Silom; Skytrain: Sala Daeng) does indeed look out over the street. It has one of the best happy hours on the Soi. On crowded Silom Soi 2, **DJ Station** (✉ 8/6–8 Silom Soi 2 , Silom ☎ 02/266–4029 Ⓜ Subway: Silom; Skytrain: Sala Daeng) draws a young crowd. Around the corner from DJ Station, **Freeman** (✉ 60/18–21 Silom Rd., Silom ☎ 02/632–8033 Ⓜ Subway: Silom; Skytrain: Sala Daeng) has a famous drag show every night at midnight and a balcony where you can watch the dance floor.

The most venerable of Bangkok's gay bars, **Telephone** (✉ 114/11–13 Silom Soi 4, Silom ☎ 02/235–5891 Ⓜ Subway: Silom; Skytrain: Sala Daeng) is hopping every night of the week. There are telephones on the table so you can chat up your neighbors.

Jazz Bars

To hear easy-on-the-ears jazz, try the Oriental Hotel's **Bamboo Bar** (✉ Oriental La., Silom ☎ 02/236–0400 Ⓜ Skytrain: Saphan Taksin). This legendary bar features international jazz musicians. **Fabb Fashion Café** (✉ Mercury Tower, 540 Ploenchit Rd., Sukhumvit ☎ 02/843–4946 Ⓜ Skytrain: Ploenchit) is the place to go for live music early in the evening.

The Foreign Correspondents Club of Thailand (✉ Maneeya Center, Ploenchit Rd., Sukhumvit ☎ 02/652–0580 Ⓜ Skytrain: Chitlom) has live music Friday night, when it's open to the public. **Witch's Tavern** (✉ Sukhumvit Soi 55, Sukhumvit ☎ 02/391–9791 Ⓜ Skytrain: Thong Lo) recently received a much-needed face-lift and has musicians on Friday, Saturday, and Sunday. The bar also serves hearty English fare.

The Arts

A contemporary arts scene is relatively new to Thailand, but the last decade has seen great changes in the fine arts: artists are branching out into all kinds of media, and modern sculpture and artwork can be increasingly found decorating office buildings, parks, and public spaces. Bangkok also offers an eclectic range of theater and dance performances such as traditional *khon* drama dances, and masterful puppet shows. Music options range from piano concertos and symphonies to rock concerts and blues-and-jazz festivals. Thai artists and performers are always exploring new styles and techniques and are definitely turning Bangkok into a hot-spot for artists.

Art Galleries

Today, artists use various media, often melding international art trends with distinctly Thai craftsmanship. To keep up with the pace of an emerging movement, galleries are popping up all over Bangkok. Exhibitions are now held in cafés, restaurants, shopping malls, foreign clubs, and even bars.

About Studio/About Cafe (⊠ 418 Maitrichit Rd., Chinatown ☎ 02/623–1742 Ⓜ Subway: Hua Lamphong) shows mixed media, sculpture, and exhibitions from up-and-coming Thai artists. **Carpediem Gallery** (⊠ 1B–1 Ruam Rudee Bldg., 566 Ploenchit Rd., Sukhumvit ☎ 02/250–0404 Ⓜ Skytrain: Ploenchit) is owned by a vivacious, charismatic Singaporean woman. Most of the artists featured are prominent and have oversize artwork.

Eat Me (⊠ Soi Phi Phat 2, off Convent Rd., Silom ☎ 02/238–0931 Ⓜ Skytrain: Sala Daeng) is a restaurant-cum-art space. By day this split-level space features a variety of exhibitions from both Thai and foreign artists. In the evening it morphs into a fusion eatery.

The lovely courtyard at the **Four Seasons Hotel Bangkok** (⊠ 155 Ratchadamri Rd., Siam Square ☎ 02/251–6127 Ⓜ Skytrain: Ratchadamri) rotates their exhibits frequently and features paintings in different media, with a greater emphasis on photos. **H Gallery** (⊠ 201 Sathorn Rd., Silom ☎ 01/310–4428 Ⓜ Skytrain: Surasak) often shows solo exhibitions from renowned artists.

Tadu Contemporary Art (⊠ Barcelona Motors Building, 99/2 Tiam Ruammit Rd., North Bangkok ☎ 02/645–2473 ⊕ www.tadu.net) exhibits an eclectic group of contemporary artists whose work is dynamic and powerful and comes in an array of media. **Tang Gallery** (⊠ B29, 919/1 Silom Rd., Silom ☎ 02/630–0977 Ⓜ Skytrain: Sala Daeng) features works by Chinese artists, including contemporary oil and watercolor paintings and ceramic sculptures.

Theater & Dance

For Thais, classical dance is more than graceful movements. The dances actually tell tales from the religious epic *Ramakien*. A series of controlled gestures convey the stories. Performances are accompanied by a woodwind called the *piphat*, which sounds like an oboe, as well as a range of percussion instruments. Many restaurants also present classical dance performances.

The **Chalerm Krung Royal Theater** (✉ 66 Charoen Krung (New Rd.), Wang Burapha, Phirom, Old City ☎ 02/222–1854) was designed in 1933 by a former student of the Ecole des Beaux-Arts in Paris. The design is Thai Deco, and it hosts traditional khon performances, a masked dance-drama based on tales from the Ramakien.

A visit to the Suan Lum Night Bazaar would not be complete without stopping at the **Joe Louis Theatre** (✉ Suan Lum Night Bazaar, Lumphini Park Ⓜ Subway: Lumphini; Skytrain: Ploenchit). Master Sakorn Yangkhiawsod grew up in the theater and is a versatile performer and puppet-maker. He has passed on the dying tradition to his nine children and two dozen grandchildren; his family is the only troupe left in Thailand keeping the art alive. Performances take place every night at 7:30 PM. Tickets are B600.

At the **National Theatre** (✉ Na Phra That Rd., Old City ☎ 02/224–1342), performances begin most days at 10 AM and 3 PM. Special performances of traditional dance start at 5:30 PM on the last Friday of each month.

Across the river, **Patravadi** (✉ 69/1 Soi Wat Rakang, Thonburi ☎ 02/412–7287) offers a dance show during dinner. There's also a theater in the restaurant showing performances from classical to contemporary. The owner, formerly a dancer, oversees all productions. The company just moved into a new building, expanding the theater and the troupe.

At the Oriental Hotel, **Sala Rim Naam** (✉ Oriental La., Silom ☎ 02/236–0400 Ⓜ Skytrain: Saphan Taksin) stages a beautiful show accompanied by an excellent dinner. **Silom Village** (✉ 286 Silom Rd., Silom ☎ 02/234–4448 Ⓜ Skytrain: Sala Daeng) appeals most to foreigners, but it also draws many Thais. The block-size complex, open 10 AM–10 PM, features performances of classical dance. The **Supatra River House** (✉ 266 Wat Rakang, Thonburi ☎ 02/411–0305 Ⓜ Skytrain: Saphan Taksin) puts on nightly traditional dance performances. Ask for their boat to pick you up at the Oriental Pier near the Saphan Taksin Skytrain stop.

The **Thailand Cultural Center** (✉ Ratchadaphisek Rd., Huay Kwang, Northern Bangkok ☎ 02/247–0028 Ⓜ Subway: Thai Cultural Center) is another place not to be missed. It hosts local and international cultural events, including opera, symphony orchestras, modern dance, and ballet. You can ask your concierge to find out what performance is showing while you're in town.

SPORTS & THE OUTDOORS

Although Thailand is home to an abundance of adventure and water sports, trekking, and boat racing, it's often difficult to find outdoor activities within Bangkok. Due to elevated temperatures, Bangkok residents generally head to malls on weekends where they can cool off, but the city does have golfing, jogging, and cycling options.

Bangkok offers one of the most intense spectator sports in the world, *muay thai* (thai kickboxing). This is the national sport of Thailand and matches are held almost every night. Even if you're not a martial arts enthusiast, the spectacle and pageantry of these matches—as well as the gambling fervor that surrounds them—make them a quintessential Bangkok experience.

Golf

There are several good golf courses in and around Bangkok. Greens fees are around B700 weekdays and B1,500 weekends, with caddy fees about B200. Book early for weekends, when tee times are harder to come by.

Krungthep Kreetha (⊠ 516 Kreetha Rd., Bangkapi ☎ 02/379–3716) is arguably the best managed course in Thailand, favored by local expats. There are 18 holes but the greens fees are high.

Navatanee Golf Course (⊠ 22 Mul Sukhaphiban 2 Rd., Bangkapi ☎ 02/376–1422), designed by the legendary Robert Trent Jones for the 1975 World Cup and recently renovated, is one of the more famous and challenging courses in Thailand. It's strictly members only on weekends, but you can tee up on weekdays. The 18-hole course is par 72.

The 27-hole, par-108 **Panya Indra** (⊠ 99/1 Moo 6, Ramindra Rd., Buengkhum ☎ 02/943–0000) offers three distinctly different championship courses. Another triple 9-hole championship course is the par-108 **Panya Park** (⊠ 46 Moo 8, Nongchok ☎ 02/989–4200); the fairway extends nearly 3,470 yards to the tree line.

Cycling

On the first Sunday of every month, the **Bangkok Tourist Bureau** (⊠ 17/1 Phra Athit Rd., Banglamphu ☎ 02/225–7612) organizes a cycling tour around the scenic klongs and temples of Thonburi. The B650 per-person price includes mountain bike rental and lunch. If you dare to rent a cycle on your own, **Pro Bike** (⊠ 237/2 Ratchadamri Rd., Lumphini Park ☎ 02/253–3384 or 02/254–1077 ⊕ www.probike.co.th Ⓜ Skytrain: Ratchadamri) is a one-stop shop for biking needs.

Health Clubs

California Fitness (⊠ Silom Rd., Silom ☎ 02/631–1122 Ⓜ Subway: Silom; Skytrain: Sala Daeng) is a multilevel space with floor-to-ceiling windows and a daily fee of B1,000. One-on-one training sessions are available.

The well-regarded **Clark Hatch Athletic Club** (⊠ Thaniya Plaza, Silom Rd., Silom ☎ 02/231–2250 Ⓜ Skytrain: Sala Daeng ⊠ Amari Watergate Hotel, 847 Petchburi Rd., Pathumwan ☎ 02/653–9000 Ⓜ Skytrain: Chitlom ⊠ Amari Atrium Hotel, 1880 New Petchburi Rd., Pathumwan ☎ 02/718–2000 Ⓜ Subway: Phetchaburi; Skytrain: Asok ⊠ Century Park Hotel, 9 Ratchaprarop Rd., Victory Monument ☎ 02/246–7800 Ⓜ Skytrain: Victory Monument) charges B300 per day for nonmembers.

With the best fitness facility of any hotel, the **JW Health Club** (⊠ JW Marriott Hotel, 4 Sukhumvit Rd., Sukhumvit ☎ 02/656–7700 Ⓜ Skytrain: Nana) has a palatial spread that would please any diehard fitness fanatic. You can choose from a variety of classes, spend time in the swimming pool, or hit the juice bar for some healthy treats. The new sleek **Westin Workout** (⊠ Westin Grande, 259 Sukhumvit Rd., Sukhumvit ☎ 02/651–1000 Ⓜ Skytrain: Asok) has a reputation as a premium fitness center, with cardio workouts, Latin dance aerobics, box-ercise, and muay thai, for B500 per day.

Horse Racing

Betting on the horses is a popular pastime in Bangkok, where a typical day at the track might involve a dozen races. Two tracks hold races on alternating Sundays. The **Royal Bangkok Sports Club** (⊠ Henri Dunant Rd. between Rama I and Rama IV Rds., Siam Square ☎ 02/251–0181 Ⓜ Skytrain: Ratchadamri) is across from Lumphini Park. The **Royal Turf Club** (⊠ North side of Phitsanulok Rd., just east of Rama V Rd., Dusit ☎ 02/280–0020) is a stone's throw from Chitlada Palace.

Jogging

If you want to run a few miles before breakfast, the small running tracks found at many hotels may be the best bet. You're safe in public parks during the day, but not at night. North of the city, **Chatuchak Park** has a loop that is 4 km (2½ mi). The well-paved paths at **Lumphini Park,** measure about 2 km (1 mi). They are popular among serious joggers. On Sukhumvit Road between Sois 22 and 24, **Queen Sirikit Park** is small but pleasant, with a jogging trail. **Sanam Luang,** the open space near the Grand Palace, is another popular park for runners.

Spas

Venues offering traditional massage are quite common in Bangkok—you can even pamper yourself while sightseeing at Wat Po. The staff at your hotel can recommend reputable therapists. If you have the time, pull out all the stops with a two-hour massage.

The pampering of **Being Spa** (⊠ 88 Sukhumvit Soi 51, Sukhumvit ☎ 02/662–6171 Ⓜ Skytrain: Thong Lo) takes place in a Thai-style house. Among the inventive treatments are a coffee-bean body scrub, and detoxifying algae and green tea body wraps.

If you're homesick for your yoga classes, **Bikram and Power Yoga Bangkok** (⊠ 14th fl., Unico House, 29/1 Soi Langsuan, Sukhumvit ☎ 02/652–1333 Ⓜ Skytrain: Chitlom) is the answer, for a drop-in rate of B500. In addition to beginner classes, there are also Power Vinyasa yoga and yoga for kids.

For those seeking greater health and mental quietude through Asian therapies, **COMO Shambhala** (⊠ Metropolitan Hotel, 27 S. Sathorn, Silom ☎ 02/625–3333 Ⓜ Subway: Lumphini; Skytrain: Sala Daeng) is the ultimate urban escape. The Metropolitan Bath starts with an invigorating salt scrub, followed by a bath and relaxing massage. In the heart of the city, **Divana Massage & Spa** (⊠ 7 Sukhumvit Soi 25, Sukhumvit ☎ 02/661–6784 Ⓜ Skytrain: Asok) has a cozy interior to make you feel right at home. All of the products used are designed by the spa and made mostly from Thai herbs.

A most relaxing massage with deliciously warm oils is available at the **Four Seasons Hotel Bangkok** (⊠ 155 Ratchadamri Rd., Siam Square

CloseUp

MUAY THAI, THE SPORT OF KINGS

THAIS ARE EVERY BIT AS PASSIONATE about their national sport as Americans are about baseball. Though it's often dismissed as a blood sport, muay thai is one of the world's oldest martial arts, and it was put to noble purposes long before it became a spectator sport.

No one knows exactly when muay thai originated, but it's believed to be over 2,000 years old. It's been practiced by kings—a few were champions—and it was used to defend the country from invaders. It's so important to Thai culture that until the 1920s, muay thai instruction was part of the country's public school curriculum.

Admittedly, some of sport's brutal reputation is well-deserved. There were very few regulations until the 1930s. Before then, there were no rest periods between rounds (at one point there were no rounds—there are stories of matches lasting hours). Protective gear was unheard of—the exception was a groin protector, an essential item when kicks to the groin were still legal. Boxing gloves were introduced to the sport in the late 1920s. Hand wraps did exist, but for some matches fighters would actually dip their wrapped hands in resin and finely ground glass to inflict more damage on their opponent.

Techniques: Muay thai was developed with the battlefield in mind and its moves mimic the weapons of ancient combat. Punching combinations, similar to modern-day boxing, turn the fists into spears that jab relentlessly at an opponent. The roundhouse kick—delivered to the thigh, ribs or head—turns the shinbone into a devastating striking surface, resembling a pike. Elbow strikes to the face and strong knees to the abdomen mimic the motion (and damage) of a battle axe. Finally, strong front kicks, using the ball of the foot to jab at the abdomen, thigh, or face, mimic an array of weapons from pikes to arrows to spears. Muay thai also includes clinching and a slew of defensive techniques—the most cringe-inducing is the basic block for an incoming kick, which results in shin-on-shin contact.

Rules: Professional bouts have five three-minute rounds, with a two-minute rest period in between each round. Fights are judged using a points system, with judges awarding rounds to each fighter. However, in muay thai, not all rounds are not given equal weight—the later rounds are more important as judges view fights as "marathons" with the winner being the fighter who's fared best throughout the entire match. The winner is determined by majority decision. Of course, a fight can also end decisively with a knock-out or a technical knock-out (wherein a fighter is conscious, but too injured to continue).

Rituals: The "dance" you see before each match is called the ram muay or wai kru (these terms are often used interchangeably, though the wai kru really refers to the homage paid to the kru or trainer). The ram muay serves to honor the fighter's supporters and his god, as well as to help him warm-up, relax, and focus. Both fighters walk around the ring with one arm on the top rope to seal out bad spirits, pausing at each corner to say a short prayer. They then kneel in the center of the ring facing the direction of their birthplace and go through a set of specific movements, often incorporating aspects of the Ramakien. Fighters wear several good luck charms, including armbands (kruang rang) and a headpiece (mongkron). The music you hear during each bout is live. Though it may sound like the tune doesn't change, the musicians actually pay close attention to the fight and the will speed up to match its pace—or to encourage the fighters to match theirs.

☎ 02/251–6127 Ⓜ Skytrain: Ratchadamri). On a street alive with street vendors, the small **Jivita Spa House** (✉ 57/155 Silom Terrace Bldg., Saladaeng Soi 2, Silom ☎ 02/635–5422 Ⓜ Subway: Silom) is an oasis of calm and regeneration. There's a variety of treatments here, but the most unusual is the Japanese Healing Stone, using crystals (not stones). You also get your choice of oils: relaxing, reviving or digestive.

A gentle massage in genteel surroundings is what you'll get at **Oriental Spa** (✉ The Oriental Hotel, 48 Oriental Ave., Silom ☎ 02/236–0400 Ⓜ Skytrain: Saphan Taksin). Amid the wood-panel sophistication of the Oriental Hotel's spa you can treat yourself to facials, wraps, and even a "jet-lag solution." **Sareerarom Tropical Spa** (✉ 117 Thong Lor Soi 10, Sukhumvit ☎ 02/391–9919 Ⓜ Skytrain: Thong Lo) is in a residential area and set around a pond. The spa offers yoga, organic cuisine, and a variety of soothing body treatments.

Thai Boxing
The national sport of Thailand draws enthusiastic crowds in Bangkok. Unlike some shows you can see in the resort areas down south, the city has the real thing. Daily matches alternate between the two main stadiums. The older **Lumphini Stadium** (✉ Rama IV Rd., Lumphini Park ☎ 02/251–4303 Ⓜ Subway: Lumphini) has matches on Tuesday and Friday at 6:30 PM and Saturday at 5 PM and 8:30 PM. The newer and larger **Ratchadamnoen Stadium** (✉ Ratchadamnoen Nok Rd., Banglamphu ☎ 02/281–4205) has bouts on Monday, Wednesday, and Thursday at 6 PM and Sunday at 5 PM. Tickets may be purchased at the gate.

Beware the hawkers outside the stadiums who will try to sell you pricey ringside seats—you'll be able to see all the action very well and get food-and-drink service at the mid-price seats in the bleachers. The only thing you're getting with the pricier tickets is a little more comfort (a folding chair versus bleacher seating or standing room). In both stadiums there are sections that seem solely reserved for the most manic of Thai gamblers; if you find yourself accidentally sitting in one of these sections, you'll be politely redirected to the farang section.

Water Sports
☾ **Siam Park** (✉ 99 Serithai Rd., Kannayao ☎ 02/919–7201) is home to the city's only water park. Parents looking for an alternative to a day of sightseeing will find this a cool reprieve. For B200, kids of all ages will be entertained in the wave pool, and on the waterslides and a log flume.

SHOPPING

Though Bangkok may not have Singapore or Hong Kong's reputation as a shopping hub, more and more tourists each year are being drawn to the Thai capital for its silk, gems, and tailor-made items. But Thailand also has a slew of other goods worth discovering: quality silverware, furniture, fine porcelain, and handmade leather goods, all at prices that put Western shops to shame. Plus, already low prices can often be haggled down even further (haggling is mainly reserved for markets, but shopkeepers will let you know if they're willing to discount). A word to the wise: to avoid getting scammed when shopping for bigger ticket items, namely jewelry, be sure to patronize reputable dealers only. Don't be fooled by a tuk-tuk driver offering to take you to a shop. This is a popular con perpetrated by shop owners, who in turn are paying drivers a commission to lure in unsuspecting tourists.

The city's most popular shopping areas are Silom Road and Surawong Road, where you can find quality silk; Sukhumvit Road, which is rich in leather goods; Yaowarat Road in Chinatown, where gold trinkets abound; and along Oriental Lane and Charoen Krung Road, which have many antique shops. The shops around Siam Square and at the World Trade Center attract both Thais and foreigners. Peninsula Plaza, across from the Regent Hotel in the embassy district, has very upscale shops. If you're knowledgeable about fabric, you can find bargains at the textile merchants who compete along Pahuraht Road in Chinatown and Pratunam Road off Phetchburi Road. You can even take the raw material to a tailor and have something made.

You can reclaim the 10% V.A.T. (Value-Added Tax) at the airport if you have a receipt. Ask shopkeepers about the V.A.T. refund—you must fill out the proper forms at the time of purchase. If you still want the convenience of duty-free shopping, try **King Power International Group** (⊠ World Trade Center, Ratchadamri Rd. ☎ 02/252–3633 Ⓜ Subway: Sukhumvit; Skytrain: Siam ⊠ Mahatun Plaza, Ploenchit Rd., Sukhumvit ☎ 02/253–6451 Ⓜ Subway: Sukhumvit; Skytrain: Ploenchit). Both branches are open daily 9:30 AM to 10:30 PM. You pay for the items at the shop, then pick them up at the airport when you leave. You need your passport and an airline ticket, and you need to make your purchase at least eight hours before leaving the country.

Markets

You can purchase virtually anything at the sprawling **Chatuchak Weekend Market** (⊠ Phaholyothin Rd., Chatuchak, Northern Bangkok Ⓜ Subway: Chatuchak; Skytrain: Mo Chit), from fountains to place in your rock garden to roosters ready to do battle. Sometimes you can find great buys on clothing, including silk items in a *mudmee* (tie-dyed before weaving) design that would sell for five times the price in the United States. Strategically placed food vendors mean you don't have to stop shopping to grab a bite. Though it's open Friday from 5 to 9 PM and weekends from 9 AM to 9 PM, the city's (some say the world's) largest market is best on weekend mornings. It's easy to reach, as it's across the street from the northern terminus of the Skytrain and near the Northern Bus Terminal.

An afternoon at JJ, as it is known by locals ("ch" is pronounced "jha" in Thai, so phonetically Chatuchak is Jatujak), is not for the faint of heart: up to 200,000 people visit each day and there are more than 8,000 vendors. But what's a little discomfort when there are such fantastic bargains to be had? Go prepared with bottles of water, comfortable shoes, and, if you can get a copy, Nancy Chandler's Map of Bangkok, which has a helpful, color-coded, stall-by-stall rendering of the market. You can order the map online at www.nancychandler.net or pick up a copy at her retail outlet in the Suan Lum Night Bazaar (the shop is at Ayut-thaya or Section C, Soi 6, #36-37).

The borders between the market's many sections can be a bit hazy (for example, the animal section spills into the silverware section), but you can keep your bearings by remembering that the outer ring of stalls has mainly new clothing and shoes, with some plants, garden supplies, and home decor thrown in for good measure. The next ring of stalls is where you can find mainly used clothing and shoes, as well as new cloth-ing, shoes, and accessories. Farther in are pottery, antiques, furniture, dried goods, and live animals. Even with a map, it's easy to get turned around in the mind-boggling array of goods, but this is also part of the joy of Chatuchak—wandering through the maze of vendors and sud-denly stumbling upon the beautiful teak table, handmade skirt, or col-orful paper lamp you'd been seeking.

The **Suan Lum Night Bazaar** (⊠ Rama IV and Wittayu (Wireless Rd.), Sukhumvit Ⓜ Subway: Lumphini; Skytrain: Ploenchit), across from Lumphini Park, is a relatively new market (it opened in 2001). It has attracted some attention, but nowhere near that of Chatuchak. This may be because at first glance Suan Lum appears gimmicky, but it does draw many locals, indicating that the prices are right and the goods go be-yond tourist knickknacks. The market is open nightly and is an attrac-tive alternative to the chaos of Chatuchak: it's far less crowded, it carries many of the same goods, and, being a night market, is far less likely to give you heat stroke. There are also a number of fun beer gar-dens within the market, as well as the famous Joe Louis Puppet The-atre if you want to catch a traditional Thai puppet show.

Hundreds of vendors jam the sidewalk each day at **Pratunam Market** (⊠ At Phetchaburi and Ratchaprarop Rds., Pathumwan Ⓜ Subway: Phetch-aburi; Skytrain: Asok). The stacks of merchandise consist mainly of in-expensive clothing. It's a good place to meet Thais, who come in the evening to sample the inexpensive Thai and Chinese street food.

In Chinatown you can find the **Thieves Market** (Nakorn Kasem) (⊠ Yaowarat and Charoen Krung Rds., Chinatown Ⓜ Subway: Hua Lamphong), where you can buy anything from housewares to porce-lains. Bargains are hard to find nowadays (you won't find anyone fenc-ing stolen goods), but these small, cluttered streets are fascinating. **Pahuraht Market** (⊠ Near Yaowarat Rd., Chinatown Ⓜ Subway: Hua Lamphong), operated mostly by Indians, is known for its bargain tex-tiles. A man with a microphone announces when items at a particular stall will be sold at half price, and shoppers surge over to bid. **Soi Sam-peng** (⊠ Parallel to Yaowarat Rd., Chinatown Ⓜ Subway: Hua Lam-phong) also has lots of fabrics—it's Bangkok's best-known and oldest textile center.

Khao San Road (⊠ Yaowarat Rd. and Charoen Krung (New Rd.), Banglamphu Ⓜ Subway: Hua Lamphong), in the middle of backpacker neighborhood Banglamphu, is closed to cars, and has some of the finest and most fun street shopping in the city. If the hip clothes, Thai sou-

CloseUp

BARGAINING FOR BARGAINS

EVEN IF YOU'VE HONED YOUR *bargaining skills in other countries, you might still come up empty-handed in Thailand. The aggressive* techniques that go far in say, Delhi, won't get you very far in Bangkok. One of the highest compliments you can pay for any activity in the Land of Smiles is calling it sanuk (fun), and haggling is no exception. Thais love to joke and tease, so approach each bargaining situation playfully. However, be aware that Thais are also sensitive to "losing face," so make sure you remain pleasant and respectful throughout the transaction.

As you enter a market stall, smile and acknowledge the proprietor. When something catches your eye, inquire politely about the price, but don't immediately counter. Keep your voice low—you're more likely to get a deal if it's not announced to the whole shop—then ask for a price just slightly below what you

want. Don't get too cavalier with your counter-offer—Thai sellers generally price their wares in a range they view as fair, so asking to cut the initial price in half will most likely be seen as an insult and might end the discussion abruptly. In most cases, the best you can hope for is 20%–30% discount.

If the price the shopkeeper offers in return is still high, turn your smile up another watt and say something like, "Can discount more?" If the answer is no, your last recourse is to say thank you and walk away. If you are called back, the price is still negotiable; if you aren't, maybe B500 wasn't such a bad price after all.

— Molly Petersen

venirs, used books, and delicious B10 pad Thai doesn't make the trip to Khao San worth it, the people-watching and energy of the place will.

Asking a taxi driver to take you to **Patpong** (✉ Silom Rd. at Soi 2, Silom Ⓜ Subway: Silom; Skytrain: Sala Daeng) may prompt a smirk, but for fake Rolex watches, imposter Louis Vuitton handbags, and Western-size clothing there's no better place than this notorious street. You can easily make a night of Patpong's great shopping, good restaurants, and happening bars and clubs.

Shopping Centers

In stark contrast to the grit and overcrowding of the markets are Bangkok's glittering high-end shopping centers. For a whirlwind tour of these facilities, hop on the Skytrain. **Peninsula Plaza** (✉ 153 Ratchadamri Rd., Sukhumvit Ⓜ Subway: Sukhumvit; Skytrain: Ratchadamri) is tucked between the Grand Hyatt Erawan and the Four Seasons Hotel Bangkok. Eerily quiet, but very elegant, it has quite a selection of imported labels, top local fashion designers, and jewelry shops.

The next stop on the line, Siam, is pay dirt for shoppers. **Gaysorn** (✉ Ratchaprasong Intersection, Siam Square Ⓜ Subway: Sukhumvit; Skytrain: Siam) may outshine all the other posh centers with its white marble and chrome fixtures. Here you can find all the requisite European labels as well as many local designers. **Siam Discovery** (⌧ 989 Rama I Rd., Siam Square Ⓜ Subway: Sukhumvit; Skytrain: Siam) is full of international labels, but has the added bonus of the most grandiose movie theater in Thailand, the Grand EGV. Across Sukhumvit, **Siam Centre** (⌧ At Phaya Thai and Rama I, Siam Square Ⓜ Subway: Sukhumvit; Skytrain: Siam) is the place to check out Bangkok's young hipsters searching for the latest fashion trends. With one-of-a-kind handmade clothing, shoes, and accessories, Siam Centre oozes style, but be prepared for the dreaded "no have big size, " as the clothes are all made to Thai proportions. An overhead walkway connects Siam Centre with the massive shopping complex **Mah Boon Krong** (MBK) (⌧ At Phaya Thai and Rama I, Siam Square Ⓜ Subway: Sukhumvit; Skytrain: Siam). It's an impressive seven stories high, and though it's no longer the biggest shopping center in Bangkok, it's still one of the busiest. It's not as stylish as Siam Centre and about as hectic as shopping can get, but it does have an entertainment center complete with a movie theater and bowling alley, and you can find everything under the sun here.

One stop east of Siam on the Skytrain is **Central Chidlom** (⌧ 1027 Ploenchit Rd., Sukhumvit Ⓜ Subway: Sukhumvit; Skytrain: Chitlom). The flagship store of Thailand's largest department store chain is not as flashy as its neighbors, but it does have a Jim Thompson silk shop. Two more Skytrain stops beyond Chidlom is **The Emporium** (⌧ Between Sukhumvit Sois 24 and 26, Sukhumvit Ⓜ Subway: Sukhumvit; Skytrain: Phrom Phong). It's glitzy, but often has sales. There's a little area on the sixth floor full of beautiful Thai silks, incense, and glassware, which are all reasonably priced.

Specialty Stores

Antiques

Thai antiques and old images of the Buddha require a special export license; check out the Thai Board of Investment's Web site at www.boi.go.th/english/ for rules on exporting, and applications to do so. Surawong Road, Charoen Krung Road, and the Oriental Plaza (across from Oriental Hotel) have many art and antiques shops, as does the River City Shopping Centre. Original and often illegal artifacts from Angkor Wat are sometimes sold there as well.

As you wander around the Old City, don't miss the small teak house that holds **123 Baan Dee** (⌧ 123 Fuengnakorn Rd., Old City ☎ 02/221–2520 Ⓜ Subway: Hua Lamphong). Antique silks, ceramics, beads, and other fascinating artifacts fill two floors. If you need sustenance, there's a small ice-cream parlor at the back. **Peng Seng** (⌧ 942 Rama IV, at Surawong Rd., Silom ☎ 02/234–1285 Ⓜ Subway: Sam Yan; Skytrain: Chong Nonsi) is one of the city's most respected dealers of antiquities. Prices may be high, but articles will most likely be genuine. **Rasi Sayam** (⌧ 32 Sukhumvit Soi 23, Sukhumvit ☎ 02/258–4195 Ⓜ Subway: Sukhumvit; Skytrain: Asok), in an old teak house in a garden, has a wonderful collection of fine Thai crafts.

Children's Shops

Bangkok Dolls (⊠ 85 Soi Ratchataphan, Makkasan District ☎ 02/235–3008) is outside of town and out of reach of public transportation, but it's well worth the taxi trip. It sells quality dolls of traditional Thai dancers and northern Thai tribes figures. At the **Pet Farm Workshop** (⊠ The Emporium Shopping Center, Sukhumvit Soi 24, Sukhumvit Ⓜ Subway: Sukhumvit; Skytrain: Phrom Phong) kids can make their own stuffed animals. From nose to tail, it's up to them.

Clothing & Fabrics

Thai silk gained its reputation only after World War II, when technical innovations made it less expensive. Two fabrics are worth seeking out: mudmee silk, produced in the northeastern part of the country, and Thai cotton, which is soft, durable, and easier on the wallet than silk.

Design Thai (⊠ 304 Silom Rd., Silom ☎ 02/235–1553 Ⓜ Subway: Silom; Skytrain: Sala Daeng) has a large selection of silk items in all price ranges. If you ask, you can usually manage a 20% discount. The **Jim Thompson Thai Silk Company** (⊠ 9 Surawong Rd. , Silom ☎ 02/234–4900 Ⓜ Subway: Silom; Skytrain: Sala Daeng) is a prime place for silk by the yard and ready-made clothes. The prices are high, but the staff is knowledgeable. Branches have opened in the Oriental Hotel and Central Chidlom shopping center. For factory-made clothing, visit the **Indra Garment Export Centre** (⊠ Ratchaprarop Rd., behind the Indra Regent Hotel, Pathumwan Ⓜ Skytrain: Phaya Thai), where hundreds of shops sell discounted items.

Napajaree Suanduenchai studied fashion design in Germany and more than two decades ago opened the **Prayer Textile Gallery** (⊠ Phayathai Rd., near Siam Sq., Siam Square ☎ 02/251–7549 Ⓜ Subway: Sukhumvit; Skytrain: Siam) in her mother's former dress shop. She makes stunning items in naturally dyed silks and cottons and in antique fabrics from the farthest reaches of Thailand, Laos, and Cambodia.

Many people who visit Bangkok brag about a custom-made suit that was completed in just a day or two, but the finished product often looks like the rush job that it was. If you want an excellent cut, give the tailor the time he needs, which could be up to a week at a reputable place. One of the best custom tailor shops in Bangkok is **Marco Tailor** (⊠ 430/33 Siam Sq., Soi 7, Siam Square ☎ 02/252–0689 Ⓜ Subway: Sukhumvit; Skytrain: Siam), which sews a suit equal to those on London's Savile Row. For women's apparel, **Stephanie Thai Silk** (⊠ 55 Soi Shangri-La, New Rd., Sukhumvit ☎ 02/233–0325 Ⓜ Subway: Sukhumvit; Skytrain: Nana) is among the city's finest shops. A skirt with blouse and jacket made of Thai silk starts at B5,000. Check out photographs of both President Bushes modeling their new suits made by **Raja Fashions** (⊠ Sukhumvit Soi 4, Sukhumvit ☎ 02/253–8379 Ⓜ Subway: Sukhumvit; Skytrain: Nana). Raja has the reputation for tailoring some of the finest men and women's fashions in Bangkok.

Electronics

If you're looking for a computer, pirated software, or any other electronic gizmo, **Panthip Plaza** (⊠ Phetchburi Rd., Sukhumvit Ⓜ Subway:

Phetchaburi; Skytrain: Asok) is the place. With hundreds of shops, Thais know it as the ultimate gadget retailer.

Flowers

After a few choice klong odors or whiffs of chili powder, **Pak Klong Talat Flower Market** (⊠ Chakraphet Rd., Chinatown Ⓜ Subway: Hua Lamphong) is a breath of fresh air. Though Thais generally come here to buy in bulk, you can spend just B100 and have enough orchids to fill your hotel room.

Food

To bring home a taste of Thailand, **Nittaya Thai Curry Shop** (⊠ Jakraphong Rd., Banglamphu Ⓜ Subway: Hua Lamphong) has pre-made, easy-to-prepare Thai curries and desserts that are packed in durable pouches. If street vendors don't do it for you and you want to pick up a few supplies, head to the posh **Emporium Supermarket** (⊠ The Emporium Shopping Center, Sukhumvit Soi 24, Sukhumvit Ⓜ Sukhumvit, Skytrain: Phrom Phong). It has a good selection of fresh fruits and vegetables.

Furniture

Along Sukhumvit Road between Sois 43 and 47, you can find shop after shop of rattan furniture. All are good quality and reasonably priced. Just across Sukhumvit you can find more shops of Asian furniture in both contemporary and traditional styles.

The best prices on a Thai take-off on the lounge chair (triangular pillows attached to mats) are at **Chatuchak Market** (⊠ Section 19 Ⓜ Subway: Chatuchak; Skytrain: Mo Chit).

Touch Wood (⊠ Sukhumvit Soi 38, Sukhumvit Ⓜ Subway: Sukhumvit; Skytrain: Thong Lo) has beautiful, high-quality restored teak furniture. If you're looking for furniture, wood carvings, old doors, or anything else for that matter **Wood Street** (⊠ Prachanarumit, Dusit Ⓜ Subway: Hua Lamphong) is the place.

Jewelry

Thailand is known for its sparkling gems, so it's no surprise that the country exports more colored stones than anywhere in the world. There are countless jewelry stores on Silom and Surawong roads. Be wary of deals that are too good to be true, as they probably are. Scams are common, so it's best to stick with established businesses.

A long-established firm is **Johny's Gems** (⊠ 199 Fuengnakorn Rd., Old City ☎ 02/224–4065 Ⓜ Subway: Hua Lamphong). If you call first, they'll send a car (a frequent practice among the city's better stores) to take you to the shop near Wat Phra Keo. You can rest assured you are getting a genuine piece from **Lin Jewelers** (⊠ 9 Soi 38 Charoen Krung (New Rd.), Old City Ⓜ Subway: Hua Lamphong), though their prices are a bit more expensive than average. **Oriental Lapidary** (⊠ 116/1 Silom Rd., Silom ☎ 02/238–2718 Ⓜ Subway: Silom; Skytrain: Sala Daeng) has a long record of good service. **Than Shine** (⊠ Sukhumvit Soi 22, Sukhumvit ☎ 02/381–7337 Ⓜ Sukhumvit, Skytrain: Thong Lo), run by sisters Cho Cho and Mon Mon, offers classic and modern designs. With top-quality gems, reliable service, and hordes of repeat clients, it's no wonder you need an appointment to peruse the huge inventory at **Uthai's Gems** (✉ 28/7 Soi Ruam Rudi, Sukhumvit ☎ 02/253–8582 Ⓜ Subway: Sukhumvit, Skytrain: Ploenchit).

Leather
It's easy to find good buys on leather goods in Bangkok, which has some of the lowest prices in the world for custom work. Crocodile leather is popular, but be sure to obtain a certificate that the skins came from a domestically raised reptile; otherwise, U.S. Customs may confiscate the goods. The River City Shopping Centre, next to the Royal Orchid Sheraton Hotel, has a number of leather shops.

For shoes and jackets, try 25-year-old **Siam Leather Goods** (✉ River City Shopping Centre, 23 Trok Rongnamkhaeng, Silom ☎ 02/639–6301 Ⓜ Subway: Sam Yan; Skytrain: Saphan Taksin). The **Chaophraya Bootery** (✉ 116 Silom Soi 4, Silom Ⓜ Subway: Silom; Skytrain: Sala Daeng) will custom-make cowboy boots in four or five days. This service is in addition to the already large inventory of ready-made leather shoes, boots, and accessories.

Music
For the best quality and widest selection of pirated CDs in town, visit **Hole in the Wall** (✉ Khao San Rd., Banglamphu). If you would rather have the real deal go to **CD Warehouse** (✉ The Emporium Shopping Center, Sukhumvit Soi 24, Sukhumvit Ⓜ Subway: Sukhumvit; Skytrain: Phrom Phong). This chain has a good selection, but the prices are not much better than back home.

Porcelain, Ceramics & Celadon
The pale green ceramic that will remind you of Thailand for years to come can be found in abundance at the **Celadon House** (✉ 8/3 Ratchadaphisek Rd., Sukhumvit Ⓜ Subway: Sukhumvit; Skytrain: Asok). This retailer carries some of the finest celadon tableware found in Bangkok. **Damrongluck Benjarong** (✉ River City Mall, Yotha Rd., Thonburi) has a huge inventory, and will make to-order dining sets, bowls, and vases. The blue-and-white porcelain may look more Chinese than Thai, but a lovely selection of dishes and more can be found at **Siamese D'art** (✉ 264 Sukhumvit Rd., Sukhumvit Ⓜ Subway: Sukhumvit; Skytrain: Phrom Phong).

Precious Metals
Chinatown is the place to go for gold. There's no bargaining, but you're likely to get a good price anyway. For bronze try **Siam Bronze Factory** (✉ 1250 Charoen Krung (New Rd.), Silom ☎ 02/234–9436 Ⓜ Subway: Sam Yan; Skytrain: Saphan Taksin). It's near the Oriental Hotel. Just around the corner from Lin Jewelers is its sister shop **Lin Silvercraft** (✉ 14 Soi Oriental Charoen Krung (New Rd.), Silom Ⓜ Subway: Sam Yan; Skytrain: Saphan Taksin). Among all the knickknacks stacked from floor to ceiling, this shop has some of the most finely crafted silver cutlery in town.

Souvenirs
For a one-stop souvenir shop, go to **Narayana Phand Pavilion** (✉ 127 Ratchadamri Rd., Sukhumvit Ⓜ Subway: Sukhumvit; Skytrain:

Ratchadamri). Thai silk, ceramics, lacquerware, and hand-tooled leather are all under one roof. It was established by the Thai government in 1941; expect to find high-quality goods, low prices, and half the crowds of the packed markets.

BANGKOK A TO Z

To research prices, get advice from other travelers, and book travel arrangements, visit www.fodors.com.

AIR TRAVEL

Dozens of airlines fly into Bangkok each day. Thai Airways, the national airline, has direct flights from the West Coast of the United States and from London. It also flies from Hong Kong, Singapore, Taiwan, and Japan.

The U.S. carrier with the most frequent flights is Northwest Airlines. It has service through Tokyo from New York, Detroit, Seattle, Dallas, San Francisco, and Los Angeles. British Airways flies nonstop to Bangkok from London. Singapore Airlines flies to Bangkok through Singapore. Japan Airlines has regular flights from New York to Bangkok with a connection in Tokyo, and Korean Air has a 1 AM flight daily from Bangkok to Los Angeles with a connection in Seoul.

Air New Zealand and Qantas both fly to Bangkok, with the latter offering several flights a day. Two Taiwanese airlines, China Airlines and Eva Air, both fly frequently through Bangkok to many points in Asia, as does Hong Kong–based Cathay Pacific.

🛪 Carriers **Air New Zealand** ✉ Charoen Krung (New Rd.), Silom ☎ 02/233-5900 Ⓜ Subway: Sam Yan; Skytrain: Saphan Taksin. **British Airways** ✉ 990 Rama IV Rd. ☎ 02/636-1747. **Cathay Pacific** ✉ 11th floor, Ploenchit Tower, Ploenchit Rd., Sukhumvit ☎ 02/263-0606 Ⓜ Subway: Sukhumvit; Skytrain: Ploenchit. **China Airlines** ✉ Peninsula Plaza, 153 Ratchadamri Rd., Sukhumvit ☎ 02/253-5733 Ⓜ Subway: Sukhumvit; Skytrain: Ratchadamri. **Eva Air** ✉ 2nd floor, Green Tower, Rama IV Rd. ☎ 02/367-3388. **Japan Airlines** ✉ 254/1 Ratchadaphisek Rd., Sukhumvit ☎ 02/692-5185 Ⓜ Subway: Phetchaburi; Skytrain: Asok. **Korean Air** ✉ 21/133 South Sathorn Rd., Silom ☎ 02/267-0985 Ⓜ Subway: Silom; Skytrain: Silom. **Northwest** ✉ 153 Ratchadamri Rd., Peninsula Shopping Plaza, 4th floor, Sukhumvit ☎ 02/254-0789 Ⓜ Subway: Sukhumvit; Skytrain: Ratchadamri. **Qantas** ✉ Charn Issara Tower, 942/51 Rama IV Rd. ☎ 02/267-5188. **Singapore Airlines** ✉ Silom Centre Bldg., 2 Silom Rd., Silom ☎ 02/236-0440 Ⓜ Subway: Silom; Skytrain: Sala Daeng. **Thai Airways** ✉ 485 Silom Rd., Silom ☎ 02/280-0060 Ⓜ Subway: Silom; Skytrain: Sala Daeng.

AIRPORTS & TRANSFERS

Foreign arrivals are scheduled to start landing at the new Suvarnabhumi Airport (pronounced Soo-wan-na-poom and also known as the Second Bangkok International Airport or SBIA) in the fall of 2005. The SBIA's seven-floor terminal makes it the largest in the world. A 10-lane road connects the SBIA, which is about 25 km (15 mi) southeast of Downtown Bangkok, to the city's outer-ring road and is linked to the Bang Na-Chonburi Expressway which leads to some of Thailand's many beaches. Until it opens, most international flights to Thailand will continue to land at Don Muang International Airport, 25 km (16 mi) north of the city.🛈 **Don Muang International Airport** ☎ 02/535-1111. **Suvarnabhumi Airport** ⊕ www.bangkokairport.org.

TRANSFERS At this writing, details on transfers from Suvarnabhumi are still sketchy, but in 2007 a city rail link between the airport and Phayathai-Makkasan will be provided. There will also be a bus terminal at the airport, as well as numerous taxi stands around the premises.

There are many ways to get into Bangkok from Don Muang, though taxi is the most convenient. A bus service costing B100 runs approximately every 30 minutes between the airport and four sectors of downtown Bangkok. A1 travels to Ratchadamri and Silom roads. A2 covers the central area that includes Chinatown. A3 travels down Sukhumvit Road. A4 weaves its way to Hua Lamphong, the main train station. A detailed listing of each route is available from the Tourist Authority of Thailand office and at the bus stop outside the arrivals hall. You can also catch local air-conditioned buses costing B25 on the main road that passes the airport.

If you take a taxi, count on a B200–B250 fare plus a B50 expressway toll charge and a B50 airport surcharge. (Taxis bound for the airport do not add the surcharge.) To make sure that your driver knows where you are headed, state your destination to the person in the kiosk near the curb. The dispatcher will write it down for the driver, who will lead you to the taxi. The expressways are often congested, meaning that the trip from the airport can take anywhere from 30 minutes to more than an hour. The driver will ask you for toll money when you reach the tolls.

Bangkok Airport Express trains make the 35-minute run every 90 minutes from 8 AM to 7 PM. Check the schedule at the information booth in the arrival hall. The fare is B45. You can also take the regular trains from 5:30 AM to 9 PM. The fare is B5 for a local train and B13 for an express. The train is not convenient for many travelers, as most hotels are not near its terminus, the Hua Lamphong train station in Chinatown.

For about B6,000 per person you can whiz into the city in a helicopter. Travex flies between the airport and several downtown hotels, including the Peninsula, Oriental, Royal Orchid Sheraton, and Shangri-La. The new expressways have greatly diminished the need for this service, however.

Note: The airport has more than its share of hustlers out to make a quick baht, many wearing uniforms and name tags that make them look official. Many try to get you to change your hotel to one that pays them a large commission, often claiming your hotel is overbooked. They will also hustle you into overpriced taxis or limousines. Do not get taken in by these ruses. Instead, follow the signs that point the way to the public taxi stand. Here, you will line up in front of a booth where an English-speaker will fill out a destination form for you. All of these taxis will use a meter.
🛈 **Bangkok Airport Express** ☎ 02/223-0341. **Travex** ☎ 02/652-2550.

BOAT & FERRY TRAVEL
Ferries (sometimes called "river buses") ply the Chao Phraya River. The fare for these express boats is based on the distance you travel; the price

ranges from B2–B25. At certain piers you must add a B1 jetty fee. The pier adjacent to the Oriental Hotel is convenient to many of the city's hotels. You can get to the Grand Palace in about 10 minutes, or to the other side of Krungthon Bridge in about 15 minutes. Local line boats run from 6 AM to 6 PM. If you are on Sukhumvit, Phetchaburi Road is a good place to catch them. These boats stop at every pier and will take you all the way to Nonthaburi, where you'll find a little island with vendors selling pottery. A trip up the river makes for a fun afternoon on days when it's too hot to trudge around the city. Under the Saphan Taksin Skytrain stop, there is a ferry stop where passengers can cross the river to Thonburi for B3.

Longtail boats (so called for the extra-long propeller shaft that extends behind the stern) operate as taxis that you can hire for about B400 an hour. The best place to hire these boats is at the Central Pier on Sathorn Bridge. Longtails for hire often quit running at 6 PM.

For a blast into Bangkok's transportation past, traditional wooden canal boats are a fun, though not entirely practical way to get around town. Klong Saen Saep, just north of Ploenchit Road, is the main boat route. The fare is a maximum B15, and during rush hour boats pull up to piers in one-minute intervals. Klong boats provide easy access to Jim Thompson's house and are a handy alternative way to get to Khao San Road during rush hour.

BUS TRAVEL TO & FROM BANGKOK

Bangkok has three major terminals for buses headed to other parts of the country. The **Northern Bus Terminal**, called Mo Chit, serves Chiang Mai and points north. The **Southern Bus Terminal**, in Thonburi, is for buses bound for Hua Hin, Ko Samui, Phuket, and points south. The **Eastern Bus Terminal**, called Ekkamai, is for buses headed to Pattaya, Rayong, and Trat provinces.

Most bus companies do not take reservations, and tickets are sold on a first-come, first-served basis. This is seldom a problem, however, because the service is so regular that the next bus is sure to depart before long. For example, VIP buses from Bangkok to Kanchanaburi depart every 15 minutes.

The air-conditioned orange-color 999 buses are the most comfortable. They have larger seats that recline. A hostess serves drinks and snacks and a movie is usually shown on longer trips. If no 999 bus is available on your route, stick with the air-conditioned blue VIP buses. They aren't as luxurious, but are still comfortable.

⚐ Bus Stations **Eastern Bus Terminal** ✉ Sukhumvit Soi 40, Sukhumvit ☎ 02/391-2504 Ⓜ Subway: Sukhumvit; Skytrain: Ekkamai. **Northern Bus Terminal** ✉ Phaholyothin Rd., behind Chatuchak Park ☎ 02/936-2852 Ⓜ Subway: Chatuchak; Skytrain: Mo Chit. **Southern Bus Terminal** ✉ Pinklao-Nakomchaisri Rd., Talingchan ☎ 02/434-7192.

BUS TRAVEL WITHIN BANGKOK

Although city buses can be very crowded, they are convenient and inexpensive. For a fare of B3.50 to B5 on the non-air-conditioned buses and B8 to B20 on the air-conditioned ones, you can travel virtually anywhere in the city. Air-conditioned microbuses, in which you are guaranteed a seat, charge B25. Most buses operate from 5 AM to around 11 PM, but a few routes operate around the clock.

The bus routes are confusing, but someone at the bus stop should know the number of the bus you need. You can pick up a route map at most bookstalls for B35. Buses can be very crowded, so be alert for pickpockets.

CAR RENTALS
Most rental agencies in the capital let you drop off the car in a different city. Of the international chains, Avis, Hertz, and National have offices at the airport and in downtown Bangkok.

🛈 Agencies **Avis** ✉ 2/12 Wittayu (Wireless Rd.), Sukhumvit ☎ 02/255-5300 Ⓜ Subway: Sukhumvit; Skytrain: Ploenchit. **Budget** ✉ 19/23 Bldg. A, Royal City Ave., ☎ 02/203-0180 🖨 02/203-0249. **Hertz** ✉ 1620 New Phetchburi Rd. ☎ 02/251-7575 Ⓜ Subway: Phetchaburi; Skytrain: Asok. **National** ✉ 727 Srinakarin Rd. ☎ 02/722-8487.

CAR TRAVEL
Thailand's highway system is good (and getting better), so driving is a more popular option than in years past. There are plenty of sights around Bangkok that are within easy driving distance.

As for driving in Bangkok—don't bother. The maze of streets is difficult enough for taxi drivers to negotiate. Throw in bumper-to-bumper traffic and you'll wish that you were on a water taxi on the river or the Skytrain soaring above the streets.

DISABILITIES & ACCESSIBILITY
Bangkok has made precious few steps toward improving things for people with disabilities. Most sights are reached by at least one daunting set of steps. This means getting around the city will be a challenge for those in a wheelchair. Your best bet is hiring a guide who can drive you from sight to sight. The good news is that most of the larger hotels have rooms that are designed for people with handicaps.

EMBASSIES
Most of the embassies in the capital are located around Lumphini Park, especially along Wittayu (Wireless Rd.). The U.S. embassy is open weekdays 7 to 4.

🛈 **Australia** ✉ 37 Sathorn Rd., Silom ☎ 02/287-2680 Ⓜ Subway: Silom; Skytrain: Chong Nonsi. **Canada** ✉ 990 Rama IV Rd., Silom ☎ 02/636-0540. **New Zealand** ✉ 93 Wittayu (Wireless Rd.), Sukhumvit ☎ 02/254-2530 up to 3 Ⓜ Subway: Sukhumvit; Skytrain: Ploenchit. **United Kingdom** ✉ 1031 Wittayu (Wireless Rd.), Sukhumvit ☎ 02/253-0191 Ⓜ Subway: Sukhumvit; Skytrain: Ploenchit. **United States** ✉ 120 Wittayu (Wireless Rd.), Sukhumvit ☎ 02/205-4000 Ⓜ Subway: Sukhumvit; Skytrain: Ploenchit.

EMERGENCIES
In case of emergency, it's a good idea to contact the Tourist Police. The force has mobile units in major tourist areas.

For medical attention, Bunrungrad Hospital, on Sukhumvit Soi 1, and Bangkok Nursing Hospital, near Silom Road, are considered the best by most expatriates. Nonthavej Hospital, not far from Don Muang International Airport, has an excellent staff accustomed to foreign patients. Other good facilities include Bangkok Adventist Hospital, Bangkok Christian Hospital, and Chulalongkorn Hospital.

Bangkok has a number of reputable dental clinics, among them 11 Dental Clinic and Thaniya Dental Centre. If you want a private dentist, the aptly-named Dr. Smile is conveniently located at the foot of Sala Daeng Skytrain stop.

There are many pharmacies in Bangkok, including Foodland Supermarket Pharmacy. Compared with the United States, fewer drugs require prescriptions. If you need one, the prescription must be written in Thai. Over-the-counter drugs do not necessarily have the same ingredients as those found elsewhere, so read the label carefully. If you cannot find a pharmacy, the ubiquitous 7-Eleven, AM/PM, and other convenience stores carry non-prescription medications.

▸ Doctors & Dentists **11 Dental Clinic** ✉ 155 Sukhumvit Soi 11/1, Sukhumvit ☎ 02/255-2279 Ⓜ Subway: Sukhumvit; Skytrain: Nana. **Dr. Smile** ✉ Silom Soi 1, Silom ☎ 02/661-1156 Ⓜ Subway: Silom; Skytrain: Sala Daeng. **Thaniya Dental Centre** ✉ 52 Silom Rd., Silom ☎ 02/231-2100 Ⓜ Subway: Silom; Skytrain: Sala Daeng.

▸ Emergency Services **Ambulance** ☎ 1669. **Fire** ☎ 199. **Police** ☎ 191. **Tourist Police** ✉ 4 Ratchadamnoen Rd., Sukhumvit ☎ 1155 Ⓜ Subway: Phetchaburi; Skytrain: Asok.

▸ Hospitals **Bangkok Adventist Hospital** ✉ 430 Phitsanulok Rd., Dusit ☎ 02/281-1422. **Bangkok Christian Hospital** ✉ 124 Silom Rd., Silom ☎ 02/233-6981, 02/233-6989 Ⓜ Subway: Silom; Skytrain: Sala Daeng. **Bangkok Nursing Home** ✉ 9 Convent Rd., Silom ☎ 02/632-0550 Ⓜ Subway: Silom; Skytrain: Sala Daeng. **Bunrungrad Hospital** ✉ Sukhumvit Soi 3, Sukhumvit ☎ 02/253-0250 Ⓜ Subway: Sukhumvit; Skytrain: Ploenchit. **Chulalongkorn Hospital** ✉ Rama IV Rd. ☎ 02/252-8181. **Nonthavej Hospital** ✉ 30/8 Ngam-wongwan Rd., Bangkhen Nonthaburi ☎ 02/589-0102.

▸ 24-Hour Pharmacies **Foodland Supermarket Pharmacy** ✉ No. 9 Patpong 2 Rd., Silom ☎ 02/233-2101 Ⓜ Subway: Silom; Skytrain: Sala Daeng ✉ 1413 Sukhumvit Soi 5, Sukhumvit ☎ 02/254-2247 Ⓜ Subway: Sukhumvit; Skytrain: Nana.

ENGLISH-LANGUAGE MEDIA

The English-language dailies, the *Bangkok Post* and *The Nation,* and the monthly *Metro* are available at most newsstands.

With two locations, Asia Books has a wide selection of books and magazines. Bookazine is a chain with a good selection and several locations, including one in the CP Tower. Kinokuniya Books has one of the city's largest selections of English-language books. And for older hard-to-find used books try Merman Books. Also try Dasa Book Cafe for great prices on second-hand titles.

▸ English-Speaking Bookstores **Asia Books** ✉ 221 Sukhumvit Soi 15, Sukhumvit ☎ 02/651-0428 Ⓜ Subway: Sukhumvit; Skytrain: Asok ✉ Peninsula Plaza, Sukhumvit ☎ 02/253-9786 Ⓜ Subway: Sukhumvit; Skytrain: Ratchadamri. **Bookazine** ✉ 313 Silom Rd., Silom ☎ 02/231-0016 Ⓜ Subway: Silom; Skytrain: Sala Daeng. **Dasa Book Cafe** ✉ 710/4 Sukhumvit Road between Sois 26 and 28, Sukhumvit ☎ 02/231-3155 Ⓜ Subway: Sukhumvit; Skytrain: Phrom Phong.

Kinokuniya Books ✉ Emporium Shopping Complex, Sukhumvit Rd., Sukhumvit ☎ 02/664-8554 Ⓜ Subway: Sukhumvit; Skytrain: Phrom Phong. **Merman Books** ✉ 191 Silom Rd., Silom ☎ 02/231-3155 Ⓜ Subway: Silom; Skytrain: Sala Daeng.

HEALTH

Use common sense to stay healthy in Bangkok. There's no need to avoid most foods, even those sold by street vendors. Simply make sure what you are eating was cooked in front of you or is still hot. Never eat food that has been allowed to cool to room temperature. The rule of thumb is to look for the vendors patronized by long lines of locals. Spicy food may be too much for sensitive stomachs, so try to take it easy your first few days. The tap water in Thailand is not potable. Most people brush their teeth with tap water and are fine, but it is recommended to avoid ice from street vendors (most restaurants, not just the high-price ones, will have filtered water for ice cubes). Travelers' diarrhea is a common ailment in Thailand, so at the first onset of symptoms head to the nearest pharmacy. Diarrhea is usually no more than a nuisance, but stay hydrated. Bottled water is available everywhere in Bangkok.

Sexual transmitted diseases should be taken seriously in Bangkok. AIDS is a big problem, especially among sex workers. Condoms are available everywhere, even from street vendors.

You might be surprised at the number of stray dogs in Bangkok. These "soi dogs, " as they're called, should be avoided. In Lumphini Park there have been reports of rabies from these mongrels. If you are bitten seek medical attention immediately, but even a lick or a scratch from a stray dog should be washed thoroughly.

MAIL & SHIPPING

All neighborhoods have at least one post office, and the staff at your hotel can tell you where to find the nearest one. The city's main post office is on Charoen Krung Road south of Chinatown. It is more efficient than smaller ones, which can have dreadfully slow service.

The major international courier services, Federal Express, DHL, and UPS, have offices in Bangkok.

🏢 Courier Services **DHL Worldwide** ✉ Grand Amarin Tower, 22nd floor, New Phetchburi Rd., Sukhumvit ☎ 02/207-0600 Ⓜ Subway: Phetchaburi; Skytrain: Asok. **Federal Express** ✉ Green Tower, 8th floor, Rama IV Rd. ☎ 02/229-8800. **UPS** ✉ Soi 44/1, Sukhumvit Rd., Sukhumvit ☎ 02/712-3300 Ⓜ Subway: Sukhumvit; Skytrain: Ekkamai.

MONEY MATTERS

Major banks all exchange foreign currency, and most have easily accessible ATMs that accept foreign bank cards. Bangkok has come great strides in the past decade, with ATMs proliferating in areas popular with tourists.

Currency exchange offices are common, but don't wait until the last minute. It's distressing to try to find one when you're out of baht.

SAFETY

For a city of its size, Bangkok is relatively safe; however, practice common sense. Do not walk alone at night down poorly lit streets. Guard your valuables, whether in a backpack or hotel room, against theft by safely stashing them away in an inside zipper pocket or safe deposit box. Do not accept food or drinks from strangers, as there have been reports of men and women being drugged and robbed or worse. Bangkok is no more dangerous for women than any other major city, but women should still take precautions to not travel alone at night (take a taxi back to your hotel if you're out late) and to make sure their hotel rooms are adequately secure.

SKYTRAIN

The Skytrain transformed the city when it opened on the king's birthday in 1999. It now has 25 stations on two lines that intersect at Siam Square. Although it covers just a fraction of the capital (it bypasses the Old City and Dusit, for example), it is surprisingly convenient for visitors. The routes above Sukhumvit, Silom, and Phaholyothin roads make traveling in those areas a breeze. If you are traveling between two points along the route, the Skytrain is by far the best way to go. The fare is B10 to B40, determined by the distance you travel. It runs from 5 AM to midnight. Although the Skytrain and subway are separate entities and use different fare and ticketing systems, the two connect at three points: Sala Daeng Station and Silom Station, Asok Station and Sukhumvit Station, and Mo Chit Station and Chatuchak Station.
🚩 **Bangkok Transit System** ☎ 02/617-7300.

SUBWAY

Five years after ground was first broken, Bangkok's M.R.T. subway system opened in August 2004. The subway stretches from Hua Lamphong Train Station to Bang Sue Train Station, stopping at 16 stations along the way. Although it only covers a small section of the city, the subway does make getting from city center out to the train stations a breeze. (What was once an hour-long affair is now a short 20-minute ride underground.) There are also convenient stops at Chatuchak, Queen Sirikit Convention Center, Thailand Cultural Center, Silom Road, and Sukhumvit Road.

The subway runs daily from 6 AM until midnight and passes every 5 minutes during rush hour and every 10 minutes during regular hours. Adult fares are B14 to B36. Fares for children and those older than 65 are 50% off the regular rates. Children whose height is less than 3 feet ride free of charge. If you plan on multiple journeys, there is also a Stored Value Card, which can be bought at ticket booths for a minimum of B100, plus a B50 deposit.

TAXIS & TUK-TUKS

Taxis can be an economical way to get around, provided you don't hit gridlock. A typical journey of 5 km (3 mi) runs about B60. Most taxis have meters, so avoid those that lack one or claim that it is broken. The rate for the first 2 km (1 mi) is B35, with an additional baht for every 50 meters after that. If the speed drops to below 4 mph, a surcharge of one baht per minute is added. Taxi drivers may take a fare without a clue as to where they are going, so having a concierge write the name of your destination and its cross streets in Thai is always a good idea, especially if you are visiting a place that is not a well-known landmark or buried in the bowels of a labyrinthine neighborhood like Chinatown.

Though colorful three-wheeled tuk-tuks are somewhat of a symbol of Bangkok, they're really only a good option when traffic is light—otherwise you can end up sitting in traffic, sweating, and sucking in car fumes. Oh, and did we mention that they're unmetered and prone to overturning? The drivers are tough negotiators, and unless you are good at bargaining you may well end up paying more for a tuk-tuk than for a metered taxi. Unscrupulous tuk-tuk drivers—all too common, especially around touristy areas—offer tours at a bargain rate, then take you directly to jewelry shops and tailors who, of course, give the drivers a commission. Don't fall for it. In many ways a tuk-tuk is not ideal, but if a trip to Bangkok does not seem complete without a spin around town in one, pay half of what the driver suggests, insist on being taken to your destination, and hold on for dear life.

At many sois you will find groups of motorcycle taxis. These "soi boys" once only took passengers down the side streets, but their operations have expanded so that they can travel anywhere in Bangkok. Fares are negotiable, usually about the same as or perhaps a little less than taxis. A trip to go the length of a street is B10. Motorbikes can be dangerous, and helmets, when available, are often nothing more than a thin sheath of plastic without a chin strap, but most locals take these taxis as part of the daily commute. Motorcycle drivers seem to know their way around the city much better than taxi drivers—they also know good side street shortcuts. The risk and discomfort limit their desirability, but motorcycles are one of the best ways to get around Bangkok, especially if you're in a hurry.

TELEPHONES
Telephone information from an English-speaking operator is available by dialing 1133. Getting through, however, can often be difficult.

TOUR OPERATORS
Virtually every major hotel has a travel desk that books tours in and around Bangkok. With only slight variations, companies usually offer half-day tours of Wat Pho, Wat Benjamabophit, and Wat Traimit; half-day tours of the Grand Palace and Wat Phra Keo; and dinners featuring traditional dance. Several established agencies are good bets. Try Diethelm, East West Siam, or World Travel Service.

🚩 Agencies **Diethelm** ⊠ Kian Gwan Bldg. 11, 140/1 Wittayu (Wireless Rd.), Sukhumvit ☎ 02/255–9150 Ⓜ Subway: Sukhumvit; Skytrain: Ploenchit. **East West Siam** ⊠ Bldg. One, 11th floor, 99 Wittayu (Wireless Rd.), Sukhumvit ☎ 02/256–6153, 02/256–6155 Ⓜ Subway: Sukhumvit; Skytrain: Ploenchit. **World Travel Service** ⊠ 1053 Charoen Krung (New Rd.), Chinatown ☎ 02/233–5900 Ⓜ Subway: Hua Lamphong.

TRAIN TRAVEL TO & FROM BANGKOK
Hua Lamphong Railway Station, the city's main station, is where you'll find most long-distance trains. Bangkok Noi Railway Station, on the Thonburi side of the Chao Phraya River, is used by local trains to Hua Hin and other nearby destinations.

🚩 Train Stations **Bangkok Noi** ⊠ Arun Amarin Rd., Thonburi ☎ 02/411-3102. **Hua Lamphong** ⊠ Rama IV Rd. ☎ 02/223-0341 Ⓜ Hua Lamphong.

VISITOR INFORMATION
Bangkok's downtown branch of the Tourist Authority of Thailand, open 8:30 to 4:30, tends to have more in the way of colorful brochures

than hard information, but it can supply useful material on national parks and various out-of-the-way destinations. A 24-hour hot line provides information on destinations, festivals, arts, and culture. You may also use the hot line to register complaints or request assistance from the tourist police. There is also a TAT branch at the international terminal at Don Muang International Airport.

🚩 Info **Tourist Authority of Thailand** ✉ 1600 New Phetchburi Rd., Sukhumvit ☎ 02/250-5500 🖷 02/694-1361 Ⓜ Subway: Sukhumvit; Skytrain: Asok.

AROUND BANGKOK

2

MOST MOBILE MARKET
Damnoen Saduak's floating vendors ⇨*p.88*

MOST INCREDIBLE INHABITANTS
Kitti's Hog-nosed bats, the world's smallest
mammals, at Sai Yok park ⇨*p.102*

COOLEST WAY TO COOL OFF
Taking a dip in Erawan Waterfall ⇨*p.101*

MOST SOBERING STRETCH OF LAND
The Death Railway at Kanchanaburi ⇨*p.95*

BEST WAY TO GET YOUR BEARINGS
Wandering amid replicas of all of Thailand's
greatest attractions ⇨*p.88*

Updated by
Howard
Richardson

IF YOU NEED RESPITE from the heat, noise, and pollution of Bangkok, the surrounding countryside offers many possibilities. When most people head south of the city, it's to make for Thailand's famous beaches, but on the way—and within three hours of the city—are two floating markets at Damnoen Saduak and Samut Songkram, a huge park with replicas of many of the country's landmarks at Muang Boran, and the town of Phetchaburi, which has many interesting temples and a few royal summer palaces.

To the west of Bangkok is Nakhon Pathom, keeper of Thailand's biggest temple. Travel for another hour and you're in Kanchanaburi, site of the famous Bridge on the River Kwai. The town juxtaposes the solemnity of war graveyards with fleets of thunderous floating discos popular with Thai weekenders. From here you can arrange jungle treks or a trip to the Myanmar border. If you're not in a hurry to get back to Bangkok, you can continue your exploration of stunning Kanchanaburi Province, with day trips to 13th century Khmer ruins, a monastery-cum-tiger sanctuary, and two national parks containing waterfalls. A little further west and you'll be on Myanmar's doorstep in Sangklaburi, where Thai, Mon, Karen, and Bangladeshi communities mix and longtail boats take you to see an underwater village.

About the Restaurants

The areas around Bangkok allow you to sample both regional and ethnic foods. Kanchanaburi and Sangklaburi have Mon, Karen, Bangladeshi, and Burmese communities, each serving specialties such as *laphae to*, a Burmese salad of nuts and fermented tea leaves. Nakhon Pathom is reputed to have the country's best version of a rice-based dessert called *khao laam*. Phetchaburi is also famous for its desserts as well as *khao chae*, a chilled rice dish soaked in herb-infused water.

About the Hotels

An overnight stay is essential in Sangklaburi and highly recommended in Kanchanaburi. Stay in Damnoen Saduak the night before you visit the floating market to avoid a very early-morning bus ride.

Luxury accommodation is in short supply in most provincial towns, so be prepared to stay at a resort on the outskirts, or lower your expectations. It's best to book ahead on weekends and national holidays in Kanchanaburi.

WHAT IT COSTS In Baht				
$$$$	$$$	$$	$	¢
RESTAURANTS over B400	B301–B400	B201–B300	B100–B200	under B100
HOTELS over B6,000	B4,001–B6,000	B2,001–B4,000	B1,000–B2,000	under B1,000

Restaurant prices are per person for a main course at dinner. Hotel prices are for a standard double room, excluding tax.

Timing

On weekends and national holidays (particularly the water festival Songkran in mid-April), Kanchanaburi and the seafood restaurants at

Samut Songkram will be packed with Thais. From November to March (the high season) the floating market has more tourists than vendors.

The waterfalls of Kanchanaburi province are at their best during or just after the rainy season (June to November).

Muang Boran

❶ *20 km (12 mi) southeast of Bangkok; 2 hrs by bus.*

Muang Boran (Ancient City) is a park with more than 100 replicas and reconstructions of the country's most important architectural sites, monuments, and palaces. The park itself is shaped like Thailand, and the attractions are placed roughly in their correct geographical position. A "traditional Thai village" within the grounds sells crafts, but don't let that put you off—the experience is surprisingly untouristy. It's possible to see a few sights on foot, but the park stretches over 320 acres, and takes about four hours to cover by car. Alternatively, rent a bicycle at the entrance for B50. Small outdoor cafés scattered throughout the grounds serve decent Thai food.

To get here by car, take the Samrong–Samut Prakan expressway and turn left at the Samut Prakan intersection onto Old Sukhumvit Road. You can also take an air-conditioned bus (number 511) from Bangkok's Southern Bus Terminal to the end of the line at Pak Nam, then transfer to a minibus (number 36). Muang Boran is well sign-posted on the left at Km 33. ⊠ *Km 33, Old Sukhumvit Rd., Samut Prakan* ☎ *02/226–1936* 🖃 *B100* ☉ *Daily 8–5.*

Damnoen Saduak

❷ *109 km (65 mi) southwest of Bangkok; 2 hrs by bus.*

The town's colorful floating market is a true icon of Thai tourism. The image is so evocative that it's become an ad agency favorite (it was used to launch Absolut Vodka's introduction to the country). Today the market, which sells mostly produce and other foods, is often infested with tourists and it bears only passing resemblance to the authentic commercial life of this canal-strewn corner of Thailand.

On the other hand, this may be your only opportunity to catch a glimpse of a fading Thai tradition. Twenty years ago many communities had floating markets, but with new roads replacing the need for canal commerce, this is one of the only ones left. And if you get here before 9 AM—when most tourists start to arrive—you can still catch a glimpse of yesteryear. Buy your breakfast from women in straw hats paddling boats laden with fruit or steaming stir-fry pans. The best way to enjoy the market is to hire a boat (holding up to six people) for around B300 per hour; after seeing the market, you can also arrange to tour the wider countryside, taking in local temples and gardens, or even travel back to Bangkok (around 3 hours). A second market, around a canal turn, sells strictly tourist souvenirs.

Into the Wild There's a huge expanse of untouched jungle in the west of Thailand around Kanchanaburi, the kick-off point for treks involving overnight stays in Karen villages, elephant riding, river rafting, and refreshing dips in waterfall pools. Rumors of tigers in the jungles near the Myanmar border are reinforced by the Tiger Temple, a forest sanctuary for cubs abandoned after their mothers were killed by poachers. There are also many caves to visit, some of them temples full of Buddha images, and one that's home to the Kitti Hog-nosed bat, the world's smallest mammal. Kaeng Krachan National Park, near Phetchaburi, is a favorite haunt of bird-watchers.

2

Shopping Adventures The region outside Bangkok offers some unique shopping experiences. Few markets are world famous, but most tourists know of Damnoen Saduak's floating market before they even set foot in Thailand, and designate it as a must-see. It's the only daily floating market left in the region southwest of Bangkok—an area with a network of more than a hundred canals—and it's a vivid reminder of village life during a time when most travel and commerce was done on the water. Kanchanaburi and Phetchaburi both have night markets, and there's an array of ethnic goods available in Sangklaburi—much of it smuggled across the Myanmar border. On the border itself there's a market at the Three Pagodas Pass checkpoint, selling mainly teak items, from small souvenirs to large pieces of furniture.

Step into Old Siam The region outside Bangkok is dripping with history. Nakhon Pathom, center of the city-states of Mon Buddhist culture in the area west of Bangkok between the 6th and 11th centuries, is Thailand's oldest seat of Buddhist learning. It has been continuously populated since the 2nd century BC, and contains one the most important religious monuments in the country. Outside Kanchanaburi, close to a Neolithic site, are the remains of a Khmer settlement. Further traces of Khmer influence are found in the architecture of Phetchaburi's temples; the city also has palaces of former Thai kings that are open to the public. Replicas of many temples and palaces are found in the huge open-air museum of Muang Boran.

Where to Stay & Eat

There are morning buses from Bangkok, but the best way to get an early start is to stay overnight. A few places are available on the main road from Samut Songkram.

¢ ✕▥ **Baan Sukchoke Country Resort.** The resort is made up of small wooden bungalows, which are a bit rickety, but clean and comfortable nonetheless. The bungalows surround a pond connected to the canal. The water is beautifully floodlit at night, and there's an outdoor restaurant serving a Thai menu (¢–$), with old boats displayed outside. The property is 3 km from the floating market; you can have the staff call a tuk-tuk or a boat (B400, up to 10 people) to take you there. ✉ 103

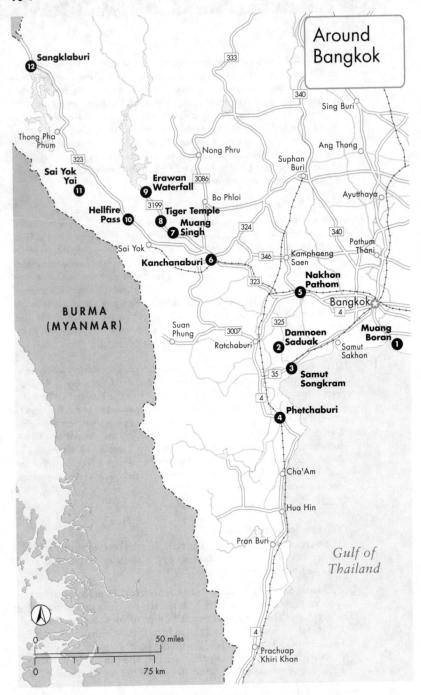

Around Bangkok

Sangklaburi 12

Thong Pha Phum

BURMA (MYANMAR)

333

340

Sing Buri

Ang Thong

Nong Phru

Suphan Buri

Ayutthaya

323

Sai Yok Yai 11

Erawan Waterfall 9   3086

Bo Phloi

Pathum Thani

340

Hellfire Pass 10   3199

Tiger Temple 8

Muang Singh 7

324

Kanchanaburi 6

346

Kamphaeng Saen

323

Nakhon Pathom 5

Bangkok

4

Sai Yok

325

Suan Phung

3007

Damnoen Saduak 2

Muang Boran 1

Ratchaburi

Samut Sakhon

35

Samut Songkram 3

4

Phetchaburi 4

Cha'Am

Hua Hin

Pran Buri

Gulf of Thailand

4

Prachuap Khiri Khan

0   50 miles

0   75 km

Moo 5, Damnoen Saduak ☎ *032/254301* ⌂ *Restaurant; no a/c in some rooms* ▭ *No credit cards.*

¢ 🖼 **Little Bird Hotel.** The large, basic rooms at this hotel are set back from the main road, so the place is quiet. The plain, municipal-looking building may be unattractive, but it's a 10-minute walk to the boats for the market and close to banks, convenience stores, and cafés. ⊠ *Moo 1/8, Damnoen Saduak* ☎ *032/254382* ⌂ *No a/c in some rooms* ▭ *No credit cards.*

Samut Songkram

❸ *72 km (45 mi) south of Bangkok; 1 ½ hrs by bus.*

The provincial town of Samut Songkram has little to recommend it, but it has many nearby attractions that make it an enjoyable day trip from Bangkok. There are terrific seafood restaurants along the waterfront at Don Hoi Lod, and a top quality *benjarong* (ceramic and bone china glazed in at least five different colors) workshop; the area is also a good base for exploring some of the surrounding villages on the canal network. **Ampawa,** for example, is a 15-minute drive away and has a **floating market** on Friday, Saturday, and Sunday evenings from 5 PM to 9 PM. It's similar to Damnoen Saduak, but smaller.

Don Hoi Lod, on the outskirts of town (about 3 km away), is named after a local clam with a tubular shell, the fossilized remains of which are found on the river banks here. Thai families flock here on weekends to eat the clams (try them with garlic and pepper) and other seafood dishes at the restaurants nestled between the trees at the mouth of the Mae Khlong River. The best times to view the fossils are March and April, when the water is low. During the rest of the year, you can also see them in the early mornings and in the evenings at low tide.

Some of Thailand's finest benjarong can be found at **Ban Pinsuwan Benjarong.** This cottage workshop was started in 1979 by Virat Pinsuwan, who adapted his skills as an antique restorer to produce traditional designs like those made during the Ayutthaya period and onward. You can watch the craftsmen work Monday through Saturday from 8 to 5, but there's an eight-month waiting list for buyers (one teacup-and-saucer set, B1,600, takes three days to make), so you can only purchase from a small selection of items. ⊠ *32/1 Moo 7, Bangchang* ☎ *034/751322.*

Phetchaburi

❹ *132 km (84 mi) south of Bangkok; 3 hrs by bus.*

This small seaport town once linked the old Thai capitals of Sukhothai and Ayutthaya with trade routes on the South China Sea and Indian Ocean. Its many wats are within or easily accessible on foot from the town center, particularly along Matayawong, Pongsuriya, and Phrasong roads.

Phetchaburi is also famous for *khao chae,* a chilled rice dish with sweetmeats once favored by royals that has become a summer tradition in posh Bangkok hotels. You can find it around the day market on Phanit Charoen Road (look for people eating at stalls from small silver bowls), along with other local specialties such as *khanom jeen thotman* (noodles with curried fish cake). The city was also a royal retreat during the reigns of Rama IV and Rama V (1851–1910) and has two palaces open to the public.

Watch out for roving gangs of monkeys that roam the streets of town, particularly around Khao Wang; some of them are cute and friendly, but it is wise to realize they are clever and cunning and should be approached with caution.

The 800-year-old Khmer-influenced **Wat Mahathat Worawihan,** on the eastern side of the Phetchaburi River, is a royal temple built approximately 800 years ago. Besides the magnificent architecture and main Buddha statue, an interesting feature of this wat is a subtle political joke. Look around the base of the Buddha statue outside the main temple. A ring of monkey-like Atlases supports the large Buddha image, but one of the monkeys is not like the others. See if you can find him!

Wat Yai Suwannaram, built during the Ayutthaya period by skilled craftsman, has a 300-year-old painting in its main hall, a library on stilts above a fishpond (to protect the documents from termites), and an axe mark above one of the temple doors, said to have been left by a Burmese invader.

The exterior wood-paneled wall of **Wat Ko Kaeo Suttharam** is considered Thailand's finest. It depicts the constellations and the ten lives of the Lord Buddha.

Wat Kam Paeng Laeng is the largest and oldest temple in Phetchaburi. It was built during the height of the Khmer empire, known as the Bayon era. Surrounded by a laterite wall, the compound includes four Khmer-style pagodas. The wat's architecture, unique among a city of a hundred-plus temples, is greatly admired by local residents.

Phra Nakhon Khiri Historical Park (aka Khao Wang) is a forested hillside area on the edge of Phetchaburi with one of King Rama IV's palaces and a series of temples and shrines. Many of these are set high on the hilltop and have good views of the surrounding plains and the first karsts (large limestone outcroppings), which are a main feature of southern Thailand, on the horizon. Monkeys are a major shoplifting hazard around the gift shops at the foot of the hill, where there's a cable car (B30) for those who don't fancy the strenuous walk. ⊠ *Khao Wang, entrance off Phetkasem Rd.* ☉ *Daily 9–4* ☞ *B40.*

Built in 1910 as a rainy season retreat by King Rama V, **Phra Ram Ratchaniwet** was modeled on a palace of Germany's Kaiser Wilhelm, and consequently has grand European architecture with art nouveau flourishes. The dining room has impressively ornate ceramic tiles. ⊠ *Thai Military Base, Ratchadamnoen Rd.* ☞ *B50* ☉ *Daily 8:30–4.*

Twenty-two km (14 mi) north of Phetchaburi is Khao Yoi. The town is best known for its unique culture, including a large population of Laotian immigrants. The **Thai Song Dam Cultural Center,** which represents the Lao Song Dam people, puts on traditional dancing shows each weekend, organized by the leader of the community. Homestays with the villagers can also be arranged through the cultural center. The region is also a popular destination for rock climbers from Bangkok (call 02/4346100 in Khao Yoi if you wish to climb while you're passing through). ☎ 032/562208.

KAENG KRACHAN NATIONAL PARK – If you have access to a car, head to Thailand's largest national park, which covers nearly half of Phetchaburi province. The park is home to bears, Indo-Chinese tigers, leopards, and more than 250 bird species, including the ratchet-tailed treepie, which is unique to Thailand. It's also possible to visit Karen villages that lie within the park's boundaries. If you wish to stay overnight, accommodation is available in bungalows (B1,500, sleep up to four people) near the visitor center, or in rented tents (B250, plus B30/person). Reservations are essential for the bungalows; call the Bangkok office. It's really best to drive here, as you'll need a car to get around the park easily. However, travel by songthaew is possible from Phetchaburi's market (B50), and taxis can take you from the visitor center to campsites and back. The last songthaew to and from Phetchaburi is at 1 PM. To get to the park by car, take Route 4 from Phetchaburi and turn right on Route 3499 at Tha Yang; the trip takes about 1½ hours. ⊠ *Route 3499, 40 mi southwest of Tha Yang* ☎ *034/459291, 02/562–0760 in Bangkok* ⊕ *www.dnp.go.th* ⊠ *B200 per person/B30 per vehicle* ⊙ *Daily 5 AM–6 PM.*

Where to Stay

Phetchaburi has no top-end hotels.

¢ ▦ **Khao Wang Hotel.** This Chinese guesthouse hotel opposite a 24-hour Internet shop has simple rooms. You may or may not enjoy the added spectacle of monkeys climbing all over your room's window grates. ⊠ *Ratchawithi Rd.* ☎ *032/425167* ▤ *No credit cards.*

¢ ▦ **Rabieng Rooms.** A cluster of small dark-wood plank buildings hold a few basic rooms that are big enough for a bed and not much else. The restaurant, which has windows that look out onto the river, serves Thai and Western food. The hotel organizes treks of varying length into nearby Kaeng Krachan National Park. ⊠ *1 Shesrain Rd.* ☎ *032/425707* ⤶ *6 rooms* ⚉ *Restaurant; no a/c, no room TVs* ▤ *No credit cards.*

¢ ▦ **The Royal Diamond Hotel.** It's a long way from town, but the Royal Diamond is Phetchaburi's only choice for those seeking a hotel instead of a guesthouse. However, it's close to Khao Wang and there are a few decent cafés nearby (try Puong Petch for sizzling seafood with hot Kariang chilies or Kway Tiao Pla VIP for a variety of fish noodle dishes). ⊠ *555 Moo 1, Phetkasem Rd., Tambon Rai-Som* ☎ *032/411061 up to 70* 🖷 *032/424310* ⤶ *58 rooms* ⚉ *Restaurant, bar, massage* ▤ *MC, V* ⧗ *BP.*

Nakhon Pathom

➎ *56 km (34 mi) west of Bangkok; 1 hr by bus.*

Reputed to be Thailand's oldest city (it's thought to date from 150 BC), Nakhon Pathom was once the center of the Dvaravati kingdom, a 6th-to 11th-century affiliation of Mon city-states. It marks the region's first center of Buddhist learning, established here about a millennium ago. Today, there would be little reason to visit if it weren't for **Phra Pathom Chedi,** the tallest Buddhist monument in the world. At 417 feet, it stands just a bit higher than the chedi at Shwe Dagon in Myanmar.

The first chedi on this site was erected in the 6th century but was destroyed in a Burmese attack in 1057. Surrounding the chedi is one of Thailand's most important temples, which contains the ashes of King Rama VI.

In the outer courtyard are four viharns facing in different directions that contain images of Lord Buddha in various postures. The terraces around the temple complex are full of fascinating statuary, including Chinese figures, a large reclining Buddha, and an unusual Buddha seated in a chair. By walking around the inner circle surrounding the chedi, you can see novice monks in their classrooms through arched stone doorways. Traditional dances are sometimes performed in front of the temple, and during Loi Krathong (a festival in November that celebrates the end of the rainy season) a fair is set up in the adjacent park. ✛ ½ km (⅓ mi) south of train station 🚋 B20 ☉ Daily 6–6.

Next to Phra Pathom Chedi is the **Phra Pathom Chedi National Museum,** which contains Dvaravati artifacts such as images of the Buddha, stone carvings, and stuccos from the 6th–11th centuries. ⊠ Khwa Phra Rd. 🚋 B30 ☉ Wed.–Sun. 9–4.

Sanam Chan Palace was built during King Rama IV's reign. The palace is closed to the public, but the surrounding park is a lovely place to relax in the shade before heading back to Bangkok. ⊠ Petchkasem Rd. west of chedi.

On the Bangkok Road out of Nakhon Pathom (toward Bangkok) is the **Rose Garden,** which is actually a park complex where herbs, bananas, and various flowers, including orchids and roses, flourish. Within the complex are traditional houses and a performance stage, where shows include dancing, thai boxing, sword fighting, and even wedding ceremonies (daily at 2:45 PM). The park is popular with Thai families and has restaurants, a hotel (from B2,100), and simple lakeside accommodations with air-conditioning, TVs, refrigerators, and private bathrooms for B700. ⊠Km 32, Petchkasem Rd. 🕿 034/32288 🖷 034/322775 ⊕ www.rose-garden. com 🚋 B20, B380 with lunch and show ☉ Daily 8–6.

Next door to the Rose Garden is the **Samphran Elephant Ground & Zoo.** The main attraction here is, of course, elephants. You can take rides on them, and also watch a 40-minute performance during which they display some of their historical roles in Thai warfare and industry. During the show elephants haul logs, play soccer, and even reenact the Yutha Harti, a 16th-century elephant-back battle between a Thai king and an invading Burmese prince. The show is very popular with Thai day-trippers and school parties. There are other attractions at the zoo, including an orchid nursery, but avoid the degrading "crocodile wrestling" show, in which practically comatose animals are tormented and dragged around by their tails. You can pay the zoo's entrance fee in dollars, but at a poor rate of exchange. ⊠ *Km 30, Petchkasem Rd.* ☎ *02/429–0361* 🖷 *02/429–0455* ⊕ *www.elephantshow.com* 🖾 *B400* ⊙ *Daily 8–5:30.*

Where to Eat

The road from Nakhon Pathom train station has several cafés, and a market where food stalls sell various one-plate Thai meals. Similar dining options can be found at the entrance of the chedi. Keep an eye out for Nakhon Pathom specialties such as *khao lam* (sticky rice, palm sugar, and black beans grilled in hollowed-out bamboo sections) and sweet, pink-flesh pomelo (a large citrus fruit). The Rose Garden has several places to eat, including a Japanese restaurant, and Samphran Elephant Ground has an open-air food court that's cheaper than the restaurant at the gate.

Kanchanaburi

❻ *140 km (87 mi) west of Bangkok; 2 hrs by bus.*

Within and around Kanchanaburi are many cave temples, museums, tribal villages, and waterfalls, along with many places to go trekking, elephant riding, and rafting; it's also the main access point to the large national parks of western Thailand. But the city is most famous for being the location of the **Bridge on the River Kwai**—a piece of the WWII Japanese "Death Railway" and subject of the 1957 film of the same name starring Alec Guinness (though the film was actually shot in Sri Lanka).

During World War II, the Japanese, who had occupied Thailand, forced about 16,000 prisoners of war and 50,000 to 100,000 civilian slave laborers from neighboring countries to construct the "Death Railway, " a supply route through the jungles of Thailand and Burma. It's estimated that one person died for every railway tie that was laid. Two cemeteries are a testament to the thousands who died here and three museums have exhibits from the period. Sure-footed visitors can walk across the Bridge on the River Kwai, of which the arched portions are original (the bombed out central sections were rebuilt after the war). Next to the bridge is a plaza with restaurants and souvenir shops.

In December Kanchanaburi holds a big fair and puts on a sound-and-light show depicting the Allied bombing of the bridge.

The **Kanchanaburi War Cemetery,** next to noisy Saengchuto Road just south of the train station, has row upon row of neatly laid-out graves: 6,982 Australian, British, and Dutch prisoners of war were laid to rest here. (The remains of the American POWs were returned to the United States during the Eisenhower administration.) A remembrance ceremony is held here every April 25, Australia's ANZAC (Australia and New Zealand Army Corps) Day.

The **Chong-Kai War Cemetery,** on the grounds of a former hospital for prisoners of war, is a serene site with simple, neatly organized grave markers of the soldiers forced to work on the railway. It's a little out of the way, and therefore rarely visited, but this graveyard is worth the trek. To get there, hire a tuk-tuk or take a ferry across the river and walk about 500 meters (⅓ mi) down the road. The cemetery will be on your left.

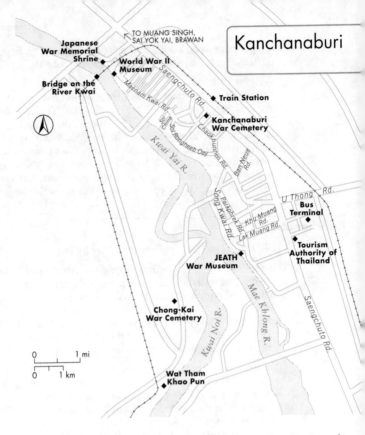

Kanchanaburi

The **Japanese War Memorial Shrine** is near the bridge, 1 km (½ mi) north-west of the Kanchanaburi War Cemetery.

About 2 km (1 mi) downriver from the bridge is the **JEATH War Museum** (JEATH is an acronym for Japan, England, America, Australia, Thailand, and Holland). The museum was founded in 1977 by a monk from the adjoining Wat Chaichumpol; it's in a replica of the bamboo huts that were used to hold prisoners of war. Among the items displayed at the museum are railway spikes, clothing, aerial photographs, newspaper clippings, and original sketches by ex-prisoners depicting their living conditions. ✉ *Wat Chaichumpol, Bantai* ☎ *034/515203* 💷 *B30* ⏰ *Daily 8–6.*

The **World War II Museum** contains memorabilia from the Japanese occupation, including weapons and vehicles. It's next to the bridge, at the site of another temporary wooden bridge once erected by prisoners (a few remains can still be seen on the river bank). Alongside the WWII artifacts is a museum of Thai history; note that in an attempt to bring in more customers, this museum bears a sign that misrepresents it as the more famous JEATH Museum, which is actually at the other end of town. ✉ *395–403 River Kwai Rd.* ☎ *034/512596* 💷 *B30* ⏰ *Daily 7–6.*

About 1 km (½ mi) southwest of the Chong-Kai War Cemetery you'll find **Wat Tham Khao Pun,** one of the best cave temples in the area. A guide at the small shrine outside the cave will direct you on where to go. Inside the cave, between the stalagmites and stalactites, are Buddhist and Hindu statues and figurines. The cave complex was used as a series of storerooms by the Japanese in WWII.

Where to Stay & Eat

Kanchanaburi is laid out along the Mae Khlong and Kwai Yai rivers. It has three areas of activity: the main road commercial district, which has a few mid-range hotels; the south end of the river, a popular Thai weekend holiday retreat with raft house accommodation, floating restaurants, and loud disco boats; and the northern riverbank, geared more toward backpackers, with guesthouses, bars, and Internet cafés. The city is busy on long weekends and public holidays, when booking ahead is essential for hotels and resorts.

$ ✕ **River Kwai Floating Restaurant.** The most attractive—and crowded—open-air restaurant in town is adjacent to the bridge. Fish dishes (fried with pungent spices or lightly grilled), soups, and curries dominate the menu. The local specialty is *yeesok,* a fish caught fresh from the Kwai Yai and Kwai Noi rivers. Another tasty choice is the *tom yum gong,* hot-and-sour shrimp soup. Note that the restaurant is often busy with tour groups. ⊠ *River Kwai Bridge* ☎ *034/512595* ▤ *No credit cards.*

¢–$ ✕ **Maenam.** The busiest of the floating restaurants at the south end of the river is built on a network of moored rafts. It serves Thai seafood standards such as red curry with "serpent head fish" (a freshwater relative of the catfish) and char-grilled prawns. As with all properties in this area, the restaurant's riverfront serenity is disrupted periodically by the incredibly loud music of the disco and karaoke boats that meander up and down the river. The restaurant also has a singer each night. ⊠ *5/7 Song Kwai Rd.* ☎ *034/514318* ▤ *MC, V.*

¢–$ ✕ **The Resort.** This relatively new bar-restaurant occupies a white Thai-style house and draws a mostly Thai clientele. Red clay-tile floors and a low-lit covered courtyard give the place a casual elegance; the garden is particularly lovely—tables are shaded by white canvas umbrellas and palm trees. The menu is standard Thai, but there are also a few unusual dishes to sample, such as deer and fried pig's appendix with garlic. ⊠ *318/2 River Kwai Rd.* ☎ *01/847–9227* ▤ *MC, V.*

¢ ✕ **Apple's Guesthouse.** The massaman curry at this quiet garden restaurant is very popular with backpackers; it's made with heaps of palm sugar, and is a good balm for stomachs struggling with chili overdose. More authentic (in other words, hotter) dishes are available on request and there's a choice of fresh (although weak) coffees. Owners Apple and Noi also teach a Thai cookery course (B900, which includes six of Noi's curry pastes to take away), which starts off with a market visit by bicycle and ends with six prepared dishes. Apple runs two- to four-day treks (minimum four people; B1,950 per person) that include a stay in a Karen village. ⊠ *52 Soi Rongheeb Oay, Chaokhunnen Rd.* ☎ *034/512017* ▤ *MC, V.*

¢ ✕▥ **Jolly Frog Guesthouse.** These bungalow rooms are small and spartan, but some are riverfront, and all are surrounded by peaceful gardens. The cheaper rooms have fans and some have shared bathrooms. The more expensive rooms have four beds each. Because it's close to bars, Internet access, and convenience stores, the Jolly Frog is popular with backpackers and it's a good place to meet people. The restaurant (¢) has Thai and Western dishes, including fish, burgers, pizzas, and a good selection of Thai vegetarian dishes. ⊠ *28 Soi China, River Kwai Rd., 71000* ☎ *034/514579* ⪦ *55 rooms* ⚐ *Restaurant* ▤ *MC, V.*

★ ¢ ✕⊞ **Little Creek.** Thai-style bungalows and a few larger chalet-style buildings on stilts are spaced around calm, bucolic grounds. The tribal-chic bungalows have peach-color walls, thatched roofs, and open-air showers. The chalets and the more expensive bungalows have air-conditioning and hot water; cheaper rooms have fans and cold water. All accommodations have verandas with bench seating. The lakeside restaurant (¢–$) has a wood-fire pizza oven and charcoal grill and serves Western and Thai food while ambient World music plays in the background. Little Creek is a 10-minute drive from town; the resort provides free taxi rides or you can rent motorcycles or bicycles. ⊠ *155 Moo 6, Parkphrek Rd., 71000* ☎ *034/510127* ⊕ *www.littlecreekhideawayvalley.com* ⪦ *50 bungalows* ⚐ *Restaurant, pool, bar, Internet* ▤ *MC, V.*

$$ ⊞ **Felix River Kwai Resort.** Kanchanaburi's first luxury hotel is a bit faded now, but it's still a good value. Polished wood floors and wicker headboards decorate the cool, airy rooms. The large pool set amid tropical gardens is a great place to relax. The hotel is within walking distance of Kanchanaburi; the River Kwai bridge is 300 meters from the hotel. Rates include a buffet breakfast. ⊠ *9/1 Moo 3, Tambon Thamakham, 71000* ☎ *034/515061, 02/655–7949 in Bangkok* 🖷 *034/ 515095* ⊕ *www.felixriverkwai.co.th* ⪦ *255 rooms* ⚐ *2 restaurants, in-room safes, cable TV, tennis courts, pool, health club, massage* ▤ *AE, DC, MC, V.*

$–$$ ⊞ **River Kwai Village.** In the jungles of the River Kwai Valley, this resort organizes elephant riding and rafting trips, as well as the usual city excursions. Most of the simple rooms, which are embellished with teak accents and colored stones embedded in the walls, are in five single-story log cabins. You have to be slightly more adventurous to stay in one of the "raftels" (rooms set on rafts floating in the river), but not that much more—they have similar amenities to the rooms on dry land. The cafeteria-style restaurant offers a combination of Thai and Western dishes, but it's more fun to eat at the casual restaurant on one of the rafts. The resort provides transportation to and from Bangkok. ⊠ *72/12 Moo 4, Tambon Thasao, Amphoe Sai Yok, 71150* ☎ *034/634454, 02/251–7552 in Bangkok* 🖷 *034/634456* ⊕ *www.bkk2000.com/rkvh* ⪦ *165 rooms, 26 raft houses* ⚐ *2 restaurants, pool, meeting rooms, travel services* ▤ *AE, DC, MC, V* ⊚ *BP.*

$ ⊞ **Kasem Island Resort.** Perched on an island in the middle of the river, this resort has one of the area's most enviable locations. You can choose between bungalows with private, hot-water bathrooms and air-conditioning, or cheaper bamboo huts on rafts, with fans and private cold-water bathrooms. All accommodations have balconies and river views. There's limited parking available on the mainland and a free ferry for guests. ⊠ *44–48 Chaichumpol Rd., 71000* ☎ *034/513359, 02/255–3604 in Bangkok* ⪦ *29 rooms, 10 bungalows, 19 raft houses* ⚐ *Restaurant, pool; no a/c in some rooms, no room phones, no TV in some rooms* ▤ *MC, V.*

$ ⊞ **Pavilion Rim Kwai Thani Resort.** This resort near the Erawan Waterfall caters to wealthy Bangkok residents who want to retreat into the country without giving up their creature comforts. Tropical flora surrounds the complex, and the River Kwai flows serenely past. The minimally furnished rooms have polished wood floors and balcony views. The large dining room serves Thai and Western dishes. ☒ *79/2 Moo 4, Km 9, Ladya-Erawan Rd., Tambon Wangdong, 71190* ☎ *034/515772* 🖷 *034/515774* 📞 *200 rooms* ♿ *Restaurant, tennis courts, pool, gym, sauna, meeting room* ▤ *AE, MC, V* ⎟◎⎟ *BP.*

¢ ⊞ **River Kwai Hotel.** On the main road through town you can find the first large-scale hotel constructed in Kanchanaburi. It's a comfortable place and very popular with tour groups, but the river is quite a distance away. Rates include a buffet breakfast. ☒ *284/4–6 Saengchuto Rd., 71000* ☎ *034/513348* 🖷 *034/511269* 📞 *150 rooms* ♿ *Restaurant, travel services* ▤ *AE, MC, V.*

¢ ⊞ **Sam's Guest House.** This property is popular with tour groups and as a launching pad for treks, which the staff here can arrange. Waterfront rooms are more expensive than those set away from the river. Motorbikes (B150 per day) and cars (B1,200 per day) are available for rent. Sam's has two other locations on the river, one with raft houses. ☒ *14/2 River Kwai Rd., 71000* ☎ *034/515956* 🖷 *034/512023* ⊕ *www.samsguesthouse.com* 📞 *36 rooms* ♿ *Restaurant; no a/c in some rooms, no room TVs* ▤ *No credit cards.*

Sports & the Outdoors

RAFTING Rafting trips on the Kwai Yai or Mae Khlong rivers, which take at least a full day, let you venture far into the jungle. The mammoth rafts, which resemble houseboats, are often divided into separate sections for eating, sleeping, and sunbathing. Be careful when taking a dip—the currents can sometimes suck a swimmer down. The cost of a one-day trip starts at about B300. Longer trips are also available. The tour companies listed below can help you arrange rafting trips, as can most guesthouses. The Tourism Authority of Thailand office on Saengchuto Road can also be of assistance.

TREKKING Jungle treks of one to four days are possible all over the region. They typically include bamboo rafting, elephant riding, visits to Karen villages, and sampling local food (sometimes a cultural performance is also included). To ensure safety and reliability, stick to tour companies with TAT (Tourism Authority of Thailand) licenses, which will be prominently displayed on the premises.

Good Times Travel's (☒ 63/1 River Kwai Rd. ☎034/624441 ⊕ www.goodtimes-travel.com) trips take in all the usual highlights, including national parks, rafting, caves, Karen village stays, and the Tiger Temple.

RSP Jumbo Travel (☒ 3/13 Chao Kun Nen Rd. ☎ 034/514906 ⊕ www.jumboriverkwai.com) offers everything from day trips to weeklong itineraries that include rafting, elephant riding, and off-road adventures. They also organize theme party nights; one of the most popular includes dinner and a Thai classical music concert at the Muang Singh Historical Park. Some tours are combined with stays at up-market hotels for those who like more comfort with their adventure.

Shopping

Blue sapphires from the Bo Phloi mines, 45 km (28 mi) north of Kanchanaburi, are for sale at many shops and stalls in the plaza near the bridge. They're generally a good buy; price is determined by the size and color of the stone, and, as usual, your bargaining skills. You'll do the best when there are few tourists around and business is slow. Stick to stalls with licenses displayed, and never buy from touts promising outrageously cheap prices. You may also want to look for deals at the small shops in the center of town.

Around Kanchanaburi Province

Kanchanaburi Province contains several of Thailand's most beautiful national parks, replete with jungles, rivers, caves, and waterfalls. You'll get the best of the waterfalls during or just after the rainy season (June to November), however, this is also when jungle trekking is the hardest. Other highlights of the region include Khmer ruins and a temple sanctuary for tigers.

Muang Singh Historical Park

❼ *45 km (28 mi) northwest of Kanchanaburi; 1 hr by train.*

King Chulalongkorn reportedly discovered this 13th- to 14th-century Khmer settlement while traveling along the Kwai Noi River. The restored remains of the city range from mere foundations to a largely intact, well-preserved monument and building complex. There are also examples of Khmer statues and pottery and a prehistoric burial site. All are now enclosed in Muang Singh Historical Park, large grounds that you can drive or cycle around with the aid of taped commentary in English, Thai, or French, available at the park's entrance. Bicycle rentals cost around B20 per hour. If you don't want to make the 45-minute drive, take the train from Kanchanaburi to Tha Kilen station (B10, one hour); the park is a 1-km (½-mi) walk (turn right when leaving the station) away. There's a small café and lodgings on the grounds. ⊠ *Tha Kilen* ☎ *034/591122* ⊠ *B40* ☉ *Daily 8:30–5.*

Ban Khao Museum, a small two-room exhibition of 4,000-year-old Neolithic remains, is a short drive away. It may be possible to hitch a lift here. ⊠ *Ban Khao* ⊠ *B30* ☉ *Wed.–Sun. 9–4.*

Tiger Temple

★ **❽** *25 km (15 mi) northwest of Kanchanaburi; 40 min by bus.*

Tiger Temple (or Wat Pa Luanta Bua Yannasampanno) is a forest monastery that houses several kinds of animals on its grounds, most notably 10 tigers that have been cared for here since 1999 and are now a major tourist attraction. Three cubs were born in 2003. The tigers are let out of their cages at 3 PM daily, when visitors arrive and line up to touch them. It's a unique attraction, but it's worth noting that the monastery has caused quite a bit of controversy in Kanchanaburi. Locals' concerns range from lack of safety to the possibility of the tigers being drugged to the presence of commercialism unbefitting a temple (entry fees have steadily increased, which the temple says is necessary to fund the creation of a larger environment for the tigers). In fact, many tour operators claim they'd rather not promote the sight, but have no choice because they can't afford to lose customers. The Tourism Authority of Thailand reports that there have been no cases of injury to visitors, but the risks are obvious, and you should think carefully before paying a visit. If you still insist on going, look for the sign posted on the right of the road to Sai Yok National Park. ⊠ *Km 21, Rte. 323* ☎ *034/531557 or 034/531558* 🖷 *B150* ☽ *Daily 8:30–5:30.*

Erawan National Park

★ ❾ *65 km (40 mi) northwest of Kanchanaburi; 1½ hrs by bus.*

Some of the most spectacular scenery of Kanchanaburi Province can be found in Erawan National Park. The main attraction is **Erawan Waterfall,** which has seven tiers; the topmost supposedly resembles the mythical three-headed elephant (Erawan) belonging to the Hindu god Indra. You'll need to make a rather steep 2-km (1-mi) hike to get to the top (it should take about two hours). Comfortable footwear is essential, although many people seem to manage in sturdy sandals. And don't forget to bring water! You can swim at each level of the waterfall, but levels two through five are the most popular. The first tier has a small café, and there are several others near the visitor center. There are also accommodations (bungalows sleeping up to eight, or tents sleeping up to six) in two locations—the ones nearest the waterfall are quieter.

Other highlights of the park include five caves. One of them, **Ta Duang**, has wall paintings, and another, **Ruea**, has prehistoric coffins.

The park is massive; the waterfall is near the main entrance—also where you can find the visitor center and accommodations—but the caves are much farther away, and accessed via a different road. About 2 km (1 mi) from the park is Erawan Village; songthaews leave from its market and travel to the park entrance and the caves (B500–B600). The bus to Erawan leaves Kanchanaburi's second bus station every 50 minutes; the trip takes 90 minutes. It stops at the Erawan Village market in the morning and at the park in the afternoon. If you arrive in the morning, take a songthaew from the market to the park. ⊠ *Km 44, Rte. 3199* ☎ *034/574222* ⊕ *www.dnp.go.th* 🖷 *B200* ☽ *Daily 8–4:30.*

Hellfire Pass

❿ *70 km (45 mi) northwest of Kanchanaburi; 2 hrs by bus.*

The museum at Hellfire Pass is a moving memorial to the Allied prisoners of war who built the River Kwai railway, 12,399 of whom died in the process. Along with a film and exhibits, there's a 4½-km (3-mi) walk along a section of the railway, including the notorious Hellfire Pass, one of the most grueling sections built. The pass got its name from the bonfires that flickered on the mountain walls as the men worked through the night. Many people do the walk in the early morning before the museum opens, and before it gets too hot. Allow 2½ hours round-trip for the walk. Take plenty of water and a snack; there's a small shack near the museum that sells drinks, but not much food. The pass can be busy at weekends (when an average of 500 people a day visit), and on ANZAC Day (April 25). ⊠ *Km 66, Rte. 323* ☎ *01/754–2098* ☽ *Daily 9–4.*

Sai Yok National Park

⓫ *97 km (62 mi) northwest of Kanchanaburi; 2 hrs by bus.*

The main attraction in Sai Yok National Park is **Sai Yok Yai waterfall,** which flows into the Kwai Noi River. The waterfall, an easy walk from the visitor center, is single tier and not nearly as spectacular as Erawan. More unique are the **bat caves** (2-km past the waterfall) that house the thumb-size Kitti's Hog-nosed bat, the world's smallest mammal, found only in these caves. You can rent flashlights at the visitor center.

There are park-run accommodations at Sai Yok Yai in tents (from B85 per person) and guesthouses (from B800 for up to four people). The private raft houses on the Kwai Noi River (B500) are more scenic options, although they sometimes catch a lot of noise from floating karaoke parties going upstream. Note that there's no electricity at these guesthouses; light is provided by oil lamp. Sai Yok View Raft guesthouse (01/ 857–2284) has more isolated raft houses (B500–B700) farther upstream. The raft houses near the waterfall also have cheap restaurants that are more pleasant than the food stalls near the visitor center.

Buses to Sai Yok Yai leave Kanchanaburi every 30 minutes from 6 AM to 6:30 PM. The two-hour trip costs B38.

Also within the national park's boundaries—though not accessible from the Sai Yok visitor center—are **Sai Yok Noi Waterfall** and other notable caves. Despite being higher than Sai Yok Yai, Sai Yok Noi has less water, but there's enough to swim in from June to November, and the area is often packed with Thai families on weekends. It's 2 km (1 mi) from Nam Tok Station, the terminus of the Death Railway. Trains leave Kanchanaburi each day at 5:52 AM and 10:20 AM, passing through thick jungles and past rushing waterfalls as they cling to the mountainside; the journey takes two hours. Alternatively, buses run to and from Kanchanaburi every 30 minutes from 6 AM to 5 PM (B25) in half the time it takes on the train. If you're driving, take Route 323; Sai Yok Noi is at Km 65. Other caves of note in the park are Lawa Cave, 1 km (½ mi) before Sai Yok Noi, and Dowadeung Cave (turn left off Route 323 after the signs for Sai Yok Yai Waterfall). ⊠ *Sai Yok Yai, Km 97, Rte. 323* ☎ *034/516163 up to 4* ⊕ *www.dnp.go.th* ⊠ *B200* ⊘ *Daily 8–4:30.*

Sangklaburi

⓬ *203 km (127 mi) northwest of Kanchanaburi; 3 hrs by bus.*

Sangklaburi is a sleepy town on a large lake created by the Khao Laem Dam. There was once a Mon village here, but when the dam was built in 1983, it was almost completely covered by water. (Some parts, including a temple, are still visible beneath the surface.) The Mon were relocated to a village on the lakeshore opposite Sangklaburi. The village has a temple with Indian and Burmese influences and a bronze-color pyramid chedi that's illuminated beautifully at night. Also in the village is a dry goods market selling Chinese and Burmese clothes and trinkets, with Mon dishes available at nearby food stalls. You can reach the village by car or boat or you can walk from Sangklaburi across the country's longest wooden bridge.

The Mon arrived here 50 years ago from Myanmar, seeking religious sanctuary, and they are not allowed to travel to other areas without permission. Due to its closeness to Myanmar's border, Sangklaburi is also home to Karen and Bangladeshi communities, and its small **night market** (from 4 PM to 7 PM) attracts itinerant ethnic stalls selling food, clothing, and trinkets. Jungle trekking and visits to Karen villages are popular activities for visitors; trips can be arranged through the guesthouses listed below. You can also cross into Myanmar at Three Pagodas Pass with a passport photo and $10 (U.S. currency only—there's an exchange facility at the border), but you cannot renew Thai visas at this checkpoint, so you won't be allowed to go any further than the Myanmar border town, Phayathonzu.

Where to Stay & Eat

There are six or seven guesthouses on the lakeside road, all with views of the wooden bridge and the Mon village—its temple's lights shimmering on the water at night. From the bus station you can reach them by motorcycle taxi (B10) or songthaew (B60). They all have restaurants, most of which offer Burmese and Mon food such as *haeng leh curry* (a country dish made of whatever ingredients are on hand, but often including pork) and the coconut-and-noodle dish *kao sawy,* usually made with chicken. Nightlife consists of a shophouse karaoke bar on the same road as the guesthouses, and a single rice soup stall at the market that sells beer and local whiskey until 2 AM.

¢ ✕🏠 **The Burmese Inn.** These homey bungalows, run by an Austrian and his Thai wife, are on a garden hillside above the lake. The rooms are filled with pictures and knickknacks and some are directly over the water. The room TVs only have Thai-language stations. The terrace restaurant (¢–$) has fish dishes and other Thai and Burmese options, including *laphae to,* a salad of nuts, beans, and fermented tea leaves. It also serves Western breakfasts, salads, and sandwiches. ✉ *52/3 Moo 3, Tambon Nongloo* ☎ *034/595146* ✉ *burmeseinn@yahoo.com* 🛏 *19 rooms* ♨ *Restaurant, boating; no a/c in some rooms* 🚫 *No credit cards.*

¢–$ 🏠 **Pornphailin Riverside.** The bungalows here are indeed on the water's edge, but note that the guesthouse is a long walk from town. All rooms have balconies and panoramic views of the lake; ask to see a couple of rooms first, as some have more windows than others. Larger rooms are less expensive on weekdays. The huge terrace restaurant serves Thai food. ✉ *60/3 Moo 1, Soi Tonpeung* ☎ *034/595332* 🛏 *21 bungalows* ♨ *Restaurant* 🚫 *No credit cards.*

¢ 🏠 **P Guest House.** Stone bungalows with narrow log ceilings are in a stepped garden that leads down to the lakeside. Rooms are mainly fan-cooled with shared bathrooms, but there are also three air-conditioned rooms with private bathrooms that cost a bit more. The latter are on the lakeside (look at all of them to get the best view). You can rent kayaks (B100 per hour) and motorcycles (B200 per day) here, and the owners also organize treks that include a longtail boat ride on the lake to see the underwater temple, elephant riding, and rafting (packages start at B900 per person, and include one night's stay at the guesthouse). The large terrace restaurant has an inexpensive Thai menu with a few Burmese dishes, as well as pastas, sandwiches, and Western breakfasts.

✉ *81/2 Moo 1, Tambon Nongloo* ☎ *034/595061* 🖷 *034/595139*
⊕ *www.pguesthouse.com* 🖘 *20 rooms* ♿ *Restaurant; no a/c in some
rooms, no room TVs* 🖃 *No credit cards.*

AROUND BANGKOK A TO Z

BUS TRAVEL

For all destinations except Sangklaburi, air-conditioned buses leave
from Bangkok's Southern Bus Terminal. Sangklaburi buses run from
Kanchanaburi.

Buses to Damnoen Saduak (2 hours, B65) leave every 20 minutes starting at 5 AM; from the station, walk or take a songthaew along the canal
for 1½ km (¾ mi) to the floating market.

Buses depart for Kanchanaburi (2 hours, B79) every 20 minutes from
5 AM–10:30 PM; for Nakhon Pathom (1 hour, B34) every hour from 5:30
AM–4 PM; for Phetchaburi (3 hours, B90) every 30 minutes from 5 AM–9
PM; for Samut Songkram (1½ hours, B45) every hour 3 AM–6:30 PM.

For buses to Muang Boran (2 hours, B30), take the 511, which leaves
every half hour from Bangkok's Southern Bus Terminal, to the end of
the line at Pak Nam. Transfer to minibus number 36 (B5), which goes
to the entrance of Muang Boran. Buses also run between Nakhon
Pathom and Damnoen Saduak.

Buses to Sangklaburi (2 hours, B79) leave Kanchanaburi every 20 minutes from 5 AM–4 PM.

Tickets are sold on a first-come, first-served basis, but services are so
frequent that it's seldom a problem finding an empty seat.
🚩 **Southern Bus Terminal** ✉ Pinklao-Nakomchaisri Rd., Talingchan, Bangkok ☎ 02/
435–5012 or 02/435-1199.

CAR TRAVEL

Thailand's highway system is improving, but Route 35, the main road
south to Samut Songkram (1 hour) and Phetchaburi (1½ hours) is
mainly a two-lane highway that can be slow going if there's heavy traffic. Add an extra half-hour to all trip times for possible delays.

On the way back to Bangkok from Phetchaburi, there are two possible
routes. Follow signs to Samut Songkram for the shorter distance (Route
35). From Samut Songkram to Damnoen Saduak is a pleasant half-hour
drive along Route 325, particularly if you go via Ampawa, which is well-
marked with signs.

Driving to Muang Boran means a trip through heavy and unpredictable
Bangkok traffic. It should take 1½ to 2 hours. West from Bangkok, allow
one hour to Nakhon Pathom on Route 4, and two hours to Kanchanaburi. To Sangklaburi it's a very rewarding 2½- to 3-hour drive from
Kanchanaburi on Route 323, along very good roads beside fields of
pomelo, corn, and banana palms, with the mist-shrouded mountains of
the Myanmar border in the distance. The last third of the journey winds
through the mountains.

In case of break downs or other road troubles it's best to call information (1133) and ask for the number of the local *tam rouat tong tiaow* (Tourist Police).

EMERGENCIES

🏥 Hospitals **Mae Khlong Song Hospital** ✉ Ratrasit Rd., Samut Songkram ☎ 034/715001. **Meung Phet Thonburi Hospital** ✉ Phetkasem Rd., Phetchaburi ☎ 032/415191. **Sanam Chan Hospital** ✉ 1194 Petchkasem Rd., Nakhon Pathom ☎ 034/219600. **Sangklaburi Hospital** ✉ Sukhaphiban 2, Sangklaburi ☎ 034/595058. **Thanakan Hospital** ✉ Saenchuto Rd., Kanchanaburi ☎ 034/622360.

HEALTH

There are no specific health hazards associated with these areas, but river, canal, and jungle environments make mosquitoes a constant irritation, so bring repellent with you. Pharmacies are common in all destinations.

MONEY MATTERS

ATMs and exchange facilities are common in all towns. In Damnoen Saduak you can find them on the main road from Samut Songkram, and in Sangklaburi there's a bank opposite the market.

SAFETY

This area is generally a very safe place to travel. Still, normal commonsense precautions should be taken when dealing with strangers, and valuables should be kept on your person at all times when traveling by bus or train. Beware of deals, particularly involving gems, that sound ridiculously cheap. They will *always* be a rip-off.

TAXIS & SONGTHAEWS

Bangkok's air-conditioned taxis are an often neglected way of accessing sights outside the city. Estimate around B500 per hour of travel, depending on your bargaining skills.

Outside of Bangkok, songthaews (open-back trucks) are the closest thing to taxis in most areas.

TOUR OPERATORS

Both Asian Trails and Diethelm Travel organize trips to the floating markets, trekking trips, home stays, river and canal trips, and bicycle tours. 🏢 Operators **Asian Trails** ✉ 9th fl., SG Tower, 161/1 Soi Mahadlek Luang 3, Ratchadamri Rd., Lumpini, Pathumwan, Bangkok ☎ 02/658-6080. **Diethelm Travel** ✉ Fl. 14 Kian Gwan 2 Bldg., 140/1 Wireless Rd., Bangkok ☎ 02/255-9150.

TRAIN TRAVEL

Most long-distance trains run from Hua Lamphong Railway Station in Bangkok. Trains to Kanchanaburi leave from Bangkok Noi Railway Station, on the Thonburi side of the Chao Phraya River. There are no trains to Damnoen Saduak, Muang Boran, Samut Songkram, or Sangklaburi.

Ten trains a day run at regular intervals to Nakhon Pathom (1½ hours, B14–B20) from 7:45 AM to 10:50 PM. The Nakhon Pathom train also stops at Phetchaburi (4 hours, B94–B114).

Two daily trains to Kanchanaburi leave Bangkok Noi Station at 7:45 AM and 1:50 PM (3 hours, B300). On weekends and holidays, a special excursion train (B75) leaves Hua Lamphong Station at 6:30 AM and returns at 7:30 PM, stopping at Nakhon Pathom and Kanchanaburi.

🚆 Train Stations **Bangkok Noi** ⊠ Arun Amarin Rd., Bangkok ☎ 02/411-3102. **Hua Lamphong** ⊠ Rama IV Rd., Bangkok ☎ 1690 hotline, 02/223-7010 or 02/225-6964.

VISITOR INFORMATION

The TAT (tourist information) office in Kanchanaburi covers Nakhon Pathom, Samut Songkram, and Sangklaburi. Phetchaburi is handled by the office in the nearby town of Cha'am.

🚆 Tourist Information **Cha'am** ⊠ 500/51 Phetkasem Rd. ☎ 032/471005. **Kanchanaburi** ⊠ 325 Saenchuto Rd. ☎ 034/577200 or 034/623691.

THE CENTRAL PLAINS

3

Updated by
Warwick
Dixon

THE STONE-STREWN PATH up the hillside doesn't look as if anyone has passed this way for ages. Could this really be the way? You glance over to your guide, who nods. After mopping the sweat from your forehead you continue your climb. At the top, the path opens onto a huge plaza with a sweeping view of the valley below. Just ahead is a stone wall, and beyond that is a spire that points heavenward. No tour buses here. This temple is yours alone.

This is the Central Plains, one of the most overlooked regions of Thailand. Some people take a side trip from Bangkok to the ancient capital of Ayutthaya, but fewer venture farther north to the even older cities at Sukhothai and Sri Satchanalai, which means that you're unlikely to encounter many other people as you wander among some of the most breathtaking ruins in the country.

Thailand was founded in 1238, when the cornerstones were laid for the towering temples at Sukhothai. The Sukhothai period was relatively brief—a series of eight kings—but it witnessed lasting accomplishments. The Thais gained their independence, which was maintained despite the efforts of Europe. King Ramkhamhaeng formulated the Thai alphabet by adapting the Khmer script to suit the Thai tonal language, Theravada Buddhism was established and became the dominant national religion, and, toward the end of the Sukhothai dynasty, such a distinctive Thai art flourished that the period is known as Thailand's Golden Age.

Thailand's most glorious period began when Ayutthaya became the kingdom's seat of power in 1350. Toward the end of the 16th century, Europeans described the city, with its 1,700 temples and 4,000 golden images of the Buddha, as more striking than any capital in Europe. In 1767 the Burmese conquered Ayutthaya and destroyed its temples with such vengeance that little remained standing. The city never recovered, and today it's a small provincial town with partially restored ruins. The site is particularly striking at sunset, when the silhouetted ruins glow orange-brown.

Although some sights are decidedly off the beaten track, it isn't difficult to reach the Central Plains. If you have more than a passing interest in Thailand's history, you won't be able to resist spending a few days rooting around in its majestic ruins. Accommodations here aren't luxurious, but a night or two in a charming guesthouse amid beautiful gardens or a bamboo hut in the middle of a rice field brings you remarkably close to the people.

About the Restaurants

Although the region is not known for its cuisine, it's possible to eat well in the Central Plains. The staples of the region are the dishes such as *tom yam* (spicy soup with lemongrass and kaffir leaves), *gaeng kiew wahn* (green curry), *panaeng* (red curry), and a number of milder Chinese dishes such

3

Numbers in the text correspond to numbers in the margin and on the Central Plains, Ayutthaya & Sukhothai maps.

If you have
1 day

If you have little time to venture into the Central Plains, the easiest trip is to **Ayutthaya** ①–⑧, which became the country's capital after Sukhothai's influence waned. You can reach the ancient city several ways, but none is more atmospheric than by longtail boat up the Chao Phraya River. If you have time, take a side trip to see the summer palace of **Bang Pa-In** ⑨.

If you have
3 days

Leave Bangkok early on a journey up the Chao Phraya River to the old capital of **Ayutthaya** ①–⑧. While you're here, take in **Bang Pa-In** ⑨, the opulent summer palace. Return to Bangkok, where you can take the train or plane to **Phitsanulok** ⑪ to see the Phra Buddha Chinnarat and the Pim Buranaket Folkcraft Museum. Board a bus for the hour-long trip to ⊞ **Sukhothai** ⑫–⑳. You need the best part of a day to see highlights of the country's first capital. The next morning take the hour's trip to **Si Satchanalai** ㉑, an ancient satellite city. In the afternoon you can grab a plane at Sukhothai for the trip back to Bangkok or Chiang Mai.

If you have
7 days

A river cruise from Bangkok to **Ayutthaya** ①–⑧ means an early start, but still remains the most enjoyable way to reach the ancient city. Spend a night in one of Ayutthaya's riverside hotels and hit the Pasak River for a memorable dinner cruise passing by the illuminated ruins of the historical park. The next day, wake early to tour the park, taking in the Ayutthaya historical center and the more prominent temple ruins.

With the afternoon fading you should head back to Bangkok via bus and take a flight to the city of **Sukhothai** ⑫–⑳ where you can study varying styles of sculpture and architecture, from Khmer-style prangs (pagodas) at Wat Phra Phai Luang to Hindu influences at Wat Sri Sawai to immense stone Buddhas at Wat Sri Chum. In the morning take a bus to **Mae Sot** ㉒ and spend an afternoon choosing a tour program and strolling around the border market and Burmese temples.

Spend the next few days in and around **Umphang** ㉓, rafting through canyons and waterfalls and camping streamside for the night. Head to the region's biggest waterfall, Thee Lor Su, where you can swim in the natural pool before trekking into the jungle and staying the night at a Karen village.

Upon returning to Mae Sot you can fly either to Chiang Mai and Northern Thailand if you have more time, or trace your way back to Sukhothai for travel back to Bangkok.

as *gaeng jeut woon sen* (noodle consommé) and the ever present *kuaytiew nahm* (noodle soup). Restaurants don't really reach dizzying heights of splendor—most are simple shophouse affairs—and you'll find that local markets, with their cheap fast food and *khao lad gaeng* (canteen-style) restaurants are just as reliable, and sometimes have more variety.

About the Hotels

Because relatively few tourists visit the Central Plains, most hotels and guesthouses cater chiefly to a business clientele. There are some top-class hotels, but most accommodations are much more modest than in Bangkok or Chiang Mai. As elsewhere in Thailand, standards of cleanliness are high and even the most basic room will invariably have fresh linen and towels.

A new phenomenon is the appearance of lodgings run by hospitable and knowledgeable local people anxious to help visitors get to know this seemingly remote region. They open up their homes to paying guests and show them around for a modest fee. Listed here are a few of the most reputable.

For budget-conscious travelers, rooms in the Central Plains are truly a bargain—even the most expensive hotels charge less than $60 a night. Don't expect the full range of facilities, however. Such refinements as room phones, TVs, and even hot water can be rare outside the cities.

WHAT IT COSTS In Baht					
	$$$$	**$$$**	**$$**	**$**	**¢**
RESTAURANTS	over B400	B300–B400	B200–B300	B100–B200	under B100
HOTELS	over B6,000	B4,000–B6,000	B2,000–B4,000	B1,000–B2,000	under B1,000

Restaurant prices are per person for a main course at dinner. Hotel prices are for a standard double room, excluding tax.

Exploring the Central Plains

With its rich soil, perfect for rice farming, and waterways connecting to the Chao Phraya River basin, the Central Plains region has long attracted settlers. The Khmer empire made it as far as Lopburi, while Ayutthaya is seen as the cultural bastion of present-day Thailand, and, to many, the soul of the country is to be found in Sukhothai and Si Satchanalai. These strongholds of architecture and culture evoke Thailand's ancient civilizations and provide the modern-day hubs for exploring the region. Journeying farther north, by combinations of minibus, bus, and songthaew, will take you from historic to geographic majesty. Within the cooler climes of the north are Mae Sot and Umphang, with their mountainous, forested isolation, natural grandeur, hill tribe villages, and ecotourism opportunities.

Timing

The driest months, between November and February, are the coolest and the busiest, with refreshing temperatures enticing travelers. From March to June, this central area, like much of Thailand, becomes almost unbearably hot; it's only slightly cooled by the rains that fall between June and early October.

3

Architecture

The optimism that accompanied the birth of the nation at Sukhothai is reflected in the art and architecture of the period. Strongly influenced by Sri Lankan Buddhism, the monuments left behind by the architects, artisans, and craftsmen of those innovative times had a light, often playful touch. Statues of the Buddha show him as smiling, serene, and confidently walking toward a better future. There were impudent touches in the temple decoration, such as the impossibly graceful elephants portrayed in supporting pillars.

The Natural World

Though the Central Plains may be known more for its man-made marvels in the historic towns of Ayutthaya and Sukhothai, the region has much of mother nature's best to gawk at as well. Not far from Phitsanulok is a great strip of rapids, only a warm-up for the challenging rafting opportunities that lie further west. Around Mae Sot you'll see everything from mountains to teak forests to extensive cave systems to Thailand's largest waterfall, Thee Lor Su. Many trekking tours leave from the remote town of Umphang.

Shopping

Because a relatively small number of travelers venture this way, there are fewer crafts for sale here than elsewhere in the country. One notable exception is around Sukhothai and Sri Satchanalai, where you can find reproductions of the pottery that was made here when this was the capital of the country.

November's amazing Loi Krathong festival sees both Ayutthaya and Sukhothai's historical parks explode with orchestrated light-and-sound shows. Domestic and international tourists eager to see this operatic event fill the towns' guesthouses and hotels, so make sure to book as soon as possible.

AYUTTHAYA & ENVIRONS

With 92% of its land used for agriculture, it isn't surprising that Ayutthaya is known as Asia's rice field. To its west is the Suphan Buri and its continuing rice paddies, while to the northeast the region borders with Lopburi, approaching the northeastern plateau with rising forested hills. The bountiful plain has been home to Thailand's most influential and ancient Kingdoms: Lopburi and Ayutthaya.

Ayutthaya and its environs represent an important historic journey that traces Thailand's most significant cultural developments from Buddhist art and architecture to modern government and language. Ayutthaya often gets the most attention, drawing day-trippers from Bangkok, but a visit to Lopburi, with its Khmer temples and French-influenced royal palace (complete with a collection of Dvaravati/Lopburi-style Buddha images), can better set the scene and lends even more historical context to the museums and ransacked ruins found at Ayutthaya's historical park and the 18th-century Royal Palace found in nearby Bang Pa-In.

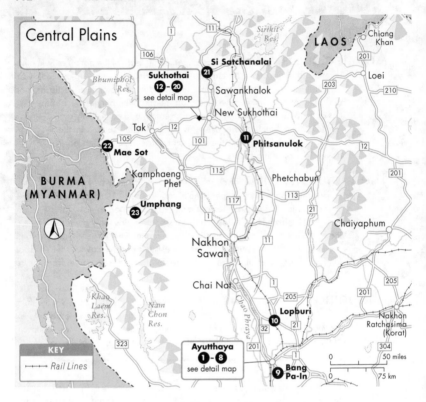

Central Plains

Si Satchanalai 21

Sukhothai 12 – 20
see detail map

Sawankhalok

New Sukhothai

LAOS

Chiang Khan

Loei

Tak

Phitsanulok 11

Phetchabun

Mae Sot 22

BURMA
(MYANMAR)

Kamphaeng
Phet

Umphang 23

Nakhon
Sawan

Chaiyaphum

Chai Nat

Lopburi 10

Nakhon
Ratchasima
(Korat)

Ayutthaya 1 – 8
see detail map

**Bang
Pa-In** 9

KEY

Rail Lines

0   50 miles
0   75 km

Ayutthaya

★ *72 km (45 mi) north of Bangkok.*

Ayutthaya was named by King Ramatibodi after a mythical kingdom
of the gods portrayed in the pages of the Ramayana. The city was completed in 1350 and was a powerhouse of Southeast Asia. The city was
originally chosen as a capital for its eminently defendable position: it
lies in a bend of the Chao Phraya River, where it meets the Pa Sak and
Lopburi rivers; to completely encircle their capital with water, early residents dug a curving canal along the northern perimeter, linking the Chao
Phraya to the Lopburi. However, Ayutthaya quickly changed from being
essentially a military base to an important center for the arts, medicine,
and technology. Trade routes opened up Siam's first treaty with a Western nation (that of Portugal in 1516) and soon after, the Dutch, English,
Japanese and, most influentially, the French, accelerated Ayutthaya's role
in international relations under King Narai the Great. After Narai's death
in 1688 the kingdom plunged into internal conflict, ultimately paving
a way for the Burmese and the last act in its story.

Today Ayutthaya is a carefully preserved World Heritage Site and a visit
provides a fascinating snapshot of ancient Siam. Scattered ruins lay tes-

tament to the kingdom's brutal demise at the hands of the Burmese in 1767. Although the modern town is on the eastern bank of the Pa Sak, most of the ancient temples are on the island. An exception is Wat Yai Chai Mongkol, a short tuk-tuk ride away.

Ayutthaya is best appreciated in historical context, and a visit to the Historical Study Center can improve the experience for a first time visitor. Certain sites are guaranteed to take your breath away, with Wat Phra Si Sanphet, Wat Yai Chaiyamongkhon, Wat Mahathat, and Wat Ratchaburana being the best. Outside of the temples, Ayutthaya's friendly guesthouses, welcoming people, and relaxing floating restaurants make for a refreshing change from Bangkok, its frenzied descendant.

a good tour

One of the more pleasant ways to take in the sights is by renting a bicycle or motorbike, tucking a copy of the "Best Map of Ayutthaya" (they're not lying) under your arm and heading off on your own. Make sure you plaster on the sunscreen or wear long sleeves though, as you'll be in the sun most of the day. To get a good sense of what you're about to dive into, first pay a visit to the **Ayutthaya Historical Study Center** ❶ on Rochana Road and see the site in miniature.

A short ride will take you to **Chao Sam Phraya Museum** ❷ on Si Sanphet Road, where the treasure vaults are worth exploring. Along the nearby Shi Khun Road are the first two sites to visit: **Wat Phra Mahathat** ❸ and **Wat Ratchaburana** ❹. Then hop back in the saddle and over to **Wat Phra Si Sanphet** ❺, just off Khlong Tho Road, to the one-time royal palace and a neck-straining stare at the mammoth Phra Mongkon Borphit image.

Head down to the river and find the ferry crossing near the River View Palace Hotel. A few baht will see you across to **Wat Phanan Choeng** ❻. After you've wandered around, scoot over to Pae Krung Kao floating restaurant for lunch. Sit down, order a cold beer, and prepare for a nice nap in the shade.

TIMING   Most people find that a morning or afternoon is sufficient to see Ayutthaya. For a three-hour tour of the sites, tuk-tuks can be hired for about B700; a three-wheel samlor (small bicycle cab) costs about B500.

What to See

❶ **Ayutthaya Historical Study Center.** This educational center, financed by the Japanese government, houses fascinating audiovisual displays about Ayutthaya. Models of the city as a rural village, as a port city, as an administrative center, and as a royal capital reveal the site's history. ⊠ *Rotchana Rd. between Si San Phet and Chikun Rds.* ☎ *035/245124* ⌨ *B100* ⊙ *Weekdays 9–4:30, weekends 9–5.*

❷ **Chao Sam Phraya National Museum.** This dated museum in spacious grounds is ostensibly a showcase for the varying styles of Buddhist sculpture, including Dvaravati (Lamphun), Lopburi, Ayutthayan and U-Thong. In truth, the artifacts are poorly presented, and the best attraction is an upstairs vault in the first building, which has relics (such as a jewel-covered sword) of two of Wat Ratchaburana's original princes. The vault is worth a visit before heading on to the temple itself. ⊠ *Rotchana Rd. at Si San Phet Rd.* ☎ *035/241587* ⌨ *B30* ⊙ *Wed.–Sun. 9–4.*

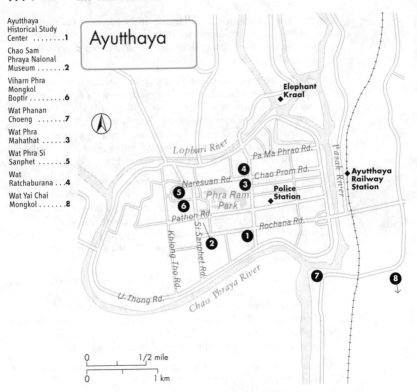

Elephant Kraal. Thailand's only intact royal kraal was built to hold and train elephants for martial service; it was last used during King Chulalongkorn's reign in 1903. The restored teak stockade acts as little other than a gateway to the Royal Elephant Kraal Village behind it, which opened in 1996 and cares for about 100 elephants. Though it looks like a working village, it's primarily a business—rehabilitating and parenting elephants for work on tours around Ayutthaya and also for TV and film productions (most recently Oliver Stone's *Alexander*). ⊠ *5 km (3 mi) north of Ayutthaya, on the Hwy. 3060 to Panead* ☎ *035/321982* ⊙ *Daily 8–5.*

6 **Viharn Phra Mongkol Bopitr.** This is one of the modern structures in the old city. The site's original temple was built in 1610. When the roof collapsed in 1767, one of Thailand's biggest and most revered bronze Buddha images (one of few that escaped the destruction wrought by the Burmese) was revealed. It lay here uncovered for almost 200 years before the huge modern viharn was built in 1951. Historians have dated the image back to 1538. ⊠ *Off Naresuan Rd.* 🎫 *Free* ⊙ *Weekdays 8–4:30, weekends 8–5:30.*

★ **7** **Wat Phanan Choeng.** This is a bustling merit-making temple complex located on the banks of the Lopburi River and is an interesting diversion from the dormant ruins that dominate Ayutthaya. A short B3 ferry ride across the river sets the scene for its dramatic origins. The temple was built in 1324 (26 years before Ayutthaya's rise to power) by a U-Thong king in atonement for the death of his fiancée. Instead of bringing his bride, a Chinese princess, into the city himself, the king arranged an escort for her. Distraught at what she interpreted to be an indifferent and lackluster welcome, the princess threw herself into the river (at the site of the current temple) and drowned. ⊠ *East of the old city* 🎫 *Free* ⊙ *Daily 8–5.*

❸ **Wat Phra Mahathat.** Building began on this royal monastery in 1374 and was completed during the reign of King Ramesuan (1388–95). Today, pleasant tree-shaded grounds contain what's left of its 140-foot brick *prang* (pagoda). The prang collapsed twice between 1610 to 1628, and again in the early 20th century, and today barely reflects its former glory. The stunted ruins and beheaded Buddhas that remain in Wat Mahathat are a result of the Burmese sacking this once revered temple in 1767. ⊠ *Naresuan Rd. at Chee Kun Rd.* 🎫 *B30* ⊙ *Daily 8–6:30.*

❺ **Wat Phra Si Sanphet.** This wat was the largest temple in Ayutthaya, as well as the place where the royal family worshipped. The 14th-century structure lost its 50-foot Buddha in 1767, when the invading Burmese melted it down for its 374 pounds of gold. The trio of chedis survived and are the best existing examples of Ayutthaya architecture; enshrining the ashes of several kings, they stand as eternal memories of a golden age. If the design looks familiar, it may be because Wat Phra Si Sanphet was used as a model for Wat Phra Keo at the Grand Palace in Bangkok. Beyond the monuments you can find a grassy field where the royal palace once stood. The foundation is all that remains of the palace that was home to 33 kings. The field is a cool, shady place in which to stop for a picnic. ⊠ *Naresuan Rd.* 🎫 *B30* ⊙ *Daily 7–6:30.*

❹ **Wat Ratchaburana.** Directly north across the road from Wat Mahathat is Wat Ratchaburana, its Khmer-style prang dominating the skyline. King Borommaracha II (Chao Sam Phraya) built this temple in 1424 to commemorate the death of his two older brothers, whose duel for the throne ironically left their younger brother as king. Their relics were buried in a crypt directly under the base of the prang, which was looted in 1957. Arrests were made, however, and the retrieved treasures can now be seen in the Chao Sam Phraya National Museum. ⊠ *Naresuan Rd. and Chee Kun Rd.* 🎫 *B30* ⊙ *Daily 8:30–4:30.*

❽ **Wat Yai Chai Mongkol.** The enormous chedi at Wat Yai Chai Mongkol, the largest in Ayutthaya, was constructed by King Naresun after he defeated the Burmese crown prince during a battle atop elephants in 1593. (A recent painting of the battle is one of the highlights of the temple.) The chedi is now leaning a bit, as later enlargements are weighing down on the foundation. The complex, dating from 1357, was totally restored in 1982. Linger a while to pay your respects to the huge Reclining Buddha. ⊠ *About 5 km (3 mi) southeast of the old city on the Ayutthaya to Bang Pa-In Rd.* 🎫 *B20* ⊙ *Daily 8–5.*

Where to Stay & Eat

If you're a romantic, you may want to stay in Ayutthaya so you can wander among the ruins at night. Since most tourists leave Ayutthaya by 4 PM, those who stay the night are treated to genuine Thai hospitality. Don't expect luxury, however; Ayutthaya has only modest hotels and simple restaurants.

$$–$$$$ ✕ **Pasak River Queen.** Enjoy a leisurely two-hour ride along the Pa Sak
★ River while filling your belly with grilled seafood and some fantastic Thai dishes. The 350-passenger boat departs nightly at 6:30 PM. There's a B79 cover charge and then dishes are ordered à la carte. The dock's a bit outside of town; it's worth booking transportation to and from the dock ahead of time. ✉ *116 Moo 2, Borpong* ☎ *035/724520, 035/724504, or 035/724519* ▭ *AE, DC, MC, V.*

$ ✕ **Tevaraj.** For good, spicy food, head for this unpretentious restaurant behind Ayutthaya's railway station. The *tom kha gai* (chicken soup with coconut) is excellent, as are the always-fresh fish dishes. ✉ *74 Wat Pa Kho Rd.* ☎ *No phone* ▭ *No credit cards.*

¢–$ ✕ **Pae Krung Kao.** If you can't resist dining outdoors beside the Pa Sak River, this is a good option near the Pridi Damrong Bridge. You can also drop by for a leisurely beer. ✉ *4 U-Thong Rd.* ☎ *035/241555* ▭ *AE, MC, V.*

$$$$ ▥ **Manohra Song.** This 60-foot rice barge built at the start of the 20th century has, with the help of lots of taste and even more money, been brought back to life as a luxury cruiser. For a day and a half, you can relax in suites decorated with rich woods like mahogany and teak and yards of flowing silks. Pampered by a private chef, you can watch the world drift by between Bangkok and Ayutthaya. ✉ *Marriott Royal Garden Riverside Hotel, 257/1–3 Charoen Nakorn Rd., Thonburi, Bangkok 10600* ☎ *02/476–0021, 02/276–0022 in Bangkok* ☎ *02/476–1120* ⊕ *www.manohracruises.com* ⌂ *4 suites* ⌂ *Dining room* ▭ *AE, MC, V.*

$ ▥ **Krungsri River Hotel.** This hotel near the train station is a welcome addition to Ayutthaya. The spacious marble-floor lobby is refreshingly cool, and the rooms, although not distinguished in any way, are clean, fresh, and filled with modern furnishings. For the best views, choose a room overlooking the river. Because Ayutthaya has few overnight visitors, try to negotiate a discounted rate. Rates include a buffet breakfast. ✉ *27/2 Rojana Rd., Ayutthaya 13000* ☎ *035/244333* ☎ *035/243777* ⌂ *200 rooms* ⌂ *Restaurant, coffee shop, minibars, cable TV, outdoor pool, gym, massage, bowling, lobby lounge, pub, meeting rooms, travel services* ▭ *AE, DC, MC, V.*

Bang Pa-In

❾ *20 km (12 mi) south of Ayutthaya.*

A popular attraction near Ayutthaya is found in the village Bang Pa-In: the extravagant **Royal Palace** set in well-tended gardens. The original structure, built by King Prusat on the banks of the Pa Sak River, was used by the Ayutthaya kings until the Burmese invasion. After being neglected for 80 years, it was rebuilt during the reign of Rama IV and became the favored summer palace of King Rama V until tragedy struck. When the king was delayed in Bangkok, he sent his wife ahead on a boat that capsized. Although she could easily have been rescued, people stood by helplessly because a royal could not be touched by a commoner on pain of death. The king could never forgive himself. He built a pavilion in her memory; be sure to read the touching inscription engraved on the memorial. 🖃 *B100* 🕙 *Tues.–Thurs. and weekends 8–3.*

King Rama V was interested in the architecture of Europe, and many Western influences are evident here. The most beautiful building, however, is the **Aisawan Thippaya,** a Thai pavilion that seems to float on a small lake. A series of staggered roofs lead to a central spire. The structure is sometimes dismantled and taken to represent the country at worldwide expositions.

Phra Thinang Warophat Phiman, nicknamed the Peking Palace, faces a stately pond. The replica of a palace of the Chinese imperial court, it was built from materials custom-made in China—a gift from Chinese Thais eager to win the king's favor. It contains a collection of exquisite jade and Ming-period porcelain.

Take the cable car across the river to **Wat Nivet Thamaprawat,** built in Gothic style. Complete with a belfry and stained-glass windows, it looks as much like a Christian church masquerading as a Buddhist temple.

Shopping

The **Bang Sai Folk Arts and Craft Centre** was set up by Queen Sirikit in 1982 to train farming families to make traditional crafts as a means of extra income. Workers at the center regularly demonstrate their techniques and a small souvenir shop offers a chance to buy their crafts. ✉ *24 km (14½ mi) south of Bang Pa-In* ☎ *035/366090 or 035/366666* 🖃 *B100* 🕙 *Weekdays 9–5, weekends 9–6.*

Lopburi

🔟 *75 km (47 mi) north of Ayutthaya, 150 km (94 mi) north of Bangkok.*

One of Thailand's oldest cities, Lopburi has been inhabited since the 4th century. After the 6th century, its influence grew under the Dvaravati rulers, who dominated northern Thailand until the Khmers swept in from the east. From the beginning of the 10th century until the middle of the 13th, when the new Thai kingdom drove them out, the Khmers used Lopburi as their provincial capital. During the Sukhothai and early Ayutthaya periods, the city's importance declined until, in 1664, King Narai made it his second capital to escape the heat and humidity of Ayutthaya. He employed French architects to build his palace; consequently, Lopburi is a strange mixture of Khmer, Thai, and Western architecture.

Lopburi is relatively off the beaten track for tourists. Few foreigners stay overnight. The rarity of foreigners may explain why locals are so friendly and eager to show you their town—and to practice their English. Samlors are available, but most of Lopburi's attractions are within easy walking distance.

Wat Phra Si Rattana Mahathat, built by the Khmers, is near the railway station. It underwent so many restorations during the Sukhothai and Ayutthaya periods that it's difficult to discern the three original Khmer prangs—only the central one is intact. Several Sukhothai- and Ayutthaya-style chedis are within the compound. ⊠ *Na Phra Karn Rd.* 🕾 *B30* ⊙ *Daily 6–6.*

Past Wat Phra Si Mahathat is **Phra Narai Ratchaniwet.** The palace's well-preserved buildings, completed between 1665 and 1677, have been converted into museums. Surrounding the buildings are castellated walls and triumphal archways grand enough to admit an entourage mounted on elephants. The most elaborate structure is the Dusit Mahaprasat Hall, built by King Narai to receive foreign ambassadors. The roof is gone, but you can spot the mixture of architectural styles: the square doors are Thai and the domed arches are Western. North of Phra Narai Ratchaniwet is the restored Wat Sao Thong Thong. Notice the windows of the viharn, which King Narai intended to imitate those found in Europe. ⊠ *Ratchadamnern Rd.* 🕾 *B30* ⊙ *Daily 8:30–4:30.*

North of Wat Sao Thong Thong is **Vichayen House,** built for French King Louis XIV's personal representative, De Chaumont. The house was later occupied by King Narai's infamous Greek minister, Constantine Phaulkon, whose political schemes eventually caused the ouster of all Westerners from Thailand. When King Narai was dying in 1668, his army commander, Phra Phetracha, seized power and beheaded Phaulkon. During the attack, Vichayen House was nearly destroyed. ⊠ *Vichayen Rd.* ⊙ *Wed.–Sun. 9–noon and 1–4.*

East on Vichayen Road is a Khmer shrine called **Phra Prang Sam Yot,** Lopburi's most famous landmark. The three prangs symbolize the sacred triad of Brahma, Vishnu, and Shiva. King Narai converted the shrine into a Buddhist temple, and a stucco image of the Buddha sits serenely before the central prang. ⊠ *Vichayen Rd.*

East of Phra Prang Sam Yot is **San Phra Kan** shrine, where a statue of King Narai was found with part of the head missing. During the Ayutthayan period the image was replaced with that of the present day Phra Kan stone Buddha image and serves as the merit-making center of Lopburi. There's not much of interest at this small, solitary shrine, except an ever-present troop of annoying monkeys. ⊠ *Vichayen Rd.*

Where to Stay & Eat

¢–$$ ✕ **White House.** A popular haunt for travelers, the White House offers a standard range of Thai and seafood dishes. The place is no frills, with simple plastic chairs and tables, but the enigmatic owner Mr. Piak gives it some character—he's a good source of information on the area. Make sure to flip through his guestbook. ⊠ *Phraya Kumjud Rd.* 🕾 *036/ 413085* ⊟ *No credit cards.*

¢–$ ✕ **Chan Chao.** For a fun night out in Lopburi's old town, try Chan Chao, a diner-style country pub that draws in crowds of music-loving locals. The extensive menu has predominantly Thai food, but there are also good steaks and other Western fare and a fiendish range of cocktails. ⊠ *3 Sorasak 1 Rd.* 🕾 *036/617174.*

$–$$ ☒ **Lopburi Inn.** This hotel has achieved a certain amount of fame by hosting an annual dinner party for the town's resident monkeys each November. It is, however, awkwardly located between the old and new cities and dated rooms and cluttered corridors means that it's not really worth the expense. The dining room serves Thai and Chinese food; a buffet breakfast is included in the rates. ✉ *28/9 Narai Maharat Rd.* ☎ *036/ 412300* 🖷 *036/412457* 🛏 *130 rooms* ⛄ *Restaurant, coffee shop, room service, cable TV, massage, laundry service, Internet* ▤ *MC, V.*

$ ☒ **Lopburi Inn Resort.** This is the best value hotel in Lopburi, with stylish rooms decorated in a modern Thai style, a good range of facilities, and a generous buffet breakfast. The only drawback is its distance from the old city and main sights (10 km), but samlors to the sights are easy enough to arrange. ✉ *17/1–2 Ratchadamnoen Rd., 15000* ☎ *036/614790, 036/420777, or 036/421453* 🖷 *036/614795* 🛏 *90 rooms* ⛄ *Restaurant, room service, cable TV, pool, gym* ▤ *AE, MC, V.*

¢ ☒ **Nett Hotel.** This clean and airy three-floor hotel is slightly cramped, but it's a good value. Its great location in the center of town and its friendly staff are also major selling points. ✉ *144 Paholyothin Rd., 15000* ☎ *036/441738 or 036/421460* 🛏 *24 rooms* ⛄ *Cable TV, laundry service* ▤ *No credit cards.*

AYUTTHAYA & ENVIRONS A TO Z

BUS TRAVEL

Buses to both Ayutthaya (B60/1½ hours) and Lopburi (B85/3 hours) leave from Mo Chit Northern bus terminal every 20 minutes between 6 AM and 7 PM. From Ayutthaya, Lopburi is another 1½ hours on the green 607 bus from Ayutthaya's bus terminal.

🚌 **Bus Stations** **Ayutthaya** ✉ Buses to Bangkok, Naresuan Rd. ✉ Main Bus Terminal, Soi Grand, Rojchana Rd. ☎ 035/335304. **Northern Bus Terminal** ✉ Khamphaeng Phet 2 Rd., Bangkok ☎ 02/937–0055 or 02/936–0667.

CAR TRAVEL

Driving to Ayutthaya from Bangkok is an easy day trip once you're out of the congestion of the big city. Kanchanaphisek Road, Bangkok's outer ring road, is the best route to take, costing around B120 in tolls. Following this road will drop you into Bang Pa-In—a good opportunity to visit the Royal Palace before continuing to Ayutthaya itself.

EMERGENCIES

🚓 **Emergency Numbers** **Ayutthaya Tourist Police** ☎ 035/241446.
🏥 **Hospital** **Ratcha Thani Hospital** ✉ 111 Moo 3, Rotchana Rd., Ayutthaya ☎ 035/335555.

HEALTH

Food from street vendors and night markets should be fine if you make sure it's still hot. In most cases, food is cooked to order, so you can observe whether the seller is cutting corners.

Locals will proudly state that no cases of malaria have been reported for years. There are still plenty of mosquitoes, so bring along plenty of repellent. If there are no screens in the window of your hotel, a mosquito net will probably be hung over the bed. If not, ask for one.

MONEY MATTERS

ATMs and exchange services are abundant in Ayutthaya, on Naresuan Road, and in Lopburi on Ratchadamnoen Road. Just follow the towering bank logos.

SAFETY

Both cities are pretty safe, with common sense being the only precaution needed. However, do beware the monkeys in Lopburi. They are a cheeky bunch and have been known to steal anything that you can't hold onto, including cameras, so keep the bananas peeled and camera straps taut.

TAXIS & TUK-TUKS

All forms of local transport are available from samlors to a few songthaews, but the brightly colored tuk-tuks are more frequently used. Tuk-tuks can be hired for an hour for around B200 or the day for around B600 to B700 and make easier work of Ayutthaya's historical sites.

TOUR OPERATORS

The Chao Phraya Express Boat Company runs a Sunday excursion from Bangkok to Bang Pa-In Summer Palace. It departs at 8 AM and arrives in time for lunch. On the return trip, the boat stops at the Bang Sai Folk Arts and Craft Centre before arriving in Bangkok at 5:30 PM. The trip costs B350.

🚩 Tour Companies **Chao Phraya Express Boat Company** ⊠ Maharat Pier, 2/58 Aroon-Amarin Rd., Bangkok ☎ 02/222–5330.

TRAIN TRAVEL

The Northeastern Line, which heads all the way up to Isan, has frequent service from Bangkok to Ayutthaya and Lopburi. Beginning at 4:30 AM, trains depart frequently (roughly every 40 minutes) from Bangkok's Hua Lamphong Station, arriving in Ayutthaya 80 minutes later. Since Don Muang International Airport lies between the two cities, many travelers returning from Ayutthaya get off at the airport to fly to their next destination.

Trains from Bangkok's Hua Lamphong Station regularly make the hour-long trip to Bang Pa-In Station, where you can catch a minibus to the palace. Three morning and two afternoon trains depart for the three-hour trip to Lopburi. Trains back to Bangkok run in the early and late afternoon. Since Lopburi is such a short distance from Bangkok, advance tickets aren't necessary, unless you want to secure a first-class sleeper.

VISITOR INFORMATION

The Tourist Authority of Thailand has an office in Ayutthaya, where you can find helpful maps and brochures. The office is open daily 8:30–4:30.

🚩 Tourist Information **Tourist Authority of Thailand** ⊠ Si Sanphet Rd. ☎ 035/246076.

SUKHOTHAI & ENVIRONS

In the valley of the Yom River, protected by a rugged mountain range in the north at Si Satchanalai and rich forest mountains in the south, lies Sukhothai, a city that holds the region's historical key. Here laterite (red porous soil that hardens when exposed to air) ruins signify the birthplace of the Thai nation and its emergence as a center for Theravada Buddhism.

North of Sukhothai is its sister city of Si Satchanalai, which is quieter and more laid-back, but no less interesting—its historical park has the remains of over 200 temples and monuments.

But before you reach these two cities, you'll come across Phitsanulok, which in many ways makes the best base for exploring the area. Despite its historical relevance as Sukhothai's capital for 25 years, the birthplace of King Narai the Great, and residence of the Ayutthayan Crown Princes, Phitsanulok has grown away from its roots. This one-time military stronghold has stamped over its past, with only a few reminders, like Wat Mahathat and the revered Phra Buddha Chinnarat image, left to hint at its prior importance. But when one thing is lost, another is gained, and Phitsanulok now serves as a center for commerce, transportation, and communication. In addition, its blend of entertainment and access to outward-bound excursions make it an enjoyable diversion.

Phitsanulok

⑪ *377 km (234 mi) north of Bangkok; 60 km (37 mi) southeast of Sukhothai.*

For a brief span in the 14th century, after the decline of Sukhothai and before the rise of Ayutthaya, Phitsanulok was the kingdom's capital. Farther back in history, Phitsanulok was a Khmer outpost called Song Kwae—today only an ancient monastery remains of that incarnation. The new city, which had to relocate 5 km (3 mi) from the old site, is a modern provincial administrative seat with few architectural blessings. There are outstanding attractions, however, such as the Phra Buddha Chinnarat inside Wat Phra Si Ratana Mahathat. And make sure to take time to walk along the Nan River, lined with numerous tempting food stalls in the evening. On the far side you can see many houseboats, which are popular among Thais. Disregarding the Naresuan Bridge, some locals still paddle across the river in small boats.

With modern conveniences, Phitsanulok is an ideal base for exploring the region. Most of the sights in Phitsanulok are within walking distance, but samlors are easily available. Bargain hard—most trips should be about B20. Taxis are available for longer trips; you can find a few loitering around the train station.

Naresuan Road runs from the railway station to the Nan River. North of this street you can find **Wat Phra Si Ratana Mahathat,** a temple commonly known as Wat Yai. Built in the mid-14th century, Wat Yai has developed into a large monastery with typical ornamentation. Particularly noteworthy are the viharn's wooden doors, inlaid with mother-of-pearl in 1756 at the behest of King Boromkot. Behind the viharn is a 100-foot prang with a vault containing Buddha relics. The many religious souvenir stands make it hard to gain a good view of the complex, but the bot is a fine example of the traditional three-tier roof with low sweeping eaves, designed to diminish the size of the walls, accentuate the nave, and emphasize the image of the Buddha.

Within the viharn is what many consider the world's most beautiful image of the Buddha, Phra Buddha Chinnarat. It was probably cast in the 14th century, during the late Sukhothai period. Its mesmerizing beauty and the mystical powers ascribed to it draw streams of pilgrims—among the most notable of them was the Sukhothai's King Eka Thossarot, who journeyed here in 1631. According to folklore, the king applied with his own hands the gold leaf that covers the Buddha. Many copies of the image have been made, with the best known residing in Bangkok's Marble Temple. ⊠ *Off Ekethosarot Rd.* ⊙ *Daily 8–6.*

★ Phitsanulok also has a little-known museum, **Pim Buranaket Folkcraft Museum,** that alone would justify a visit to the city. In the early 1980s, Sergeant-Major Khun Thawee traveled to small villages, collecting traditional tools, cooking utensils, animal traps, and handicrafts that were rapidly disappearing, and crammed them into a traditional house and barn. For a decade nothing was properly documented; visitors stumbled around tiger traps and cooking pots, with little to help them decipher what they were looking at. But Khun Thawee's daughter came to the rescue and now the marvelous artifacts are systematically laid out. You can now understand the use of everything on display, from the simple wood pipes hunters played to lure their prey to elaborately complex rat guillotines. The museum is a 15-minute walk south of the railway station, on the east side of the tracks. ⊠ *Wisut Kasat Rd.* 🖅 *B50* ⊙ *Tues.–Sun. 8:30–4:30.*

Where to Stay & Eat

Phitsanulok has a good range of dining options, from its popular pontoon and riverside restaurants to some great little daytime canteen-style restaurants near the central clock tower on Phayalithai Road. The Muslim restaurants on Pra Ong Dam Road, opposite the town's mosque, are great for curry and roti breakfasts. The new night bazaar promenade banking the Nan River contains some basic early-evening places to enjoy the sunset, including the infamous "flying vegetable restaurant, " where you can have the province's famed *pak bung fire dang* (stir-fried morning glory). And the veggies do fly here—when the cooks finish their stir-frying, they fling the food to waiters, who deftly catch the food on their plates. Sanambin Road has some well-priced seafood joints, while Akathodsarod Road near Topland Hotel is a good bet for late-night noodles.

$$–$$$$ ✕**Boo Bpen Seafood.** Although not actually on the river, this upbeat seafood restaurant still has the edge on the competition because of its spacious bench seating and pleasant garden atmosphere created by abundant greenery and colored lights. There's a small central stage where live bands play. House specialties include *gai khua kem* (roasted chicken with salt) and *boo nim tort gratium* (crab fried in garlic) and are worth a nibble, but for something a bit more substantial, the barbecue prawns are a must, sampled with the chili, lime, and fish sauce dip. ⊠ *Sanambin Rd.* ▭ *No credit cards.*

¢–$$ ✕ **Phraefahthai.** This floating teak Thai-style house on the Nan River is the more popular of the two pontoon eateries in Phitsanulok; it draws the majority of tourists, as well as local businessmen and their families. It's strikingly lit up at night, impossible to miss from anywhere on the river. It has areas for all occasions from large groups to intimate riverside seating. An extensive menu in English makes it the most comfortable riverside experience. The emphasis is on fresh seafood—the *pla taptim* (St. Peter's fish, a delicious freshwater fish) is particularly recommended, served steamed with a spicy lemon and lime sauce. ⊠ *60 Wangjan Rd.* ☎ *055/242743* ⊟ *AE, DC, MC, V.*

$–$$$ 🏨 **La Paloma.** This vast complex is Phitsanulok's best value high-end option. Rooms are clean and comfortable, with soft floral upholstering against classic dark-wood stain. A good selection of English-language TV channels help make it a comfy retreat. The location, however, isn't the best, with the center of the city a brisk 20-minute walk away and few independent dining or drinking options nearby. ⊠ *103 Srithumtripdork Rd.* ☎ *055/217930* 🖨 *249 rooms* ⚐ *Restaurant, coffee shop, minibars, cable TV, pool, massage, billiards, laundry service, business services, convention center* ⊟ *MC, V.*

$–$$ 🏨 **Phitsanulok Thani Hotel.** This fresh-faced hotel has a friendly and helpful staff. A nicely designed marbled foyer based around a small fountain leads to less attractive, though comfortable, rooms. Although away from the town center, the area around the hotel has a pulse of its own, with plenty of good restaurants and pubs to choose from. Local transport to other areas of the city is easy to find as well. ⊠ *39 Sanambin Rd., 65000* ☎ *055/211065 up to 69 or 055/212631 up to 34* 🖨 *055/211071 or 055/ 212630* ⊕ *www.phitsanulokthani.com* 🖨 *110 rooms* ⚐ *Restaurant, minibars, cable TV, spa, lobby bar, meeting rooms* ⊟ *AE, DC, MC, V.*

$ 🏨 **Grand Riverside Hotel.** The new kid on the block, completed in early 2003, is a fine looking hotel. The foyer is grand, with a spiral staircase that leads up to well-appointed rooms. It's a great base for Phitsanulok and is within walking distance of restaurants, bars, and the city's main temple. ⊠ *59 Praroung Rd., 65000* ☎ *055/216420 or 055/232777* 🖨 *055/23278* 🖨 *81 rooms* ⚐ *Restaurant, minibars, cable TV, in-room dataports, lobby lounge, Internet* ⊟ *MC, V.*

$ 🏨 **Pailyn Hotel.** The rooms at this white high-rise are quite large, with picture windows adding plenty of light—rooms on the higher floors have the best view of the river. The large lobby and coffee shop are full of activity in the morning as tour groups gather, as well as in the evening when the disco attracts the local teenagers. It's in downtown Phitsanulok, within walking distance of most of the city attractions. ⊠ *38 Baromatrailokart Rd., 65000* ☎ *055/252411, 02/215–7110 in Bangkok* 🖨 *055/225237* 🖨 *125 rooms* ⚐ *2 restaurants, coffee shop, minibars, cable TV, massage, sauna, spa, nightclub, meeting rooms, travel services* ⊟ *MC, V.*

¢–$ 🏨 **Rajapruk Hotel.** From the exterior, the Rajapruk looks like a run-down relic from the cold war. Fortunately the interior fares slightly better, though the rooms are basic and not very memorable. There's also a guesthouse at the back of the main building offering cheaper, but inferior, rooms with fans instead of air-conditioning. ⊠ *99/9 Pha-Ong Dum Rd.* ☎ *055/*

258477, 02/251–4612 in Bangkok 🖷 *055/212737* 🛏 *110 rooms* 🍴 *Restaurant, coffee shop, refrigerators, cable TV, pool, hair salon, laundry service* 🟰 *AE, DC, MC, V.*

¢ 🏠 **Phitsanulok Youth Hostel.** This is the only real guesthouse in Phitsanulok. Despite the name, you wouldn't associate this with any of the other youth hostels found in Thailand. Rooms range from basic raised mattresses with shared hot-water showers in the dorm room to rustic private rooms with antique wooden furnishings. It's set back from the road in beautifully green grounds; the teak pavilion with its woven reed hammocks is a welcome relief in this bustling city. Plans are in progress to add 40 more Thai-style bungalows, a swimming pool, and a spa with massage by 2006. ✉ *38 Sanambin Rd., 65000* 🕿 *055/242060* 🖷 *055/ 210864* ⊕ *www.tyha.org* 🛏 *240 rooms* 🍴 *Restaurant, laundry service, car rental.*

Nightlife

Phitsanulok has some fun options if you want to throw back a few beers or hear some live music. Located over Ekathosarok Bridge, just behind the visible 7-Eleven outlet, is **Phitsanulok Bazaar.** Not to be mistaken for the night bazaar, this is a small horseshoe-shape nightlife area with about 10 bars to pick from, along with the small Discovery nightclub. It's easily reached and a great place to start the evening. Good choices include the English-run Phitsanulok Sports Bar for a few games of pool, and the larger Muen Tamling for some live music and friendly banter with the locals. Things get started around 6 PM and go until about 1 AM.

Sanuk Neuk (✉ Baromtri Loknard Rd.) has to be Phitsanulok's best pub. Set in an old wooden corner house, it has an open-air café vibe, and is a great place to soak up the atmosphere and meet locals. Small cushioned sofas and collapsible beer-sponsored seats spread out from a small stage. Good local singers bring the place alive with selections of modern Western and Thai hits that keep the twenty- to thirtysomething crowd well entertained. It's about 1 km (½ mi) out of town along Boromtrailokanart Road—all the local drivers should know it.

Sports & the Outdoors

WHITE-WATER RAFTING   Outside of Phitsanulok, off Highway 12, is the best strip for rafting in the immediate region—a 9-km (5½-mi) route along the Keg River. This is an accessible and solid place to get your feet wet before heading off to more challenging options in the surrounding provinces. **Pop Tour** (✉ 50/39 Phra Ong Khao Rd. 🕿 01/6803939 Mr. Pop, 01/7070440 Miss Som 🖷 055/247136 ⊕ www.poptour.com) is the only rafting operator in Phitsanulok. The cost is B750 per person for a one- to two-hour ride. Buses transport groups from Phitsanulok to Ban Ta Kham village, where the rafts will be waiting. Technically, trips can be had any day of the week, but unless you're traveling with a large group, you might have trouble arranging one on weekdays, which are typically slow (there's a minimum of five people required per trip). On the weekend, however, there's enough interest that you can just turn up and join in with any one of the tours taking the plunge. Always call in advance to confirm trip times. The company operates from July to October, when you can expect up to Grade 5 rapids.

Sukhothai

Fodor's Choice ★ *56 km (35 mi) northwest of Phitsanulok, 427 km (265 mi) north of Bangkok; 1 hr by bus from Phitsanulok.*

Sukhothai, which means "the dawn of happiness, " holds a unique place in Thailand's history. Until the 13th century most of Thailand consisted of many small vassal states under the thumb of the Khmer Empire based in Angkor Wat. But the Khmers had overextended their reach, allowing the princes of two Thai states to combine forces. In 1238 one of the two princes, Phor Khun Bang Klang Thao, marched on Sukhothai, defeating the Khmer garrison commander in an elephant duel. Installed as the new king of the region, he took the name Sri Indraditya and founded a dynasty that ruled Sukhothai for nearly 150 years. His youngest son became the third king of Sukhothai, Ramkhamhaeng, who ruled from 1279 to 1299. Through military and diplomatic victories he expanded the kingdom to include most of present-day Thailand and the Malay peninsula.

By the mid-14th century Sukhothai's power and influence had waned, and Ayutthaya, once its vassal state, became the capital of the Thai kingdom. Sukhothai was gradually abandoned to the jungle, and a new town grew up about 14 km (9 mi) away. New Sukhothai, where all intercity buses arrive, is a quiet market town where most inhabitants are in bed by 11 PM.

In 1978 a 10-year restoration project costing more than $10 million created the Sukhothai Historical Park. The vast park (70 square km [27 square mi]) has 193 historic monuments, of which about 20 can be classified as noteworthy and six have particular importance.

Sukhothai is the busiest during the Loi Krathong festival, which falls each year on the full moon in November. Its well-orchestrated, three-day light-and-sound show is the highlight. During this time you can find most of the town's hotels and guesthouses booked up weeks in advance.

a good tour

Frequent songthaews from New Sukhothai will take you to the old city for about B10. You'll be dropped on the main street just outside the park entrance, about 500 yards from the **Ramkhamhaeng National Museum ⑫**. This repository of some of Sukhothai's greatest treasures should be your first stop.

Because the sights are so spread out, the best way to explore the park is by bicycle; you can rent one along the main street. You can also book a tour with a guide. Either way, bring a bottle of water with you—the day will get hotter than you think. Head first to **Wat Mahathat ⑬**, the spiritual center of the old city. More than 200 structures are a part of this massive complex. It's quite a contrast to the adjacent site of the **Royal Palace ⑭**, where almost nothing remains. To the south is one of the city's most fascinating structures, **Wat Sri Sawai ⑮**. Because of its Hindu images in the stonework, many believe the three-prang temple was here before construction began on the city itself. To the north of Wat Mahathat is **Wat Sra Sri ⑯**, which is built on a pair of islands in a tranquil lake.

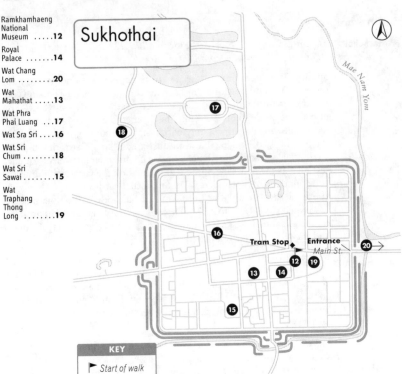

KEY

▶ *Start of walk*

Just beyond the northern city walls is **Wat Phra Phai Luang** ⓱, second in importance to Wat Mahathat. Look for the remains of what was an immense reclining Buddha. Southwest of Wat Phra Phai Luang is **Wat Sri Chum** ⓲, worth visiting for its sheer size. The Buddha statue seated within is one of the most impressive in the old city.

On the eastern side of the old city the most notable temple is **Wat Traphang Thong Lang** ⓳. On the walls are well-preserved carvings that depict the Buddha preaching. To the east is **Wat Chang Lom** ⓴, where you can still make out the stone elephants that once supported the temple.

TIMING   Depending on your means of transportation, this tour could take a few hours or the better part of a day. It's best to come in the late afternoon to avoid the midday sun and enjoy the late evening's pink-and-orange hues. Crowds generally aren't a problem.

What to See

▶ ⓬ **Ramkhamhaeng National Museum.** Most of the significant artifacts from Sukhothai are in Bangkok's National Museum, but this open, airy museum has more than enough fine pieces to demonstrate the gentle beauty of this period. Here you can learn about how refinements in the use of bronze let artisans create the graceful walking Buddhas found here. A relief map gives you an idea of the layout of the old city.

✉ *Jordvithikong Rd., just before entrance to historical park* 🚌 *B30* ⏱ *Daily 9–4.*

⑭ Royal Palace. Thais imagine Sukhothai's government as a monarchy that served the people, stressing social needs and justice. Slavery was abolished, and people were free to believe in their local religions, Hinduism and Buddhism (often simultaneously), and to pursue their trade without hindrance. In the 19th century a famous stone inscription of King Ramkhamhaeng was found among the ruins of the palace across from Wat Mahathat. Sometimes referred to as Thailand's Declaration of Independence, the inscription's best-known quote reads: "This city Sukhothai is good. In the water there are fish, in the field there is rice. The ruler does not levy tax on the people who travel along the road together, leading their oxen on the way to trade and riding their horses on the way to sell. Whoever wants to trade in elephants, so trades. Whoever wants to trade in horses, so trades." ✉ *In the Old City* 🚌 *B30* ⏱ *Daily 8–4:30.*

⑳ Wat Chang Lom. Located south of the park off Chotwithithong Road, this is regarded as one of Sukhothai's oldest monasteries. Its bell-shape pagoda, thought to have been built some time in the latter part of the 14th century, is of Sri Lankan influence and is perched on a three-tiered square base atop now-damaged elephant buttresses (a few have been reconstructed). In front of the chedi are a viharn and solitary pillars; the remains of nine other chedis have been found within this complex. ✉ *Chotwithithong Rd., about 4 km (2 ½ mi) before entrance to historical park, reached by turning north down a small lane over a smaller bridge.*

⑬ Wat Mahathat. Sitting amid a tranquil lotus pond, Wat Mahathat is the largest and most beautiful monastery in Sukhothai. Enclosed in the compound are some 200 tightly packed chedis, each containing the funeral ashes of a nobleman. Towering above them is a large central chedi, notable for its bulbous, lotus-bud prang. Wrapping around the chedi is a frieze of 111 monks, their hands raised in adoration. Probably built by Sukhothai's first king, Wat Mahathat owes its present form to King Lö Thai, who in 1345 erected the lotus-bud chedi to house two important relics brought back from Sri Lanka by the monk Sisatta. This Sri Lankan–style chedi became the symbol of Sukhothai and classical Sukhothai style. Copies of it were made in the principal cities of its vassal states, signifying a magic circle emanating from Sukhothai, the spiritual and temporal center of the empire. ✉ *In the Old City* 🚌 *B30* ⏱ *Daily 8:30–4:30.*

⑰ Wat Phra Phai Luang. This former Khmer structure, once a Hindu shrine, was converted to a Buddhist temple. Surrounded by a moat, the sanctuary is encircled by three laterite prangs, similar to those at Wat Sri Sawai—the only one that remains intact is decorated with stucco figures. In front of the prangs are the remains of the viharn and a crumbling chedi with a seated Buddha on its pedestal. Facing these structures is the *mondop* (a square structure with a stepped pyramid roof, built to house religious relics). It was once decorated with Buddha images in four different poses. Most of these are now too damaged to be recognizable;

LOI KRATHONG

ON THE FULL MOON OF THE 12TH LUNAR MONTH, when the tides are at their highest and the moon at its brightest, the Thais head to the country's waterways to celebrate Loi Krathong, one of Thailand's most anticipated and enchanting festivals.

Loi Krathong was influenced by Diwali, the Indian lantern festival that paid tribute to three Brahman gods. Thai farmers adapted the ceremony to offer tribute to Mae Khlong Kha, the goddess of the water, after harvest to thank her for blessing the land with water—and to appease her for the dirtying of her rivers and canals.

Ancient Sukhothai is where the festival's popular history began, with a story written by King Rama IV in 1863 that has become a part of the consciousness of modern Thais. The story concerns Naang Noppamart, the daughter of a Brahman priest who served in the court of King Li-Thai, grandson of King Ramkhamhaeng the Great. She was a woman of exceptional charm and beauty who soon became his queen. She's said to have secretly fashioned a krathong (a small float used as an offering), setting it alight by candle in accordance with her Brahmanist rites. The king, upon seeing this curious, glimmering offering embraced its beauty, adapting it for Theravada Buddhism and thus creating the festival of Loi Krathong.

Krathong were traditionally formed by simply cupping banana leaves and offerings such as dried rice and betel nut were placed at the center along with three incense sticks representing the Brahman gods. Today krathong are more commonly constructed by pinning folded banana leaves to a buoyant base made of a banana tree stem; they're decorated with scented flowers, orange candles (said to be representative of the Buddhist monkhood), and three incense sticks, whose meaning was changed under Li-Thai to represent the three forms of Buddhist existence. For a while, Styrofoam was a popular float, but thankfully these non-biodegradable imitations were banned for polluting Mae Khlong Kha's waters.

The ceremony has, of course, evolved, and contemporary desires have begun to inform it. Young Thai couples, "loi" their "krathong" to bind their love in an act almost like that of a marriage proposal, while others use the ceremony more as a way to purge any bad luck or resentments they may be harboring. Today Loi Krathong also commonly represents the pursuit of material gain, with silent wishes placed for a winning lottery number or two. The festival remains Thailand's most romantic vision of tradition, with millions of Thais sending their hopes floating down the nearest waterway, creating a shimmering wave of national unity.

Although it's celebrated nationwide, with events centered around cities such as Bangkok, Ayutthaya, Chiang Mai, and Tak, the festival's birthplace of Sukhothai remains the focal point. The historical park serves as a kind of Hollywood backlot, with hundreds of costumed students and light, sound, and pyrotechnic engineers, preparing for the fanfare of the annual show. With the historical park lit and Wat Mahathat as its stage, the show reenacts the story of Sukhothai and the legend of Loi Krathong with a spectacular finale that includes hundreds of fireworks.

— Warwick Dixon

only the reclining Buddha still has a definite form. ⊠ *North of Old City walls on Donko Rd., opposite from Tourist Information Center* 📞 *B30* 🕓 *Daily 8:30–4:30.*

16 **Wat Sra Sri.** Another one of Sukhothai's noteworthy attractions is this peaceful temple that sits on two connected islands encircled by a lotus-filled lake. The rolling mountains beyond add to the monastery's serenity. The lake, called Traphong Trakuan Pond, supplied the monks with water and served as a boundary for the sacred area. A Sri Lankan–style chedi dominates six smaller chedis, and a large, stucco, seated Buddha looks down a row of columns, past the chedis, and over the lake to the horizon.

Especially wondrous is the walking Buddha beside the Sri Lankan–style chedi. The walking Buddha is a Sukhothai innovation and the most ethereal of Thailand's artistic styles. The depiction of the Buddha is often a reflection of political authority and is modeled after the ruler. Under the Khmers, authority was hierarchical, but the kings of Sukhothai represented the ideals of serenity, happiness, and justice. The walking Buddha is the epitome of Sukhothai's art; he appears to be floating on air, neither rooted on this earth nor placed on a pedestal above the reach of the common people. Later, after Ayutthaya had become the capital, statues of the Buddha took on a sternness that characterized the new dynasty. ⊠ *In the Old City* 📞 *B30* 🕓 *Daily 8:30–4:30.*

18 **Wat Sri Chum.** Like many other sanctuaries, Wat Si Chum was originally surrounded by a moat. The main structure is dominated by a breathtaking statue of the Buddha in a seated position. The huge stucco image is one of the largest in Thailand, measuring 37 feet from knee to knee. Enter the mondop through the passage inside the left inner wall. Keep your eyes on the ceiling: more than 50 engraved slabs illustrate scenes from the *Jataka,* which are stories about the previous lives of Lord Buddha. ⊠ *East of Old City walls* 📞 *B30.*

15 **Wat Sri Sawai.** Sukhothai's oldest structure may be this Khmer-style one, which has three prangs—similar to those found in Lopburi—surrounded by a laterite wall. The many stucco Hindu images and scenes suggest that Sri Sawai was probably first a Hindu temple, later converted to a Buddhist monastery. Historians believe that Brahmanism probably played an important role throughout the Sukhothai period. ⊠ *In Old City* 📞 *B30* 🕓 *Daily 8:30–4:30.*

19 **Wat Traphang Thong Lang.** The square mondop of Wat Traphang Thong Lang is the main sanctuary, the outer walls of which boast beautiful stucco figures in niches—some of Sukhothai's finest art. The north side depicts the Buddha returning to preach to his wife. On the west side he preaches to his father and relatives. Note the figures on the south wall, where the story of the Buddha is accompanied by an angel descending from Heaven. ⊠ *Just north of Old City walls* 📞 *B30* 🕓 *Daily 8:30–4:30.*

Where to Stay & Eat

Eating out in Sukhothai means mostly cheap, local restaurants, food stalls, and the night market. The exception is the not-to-be-missed Dream Café with its collection of local ceramic artifacts.

$ ✕ Dream Café. While waiting for your meal, you can feast your eyes on
Fodor'sChoice   the extraordinary collection of antiques that fill this charming restau-
★   rant. This is Sukhothai's finest restaurant, and possibly the best in the
entire Central Plains. The rustic tile floor, the glowing teak tables and
chairs, and the nooks and crannies packed with fascinating odds and
ends—everything from old lamps to fine ceramics—combine in a perfect harmony. The traditional food is excellent, too, especially the pork
spare ribs with tamarind-stem spicy soup and the Sukhothai fondue. If
you can't bear to leave this paradise, behind the restaurant are five romantic rooms, aptly named Cocoon House, set in a fairy-tale garden.
⊠ 86/1 Singhawat Rd. ☎ 055/612081 🖶 055/622157 ▤ MC, V.

★ **$ ▥ Pailyn Sukhothai Hotel.** The staff is proud to point out that King Bhu-
mibol Adulyadej has spent the night here; indeed, it's the only luxury
hotel near Sukhothai. It's a vast building with a subtle contemporary
Thai look, including a typical stepped roof. Rooms are large, comfortable, and reasonably decorated, though the highly varnished bamboo
bedframes and chairs look kind of tacky. The airy central atrium and
the pool are a welcome sight after a day exploring the dusty ruins It's
halfway between New Sukhothai and the Old City, so transport can be
a problem. ⊠ Jarodvithithong Rd., 64210 ☎ 055/633336 up to 9, 02/
215–5640 in Bangkok 🖶 055/613317 ☞ 238 rooms ♨ 3 restaurants,
minibars, cable TV, pool, health club, massage, sauna, travel services
▤ MC, V.

¢–$ ▥ Lotus Village. The lotus-flower ponds that dot the lush gardens of this
attractive Thai-style lodging give the place its name. It's run by a charming French-Thai couple who are happy to help organize tours of Sukhothai
and the surrounding area. The teak bungalows—some with fans, others
with air-conditioning—are comfortably furnished and have private verandas. The inn is tucked away near the Yom River. It's best reached
via Rajuthit Road, which runs along the river from the center of town.
There's a breakfast room but no restaurant. ⊠ 170 Ratchathani Rd.,
64000 ☎ 055/621484 🖶 055/621463 ⊕ www.lotus-village.com ☞ 10
rooms ♨ Laundry service, Internet, travel services ▤ No credit cards.

¢–$ ▥ Thai Village House. This cluster of thatched bungalows is usually
jammed with tour groups. The hotel's advantage is its location—a five-
minute bicycle ride from the Old City. Rooms, most of which are air-
conditioned, have two queen-size beds, but little else. The open-air
dining room is pleasantly relaxing. ⊠ 214 Jarodvithithong Rd., Muang
Kao, 64000 ☎ 055/611049 or 055/612075 🖶 055/612583 ☞ 123
rooms ♨ Restaurant, shops ▤ MC, V.

★ **¢ ▥ Number 4 Guest House.** It's a bit difficult to find this lodging on the
outskirts of town (even taxi drivers sometimes scratch their heads), but
once you're here you will wonder how you could have stayed elsewhere. These bamboo bungalows are set in an overgrown garden where
golden bananas and scarlet birds of paradise hang just outside your door.
Just beyond are seemingly endless rice fields. On your veranda is a comfortable day bed, while inside is delightfully worn antique furniture. There's
no dining room, but the hosts are happy to cook you dinner and serve
it in the garden. The guesthouse is west of the Yom River, off Charodvithitong Road. ⊠ 140/4 Soi Khlong Mae Lumpung Rd., 64000 ☎ 055/
610165 ☞ 13 rooms ♨ Travel services ▤ No credit cards.

¢ 🏨 **Rajthanee Hotel.** The traditional Thai entrance of this well-run hotel leads into a modern building. There's a terrace where you can also enjoy a Thai whiskey and a stylish restaurant that serves good Asian cuisine. Comfortable rooms (standards and slightly larger deluxe rooms) are clean and practically furnished with a few trimmings such as woven headboards, which help soothe the eyes from the ever-present glare of lacquer. The newly constructed swimming pool is proving a welcomed addition to this hotel as is its karaoke bar that lights up like a lava lamp at night. ✉ *229 Jarodvithitong Rd., 64000* ☎ *055/611031 or 055/611308* ↪ *83 rooms* 🍴 *Restaurant, café, minibars, cable TV, pool, lounge, meeting rooms* ▭ *AE, MC, V.*

Si Satchanalai

㉑ *80 km (50 mi) north of Sukhothai.*

With its expanse of neatly mown lawns, Sukhothai is sometimes criticized for being too well groomed. But Si Satchanalai, spread out on 228 acres on the banks of the Mae Yom River, remains a quiet place with a more ancient, undisturbed atmosphere. It isn't difficult to find the ruins of a temple where you won't be disturbed for hours.

Most visitors to Si Satchanalai reach it as part of a tour from Sukhothai (most hotels can set you up with a guide). If you want to go on your own, hop on a bus bound for the town of Sawankhalok. Take a taxi to the historical park, asking the driver to wait while you visit the various temples. You can also tour the site by bicycle or on top of an elephant, if that's your choice of transportation. Accommodations near the park are only relatively expensive bungalows, so most visitors stay in Sukhothai.

Si Satchanalai, a sister city to Sukhothai, was governed by a son of Sukhothai's reigning monarch. Despite its secondary position, the city grew to impressive proportions, and no less than 200 of its temples and monuments survive, most of them in a ruined state but many well worth seeing. Near the entrance, **Wat Chang Lom** shows strong Sri Lankan influences. The 39 elephant buttresses are in much better condition than at the similarly named temple in Sukhothai. The main chedi was completed by 1291. As you climb the stairs that run up the side, you can find seated images of the Buddha. The second important monument, **Wat Chedi Jet Thaew,** is to the south of Wat Chang Lom. The complex has seven rows of ruined chedis, some with lotus-bud tops that are reminiscent of the larger ones at Sukhothai. The chedis contain the ashes of members of Si Satchanalai's ruling family. **Wat Nang Phya,** to the southeast of Wat Chedi Jet Thaew, has well-preserved floral reliefs on its balustrade and stucco reliefs on the viharn wall. As you leave the park, stop at **Wat Suam Utayan** to see a Si Satchanalai image of Lord Buddha, one of the few still remaining.

Sukhothai grew wealthy on the fine ceramics it produced from the rich earth around the neighboring town of Sawankhalok. The ceramics were so prized that they were offered as gifts from Sukhothai rulers to the imperial courts of China, and they found their way as far as Japan. Fine examples of 1,000-year-old Sawankhalok wares are on display at the

Sawankhalok Museum, about 1 km (½ mi) from the town. ✉ *Phitsanulok Rd., Sawankhalok* ☎ *B40* ⊙ *Weekdays 10–6, weekends 10–8.*

Where to Eat

Si Satchanalai's historical park has plenty of basic eating options. Kaeng Sak restaurant at the entrance will offer a bit more variety, with some good Chinese and European dishes.

¢–$ ✕ **Wang Yong Resort.** For a more leisurely meal, walk just east of the historical park and you can find the pleasant riverside Wang Yong Resort, an expensive riverside resort with attractive grounds and scenic hills as a backdrop. The restaurant is in an open-side antique wooden pavilion on the riverbank; it serves up some delectable Thai dishes such as *neua tord krapao grob* (crispy fried beef and holy basil) and *yam gai tua pu* (chicken and bean salad). ✉ *78/2 Suwanthanas Rd.* ☎ *055/631380* ▭ *MC, V.*

SUKHOTHAI & ENVIRONS A TO Z

AIR TRAVEL

All air traffic to the Central Plains radiates from Bangkok, with the exception of daily flights from Chiang Mai to Sukhothai and thrice-weekly flights between Chiang Mai and Phitsanulok, all on Thai Airways. There are several Thai Airways flights daily from Bangkok to Sukhothai and Phitsanulok. Sukhothai is roughly equidistant between its own airport (a beautiful open-air terminal built by Bangkok Airways but also used by Thai Airways) and the one in Phitsanulok, which is less than an hour away by taxi or bus.

🛦 **Bangkok Airways** ✉ 10 Moo 1, Jarodvithithong Rd., Sukhothai ☎ 055/633266. **Thai Airways** ✉ Singhawat Rd., Sukhothai ☎ 055/613075 or 055/610578.

🛦 Airports **Phitsanulok Airport** ☎ 055/301002. **Sukhothai Airport** ☎ 055/647220 up to 5.

BUS TRAVEL

Buses to Sukhothai depart from Bangkok's Northern bus terminal (Mo Chit) daily from 7:30 AM to 11 PM, leaving roughly every 20 minutes. There are five main companies to choose from but all charge B256 for first-class air-conditioned buses and B199 for second-class air-conditioned buses. The journey takes about seven hours. Buses from Sukhothai's new bus terminal on the bypass road depart at the same times and and for the same prices.

Phitsanulok's main bus terminal, on Highway 12, is the stop before Sukhothai, shaving 1½ hours off the journey and around B40 off the ticket price. The terminal also has buses for travel to Chiang Mai via Lampang or via Phrae and Phayao and to Khon Kaen via Lomsak.

Between Phitsanulok and Sukhothai there are regular, non-air-conditioned buses for B23, which depart roughly every hour; the trip takes about 1½ hours. To get to Si Satchanalai from Sukhothai takes 1½ hours and costs B36.

🚍 Bus Stations **Phitsanulok** ✉ Mittaparp Rd. ☎ 055/242430 or 055/242030. **Sukhothai** ✉ Bypass Rd. ☎ 055/614529.

CAR RENTAL

Agencies with drop-off services, such as Avis or Budget, will be your best option around this area—they both have desks at the airport in Phitsanulok. Costs for renting economy cars up to SUVs range from B1,500 to B3,500 per day without drivers. For chauffeur driven services, figure on an additional B500. Bigger hotels in Phitsanulok offer chauffeur services at similar prices, but are more tour-orientated and generally offer no more than one day trip.

🔓 Agencies **Avis** ✉ Phitsanulok Airport ☎ 055/242060. **Budget** ✉ Phitsanulok Airport ☎ 055/258556.

CAR TRAVEL

A car is a good way to get between the three towns. Highway 12 from Phitsanulok leads to Sukhothai and is a long, straight, and reasonably comfortable 59-km (1-hour) drive.

To get to the region from Bangkok, take the four-lane Highway 117; the drive takes about four hours.

EMERGENCIES

🔓 In Phitsanulok **Phitsanuwej Hospital** ✉ Khun Piren Rd. ☎ 055/21994. **Police** ☎ 055/258777.

🔓 In Sukhothai **Police** ☎ 055/613611. **Sukhothai Hospital** ✉ Charodvithitong Rd. ☎ 055/611782.

MONEY MATTERS

You'll have no difficulty finding ATM machines or exchange kiosks in Phitsanulok and Sukhothai. Sukhothai's banks are mainly on Sriintharathid Road, while Naresuan Road has most of Phitsanulok's banks.

SAFETY

Phitsanulok and Sukhothai prove safe and friendly as long as you keep your valuables hidden and secure.

TAXIS, SAMLORS & SONGTHAEWS

A cheap, cramped, tin-can bus service is available for use in Phitsanulok, but unless ovens are your thing, you're best off using the motorized samlors or the more ecofriendly pedal-powered ones, which are faster and more laid-back than the bus respectively. Sukhothai is without public bus routes, but is similar to Phitsanulok with most of the population getting around in souped-up samlors or songthaews.

TOUR OPERATORS

In Sukhothai, Dhanasith Kampempool's one-man agency is *the* place to go for a tour of the area. Dhanasith (or Tom, as he prefers to be called) studied and worked for more than 20 years in the United States. His English is, of course, perfect. His office is next to the Vitoon Guesthouse in Old Sukhothai: just tell Tom what you want to see and where you want to go and he'll arrange it.

🔓 Tour Companies **Dhanasith Kampempool** ✉ 49 Moo 3, Jarodvithithong Rd., Old Sukhothai ☎ 055/697045 or 055/633397 🖨 055/633397.

TRAIN TRAVEL
The train is the most enjoyable way to see the region; you'll travel through a number of destinations including historic Lopburi and Ayutthaya on the way to the station at Phitsanulok. Trains depart from Bangkok and Chiang Mai seven times daily with the journey taking approximately six hours from either city, and costing between B129 for third-class car (with fans) and B974 for a private first-class sleeper.

VISITOR INFORMATION
The Tourist Authority of Thailand's office in Phitsanulok has maps and brochures, and is open daily between 8:30 AM and 4:30 PM.
🚩 Tourist Information Phitsanulok ⊠ 209/7–8 Boromtrailokanat Rd. ☎ 055/231063.

TAK PROVINCE: MAE SOT & ENVIRONS

Often overlooked, Tak province is finally beginning to find its feet as a destination, mainly because of the wonderful trekking opportunities on offer in the region.

Famed for its teak forests, the province is home to an incredible number of plants and animals, including Thailand's last remaining wild cattle and the last 50 remaining wild water buffalo. Umphang National Park and Thung Yai Naresuan Wildlife Sanctuary are two definite highlights in this, Thailand's largest forest region.

Although the provincial hub city of Tak has little of interest for travelers, it's an inevitable transit point coming from other provinces in the Central Plains. From here, you can head off to Mae Sot and Umphang, where you have the opportunity to sample some of the country's more diverse cultural mixes, as well as outstanding natural beauty.

Mae Sot borders Myanmar and is a cultural melting pot, with Karen and Burmese peoples creating a vibrant mix rarely seen elsewhere in Thailand. It's also the best place to base yourself, with a range of guesthouses and tour companies preparing you for further exploration of Umphang's natural riches.

Umphang is the key to this area's spectacular tourist attractions; the small, peaceful town is your launching pad for white-water rafting tours that will take you through national parks and along gorges and ravines, passing hill tribe communities on your way to the ultimate goal of Thee Lor Su waterfall.

Mae Sot

❷ *83 km (51 mi) west of Tak city, 506 km (312 mi) north of Bangkok.*

At Mae Sot, which borders Myanmar to its west, you can find an interesting mix of local Thais, a dominant Burmese workforce, and the Karen refugees who live an ambiguous life in their 10,000-strong community, stuck between two worlds. It's definitely a frontier town, complete with black-market gems and timber smuggling, but it also provides the gateway for the natural sights of Tak province.

Wattanaram Monastery, a Tai Yai temple dating back to 1867, was built in Myanmar by a merchant from Tongchai. A typically Burmese wat, it's notable chiefly for its ornate gold-plate bronze Buddha image (Phra Phutta Maha Muni), which measures 6½ feet by 6½ feet and is encrusted with small precious stones, adding to its prestige. There's also a long 90-foot white concrete reclining Buddha behind the ordination hall. For men, there's an herbal sauna service available daily from 8–7. The temple is 3 km (2 mi) west of Mae Sot on Route 1085.

Aside from its miniature Mon-style pagoda—precariously mounted on a boulder and overhanging a 300-meter cliff—the forest temple of **Wat Phra That Hin Kew** is not really much to look at. There is, however, a fantastic view out over the Moei River and Myanmar's forested bank, which you'll feel you've earned after a good 20-minute hike up the complex's 413 stairs. It's about 11 km (7 mi) north of town; take the 1085 road heading north and follow the signs.

<table>
<tr>
<td>off the
beaten
path</td>
<td>

WAT DON KAEO – In Ban Maetao, 33 km (20 mi) north of Mae Sot, Wat Don Kaeo houses one of only three white-marble Buddha images in the world. This beautifully crafted sculpture is approximately 50 inches wide and 60 inches tall and is an example some of Myanmar's finest craftsmanship. It was supposedly bought by a villager for 800 rupees and, via boat, horse cart, and mountain passes was brought to this temple in 1922.

</td>
</tr>
</table>

Rim Moei Market lies on the Thai side of the Moei river and sells all sorts of imported goods such as jade, rubies, garnets, and fake cosmetics and clothes. But the market is really renowned for is its furniture—teak wood smuggled in from Myanmar, as well as by more legal means from Phrae, supply the surrounding workshops with these scarce materials. Anything from colonial-style cabinets and four-poster beds to contemporary bed boxes and work desks can be bought or made to order. Great bargains are available.

The second Thai-Myanmar Friendship Bridge, built in 1996, is 6 km (4 mi) east of town. Crossings into the eastern frontier town of **Myawady** give a brief taste of Myanmar, but with no safe access routes incountry, return to Thailand is unavoidable. The border is open daily 8–6. No visa is required, but you will be required to pay a B500 fee upon arrival in Myanmar. Myawady is a refreshing but chastening change from Thailand, noticeable as soon as you cross. Warm welcomes in English greet you, along with motorbikes with homemade sidecars. Guided tours of the nominal attractions here are cheap at around B200, and even if the temples aren't spectacular, it's an interesting experience nonetheless. The town occasionally erupts into a political flashpoint as the KNU slug it out with the Yangon-based government, sometimes resulting in the temporary closure of the bridge.

Tens of thousands of Karen have been driven into **refugee camps** in Northern Thailand by the Burmese government-backed military attacks on their Burmese villages. Karen villagers live in terror of these attacks, as they're generally being presented with two simple options: stay and work in labor camps on the government's oil pipelines or flee into the forest, where they'll be branded as enemies of the state and consequently hunted and killed. Some stand up and fight as guerrillas for the KNU, but the majority try to cross the border into Thailand, where they are recognized as political refugees. The largest Karen camp, **Bargor**, is about 40 km (25 mi) north of Mae Sot on the 1085 road to Mae Rammat. It's an arresting sight, with thousands of traditional split-bamboo huts staggered (some on stilts) over a hill range that stretches for 4 km (2½ mi). There are small checkpoints at each end, but villagers are allowed to leave during the day to farm the fields and travel into Mae Sot. You won't be able to visit this town without a guide.

Where to Stay & Eat

Mae Sot is often used as a one- or two-night stopover for trips into Umphang and therefore has a good range of cheap, friendly guesthouses, as well as some not-so-special mid-range hotels. In addition to a few good restaurants, you can always find cheap, basic eats at the markets on Intarakeeree and Prasartwithee Roads.

¢–$$ ✕ **Chicago.** This indoor, air-conditioned homage to the Beatles is something of an anomaly in Mae Sot. It's a small but well-stocked Japanese restaurant with a vast picture menu that seems to have a little bit of every type of Japanese food. The owner speaks great English; as you see on the wall, he's a successful owner of a Thai restaurant based in Chicago (no, he didn't call it Mae Sot). Overall, it's a pleasant place for a bottle of sake and some sushi. ⊠ *35 Prasart Vitti Rd.* ☎ *055/542333* ▭ *No credit cards.*

¢–$ ✕ **Bai Fern Restaurant & Guesthouse.** This is Mae Sot's only real Western restaurant, and for being in such a remote location, it does a good job. Wooden tables and chairs fill this guesthouse's ground floor, where you can tuck into the likes of New Zealand tenderloin steaks, salmon, and the old standbys of pizza and pasta. This is a popular stop for travelers, resident foreigners and Thai's alike, making it one of the busier and more sociable places in town. ⊠ *660 Intarakeeree Rd.* ☎ *055/533343 or 09/8584186* ▭ *No credit cards.*

¢–$ ✕ **Khaomao Khaofang.** The location, about 5 km (3 mi) from the town center, really shouldn't dissuade you from enjoying one of the most beautiful restaurants in Thailand. This is like a national park of restaurants with spacious, forested grounds—thick-cut varnished teak wood tables are arranged under a variety of open-air pavilions, which are nearly buried in lush vegetation. It's a stunner, but the food is pricey and doesn't match up to the quality setting. The house specialties are all appetizers such as *moo khao mao* (fried pork with rice grain), *muang gai gorp* (crispy chicken wrapped in pendant leave), and *gai tort grua* (deep-fried chicken with salt). ⊠ *382 Moo 9, Maepa* ☎ *055/532483 or 055/533607* ▭ *AE, MC, V.*

$–$$ ▥ **Central Mae Sot Hill Hotel.** The biggest and brightest hotel in Mae Sot has spacious rooms done in a contemporary Thai design, with nice wood furnishings and marble-trim bathrooms. The courtyard surrounding the large pool is a pleasant place to get a massage or to just relax with a cocktail in hand. ⊠ *100 Asia Rd., 63110* ☎ *053/532601* *up to 8* 🖷 *053/532600* ⊕ *www.centralhotelsresorts.com* ⟿ *114 rooms* ⚘ *Restaurant, minibars, cable TV, tennis courts, outdoor pool, gym, massage, sauna, lobby bar, Internet, meeting rooms, airport shuttle, car rental, travel services* ▤ *AE, DC, MC, V.*

¢ ▦ **Ban Thai Guesthouse.** Follow the signpost down a small lane past the Fortune guesthouse and you can find this converted white wooden Thai house. Rooms are very clean and surprisingly cool, with dark varnished floors and furniture. It's popular with expats and long-term tourists, it's a good spot to pick up some info on the area. ⊠ *740/1 Intarakeeree Rd., 63110* ☏ *053/531590, 02/9418878 in Bangkok* 🖷 *053/534798* ⟿ *12 rooms* ⚘ *Massage, laundry service* ▤ *No credit cards.*

¢ ▦ **No. 4 Guesthouse.** This one-man show from Mr. Oom is Mae Sot's original guesthouse (it opened in the late '80's). The rooms are basic (mosquito net and fan) but it's all about the trekking here—Mr. Oom and his guides won the 2004 Tourist Authority of Thailand's "Trekking Award for the North." There's a dangerously comfortable, small chill-out lounge downstairs in which to chat about the trip ahead or to loll unconscious upon your return. ⊠ *736 Intarakeeree Rd., 63110* ☏ *053/544976 or 01/7852095* 🖷 *053/544976* ⊕ *www.geocities.com/ no4guesthouse/* ⟿ *6 rooms* ⚘ *Travel services* ▤ *No credit cards.*

¢ ▦ **PIN Guesthouse.** This two-story building is pretty homely from the outside, but all rooms are extremely comfortable, with straw mats and bamboo beds. There's also a pleasant, spacious balcony with seating outside the second floor rooms. ⊠ *102 Asia Rd., 63110* ☏ *053/534651* ⟿ *14 rooms* ⚘ *Minibars, cable TV, laundry service* ▤ *No credit cards.*

Umphang

㉓ *164 km (100 mi) south of Mae Sot, 249 km (150 mi) southeast of Tak city*

Umphang is Tak province's largest district. It's landlocked in the Tano Thongchai mountain range, with the high mountains making up 97% of the area; there's only one access road to it from Mae Sot. Dense rain forest rich with bamboo and teak abuts the Thungyai Naresuan and Huai Kha Kaeng wildlife sanctuaries, as part of the Western Forest range (the largest in Southeast Asia), which due to its importance as a conservation area was classified as a World Heritage Site.

The district's distinct geography and culture is everpresent. The town is a center for ecotreks to hill tribe villages and some of the oldest remaining rain forest left in the country, as well as rafting expeditions along the Mae Khlong river to Thailand's largest and most spectacular waterfall, Thee Lor Su.

"Umphang, " adapted from the Karen word "umpha, " refers to the border pass that the Burmese were required to have to trade with this Thai village. The document was folded, sealed, and placed inside a bamboo cane to prevent wear; its story has become an important part of Umphang's heritage. Today, rubber boats and canoes have replaced the bamboo rafts once used on the rivers and local Karen guides are employed counteracting logging activities.

Umphang town itself is a sleepy and seasonal one with 3,000 residents of mainly Karen, Mon, and Thai. The small cluster of streets is a sight for sore eyes after a twisting four-hour songthaew ride from Mae Sot.

At almost 6 km (3½ mi), **Tham Takobi** (meaning "Flat Mangoes" in Karen dialect) is Thailand's fourth-longest cave complex. The cave has three levels; the lowest and narrowest is for the more adventurous (it gets very dark and narrow in parts) and follows an active stream through the system's entire length. The main tourist cave, on the other hand, is 82 feet above the streamline; it's a big, comfortable space to explore, plastered with stalagmites and stalactites, which are lit up. There's also another cave 98 feet above the main one. There are a total of 15 entrances poking out of the caves but the well-marked tourist entrance is the recommended choice.

Takobi is an easy 2-km (1-mi) walk from Umphang town, making it an accessible and enjoyable half-day excursion. If you intend to walk the full lower level, make sure to give yourself an early start as it will take most of the day. Also take into account that the stream is seasonal: the chambers are flooded from June through December, rendering the lower cave inaccessible. Good shoes, plenty of bottles of water, and a flashlight are essential. 🎟 *Free* ⏰ *8:30–5.*

Considered one of Southeast Asia's most spectacular falls and Thailand's largest, **Thee Lor Su Waterfall** is in the Umphang Wildlife Conservation Area. The valley's river, tracking its way from Huai Klotho, cascades down a 984-ft limestone cliff into a green translucent pool; the clearing is surrounded by virgin mountain forest. The waterfall is a 30-minute walk from the conservation area's headquarters. Note that though the conservation area is open year-round, the park's roads are unusable from May to November because of flooding; the best months to visit are August through October. Rafting tours are the most rewarding means of seeing Thee Lor Su and its surrounding area, with programs readily available from agents in Umphang, as well as in Mae Sot. ⊠ *27 km (17 mi) from Umphang* 🎟 *B300* ⏰ *Daily 8:30–6:30.*

FodorśChoice
★

Where to Stay & Eat

Umphang's about as basic as it gets when it comes to eating options. Noodle soup and basic rice dishes are the staples, but places such as the Phu Doi Restaurant liven things up a bit. Bigger resorts such as Tukasu Cottage have pleasant grounds for a meal and the market adjacent to the main road can supply you with some good Umphang home cooking.

¢–$ 🏠 **Thee Lor Su Riverside.** This resort 3 km (2 mi) uphill from town is set in spacious, beautifully tended gardens, and is a great way to start your Umphang experience. There are ten log bungalows of varying sizes for groups as small as two or as large as ten. Rooms are cozy, with glowing varnished wood and plenty of blankets and cushions on long communal mattresses. Gas-powered hot-water heaters in the tiled bathrooms mean you're guaranteed a hot shower on a cool morning. The larger communal house, where evening barbecues take place, is the center of activities—here you can arrange one of their popular rafting tours (one includes a flight over Thee Lor Su in a Cessna before your rafting begins). ✉ *Hwy. 1090, 63170* ☎ *055/561010, 038/312050, or 01/8620533* ⚓ *10 bungalows* ⛓ *Travel services* ▭ *No credit cards.*

¢–$ ▦ **Tukasu Cottage.** Even from the stylish green sign, you can tell that something special awaits. Flowering plants and lush foliage lead you along the grounds to contemporary hill tribe–inspired bungalows. A combination of split-bamboo and dried-grass roofs cover cozy brick and wood rooms. Prices are high, as with many of the resorts in Umphang, but the proximity to town and smart accommodations make it a good choice. ✉ *40 Moo 6, 63170* ☎ *055/561295or 01/8258238* ⊕ *www. tukasu.com* ⚓ *12 bungalows* ⛓ *Restaurant, travel services* ▭ *No credit cards.*

TAK PROVINCE: MAE SOT & ENVIRONS A TO Z

AIR TRAVEL

Mae Sot has a small airport serving only Chiang Mai. Flights are Monday, Wednesday, and Friday, with one flight per day. Tickets can be purchased at Mae Sot airport as well as at Chiang Mai airport through Phuket Air.

🛪 **Airlines Phuket Air** ✉ Mae Sot Airport, Mae Sot ☎ 055/544652 up to 4 ✉ Chiang Mai Airport, Chiang Mai ☎ 053/904494.

BICYCLES & MOTORBIKES

This is a good way to see Mae Sot. Bai Fern Guesthouse rents bicycles for B50 a day and 100cc motorbikes for B100 a day. A passport will be required as a deposit for motorbikes.

BUS TRAVEL

Mae Sot only has bus service to and from Bangkok. Cherd Chai Travel has first-class air-conditioned buses that leave from the old bus station on Chidwana Road at 9 PM for the eight-hour journey to Bangkok (B310); the bus also stops outside the Siam Hotel in town at 9:30 PM. It also has smaller second-class air-conditioning buses departing at 5:40 PM (6 PM outside Siam hotel) for B241. Tanjit Tour provides a luxury 32-seat VIP bus for B350 that leaves at 9:30 PM from Intarakeeree Road, 50 feet from the police station.

Minibuses are the main link between Tak city and Mae Sot. For B44 they take you from the Tak bus terminal to the old bus station on Chidwana Road. Going both ways, minibuses depart every 30 minutes 6:30–6; the journey takes 1½ hours.

🚌 **Bus Stations Cherd Chai Travel** ☎ 055/546856 or 09/7089448. **Tanjit Tour** ✉ Intarakeeree Rd., 50 m from the police station ☎ 055/531835

CAR TRAVEL

Bai Fern Guesthouse in Mae Sot rents pick-up trucks for B1,200 per day.

EMERGENCIES

🚨 **Police** ✉ Mae Sot ☎ 055/563937. **Mae Sot Hospital** ✉ 175/16 Seepharnit Rd., Mae Sot ☎ 055/531229 or 055/531224.

MONEY MATTERS

The majority of banks with ATMs and exchange services are easily located on Intarakeeree Road, but make sure to take enough cash with you for a trip down to Umphang, because there are no exchange counters or ATMs in that small town.

SAFETY

Rubies, brought in from Burmese mines, are a big draw at Mae Sot, but unless you know what you're looking at, you might find yourself with substandard or fake gems as scams on unsuspecting visitors are common.

SONGTHAEWS

This is the main form of travel in Mae Sot. Songthaews to Umphang are blue and can be found on Ratchaganratchadamri 2 Road, ⅓ mi from the Telecommunications building. The long four-hour ride is B100; songthaews leave every hour from 7:30–5:30. Orange songthaews from the old bus station on Chidwana Road go to Mae Sariang, making stops in Mae Hong Son and Chiang Mai, but it's an arduous six-hour trip (though it is only B150). They run from 6:30 to 5:30.

If you're looking simply to get to the Thai/Myanmar border, however, jump on one at Prahsartwithee Road, 60 feet from Siam Hotel. Hop on as they come along and expect to pay B10. For around B50 you can charter one privately.

TOUR OPERATORS

Eco-trekking options are abundant in Mae Sot and Umphang with a number of programs available. Most center around Umphang's Thee Lor Su waterfall and range from two-day tours (B5,500) to seven-day experiences (B19,000). You can raft, trek, and ride elephants around the area, taking in Karen villages, caves, mountain peaks, and waterfalls.

One-day or half-day tours around Mae Sot are also available and are a good way to see the main sights. Tours are typically around B1,500 for a full day or B350 for a half day.

Mae Sot's brightest and best-organized tour operator works out of an office directly next to DK Hotel. They provide a number of tours including a standard itinerary to Thee Lor Su waterfall, as well as the newer Mae Sot to Kee district white-water rafting route. All of their tours can be found along with prices, photographs, and previous travelers' comments on their fantastic Web site.

No. 4 Guesthouse and Mr. Oom are another secure option in Mae Sot. Mr. Oom is a true adventurer and he can put together customized tours if none of his standard tours meet your needs.

The other big tour company in the area is Thee Lor Su Riverside based in the resort of the same name in Umphang. This is the more popular tour company for domestic Thai tourists and they have a unique tour of Thee Lor Su waterfall. It involves an initial flight over the falls and its surrounding area in a Cessna. After the first night's stay, you leave early and the rafting begins. A 3 day/2 night program costs B5,500, but there has to be a minimum of five people for the trip to happen. Book well in advance. The one disadvantage to this company is that unlike its competitors, it can't guarantee English-speaking guides.

🔗 Tour Companies **Max One Tour** ✉ 269/2 Intarakeeree Rd., Mae Sot ☎ 055/542941 or 055/542942 🖷 055/543142 ⊕ www.maxonetour.com. **No. 4 Guesthouse** ✉ 736 Intarakeeree Rd., Mae Sot ☎ 055/544976 or 01/7852095 ⊕ www.geocities.com/no4guesthouse/. **Thee Lor Su Riverside Resort** ✉ Hwy. 1090, Umphang ☎ 055/561010, 038/312050, or 01/8620533.

VISITOR INFORMATION

There's no official tourist information center in Mae Sot, so your best option is contacting the No. 4 Guesthouse or Max One Tour—both have a wealth of local information and advice on what to do, as well as helpful maps of Mae Sot and the Umphang area.

NORTHERN
THAILAND

4

BEST LIGHT AT THE END OF THE TUNNEL
Glittering Wat Phra That Doi Suthep,
reached via a mere 304 steps ⇨ *p.159*

BEST "ONLY IN THAILAND" EVENT
Listening to an elephant orchestra ⇨ *p.181*

STRANGEST TRIP
The Hall of Opium's simulated high ⇨ *p.213*

MOST ENLIGHTENING ECO-TRIP
Trekking to visit remote hill tribes ⇨ *p.208*

BEST WAY TO DO A 360
Traveling the Mae Hong Son loop,
the country's best scenic drive ⇨ *p.194*

Updated by
Robert Tilley

AS LATE AS 1939 Northern Thailand was a semi-autonomous region of Siam, with a history rich in tales of kings, queens, and princes locked in dynastic struggles and wars of conquest and defense. Even today, a journey through Northern Thailand feels like venturing into a different country than the one ruled by far-off Bangkok. The landscape, the language, the architecture, the food, even the people are all quite distinct. This is hardly surprising, since the ancestors of today's Northern Thai people came from China, and the point where they first crossed the mighty Mae Khong River, Chiang Saen, became a citadel-kingdom of its own as early as 773. Nearly half a millennium passed before the arrival of a king who was able to unite the peoples of the far north and give them a cohesive identity—citizens of the new realm of Lanna ("a thousand rice fields").

The fabled ruler King Mengrai (1259–1317) also established a dynasty that lasted two centuries. Mengrai's first capital was Chiang Rai, but at the end of the 13th century he moved his court south and in 1296 founded a new dynastic city, Chiang Mai. Two friendly rulers, King Ngarm Muang of Phayao and King Rama Kampeng of Sukhothai, helped him in the huge enterprise, and the trio sealed their alliance in blood, drinking from a chalice filled from their slit wrists. A monument outside the city museum in the center of Chiang Mai's old city commemorates the event. Nearby, another monument marks the spot where King Mengrai died, in 1317, after being struck by lightning in one of the fierce storms that regularly roll down from the nearby mountains. Such is the fascinating lore of Chiang Mai, a city whose ancient walls and bulwarks breathe history.

Lanna power was weakened by waves of attacks by Burmese and Lao invaders, and for two centuries—from 1556 to the late 1700s—Lanna was virtually a vassal Burmese state. The capital was moved south to Lampang, where Burmese power was finally broken and a new Lanna dynasty, the Chakri, was established under King Rama I. The courageous commander of the Lanna forces in Lampang, Kawila, was made a "Chao" or lord of the realm—a title that eventually passed to the last ruler of Chiang Mai, Chao Keo Nawarat. A Bangkok-appointed governor replaced him in 1939.

Chiang Mai is the natural capital of the north. The old walled city with newer neighborhoods spreading in every direction is no smaller version of Bangkok, but a bustling metropolis in its own right. Chiang Mai lays claim to a longer history, richer culture, tastier cuisine, and friendlier people than the country's capital—opinions that only longtime visitors can confirm or dismiss.

Chiang Mai, nearby Lamphun (also at the center of Lanna-Burmese struggles), and Lampang are full of reminders of this rich history. Lampang's fortified Wat Lampang Luang commemorates with an ancient bullet hole the spot where the commander of besieging Burmese forces was killed. In the far north, the Chiang Saen, site of the region's first true kingdom, is being excavated, its 1,000-year-old walls slowly taking shape again.

From Chiang Mai, the highways and byways extend into mountains that appear on the map but are often hidden in the haze that descends on the city for much of the year. To the north is Chiang Rai, a regal capital 30 years before Chiang Mai was built. This quieter, less-developed town is slowly becoming a base for exploring the country's northernmost reaches. Chiang Saen is on the edge of the fabled Golden Triangle, an irresistible draw for many visitors to Thailand. This mountainous region, bordered by Myanmar to the west and Laos to the east, was once ruled by the opium warlord Khun Sa, whose home town, Ban Sop Ruak, has a magnificent museum, the Hall of Opium, tracing the story of the spread of narcotics. The opium trade still flourishes in the more remote parts of the region, despite determined efforts by government officials and police to stamp it out.

Chiang Mai and Chiang Rai are ideal bases for exploring the hill tribe villages, where people live as they have for centuries. The communities closest to the two cities have been overrun by tourists, but if you strike out on your own with a good map you may still find some that haven't become theme parks. Most of the villages are bustling crafts centers where the colorful fabrics you see displayed in Bangkok shop windows take shape before your eyes. The elaborately costumed villagers descend into Chiang Mai and Chiang Rai every evening to sell their wares in the night markets that transform thoroughfares into tented bazaars.

There's also plenty of excitement, from riding elephants into the mountains to rafting down the rivers that cut deep into the jungle-swathed hills. Here you can find Thailand's highest mountain, Doi Inthanon, regarded as an eastern buttress of the Himalayas. You can trek to the foot of the mountain and still be back at your hotel in time for a sumptuous dinner followed by a night on the town.

Exploring Northern Thailand

On a world map, Northern Thailand appears to be a very remote area of Asia, far from the country's capital, Bangkok, or other major regional centers. In fact, this region bounded on the north, east, and west by Myanmar and Laos is easily accessible, its main cities and towns linked with Bangkok by frequent and reliable air services and connected regionally by a network of highways. An excellent regional bus service also links every town and most villages, however remote.

Chiang Mai is Northern Thailand's self-described "hub, " although the country's main north–south artery, the Highway 1, bypasses the city and actually connects Bangkok with Chiang Rai and the Golden Triangle in the far north. An arm of the motorway, Highway 11, branches off for Chiang Mai at Lampang, itself a major transport hub with long-distance bus terminal, railroad station, and airport. There are several flights a day from Bangkok to Chiang Mai and Chiang Rai, and daily flights from the capital to Lampang, Mae Hong Son, and Nan.

From Chiang Mai you can reach the entire region on well-paved roads, with travel times not exceeding eight hours or so. The journey on serpentine mountain roads to Mae Hong Son, however, can be very tiring, requiring a stopover in either the popular resort town of Pai or quieter, more sedate Mae Sariang. Similarly, Chiang Rai offers a convenient stopover on the road north to the Golden Triangle.

To get a feeling for Northern Thailand, it would be ideal to spend at least a week or two. This would allow time to make a trek to one or two hill tribe villages.

Numbers in the text correspond to numbers in the margin and on the Northern Thailand, Chiang Mai, Near Chiang Mai, Mae Hong Son, Chiang Rai, and Golden Triangle maps.

If you have 2–3 days

Spend your first day exploring the streets and lanes of central ▣ **Chiang Mai** ❶– ❿. In the morning you can poke around Wat Phra Singh and the other sights in the Old City. Flag down a songthaew and check out the crafts stores that line several kilometers of Sankamphaeng Road in the afternoon. After a hard day of shopping, treat yourself to the luxury of a Thai massage. On the second day rise early and drive up to **Wat Phra That Doi Suthep** ⓭, the breathtaking temple overlooking Chiang Mai. In the afternoon, visit the Elephant Training Center at Mae Sa and then, if there's time, stop by **Wat Chedi Yot** ❽ and the **National Museum** ❾. For the evening's entertainment, wander among the stalls at the justifiably famous Night Bazaar. If you have a day to spare, head south to see the wats of **Lamphun** ⓴ and the markets of **Pa Sang** ⓳, then continue on to see the Burmese and Chinese architecture at ▣ **Lampang** ㉑, visiting the famous Elephant Conservation Center on the way.

If you have 5 days

On your first two days, cover the major sights in and around ▣ **Chiang Mai** ❶– ❿. On the third day, fly to ▣ **Mae Hong Son** ㉗– ㉚ and take a tour of a nearby Karen village. Set out the next day (by hired car or bus) for ▣ **Chiang Rai** ㉞– ㊱. Be sure to take a ride on the Mae Kok River in a longtail boat. You might want to consider overnighting in **Tha Ton** or **Chiang Dao.** On the fifth day make a circular tour to **Chiang Saen** ㊲ to see its excavated ruins, then to **Ban Sop Ruak** ㊴ to learn about the opium lords at the magnificent new Hall of Opium. Finally head to **Mae Sai** ㊵ for a look at Burmese crafts in the busy local markets.

If you have 7 days

If you're lucky enough to have a week or more in Northern Thailand, you have plenty of time to stay for a few nights with a hill tribe family. Treks to these mountain villages, most often on the back of an elephant, can be arranged from Chiang Mai, Chiang Rai, Mae Hong Son, and other communities.

Lampang, with its laid-back style of life and glittering temples, is less than two hours' drive south from Chiang Mai, but is also a convenient and comfortable center from which to explore the nearby national parks and lakes. A three-hour drive southwest from Chiang Mai brings you to the summit of Thailand's highest mountain, Doi Inthanon. Nan, whose temples rival those of Chiang Mai and Lampang, sits in a remote valley with few routes in and out—if you're traveling there from Bangkok, it's advisable to do one leg of the journey by air.

Timing

Northern Thailand has three seasons. The region is hottest and driest from March to May. The rainy season runs from June to October, with the wettest weather in September. Unpaved roads are often impassable at this time of year. The best season to visit is in the winter months from November to March, when days are warm, sunny, and generally cloudless, and evenings and nights pleasantly cool. At higher altitudes it can then be quite cold in the evening, so take a sweater if you're heading to the mountains. It's advisable to book hotel accommodation a month or two ahead of the Christmas and New Year holiday periods and the Songkran festival, which falls in April.

Trekking

In the 1960s a few intrepid travelers in Northern Thailand started wandering through the countryside, finding rooms at the hill tribe villages. By 1980 tour companies were organizing guided groups and sending them off for three- to seven-day treks. The level of difficulty of a Northern Thailand trek varies: you might traverse tough, hilly terrain for several hours or travel mostly by pick-up and hike just the last few miles. Days are spent walking forest trails between villages, where you can sleep overnight. Accommodations are in huts, where the bed can be a wooden platform with no mattress. Food is likely to be a bowl of sticky rice and stewed vegetables. Travel light, but be sure to wear sturdy hiking shoes and to pack a sweater. Mosquito repellent is a must.

Always use a certified guide. It's important to pick one who's familiar with local dialects and who knows which villages are not overrun with tour groups. It's also imperative that you discuss the route; that way you'll know what to expect. You can usually tell whether the guide is knowledgeable and respects the villagers, but question him thoroughly about his experience before you sign up. The best way to select a tour that is right for you is to talk to other travelers. Guides come and go, and what was true six months ago may not be today. The charge for a guided trek is around B800 per day.

Try and avoid the hot months of April and May, when trekking can be sweaty work even at high altitudes. The best time of year to make for the hills is the cool, dry season, between November and March.

Trekking is more than a popular pastime in Northern Thailand—it's big business. Some of the more accessible villages, particularly those inhabited by the long-necked women of the Karen people, have consequently come to resemble theme parks. Be clear about what you expect when booking a trek. Insist on the real thing, perhaps offering a bit more to achieve it. Better still, ask your hotel to recommend a good local guide. Gather as much information as you can from those who have just returned from a trek. Their advice will save you time, money, and frustration.

About the Restaurants

The cuisine in the northern part of the country differs significantly from the rest of Thailand, although most restaurants serve both types. Locals prefer the glutinous *khao niao* (sticky rice), using handfuls of it to

4

Natural Wonders
You don't have to venture far outside of Chiang Mai, the region's major city, before you're introduced to the region's natural beauty. Doi Suthep National Park, easily reached from the city center, has a bunch of hiking trails up its main peak, and a spectacular set of hot springs is also very close to the city. Southwest of Chiang Mai is Doi Inthanon, Thailand's highest mountain, contained in a national park of staggering beauty. The drive along the Mae Hong Son loop will take you past more mountain ranges and thick teak forests. The mountains immediately north and west of Chiang Rai have some of the regions most beautiful waterfalls: Huai Mae Sai, Pong Pha Bat and the 70-meter high Khun Kon. All are within an hour's drive and any one is an ideal picnic destination.

Shopping
The region is world famous for its silks, of course, but a stroll through the night markets of Chiang Mai and Chiang Rai will uncover an astonishing range of handicrafts, many of them originating in the nearby hill tribe villages. Hand-painted ceramics, delicately woven fabrics, carefully tooled leather—the list is almost endless. Chiang Mai has a silversmith district where exquisite pieces are found for incredibly low prices. The city is also famous for its lacquered umbrellas, and a visit to one of the local workshops should be on every itinerary. Some of the smaller border towns have unusual imported goods—in Chiang Khong, for instance, you can find fine lace from Laos. Mai Sai, on the Myanmar border, is the place to find Burmese rubies and other precious and semi-precious stones.

Temples
Chiang Mai's glittering Wat Phra That Doi Suthep, high on a mountain overlooking the city, has so many gold surfaces it can be hard to look at when the sun's strong. Nearby Lamphun's Wat Phra That Hariphunchai is an equally dazzling complex, with a copper-covered chedi and large bronze images of the Buddha. Wat Pumin in Nan is worth a visit for its unusual murals alone, but it's also one of the best examples of folk architecture in the north.Chiang Rai's four most famous temples together offer a fascinating introduction to the beauties of Lanna architecture. Wat Doi Tong—or Wat Phra That Doi Chom Thong, to give it its full name—actually predates the founding of Chiang Rai and is supposedly the place where King Mengrai first surveyed the site of his future capital. It's one of many temples built on vantage points around Chiang Rai. A visit to Wat Phra That Pha-Ngao, on the main road between Chiang Saen and Chiang Khong, is especially recommended for the fine view it affords of the Mae Khong river below.

---

scoop up delectable sauces and curries, but you'll have no problem ordering plain *khao suay* (steamed rice) or fragrant jasmine rice. A truly northern and very popular Muslim specialty, which has taken root in the north is *khao soy*, a delicious pork or chicken curry with crispy and soft noodles, served with pickled cabbage and onions. Lively debates take place at Chiang Mai dinner tables on the best restaurants to find khao soy, and at least one establishment—"Just Khao Soy" in Chiang Mai—serves only this one dish.

Another scrumptious northern specialty is *hang led,* a succulent pork curry spiced with ginger. Chiang Mai's sausages are nationally famous— try *sai ua* (crispy pork sausage) and *mu yo* (spicy sausage). Noodles of nearly every variety can be bought for a few baht from food stalls everywhere, and some fried-noodle dishes, particularly pad thai, have found their way onto many menus. Other northern dishes to try include *nam pik ong* (pork, chilies, and tomatoes), *gaeng ke gai* (chicken curry with chili leaves and baby eggplant and *kap moo,* crispy pork served with *nam pik num,* a mashed chili dip. Western food is served at all larger hotels, although the local version of an "American" or "English" breakfast can sometimes be a bit of a shock.

About the Hotels

Chiang Mai is in the midst of a major hotel building program, with seven new five-star luxury establishments and two four-star ones due to open by 2006, adding more than 1,000 new rooms to the city's capacity. The feverish building program is a centerpiece of Chiang Mai's long-term plan to become a regional business and tourism hub. There's a definite trend toward smaller, "boutique" hotels and away from anonymous tower blocks. High-rises are banned from the Old City. The low-eaved Lanna style of construction exactly meets the requirements of the ban, and two exquisite recent additions to the accommodation scene—the Rachamankha and the Tamarind Village—have been designed to combine the distinctive, restrained Lanna look (whitewashed walls, dark wood, low multiple eaves). The Four Seasons, in the hills outside Chiang Mai, is another trailblazer in this class and is among the finest hotels in all of Southeast Asia. Two resorts in the Golden Triangle—the Anantara and the Imperial—are among Thailand's best.

Prices in the high season (November–March) are high and hit Bangkok levels (in excess of B10,000), but 75% reductions are common in other months. Resorts near Chiang Mai offer a range of outdoor activities that surpass those in Bangkok. Golfers, in particular, are sure to be pleased. Resorts in nearby towns such as Chiang Rai, Chiang Saen, and Mae Sai are less expensive, and those in distant villages like Phrae and Nan are downright cheap.

Smaller hotels and guesthouses range from simple accommodations with fan-cooled rooms and shared baths to stylish establishments with lovely gardens and homey rooms. The cheapest can be quite simple indeed—perhaps a bit shabby, but never dirty—while spending a bit more will get you home-away-from-home comfort.

WHAT IT COSTS In baht				
$$$$	**$$$**	**$$**	**$**	**¢**
RESTAURANTS over B400	B300–B400	B200–B300	B100–B200	under B100
HOTELS over B6,000	B4,000–B6,000	B2,000–B4,000	B1,000–B2,000	under B1,000

Restaurant prices are per person, for a main course at dinner. Hotel prices are for a standard double room, excluding tax.

CHIANG MAI & ENVIRONS

Chiang Mai, known as the "Rose of the North, " has ambitious plans: it wants to expand beyond its role as a provincial capital to become a gateway to Myanmar, Laos, and western China. New luxury hotels are shooting up, attracting more business and leisure travelers. The airport is being expanded to accommodate more and larger airplanes, and already there has been an increase in the number of direct flights from Europe and Asia. And although the country's main highway, the Highway 1, bypasses Chiang Mai as it runs between Bangkok and Chiang Rai, officials have made sure the city is at the center of a spider's web of highways reaching out in all four directions of the compass, with no major city or town more than a day's drive away.

It's a long way between Bangkok and Chiang Mai—about 550 km, or 342 mi—but there are several very comfortable options for making the journey. Because of the distance, most visitors decide to fly from Bangkok to Northern Thailand. The 70-minute flight to Chiang Mai and the 90-minute flight to Chiang Rai are relatively inexpensive. (If you have the time to shop around, you can arrange flights with most travel agents for as low as $25.) The airports of both Chiang Mai and Chiang Rai are a 10–15 minute taxi ride from city centers. Express trains and long-distance buses take either an entire day or night to cover the distance. Trains are among the most comfortable in Southeast Asia, and even second-class sleeper accommodations compare favorably with American and European standards. Long-distance buses—the most comfortable are termed VIP—have fully reclinable seats, hostesses serving snacks and drinks, and TV (although they usually show absurd Thai comedies). The bus fare (less than $20) includes lunch or supper at a stop along the way.

Regional buses connect Chiang Mai to nearby towns such as Lamphun and Lampang, which make them easy excursions. The Golden Triangle and the mountains near the Myanmar border, home of many hill tribes, are farther afield, but are readily accessible by air or by bus.

Chiang Mai

696 km (430 mi) north of Bangkok.

Chiang Mai's rich history stretches back 700 years to the time when several small tribes, under King Mengrai, banded together to form a new nation called Anachak Lanna Thai. Their first capital was Chiang Rai, but after three decades they moved it to the fertile plains near the Mae Ping River to a place they called Napphaburi Sri Nakornping Chiang Mai.

The Lanna Thai eventually lost their independence to Ayutthaya and, later, to Myanmar. Not until 1774—when the Burmese were finally driven out—did the region revert to the Thai kingdom. After that, the region developed independently of southern Thailand. Even the language is different, marked by a more relaxed tempo. In the last 50 years the city has grown beyond its original borders; the provincial capital has exploded beyond its moated city walls, expanding far into the neighboring countryside.

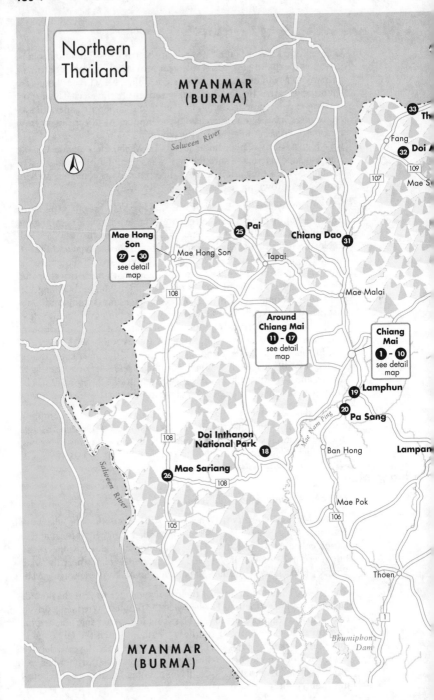

Northern Thailand

MYANMAR
(BURMA)

Salween River

33 Th

Fang

32 Doi

109

Mae S

107

25 Pai

Chiang Dao

31

Mae Hong Son
27 – **30**
see detail map

Mae Hong Son

Tapai

Mae Malai

108

Around Chiang Mai
11 – **17**
see detail map

Chiang Mai
1 – **10**
see detail map

19 **Lamphun**

20 **Pa Sang**

Mae Nam Ping

Doi Inthanon National Park
18

Ban Hong

Lampan

108

26 **Mae Sariang**

108

Mae Pok

106

105

Salween River

Thoen

1

Bhumiphon Dam

MYANMAR
(BURMA)

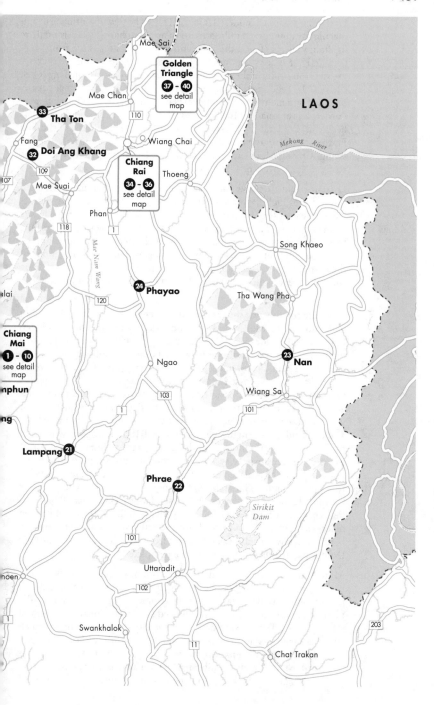

First impressions of modern Chiang Mai can be disappointing. The immaculately maintained railroad station and the chaotic bus terminal are in shabby districts, and the drive into the city center is far from spectacular. First-time visitors ask why they can't see the mountains that figure so prominently in the travel brochures. Once you cross the Ping River, Chiang Mai begins to take shape. The Old City is roughly one mile square, bounded by a moat where fountains splash and locals stroll along a flower-bordered promenade. Much of the wall that once encircled the city has been restored, and the most important of its five original gates, called Pratou Tapei, fronts a broad square where markets are constantly in full swing. Chiang Mai's brooding mountain, Doi Suthep, is now in view, rising in steps over the Old City.

Enter the Old City and you're in another world. Buildings more than three stories high have been banned, and guesthouses and restaurants vie with each other for the most florid decoration. Many of the streets and *sois* (alleys) have been paved with flat, red cobblestones. Strolling these narrow lanes, lingering in the quiet cloisters of a temple, sipping hill tribe coffee at a wayside stall, and fingering local fabrics in one of the many boutiques are among the chief pleasures of a visit to Chiang Mai. Whenever you visit, there's bound to be a festival in progress.

The Old City

Covering roughly one square mile, the patchwork of winding lanes that make up Chiang Mai's Old City is bounded by remains of the original city wall and a wide moat. Connected by about half a dozen major thoroughfares, this system of one-way streets can be confusing for a newcomer. The plan, however, keeps traffic moving quite effectively around the moat, which is crossed by bridges at regular intervals. The compact Old City can be explored easily on foot or by bicycle. Tuk-tuks and songthaews cruise the Old City and can easily be flagged down if you tire or want to take a trip outside the ancient walls. Count on paying B50 for a tuk-tuk ride to the night market area or B10 if a songthaew is going that way. Under a multimillion dollar program to improve the sometimes chaotic transport system, the songthaews are gradually being phased out, to be replaced by metered taxis. It will take a few years before taxis are a familiar sight on Chiang Mai roads, but you can have your hotel arrange one for you. The basic charge is B30, plus a B20 booking fee. If you hire a taxi for a day (B1,000–B1,400, depending on mileage), negotiate the price in advance or, better yet, arrange it the evening before and have the driver collect you from your hotel in the morning. Do not pay the driver until you have completed the trip.

Motorcycles are a cheap and popular option. Rental agencies are numerous, and most small hotels have their own agency. A car and driver is the most convenient way to visit the temples outside the city. If you're planning on driving yourself you'll need an international license—and strong nerves. Try to avoid driving in the city during rush hour, which starts as early 7 AM in the morning and 3 PM in the afternoon, and pay special attention to no-parking restrictions (usually 9 AM–noon and 3 PM–6 PM). Many streets prohibit parking on alternate days, but the explanatory signs are in Thai. Your best bet is to note on which side of the street vehicles are parking. Chiang Mai's traffic police are merciless and clamp and tow away vehicles parked illegally. Parking lots are numerous and charge only about B20 for all-day parking.

a good tour

Start your tour at the Tha Pae Gate, which leads through the ancient city walls into the oldest part of Chiang Mai. Head west on Ratchadamnoen Road, turning north on Ratchaphakhina Road. After a few blocks you reach **Wat Chiang Man** ❶, the oldest temple in Chiang Mai. Check out the pair of Buddha statues in the viharn. Backtrack down Ratchaphakhina Road and head west on Ratchadamnoen Road. At the next set of traffic lights, at the corner of Phra Pokklao Road you'll find a shrine and plaque commemorating Chiang Mai's founder, King Mengrai, who, say the history books, was struck dead by lightning at this spot. Continue on down Phra Pokklao Road for 200 yards and King Mengrai's statue stands, together with two provincial rulers who helped him found Chiang Mai, in front of the city museum, which also once housed a local ruler. Retrace your path along Phra Pokklao Road, and between Rajmankha and Ratchadamnoen roads, stands **Wat Chedi Luang** ❷. Most striking is the ruined chedi. A bit farther west is **Wat Phra Singh** ❹, whose colorfully decorated viharn typified Lanna Thai architecture.

Several other worthwhile temples are outside the city walls. To the east is the serene **Wat Chaimongkol** ❺. It's an easy walk from the Tha Pae Gate if the sun isn't too strong. You'll want to take a tuk-tuk to **Wat Suan Dok** ❻, one of the largest temples in the region. A bit farther away are the verdant grounds of **Wat Umong** ❼.

Most temple complexes open as early as 6 AM and don't close until 6 or 8 PM, although the hours can be irregular and you might find the doors locked for no reason. If that's the case, approach any monk and explain you'd like to visit. He'll normally open up. There's no admission charge, but leave some small change in one of the collection boxes found throughout the compound. (By making a donation you're also "making merit" and easing your journey to the hereafter.) Candles, incense, and lotus blossoms are another source of income for the temples. In some temples, caged birds are for sale—you're expected to set them free, another means of making merit.

TIMING If you don't venture beyond the city walls, you can see the three main temples in a few hours. If you want to visit the nearby wats, plan on at least half a day.

What to See

❸ **Chiang Mai City Art & Cultural Center.** The handsome city museum is housed in a colonnaded palace that was the official residence of the last local ruler, Chao Inthawichayanon. Around its quiet central courtyard are 15 rooms with exhibits documenting the history of Chiang Mai. The palace was built in 1924 in the exact center of the city, site of the ancient city pillar that now stands in the compound of nearby Wat Chedi Luang. In front of the museum sits a statue of the three kings who founded Chiang Mai. ✉ *Phra Pokklao Rd.* ☎ *053/217793 and 053/219833* 🎟 *B30* ⏲ *Tues.–Sun. 8:30–5.*

Chiang Mai

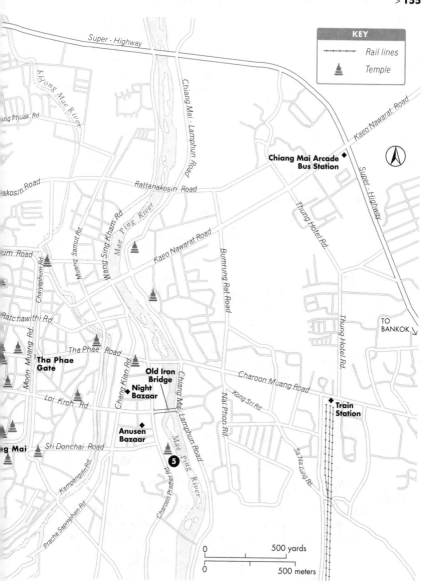

KEY

┽─┼─┼─ Rail lines

▲ Temple

Super - Highway

Khlong Mae River

ng Phuak Rd

Chiang Mai - Lamphun Road

Kaeo Nawarat Road

akosin Road

Rattanakosin Road

Chiang Mai Arcade Bus Station ◆

Super - Highway

Mae Ping River

um Road

Wang Sing Kham Rd

Muang Samut Rd

Kaeo Nawarat Road

Bumrung Rat Road

Thung Hotel Rd

Chaiyaphum Rd

Ratchawithi Rd

Tha Phae Road

TO BANKOK

Moon Muang Rd.

Tha Phae Gate

Chiang Klan Rd

Old Iron Bridge

Chiang Mai - Lamphun Road

Charoon Muang Road

Thung Hotel Rd

Loi Kroh Rd

Night Bazaar

Kong Sri Rd

Nai Phon Rd.

Train Station ◆

Anusen Bazaar

Sri Donchai Road

Mae Ping River

Sa Na Luang Rd

g Mai

Kampaengdin Rd

⑤

Charoon Muang Rd

Practa Sapmphan Rd

0		500 yards
0		500 meters

⑩ Chiang Mai Tribal Museum. This museum has more than 1,000 pieces of traditional crafts from the hill tribes living in the region. The varied collection—farming implements, hunting traps, weapons, colorful embroidery, and musical instruments—is one of the finest in the country. Its in Ratchangkla Park, off the road to Mae Rim, about 1 km (½ mi) from the National Museum. ⊠ *Ratchangkla Park, Chotana Rd.* ☎ *053/ 210872* 🖼 *Free* ⊙ *Daily 9–4.*

☺ Museum of World Insects & Natural Wonders. Save a visit to this offbeat museum for a rainy day. Children love its oddball collection of creepy-crawlies, which include enormous centipedes, beetles, moths, and gaudy butterflies. ⊠ *72 Soi 13, Nimmanhemin Rd.* ☎ *053/211891* 🖶 *053/ 410916* 🖼 *B100* ⊙ *Daily 8:30–4:30.*

❾ National Museum. This Northern Thai–style building contains many statues of Lord Buddha, including a bust that measures 10 feet. There's also a huge Buddha footprint of wood with mother-of-pearl inlay. The exhibits have been skillfully arranged into topics such as the early history of the Lanna region, the founding of Chiang Mai, and the development of city's distinctive art forms. The centerpiece of one display is a regal bed covered with mosquito netting that was used by an early prince of Chiang Mai. ⊠ *Chiang Mai-Lampang Rd.* ☎ *053/221308* 🖶 *053/408568* 🖼 *B30* ⊙ *Daily 9–4.*

Sbun-nga Museum. More than 1,000 rare textiles from the royal courts of Thailand and Myanmar are displayed in this important museum, the largest of its kind in the country. The museum is part of the Old Chiang Mai Cultural Center. Combine a visit to the museum with a buffet lunch at the modest restaurant, which serves Northern Thai specialties from clay pots. ⊠ *Wualai Rd.* ☎ *053/200655* 🖼 *Free* ⊙ *Thurs.–Tues. 10:30–6:30.*

★ ❺ Wat Chaimongkol. Although rarely visited, this small temple is well worth the journey. Its little chedi contains holy relics, but its real beauty lies in the serenity of the grounds. Located outside the Old City near the Mae Ping River, it has only 18 monks in residence. ⊠ *Charoen Prathet Rd.*

❷ Wat Chedi Luang. In 1411 King Saen Muang Ma ordered his workers to
FodorsChoice build a chedi "as high as a dove could fly." He died before the structure was finished, as did the next king. During the reign of the following king, an earthquake knocked down about a third of the 282-foot spire. Wat Chedi Luang is now a superb ruin. Don't miss the naga balustrades at the steps to the viharn, considered the finest of their kind. ⊠ *Phra Pokklao Rd. between Rajmankha and Ratchadamnoen Rds.*

> **need a break?** Chiang Mai has no shortage of massage parlors (the respectable kind) where the aches of a day's strenuous sightseeing can be kneaded away with a traditional massage. The full body massage takes two hours and costs around B200. Your hotel can usually organize either an in-house massage or recommend one of the city's numerous centers. One of the best massage parlors is **O. T. Traditional Thai Massage Center** (⊠ 459/100 Charoenmuang Rd. ☎ 053/302665), at the Charoenmuang Bazaar. **Petngarm Hat Wast** (⊠ 33/10 Charoen

Prathet Rd. ☏ 053/270080), in the Diamond Hotel, offers a range of traditional and herbal massages. Good massages with or without herbs are given at **Suan Samoon Prai** (✉ 105 Wansingkham Rd. ☏ 053/252716).

8 **Wat Chedi Yot.** Wat Photharam Maha Viharn is more commonly known as Wat Chedi Yot, or Seven-Spired Pagoda. Built in 1455 it's a copy of the Mahabodhi temple in Bodh Gaya, India, where the Buddha is said to have achieved enlightenment. The seven intricately carved spires represent the seven weeks that he subsequently spent there. The sides of the chedi have striking bas-relief sculptures of celestial figures, most of them in poor repair but one bearing a face of hauntingly contemporary beauty. The temple is just off the highway that circles Chiang Mai, but its green lawns and shady corners are strangely still and peaceful. ✉ *Super Hwy. between Huai Kaeo Rd. and Chang Puak Rd.*

1 **Wat Chiang Man.** Chiang Mai's oldest monastery, dating from 1296, is typical of Northern Thai architecture. It has massive teak pillars inside the bot, and two important images of the Buddha sit in the small building to the right of the main viharn. They are supposedly on view only on Sunday, but sometimes the door is unlocked. ✉ *Ratchaphakhina Rd.*

★ **4** **Wat Phra Singh.** In the western section of the Old City stands Chiang Mai's principal monastery, Wat Phra Singh. The beautifully decorated wat contains the Phra Singh Buddha, with a serene and benevolent expression that is enhanced by the light filtering in through the tall windows. Note the temple's facades of splendidly carved wood, the elegant teak beams and posts, and the masonry. Don't be surprised if a student monk approaches you—he doubtless wants to practice his English. ✉ *Phra Singh Rd. and Singharat Rd.*

6 **Wat Suan Dok.** To the west of the Old City is one of the largest of Chiang Mai's temples, Wat Suan Dok. It's said to have been built on the site where bones of Lord Buddha were found. Some of these relics are believed to be inside the chedi; others were transported to Wat Phra That Doi Suthep. At the back of the viharn is the bot housing Phra Chao Kao, a superb bronze Buddha figure cast in 1504. Chiang Mai aristocrats are buried in stupas in the graveyard. ✉ *Suthep Rd.*

7 **Wat Umong.** The most unusual temple in Chiang Mai is Wat Umong, dating from 1296. According to local lore, a monk named Jam liked to go wandering in the forest. This irritated King Ku Na, who often wanted to consult with the sage. So he could seek advice at any time, the king built this wat for the monk in 1380. Along with the temple, tunnels were constructed and decorated with paintings, fragments of which may still be seen. Beyond the chedi is a pond filled with hungry carp. Throughout the grounds the trees are hung with snippets of wisdom such as "Time unused is the longest time." ✉ *Off Suthep Rd., past Wat Suan Dok.*

Near Chiang Mai

Beyond the highway that surrounds Chiang Mai you will find plenty to hold your attention. The most famous sight is Wat Phra That Doi Suthep, the mountaintop temple that overlooks the city.

MONK CHAT

If you're like most people, a visit to Chiang Mai's numerous temples is likely to leave you full of unanswered questions. Head to Wat Suan Dok or Wat Chedi Luang, where help is at hand. The monks and novice monks who reside in the two temples eagerly welcome foreign visitors for chats about the history of their temples, the Buddhist faith, and Thai history and culture. Their enthusiasm isn't totally altruistic—they're keen to practice their English.

The talkative monks at Wat Suan Dok are all students of a religious university attached to the temple. Their "monk chat" takes place 5:30–7:30 PM on Monday, Wednesday, and Friday. Their counterparts at Wat Chedi Luang can be approached Monday to Saturday noon–6:30 PM as they relax under the trees of their parklike compound. They urge foreign visitors to converse with them about Lanna culture, life in a monastery, or, as one monk put it, "anything at all."

What to See

12 Chiang Mai Night Safari. Modeled on Singapore's famous game park, the Chiang Mai Night Safari realized the long-held dream of Thaksin Shinnawatra, the country's prime minister. The 100-acre reserve on the edge of the Suthep-pui National Park, 10 km (6 mi) from downtown Chiang Mai, has more than 100 species of wild animals, including tigers, leopards, jaguars and elephants. You view them from the safety of your car as they prowl the grounds after dark. ⊠ *Km 10, Chiang-Mai Hod Rd.* ☎ *B800* ⊗ *Daily 6 PM–midnight.*

☉ Chiang Mai Zoo. On the lower slopes of Doi Suthep, this zoo's cages and enclosures are spaced out along paths that wind leisurely through shady woodlands. If the walk seems too strenuous you can hop on an electric trolley that stops at all the sights. The most popular animals are two giant pandas, Lin Hui and Chuang Chuang—the only ones in captivity in Southeast Asia. ⊠ *100 Huai Kaeo Rd.* ☎ *053/221179* ☎ *B30* ⊗ *Daily 9–5.*

13 Doi Suthep National Park. You don't have to head to the distant mountains to go trekking during your stay in Chiang Mai. Doi Suthep, the 3,500-foot peak that broods over the city, has its own national park with plenty of hiking trails to explore. One of these paths, taken by pilgrims over the centuries preceding the construction of a road, leads up to a gold-spired wat. It's a half-day hike from the edge of the city to the temple compound. Set off early to avoid the heat of the midday sun. If it's not a public holiday, you'll probably be alone on the mountain.

An easy hike lasting about 45 minutes brings you to one of Chiang Mai's least known but most charming temples, **Wat Pha Lat.** This modest ensemble of buildings is virtually lost in the forest. Make sure to explore the compound, which has a weathered chedi and a grotto filled with images of the Buddha. After you leave Wat Pha Lat, the path becomes steeper. After another 45 minutes you emerge onto the mountain road,

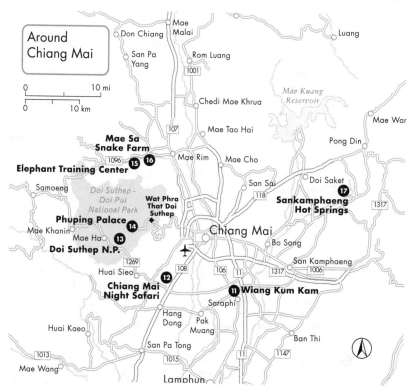

Around Chiang Mai

0 ———— 10 mi
0 ———— 10 km

Don Chiang
Mae Malai
Luang
San Pa Yang
Rom Luang
1001
Mae Kuang Reservoir
Chedi Mae Khrua
Mae War
107
Mae Tao Hai
Pong Din
Mae Sa Snake Farm
1096 **15 16**
Mae Rim
Mae Cho
Elephant Training Center
Samoeng
San Sai
Doi Saket
17
Doi Suthep – Doi Pui National Park
Wat Phra That Doi Suthep
118
Sankamphaeng Hot Springs
1317
Phuping Palace
14
Chiang Mai
Mae Khanin
Mae Ha **13**
Bo Sang
Doi Suthep N.P.
1269
San Kamphaeng
Huai Sieo
108
106
11
1317
1006
12
Chiang Mai Night Safari
11 Wiang Kum Kam
Saraphi
Hang Dong
Pak Muang
Ban Thi
Huai Kaeo
1013
San Pa Tong
1015
11
1147
Mae Wang
Lamphun

where you can flag down a songthaew if you can't take another step. Otherwise follow the road for about 200 yards and pick up the path in a break in the forest. The trail leads inexorably upward, emerging just below the naga-flanked staircase that leads to Wat Pra That. A funicular can carry you to the top, but the true pilgrim's way is up the majestic steps. Your reward is a breathtaking view from the temple's leafy terrace.

Fodor's Choice
★
The trail begins at the entrance of the national park, reached by a five-minute ride in one of the songthaews that wait for passengers at the end of Suthep Road, near the entrance to Chiang Mai Zoo. **Wat Phra That Doi Suthep** is perched on the top of 3,542-foot Doi Suthep. You can find songthaews to take you on the 30-minute drive at Chuang Puak Gate or at the Central Department Store on Huai Kaeo Road. When you arrive, you are faced with an arduous but exhilarating climb up the broad staircase leading to the temple compound. The 304-step staircase is flanked by 16th-century tiled balustrades taking the customary form of *nagas* (mythical snakes believed to control the irrigation waters in rice fields). If you find the ascent too daunting, there's also a short ride up the funicular railway.

As in so many chapters of Thai history, an elephant is closely involved in the foundation of Wat Phra That, Northern Thailand's most revered temple and one of only a few enjoying royal patronage. The elephant was dispatched from Chiang Mai carrying religious relics from Wat Suan Dok. Instead of ambling off into the open countryside, it stubbornly climbed up Doi Suthep. When it finally came to rest, and after turning in a pattern of circles given symbolic significance by the party accompanying it, the solemn decision was made to establish a temple on the site that would contain the relics. Over the centuries the temple compound grew into the glittering assembly of chedis, bots, viharns, and frescoed cloisters you see today. The vast terrace, usually smothered with flowers, commands a breathtaking view of Chiang Mai, spread out like an apron on the plain below.

Constructing the temple was quite a feat—until 1935 there was no paved road to the temple. Workers and pilgrims alike had to slog through thick jungle. The road was the result of a vast community project—individual villages throughout the Chiang Mai region contributed the labor, each laying 1,300-foot sections. ⊠ *Huay Kaew Rd.* 🚌 *B200* ⊙ *Daily 6–6.*

🖑 ⓯ **Elephant Training Center.** Animal shows aren't everybody's idea of fun, but the Elephant Training Center, about 20 km (12 mi) northwest of Chiang Mai, is actually quite entertaining. The big fellows are treated well and seem to enjoy showing off their skills. They certainly like the dip they take in the river before demonstrating log-rolling routines and giving rides around the grounds. ⊠ *Between Mae Rim and Samoeng* 🚌 *B500* ⊙ *Daily 8:30–noon.*

⓰ **Mae Sa Snake Farm.** If you're fascinated by slithering creatures, you'll find them not only at Chiang Mai Zoo but at this snake farm north of Chiang Mai (take Chotana Road north to Mae Rim, then head west to Samoeng). There are cobra shows at 11:30 AM, 2:15 PM, and 3:30 PM), during which the snakes are "milked" for their venom. ⊠ *Mae Rim-Samoeng Rd.* 🕾 *053/860719.*

> **need a break?** If you're visiting the Elephant Training Center or the Mae Sa Snake Farm, stop for lunch at **Mae Sa Valley Resort** (⊠ Mae Rim-Samoeng Rd. 🕾 053/291051 🖷 053/290017). It's a pretty place, with thatched cottages in beautifully tended gardens. The owner's honey-cooked chicken with chili is particularly good.

⓮ **Phuping Palace.** The summer residence of the royal family is a serene mansion that shares an exquisitely landscaped park with the more modest mountain retreats of the crown prince and princess. The palace itself cannot be visited, although the gardens are open Friday, weekends, and public holidays, unless any of the royal family is in residence (usually in January). Flower enthusiasts will swoon at the sight of the roses—among the lovely blooms is a variety created by the king himself. A rough, unpaved road left of the palace brings you after 4 km (2½ mi) to a village called Doi Pui Meo, where most of the Hmong women seem busy creating finely worked textiles. On the mountainside above the village are two tiny museums documenting hill tribe life and the opium trade. ⊠ *Off Huai Kaeo Rd., 6 km (4 mi) past Wat Phra That Doi Suthep.*

⑰ Sankamphaeng Hot Springs. Among the most spectacular in Northern Thailand, these hot springs include two geysers that shoot water about 30 meters into the air. The spa complex, set among beautiful flowers, includes an open-air pool and several bathhouses of various sizes. There's a rustic restaurant with a view over the gardens and small chalets with hot tubs are rented either by the hour (B200) or for the night (B800). Tents and sleeping bags can also be rented for B80. The spa is 35 mi north of Chiang Mai, beyond the village of San Kamphaeng. Songthaews bound for the spa leave from the riverside flower market in Chiang Mai. ⊠ *Moo 7, Tambon Ban Sahakorn Mae-On* ☎ *053/929077 or 053/929099* ⊠ *B20* ☉ *Daily 8–6.*

⑪ Wiang Kum Kam. When King Mengrai decided to build his capital on the Ping River, he chose a site a few miles south of present-day Chiang Mai. He selected a low-lying stretch of land, but soon realized the folly of his choice when the river flooded during the rainy seasons. Eight years after establishing Wiang Kum Kam, he moved to higher ground and began work on Chiang Mai. Wiang Kum Kam is now being excavated, and archaeologists have been amazed to uncover a cluster of buildings almost as large as Chiang Mai's Old City. Chiangmai Cattleya Tour & Travel Services offers morning and afternoon tours for B700. ⊠ *4 km (2½ mi) south of Chiang Mai on the old Chiang Mai-Lamphun Rd.* ☎ *No phone* ⊠ *Free.*

Where to Eat

All of the city's top hotels serve reasonably good food, but for the best Thai cuisine go to the restaurants in town. Several good restaurants serving Northern Thai cuisine are across from the Rincome Hotel on Nimanhaemin Road, about 1½ km (1 mi) northwest of downtown. Also try the food at the Anusan Market, found near the Night Bazaar.

★ $ ✕ **Antique House.** Built in 1870, this teak-beamed home is one of Chiang Mai's true treasures. It's furnished with the antiques from Chiang Mai's finest shops. If you like the chair you're sitting on or the table in front of you, it's possible to add to your (surprisingly modest) bill an order for a replica from a local workshop. The menu, of course, is authentic northern cuisine. A big surprise is the wine list—small but very interesting, with some real finds for oenophiles. ⊠ *71 Charoen Prathet Rd.* ☎ *053/276810* 🖷 *053/213058* ☰ *MC.*

$ ✕ **Chiengmai Gymkhana Club.** The son of the author of *Anna and the King of Siam* was among the founders of Chiang Mai's delightfully eccentric Chiengmai Gymkhana Club. Harking back to when it was founded, the club insists on keeping the spelling of the city used back in 1898. Polo isn't played as often now, but a very horsey crowd gathers regularly at the restaurant for lunch and dinner. Visitors are more than welcome. The food is remarkably good, with a variety of local and foreign dishes. Sporty types can enjoy a round of golf on the 9-hole course or a set or two of tennis. ⊠ *349 Chiang Mai-Lamphun Rd.* ☎ *053/241035 or 053/247352* ☰ *No credit cards.*

$ ✕ **The Gallery.** This riverside restaurant doubles as an art gallery, so you can admire outstanding contemporary works while waiting for your order. It's a very civilized place indeed, filled with choice antiques. There are

BACK TO SCHOOL

F SPENDING TIME IN MONASTERIES
MAKES YOU WONDER *about the lives of
the monks, or if you find yourself so
enthralled by delicious dishes that you
want to learn how to prepare them, you're
in luck. Chiang Mai has hundreds of
schools offering classes in anything from
aromatherapy to Zen Buddhism.
Alternative medicine, cooking, and
massage are the most popular courses, but
by no means the most exotic. In three
weeks at the Thailand's Elephant
Conservation Center near Lampang you
can train to become a fully qualified
mahout, though you might have difficulty
finding an elephant to look after when you
return home.*

Alternative Therapies: *Reiki, an ancient
Tibetan healing practice, is based on the
belief that therapeutic energy can be
passed from the hands of one person into
the body of another.* **Kun Chaba** *(☎ 01/
029–5833) holds two-day workshops in
her home in the Old City.*

Cooking: *Chiang Mai has dozens of
classes—some in the kitchens of
guesthouses, others fully accredited
schools—teaching the basics of Thai
cuisine. Among the best cooking classes is
the* **Baan Thai Home Cooking Course**
*(✉ 11 Ratchadamnoen Rd. ☎ 053/
357339).* **Chiang Mai Cookery School,**
*(✉ 1–3 Moon Muang Rd. ☎ 053/
206388) offers one-day courses for about
B800. One of the city's most popular
budget lodgings,* **Gap's House** *(✉ 4
Ratchadamnoen Rd., Soi 3 ☎ 053/
278140) also runs an excellent cooking
school. A trek through the mountains
usually involves eating simple meals
cooked over an open fire. One Chiang
Mai cooking course teaches how to
prepare these simple, flavorful meals. The
so-called "jungle course" is organized by*
Smile House *(✉ 5 Ratchamanka Rd., Soi 2
☎ 053/208661) and costs about B800.*

Dancing: *Surprise your friends by learning
the ancient art of Thai dancing at the* **Thai
Dance Institute** *(✉ 53 Kaokrang Rd.,
Nuanghoy ☎ 053/801375). A two-hour
course teaching you a few of the graceful
movements costs B800.*

Jewelry: *One- to five-day courses in
jewelry making are offered at* **Nova Artlab**
*(✉ 201 Tha Pae Rd. ☎ 053/273058
⊕ www.nova-collection.com). This is a
"multidisciplinary center, " so you can also
study sculpture, leatherwork, painting, and
photography. The cost is B1,100 per day.*

Language: *The* **American University Alumni**
*(✉ 73 Ratchadamnoen Rd. ☎ 053/
278407) has been teaching the Thai
language to foreigners for more than 20
years. Charges vary according to the
duration of the course and the number of
pupils.* **Corner Stone International**
*(✉ 178/233 Moo 7, Nhongkwai, Hang
Dong ☎ 053/430450) has both group
and individual instruction.*

Massage: *Held at the Chiang Mai
University Art Museum, the* **Thai Massage
School** *(✉ Nimmanhaemin Rd. ☎ 053/
907193 ⊕ www.tmcschool.com) is
authorized by the Thai Ministry of
Education. Courses lasting two to five
days cost B2,560 to B4,800.*

Yoga: *The* **Yogasala** *(✉ 48/1 Ratchamanka
Rd. ☎ 05/208452 ⊕ www.cmyogasala.
com) has a five-day yoga course that costs
B1,500.* **The Yoga Center** *(✉ 65/1 Arak
Rd. ☎ 061/927375) has five-day
workshops costing B1,800. The 90-minute
"open classes" on Tuesday, Thursday, and
weekends cost B200.*

performances of classical northern music by a small orchestra during the week, while Saturday is for jazz fans. If the music isn't your thing, you can escape to a quiet table on one of the terraces descending to the Mae Ping River. Don't miss the *nam prik ong* (spicy pork dip). ⊠ *25–29 Charoen Rat Rd.* ☎ *053/248601* ▭ *AE, DC, MC, V.*

$ ✕ **The Good View.** Of the three terraced restaurants along the Mae Ping River, this one has the best views. Its vast open-air dining room can get as noisy as a German beer hall, particularly when the band gets going, but the atmosphere is always good-humored. The menu is a mix of moderately priced Thai and international dishes. The dessert menu is totally Thai, though, and has such treats as pineapple-stuffed *rambutan* (an exotic Thai fruit). ⊠ *13 Charoen Rat Rd.* ☎ *053/302764* ▭ *MC, V.*

$ ✕ **Just Khao Soy.** Northern Thailand's favorite dish, *khao soy,* has been turned into a work of art at Shane Beary's stylish, brick-floored restaurant one block from the river. The eponymous dish—a bowl of meat soup topped up with crispy fried noodles—is served on an artist's palette, with the various condiments taking the place of the paint pots. Diners are issued aprons—eating khao soy can be messier than tackling lobster. ⊠ *108/2 Charoenphrathet Rd.* ☎ *053/818641* ▭ *DC, MC, V.*

$ ✕ **La Gondola.** Chiang Mai has more than a dozen Italian restaurants, but La Gondola is regarded as one of the best. A glassed-in dining room is bordered on two sides by a terrace overlooking the river. There's something festive about the white-and-gold decor, matched by crisp table linens and sparkling table settings. The pasta certainly has no match elsewhere in Chiang Mai, and it would be hard to find a more comprehensive wine list. Reservations are advised on weekends. ⊠ *Rimping Condominium, 201/6 Charoen Rat Rd.* ☎ *053/306483* ▭ *AE, DC, MC, V.*

$ ✕ **Mango Tree Café.** A mango-yellow sign welcomes you to this small restaurant, where you can sip a coffee while you leaf through one of the newspapers and magazines or settle in for a full meal. The atmosphere isn't your typical Thai, but the menu is—try the fried fish with chilli sauce or the curried crab. ⊠ *8/2 Loi Khroa Rd.* ☎ *053/208292* ▭ *No credit cards.*

$ ✕ **The Riverside.** Housed in a century-old teak house on the banks of the Mae Ping River, this casual restaurant serves Western favorites given some extra zing by the Thai chef. The conversation-laden atmosphere attracts young Thais as well as Westerners, and with lots of beer flowing the food gets only partial attention. Choice tables are on the deck, where you're treated to views of Wat Phra That, a golden-spired temple that sits on the summit of distant Doi Suthep. There's live light jazz and pop music after 7 PM. ⊠ *9–11 Charoentat Rd.* ☎ *053/243239* ⚑ *Reservations not accepted* ▭ *No credit cards.*

$ ✕ **Whole Earth.** On the second floor of an attractive old house, this longtime favorite serves delicious and healthy foods. It's mostly vegetarian fare, but there are a few meat dishes for the carnivorous, such as *gai tahkhrai* (fried chicken with lemon and garlic). Many of the favorites here, including the tasty eggplant masala, are Indian dishes. The dining room is air-conditioned, and the garden terrace that surrounds it takes full advantage of any breezes. The service is sometimes slow. ⊠ *88 Sridonchai Rd.* ☎ *053/282463* ⚑ *Reservations not accepted* ▭ *No credit cards.*

Where to Stay & Eat in Chiang Mai

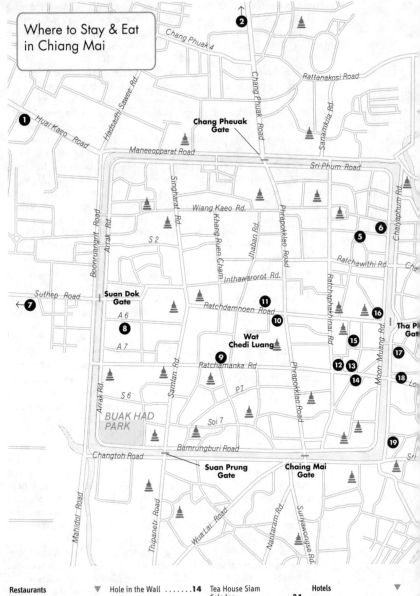

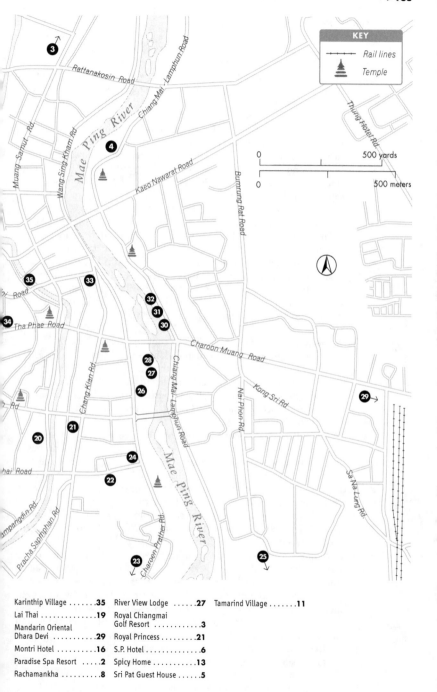

¢–$ ✕ **Hole in the Wall.** The name is something of a misnomer—the Hole in the Wall is open and airy. This pub has a gracefully curved bar, beamed ceiling, and half-timbered walls edged with brick. In the corner is the obligatory dartboard. The food is defiantly English, meaning you can opt for a slab of fish and chips or a plate of shepherd's pie. But judging from the compliments scrawled in many languages across one wall, it seems to find international favor. ✉ *39/7–8 Ratchamanka Rd.* ☎ *053/ 283824* ▭ *No credit cards.*

★ ¢–$ ✕ **Tea House Siam Celadon.** Escape the hustle and bustle of busy Tapei Road by stepping into the cool interior of this exquisitely restored century-old Chinese merchant's house. You enter through a showroom of fine celadon pottery and an adjoining courtyard flanked by tiny boutiques selling Lanna fabrics. The fan-cooled tearoom is a teak-floored salon furnished with wrought iron and glass. The menu is limited, mostly sandwiches and salads, but the pastries are among Chiang Mai's best. ✉ *158 Tha Pae Rd.* ☎ *053/234518* ▭ *AE, MC, V* ☽ *No dinner.*

¢–$ ✕ **Tha Nam.** The Ping River meanders past the outdoor terrace of this rambling old Thai house. The upper floor, where a classical trio plays for evening diners, is so old and creaking that it tilts like the main deck of a schooner in a storm. The lower terrace is a lush tropical garden, shaded by enormous trees older than the house itself. The extensive menu is packed with Thai specialties—try the *hang le* (pork curry with ginger) or the chicken wrapped in pandanus leaves. ✉ *43/3 Moo 2, Chang Klan Rd.* ☎ *053/275125* 🖷 *053/282988* ▭ *AE, MC, V.*

¢–$ ✕ **The Wok.** One of Chiang Mai's best cooking schools is fronted by this excellent restaurant. If the ancient teak house at the heart of the establishment is crowded, grab a table in the shrub-festooned garden. The menu is packed with local specialties like *nam prik ong* (minced pork dip), and the puddings are a delight—particularly the black rice and the pumpkin in coconut milk. ✉ *44 Ratchamanka Rd.* ☎ *053/208287* ▭ *AE* ☽ *No lunch Mon.*

¢–$ ✕ **The Writers Club & Wine Bar.** You don't have to be a journalist to dine at Chiang Mai's unofficial press club—the regulars include not only media types but anyone from hard-up artists and eccentric local characters to successful entrepreneurs. Local venison, wild boar, and rainbow trout from Thailand's highest mountain range frequently appear on the ever-changing menu, and the house wines are that rare vintage—good and sensibly priced. Reservations are recommended on Friday and Sunday. ✉ *141/3 Ratchadamnoen Rd.* ☎ *01/928–2066* ▭ *No credit cards* ☽ *Closed Sat.*

¢ ✕ **Arun Rai.** Chef Khun Paichit smiles when she says that some travelers have been so taken with her food that they return again and again during their stay in Chiang Mai. For more than 30 years she has prepared such traditional northern dishes as frogs' legs fried with ginger, and she's added to the menu at about the same rate as the size of her dining room. Try the *tabong* (boiled bamboo shoots fried in batter) and *sai ua* (pork sausage with herbs). ✉ *45 Kotchasarn Rd.* ☎ *053/276947* 🖆 *Reservations not accepted* ▭ *No credit cards.*

★ ¢ ✕ **Huen Phen.** The small rooms in this restaurant, once a private home, are full of handicrafts that are typical of the region. Select a table in any of the dining rooms or out among the plants of the garden. The house and garden are open only in the evening; lunch is served in a streetfront extension packed daily with hungry Thais. The *kaeng hang led* (northern pork curry) with *kao nio* (sticky rice) is a specialty. The *larb nua* (spicy ground beef fried with herbs) and deep-fried pork ribs are two more dishes you won't want to miss. ⊠ *112 Ratchamanka Rd.* ☎ *053/ 277103* ▭ *MC, V.*

Where to Stay

Chiang Mai's top hotels rival those in Bangkok, with prices about half what you'd expect to pay in the capital (although in January and February surcharges tend to close the gap). The west side of Chiang Mai, toward Wat Phra That Doi Suthep, is where you'll find several of the most expensive hotels; it's a quieter part of the city, but also far from many points of interest. Unlike in Bangkok, the luxury hotels do not enjoy a monopoly on river frontage, and some charming and modestly priced guesthouses are right on the water. There are also small hotels within the walls of the Old City that are cheap and ideally located for sightseeing.

Some unscrupulous taxi and tuk-tuk drivers will try to get you to change your hotel for one they recommend (and which gives them a commission). It's seldom a good idea, as you won't have any idea about the quality of the establishment. Remain firm and insist on being taken to your original destination.

$$$$ 🖼 **The Chedi.** The city's newest waterfront hotel sits in isolated splendor between the Mae Ping River and one of the city's busiest streets. Rooms and suites have their own private courtyard entrances and terraces overlooking either the river or the mountains. Suites have access to a lounge serving complimentary breakfast, afternoon tea, and evening cocktails and canapes. ⊠ *144/1 Charoen Prathet Rd. 50200* ☎ *053/ 904555* 🖷 *053/904777* ⊕ *www.ghmhotels.com* ↝ *84 rooms* ♻ *Restaurant, room service, IDD phones, minibars, cable TV with movies, pool, gym, spa, babysitting, dry cleaning, laundry service, business services, travel services* ▭ *AE, DC, MC, V* ⊙ *BP.*

$$$$ 🖼 **Four Seasons.** Formerly the Regent, the magnificent Four Seasons stands
Fodor'sChoice on a hilltop above the lush Mae Rim Valley. It commands a view of ver-
★ dant mountains, tropical gardens, and its own manicured rice paddies. The accommodations are in clusters of Lanna-style buildings. Each suite has an outdoor *sala* (gazebo) ideal for breakfast or cocktails. Rooms of polished teak are furnished with richly colored fabrics and traditional art. The restaurant, which serves beautifully presented Thai dishes, overlooks the valley. ⊠ *Mae Rim-Samoeng Old Rd., 50180* ☎ *053/298181, 800/545-4000 in U.S* 🖷 *053/298190* ⊕ *www. fourseasons.com* ↝ *67 suites* ♻ *2 restaurants, room service, IDD phones, minibars, cable TV, 2 tennis courts, pool, health club, bar, laundry service, business services* ▭ *AE, DC, MC, V.*

★ **$$$$** 🖼 **Mandarin Oriental Dhara Devi.** This extraordinary resort is one of the most lavish in Southeast Asia. Regal in scale and style, it's a huge contrast to the shabby neighborhood guests must navigate to reach it. Even the most modest of its accommodations is palatial. The "residences"— really free-standing villas, many with private pools—are grouped around landscaped rice fields worked by buffaloes. Concerts are given in the cultural center (with a library of 5,000 volumes) or in the outdoor amphitheater. A temple and weathered chedi were built to add historical character. Even if you're not staying the night, visit the pavilionlike King's Room—so named because the king dined here. ⊠ *51/4 Chiang Mai-Sankampaeng Rd., Moo 1, Tambon Tasala, 50000* 🕾 *053/888888* 🖷 *053/888999* ⊕ *www.mandarinoriental.com* ⇒ *101 suites, 34 residences* ♢ *2 restaurants, café, room service, IDD phones, in-room hot tubs, kitchens, minibars, cable TV with movies, 2 tennis courts, pools, lake, health club, hair salon, massage, spa, squash, 2 bars, lobby lounge, lounge, piano bar, concert hall, theater, library, shops, dry cleaning, laundry facilities, concierge, business services, convention center, airport shuttle, travel services* ⊟ *AE, DC, MC, V.*

★ **$$$$**   🏨 **Rachamankha.** On a quiet lane near Wat Pra Singh, the Rachamankha is one of the newest of the city's luxury resorts. Visually an extension of the temple compound, the hotel is a series of hushed brick courtyards enclosed by triple-eaved Lanna-style buildings. Most of the rooms, all furnished with Lanna or Chinese antiques, are set along green lawns planted with tall palms and fragrant frangipani. Collections of rare 19th-century Lanna scripture boxes and Burmese manuscript chests stand guard outside the rooms. The courtyard swimming pool is a blue haven of peace. The lounge is a replica of a Chinese reception hall, its beamed and tiled ceiling supported by massive crimson wood columns. ⊠ *Ratchamanka Rd., Soi 9, 50200* 🕾 *053/904111* 🖷 *053/904114* ⊕ *www.rachamankha.com* ⇒ *21 rooms, 1 suite* ♢ *Restaurant, room service, IDD phones, cable TV with movies, pool, bar, dry cleaning, laundry services, business center, airport shuttle, car rental, travel services* ⊟ *AE, DC, MC, V* ⊺⊙⊺ *CP.*

$$$ 🏨 **Tamarind Village.** A canopy of towering, interlaced bamboo leads to the main entrance of this stylish, village-style hotel in the center of the Old City. Beyond the entrance is a blue pool, embraced by whitewashed corridors that lend a feeling of contemplative peace. Rooms, furnished in tones of cream and teak, surround a garden dominated by a venerable old tamarind tree. An excellent restaurant fits snugly into one corner of the complex. ⊠ *50/1 Ratchadamnoen Rd., 50200* 🕾 *053/418898* 🖷 *053/418900* ⊕ *www.tamarindvillage.com* ⇒ *40 rooms* ♢ *Restaurant, room service, minibars, cable TV, pool, dry cleaning, laundry service* ⊟ *AE, MC, V.*

$$–$$$ 🏨 **Royal Chiangmai Golf Resort.** Although this luxurious resort in the hills about 25 km (18 mi) outside Chiang Mai is geared for golfers (greens fees are included in the room rate), visitors who value tea over tee are also pampered—and receive a B1,000 rebate if they renounce the pleasure of playing the resort's fine 18-hole course. The luxuriously appointed rooms, in gleaming white wings that embrace a large swimming pool, overlook either the golf course or the surrounding rolling countryside. ⊠ *169 Moo 5, Prao Rd., 5000* 🕾 *053/849301, 02/233–7950 in Bangkok* 🖷 *053/849310* ⊕ *www.royalchiangmai.co.th* ⇒ *60 rooms* ♢ *Restaurant, IDD phones, minibars, 18-hole golf course, pool, gym, massage, sauna, airport shuttle* ⊟ *AE, MC, V.*

$$ 🏨 **Chiang Mai Orchid.** With teak pillars lining the lobby, the Chiang Mai Orchid is a grand hotel in the old style. The rooms are tastefully furnished and trimmed with hardwoods. The lavish honeymoon suite is often used by the crown prince. You can dine at either the formal Le Pavillon, which serves French fare, or at Puping, where you can enjoy Chinese favorites. The more informal Mae Rim Café features a buffet. You'll want to stop for a cocktail in the lobby bar where a pianist plays nightly, or the cozy Opium Den. The hotel is a 10-minute taxi ride from the center of Chiang Mai. ⊠ *23 Huai Kaeo Rd., 50000* ☎ *053/222099, 02/714–2521 in Bangkok* 🖷 *053/221625* ⊕ *www.chiangmaiorchid. com* ⟳ *364 rooms* ⏦ *2 restaurants, coffee shop, room service, IDD phones, minibars, cable TV, pool, health club, hair salon, massage, sauna, 2 bars, dry cleaning, laundry service, business services, meeting rooms, travel services* ▱ *AE, DC, MC, V.*

$$ ▦ **Imperial Mae Ping.** The elegant curved facade of the Imperial Mae Ping resembles the side of a luxury cruise ship tethered to the center of Chiang Mai. Everything about the hotel is vast, from the extensive gardens to the marble, mirrored, and pillared lobby. Rooms are furnished in shades of softly-lit ocher. Two of the floors have butlers assigned to each room. Four restaurants serve Thai, Chinese, Japanese and Western food, and in late 2004 a beer garden tapped its first barrel. ⊠ *153 Sridonchai Rd., 50100* ☎ *053/283900, 02/261–9460 in Bangkok* 🖷 *053/270181* ⊕ *www.imperialhotels.com/maeping/* ⟳ *336 rooms, 35 suites* ⏦ *4 restaurants, coffee shop, room service, IDD phones, minibars, cable TV, pool, massage, bar, beer garden, dry cleaning, laundry service, meeting rooms, travel services* ▱ *AE, DC, MC, V.*

$$ ▦ **Royal Princess.** This centrally located hotel is ideal if you'd like to step out of the lobby and into the tumult of downtown Chiang Mai. The bustling Night Market is right at the front door and the famous Night Bazaar is barely a block away. Rooms have been upgraded and reflect the light, airy atmosphere of the lobby, where a pianist or a Thai trio play nightly. The swimming pool and its tropical garden terrace and bar are a welcome retreat after a day's sightseeing or shopping. A café and two restaurants offer a range of Thai, Chinese, and Japanese dishes, as well as some international favorites. ⊠ *112 Chang Klan Rd., 50000* ☎ *053/281033* 🖷 *053/281044* ⊕ *www.royalprincess.com* ⟳ *182 rooms, 16 suites* ⏦ *2 restaurants, café, 2 bars, room service, IDD phones, minibars, cable TV, pool, massage, dry cleaning, laundry service, meeting rooms, airport shuttle, travel services* ▱ *AE, DC, MC, V.*

$–$$ ▦ **Paradise Spa Resort.** Nina Boonsirithum graduated from Washington State University with a degree in interior design, and her background shows in the exquisitely attractive layout of this lakeside retreat near Chiang Mai. Ask for one of the special spa rooms, which have huge marble sunken baths and luxurious furnishings. Richly colored fabrics are used throughout, complemented by fine carvings. The airy restaurant has an adjacent antiques shop stocked with items that caught Boonsirithum's expert eye. ⊠ *43/1 Moo 6, Tambon Maerim, 50000* ☎ *053/ 860463* 🖷 *053/860468* ⊕ *www.paradisesparesort.com* ⟳ *50 rooms* ⏦ *Restaurant, cable TV, spa, bar* ▱ *MC, V.*

$ ▦ **Karinthip Village.** A statue of a mythical winged elephant welcomes you at the entrance of the Karinthip, one of many traditional Lanna touches that distinguish the hotel from others in this otherwise rather shabby corner of town. Chinese influences are also present, particularly in the furnishings of many of the rooms. For an extra B1,000 or so you can sleep in a Lanna-style four-poster, while B6,000 suites have whirl-pool bath tubs and crimson-and-pink bedrooms complete with Chinese-style lounge chairs. ⊠ *50/2 Changmoikao Rd., 50300* ☎ *053/235414 or 053/874302* 📠 *053/874306* ⊕ *www.karinthipville.com* 💬 *62 rooms, 5 suites* ⚐ *Restaurant, pool, bar, laundry service, travel services* ▭ *AE, DC, MC, V.*

★ $ ▦ **River View Lodge.** Facing a grassy lawn that runs down to the Mae Ping River, this lodge lets you forget the noise of the city. The restful rooms have terra-cotta floors and locally made wood furniture; some have private balconies overlooking the river. Although it couldn't be called luxurious, there's a restful simplicity here that's a far cry from the uniformity of many of the city's hotels. The small restaurant has an adequate menu, and the veranda overlooking the pool is a good place for afternoon tea. After dark, it's an easy 10-minute walk to the Night Bazaar. ⊠ *25 Charoen Prathet Rd., Soi 4, 50100* ☎ *053/271109* 📠 *053/ 279019* ⊕ *www.riverviewlodgch.com* 💬 *33 rooms* ⚐ *Restaurant, IDD phones, in-room safes, pool, laundry service* ▭ *MC, V.*

★ ¢   ▦ **Galare Guest House.** This pleasant guesthouse on the Mae Ping River has a location that is the envy of many of the city's top hotels—its gardens lead right down to the river. Even better, it's a short walk to the Night Bazaar. The teak-paneled rooms are simply but adequately furnished and overlook a tidy garden. The terrace restaurant faces the river. The staff is happy to assist with all travel requirements, from bus, train, and plane tickets to visas to Myanmar and Laos. ⊠ *7 Charoen Prathet Rd., Soi 2, 50100* ☎ *053/818887* 📠 *053/279088* 💬 *35 rooms* ⚐ *Restaurant, refrigerators, cable TV, laundry service, travel services* ▭ *MC, V.*

¢   ▦ **Gap's House.** This collection of traditional wooden houses resembling a little village sits on a quiet lane within the walls of the Old City. Room 5 is among the best, as it overlooks a pretty little flower garden. The main house, which has a quiet corner for reading and relaxing, is practically submerged in flowers and shrubs, enhancing the rustic look of the place. Rooms are furnished in an eclectic mix of old and new, with some genuine antiques here and there. Gap's own cooking school is among Chiang Mai's best, and you can sample its quality at the daily vegetarian buffet served up for guests. It's one of the city's most popular guesthouses, so early booking is advised. ⊠ *4 Ratchadamnoen Rd., Soi 3, 50200* ☎ *053/278140* 💬 *18 rooms* ⚐ *Bar* ▭ *MC, V.*

★ ¢   ▦ **Lai Thai.** This rambling guesthouse on a busy thoroughfare just outside the moat is a budget travelers' favorite, so book far ahead. Rooms, some of them cooled with lazily turning fans, are huddled around a courtyard with a small swimming pool. The adjacent open-air restaurant is also always buzzing with activity—this is the place to pick up helpful hints from seasoned travelers. The staff is happy to arrange excursions in the area, but the prices are a bit higher than you'll find at nearby travel agencies. ⊠ *111/4–5 Kotchasarn Rd., 50100* ☎ *053/271725* 📠 *053/ 272724* 💬 *120 rooms* ⚐ *Restaurant, IDD phones, minibars, cable TV, pool, laundry facilities, travel services* ▭ *AE, DC, MC, V.*

¢   ▦ **Montri Hotel.** Next to the Tha Pae Gate, this hotel's view of the moat makes up what it lacks in creature comforts with an unrivaled location. It's adjacent to the bars and restaurants on Tha Pae Road and Loi Khroa Road and is an easy walk to the Night Bazaar. Most of the rooms lack a view of the moat, but they are quiet. ✉ *2–6 Ratchadam-noen Rd., 50200* ☎ *053/211069 or 053/418480* 🖷 *053/217416* 🌐 *www.norththaihotel.com/montri.html* 🖙 *75 rooms* ⚐ *Restaurant, refrigerators, cable TV, laundry service, airport shuttle, travel services* ▭ *MC, V.*

★ ¢ ▦ **S. P. Hotel.** The friendliness of the welcome at this very attractive boutique hotel on the edge of the Old City is almost overwhelming. The lodging has the sophisticated air of a big city hotel, from the plush elegance of the little lobby to the romantic, pastel-shaded decor of the rooms. ✉ *7/1 Moon Muang Rd., Soi 7, 50200* ☎ *053/214522* 🖷 *053/223042* 🌐 *www.chiangmaisphotel.com* 🖙 *60 rooms* ⚐ *Restaurant, refrigerators, cable TV* ▭ *AE, MC, V.*

¢ ▦ **Spicy Home.** The incredibly low rates at this very friendly little guesthouse include an evening meal, making this an incredible deal. Kun Mim, who runs the place, is an excellent cook and has a small business on the side teaching Thai cooking. The evening meals around her dining table attract not only paying guests but friends as well, so they are a great way of breaking the ice on a first visit to Chiang Mai. Rooms are basic but functional and clean—there are only four, so it's essential to book ahead. ✉ *42/1 Ratchamanka Rd., 50200* ☎ *09/5566727* 🖙 *4 rooms* ▭ *No credit cards.*

¢ ▦ **Sri Pat Guest House.** This family-run establishment is one of the best deals in the Old City. The spotlessly clean and stylishly furnished little hotel sits on a cobbled lane a short walk from the moat. The light and airy rooms have twin beds with crisp linens and tiled baths. Som Pet market, with its jumble of stalls selling every kind of fresh produce, is just around the corner. ✉ *16 Moon Muang Rd., Soi 7, 50200* ☎ *053/218716* 🖷 *053/218718* 🌐 *www.chiangmaishotel.com* 🖙 *18 rooms* ⚐ *Restaurant* ▭ *No credit cards.*

Nightlife

This being Thailand, Chiang Mai has its share of Bangkok-style hostess bars, although nudity is taboo. If you don't want to be hassled, there are also dozens of places where you can grab a beer and listen to live music. Many restaurants, such as the Riverside, double as bars later in the evening.

BARS The western end of Loi Khroa Road, the southern end of Moon Muang Road, and the vast **Bar Beer Center** next to the Top North Hotel on Moon Muang Road have bars where the "working girls" usually outnumber the customers, but pool tables and dartboards are valid rival attractions.

Chiang Mai is proud to be the home of one of the world's top English-style pubs. Step through the gnarled door of **The Pub** (✉ 189 Huai Kaeo Rd. ☎ 053/211550) and you could be anywhere in rural England. The bar area is hung with the usual pub paraphernalia and there's a large hearth where a log fire burns on cold evenings. The clientele is drawn mostly from Chiang Mai's large expat community. Foreign residents also favor the rather shabby **Red Lion** (✉ 123 Loi Khroa Rd. ☎ 053/818847).

No city is complete without its Irish pubs, and Chiang Mai has two. They're popular with expats and locals alike.

O'Malley's Irish Pub (⊠ Anusan Market, Chang Klan Rd. ☎ 053/271921) serves draught Guinness. Regulars say it's Chiang Mai's most authentic Irish bar. **U.N. Irish Pub & Restaurant** (⊠ 24 Ratjawittee Rd. ☎ 053/214554) has a nightly entertainment program, varying from live music to movies, from quiz games to live sports. The upstairs bar, with French doors onto the street, and an small side garden are cool places to while away a warm evening.

Most bars serve wine, but two have made it their specialty: **Darling** (⊠ 49/21 Huai Kaeo Rd. ☎ 053/227427) is a chic place on a busy main road, compared by many to a smart New York bar. The owner imports his own wine. **The Writers Club & Wine Bar** (⊠ 141/3 Ratchadamnoen Rd. ☎ 01/928–2066) is Chiang Mai's unofficial press club but open to anyone who enjoys networking in good company. The decor is "eclectic colonial."

DANCE CLUBS   Chiang Mai finally has a dance club to rival the best ones in Bangkok. **X-Zone** (⊠ Osathapan Rd. ☎ 053/302989) is a warren of bars, dance floors, and show stages. It's tucked away behind the Rim Ping Supermarket on the Chiang Mai-Lamphun Road. **Bubbles** (⊠ Charoen Prathet Rd. ☎ 053/270099) is Chiang Mai's liveliest disco, packed nightly with the city's "tuppies" (Thai yuppies). It adjoins the Pornping Tower Hotel.

In the Chiang Mai Orchid Hotel, **Club 66** (⊠ 100–102 Huai Kaeo Rd. ☎ 053/222099) caters to a stylish, sophisticated crowd. For sophisticated dining and dancing, try the Empress Hotel's **Crystal Cave Supper Club** (⊠ 199/42 Chang Klan Rd. ☎ 053/270240).

CABARET   In the Las Vegas–style cabaret show staged nightly at the **Simon Chiang Mai** (⊠ 177 G Bldg., Chang Phuak Rd. ☎ 053/410321) the girls are actually boys. The costumes and sets are so spectacular, and the dance routines so decorous, that people take the whole family. The theater isn't easy to find, tucked behind the Novotel Hotel in the Chang Phuak district. Performances are at 7:30 PM and 9:30 PM.

KHANTOKE   Khantoke (or kantoke) originally described a revolving wooden tray on which food is served, but it has now come to mean an evening's entertainment combining a seemingly endless menu of northern cuisine and presentations of traditional music and dancing. With sticky rice, which you mold into balls with your fingers, you sample delicacies like *kap moo* (spiced pork skin), *nam prik naw* (a spicy dip made with onions, cucumber, and chili), and *kang kai* (a chicken and vegetable curry).

Among the best of places offering khantoke is the sumptuously templelike **Khum Khantoke** (⊠ Chiang Mai Business Park, 139 Moo 4, Nong Pakrung ☎ 053/304121). Another popular place for khantoke is **Kantoke Palace** (⊠ 288/19 Chang Klan Rd. ☎ 053/272757). At **Khum Kaew Palace** (⊠ 252 Phra Pokklao Rd. ☎ 053/214315), an authentic northern Thai house, you sit cross-legged on the floor or at long tables. The **Old Chiang Mai Cultural Center** (⊠ 185/3 Wualai Rd. ☎ 053/275097), resembling a hill tribe village, has nightly classical music and dancing after a big dinner. A traditional Northern Thai buffet is also served daily—a bargain at B60.

MUSIC   You don't have far to go to enjoy live music in Chiang Mai—wherever you're staying there's bound to be a nearby bar or restaurant where either Thai folk music or Western jazz, rock, and blues can be heard. Thai rock is the specialty of the vast beerhall called **Sai Lom Joi** (✉ 125 Chang Klan Rd. ☎ 053/247531). **Tha Nam** (✉ 43/3 Moo 2, Chang Klan Rd. ☎ 053/275125) has nightly performances of Thai classical music. Salsa and other Latin rhythms throb nightly at the **Rasta Café** (☎ 01/8829691), one of a string of small bars crammed into a rough alley off Ratchakinai Road.

The east bank of the Ping River between Nawarat Bridge and Nakorn Ping Bridge resounds nightly with live music. Most of the decibels come from **The Riverside** (✉ 9–11 Charoen Rat Rd. ☎ 053/243239). Next door, **The Good View** (✉ 13 Charoen Rat Rd. ☎ 053/221863) has a variety of bands that play nightly. Farther along the river bank, **The Gallery** (✉ 25–29 Charoen Rat Rd. ☎ 053/248601) hosts the Menam String Band, which performs early every evening except Tuesday. At 9 PM on Saturday they give the stage to Teh and Friends' Jazz Band. A few doors down, crowds pack in nightly to hear one of Chiang Mai's finest guitarists, Lek, at **The Brasserie** (✉ 31 Charoen Rat Rd. ☎ 053/241665).

Sports & the Outdoors

AMUSEMENT   Children can't get enough of the **Red Bull** (✉ Huai Kaeo Rd.), an amuse-
PARKS   ment park next to Chiang Mai's Central Department Store. The rides are exhilarating enough to keep parents amused.

BOATING   **Two-hour cruises** along Chiang Mai's Ping River depart daily between 8:30 AM and 5 PM from the **River Cruise Seafood Restaurant** (✉ Charoen Prathet Rd. ☎ 053/274822) landing at Wat Chai Mongkol, Charoen Prathet Road. A "dinner cruise" sets off nightly at 7:30 PM.

For a taste of how the locals used to travel along the Ping River, take a ride in a **scorpion-tail boat** (✉ Charoen Rat Rd. ☎ 01/960–9398 ⊕ http://scorpiontailvessel.tripod.com). The large rudder at the stern of this sturdy Siamese craft gives it its name. Trips depart daily, 8 AM–5 PM, from the Sri-Khong jetty next to the Sri-Khong temple on Charoen Rat Road, between the Nakon Ping Bridge and the Rattanagosin Bridge.

GOLF   Chiang Mai is ringed by championship golf courses that will challenge players of all levels. **Northern Express Tour** (✉ Chiang Mai–Lamphun Rd., Soi 9, Nong Hoi ☎ 09/8507344) has a "tee off service" that delivers golfers to any one of four courses near Chiang Mai. The service costs B800.

There's a 9-hole course at the **Chiengmai Gymkhana Club** (✉ 349 Chiangmai-Lamphun Rd. ☎ 053/241035 or 053/247352). Greens fees are B400 per day. The facility is a 10-minute drive from the city center.

Between the airport and the city center there's a two-tier driving range, with a good restaurant and coffee shop. (✉ 3 Ormmuang Rd.).

HORSEBACK   North of Chiang Mai, **J & T Happy Riding** (✉ Maerim-Samoeng Rd. ☎ 05/
RIDING   0361227) sponsors trail rides through the beautiful Mae Sa valley. Beginners are welcome. The stables are opposite the Mae Sa Orchid Farm.

ROCK CLIMBING   You can go rock climbing right in the center of Chiang Mai at The Peak, a three-story-tall artificial rock face. **The Peak Rock Climbing School**

(✉ 282 Chang Klan Rd. ☎ 053/800567 ⊕ www.thepeakadventure. com) offers climbs for first-timers costing B200 and three-day courses for more advanced climbers costing B5,800. A four-day tour that includes climbs up rock faces in the Pai and Mae Hong Son areas costs B7,100. The facility is on Chang Klan Road behind the Night Bazaar.

SPAS Chiang Mai has dozens of spas specializing in Thai massage and various treatments involving traditional herbs and oils.

The Oasis Spa (✉ 102 Sirimuangkalajan Rd. ☎ 053/227494 ⊕ www. chiangmaioasis.com) offers many different types of massage from Swedish to traditional Thai massage and a slew of mouth-watering body scrubs like Thai coffee, honey and yogurt or orange, almond, and honey.

At the **Ban Sabai Spa Village** (✉ 17/7 Charoen Prathet Rd. ☎ 053/285204) you can get your massage in a wooden Thai-style house or in a riverside sala. Treatments of note include a steamed herb massage, wherein a bundle of soothing herbs is placed on the body, and various fruit-based body masques like honey tamarind or pineapple.

Shopping

Day-to-day life in Chiang Mai seems to revolve around shopping. The delightful surprise is that you don't have to part with much of your hard-earned money—even the most elaborately crafted silver costs a fraction of what you'd expect to pay at home. Fine jewelry, weighed and priced at just above the current market value, pewter, leather, and silk are all on display all around the city.

Fodor'sChoice The justifiably famous **Night Bazaar,** on Chang Klan Road, is a kind of
★ open-air department store filled with stalls selling everything from inexpensive souvenirs to pricey antiques. In the afternoon and evening traders set up tented stalls, known as the Night Market, along Chang Klan Road and the adjoining streets. You're expected to bargain, so don't be shy. Do, however, remain polite. Many vendors believe the first and last customers of the day bring good luck, so if you're after a real bargain (up to 50% off) start your shopping at 9 PM.

Another permanent bazaar, the **Kalare Night Bazaar,** is in a big entertainment complex on the eastern side of the Night Market on Chang Klan Road; it's clearly marked. It's packed with boutiques, stalls, cheap restaurants, and a beer garden featuring nightly performances of traditional Thai dances. If you're in Chiang Mai on a Sunday, make for the so-called **Walking Street Market** on Ratchadamnoen Road. It's cheaper than the market on Chang Klan Road, and when the lanterns are lit at sundown it calls to mind a Mediterranean corso.

ANTIQUES If you follow certain common sense rules—examine each item very carefully for signs of counterfeiting (new paint or varnish, tooled damage marks) and ask for certificates of provenance and written guarantees that the goods can be returned if proved counterfeit—shopping for antiques should present few problems. Reputable stores will *always* give certificates of provenance, aware that penalties for dishonest trading are severe (if you're ever in doubt about a deal contact the Tourist Police). The Night Bazaar in Chiang Mai has one floor packed with antiques, many of which were manufactured yesterday (and hence come with no guarantee of authenticity). Some stalls have the genuine article, among them **Lanna Antiques** (✉ Chang Klan Rd.). It's the second booth on the second floor.

The road south to Hang Dong (take the signposted turning before the airport) is lined with antiques shops. Just outside Hang Dong you'll reach the craft village of Ban Tawai. You could spend an entire morning or afternoon rummaging through its antiques shops and storerooms.

HANDICRAFTS   For local handicrafts, head to two of Chiang Mai's main shopping streets, Tha Pae Road and Loi Khroa Road. Across the Nawarat Bridge, Charoen Rat Road is home to a row of refurbished old teak houses with a handful of boutiques selling interesting crafts such as incense candles and carved curios. Farther afield, along Nimmanhaemin Road near the Amari Rincome Hotel, a whole neighborhood of crafts shops has developed. The first lane on the left, Soi 1, has some of the most rewarding.

★   In an effort to encourage each *tambon* (community) to make the best use of its special skills, the government set up a program called **OTOP** (✉ 29/19 Singharat Rd. ☎ 053/221174 or 053/223164 ⊕ www.depthai. go.th). The program, which stands for "One Tambon, One Product, " has been a great success, especially in Northern Thailand, which has a long and active local handicraft tradition. The center has a two-story showroom with a collection that rivals many of the city's galleries and museums. The ground floor has an exquisite display of furniture and decorative items constructed in polished teak, mango, bamboo and upholstered with rattan, water hyacinth, or hand-woven textiles. Upstairs are smaller items—baskets, carvings, ceramics, textiles, and a display of rocking horses fit for the nursery of a young prince.

The money you pay for a woven mat or carved mask goes directly to the local communities at the **Hilltribe Products Promotion Center** (✉ 21/ 17 Suthep Rd. ☎ 053/277743). Here you can discover a wide range of handicrafts by Akha, Hmong, Karen, Lahu, Lisu, and Yao people in their native villages. Chiang Mai's largest handicrafts retail outlet is called the **Northern Village** (✉ Hang Dong Rd. and Mahidol Rd.). The massive store takes up two floors of the Central Airport Plaza Shopping Center. The selection here is astounding: silks and other textiles, ceramics, jewelry, carvings.

For two of Chiang Mai's specialties, lacquerware and exquisite paper products, take a taxi or songthaew to any of the outlets along San Kamphaeng Road (also known as the Golden Mile). Large emporiums that line the 10-km (6-mi) stretch sell a wide variety of items. Whole communities here devote themselves to their traditional trades. One community rears silkworms, for instance, providing the raw product for the looms humming in workshops. Among the crafts you can find are hand-painted umbrellas made from lacquered paper and tree bark. Hundreds are displayed at the **Umbrella Making Center** (✉ 11/2 Moo 3, Bor Sang ☎ 053/338324). The artists at the center will paint traditional designs on anything from a T-shirt to a suitcase—travelers have discovered that this is a very handy way of helping identify their luggage on an airport carousel.

Outside of the city center, the highways running south and east of Chiang Mai—those leading to Hang Dong and San Kamphaeng—are lined for several miles with workshops stocked with handicrafts of every description. They're a favorite destination for tuk-tuk drivers, who receive commission on goods bought by their passengers. Be very specific about what you're looking for before setting out—otherwise you might find yourself ferried to an expensive silverware outlet when all you want to buy is an inexpensive souvenir. Beyond the Hang Dong–Ban Tawai junction is a large Lanna-style crafts center called **Baan Mai Kham** (⊠ 122 Chiang Mai–Hod Rd. ☎ 04/0405007). At workshops you can see teak, mango, rattan, and water hyacinth being worked into an astonishing variety of attractive and unusual items. If you get carried away by a heavy teak piece of furniture, the dealers here will arrange for transport.

JEWELRY   Chiang Mai is renowned for its gems and semi-precious stones. Avoid unscrupulous dealers at the Night Market and head to any of the more reputable stores. If gold is your passion, head for the Chinese district. All the shops that jostle for space at the eastern end of Chang Moi Road are reliable, invariably issuing certificates of authenticity. The prices are also reasonable.

The city's silver district, Wualai Road, is lined for several hundred yards with shops where you can sometimes see silversmiths at work. **Thongyon Silverware** (⊠ 1 Soi 7, Wualai Rd. ☎ 053/202796) has been in business for more than 16 years, so you're assured of reliable service.

A very attractive Chiang Mai specialty features orchid blooms or rose petals set in 24-karat gold. There's a spectacular selection at the **Royal Orchid Collection** (⊠94–120 Charoen Muang Rd., 2nd fl. ☎053/245598).

Reliable jewelry shops include **Nova** (⊠ 201 Tha Pae Rd. ☎ 053/273058) (a jewelry school is also attached to the shop), the long-established **Shiraz** (⊠ 170 Tha Pae Rd. ☎ 053/252382) (ask for Mr. Nasser), **Sherry** (⊠ 59/2 Loi Khroa Rd. ☎ 053/273529), and **Supreme Jewelry** (⊠ Chiang Inn Plaza, 100–6 Chang Klan Rd. ☎ 053/281341).

PAPER   The groves of mulberry trees grown in Northern Thailand aren't only used to feed the silkworms—their bark, called *saa,* produces a distinctive, fibrous paper that is fashioned into every conceivable form: writing paper and envelopes, boxes, book covers, and picture frames. In Chiang Mai, **HQ PaperMaker** (⊠ 3/31 Samlan Rd. ☎ 053/814717) is the biggest and best outlet. Its first floor is a secluded gallery whose works include paintings done by elephants at the Elephant Conservation Center near Lampang. **G-Create** (⊠ 230/43 Chiang Mai-San Kamphaeng Rd. ☎ 053/330429) also has a wide selection of saa paper products.

TEXTILES   Chiang Mai and silk are nearly synonymous, and here you can not only buy the product but also to see it being manufactured. Several companies along San Kamphaeng Road open their workrooms to visitors and explain the process of making fine silk, from the silkworm to the loom. These shops are a favorite destination of package tours, so prices tend to be higher than in other parts of town or at the Night Market.

Silk and other local textiles can be reliably bought at **Chanok Silk Group** (⊠ In the Chiang Inn Plaza,100-6 Chang Klan Rd.), **Studio Naenna** (⊠ Soi 8, 138 Huai Kaeo Rd. ☎ 053/226042), and **Vaniche** (⊠ 133 Boon-raksa Rd. ☎ 053/262786).

Textiles woven in hill tribe villages can be found at **Nicha** (⊠ 86/1 Charoen Rat Rd. ☎ 053/2880470).

---

en route   About 3 km (2 mi) south of Chiang Mai, on the main road to Lamphun, is one of the most curious cemeteries in Southeast Asia. It's the **Foreign Cemetery**, a plot of land given to the expatriate community by King Chulalongkorn in the late 19th century to be held in perpetuity for the internment of foreign residents. The oldest grave contains the remains of an English soldier who rode alone into Chiang Mai from northern China and died of dysentery before he could relate to the curious locals what he was doing there. A bronze statue of Queen Victoria, empress of much of Asia at that time, watches over his tombstone and those of several Americans, most of them missionaries and teachers.

Doi Inthanon National Park

18 *90 km (54 mi) southwest of Chiang Mai.*

Doi Inthanon, Thailand's highest mountain (8,464 feet), rises majestically over a national park of staggering beauty. Many have compared the landscape with that of Canada—only the 30 villages that are home to 3,000 Karen and Hmong people remind you that this is indeed Asia. The reserve is of great interest to nature lovers, especially birders who come to see the 362 species that nest in its thick forests of pines, oaks, and laurels. Red-and-white rhododendron run riot here, as do other plants found nowhere else in Thailand.

A 48-km (30-mi) toll road winds to the mountain's summit, where the ashes of Chiang Mai's last ruler, King Inthawichayanon, are contained in a stupa that draws hundreds of thousands of pilgrims annually. Hiking trails penetrate deep into the park, which has some of Thailand's highest and most beautiful waterfalls. The Mae Klang Falls, just past the turnoff to the park, are the most accessible, but the most spectacular are the Mae Ya Falls, the country's highest, and the Siribhum Falls, which plunge in two parallel cataracts from a 500 meter-high cliff above the Inthanon Royal Research Station. The station's vast nurseries are a gardener's dream, filled with countless varieties of tropical and temperate plants. Rainbow trout—unknown in the warm waters of Southeast Asia—are raised here in tanks fed by cold streams plunging from the mountain's heights, then served at the station's restaurant. The national park office provides maps and guides for trekkers and bird-watchers. It also has accommodations available (B1,000 for a two-person chalet, B8,000 for a villa for up to eight people). ⊠ *Amphur Chomthong, 50160* ☎ *053/355728* ⊕ *www.dnp.go.th* ⊠ *B30 per person, B200 per car* ⊙ *Daily 9–6.*

Lamphun

⑲ *26 km (16 mi) south of Chiang Mai.*

Lamphun claims to be the oldest existing city in Thailand (but so does Nakhon Pathom). Originally called Nakhon Hariphunchai, it was founded in AD 660. Its first ruler was a queen, Chamthewi, who has a special place in Thailand's pantheon of powerful female leaders. There are two striking statues of her in the sleepy little town, and one of its wats bears her name. Queen Chamthewi founded the eponymous dynasty, which ruled the region until 1932.

Lamphun and the countryside surrounding it are known throughout Thailand for the *lamyai,* a sweet cherry-size fruit with a thin shell. In this region it's a big business. In the nearby village of Tongkam, the "10,000-baht lamyai tree" is said to net its owner that sum each year. A good time to visit is during the annual lamyai festival, which brings the town to a halt in the first week of August. There are parades, exhibitions, a beauty contest, and copious quantities of lamyai wine. Buy yourself a jar of lamyai-flower honey—reputed to have exceptional healing and aphrodisiac powers. You can find it on sale throughout the town.

Minibus songthaews (B10) travel from Chiang Mai to Lamphun. It's also a pleasant day's trip to drive south on Highway 106, a shady road lined by 100-foot rubber trees.

★ Lamphun's architectural treasures include two monasteries. About 2 km (1 mi) west of the town's center is **Wat Chamthewi**, often called the "topless chedi" because the gold that once covered the spire was pillaged sometime during its history. Work began on the monastery in AD 755, and despite a modern viharn added to the side of the complex, it retains an ancient weathered look. Suwan Chang Kot, to the right of the entrance, is the most famous of the two chedis, built by King Mahantayot to hold the remains of his mother, the legendary Queen Chamthewi. The five-tier sandstone chedi is square; on each tier are Buddha images that get progressively smaller. All are in the 9th-century Dvaravati style, though many have obviously been restored. The other chedi was probably built in the 10th century, though most of what you see today is the work of 12th-century King Phaya Sapphasit. You probably want to take a samlor down the narrow residential street to the complex. Since this is not an area where samlors generally cruise, ask the driver to wait for you. ⊠ *Lamphun–San Pa Tong Rd.*

Fodor'sChoice The temple complex of **Wat Phra That Hariphunchai** is dazzling. Through
★ the gates, guarded by ornamental lions, is a three-tier, sloping-roof viharn, a replica of the original that burned down in 1915. Inside, note the large Chiang Saen–style bronze image of the Buddha and the carved *thammas* (Buddhism's universal principals) to the left of the altar. As you leave the viharn, you pass what is reputedly the largest bronze gong in the world, cast in 1860. The 165-foot Suwana chedi, covered in copper and topped by a golden spire, dates from 847. A century later, King Athitayarat, the 32nd ruler of Hariphunchai, added a nine-tier umbrella, gilded with 14 pounds of gold. At the back of the compound—where

you can find a shortcut to the center of town—there's another viharn with a standing Buddha, a sala housing four Buddha footprints, and the old museum. ⊠ *Inthayongyot Rd.* 🎫 *Free* ☉ *Wed.–Sun. 8:30–4.*

Just outside Wat Phra That Hariphunchai, the **National Museum** has a fine selection of Dvaravati-style stuccowork. There's also an impressive collection of Lanna antiques. ⊠ *Inthayongyot Rd.* ☎ *053/511186* 🎫 *B10* ☉ *Wed.–Sun. 9–4.*

Lamphun has one of the region's most unusual cemeteries—literally an elephant's graveyard—called **Ku Chang.** The rounded chedi is said to contain the remains of Queen Chamthewi's favorite war elephant. ⊠ *Ku Chang Rd.*

Where to Stay & Eat

¢–$ ✕ **Add Up Coffee Bar.** This attractive riverside haunt, next door to the visitor information center, is more than just a coffee shop. Serpent's head fish from the adjacent river Kwang is one of the highly recommended dishes from the sizeable and varied menu. The freshly made pastries are worth the visit. One corner of the bright, airy establishment serves as a workshop for the owner's sister, who makes tapestry cushions and wall hangings decorated with Lanna themes. ⊠ *Lobmuangnai Rd. 22* ☎ *053/530272* ▭ *No credit cards.*

¢–$ ✕ **Lamphun Ice.** The odd name of this restaurant seems to come from its origins as an ice-cream parlor. The interior has cozy booths that give it the feel of a vintage soda fountain. The Asian food served here is the real thing—try the sensational Indian-style crab curry. ⊠ *Opposite southern gate of Wat Phra That Hariphunchai* ☎ *053/560909* ▭ *No credit cards.*

¢–$ ✕ **Ton Fai.** This restaurant, named for the colorful flame tree, occupies an ancient house and its shady backyard. Inside you can climb the stairs to a teak-floored dining room with tables set beneath the original rafters. The room is cooled by the breeze that wafts in from the nearby river through the shuttered windows. The menu is simple, but has plenty of tasty Northern Thai specialties like nam pik om. ⊠ *183 Chaimongkol Rd., Tambon Nai Muang* ☎ *053/530060* ▭ *No credit cards.*

¢ 🏨 **Supamit.** From this hotel's fifth-floor restaurant you have fine views of Wat Chamthewi, located on the opposite side of the street. Lamphun's best hotel, Supamit has rooms that are clean and comfortable. After a day touring the city's temples the airy lobby offers a cool and soothing retreat. ⊠ *Chamthewi Rd.* ☎ *053/534865* 📠 *053/534355* 🛏 *50 rooms* ♨ *Restaurant, bar* ▭ *MC, V.*

Pa Sang

⑳ *12 km (7 mi) south of Lamphun, 38 km (19 mi) south of Chiang Mai.*

At one time every other shop in this little town offered locally designed and woven cloth in traditional Lanna designs, but now these eye-catching fabrics are harder to find. However, you can still find fine examples of local work in the market. Even if you're not shopping for textiles, a visit to Pa Sang takes you through some beautiful countryside, much of it part of the Khun Tan National Park.

About 5 km (3 mi) south of Pa Sang is **Wat Phra Bhat Tak Pha,** commonly known as the Temple of the Buddha's Footprint. You can climb the 600 steps to the hilltop chedi, but the main attraction here is the two huge imprints representing Lord Buddha's foot, found indented in the floor inside the temple. As you enter, buy a piece of gold leaf to affix in the imprint. ⊠ *Pa Sang-lee Rd.*

The highway between Chiang Mai and Lampang runs through the mountainous **Doi Khun Tan National Park,** a wild upland area of great natural beauty. Since the Bangkok–Chiang Mai railroad also crosses the area, the park is run by Thailand's Royal State Railway. It has its own railroad station, an immaculately kept halt at the northern end of the country's longest railroad tunnel. A small chedi near its entrance contains the ashes of the German engineer who led construction work on tunneling through the mountain in the early years of the 20th century. When World War I broke out in 1914, Emil Eisenhofer was repatriated, but was so taken with Thailand (or Siam as it then was) that he returned after the war and he and his German wife made their home in Bangkok. His last wish was for his remains—and those of his wife—to be buried at the site of his greatest professional accomplishment. Floral tributes are regularly placed on his chedi by passing travelers.

The park has a small resort of six bungalows, the **Khun Tan Nature Land Resort** (⊠ Tambon Si Bua Ban ☎ 053/561030). The bungalows cost B800–B3,000. There's a second small resort just off the Chiang Mai-Lamphun Highway, near the entrance to the park: **Kuntan Viewpoint Resort** (☎ 053/80222 🖷 053/278396). It has 20 chalets, grouped around a small lake, costing B1,000. The resort's restaurant has a fascinating gallery of photographs documenting the construction of Eisenhofer's tunnel.

Lampang

㉑ *65 km (40 mi) southeast of Lamphun, 91 km (59 mi) southeast of Chiang Mai.*

At the end of the 19th century, when Lampang was a thriving center of the teak trade, the well-to-do city elders gave the city a genteel look by buying a fleet of English-built carriages and a stable of nimble ponies to pull them through the streets. Until then, elephants had been a favored means of transport—a century ago the number of elephants, employed in the nearby teak forests, nearly matched the city's population. The carriages arrived on the first trains to steam into Lampang's fine railroad station, which still looks much the same as it did back then. More than a century later, the odd sight of horse-drawn carriages still greets visitors to Lampang. The brightly painted, flower-bedecked carriages, driven by hardened types in Stetson hats and cowboy boots, look very touristy, but the locals also use them to get around the city. They pay considerably less than the B150 for a short city tour visitors are charged.

Apart from some noteworthy temples, not much else remains of Lampang's prosperous heyday. An ever-dwindling number of fine teak homes can be found among the maze of concrete. Running parallel to the south bank of the Wang River is a narrow street of ancient shops that once belonged to the Chinese merchants who catered to Lampang's prosperous populace. The riverfront promenade is a pleasant place for a stroll; a handful of cafés and restaurants with terraces overlooks the water.

Workers from Burma were employed in the region's rapidly expanding logging business, and these immigrants left their mark on the city's architecture. Especially well preserved is **Wat Sri Chum,** a lovely Burmese temple. Pay particular attention to the viharn, as the eaves are covered with beautiful carvings. Inside you can find gold-and-black lacquered pillars supporting a carved-wood ceiling. To the right is a bronze Buddha cast in the Burmese style. Red-and-gold panels on the walls depict temple scenes. ⊠ *Sri Chum Rd.*

Near the banks of the River Wang is **Wat Phra Kaeo Don Tao,** dominated by its tall chedi, built on a rectangular base and topped with a rounded spire. More interesting, however, are the Burmese-style shrine and adjacent Thai-style sala. The 18th-century shrine has a multitier roof. The interior walls are carved and inlaid with colored stones; the ornately engraved ceiling is painted with enamel. The sala, with the traditional three-tier roof and carved-wood pediments, houses a Sukhothai-style reclining Buddha. Legend has it that the sala was once home to the Emerald Buddha, which now resides in Bangkok. In 1436, when King Sam Fang Kaem was transporting the statue from Chiang Rai to Chiang Mai, his elephant reached Lampang and refused to go farther. The Emerald Buddha is said to have remained here for the next 32 years, until the succeeding king managed to get it to Chiang Mai. ⊠ *Phra Kaeo Rd.*

Fodor's Choice Near the village of Ko Khang is **Wat Phra That Lampang Luang,** one of
★ the most venerated temples in the north. It's also one of the most striking. Surrounded by stout laterite defense walls, the temple has the appearance of a fortress—and that's exactly what it was when the legendary Queen Chamthewi founded her capital here in the 8th century. The Burmese captured it two centuries ago, but were ejected by the forces of a Lampang prince (a bullet hole marks the spot where he killed the Burmese commander). The sandy temple compound has much to hold your interest, including a tiny chapel with a hole in the door that creates an amazing, inverted photographic image of the Wat's central, gold-covered chedi. The temple's ancient viharn has a beautifully carved wooden facade; note the painstaking workmanship of the intricate decorations around the porticoes. A museum has excellent wood carvings, but its treasure is a small emerald Buddha, which some claim was carved from the same stone as its counterpart in Bangkok. ⊠ *15 km (9 mi) south of Lampang* 🎫 *Free* 🕙 *Tues.–Sun. 9–4.*

On the main highway between Lampang and Chiang Mai is Thailand's
🅒 internationally known **Elephant Conservation Center.** So-called training
Fodor's Choice camps are scattered throughout the region, but many of them are little
★ more than overpriced sideshows. This is the real thing: a government-supported research station. Here you can find the special stables that house the white elephants owned by the king. The 36 "commoner" elephants (the most venerable are over 80) get individual care from more than 40 mahouts. The younger ones evidently enjoy the routines they perform

CloseUp

THAILAND'S ELEPHANTS

THE UNITED STATES HAS ITS EAGLE. Britain acquired the lion. Thailand's symbolic animal is the elephant, which has played an enormous role in the country's history through the ages.

Though the elephant no longer appears on the national flag, as it did when Thailand was Siam, it's still a central figure in the history and culture of the region. It's a truly regal beast—white elephants enjoy royal patronage and several are stabled at the National Elephant Institute's conservation center near Lampang.

But the elephant is also an animal of the people, domesticated some 2,000 years ago to help with the heavy work and logging in the teak forests of Northern Thailand. Elephants were in big demand by the European trading companies, which scrambled for rich harvests of teak in the late 19th century and early 20th century. At one time there were more elephants in Lamphang than people.

But elephants had other uses, more dangerous even than their work in the forest. Early on warrior rulers recognized their usefulness in battle, and "Elephants served as the armored tanks of premodern Southeast Asian armies, " according to American historian David K. Wyatt. The director of the mahout training program at the Lampang conservation center believes he is a reincarnation of one of the foot soldiers who ran beside elephants in campaigns against Burmese invaders.

Paradoxically, while many of Thailand's elephants enjoy royal status, the gentle giant is under threat from the march of progress. Ivory poaching, a cross-border trade in live elephants, and urban encroachment have reduced Thailand's elephant population from about 100,000 a century ago to just 2,500 today. Despite conservation efforts, even these 2,500 face an uncertain future as mechanization

and a 1988 government ban on private logging threw virtually all elephants and their mahouts out of work. Hundreds of mahouts took their elephants to Bangkok and other big cities to beg for money and food. The sight of an elephant begging for bananas curbside in Bangkok makes for an exotic snapshot, but the photo hides a grim reality. The elephants are kept in miserable urban conditions, usually penned in the tiny backyards of city tenements. It's been estimated that the poor living conditions, unsuitable diet and city pollution combine to reduce their life expectancy by at least five years.

A nationwide action to rescue the urban elephants and resettle them usefully in the country—mostly in Northern Thailand—is gathering pace, though. The National Elephant Institute near Lampang is a leader in this field, thanks largely to the efforts of an American expert, Richard Lair, and two young British volunteers. The 40 or so elephants who have found refuge at the center actually pay for their keep by working at various tasks, from entertaining visitors with shows of their logging skills to providing the raw material (dung) for a paper-making plant. The center has a school of elephant artists, trained by two New York artists, and an elephant orchestra. The art they make sells for $1,000 and more on the Internet, and the orchestra has produced two CDs. Several similar enterprises are dotted around Northern Thailand. All are humanely run. The alternative—a life on the streets of Bangkok—is just too depressing to consider.

–Robert Tilley

for the tourists—not only the usual log-rolling, but painting pictures (a New York auction of their work raised thousands of dollars for the center). There's even an elephant band (its trumpeter is truly a star). The elephants are bathed every morning at 9:30 and perform at 10 and 11, with an additional 1:30 show on weekends and holidays. You can even take an elephant ride through the center's extensive grounds, and if you fancy becoming a mahout you can take a residential course in elephant management. Admission is free, but performances cost B50. ⊠ *Baan Tung Kwian* ☎ *054/228034 or 054/229042* ⊠ *Free* ⊙ *Daily 8–4.*

Where to Stay & Eat

¢–$ ✕ **Krua Bangkok.** The management of this riverside restaurant has introduced Vietnamese dishes to its mostly Thai menu. It was a good move, as the Vietnamese-style eggrolls are the best this side of Hanoi. You dine either indoors beneath massive teak beams and slowly revolving fans or on the flagstone terrace overlooking the Wang river. A Thai group plays folk music every night. ⊠ *340 Tipchang Rd.* ☎ *054/310103* ⊟ *AE, MC.*

¢–$ ✕ **Riverside.** A random assortment of wooden rooms and terraces gives this place an easygoing charm. Perched above the sluggish Wang River, it's a great place for a casual meal. The moderately priced Thai and European fare is excellent, and on weekends the remarkable chef serves up the best pizza east of Italy. Most nights a live band performs, but there are so many quiet corners that you can easily escape the music. There are a handful of rooms on the lower floor if you want to stay over for the authentic American breakfast. ⊠ *328 Tipchang Rd.* ☎ *054/221861* ⊟ *054/227005* ⊟ *AE, MC, V.*

¢ ✕ **Kelang Golf Club.** You don't have to be a golfer to enjoy a simple meal at Lampang's lovely links, located about 3 km (2 mi) northeast of town. The airy terrace overlooks the club's driving range, so you can admire the skills of the city's well-heeled businessmen as they practice their swings during their lunch breaks. ⊠ *Km 3, Chiang Rai Rd.* ☎ *054/225941* ⊟ *No credit cards.*

$ 🏠 **Lampang River Lodge.** Facing the Wang River, this lodge is nestled in a tropical forest. The simple but comfortable rooms are in Thai-style wooden pavilions near a small lake where you can rent boats. The vast, airy restaurant is often crammed with tour groups, but you shouldn't have a problem securing a quiet corner. To get away from the crowds, totter over the swaying bridge to the riverside bar. The complex is 6 km (4 mi) south of Lampang. ⊠ *330 Moo 11, Baan Klang Rd., Tambon Champoo 52000* ☎ *054/334795* ⊟ *054/226922* 🛏 *47 rooms* ⚐ *Restaurant, bar, laundry service* ⊟ *AE, MC, V.*

¢ 🏠 **Asia Lampang.** Although this hotel sits on a bustling street, most of the rooms are quiet enough to ensure a good night's sleep. Some are newly renovated, so ask to see a few before you decide. The airy terrace is just the place to relax on a warm evening. If you fancy singing along with the locals, there's a delightfully named karaoke room, the Sweety Music Room. ⊠ *229 Boonyawat Rd., 52100* ☎ *054/227844* ⊟ *054/224436* 🛏 *71 rooms* ⚐ *Restaurant, bar, laundry service, business services, convention center* ⊟ *MC, V.*

¢ 🏠 **Boonma Guesthouse.** An ancient mansion was dismantled and its timbers recycled to make this charming little Lanna-style guesthouse in the heart of Lampang's Chinese quarter. Insist on one of the two upstairs rooms in the main house—they're large and denlike, with creaking teak floors and raftered ceilings. They share a country houselike lounge where antlers hang on the weathered walls. ⊠ *256 Taladkao Rd., Tambon Suandok, 52100* ☎ *054/322653 or 054/218394* ⊃ *8 rooms* � ⟁ *Café* ⊟ *No credit cards.*

¢ ▦ **Lampang Wiengthong.** One of the city's best hotels, this modern highrise has a number of luxuriously appointed rooms and suites. Its "Drinks Palace" features live music most nights. The Wiengthip coffee shop and Wiengpana restaurant rank among Lampang's smartest eateries. ⊠ *138/109 Phaholyothin Rd., 52100* ☎ *054/225801* ⊟ *054/225803* ⊃ *235 rooms* ⟁ *Restaurant, coffee shop, pool, piano bar, laundry service, business services, convention center* ⊟ *AE, MC, V.*

¢ ▦ **Pin.** This boutique-style hotel is on a quiet lane between the busy main street and the river. Rooms are decorated in pastel shades. The more expensive rooms are more comfortable, each with its own private sitting room. ⊠ *8 Suandok Rd., 52100* ☎ *054/22159, 054/22884, or 054/322283* ⊟ *054/32286* ⊕ *www.travelideas.net* ⊃ *50 rooms* ⟁ *Restaurant, bar, laundry service, business services, parking* ⊟ *MC, V.*

Shopping

Lampang is known for its blue, white, and orange pottery, much of it incorporating the image of a cockerel, the city's emblem. If you're driving you can find the best bargains at markets a few miles south of the city on the highway to Bangkok, or north of the city on the road to Chiang Mai. In Lampang, Phaholyothin Road has several small showrooms. The best place for pottery is **Srisawat Ceramics** (⊠316 Phaholyothin Rd. ☎ 054/225931).

CHIANG MAI & ENVIRONS A TO Z

AIR TRAVEL

In peak season, flights to Chiang Mai are heavily booked. Thai Airways has almost hourly flights from 7 AM to 9 PM from Bangkok (70 minutes, B2,170) and two direct flights daily from Phuket (110 minutes, B4,640). Bangkok Airways has one daily flight (three on Tuesday and Saturday) from Bangkok for the same price. Three new budget airlines offer flights for as little as B900: Orient Thai Airlines (three flights daily), Air Asia (two flights daily), and Nokair (five flights daily). They are easiest booked online or at travel agencies.

Thai Airways has two daily flights from Bangkok to Lampang (1 hour). ◪ Carriers **Air Asia** ⊕ www.airasia.com. **Bangkok Airways** ⊠ 2nd fl., Chiang Mai International Airport, Chiang Mai ☎ 053/281519. **Nokair** ⊕ www.nokair.co.th. **Orient Thai Airlines** ⊕ www.orient-thai.com. **Thai Airways** ⊠ 240 Phra Pokklao Rd., Chiang Mai ☎ 053/210210.

AIRPORTS & TRANSFERS

Chiang Mai International Airport is about 10 minutes from downtown, a B80 taxi ride. Lampang Airport is just south of downtown. Songthaews run to city centers for around B50.
◪ **Chiang Mai International Airport** ☎ 053/270222. **Lampang Airport** ☎ 054/218199.

BUS TRAVEL

So-called VIP buses ply the route between Bangkok and Chiang Mai, stopping at Lampang on the way. The privately operated coaches depart Bangkok's Northern Bus Terminal at Mo Chit almost hourly. For around B400–B500 you get a very comfortable 10-hour ride in a modern bus with reclining seats, blankets and pillows, TV, on-board refreshments—a lunch or dinner is even included in the ticket price. You can take cheaper buses, but the faster service is well worth a few extra bahts.

Chiang Mai's Arcade Bus Terminal serves Bangkok, Mae Hong Son, and destinations within Chiang Rai province. Chiang Phuak Bus Terminal serves Lamphun and destinations within Chiang Mai province. From Lampang, air-conditioned buses leave for Lamphun, Phrae, and Nan.

The easiest way to reach Lamphun from Chiang Mai is to take the minibuses that leave every 20 minutes from across the Tourism Authority of Thailand office on Lamphun Road. Both air-conditioned and non-air-conditioned buses connect Lampang to cities in the north as well as to Bangkok. Lampang's bus station is 2 km (1 mi) south of the city, just off the main highway to Bangkok.

⚏ Bus Stations **Arcade Bus Terminal** ⊠ Super Hwy. and Kaew Nawarath Rd., Chiang Mai ☎ 053/274638 or 053/242664. **Chiang Phuak Bus Terminal** ⊠ Rattanakosin Rd., Chiang Mai ☎ 053/211586. **Lampang Bus Terminal** ⊠ Chantasurin Rd., Lampang ☎ 054/227410.

CAR RENTALS

Two major car-rental agencies in Chiang Mai are Avis and Hertz. Budget has a good range of four-wheel-drive vehicles for trips off the beaten path.

⚏ Agencies **Avis** ⊠ Chiang Mai International Airport ☎ 053/201574 ⊠ Mae Hong Son ☎ 053/620457. **Budget** ⊠ Chiang Mai ☎ 053/202871. **Hertz** ⊠ 90 Sridonchai Rd., Chiang Mai ☎ 053/279474.

CAR TRAVEL

The roads south of Chiang Mai or between Chiang Mai and Chiang Rai are no problem for most drivers. Even the Mae Rim route north of Chiang Mai is perfectly drivable.

EMERGENCIES

⚏ Emergency Numbers **Police** ☎ 191. **Tourist Police** ⊠ 105/1 Chiang Mai–Lamphun Rd., Chiang Mai ☎ 1669 or 053/248130.

⚏ Hospital **Lanna Hospital** ⊠ 103 Super Hwy., Chiang Mai ☎ 053/357234.

HEALTH

Chiang Mai has an abundance of modern hospitals that are well-equipped to handle every complaint. The cost is a fraction of what you'd pay in the United States or Europe, and if you're covered by an international insurance company you normally won't even see a bill. Standards of care are very high indeed—there's no need to fear contaminated surgical implements or hypodermic needles. Doctors and nurses usually speak English. Qualified help can also be found at pharmacies, particularly in Chiang Mai, where you can often find a doctor behind the counter.

INTERNET

Internet cafés are on virtually every street corner in Chiang Mai, and you'll have no trouble locating one in the region's smaller towns. Charges vary enormously, ranging from B15 an hour to B2 a minute. Sometimes a half hour's Internet use includes a free cup of coffee. Rates in hotel business centers are much higher than in Internet cafés.

MAIL & SHIPPING

Post offices are normally open weekdays 8:30 to 4:30 and for a few hours Saturday morning. Chiang Mai's main post office is also open Sunday 9–noon.

🔳 Post Offices **Chiang Mai** ⊠ 402 Charoenmuang Rd. ☎ 053/241070. **Lampang** ⊠ Tipchang and Thibpawan Rds. ☎ 054/224069.

MONEY MATTERS

Banks are swift and professional in all the region's major cities, and you can expect friendly assistance in English. ATMs are everywhere to be found and are clearly marked, as Thais have a predilection for machine banking. Instructions for using the machines are in English.

SAFETY

If you use common sense, Chiang Mai and other communities in Northern Thailand are as safe as anywhere in the world. Leave your passport and other important documents, jewelry and watches, and large amounts of cash or traveler's checks in the hotel safe (even modest guesthouses have one). Keep a copy of your passport's relevant pages on you at all times, as police can demand proof of identification and levy a fine if you can't produce it. Always walk with shoulder bags and handbags on your side away from the street, as Chiang Mai has its share of motorcycle snatch-and-grab thieves.

TAXIS & TUK-TUKS

Metered taxis are being introduced gradually in Chiang Mai, replacing the noisier, dirtier songthaews. If you manage to flag down one of the small fleet of taxis the basic charge is B30—reckon on paying around B50 for a ride across the Old City. Tuk-tuks are generally cheaper, but you are expected to bargain with the driver—offer B20 or so less than the driver demands. The songthaews that trundle around the city on fixed routes are the cheapest form of transport—just B10 if your destination is on the driver's route. If he has to make a detour you'll be charged an extra B20 or so—settle on the fare before you get in. If your Thai is limited, just hold up the relevant number of fingers. If you hold up three and your gesture evokes the same response from the driver, you'll be paying B30. Drivers of taxis and songthaews are scrupulously honest, at least in Chiang Mai.

TOURS OPERATORS

Every other storefront in Chiang Mai seems to be a tour agency, and not all of them are professionally run. You'd be wise to pick up a list of agencies approved by the Tourism Authority of Thailand before choosing one. Prices vary quite a bit, so shop around, and carefully examine the offerings. Each hotel also has its own travel desk with ties to a tour operator. The prices are often higher, as the hotel adds its own surcharge.

Chiang Mai's Trekking Club is an association of 87 licensed guides with enough experience between them to manage the most demanding customer. "Tell us what you want and we can arrange it" is the club's boast. The club has its own café where you can meet the guides over a drink.

Summit Tour and Trekking and Top North also offer good tours at reasonable prices. World Travel Service is another reliable operator. Chiangmai Cattleya Tour & Travel Services has morning and afternoon tours of Wiang Kum Kam for B700.

🔳 **Chiangmai Cattleya Tour & Travel Services** ✉ Hillside Plaza and Condotel 4, 50 Huai Kaeo Rd., Chiang Mai ☎ 053/223991. **Summit Tour & Trekking** ✉ Thai Charoen Hotel, Tapas Rd., Chiang Mai ☎ 053/233351. **Top North** ✉ 15 Soi 2, Moon Muang Rd., Chiang Mai ☎ 053/278532. **Trekking Club** ✉ 41/6 Loi Khroa Rd., Soi 6, Chiang Mai ☎ 053/818519. **World Travel Service** ✉ Rincome Hotel, Huai Kaeo Rd., Chiang Mai ☎ 053/221044.

TRAIN TRAVEL

The State Railway links Chiang Mai to Bangkok and points south. As the uninteresting trip from Bangkok takes about 13 hours, overnight sleepers are the best choice. The overnight trains are invariably well maintained, with clean sheets on the rows of two-tier bunks. Parting with a few extra baht for a first-class compartment is strongly recommended. In second-class, you could find yourself kept awake all night by partying passengers.

Trains for the north depart from Bangkok's Hualamphong Railway Station and arrive in the Chiang Mai Railway Station. Overnight sleepers leave Hualamphong at 3 PM, 6 PM, 8 PM, and 10 PM, arriving at 5:35 AM, 7:20 AM, 9:05 AM, and 1:05 PM. Return trains leave at 2:50 PM, 4:25 PM, 5:25 PM, and 11:30 PM and arrive in Bangkok at 5:55 AM, 6:25 AM, 6:50 AM, and 2:55 PM. The second-class carriages (the fare is B421–B681) are reasonably comfortable. First-class carriages (B1,193) are recommended if you value a good night's sleep. The Nakornping Special Express (no first-class coaches) leaves Bangkok at 7:40 PM and arrives in Chiang Mai at 8:25 AM. The return trip departs at 9:05 PM and arrives in Bangkok at 9:40 AM.

Most Bangkok–Chiang Mai trains stop at Lampang and at Lamphun, where a bicycle samlor can take you the 3 km (2 mi) into town for about B30. The train to Lampang from Chiang Mai takes approximately 2½ hours; from Bangkok, it takes 11 hours.

🔳 Train Station **Chiang Mai Station** ✉ Charoenmuang Rd. ☎ 053/245563.

VISITOR INFORMATION

In Chiang Mai you can find an office of the Tourist Authority of Thailand on Chiang Mai-Lamphun Road. It's in a small building on the eastern bank of the Mae Ping River, opposite the New Bridge.

🔳 Tourist Information **Tourist Authority of Thailand** ✉ 105/1 Chiang Mai-Lamphun Rd., Chiang Mai ☎ 053/248604.

NAN & ENVIRONS

Visitors looking for off-the-beaten track territory usually head north from Chiang Mai and Chiang Rai to the Golden Triangle or west to Mae Hong Son. Relatively few venture east, toward Laos, but if time permits, it's a region that's well worth exploring. The center of the region is a provincial capital and ancient royal residence, Nan, some 70 km (42 mi) from the Laotian border. The city is very remote; roads to the border end in mountain trails and there are no frontier crossings, although there are ambitious, long-term plans to run a highway through the mountains to Luang Prabang.

Two roads link Nan with the west and the cities of Chiang Mai, Chiang Rai, and Lampang—they are both modern highways that sweep through some of Thailand's most spectacular scenery, following river valleys, penetrating forests of bamboo and teak, and skirting upland terraces of rice and maize. Hill tribe villages sit on the heights of the surrounding Doi Phu Chi mountains, where dozens of waterfalls, mountain river rapids, and revered caves beckon travelers with time on their hands. Here you can find Hmong and Lahu villages untouched by commercialism, and jungle trails where you, your elephant, and mahout beat virgin paths through the thick undergrowth.

The two routes from Chiang Mai to Nan pass through a pair of ancient towns, Phayao or Phrae, both of them worth an overnight stay. Phrae is center of Thailand's richest teak-growing region and Phayao sits on a beautiful lake. The region has three wild, mountainous national parks, Doi Phak Long, 20 km (12 mi) west of Phrae on Route 1023; Doi Luang, which reaches into the outskirts of Phayao; and Doi Phukku, on the slopes of the mountain range that separates Thailand and Laos, some 80 km (48 mi) northeast of Nan.

Nan

❷❸ *318 km (200 mi) southeast of Chiang Mai, (270 km (167 mi) southeast of Chiang Rai, 668 km (415 mi) northeast of Bangkok.*

Near the border of Laos lies the city of Nan, a provincial capital founded in 1272. According to local legend, the Lord Buddha, passing through Nan valley, spotted an auspicious site for a temple to be built. By the late 13th century Nan was brought into Sukhothai's fold, but it maintained a fairly independent status into the 20th century. Only in the last two decades have modern roads been cut from Phayao and Phrae to bring this region into closer communication with authorities in Bangkok.

Nan is rich in teak plantations and fertile valleys that produce rice and superb oranges. The town of Nan itself is small; everything is within walking distance. Daily life centers on the morning and evening markets. The Nan River, which flows past the eastern edge of town, draws visitors at the end of Buddhist Lent, in late October or early November, when traditional boat races are held. The longtail boats are all carved out of a single tree trunk, and at least one capsizes every year, to the delight of the locals. A few weeks later, in mid-December, Nan honors its famous fruit crop with a special Golden Orange and Red Cross Fair— there's even a Miss Golden Orange contest. It's advisable to book hotels ahead of time for these events.

To get a sense of the region's art visit the **National Museum,** a mansion built in 1923 for the prince who ruled Nan, Chao Suriyapong Pharittadit. The house itself is a work of art, a synthesis of overlapping red roofs, forest green doors and shutters, and brilliant white walls. There's a fine array of wood and bronze Buddha statues, musical instruments, ceramics, and other works of Lanna art. The revered "black elephant tusk" is also an attraction. The 3-foot-long, 40-pound tusk is actually dark brown in color, but that doesn't detract at all from its special role as a local good luck charm. ⊠ *Phalong Rd.* ☎ *054/710561* 🚇 *B30* ⊘ *Daily 9–5.*

Fodor'sChoice
★ Nan has one of the region's most unusual and beautiful temples, **Wat Pumin,** whose murals alone make a visit to this part of Northern Thailand worthwhile. It's an economically constructed temple, combining the main shrine hall and viharn, and qualifies as one of Northern Thailand's best examples of folk architecture. To enter, you climb a flight of steps flanked by two superb nagas, their heads guarding the north entrance and their tails the south. The 16th-century temple was extensively renovated in 1865 and 1873, and at the end of the 19th century murals picturing everyday life were added to the inner walls. Some have a unique historical context—like the French colonial soldiers disembarking at a Mae Khong riverport with their wives in crinolines. A fully rigged merchant ship and a primitive steamboat are portrayed as backdrops to scenes showing colonial soldiers leering at the pretty local girls corralled in a palace courtyard. Even the conventional Buddhist images have a lively originality, ranging from the traumas of hell to the joys of courtly life. The bot's central images are also quite unusual—four Sukhothai Buddhas locked in conflict with the evil Mara. ⊠ *Phalong Rd.* 🚇 *Free* ⊘ *Daily 8–6.*

Nan is dotted with other wats. **Wat Hua Wiang Tai** (⊠ Sumonthewarat Rd.) is the gaudiest, with a naga running along the top of the wall and lively murals painted on the viharn's exterior. **Wat Suan Tan** (⊠ Tambon Nai Wiang) has a 15th-century bronze Buddha image. It's the scene of all-night fireworks during the annual Songkran festival. **Wat Ming Muang** (⊠ Suriyaphong Rd.) contains the city pillar. **Wat Chang Kham** (⊠ Suriyaphong Rd.) has one of only seven surviving solid-gold Buddha images from the Sukhothai period. Its large chedi is supported by elephant-shape buttresses.

Where to Stay & Eat

¢–$ ✕ **Suriya Garden.** This substantial restaurant on the banks of the Nan river is a larger version of the nearby Ruen Kaew, with a wooden deck overlooking the water. Like its neighbor, it has added some interesting specialties to its conventional Thai menu—Chinese-style white bass or pig's hoofs, for instance. A band and solo vocalists perform nightly. ⊠ *9 Sumondhevaraj Rd.* ☎ *054/710687* 🚇 *MC, V.*

¢ ✕ **Ruen Kaew.** Its name means Crystal House, and this riverside restaurant really is a gem. Guests step in through a profusion of bougainvillea onto a wooden deck directly overlooking the Nan River. A Thai band and singers perform from 6:30 PM every night. The Thai menu has some original touches—the chicken in a honey sauce, for instance, is a rare delight. ⊠ *1/1 Sumondhevaraj Rd.* ☎ *054/710631* 🖃 *V.*

$ ▥ **The City Park Hotel.** Nan's top hotel is a low-rise, ranch-style complex of buildings on the outskirts of the city, set in 12 acres of gardens. Rooms overlook either the gardens or the landscaped pool, and all have private balconies. The Chumpoo-Thip restaurant serves fresh produce from the hotel's own kitchen garden, where guests can walk and learn about the herbs and spices that season Thai cuisine. ⊠ *99 Yantarakitkosol Rd., 55000* ☎ *054/741343 up to 52* 🖶 *054/773135* ⊕ *www.thecityparkhotel.com* ⬠ *129 rooms* ⚬ *Restaurant, room service, cable TV, minibars, tennis court, pool, laundry service, car rental* 🖃 *AE, MC, V.*

¢ ▥ **Dhevaraj.** Built around an attractive interior courtyard, which is romantically lit for evening dining, the Dhevaraj has all the comforts and facilities of an top-class hotel. Rooms are cozily furnished and the bed linen is high quality. The location couldn't be better, across from the city market and within a short walk of all the sights. A welcome plate of fresh fruit in your room is a nice touch, but it's advisable to shun the complimentary "American" breakfast (congealed fried eggs, warped ham, and tasteless sausage) for a cup of Thai rice soup at the market. ⊠ *44 Sumondhevaraj Rd., 55000* ☎ *054/710094* 🖶 *054/710212* ⬠ *154 rooms* ⚬ *Restaurant, coffee shop, laundry services* 🖃 *MC, V.*

¢ ▥ **Nan Fah Hotel.** A reminder of the past, this old wooden Chinese hotel is worth a visit even if you're disinclined to stay in its rather dark rooms. The wide-plank floors are of a bygone age. A balcony overlooking the street is a great place to take in the town. Marvelous antiques are scattered around the hotel, and the delightful owner is happy to sell you some in the shop in the lobby. A live band plays in the restaurant at night, so if you're planning on turning in early, ask for a room at the back of the hotel. ⊠ *436–440 Sumondhevaraj Rd., 55000* ☎ *054/710284* 🖶 *054/751087* ⬠ *14 rooms* ⚬ *Restaurant, lounge, shop, travel services* 🖃 *No credit cards.*

Sports & the Outdoors

Nan is the ideal center from which to embark on treks through the nearby mountains, as well as raft and kayak trips along the rivers that cut through them. Khun Chompupach Sirsappuris has run Nan's leading tourist agency, **Fhu Travel and Information** (⊠ 453/4 Sumondhevaraj Rd. ☎ 054/710636 or 01/2877209 🖶 054/775345 ⊕ www.fhutravel.com) for nearly 20 years and knows the region like her own backyard. She speaks fluent English, and has an impressive Web site describing tours and prices.

Phrae

❷ *110 km (68 mi) southeast of Lampang, 201 km (125 mi) southeast of Chiang Mai, 118 km (73 mi) southwest of Nan.*

A market town in a narrow valley, Phrae is well off the beaten path. The town's recorded history starts in the 12th century, when it was called

Wiang Kosai, the Silk City. It remained an independent kingdom until the Ayutthaya period. Remains of these former times are seen in the crumbling city walls and moat, which separate the Old City from the new commercial sprawl.

On the northeastern edge of town stands **Wat Chom Sawan,** a beautiful monastery designed by a Burmese architect and built during the reign of King Rama V (1868–1910). The bot and viharn are combined to make one giant sweeping structure. Phrae's oldest building is **Wat Luang,** within the old city walls. Although it was founded in the 12th century, renovations and expansions completely obscure so much of the original design that the only original section is a Lanna chedi with primitive elephant statues. A small museum on the grounds contains sacred Buddha images, swords, and texts.

On a hilltop in Tambon Pa Daeng, 10 km (6 mi) southeast of Phrae, stands another ancient temple, **Wat Phra That Cho Hae.** It was built in the late 12th century, and its 108-foot chedi is coated in gold. The chedi is linked to a viharn, a later construction, that contains a series of murals depicting scenes from the Buddha's life. The revered Buddha image is said to increase a woman's fertility. Cho Hae is the name given to the cloth woven by the local people, and in the fourth lunar month (June) the chedi is wrapped in this cloth during the annual fair. About 2 km (1 mi) from Wat Cho Hae is another smaller wat, **Wat Phra That Chom Chang,** whose chedi is said to contain a strand of Lord Buddha's hair.

Phrae is renowned in Northern Thailand for its fine teak houses. There are many to admire all over the city, but none to match what is claimed to be the world's largest teak structure, the **Ban Prathap Chai,** in the hamlet of Tambon Pa Maet near the southern edge of Phrae. Like many such houses, it's actually a reconstruction of several older houses—in this case, nine of them supported on 130 huge centuries-old teak posts. The result is remarkably harmonious. A tour of the rooms open to public view give a fascinating picture of bourgeois life in the region. The space between the teak poles on the ground floor of the building is taken up by stalls selling a variety of handicrafts, including much carved teak. The B30 admission charge includes a carved elephant key ring—a charming touch.

Where to Stay & Eat

For a quick bite, there's a night market at Pratuchai Gate with numerous stalls offering cheap, tasty food.

¢ ✕ **Ban Jai.** For authentic Lanna cuisine, you can't do better than this simple but superb restaurant. You're automatically served *kanom jin* (Chinese noodles) in basketwork dishes, with a spicy meat sauce, raw and pickled cabbage, and various condiments. If that's not to your taste, then order the *satay moo,* thin slices of lean pork on wooden skewers, served with a peanut sauce dip. In the evenings, every table has its own brazier for preparing the popular northern specialty, *moo kata,* a kind of pork stew. The open-sided, teak-floored dining area is shaded by ancient acacia trees, making it a cool retreat on warm evenings. ✉ *Chatawan Rd. 3* ☎ *No phone* ▭ *No credit cards.*

$ ⊡ **Maeyom Palace Hotel.** Phrae's top hotel is scarcely palatial, but has comfortable, well-appointed rooms at a modest price. There are plenty of amenities, including a very pleasant pool and an outdoor bar. Rooms have Lanna touches, such as distinctive carvings on the walls. The two restaurants serve a comprehensive menu of Thai and European dishes; the more elegant of the two, the Maeyom, has an impressive wine list, including the best Thai vintages, and a menu that features such fine European specialties as beef rolls with mushroom filling. ⊠ *181/6 Yantarakijkosol Rd., 54000* ☎ *054/521028 up to 35* 🖷 *054/522904* ✐ *wccphrae@hotmail.com* ➷ *104 rooms* ⏃ *2 restaurants, IDD phones, minibars, cable TV, in-room VCRs, pool, dry cleaning, laundry service, Internet, meeting rooms* ⊟ *AE, MC, V.*

¢ ⊡ **Nakorn Phrae Tower.** A curious but effective combination of a conventional high-rise and a Lanna-style aesthetic distinguishes this very comfortable central Phrae hotel. Traditionally dressed staff (the women in sarongs) offer a friendly welcome, and the Lanna touches extend to decorative features of the rooms, where local woods frame the beds and work areas. Phrae has very little nightlife, so the piano-player in the lounge bar is a very popular local performer. ⊠ *3 Muanghit Rd., 54000* ☎ *054/ 521321* 🖷 *054/523503* ➷ *139 rooms* ⏃ *Restaurant, bar, lounge, laundry service, meeting rooms* ⊟ *AE, DC, MC, V.*

Phayao

❷④ *150 km (90 mi) northeast of Chiang Mai, 160 km (96 mi) north of Lampang, 188 km (116 mi) northwest of Nan.*

Nearly as old as Chiang Mai and Chiang Rai, Phayao was for several centuries the center of a powerful kingdom, acquiring great prosperity and influence during the 13th-century reign of King Ngum Muang (who helped found Chiang Mai). A statue of the monarch stands in the municipal park that borders a natural lake called Kwan Phayao, which attracts anglers from as far as Bangkok. The hyacinth-studded lake is ringed by a breezy promenade bordered by restaurants, cafés, and bars. If you're staying the night, make sure to see the sunset over the still, mountain-backed lake. One of the region's most impressive monasteries, **Wat Sri Khom Kham,** stands on the shores of Kwan Phayao. It's reputed to have been founded after a visit to the site by Lord Buddha.

Where to Stay & Eat

¢–$ ✕ **Sang Chan.** Of all the restaurants bordering the lake, Sang Chan is probably the best. Fishing nets draping the exterior signal what to expect on the menu—lake fish predominate, and the freshly caught tilapia with garlic and pepper is a treat. The pillared dining room, its walls almost entirely of glass, has a pleasantly Italianate feeling. On warm evenings it's an unforgettable experience to watch the sun set over the lake from the garden terrace. ⊠ *17/4 Chai Kwan Rd.* ☎ *053/431971* ⊟ *MC, V.*

$ ⊡ **Gateway Hotel.** The pink facade of the town's only international-class hotel is a local landmark. It stands back from the lake, giving rooms on the upper floors views of the water and the distant mountains. The pastel shade of the stark exterior is matched by the subdued tones of the interior decor, though there are colorful Lanna touches such as fabrics and wall-hangings. ⊠ *7/36 Pratuklong 2 Rd., 56000* ☎ *053/411333* 🖷 *053/410519* ✉ *info@chiangraihotel.or.th* ➲ *108 rooms* ⌂ *Restaurant, bar, pool, gym, massage, billiards, bar, laundry service, convention center, travel services* ▤ *AE, DC, MC, V.*

NAN & ENVIRONS A TO Z

AIR TRAVEL
Thai Airways has one flight daily from Bangkok to Nan, leaving Don Muang airport at 11 AM and returning from Nan at 1:30 PM. The flight takes a little over an hour.

AIRPORTS & TRANSFERS
Songthaews meet incoming flights and charge about B50 for the 3-km (2-mi) drive into central Nan.
🚩 **Nan Airport** ⊠ Thawangpha Rd. ☎ 054/710377.

BUS TRAVEL
Several air-conditioned buses leave Bangkok and Chiang Mai daily for Nan, stopping en route at Phrae. The journey from Bangkok to Nan takes 11 hours and costs B400 to B600; it's 8 hours from Chiang Mai to Nan and the cost is B300 to B400.

From Lampang, air-conditioned buses leave for Phrae (3 hours) and Nan (5 hours). There's local bus service between Nan, Phrae, and Phayao.

HEALTH
Nan Hospital on Thawangpha Road is equipped to treat most conditions, but in the case of serious illness it's advisable to make for Chiang Mai. Take a basic medical kit on any tour into the mountains, and make sure it includes sufficient supplies of mosquito repellent.

INTERNET
Nan, Phayao, and Phrae each have several Internet cafés, and all listed hotels have business facilities.

MONEY MATTERS
You'll have no problem finding banks with ATMs in this region.

TAXIS & TUK-TUKS
City transport in Nan, Phrae, and Phayao is provided by a combination of tuk-tuks, songthaews, and samlors (bicycle rickshaws). All are cheap and trips within a city should seldom exceed B30.

TOUR OPERATORS
All of the companies listed below offer the same types of trips, which range from city tours of Nan and short cycling tours of the region to jungle trekking, elephant riding, and white-water rafting.
🚩 **Fhu Travel** ⊠ 453/4 Sumondhevaraj Rd., Nan ☎ 054/710636 🖷 054/775345 ⊕ www. fhutravel.com. **Inter Tours** ⊠ 10/10 Khaluang Rd., Nan ☎ 054/710195. **River Raft** ⊠ 50/6 Norkam Rd., Nan ☎ 054/710940.

TRAIN TRAVEL

Nan is not on the railroad route, but a comfortable way of reaching the city from Bangkok is to take the Chiang Mai-bound train and change at Den Chai to a local bus for the remaining 146 km (87 mi) to Nan. The bus stops en route at Phrae.

VISITOR INFORMATION

Tourist information about Nan province, Nan itself, Phayao, and Phrae is handled by the Tourism Authority of Thailand's regional office in Chiang Rai.

🛈 **TAT** ⊠ 448/16 Singhaklai Rd., Chiang Rai ☎ 053/744674–5 🖷 053/717434.

THE MAE HONG SON LOOP

If you're driving to Mae Hong Son, the only way to get there is along a mountainous stretch of road known to adventure travelers as "The Loop." The route runs from Chiang Mai to Mae Hong Son via Pai if you take the northern route, and via Mae Sariang if you take the southern route. Which route offers the best views is the subject of much heated debate. Most people hedge their bets by taking one route to get there and the other to return. The entire loop is 615 km (369 mi) long. Allow at least four days to cover it—longer if you want to leave the road occasionally and visit the hot springs, waterfalls, and grottos found along the way.

Pai

㉕ *160 km (100 mi) northwest of Chiang Mai, 110 km (66 mi) east of Mae Hong Son.*

Over the past decade, exhausted backpackers began looking for a stopover along the serpentine road between Chiang Mai and Mae Hong Son. They discovered Pai, a dusty little town in a remote valley not far from the border of Myanmar. It's now filled with art galleries and souvenir shops, coffee houses and restaurants, guesthouses and villas. Somehow it has managed to not get too overdeveloped and has retained its slightly off-the-beaten-path appeal.

Pai has a sizeable Muslim population, which is why some of the guesthouses post notices asking foreign visitors to refrain from public displays of affection. Immodest clothing is frowned upon, so bikini tops and other revealing items are definitely out. The few music bars close early, meaning that by midnight the town slumbers beneath the tropical sky. Nevertheless, quiet partying continues behind the shutters of the teak cabins that make up much of the tourist lodgings. This is, after all, backpacker territory.

Although Pai lies in a flat valley, a 10-minute drive in any direction brings you to a rugged mountain terrain with stands of wild teak, groves of towering bamboo, and clusters of palm and banana trees. At night, the surrounding forest seems to enfold the town in a black embrace. As you enter Pai from the direction of Chiang Mai, you'll cross the so-called World

War II Memorial Bridge, which was stolen from Chiang Mai during the Japanese advance through Northern Thailand and rebuilt here to carry heavy armor over the Pai River. When the Japanese left, they neglected to return the bridge to Chiang Mai. Residents of that city are perfectly happy, as they eventually built a much handsomer river crossing.

Where to Stay & Eat

¢–$ ✕ **Baan Pai.** The town's central meeting point is this airy, teak restaurant. Dishes such as spaghetti tend to crowd out the Thai specialties, but the customers seem to come to this friendly hangout more for the atmosphere than for the food. ⊠ *7 Moo 3, Baan Pakham, Tambon Viengtai* ☎ *053/699912* ⊟ *MC, V.*

¢ ✕ **All About Coffee.** One of Pai's historic merchant houses has been converted into a coffee shop that could grace any fashionable city street. More than 20 different kinds of java are on the menu, which is also packed with delicacies from the café's own bakery. The mezzanine floor has a gallery of works by local artists. ⊠ *Chaisongkram Rd.* ☎ *No phone* ⊟ *No credit cards.*

¢ ✕ **Edible Jazz.** Try the burritos at this friendly little café. The international menu matches the flavor of the music. It's one of few places in Pai where you can hear live jazz. ⊠ *Tambon Viengtai* ☎ *053/232960* ⊟ *No credit cards.*

¢ ✕ **House of Glass.** Glass isn't much in evidence at this open-air restaurant, but modern touches like picture windows would probably spoil its unique character. The buffet is an unbeatable value—pumpkin soup, various curries, fish and chips, and fresh fruit, all for B69. ⊠ *Tambon Viengtai* ☎ *No phone* ⊟ *No credit cards.*

$$ ✕▥ **Belle Villa.** The town's finest accommodation is this exquisite little resort. The 24 teak chalets (traditional outside, pure luxury inside) are perched on stilts in a tropical garden that blends seamlessly with the neighboring rice paddies and the foothills of the nearby mountains. A thatched-roof reception area adds an additional exotic touch. The terrace restaurant, overlooking the pool and a lotus-covered pond, is one of the region's best, serving fish from the Pai River and lamb from New Zealand. ⊠ *113 Moo 6, Huay Poo-Wiang Nua Rd., Tambon Wiang Tai, 58130* ☎ *053/698226, 02/6932895 in Bangkok* 🖷 *053/698228* ⊕ *www.bellevillaresort.com* 📶 *24 chalets* ⚴ *Restaurant, IDD phones, minibars, cable TV, pool, pond, bar, shop, playground, laundry service* ⊟ *AE, DC, MC, V.*

FodorsChoice ★

¢ ▥ **Brook View.** The brook babbles right outside your cabin window if you insist on one of the rooms with a view at this well-run little resort. The teak cabins are tiny, but scrupulously clean. Those at the water's edge have terraces where you can soak up the uninterrupted view of sugarcane fields and the mountains beyond. ⊠ *132 Moo 1, Tambon Wiang Tai, 58130* ☎ *053/699366* ✑ *brookviewpai@yahoo.com* 📶 *12 rooms* ⚴ *Massage, sauna, travel services* ⊟ *No credit cards.*

Nightlife

In high season, Pai is packed with backpackers looking for a place to party. Most of them congregate at **Bepop** (⊠ 188 Moo 8, Tambon Viengtai ☎ 053/698046). Bands perform there nightly beginning at 9:30.

CloseUp

VANISHING TEAK FORESTS

F YOU DRIVE ALONG THE HIGHWAYS AND BYWAYS of Northern Thailand, you'd be forgiven for dismissing fears that the region's great forests are in trouble. Great swaths of tropical forest clothe the mountain sides. Even teak, the most threatened of Thai trees, seems abundant.

But fly above this region—on scheduled services from Bangkok to Chiang Mai, Chiang Rai or Nan—and the damage done through decades of mismanaged deforestation and illegal logging is plain to see. Most of what teak there is grows in new plantations, a pathetic imitation of the great teak forests that once brought prosperity to the north.

Long before the logging companies moved in, teak was regarded as a very special tree, the home of spirits of the forest. Teak wood was reserved for palaces, the homes of wealthy citizens and temples.

In 1988, the Thai government acted to halt the depredation of the country's forests and banned all private logging. Teak growing is now firmly in the hands of the government's Forestry Department, which does sterling work to protect and nurture the forests. If you buy teak products now in Thailand the wood must by law come from government-controlled forests or from outside the country—mostly from Myanmar and Indonesia.

Carved teak ornaments in the night markets of Chiang Mai and Chiang Rai are consequently becoming rarer, replaced by products made from alternatives like redwood, rosewood, bamboo, and mango. Mango is the big surprise—although for long a revered tree (and not only for its luscious fruit), the mango was never considered a commercially viable wood. Expertly dried and treated, mango wood is very attractive indeed. You can recognize mango because of its glistening, darkly polished luster. Bamboo and coconut palm are other modest, inexpensive woods that can be worked into beautiful products. Bamboo, of course, is easily identified by its cylindrical form, which can be polished into elegant flower vases and containers. Coconut palm is also easy to spot because of its speckled, golden and brown glow.

—Robert Tilley

Sports & the Outdoors

While in Pai, you can join a white-water rafting trip sponsored by **Pai in the Sky Rafting** (✉ 114 Moo 3, Tambon Viengtai ☎ 053/699090). The two-day outing on the Khong River sends you through steep-sided gorges, past spectacular waterfalls, and over 15 sets of rapids. An overnight stop is made at the "Pai in the Sky" camp, near the confluence of the Pai and Kohong rivers, before reaching the end point outside Mae Hong Son. The trips are made daily June to February, when the rivers are at their peak.

Mae Sariang

㉖ *175 km (105 mi) southwest of Chiang Mai, 140 km (85 mi) south of Mae Hong Son.*

The southern route of the Loop runs through Mae Sariang, a neat little market town that sits beside the Yuam River. With two very comfortable hotels and a handful of good restaurants, the town makes a good base for trekking in the nearby Salawin National Park or for boat trips on the Salawin River, which borders Myanmar.

Near Mae Sariang, the road winds through some of Thailand's most spectacular mountain scenery, with seemingly endless panoramas opening up through gaps in the thick teak forests that lines the route. You'll pass hill tribe villages where time seems to have stood still and Karen women go to market proudly in their traditional dress. In the village of Khun Yuam, 100 km (60 mi) north of Mae Sariang, you can find one of the region's most unusual and, for many, most poignant museums, the **World War II Memorial Museum.** The modest little building commemorates the hundreds of Japanese soldiers who died here on their chaotic retreat from the Allied armies in Myanmar. Locals took in the dejected and defeated men. A local historian later gathered the belongings they left behind: rifles, uniforms, cooking utensils, personal photographs, and documents. They provide a fascinating glimpse into a little-known chapter of World War II. Outside is a graveyard of old military vehicles, including an Allied truck presumably commandeered by the Japanese on their retreat east. ✉ *Mae Hong Son Rd.* 🖅 *B10* ⊙ *Daily 8–4.*

Where to Stay & Eat

¢ ✕🏠 **Riverside.** This restaurant, on the open-air terrace of an inexpensive guesthouse, is on a bend of the Yuam River, commanding an impressive view of rice paddies and the mountains beyond. The menu is simple, but the panoramic view is reason enough to eat here. The guesthouse, a rambling wooden building cluttered with antique bits and bobs ranging from worm-eaten farm implements to antlers, has 18 reasonably comfortable rooms (B180–B350). ✉ *85 Langpanich Rd.* ☎ *053/681188 or 053/682592* 🖷 *053/681353.*

¢ 🏠 **Riverhouse Hotel.** Cooling breezes from the Yuam River waft through the open-plan reception area, lounge, and dining room of this attractive hotel. Rooms are a simple but elegant synthesis of white walls, dark woods, and plain cotton drapes, with small terraces overlooking the river (room No. 23 has a lamyai tree growing through its outside deck). The 12 rooms are quickly taken in high season, so if the hotel is full the nearby, larger Riverhouse Resort (under the same management) is recommended. It's more expensive (B1,200) but has more facilities. ⊠ *77 Langpanich Rd., 58110* ☎ *053/621201* 🖷 *053/621202* ⊕ *www.riverhousehotels.com* 🛏 *12 rooms* ♻ *Restaurant, laundry service, travel services* ▭ *No credit cards.*

Mae Hong Son

245 km (147 mi) northwest of Chiang Mai via Pai, 368 km (230 mi) via Mae Sariang.

Stressed-out residents of Bangkok and other cities have transformed this remote, mountain-ringed market town into one of Northern Thailand's major resort areas. Some handsome hotels have arisen in recent years to cater for them and their families. Overseas travelers also love the town because of its easy access to some of Thailand's most beautiful countryside.

For a small town, Mae Hong Son has some notable temples, thanks to immigrants from nearby Myanmar, where Burmese architecture and decorative arts were historically more advanced. Two of the temples, Wat Chong Kham and Wat Kham Klang, sit on the banks of a placid lake in the center of town, forming a breathtakingly beautiful ensemble of golden spires. Within a short drive are dozens of villages inhabited by the Karen, the so-called "long-neck" people. Fine handicrafts are produced in these hamlets, whose inhabitants trek daily to Mae Hong Son to sell their wares at the lively morning market and along the lakeside promenade.

Although Mae Hong Son offers a welcome cool retreat during the sometimes unbearably hot months of March and April, the mountains can be obscured during that part of the year by the fires set by farmers to clear their fields. One of the local names for Mae Hong Son translates as "City of the Three Mists." The other two are the clouds that creep through the valleys in the depths of winter and the gray monsoons of the rainy season.

a good walk For a giddy view of Mae Hong Son and the surrounding mountains, take a deep breath and trudge up Doi Kong Mu, a hill on the western edge of town. It's well worth the effort—from here you can see the mountains on the border of Myanmar (it's particularly lovely at sunset). There's another shade of gold to admire—a flame-surrounded white-marble Buddha in a hilltop temple called **Wat Phra That Doi Kong Mu** ㉗.

In the center of town, a pair of the region's fine temples sit on the southern edge of a lily-strewn lake called Jong Kham. **Wat Chong Klang** ㉘ and **Wat Chong Kham** ㉙ both overlook the serene lake. A short walk up Panishwatana Road leads you to **Wat Hua Wiang** ㉚, which holds the region's most honored image of the Buddha.

TIMING Because Mae Hong Son is so compact, this walk should only take a few hours.

Sights to See

★ ♻ **Thampla-Phasua Waterfall National Park.** About 16 km (10 mi) from Mae Hong Son, this park has one of the region's strangest sights—a grotto

with a dark, cisternlike pool overflowing with fat mountain carp. The pool is fed by a mountain stream that is also full of thrashing fish fighting to get into the cave. Why? Nobody knows. It's a secret that draws thousands of Thai visitors a year. Some see a mystical meaning in the strange sight. The cave is a pleasant 10-minute stroll from the park's headquarters. ⊠ *70 Moo 1, Huay Pa* ☎ *053/619036* 🖃 *Free.*

②⑨ Fodor'sChoice ★ **Wat Chong Kham.** A wonderfully self-satisfied Burmese-style Buddha, the cares of the world far from his arched brow, watches over the temple, which has a fine pulpit carved with incredible precision. ⊠ *Chamnansathit Rd.*

②⑧ **Wat Chong Klang.** This temple is worth visiting to see a collection of figurines brought from Myanmar more than a century ago. The teakwood carvings depict an astonishing range of Burmese individuals, from peasants to nobles. ⊠ *Chamnansathit Rd.*

③⓪ **Wat Hua Wiang.** Mae Hong Son's most celebrated Buddha image—one of the most revered in Northern Thailand—is inside this temple. Its origins are clear—note the Burmese-style long earlobes, a symbol of the Buddha's omniscience. ⊠ *Panishwatana Rd.*

㉗ Wat Phra That Doi Kong Mu. On the top of Doi Kong Mu, this temple has a remarkable view of the surrounding mountains. The temple's two chedis contain the ashes of 19th-century monks. ⊠ *West of Mae Hong Son.*

Where to Stay & Eat

¢–$ ✕ **Bai Fern.** Mae Hong Son's main thoroughfare, Khunlumprapas Road, is lined with inexpensive restaurants serving local cuisine. Bai Fern is among the best. In the spacious dining room you eat in typical Thai style, amid solid teak columns and beneath whirling fans. Among the array of Thai dishes, pork ribs with pineapple stands out as a highly individual and tasty creation. ⊠ *87 Khunlumprapas Rd.* ☎ *053/611374* ▭ *MC, V.*

¢–$ ✕ **Moom Sabei.** This open-air restaurant and bar opposite Rooks Holiday Hotel & Resort has folk music during the evenings that makes it a favorite with locals. "Thai fondue"—pork stewed on open braziers—is a specialty here and it goes well with the beers on tap. Japanese sukiyaki is also on the surprisingly cosmopolitan menu. ⊠ *117/30 Khunlumprapas Rd.* ☎ *053/613838* ▭ *No credit cards.*

★ $$ 🏨 **Imperial Tara Mae Hong Son.** Set amid mature teak trees, this fine hotel was designed to blend in with the surroundings. Bungalows in landscaped gardens have both front and back porches, giving the teak-floored and bamboo-furnished rooms a light and airy feel. Golden Teak, which serves excellent Thai, Chinese, and European dishes, has a glassed-in section for chilly mornings and evenings. The restaurant and bar face the valley, as does the beautifully landscaped pool area. ⊠ *149 Moo 8, Tambon Pang Moo, 58000* ☎ *053/611473, 02/261–9000 in Bangkok* 🖨 *053/611252, 02/261–9546 in Bangkok* ⊕ *www.imperialhotels. com/taramaehongson/* ➮ *104 rooms* ⌂ *Restaurant, minibars, cable TV, pool, gym, sauna, bar, shop, business services, travel services* ▭ *AE, DC, MC, V.*

$–$$ 🏨 **Rooks Holiday Hotel & Resort.** If you're looking for a quiet retreat, this resort should not be your top choice. A favorite with tour groups, the hotel has a disco that pulsates until the wee hours. Set in attractive tropical gardens that border a large pool, it has rooms with private balconies. ⊠ *114/5–7 Khunlumprapas Rd., 58000* ☎ *053/611390* 🖨 *053/611524* ➮ *114 rooms* ⌂ *Restaurant, minibars, cable TV, pool, billiards, nightclub, travel services* ▭ *AE, DC, MC, V.*

$ 🏨 **Rim Nam Klang Doi.** This retreat, about 5 km (3 mi) outside Mae Hong Son, is an especially good value. Some of the cozy rooms overlook the Pai River, while others have views of the tropical grounds. A minivan shuttles you to town for B100. ⊠ *Ban Huay Dua, 58000* ☎ *053/ 224339* 🖨 *053/612086* ➮ *39 rooms* ⌂ *Restaurant, pool* ▭ *MC, V.*

¢ 🏨 **Piya.** Eleven small bungalows, all huddled around a tree-shaded tropical garden, make up this friendly guesthouse. Sadly, none faces placid Lake Jong Kham, which is just across the road, but their secluded position at least ensures peace and quiet. One drawback: windows of the rooms are sealed because of the air-conditioning, so don't expect fresh air and the sound of birds singing. Rooms are simply furnished, and the dining area is also spartan, but at least it overlooks the lake. ⊠ *1 Soi 6, Khunlumprapas Rd., 58000* ☎ *053/611260* 🖨 *053/612308* ➮ *11 rooms* ⌂ *Restaurant* ▭ *No credit cards.*

¢ 🏠 **Tong Jai.** Resort hotels are mercifully absent from the banks of Mae Hong Son's placid Jong Kham Lake. It is lined on one side by simple guesthouses, of which Tong Jai is the best. Rooms are very basic, but also very clean. Two of the rooms—Nos. 1 and 2—have uninterrupted views of the lake, the golden-spired wats on its shore, and the mountains beyond. ⊠ *38 Udomchaonites Rd., 58000* ☎ *053/611136* 🛏 *11 rooms* ⚠ *No a/c, no room phones, no room TVs* 🖃 *No credit cards.*

Sports & the Outdoors

TREKKING Many people come to Mae Hong Son to visit the villages belonging to the Karen people, whose women often extend their necks to unbelievable lengths by wrapping more and more brass bands around them starting at adolescence. Most of the Karen people—an estimated 3,000 families—still live in Myanmar. In Thailand there are three villages, all near Mae Hong Son, with a total of more than 30 families, all of whom are accustomed to posing for photographs. Some visitors find there's an ethical dilemma in visiting these villages, as tourism may perpetuate what some find to be a rather barbaric custom. At the same time, tourist dollars also help to feed these people, many of whom are refugees from the unrest in Myanmar and who enjoy no civil rights in Thailand (they are not recognized as an ethnic hill tribe by the Bangkok government). With as many as 150 tourists visiting each day during the peak season, a village can make good money by having their long-necked women pose for snapshots.

THE MAE HONG SON LOOP A TO Z

AIR TRAVEL

Thai Airways has a daily flight from Bangkok to Mae Hong Son. It also has five flights daily between Chiang Mai and Mae Hong Son (35 minutes, B765). Note that in March and April, smoke from slash-and-burn fires often prevents planes from landing at the airport in Mae Hong Son.

AIRPORTS & TRANSFERS

The Mae Hong Son Airport is at the town's northern edge. Songthaews run to the city center for around B50.
🚩 **Mae Hong Son Airport** ☎ 053/612057.

BUS TRAVEL

Chiang Mai's Arcade Bus Terminal serves Mae Hong Son.
🚩 **Bus Stations Arcade Bus Terminal** ⊠ Super Hwy. and Kaew Nawarath Rd., Chiang Mai ☎ 053/274638 or 053/242664.

CAR RENTALS

If you're going to rent a car, you'll probably do it in Chiang Mai, but Avis also has an office at Mae Hong Son airport, if needed.
🚩 **Avis** ⊠ Mae Hong Son ☎ 053/620457.

CAR TRAVEL

The road to Mae Hong Son from has more than 1,200 curves, so make sure your rental car has power steering. The most comfortable way to travel the route and enjoy the breathtaking mountain scenery is to let somebody else do the driving. A road called the Loop takes you there from either direction; the northern route through Pai (6 hours) is a more attractive trip; the southern route through Mae Sariang (8 hours) is easier driving.

EMERGENCIES

🔳 Emergency Number **Tourist Police** ✉ Rajadrama Phithak Rd., Mae Hong Son ☎ 053/611812.

🔳 Hospital **Srisangwarn Hospital** ✉ Singhanat Bamrung Rd., Mae Hong Son ☎ 053/611259 or 053/612520.

INTERNET

Internet cafés are easy to find in Mae Hong Son.

MONEY MATTERS

You'll have no problem finding banks with ATMs in Mae Hong Son.

THE ROAD TO CHIANG RAI

Winding your way from Chiang Mai to Chiang Rai, the hub of the fabled Golden Triangle, will take you past Chiang Dao, best known for its astonishing cave complex; Tha Ton, a pretty riverside town on the Myanmar border, which has many outdoor activities; and Doi Ang Khang, a small, remote settlement—with one very fancy resort.

Chiang Dao

★ ③ *72 km (40 mi) north of Chiang Mai.*

Near the village of Chiang Dao, north of Chiang Mai, you can find Thailand's most spectacular caves. This complex of cathedral-proportioned caverns penetrate more than 2 km (1 mi) into Doi Chiang Dao, an astonishing 7,500-foot mountain that leaps up almost vertically from the valley floor. About half the caves have electric lights, but make sure you have a flashlight in your pocket in case there's a power failure. If you want to explore more of the mountain, hire a guide.

Lodging

¢ 🔲 **Rim Doi Resort.** Rim Doi means "on the edge of the mountain, " so it's fitting that two extraordinary peaks loom over this peaceful little resort near Chiang Dao. After a day exploring the nearby caves or venturing into the mountains, it's just the place to relax and prepare for the journey farther north. Be careful, as you'll probably be tempted to stay longer than just a night. Just B200 buys you a comfortable bed in a rustic bungalow, while a more stylish room in a modern extension overlooking a placid lake is an unbeatable B350. ✉ *46 Moo 4, Muang Ghay* ☎ *053/375028* 🖷 *053/375029* 🛏 *40 rooms* ⌂ *Restaurant, café, lake, bar* 🖃 *MC, V.*

Doi Ang Khang

③ *60 km (36 mi) north of Chiang Dao.*

North of Chang Dao lies one of the most remote corners of Northern Thailand. Literally at the end of the road, the only thing beyond Doi

Ang Khang is the jungle. Ang means "bowl, " which aptly describes the location of this small settlement. Here you can find a large agricultural research station, an important part of a governmental project to wean villagers away from opium production. The fields, orchards, and hothouses sit in the shadow of towering peaks.

Where to Stay

$$–$$$ ⊞ **Ang Khang Nature Resort.** Amari, which normally runs luxurious city hotels, manages this stylish country resort in the mountains near Doi Ang Khan. Rooms have all the comforts of Amari's downtown digs, with teak furnishings and locally woven fabrics. All rooms have private balconies, many of them with spectacular views of the mountains. ⊠ *1/1 Moo 5 Baan Koom, Tambon Mae Ngon, Amphoe Fang, Doi Ang Khang, 50320* ☎ *053/450110* 🖷 *053/450120* ⊕ *www.amari.com/ angkhang* ⟱ *76 rooms* ♿ *Restaurant, IDD phones, minibars, cable TV, mountain bicycles, laundry service, Internet* ⊟ *AE, DC, MC, V.*

Tha Ton

③③ *90 km (54 mi) north of Chiang Dao.*

North of Chiang Dao lies the pretty town of Tha Ton, which sits on the River Kok right across the border from Myanmar. The local temple, Wat Tha Ton, is built on a cliff overlooking the town. From the bridge below, boats set off for trips on the River Kok, some of them headed for Chiang Rai, 130 km (78 mi) away. This small resort town is a pleasant base for touring this mountainous region. An interesting side trip from Tha Ton takes you 45 km (27 mi) northeast on Highway 1089 to **Mae Salong,** where descendants of Chinese Nationalist soldiers who fled Mao Tse Tung's forces made their home near the top of a mountain called Doi Mae Salong. The slopes of the mountain are now covered with fruit orchards and coffee plantations. Visit in December and January and you can find the area smothered in cherry blossoms.

Where to Stay

$$ ⊞ **Maekok River Village Resort.** Every possible activity—from hiking to canoeing, from practicing your golf swing to mastering the basics of Thai cuisine—can be arranged at this friendly, comfortable hotel. The resort describes itself as "the adventure tour base designed with families in mind." Kids love many of the more unusual offerings, such as learning how to ride an elephant. Rooms are as large as apartments, but if you need more space there are also nine family villas. ⊠ *84 Moo 3, Ban Thaton, Amphoe Mae Ai, 50280* ☎ *053/459328* 🖷 *053/459329* ⊕ *www.track-of-the-tiger.com* ⟱ *29 rooms* ♿ *3 restaurants, room service, IDD phones, refrigerators, cable TV, pool, gym, hair salon, sauna, bicycles, 2 bars, recreation room, shop, playground, laundry facilities, business services, Internet, car rental, travel services.*

CHIANG RAI & THE GOLDEN TRIANGLE

It was an American who first gave the name "Golden Triangle" to the corner of Southeast Asia where the borders of Thailand, Burma, and Laos meet. U.S. Assistant Secretary of State Marshall Green coined the

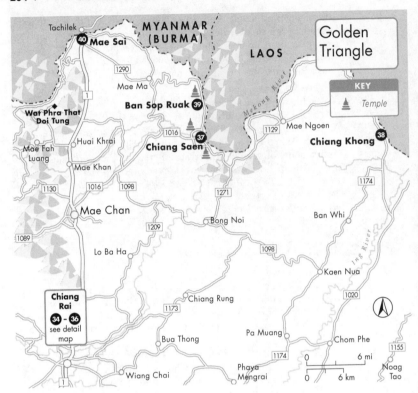

term in 1971 during a preview of the historic visit by President Richard Nixon to China. The Nixon Administration was concerned about the rise of heroin addiction in the United States and wanted to stem the flow of opium from China, Thailand, Burma, and Laos. The greatest source of opium in those years was the wild territory where the Mae Khong and Ruak rivers formed porous borders between Thailand and its two neighbors—the "golden triangle" drawn by Green on the world map.

The region's involvement in the lucrative opium trade began in the late 19th century, when migrating hill tribes introduced poppy cultivation. For more than 100 years the opium produced from poppy fields was the region's main source of income. Even today, despite vigorous official suppression and a royal project to wean farmers away from the opium trade, the mountains of the Golden Triangle conceal isolated poppy plantations. Scarcely a week goes by without a bloody clash between Thai police and suspected opium traders.

Despite its associations with the opium trade, the "Golden Triangle" is still regarded as a geographical area, varying in size and interpretation from the few square meters where the borders of Thailand, Burma, and Laos actually meet to a 40,000 square km region where the opium-yielding poppies are still cultivated. That region includes much of Thailand's Chiang Rai province, where strenuous and sometimes controversial police raids have severely curbed opium production and trade. The royal program to encourage farmers to plant alternative crops is also paying dividends.

Whatever the size of the actual triangle is thought to be, its apex is the riverside village of Ban Sop Ruak, once a bustling center of the region's opium trade. An archway on the Mae Khong riverbank at Ban Sop Ruak invites visitors to step symbolically into the Golden Triangle, and a large golden Buddha watches impassionately over the river scene. In a nearby valley where poppies once grew, stands a huge museum, the Hall of Opium, which describes the history of the worldwide trade in narcotics.

This fabled area is a beautiful stretch of rolling uplands that conceal remote hill tribe villages and drop down to the broad Mae Khong, which is backed on its far side by the mountains of Laos. Although some 60 km (36 mi) to the south, Chiang Rai is its natural capital and a city equipped with all the infrastructure for touring the entire region.

Chiang Rai

180 km (112 mi) northeast of Chiang Mai, 780 km (485 mi) north of Bangkok.

Once again, an elephant played a central role in the foundation of an important Thai city. Legend has it that a royal elephant ran away from its patron, the 13th-century king Mengrai, founder of the Lanna kingdom. The beast stopped to rest on the banks of the Mae Kok River. The king regarded this as an auspicious sign and in 1256 built his capital, Chiang Rai, on the site. But little is left from those heady days: the Emerald Buddha that used to reside in Wat Phra Keo is now in Bangkok's Grand Palace, and a precious Buddha image in the 15th-century Wat Phra Singh has long since disappeared.

Chiang Rai attracts more and more visitors each year, and it's easy to see why. Six hill tribes—the Akha, Yao, Meo, Lisu, Lahu, and Karen—all live within Chiang Rai province. Each has different dialects, customs, handicrafts, and costumes, and all still venerate animist spirits despite their increasing acquaintance with the outside world. As in Chiang Mai, they make daily journeys to the markets of Chiang Rai. The best of these is a night bazaar, just off Phaholyothin Road, which has a cluster of small restaurants and food vendors.

a good walk

Doi Tong, a modest hill on the northeastern edge of Chiang Rai, is a great way to learn the lay of the land. From the grounds of a 13th-century temple called **Wat Doi Tong** ㉞ you have a fine view of the Mae Kok River and the mountains beyond. Down the hill you soon reach Trairat Road, where you find **Wat Phra Keo** ㉟, once home to the famed Emerald Buddha. A copy now resides here. On Singhaklai Road is **Wat Phra Singh** ㊱, known for its restful atmosphere.

TIMING Chiang Rai has very few sights of note, so a leisurely walk around town will take at most a few hours.

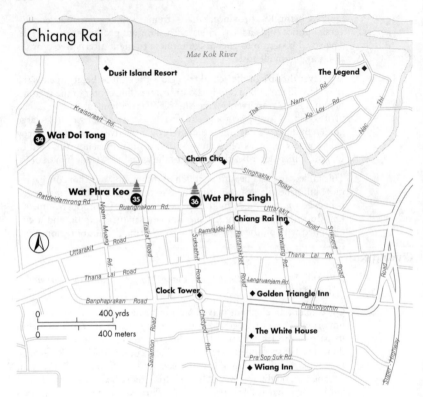

Chiang Rai

Mae Kok River

Dusit Island Resort

The Legend

Wat Doi Tong

Cham Cha

Wat Phra Keo

Wat Phra Singh

Chiang Rai Inn

Clock Tower

Golden Triangle Inn

The White House

Wiang Inn

| 0 | 400 yrds |
| 0 | 400 meters |

Sights to See

34 Wat Doi Tong. Near the summit of Doi Tong, this temple overlooks the Mae Kok River. The ancient pillar that stands here once symbolized the center of the universe for devout Buddhists. The sunset view is worth the trip. ⊠ *Winitchaikul Rd.*

35 Wat Phra Keo. The Emerald Buddha, which now sits in Thailand's holiest temple, Wat Phra Keo in Bangkok, is said to have been discovered when lightning split the chedi housing it at this similarly named temple at the foot of the Doi Tong. A Chinese millionaire financed a jade replica in 1991—although it's not the real thing, the statuette is still strikingly beautiful. ⊠ *Trairat Rd.*

36 Wat Phra Singh. This 14th-century temple is worth visiting for its viharn, distinguished by some remarkably delicate wood carving and for colorful frescoes depicting the life of Buddha. A sacred Indian Bhoti tree stands in the peaceful temple grounds. ⊠ *Singhaklai Rd.*

Where to Eat

¢–$ ✕ Kasalong. Chiang Rai's best seafood restaurant is a 15-minute tuk-tuk drive south of the city, but the journey is worth it. A large variety of seafood and lake fish is prepared according to Thai or Chinese recipes. The *tabtim* (sweet-tasting lake fish) in garlic and pepper sauce is particularly recommended. Although the restaurant sits on the busy superhighway, opposite the Big C megastore, you dine in a pleasant garden setting. ✉ *556/13 Superhighway Rd.* ☎ *053/754908* 🝙 *MC, V.*

¢ ✕ **Cham Cha.** Climb the stairs at this busy restaurant to avoid the lunchtime crowds and take a first-floor table overlooking the garden dominated by the handsome cham cha tree, which gives it its name. Avoid the Western dishes on the menu and go for traditional Northern Thai specialties such as *tom djuet,* a delicious soup laced with tofu and tiny pork dumplings. You can find the restaurant next to the Chiang Rai tourist office. ✉ *447/17 Singhaklai Rd.* ☎ *053/744191* 🝙 *No credit cards* 🕓 *No dinner. Closed Sun.*

¢ ✕ **Hawnariga.** The name of this traditional Thai restaurant means "Clock Tower, " and that's just where it's located, in the center of town. Orchids hang from the thatched palm-leaf roof of the large, open-sided restaurant. Two fish ponds are connected by a brook that skirts the tables, and they provide fat *tabtim* for the menu. ✉ *402/1–2 Banpapragarn Rd.* ☎ *053/711062* 🝙 *V.*

Where to Stay

$$–$$$$ 🏨 **The Legend.** This newer hotel could truly become something of a local legend. It's built in exclusively Lanna style on an island in the Mae Kok River, just a short walk from the city center. Rooms are furnished with exquisite Northern Thai antiques and reproductions, while public areas are a Lanna-style mixture of whitewashed walls, brickwork, and dark teak. The airy restaurant and landscaped swimming pool are on the river bank, with views of the mountains beyond. For real seclusion, book one of the villas, which have their own private pools. ✉ *124/15 Kohloy Rd., A. Muang, 57000* ☎ *053/910400 or 053/719649* 📠 *053/719650* ⊕ *www.thelegend-chiangrai.com* 📨 *79 rooms* ♨ *Restaurant, IDD phones, minibars, cable TV, pool, spa, bar, business center, travel services, parking* 🝙 *AE, DC, MC, V.*

$$–$$$$ 🏨 **Rimkok Resort.** Because it's across the Mae Kok River, and a taxi ride from town, this quiet hotel has more appeal for tour groups than for independent travelers. The main building is designed in modern Thai style with palatial dimensions—a long, wide lobby lined with boutiques leads to a spacious lounge and dining room. Rooms are in wings on either side, and most have views of the river from picture windows. ✉ *6 Moo 4 Chiang Rai-Tathon Rd., Rimkok Muang, 57000* ☎ *053/716445 up to 60, 02/279–0102 in Bangkok* 📠 *053/715859* ⊕ *www.rimkokresort. com* 📨 *256 rooms* ♨ *4 restaurants, IDD phones, minibars, cable TV, pool, hair salon, bar, nightclub, shops, meeting rooms, car rental* 🝙 *AE, DC, MC, V.*

★ $$ 🏨 **Dusit Island Resort.** This gleaming white high-rise, which sits on an island in the Mae Kok River, has tons of amenities. On the premises you can find the largest outdoor pool in Northern Thailand. The complex's three wings all have rooms overlooking the shore. The spacious rooms, filled with modern renditions of traditional Thai furnishings, have unexpected extras like large marble baths. The Peak grills up delicious steaks, while Chinatown stir-fries Cantonese fare. The casual Island Café, where a buffet breakfast is served, serves Thai food all day. All three dining rooms have impressive views. ✉ *1129 Kraisorasit Rd., 57000*

THE HILL TRIBES: "OWNERS OF THE MOUNTAINS"

ONE OF THE MAIN ATTRACTIONS OF TREKKING in Northern Thailand is meeting and staying with the hill tribe people who populate the more remote mountain areas. Some day trips include brief stops at villages, which are little more than Disneyland-type theme parks. But if you book a trek of three days or more you're sure to encounter authentic hill tribes living as they have for centuries.

Many hill tribe people claim they are victims of official discrimination, and it's indeed difficult for the majority to win full Thai citizenship because so many originate from beyond Thailand's borders. But the Thais themselves normally treat this exotic minority in their midst with respect and some measure of sympathy—it's significant that in the Thai language they are not described as "tribes" but as Chao Khao ("owners of the mountains").

For all the rigors of their hard existence, they're good-humored and friendly people who warmly welcome visitors. Whenever Westerners call to stay they usually organize a spontaneous party at which home-brewed whisky flows copiously. "There was a birthday party in every one of the three villages we stayed at, " mused one trekker, back in Chiang Mai, "that's some coincidence, isn't it?" If you stay overnight in a hill tribe village you'll be invited to share the community's simple food and sleep on the floor in one of their basic huts.

Before you leave on your trek, ask the tour operator to identify the hill tribes you'll be visiting and to describe their culture and traditions. It'll add greatly to the pleasure of your visit. There are nine hill tribes living in the mountains of Northern Thailand. They number about half a million, a mere 1% of Thailand's population. Most of them are descendants of migratory peoples from ancient Burma and China—one tribe, the Mien (called Yao by the Thais), write in Chinese script and follow Chinese Taoist religious rites.

Half of Thailand's hill tribe population are **Karen,** who mostly inhabit the mountainous northern and northwestern regions bordering Burma. They're not only the most numerous hill tribe people but also the most interesting, many of them sharing a common aim of the Karen people of eastern Myanmar: the establishment of an autonomous state. Hopes of eventual independence, fueled by empty British colonial promises, pushed many Karen onto the allied side during Japan's World War II invasion of Southeast Asia. There are old soldiers in the West who remember Karen courage with gratitude.

Western missionaries brought Christianity to the Karen in colonial Burma, and today the Christian faith is followed in many communities over the border in Thailand. Traditionally, though, the Karen hold animist beliefs, usually mingled now with Buddhist practices.

The Karen are the most settled of the hill tribes, living in permanent villages of well-constructed houses and farming plots of land that leave as much of the forest as possible undisturbed. (The slash-and-burn farming methods of some other hill tribes bring them constantly into conflict with the authorities.) Though the long-neck Karen women receive the most attention, all Karen women are skilled weavers. Styles of dress vary throughout all the distinct groups, but unmarried women generally wear loose, white blouses, while married women wear bold colors (a lot of blue and red).

The next most populous hill tribe are the **Hmong.** You'll recognize the women of this group at work in the night markets of Chiang Mai and Chiang Rai by their colorful costumes and heavy silver jewelry. There are two divisions of Hmong, White and Blue; White Hmong women wear baggy black pants and blue sashes, while Blue Hmong women wear knee-length pleated skirts. There are 80,000 Hmong in Thailand, although numbers will drop as many are being resettled in the United States, mainly in California, near Fresno— the reward for Hmong assistance to American forces in neighboring Laos during the Vietnam War.

The Hmong of Thailand have been progressively weaned away from cultivating their traditional crop, the opium-producing poppy, and today most Hmong communities farm profitable alternatives such as coffee and tea.

The poor cousins of the Hmong, the 33,000-strong **Akha,** also thrived on opium-production, shielded from outside interference and control by the relative inaccessibility of the remote mountain-top sites they chose for their settlements. They're of Tibetan origin and a gentle, hospitable people, whose women wear elaborate headdresses decorated with silver, beads, and feathers. Every Akha village is defined by a set of wooden gates, which are often decorated with charms meant to ward off evil spirits.

The tribe you're most likely to meet on day trips out of Chiang Mai and Chiang Rai are the businesslike **Lisu.** More than any other hill tribe, this 25,000-strong community has recognized the earning power of tourism, and as tourist buses draw up Lisu women scramble to don their multicolor costumes and line up for photographs.

No matter which tribe you visit, remember that the people of these villages tend to be more conservative, so be respectful and follow a few simple guidelines. Dress modestly. Keep a respectful distance from religious ceremonies or symbols—don't touch any talismans unless given permission to do so. Avoid loud or aggressive behavior and public displays of affection. And although charging tourists for snapshots is a big business for some of the villages, always ask permission before taking a person's picture.

–Robert Tilley

☎ *053/715777, 02/238–4790 in Bangkok* 🖷 *053/715801, 02/238–4797 in Bangkok* ⊕ *www.chiangrai.dusit.com* ⤳ *176 rooms* ⌂ *3 restaurants, minibars, cable TV, 2 tennis courts, pool, health club, hair salon, massage, 4 bars, nightclub, shops, meeting rooms, airport shuttle, car rental* 🖃 *AE, DC, MC, V.*

$–$$ 🏨 **Chiang Rai Inn.** All the accommodations at this Lanna-style hotel, near the bus station, look out over a cool, palm-shaded courtyard. Some of the comfortable rooms have sitting areas. The casual restaurant, furnished in cane and bamboo, serves an excellent choice of Northern Thai dishes. ⊠ *661 Uttarakit Rd., 57000* ☎ *053/71700 up to 3* 🖷 *053/711483* ⤳ *77 rooms* ⌂ *Restaurant, minibars, laundry facilities, convention center* 🖃 *MC, V.*

$–$$ 🏨 **Little Duck Hotel.** The first luxury resort in downtown Chiang Rai, Little Duck combines modern convenience with traditional Lanna design. There are even a few touches of Tibetan arts that make the place eclectic. The rooms are bright and cheery, with light-wood furnishing. Service is brisk and businesslike, as befits a hotel that handles many conventions. The travel desk organizes excursions into the neighboring hills. ⊠ *199 Phaholyothin Rd., 57000* ☎ *053/715620 up to 38* 🖷 *053/715639* ⤳ *330 rooms* ⌂ *2 restaurants, coffee shop, tennis court, pool, laundry service, meeting rooms, travel services* 🖃 *AE, DC, MC, V.*

$ 🏨 **Wiang Inn.** In the heart of downtown, this low-slung hotel is among the best in central Chiang Rai. Spacious rooms are decked out in dark woods and fine fabrics. Outside is a small outdoor pool surrounded by exotic greenery. The Golden Teak restaurant serves Thai, Chinese, and other fare. ⊠ *893 Phaholyothin Rd., 57000* ☎ *053/711533–5* 🖷 *053/711877* ⊕ *www.wianginn.com* ⤳ *260 rooms* ⌂ *Restaurant, coffee shop, minibars, cable TV, pool, health club, massage, nightclub, business services, travel services* 🖃 *AE, DC, V.*

¢ 🏨 **Ben's Guest House.** This family-run inn has repeatedly won accolades for its first-rate accommodations. The steep-eaved Lanna-style home is at the end of a quiet lane on the western edge of town. Transportation into Chiang Rai is easy to arrange. ⊠ *35/10, San Khon Noi Rd., Soi 4, 57000* ☎ *053/716775* ⤳ *22 rooms.*

¢ 🏨 **Golden Triangle Inn.** Don't confuse this cozy guesthouse with the backpackers' hangout at Ban Sop Ruak. This comfortable little place is all too popular—advance reservations are necessary—because of its ideal location in the center of town. Wood-ceiling rooms are cooled by slowly turning fans. The café serves Thai and Western fare, while the terrace bar has a wide range of fruity drinks. Next door is a travel agency that arranges treks into Laos. ⊠ *590–2 Phaholyothin Rd., 57000* ☎ *053/711339* 🖷 *053/713963* ⤳ *39 rooms* ⌂ *Restaurant, fans, bar, travel services; no a/c* 🖃 *No credit cards.*

★ ¢ 🏨 **The White House.** The charming Indian-Thai couple who run this attractive inn are justifiably proud of what they regard as their own home. Rooms are huddled around a courtyard. Nearby is a small pool and an open-air café. The owners also run an efficient travel service and a modest business center. ⊠ *789 Phaholyothin Rd., 57000* ☎ *053/713427 or 053/744051* 🖷 *053/713427* ⤳ *36 rooms* ⌂ *Restaurant, café, pool, business services, travel services* 🖃 *MC.*

Sports & the Outdoors

Chiang Rai is an excellent base from which to set out on tours trekking through the nearby mountains or canoeing and rafting on the region's rivers. Tour operators charge about B800 a day (including overnight stops in hill tribe villages).

Both Inbound-Outbound and Four Lens offer longtail boat trips on the Kok River, but if you want something more adventurous, catch a bus to the border town of Tha Thon and board a longtail boat there and ride the rapids to Chiang Rai. The 130-km (78-mi) trip takes four hours by high-powered longtail boat, or two days by raft. The trip takes you through one of the region's most remote areas, through gorges and thick jungle and past hill tribe villages.

Four Lens Tour (⊠ 131/6 Moo 13, Mae Korn Intersection ☎ 053/700617 up to 20 🖷 053/700796 ⊕ www.4lens.com) and **Inbound-Outbound Tour Service** (⊠ 199/38 Phaholyotin Rd. ☎ 053/715690 🖷 053/715691) offer a range of local tours, from river rafting and canoeing to treks to hilltribe villages.

GOLF Chiang Rai has one of Northern Thailand's finest golf courses, the **Santiburi Country Club** (⊠ 12 Moo 3, Huadoi-Sobpao Rd. ☎ 053/662821 up to 6 🖷 053/717377), laid out by the celebrated Robert Trent-Jones Jr. The par-72, 18-hole course is set among rolling hills 10 km (6 mi) outside Chiang Rai. The ranch-style clubhouse has an excellent restaurant and coffee shop and the facilities also include a sauna. Visitors are welcome and clubs, carts, and shoes can be rented. Reservations are requested.

en route | If you're traveling north from Chiang Rai on Highway 110, watch for the left-hand turn at Km 32 to **Doi Tung.** The road winds 42 km (25 mi) to the summit, where an astonishing view opens out over the surrounding countryside. The temple here, Wat Phra That Doi Tung, founded more than a millennium ago, is said to be the repository of some important relics of the Buddha, including a collarbone. The shrine attracts pilgrims from as far away as India and China, for whom its huge Chinese Buddha figure is a vastly important symbol of good fortune. On the mountain slopes below the temple is the summer home built for the king's late mother. The fine mansion is closed to the public, but the gardens, an explosion of color in all seasons, are often open.

Some 90 km (54 mi) due east of Chiang Rai is perhaps the region's most beautiful national park, **Phu Sang,** which has one of Thailand's rarest natural wonders, cascades of hot water. The temperature of the water that tumbles over the 85-foot high falls never drops below 91 degrees, and a nearby pool is even warmer. The park has some spectacular caves and is crisscrossed by nature trails teeming with bird life. One hour's drive north lies the mountainous border with Laos, straddled by 5,730-foot high Phu Chee Fah, a favorite destination for trekkers and climbers. You reach the Phu Sang National Park via Thoeng, 70 km (42 mi) east of Chiang Rai on

Route 1020. The park rents lodges for B800 to B1,000 a night. Call 054/401099 for reservations.

Chiang Saen

❸❼ *59 km (37 mi) north of Chiang Rai, 239 km (148 mi) northeast of Chiang Mai, 935 km (581 mi) north of Bangkok.*

On the banks of the Mae Khong River sits Chiang Saen, a one-road town that in the 12th century was home to the future King Mengrai. Only fragments of the ancient ramparts survived the incursion by the Burmese in 1588, and the rest of the citadel was ravaged by fire when the last of the Burmese were ousted in 1786. The government-financed excavation project now under way is well worth visiting. Chiang Saen is now being developed as a major Mae Khong river port, and it's the embarkation point for river trips to Burma, Laos, and China.

Only two ancient chedis remain standing to remind the visitor of Chiang Saen's ancient glory. Just outside the city walls is the oldest chedi, **Wat Pa Sak**, whose name refers to the 300 teak trees that were planted in the surrounding area. The stepped temple, which narrows to a spire, is said to enshrine holy relics brought here when the city was founded. Inside the city walls stands the imposing octagonal **Wat Phra That Luang.** Scholars say it dates from the 14th century.

Next door to Wat Phra That Luang is the **National Museum**, which houses artifacts from the Lanna period, as well as some Neolithic discoveries. The museum also has a good collection of carvings and traditional handicrafts from the hill tribes. ☎ *053/777102* 💷 *B30* 🕐 *Wed.–Sun. 9–4.*

Where to Stay

$ 🏨 **Chiang Saen River Hill Hotel.** Part of the Old City wall guides the way to this stylish, quietly located hotel, a short walk from the local boat jetty. Rooms are attractively decorated with Lanna arts and crafts, including the odd old cart wheel or two. The nightly buffet supper is "spiced down" to suit the tastes of the tour groups who favor this hotel, but it's a hearty, diverse meal. ⊠ *714 Moo 3, Tambon Wiang, 57150* ☎ *053/650826, 053/777396* 📠 *053/650829* ✉ *chiangsaen@hotmail.com* 🛏 *60 rooms* 🍴 *Restaurant, bar, parking* ▭ *No credit cards.*

★ ¢ 🏨 **Gin's Guest House.** A local lawyer, Kun Gin ("as in the drink"), and his wife run this charming guesthouse, which is a true home away from home. Rooms are just as you'd expect to find in your favorite aunt's country retreat. Some have large hearths for chilly nights. Kun Gin's a mine of local information and can organize everything from a trip across the nearby Mae Khong to a two-night cruise to China. If the house is full in high season you'll be lodged in bivouac-style wooden chalets in the extensive, tree-shaded garden. So early booking is recommended. ⊠ *Ban Sop Ruak Rd., 57150* ☎ *053/650847* 🛏 *9 rooms* ▭ *No credit cards.*

Chiang Khong

38 *53 km (33 mi) northeast of Chiang Rai.*

The recently paved road east out of Chiang Saen parallels the Mae Khong River en route to Chiang Khong, a town with magnificent views across the river to Laos. Songthaews ply the route, but you can also hire a speedboat to go down the river, a thrilling three hours of slipping between the rocks and rapids. Not too many tourists make the journey, especially to villages inhabited by the local Hmong and Yao tribes. The rugged scenery along the Mae Khong River is actually more dramatic than that around the Golden Triangle.

Across the river from Chiang Khong is the Laotian town of **Houay Say,** where you can find beautiful antique Laotian textiles. Thais are permitted to cross the river, but foreigners require visas. Numerous guesthouses in Chiang Khong accommodate overnight visitors. A 15-day visa can be acquired in Chiang Khong from **Ann Tour** (✉ 6/1 Moo 8, Saiklang Rd. ☎ 053/655198).

Ban Sop Ruak

39 *8 km (5 mi) north of Chiang Saen.*

Ban Sop Ruak, a village in the heart of the Golden Triangle, was once the domain of the opium warlord Khun Sa. More than a decade ago, government troops forced him back to Burmese territory, but his reputation still draws those eager to see evidence of the man who once held the region under his thumb.

Opium is so linked to the history of Ban Sop Ruak that the small town now has two museums devoted to the subject. The smaller one, **Opium Museum,** is in the center of town. A commentary in English details the growing, harvesting, and smoking of opium. Many of the exhibits, such as carved teak opium boxes and jade and silver pipes, are fascinating. ⛶ *B30* ⏲ *Daily 7–6.*

Fodor'sChoice ★ Opened in 2004, the magnificent **Hall of Opium** is a dazzling white stucco, glass, marble, and aluminium building nestling in a valley above the Mae Khong. The site of the museum is so close to former poppy fields that a plan is still being considered to extend the complex to encompass an "open-air" exhibit of a functioning opium plantation. The museum traces the history of the entire drug trade (including a look at how mild stimulants like coffee and tea took hold in the West). It even attempts to give visitors a taste of the "opium experience" by leading them through a 500-foot-long tunnel where synthetic aroma traces of the drug and atmospheric music waft between walls bearing phantasmagoric bas relief scenes.

The entrance tunnel emerges into a gallery of blinding light, where the nature of the opium-producing poppy is vividly described on an information panel erected in front of an imitation field of the insidiously beautiful flower. It's an arresting introduction to an imaginatively designed and assembled exhibition, which reaches back into the mirky history of

CloseUp

SPIRITED THAILAND

HE ANIMIST BELIEFS of many of the region's hill tribe people have mingled with traditional Buddhism.

If you're touring rural areas of the north, you might be lucky enough to witness one of the many festivals in which invisible spirits play major roles. The most impressive of these is Wat Pa, or "Tree Ordination," during which threatened trees, such as teak, are ritually dressed in saffron robes, making them holy and theoretically immune from destruction by illegal loggers. The ritual is led by monks, who hand out the robes to villagers, who then select a tree and "dress" it.

Spirits are widely believed to live in the forests, and whenever a tree is felled a ceremony of contrition has to take place. When a house is built, offerings to the spirits who once owned the timber are placed in all four corners. The garden will

usually have a "spirit house," an elaborate dollhouse to act as home for the spirits of the land on which a new house is built. If the house is extended then the spirit house is enlarged, too. You'll find spirit houses everywhere, from gardens to gas stations. On the Lampang-Chiang Mai highway there's a veritable city of them at a point in the mountains believed to be thickly populated by spirits.

Spirits are invoked at most family ceremonies from homecomings to weddings to funerals. Their influence is particularly valued in time of illness— villagers firmly believe that most maladies arise when a body "loses" one of the spirits assigned to protect it. A medicine man is commonly called upon to conduct a ceremony in which thread is wound around the patient's wrist, in the belief that the absent spirit is then reattached to the suffering body.

the opium trade and takes a long, monitory look into a potentially even darker future. The Hall of Opium is so large in scope and scale that two days are hardly enough to take it all in. A visit is ideally combined with an overnight stay, either at the Hall's own Greater Mae Khong Lodge (double rooms from B1,800 including breakfast) or, for a sheer splurge, at the luxurious Anantara Resort and Spa, just across the road. ⌨ *B300* ☉ *Thurs.–Sun. 10–3:30.*

Even if you don't stay overnight, pay a visit to the sumptuous **Imperial Golden Triangle Resort,** which has the best views over the confluence of the Mae Sai, Ruak, and Mekong rivers. Beyond you can see the hills of Myanmar and Laos.

Where to Stay

$$$–$$$$ ▨ **Anantara Golden Triangle.** The former Baan Boran hotel has been given
Fodor'sChoice a complete face-lift and is now one of the Golden Triangle's top addresses.
★ Mythical figures line your way to a palatial entrance, which leads into a vast, open-plan, two-floor area encompassing an excellent restaurant, opulently furnished lounge and reputedly the longest bar in Northern Thailand. Rooms are luxuriously furnished in indigenous woods and draped with handmade Thai fabrics. Louvered glass doors lead to bathrooms with terra-cotta tubs big enough for a pool party. Picture win-

dows opening onto private balconies command spectacular views of the confluence of the Mae Khong and Ruak rivers. The former Opium Den Bar has become the best Italian restaurant north of Chiang Mai. ☒ *Chiang Saen, 57150* ☏ *053/784084, 02/476–0022 in Bangkok* ⎙ *053/784090, 02/653–2208 in Bangkok* ⊕ *www.anantara.com* ⤴ *106 rooms, 4 suites* ⚷ *2 restaurants, room service, IDD phones, in-room safes, minibars, cable TV, 2 tennis courts, pool, health club, squash, 2 bars, laundry service, meeting rooms, airport shuttle, car rental, travel services* ▭*AE, DC, MC, V.*

$–$$ ▣ **Imperial Golden Triangle Resort.** From the superior rooms in this high-eaved, Lanna-style hotel you are treated to magnificent views of three rivers rushing together. The smart restaurant, the Border View, lives up to its name, but the best way to enjoy the panorama is to soak it up with a glass of Mae Khong whisky on the terrace. Classical Thai dance is performed in the evening during high season. ☒ *222 Ban Sop Ruak* ☏ *053/784001, 02/261–9000 Bangkok reservations* ⎙ *053/784006 or 02/261–9518* ⊕ *www.imperialhotels.com* ⤴ *74 rooms* ⚷ *2 restaurants, minibars, cable TV, pool, travel services* ▭ *AE, DC, MC, V.*

¢ ▣ **Golden Home** The Mae Khong River is just across the road from this small resortlike guesthouse. There are just seven wooden cabins, each with a tiny terrace overlooking a flower-smothered yard. The night market that borders the river is a short walk away. ☒ *41 Moo 1, Wiang, Chiang Saen, 57150* ☏ *053/784205* ⤴ *9 cabins* ⚷ *TV, refrigerators, parking* ▭ No credit cards.

Mae Sai

❹ *25 km (15 mi) west of Ban Sop Ruak, 60 km (36 mi) north of Chiang Rai.*

From Ban Sop Ruak you can travel west on a dusty road to Mae Sai, a town that straddles the Mae Sai River. At this market town the merchants trade goods with the Burmese. For the best view across the river into Burma, climb up to **Wat Phra That Doi Wao**—the 207-step staircase starts from behind the Top North Hotel.

Foreigners may cross the river to visit **Tha Kee Lek** on a one-day visa, obtainable at the bridge for $10. It's a smaller version of Mae Sai, but with no less than three casinos, packed with Thai gamblers. For $30 you can get a three-night visa that lets you travel 63-km (39-mi) north to **Kengtung,** a quaint town with colonial-era structures built by the British alongside old Buddhist temples.

Where to Stay & Eat

¢ ✕**Rabiang Kaew.** Set back from the main road by a wooden bridge, this restaurant built in the Northern style has an unmistakable charm. Antiques adorning the dining room add to its rustic style. The Thai fare is tasty and expertly prepared. ☒ *356/1 Phaholyothin Rd.* ☏ *053/731172* ▭ *MC, V.*

¢ ▣**Mae Sai Guest House.** Backpackers rank this riverside guesthouse, about 1 km (½ mi) west of the bridge, as the best in Mae Sai. It's certainly among the cheapest, with a bungalow without air-conditioning costing just B80. A small garden area surrounds the main building, which houses a casual dining room. ✉ *688 Wiengpangkam, 57130* ☎ *053/732021* 🛏 *20 bungalows* ▭ *No credit cards.*

¢ 🏨 **Northern Guest House.** When the Mae Sai Guest House is full, this is a good second choice. The rooms are small (there's just enough room for a bed) but clean. A few have their own bath. The veranda-style dining room is pleasant in the evenings, as the river flows at the edge of the garden. ✉ *402 Tumphajom Rd., 57130* ☎ *053/731537* 🛏 *26 cottages, some with bath* ⚿ *Dining room* ▭ *No credit cards.*

¢ 🏨 **Wang Thong.** This riverside hotel was originally intended to cater for business executives trading across the nearby Thai-Burmese border, but now the guests are mostly travelers. Choose a room high up on the river side so you can spend an idle hour or two watching the flowing waters and the flowing pedestrian traffic across the bridge. Its rooms are modern and functional. ✉ *299 Phaholyothin Rd., 57130* ☎ *053/733388* 🖷 *053/733399* 🛏 *150 rooms* ⚿ *Restaurant, coffee shop, cable TV, in-room VCRs, pool, bar, pub, dance club, laundry service, business services* ▭ *MC, V.*

Shopping

Thais take household goods and consumer products across the river, where the Burmese trade them for sandalwood, jade, and rubies. Though you may want to see Myanmar, the prices and quality of the goods will not be better than in Mae Sai. Near the bridge, **Mengrai Antique** (✉ Phaholyothin Rd. ☎ 053/731423) has a matchless reputation.

Rubies aren't the only red gems here. Mae Sai is also justifiably proud of its sweet strawberries, which ripen in December or January.

THE GOLDEN TRIANGLE A TO Z

AIR TRAVEL
Thai Airways has five daily flights from Bangkok to Chiang Rai.
🛈 Carriers **Thai Airways** ✉ 240 Phra Pokklao Rd., Chiang Mai ☎ 053/211044.

AIRPORTS & TRANSFERS
Chiang Rai International Airport is 6 km (4 mi) northeast of the city. Incoming flights are met by songthaews and tuk-tuks, which charge about B50 for the journey to central Chiang Rai.
🛈 Airport Information **Chiang Rai International Airport** ☎ 053/793048.

BOAT & FERRY TRAVEL
At Tha Thon, a pretty little riverside border town, longtail boats and rafts set off daily for the 130-km (78-mi) trip downstream to Chiang Rai. High-powered longtail boats leave from a pier near the town bridge at 12:30 PM and take about five hours to negotiate the bends and rapids of the river, which passes through thick jungle and past remote hill tribe villages. The fare is B160. For a more leisurely ride to Chiang Rai, board a raft, which takes two days and nights to reach Chiang Rai, overnighting in hill tribe villages. Fares are around B1,000. Take bottled water, an inflatable cushion, and (most importantly) a hat or umbrella to shade you from the sun. The best time to make the trip is during Oc-

tober and November, when the water is still high and the risk of rainy season flooding is past.

BUS TRAVEL
Destinations in Chiang Rai and the Golden Triangle are serviced by buses that leave regularly from Chiang Mai's two terminals. Buses to Chiang Rai leave regularly between 8 AM and 7:15 PM from Bangkok's Northern bus terminal and between 6:15 AM and 5 PM from Chiang Mai's Arcade terminal. The VIP bus trip from Bangkok costs B700, the air-conditioned A1 service costs B452; from Chiang Mai the fare is B139. It's an exhausting journey of at least 12 hours from Bangkok. The journey from Chiang Mai takes between three and four hours.

⛟ Bus Stations Chiang Rai Bus Terminal ⊠ Prasopsook Rd., Chiang Rai ☎ 053/711369.

CAR RENTALS
In Chiang Rai, the most prominent companies are Avis, National, and Budget. Budget has a good range of four-wheel-drive vehicles for trips off the beaten path.

⛟ Agencies Avis ⊠ Chiang Rai International Airport ☎ 053/793827 ⊠ Dusit Island Resort Hotel ☎ 053/715777. **Budget** ⊠ Golden Triangle Tours, Chiang Rai ☎ 053/740442. **National** ⊠ Wangcome Hotel ☎ 053/719233.

CAR TRAVEL
Roads are well paved throughout the Golden Triangle, presenting no problem for drivers. The area is bisected by the main north-south road, Highway 110, and crisscrossed by good country roads.

EMERGENCIES
⛟ Overbrooke Hospital ⊠ Singhaklai Rd., Chiang Rai ☎ 053/711366. **Police** ☎ 053/711444 in Chiang Rai.

HEALTH
Malaria and other mosquito-borne diseases are virtually unknown in the urban centers in the north, but if you're traveling in the jungle during the rainy season that stretches from May to August you might want to take antimalarials for your own comfort and peace of mind. If trekking in the mountains and staying at hill tribe villages pack mosquito repellent. It's advisable also to spray your room about a half hour before turning in, even if windows have mosquito screens and you're sleeping under mosquito nets. Some treks are particularly arduous, so find room in your backpack for lotions to soothe aching muscles. A small first-aid kit is also advisable.

Hospitals are found in every major city. Even the simplest village clinic is clean and well-equipped, so you need have no fear of contaminated surgical implements or hypodermic needles. Doctors almost invariably speak English.

INTERNET
Internet cafés are on virtually every street corner in Chiang Rai, and you'll have no trouble locating one in the region's smaller towns. Charges vary enormously, ranging from B15 an hour to B2 a minute. Sometimes a

half hour's Internet use includes a free cup of coffee. Rates in hotel business centers are much higher than in Internet cafés.

MAIL & SHIPPING
Post offices are normally open weekdays 8:30 to 4:30 and for a few hours on Saturday morning.

🚩 Post Offices **Chiang Rai** ✉ 21 Uttarakit Rd. ☎ 053/711444.

MONEY MATTERS
Banks are swift and professional in all the region's major cities and in tourist destinations such as the Golden Triangle, and you can expect friendly assistance in English. ATMs are everywhere to be found and are clearly marked.

TAXIS & TUK-TUKS
Tuk-tuks are the common way of getting around Chiang Rai, and a trip across town costs B40–B50. Songthaews can also be hailed on the street and hired for trips to outlying areas. The fare inside the city is B10—farther afield is a matter of negotiation.

TOUR OPERATORS
The major hotels in Chiang Rai and the Golden Triangle Resort in Chiang Saen organize minibus tours of the region. Their travel desks will also arrange treks to the hill tribe villages. Should you prefer to deal directly with a tour agency, try Golden Triangle Tours or Track of the Tiger, a pioneer of "soft adventure tourism" in Northern Thailand. Its very comprehensive program, concentrated in the Chiang Rai region, covers mountain biking, canoeing, rafting, rock climbing, river barge cruises, trekking, botany trails, golf and cooking courses.

Dapa Tours is a nonprofit company run by Akha people to raise money for their villages.

🚩 **Dapa Tours** ✉ 115 Moo 2, Rimkok Rd., Chiang Rai ☎ 053/711354. **Golden Triangle Tours** ✉ 590 Phaholyothin Rd., Chiang Rai ☎ 053/711339. **Track of the Tiger** ✉ Maekok River Village Resort, Box 3, Mae Ai, Chiang Mai ☎ 053/459355 📠 053/459329 ⊕ www.maekok-river-village-resort.com.

VISITOR INFORMATION
For information in Chiang Rai try the Tourist Information Center on Singhakhlai Road.

🚩 Tourist Information **Tourist Information Center** ✉ Singhakhlai Rd., Chiang Rai ☎ 053/744674.

ISAN

5

Updated by
Ivan Benedict
New and
Warwick
Dixon

A LAND RENOWNED AS THE TRUE TRADITIONAL THAILAND, Isan is widely credited with giving the country its famous cuisine, musical soul, and sense of good-natured fun in the face of adversity. It's been long neglected by local and international tourists, but the region nevertheless has a wealth of both natural and cultural attractions, which are becoming increasingly accessible. The cities are bustling and experiencing steady development, while the countryside still stays close to its roots, so you can witness age-old traditions and marvel at the vast tracks of luscious rice fields where the water buffalo still roam. This is the country's rice belt, where subsistence farmers work the fields so diligently that they provide for not only their country's needs but also for those of neighboring countries. These fertile fields, which cover an area bigger than Portugal, are the heart (and many say, the soul) of Thailand.

Comprising about a third of Thailand's total area, Isan is nevertheless the country's poorest region. Life here can be difficult, depending for the most part on the fickleness of the monsoons. The people of the Northeast, burned by the scorching sun and drenched by the torrential rains, are straightforward and direct, passionate and fun-loving. Their food is hot and spicy, their festivals are robust, and their regional language is very similar to that of Laos. The new bridge over the Mae Khong River at Nong Khai has stimulated trade between Thailand and Laos, and you can find interesting goods there and at Mukdahan. The handmade lace and tie-dyed cottons may tempt you, as may such oddities as large washbowls made of aluminum recycled from U.S. aircraft shot down during the Vietnam War. Nong Khai is also a good source for silver. For *mudmee* silk, try Udon Thani and its nearby silk-weaving villages.

Tour buses are rare on the roads of the sprawling northeast plateau. Consequently, the few travelers you see here are in search of the relatively undisturbed culture or remnants of its fascinating history. The region's chief attractions are its Khmer ruins, most of which have been only partially restored. Others come for its pristine nature reserves, such as Phu Kra Dueng National Park and Khao Yai National Park. Still others come to see the Mae Khong River, which borders the region to the north and east.

The good news is that even on a short trip you can get a sense of the region. If you are short on time, you may want to limit your visit to Nakhon Ratchasima, a four-hour journey by train from Bangkok. The town can serve as a base for trips to the nearby Khmer ruins at Phimai. Surin, Buri Ram, and Si Saket, a little farther away, are also good bases from which to visit more ruins.

Foreigners can cross into Laos at Nong Khai, Nakhon Phanom, and Mukdahan. You'll need a Laotian visa costing $30, which can be obtained from the Laotian Embassy in Bangkok, the consulate in Khon Kaen, or directly at the Friendship Bridge. Some hotels and guesthouses in Nong Khai can also obtain visas for an added fee.

About the Restaurants

Dining out in Isan offers no great variation, restaurant-wise, from the rest of the country. Night markets and street vendors are popular,

If you have	
3 days	From Bangkok, take an early-morning flight to 🔲 **Nakhon Ratchasima** ①, a city also known as Korat. Visit Prasat Hin Phimai, the late 11th-century Khmer sanctuary. In the evening, be sure to explore the Night Bazaar. On the next day take a car or bus to Prasat Hin Khao Phanom Rung, a supreme example of 12th-century Khmer architecture, and its neighboring predecessor Prasat Muang Tam. Spend the night in 🔲 **Buri Ram** ④, making sure to visit the Night Bazaar here and perhaps listen to some local musicians at one of the city's live music venues. On your third day, return to Bangkok.

5

If you have	
5 days	Travel up to 🔲 **Nakhon Ratchasima** ① by bus and head to **Khao Yai National Park.** ② See the waterfalls and monkeys and other wild animals that visit the salt licks. After a short trek return to the city to stay overnight. Make a quick stop at the Ya Mo Monument to listen to a Pleng Korat performance before resting up and venturing to one the city's many fine restaurants and strolling in the night bazaar. Next day go to **Phimai** ③ in the morning to see the Khmer ruins and banyan trees. After lunch head to Prasat Phanom Rung in **Buri Ram** ④, followed by a visit to nearby Prasat Muang Tham. Spend the night in Buri Ram, making sure to visit the night bazaar and enjoy some local rock ballads in a restaurant or bar. On the third day, head to **Prasat Ta Muen** on the Surin Khmer border, then go to Chom Jom market before going to **Surin** ⑤. Next day head to Ban Kwaow Sinarin village for some silver and textile shopping, and after lunch take a trip to Khao Phra Viharn, over the Cambodian border from Si Saket, to see this magical cliff-top prasat. After your visit here, spend the night in 🔲 **Ubon Ratchathani** ⑦, where the next morning you can visit some temples or take a trip to Chom Mek market in Laos before heading back to Bangkok.

---

cheaper options, and provide staple quick fillers. There are also more up-market affairs such as wooden, garden restaurants and modern and fashionable establishments where people can enjoy a more elaborate, pricier selection, often in conjunction with live music or relaxing by a fish pond or river. The differences you can find in this region are more closely related to the food on offer, which shares influences with Laotian and Vietnamese fare.

The cuisine of Isan, the country's easternmost region, is nationally famous for its fiery, chili-based salads and soups. Much is made from a limited range of staples that can be grown in the region's extreme climate—hot and dry until heavy rains flood the fields from May through October. The region is poor and the people have learned to make a little go a long way, but, as in other such regions, necessity has proven to be a virtue.

Always on the table is the glutinous *khao niao* (sticky rice), which is preferred to the more refined *khao suay* (steamed rice). An Isan cook is also more generous with spices, and herbs like basil and mint are liberally added to meat dishes. An especially tasty dish is *nua namtok,* which is sliced beef lightly grilled and garnished with shallots, dried chilies, lemon juice, and fresh mint leaves. Pork is popular, eaten in a style called *moo pan* (beaten flat and roasted over charcoal) and another called *moo yor* (ground and wrapped in a banana leaf).

Each province claims to have the best *gai yang* (roast chicken), but Si Saket and Udon Thani brag the loudest. Especially popular in Korat is *sai krog Isan,* a sausage filled with minced pork, garlic, and rice. It's usually cooked and eaten with sliced ginger, dry peanuts, and grilled chilies. But be warned—it's *very* spicy. The locals douse just about everything with *balah,* a vile-smelling but tasty fermented fish sauce that is certainly worth trying.

About the Hotels

Because relatively few tourists visit Isan, most hotels and guesthouses cater chiefly to a business clientele. There are some top-class hotels in larger towns like Nakhon Ratchasima, Khon Kaen, and Udon Thani, but most accommodations are much more modest. As elsewhere in Thailand, standards of cleanliness are high and even the most basic room will invariably have fresh linen and towels.

Isan is a bargain—even the most expensive hotels charge less than $60 a night. Remember that such refinements as room telephones, TVs, and even hot water can be rare outside the cities.

WHAT IT COSTS In Baht				
$$$$	**$$$**	**$$**	**$**	**¢**
RESTAURANTS over B400	B300–B400	B200–B300	B100–B200	under B100
HOTELS over B6,000	B4,000–B6,000	B2,000–B4,000	B1,000–B2,000	under B1,000

Restaurant prices are per person, for a main course at dinner. Hotel prices are for a standard double room, excluding tax.

Exploring Isan

The vast swath of Thailand known as Isan has often been characterized, if not stigmatized, by the existence of the Korat plateau, which makes up the heartland of the region. In truth the heart of Isan is somewhat flat and featureless, but this can not be said of the entire region. Travelers to Isan have the option of visiting the mountains of Nakhon Ratchasima and Loei, experiencing the traditional life of the provinces along the length of the Mae Khong River from Nong Kai or visiting the wealth of Khmer architecture found in the southern stretch of the region bordering Cambodia. In the best of all possible worlds you'd take two weeks in order to visit all these destinations on a circular route round the entire region.

All the region's cities are accessible by bus from the major centers of Nakhon Ratchasima, Udon Thani, and Ubon Ratchathani, all of which are easily reached from Bangkok. There are two train routes from Bangkok, both running through Nakhon Ratchasima, where the line splits—one way to Udon Thani via Khon Kaen, the other heading to

Architecture

The Khmer influence is evident in the occasional *prasat,* or tower, that dots the region. The prasat wasn't a royal residence, but rather a retreat for those traveling from the Khmer temple of Angkor in present-day Cambodia. A few retreats have been restored, but many are just ruins redolent of their rich past. The finest examples of restored and atmospherically rich prasats in Thailand can be found at Phimai in Nakhon Ratchasima province and at Phanom Rung in Buri Ram province.

Natural Wonders

Two of the country's most popular national parks are found in Isan. Misty Phu Kra Dueng National Park, in mountainous Loei province, is where you can find a profusion of wildflowers in spring. Khao Yai National Park, southwest of Korat, is so expansive that it extends into four provinces. Another favorite is Ban Phue, northwest of Udon Thani, a 1,200-acre park covered with rocks of all sizes, some shaped into Buddhist and Hindu mythical figures.

5

Shopping

Villagers in the country's northeastern reaches have a rich tradition of handicrafts. Nakhon Ratchasima has a night market offering a big variety of local handicrafts. The village of Renu Nakhon produces cheerful quilted blankets and intricately patterned ceramics. Pottery made with rust-color clay is found in the village of Ban Kwian. Straw baskets are woven at Ban Butom, and Ban Choke produces fine silver bracelets and necklaces. Along the Mae Khong River you can find markets, like the one in Mukdahan, that sell crafts brought over from Laos; look for fine handmade embroidery and lace. The villagers of Chonnabot weave high-quality mudmee silk, as do those who live around Si Chiang. More silk comes from Chiang Khan and from villages south of Nakhon Ratchasima and around Buri Ram and Surin.

Ubon Ratchathani via Buri Ram, Surin, and Si Saket. Tour companies are not common in the area, but it's possible to rent a car or hire a driver in the larger cities. The ubiquitous songthaews are found all over, but for short trips locals tend to prefer motorbike taxis and peddle-powered samlors over tuk-tuks. Most of Bangkok's taxi drivers come from Isan but you rarely find a car taxi here.

Timing

The ideal months to visit the Isan region are the cooler winter months between November and February, when temperatures are more agreeable and flora more abundant. But this major rice bowl of Thailand looks its best when the vast plains are filled with the calming sight of rice fields in full production, which happens August through December.

The region is not affected by the traditional high season, either in terms of costs or volume of visitors, but you should be prepared for crowds and steep accommodation price rises during major public festivals. It's also worth bearing in mind that discounts are prevalent during the off-season, particularly the rainy season, June through October.

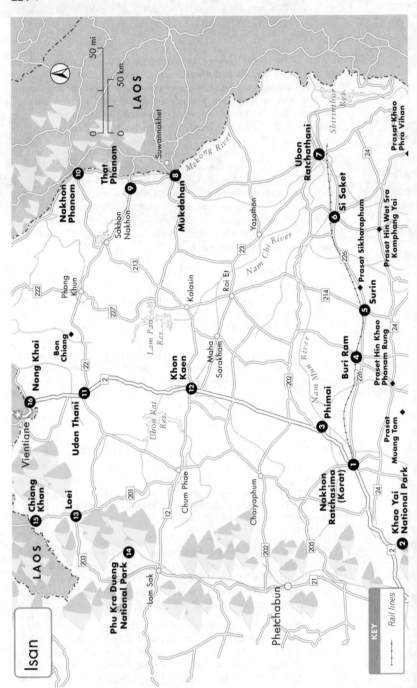

Isan

LAOS

50 mi

50 km

Nakhon Phanom

That Phanom

Suwannakhet

Mekong River

Sakhon Nakhon

Mukdahan

Ubon Ratchathani

Si Saket

Prasat Sikharaphum

Shirinthor Res.

Prasat Khao Phra Vihan

24

Prasat Hin Wat Sra Kamphang Yai

226

Surin

Yasothon

Nam Chi River

23

Roi Et

Kalasin

214

Buri Ram

Prasat Hin Khao Phanam Rung

24

213

Phang Khun

222

227

Lam Pao Res.

Maha Sarakham

Khon Kaen

202

Nam Mun River

Prasat Muang Tam

226

Bon Chiang

22

Nong Khai

2

Udon Thani

11

Khon Kaen

12

Ubon Rat Res.

Phimai

3

Nakhon Ratchasima (Korat)

1

24

Vientiane

16

Chiang Khan

15

Loei

13

201

Chum Phae

12

Chaiyaphum

205

Khao Yai National Park

2

LAOS

Phu Kra Dueng National Park

14

Lom Sak

203

202

21

Phetchabun

KEY

Rail lines

NAKHON RATCHASIMA & ENVIRONS

The provinces stretching from Nakhon Ratchasima through Buri Ram, Surin, Si Saket and to Ubon Ratchathani are commonly known as Lower Isan, a geographical reference rather than a social comment. The area is particularly renowned for its unmissable Khmer architecture and the continued influence of Khmer culture, particularly with regard to minority dialects and a musical style called *kantrum* (traditional music with singing in the Khmer language), which can be found east of Nakhon Ratchasima.

A trip to this part of the country would not be complete without visiting the famous Khmer prasats in Phimai, Buri Ram, Surin, and Si Saket. Here ruins have intricate engravings cut from sandstone and towering structures fashioned in laterite, which are somewhat more imposing than the soft touches of limestone stucco and red brick found in equivalent historical sites in the Central Plains.

The national park of Nakhon Ratchasima and the rivers of Ubon Ratchathani offer some variety to your trip, and while on your travels you may like to take advantage of the opportunity to buy the fine silks produced here or enjoy some of the local Thai folk rock ballads, known as *pleng per chavit* (songs for life), played in the bars. You'll find the people of the region proud but friendly and above all brimming with life. For chili lovers, the food is to die for, and if you're lucky enough to be here during the rice production period, the harmonious pace of rural life among the vast swaths of rice fields will provide you with an unforgettable image of traditions and culture in practice.

Nakhon Ratchasima

❶ *259 km (160 mi) northeast of Bangkok.*

Considered the gateway to the Northeast, Nakhon Ratchasima (popularly known as Korat) is the largest city in Isan and the second largest city in Thailand. Its size resulted from the need for a strong frontier city to govern the towns of the vast northeastern plateau. Nakhon Ratchasima is a modern mini-metropolis, complete with huge shopping malls and a few high-rise hotels. However, it has a very distinct culture (its own dialect and musical style, for example) and sense of self, which grew out of its prestigious past. Indeed many people in the city will describe themselves as Korat people as opposed to Isan people. Above all the city reveres its beloved *Ya Mo,* short for Thao Suranaree, a local woman who led her people to victory over the invading Laotians. Her monument can be found in front of Phratu Chumpol, one of the four gates leading into the old city, and homage is paid to her throughout the city.

The city is also home to the Thai second army and air force. The city hosts annual U.S. army exercises, called "Cobra Gold, " from November through December, when the city's hotels and nightspots fill with American servicemen and women.

Where to Eat

$–$$ ✕ **Texas.** As its name suggests, this is a Western-style restaurant, steaks being the main draw. Diners also come to enjoy the pop–rock band that plays here nightly at 9:30. The staff is friendly and there's a good cocktail list. ✉ *49 Jomsurangyath Rd., Naimuang* ☎ *044/342837* ▭ *V* ✺ *No lunch*.

¢–$ ✕ **Ton Som Restaurant.** You feel like you're walking into someone's living room at this homey restaurant. The well-traveled owner, Rampai, and her friends have decorated Ton Som with ornaments from around the world. Rampai professes to be one of the first to invent spicy, Thai-style toppings for pizzas, which you can find here. Another favorite dish here is *pla chon kua takrai*, fried fish cooked with local herbs. ✉ *125–129 Watcharasarit Rd.* ☎ *044/252275* ▭ *AE, DC, MC, V.*

¢ ✕ **Sumlanlap Restaurant.** Popular with locals, this restaurant serves up a selection of local Isan dishes, of which *laab phet*, a spicy duck dish, is a particular hit. The restaurant has basic furnishings and cement floors, but the fine fare at very reasonable prices more than makes up for the lack of ambience. If you feel brave, you can try the cow penis salad (be sure to let us know what it's like). ✉ *159/1 Watcharasarit Rd.* ☎ *No phone* ▭ *No credit cards.*

Where to Stay

$–$$ ⊞ **Hermitage Resort & Spa.** The hotel's name is a bit misleading—it sounds like a secluded retreat, but it's really only 3 km (2 mi) from town. However, the palatial seven-story hotel is set in a garden, so you might just feel like you're out in the country. Rooms, some of them with attractive oriel windows, are tastefully furnished with fabrics and indigenous woods. Follow up a workout at the health club with a traditional Thai massage at the spa. ✉ *725/2 Thaosura Rd., 3000* ☎ *044/247444* 🖷 *044/247463* ↴ *139 rooms* ♿ *Restaurant, coffee shop, room service, minibars, cable TV, pool, fitness classes, gym, health club, massage, sauna, bar* ▭ *AE, DC, MC, V.*

$–$$ ⊞ **Royal Princess.** Regal it's not, but this gleaming nine-story showplace does have finely furnished guest rooms complete with executive desks and comfortable chairs. The expansive lobby with eye-catching silk souvenir shops gives way to a comfortable lounge. A small garden and pool offer some relief from the glare of the noonday sun. The formal restaurant serves the best Cantonese food in town. ✉ *1/37 Suranarai Rd., 3000* ☎ *044/256629* 🖷 *044/256601* ⊕ *www.royalprincess. com* ↴ *186 rooms* ♿ *Restaurant, coffee shop, minibars, cable TV, pool, health club, laundry service, business services, meeting rooms* ▭ *AE, DC, MC, V.*

$ ⊞ **Ratchapruk Grand Hotel.** The dark, polished granite lobby of this modern high-rise leads to a relaxing lounge. Check out the signed photos of Thai celebrity guests behind the front desk. The light and airy rooms are decorated mostly in primrose and pale woods; Japanese-style window screens can be opened to provide a commanding view of the city. The hotel is popular with visiting U.S. forces during November and December. ✉ *311 Mittraphat Rd., 3000* ☎ *044/26122* ↴ *159 rooms* ♿ *Restaurant, minibars, cable TV, pool, gym, bar, laundry service, meeting rooms, services* ▭ *AE, DC, MC, V.*

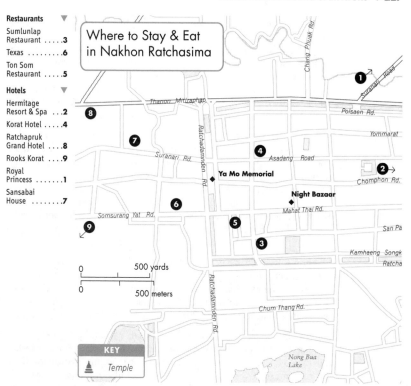

Where to Stay & Eat
in Nakhon Ratchasima

$ 🏨 **Rooks Korat.** Even if you're not an avid golfer, you might enjoy this
country club about 28 km (17 mi) southwest of Nakhon Ratchasima.
The cozy, comfortable rooms look inexplicably like beach chalets and
have private patios that overlook the par-72 golf course. Furnishings
are minimal—in case you should need a little extra putting practice, there's
grass-green carpeting throughout. The terrace beside the pool is a pleasant spot for dinner; try the crispy free-range chicken. ⊠ 622 M.12,
Korat–Pakthonchai Rd., 30000 🖼🖼 044/249060 or 044/249061 🛏 20
rooms ⚏ Restaurant, golf course, pool ▤ MC, V.

¢   🏨 **Korat Hotel.** This is one of the city's oldest hotels and probably its
most famous. Upon entering the lobby, you'll be greeted by a life-size
bronze of Luang Por Koon, the province's most famous monk. The lobby
opens up into a 24-hour dining area with soothing polished stone
floors, mini-chandeliers, and oil paintings hanging on the walls. The
rooms have an old-world feel with fretwork panels and more framed
oil paintings. The hotel's beer garden is a great place to relax with a
drink and enjoy the barbecued seafood on offer. The booming Speed
2 nightclub attracts all the young and trendy locals. ⊠ 191 Asdang Rd.,
30000 ☎ 044/257057 🖨 044/242260 🛏 105 rooms ⚏ Restaurant,
coffee shop, minibars, cable TV, hair salon, massage, bar, night club,
laundry service, travel service ▤ MC, V.

¢ ⊞ **Sansabai House.** For the budget traveler, this intimate hotel is a real find. The hotel's two buildings have been completely refurbished and the place feels fresh throughout, from the wicker sofas and chairs in the lobby to the bright, clean rooms. Only a 20-minute walk from the city's Suranaree monument and five minutes from Bus Station 1, it's well-positioned for exploring the city, old and new. ⊠ *335 Suranaree Rd., 30000* ☎ *044/255144* 🖷 *044/255144* ➳ *40 rooms* ⚬ *Minibars, cable TV, lobby lounge, laundry service* ☰ *No credit cards.*

Nightlife & the Arts

For cultural shows, head to the Suranaree Monument on Ratchadamnoen Road, in front of Chumpol Gate. Here you can find regular performances of *Pleng Korat,* an oratory sung on request here in a style unique to the province. Performers wear traditional costume and can be enticed into singing for about B400 for a half-hour performance. *Pleng Korat* was a favorite of the famous Suranaree and is still popular with merit-making Buddhists, as well as and passing tourists. The performers usually pack up by 6 PM.

Nakhon Ratchasima has a lively nightlife (though many places close at 1 AM), much of which is concentrated on Jomsurangyath Road, near the edge of the old city. For those who want to dance around the tables to a mix of dance tracks or watch a live pop stage performance replete with dancers, head to **Speed 2** in the Korat Hotel on Asdang Road.

Another good street to try is Yomraj Road, within the old city, where you can find a number of bars and restaurants. **Bule' Saloon Pub and Restaurant** (⊠ 264 Yomraj Rd. ☎ 044/256538) is a longtime favorite for Western rock music lovers in the city. You'll feel like you're in a mountain lodge as you sit back and listen to the fine guitar licks of the owner. It's one of the few places outside of Bangkok where you can hear bands play a repertoire that includes Pink Floyd, Led Zeppelin, and the Rolling Stones.

You spot the lively **Coco Beat Pub and Restaurant** (⊠ Yomraj Rd. ☎ 044/247993) by its waterfall effect windows. Inside you'll be wowed by the owner's unique decorating taste—a kitschy mishmash of decors—and the fine covers of Thai and Western pop songs coming from the marvelous live band. The crowd is mainly made up of the well-to-do local party set. Coco Beat's sister restaurant, Huaplee, across the road, is a favorite amongst the city's diners and will provide a good foundation for the club's cocktails.

Long Tiem (⊠ 38 Suranara Rd. ☎ 044/272198) is pub and restaurant set in a wooden Thai-style house with an enormous beer garden. It's a great choice for those who prefer the local Thai rock known as *pleng per chavit* (songs for life). A dreadlocked tattoo artist located to the rear of the establishment can provide you with the ultimate souvenir of your evening.

Shopping

Between 6 and 9 PM head to Nakhon Ratchasima's **Night Bazaar**, on Manat Road in the center of town. A block-long street is taken over by food stands and vendor stalls and is crowded with locals. If you're looking to buy local products during the day, head to the **Suranaree Monument.** The shops and stalls facing the monument sell local wares and souvenirs at reasonable prices. Typical buys are locally produced silks, pottery, and *kao tang* rice snacks.

A side trip to **Pak Thongchai Silk and Cultural Centre,** 32 km (20 mi) south of Korat, offers a chance to see how locals make silk, from the raising of silkworms to the spinning of thread and the weaving of fabric. You can buy silk at some 70 factories in the area. A bus from Bus Station 1 will take you to Pak Thongchai, leaving every hour (B50 one-way). It will drop you at the market and you can explore the surrounding lanes for silk outlets and factories.

For ceramics, drive out to the village of **Ban Dan Kwian,** 15 km (10 mi) southwest of Nakhon Ratchasima. The rust-color clay here is used for reproductions of classic designs. The village can be easily reached by taking a songthaew from Kamhang Songkram Road, near to the police station. Trucks leave every 20 minutes and cost a nominal B20.

Khao Yai National Park

❷ *130 km (80 mi) southwest of Nakhon Ratchasima.*

This is Thailand's oldest national park (established in 1962). The reserve covers 2,168 square km (833 square mi) and spreads over four provinces. It's a frequent destination for Thais seeking to escape Bangkok and on weekends the park can feel crowded.

On entering the park and winding your way up into the forested hills, you'll soon find yourself confronted by pleading monkeys loitering on the road in search of handouts. But these are not the only wildlife you'll likely to encounter here—of particular note are the wild elephants, tigers, and barking deer that can sometimes be observed at the salt licks.

Trekking trails, bicycle paths, view points, and bird-watchtowers are prolific in this huge evergreen forest and many of the park's splendid waterfalls are easily accessible by car or bicycle. It's particularly easy to get around, and frequent information points and warning signs such as "Cobra Crossing" will help keep you from harm's way (though evening strolls are still not advised). Hiking trails leaving from the park headquarters are 1 km to 8 km (½ mi to 5 mi) in length, so you can choose a route that suits your fitness and time available.

The park provides a variety of cabin accommodations at reasonable rates, though many prefer to camp at one of the park's two designated sites. Tents and bedding, along with bicycles, are available for hire on-site. If you don't wish to sleep under the stars there are several resorts located along Thanarat Road, which leads to the park entrance. The park's headquarters, next door to the large and informative visitor center, can help arrange lodgings, as well as guided treks, including a night-time safari.

From Nakhon Ratchasima take a bus from Bus Station 1 to Pak Chong for B50 baht; buses leave hourly. At Pak Chong take a local songthaew to the park's entrance. Note that it's another 20 km (12 mi) from the park entrance to the visitor center, so it's best to negotiate a ride into the heart of the camp or else you'll need to hire an additional taxi at the entrance. ⊠ *Khao Yai National Park, Pakchong District, Nakhon Ratchasima* ☎ *B200* ⊙ *Daily 8–8.*

Phimai

❸ *60 km (37 mi) northeast of Nakhon Ratchasima.*

Phimai is famous for its magnificent Khmer architecture, its tough muay thai boxers, and its locally produced noodles. It's also a restful break from the often hectic pace of Nakhon Ratchasima. The town's quiet streets come to life with the arrival of tour buses ferrying tourists to this most famous Khmer *prasat* (tower) site, but it's still possible to rent a bicycle and explore the area in relative peace. Phimai is dotted with the remnants of ancient edifices, walls, and gates, and the sense of history surrounding this friendly town will not be lost on you.

The Phimai festival, held on the second weekend of November, brings the crowds to see boat races and cultural shows, so it's best to book in advance if you wish to stay overnight at this time.

Phimai can easily be reached by bus from Bus Station 1 in Nakhon Ratchasima. Buses depart regularly and cost B26.

Fodor'sChoice **Prasat Hin Phimai,** in the center of town, is one of the great Khmer structures in Isan. Built sometime in the late 11th or early 12th century (believed to pre-date Angkor Wat), it has been carefully restored and frequently appears in music videos and movies. To enter the prasat is to step back eight centuries. By the time you pass through the external sandstone wall and the gallery, you're swept up in the creation and destruction of the Brahman gods engraved on the lintels. A quartet of *gopuras* (gate towers) guard the entrances, with the main one facing south toward Angkor. The central white sandstone prang, towering more than 60 feet, is flanked by two smaller buildings, one in laterite, the other in red sandstone. The combination of pink and white is exquisite, especially in the light of early morning and late afternoon. The principal prasat is surrounded by four porches whose external lintels depict Hindu gods and scenes from the Ramayana. Inside, the lintels portray the religious art of Mahayana Buddhism.

The excellent museum here contains priceless treasures from the Dvaravati and Khmer civilizations—notably great works of Khmer sculpture. The museum's masterpiece is a stone statue of King Jayavarman VII of Angkor Thom, found at Prasat Hin Phimai. ⊠ *Tha Songkran Rd.* ☎ *044/471167* ☎ *B30* ⊙ *Tues.–Sun. 9–4.*

From Prasat Hin Phimai, take a 2-km (1-mi) excursion to the village of **Sai Ngam,** home of the world's largest banyan tree. It's said to be more than 350 years old, which is easy to believe if you examine its mass of intertwined trunks. The site is both intriguing and mysterious as you wind along raised foot paths in the shade of this vast natural phenomenon; it was once believed that the roots of the tree stretched as far as the center of town. The adjoining food stalls make it a favorite picnic spot for Thai families and across the lake you'll see a faithful reconstruction of a traditional northeastern house.

Where to Stay & Eat

¢ ✕ **Baiteiy Restaurant.** This wonderful, relaxing restaurant is only five minutes from the prasat and is within sight of the Khmer marvel. Naturally, the theme here is ancient Khmer—the walls are made of local laterite bricks, the ceiling is made of bamboo, and Khmer designs and engravings are all around. The restaurant serves traditional Thai fare with some emphasis on local dishes, such as stir-fried Phimai noodles. The staff is friendly and informative. You can also rent bicycles here for a few hours or by the day. ⊠ *246/1 Jomsudasaded Rd.* ☎ *044/471725* ▤ *MC, V.*

¢ ▦ **Phimai Inn Hotel.** This friendly hotel is a good value, and it manages to pack in many of the facilities you'd expect from a top hotel at very modest rates. Many of its rooms have recently been refurbished with wooden furnishings and pale pastel hues. It's on the bypass on the edge of town. ⊠ *33/1 Bypass Rd.* ☎ *044/287228-9* ▤ *044/471175* ⤳ *80 rooms* ♻ *Restaurant, coffee shop, minibars, cable TV, pool, laundry service.* ▤ *No credit cards.*

Buri Ram

❹ *90 km (56 mi) east of Nakhon Ratchasima.*

The provincial capital of Buri Ram lies between Nakhon Ratchasima and Surin and is a good gateway for those visiting the nearby Khmer prasats, some of the finest in the country. Founded in the late 18th century by the first king of the Chakri dynasty, this somewhat neglected city, which translates as "City of Pleasantness, " is turning a corner, as evidenced by the recent $1 million conversion of an ancient moat into an attractive public park.

More peaceful than its neighboring cities, Buri Ram provides an opportunity to pick up some bargain silk products and sample the Isan lifestyle by eating local specialties such as *som tum* (spicy papaya salad) at the bustling Night Bazaar, or listening to local folk rock in one of the city's live country music venues.

Fodor'sChoice The restored hilltop shrine of **Prasat Hin Khao Phanom Rung,** 65 km (40
★ mi) from the city, is a supreme example of Khmer art. The approach to the prasat sets your heart thumping—you cross an imposing bridge and climb majestic staircases to the top, where you're greeted by a magnificent reclining Vishnu lintel. This architectural treasure hit the headlines when it mysteriously disappeared in the 1960s, then reappeared at the Chicago Art Institute. After 16 years of protests it was finally returned to its rightful place. Step under the lintel and through the portal into the double-walled sanctuary. Intricate carvings in a style similar to those found in Lopburi cover the interior walls, and in the center of the prasat stands the great throne room dedicated to Lord Shiva.

Built in the 12th century under King Suriyaworamann II, one of the great Khmer rulers, it was restored in the 1980s at a cost of $2 million. It's one of the few Khmer sanctuaries without later Thai Buddhist additions. For insight into this and other nearby Khmer architecture it's well worth having a look in the visitor center, which can be found beyond the souvenir stalls, along the shaded path where you catch your first glimpse of the prasat. The center has commendably clear information; the exhibits that shed light on the magnificent stone carvings found at Phanom Rung are particularly recommended. ☎ *044/631746* ☞ *B40* ☉ *Daily 6–6.*

Scattered around the area are other Khmer prasats in various stages of decay, many of them overgrown by vegetation. One of these has been rescued by Thailand's Department of Fine Arts. **Prasat Muang Tam** is only a couple of miles from the base of Phanom Rung hill. It's estimated to be 100 years older than its neighbor, starting off as a 10th-century Hindu sanctuary. Its main building symbolically represents the universe, with lesser towers emanating from the center. Today four towers remain, all containing carvings of Shiva and his consort Uma, Varuna on a swan, Krishna with cows, and Indra on the elephant Erawan. The complex is flanked by ceremonial ponds, with five-headed nagas lying alongside. ⊠ *8 km (5 mi) southeast of Prasat Hin Khao Phanom Rung* ☎ *044/631746* ☞ *B40* ☉ *Daily 6–6.*

Where to Eat

If you really want to mix it up with the locals and get a sense of how most people dine out in Buri Ram, head to the new Night Bazaar (4 PM to 11 PM) at the end of Romburi Road. There's plenty of cheap, ready-to-order food, along with a vast selection of fresh produce. It's at its best after 6 PM.

$ ✕ **Bamboo Bar & Restaurant.** This simple country-style restaurant in the heart of town is only minutes from the train station and even closer to the city's night spots. You'll find mainly staple Western dishes—the baguettes are particularly popular. It's a good place to meet the local expat crowd, kick back in front of some cable TV, and get some tips on what to do and see in the area. ⊠ *14/13 Romburi Rd.* ☎ *044/625577* ⊟ *No credit cards.*

¢–$ ✕ **Phu Tawan.** A popular evening eatery, Phu Tawan is a must for Thai folk rock music lovers. A booming band plays to an excitable local crowd who spend all evening jumping up to dance and sing along with the musicians. It's only a minute's walk from the Thepnakorn Hotel. Recommended dishes are the local spicy pork dish *laab moo* and *yam takrai,* a lemongrass and fish salad. ⊠ *Satuk Rd.* ☎ *044/617123* ⊟ *No credit cards.*

Where to Stay

$ ▦ **The Thepnakorn Hotel.** This is as close as Buri Ram has to a top-end hotel and the best place to rest up while investigating the nearby ruins. The English-speaking staff will give you a warm welcome, which sets the tone for this friendly hotel. It's a 5- to 10-minute tuk-tuk ride from the center of town. ⊠ *139 Jira Rd., 31000* ☎ *044/613400 up to 2* 📠 *044/613402* ⊕ *www.thepnakorn.com* ✍ *144 rooms* ⚒ *Restaurant, coffee shop, room service, minibars, cable TV, massage, billiards, bar, lobby lounge, shop, laundry service, convention center, travel services* ⊟ *MC, V.*

¢ ▦ **Fhean Fha Palace Mansion.** The Fhean Fha is primarily an apartment block, but the place also operates as a hotel. It's in the center of town and is Buri Ram's biggest bargain. Tucked down a narrow side street, it's only a short walk from the park and the Night Bazaar. ⊠ *240/9 Jira*

Rd., Soi 13, 31000 ☎ 044/617112 ⇆ 40 rooms � Restaurant, mini-bars, cable TV, hair salon, laundry service ▤ No credit cards.

¢ ▥ **Vongthong Hotel.** Although not the prettiest of hotels, the Vongthong has decent rooms furnished in a Thai style with marble floors and tapestries hanging from the walls. It's only a few blocks from the railway station. ⊠ *512/1 Jira Rd., 31000 ☎ 044/620860 up to 2 ✉ 044/620859 ⇆ 71 rooms ⠯ Restaurant, coffee shop, room service, mini-bars, cable TV, massage, billiards, lobby lounge, laundry service, convention center ▤ MC, V.*

Surin

❺ *52 km (30 mi) east of Buri Ram, 198 km (119 mi) east of Nakhon Ratchasima.*

With its Phanom Don Rak mountain range bordering Cambodia to the south, Surin has always been heavily influenced by Cambodian culture, and a large proportion of the local population speaks a Khmer dialect. Its strategic location also made Surin an assembly point for the elephant armies during the early Rattanakosin period; to this day the city is best known for its elephants. Everywhere you look in this bustling city you'll see homage paid to these noble creatures in the form of sculptures, art work, and even street lamp motifs. In addition, it shares with its neighboring provinces a wealth of ancient Khmer structures, found outside the city in varying states of decay or restoration.

Surin is famous, above all, for its annual Elephant Roundup, held the third week of November. The impressive show includes elephants performing tricks while their mahouts reenact scenes of capturing them in the wild. The main show is held at the **Sri Narong Stadium,** in town, and starts at 7:30 AM. Ticket prices start at B300, rising to B500 if you're seated in the stands with the sun at your back. If you'd like to get up close to the animals you can take a short ride on the elephants for a small fee at the end of the performance and you can also hand-feed them in the paddock to the rear of the stadium. The town is packed with visitors at roundup time, so make sure you have a hotel reservation if you plan to join them.

If you want to see elephants the rest of the year, head to Ta Klang, a village 60 km (37 mi) north of Surin. The village is home to the Suay people (also known as Kui), who migrated from southern Cambodia several centuries ago. Until recently, groups of Suay would venture into Cambodia to capture wild elephants and train them for the logging industry. But as elephants have been replaced by heavy machinery, the animals and their mahouts have become little more than tourist attractions. The village has an **Elephant Study Center,** but it has little information, and public performances are now only given on a prebooked basis for large groups. A trip here may disappoint, so it's best to take a guided tour with Khun Pirom of Pirom Guest House, who can take you to the homes of the villagers to see how they tend these magnificent animals.

Other than during roundup time, you find limited numbers of elephants in Ta Klang village; during most of the year their handlers take them to neighboring towns and to tourist areas throughout the country to perform. Sometimes mahouts make money simply by charging tourists a small fee to hand-feed the elephants in the streets. Until there's any effective legislation on the matter, it's up the individual as to whether or not they want to support a practice that has elephants wandering busy, polluted city streets.

There's much well-founded concern from animal rights groups about the well-being of animals used in tourist attractions, but so far an alternative place for the elephant in Thai society or in the wild has not been found. Without their elephants, the Suay people's age-old culture and way of life would be lost and the elephants they handle would have little or nothing to eat. So, as things stand, by seeing the Elephant Roundup visitors help to preserve the elephants and their handler's culture in a slightly perverse, but nonetheless effective, way. After all, this show is not about profit for a private organization—all proceeds go to help the elephants it celebrates. It's encouraging that, as a rule, the elephants of Surin are healthy and well cared for, despite difficult conditions. An elephant clinic in Surin provides for the health of the elephants and trips are made by vets to the village of Ta Klang.

On the road between Si Saket and Surin is **Prasat Sikhoraphum,** a five-prang Khmer pagoda built in the 12th century. The central structure has engraved lintels depicting Shiva, as well as carvings of Brahma, Vishnu, and Ganesha. The bus (no. 3) from Nakhon Ratchasima stops at Surin bus station, which has a regular bus service to the site's adjoining village. ✉ *36 km (24 mi) east of Surin* 🎫 *B40* ⏲ *Daily 6–6.*

Nestled amidst thick vegetation beside the Cambodian border, 75 km from the far south of the city, is a series of three prasats collectively known as **Prasat Ta Muean.** All lie on an ancient road stretching from Phimai to Angkor. The first prasat you see is Prasat Ta Muean, built in the Jayavarman VII period of the late 12th century and believed to be one of 17 rest stops made for pilgrims traveling the route. The second smaller site, Prasat Ta Muean Tot, acted as an ancient hospital and was also constructed in the 12th century. But these are only teasers for what lies farther on, directly beside the Cambodian border: Prasat Ta Muean Thom.

Thom means big, and Prasat Ta Muean Thom is indeed the largest of the three sites. It was constructed in the 11th century, making it the oldest of the sites as well. The contrasting textures and colors of the soft pink sandstone towers and the rugged grey laterite of the viharns set against the rich green backdrop of the forest behind are something to behold.

The prasat's survival over the ages is made particularly poignant by the existence of unexploded grenades and land mines in the vicinity, left over from more troubled times. Some have even reported the distant crack of gunfire, and the area is kept a close eye on by the Thai army, whose checkpoints you'll pass on your approach to the area. For these reasons it's strongly advised that visitors don't wander off into the forest and that they admire the structures at Prasat Ta Muean Thom from cleared paths only.

Prasat Ta Muean is situated on a newly surfaced road, but it's still a bit isolated and is often a difficult place to get to via public transportation (at any rate, it can be a slow trip). Therefore it's best to drive or take a tour provided by Saren Travel or Khun Pirom at Pirom Guest House (⇨ *see* Tour Operators *in* Nakhon Ratchasima & Environs A to Z, below).

Where to Eat

The small but busy provincial capital of Surin has plenty of standard shophouse-style eateries where you can order basic rice or noodle dishes. Sirirat Road has many late-night dining spots, but if you want to mix with the locals in the evenings head to the Night Bazaar on Krung Sri Nai Road between 5 PM and 11 PM.

¢–$ ✕ **Farang Connection.** If you have a craving for some Western fare, this foreigner-run restaurant is the place to go. Only a minute's walk from the bus station, the small restaurant acts as a meeting point for expats and provides additional services such as motorbike rental, Internet, and tour services. The upper level also has a big screen TV and a dart board. ✉ *257/11 Jitbumroong Rd.* ☎ *044/511509* ⊟ *No credit cards.*

¢–$ ✕ **Larn Chang.** This delightful, wooden house restaurant is by a small lake. You can have a relaxing Thai meal in the restaurant's garden. The manager recommends the *gai phet mamuang* (stir-fried chicken and cashew nuts, with a dash of spices). The restaurant is open until 1 AM. ✉ *199 Seepatai Samon Rd.* ☎ *044/52869* ⊟ *No credit cards.*

¢–$ ✕ **Samrubtonkreang.** With dark-wood paneling and tons of old photos on the walls, this classic Thai restaurant from yesteryear has quite an atmosphere. It's very popular with tourists. Try the traditional Thai dishes, such as *nam prik long rua*, a thick chili sauce eaten with fresh vegetables. ✉ *201/44–46 Jitbumroong Rd.* ☎ *044/515015* ⊟ *MC, V.*

¢ ✕ **Che Took Restaurant.** With a constant stream of customers passing underneath its thatched-straw roof, Che Took is a bit frenetic. But it's popular for a reason: it's won many awards for the high quality of its food, which includes Isan and Thai-style steak dishes. ✉ *Lukmuang Rd.* ☎ *06/865–8893* ⊟ *No credit cards.*

Where to Stay

¢ ▥ **Phet Kasem Hotel.** This longtime favorite surrounds you with Khmer art reproductions as you enter its two-tier lobby area. Rooms are furnished with wood and colorful Thai fabrics; the bathrooms have marble floors. The pool and terrace buffet area are favorite gathering points in the evening. The staff is charming and friendly. ✉ *104 Jitbamroong Rd., 32000* ☎ *044/511274* 🖷 *044/514041* ⇌ *162 rooms* ⚐ *Restaurant, coffee shop, minibars, cable TV, pool, massage, billiards, lobby lounge, laundry service, meeting rooms* ⊟ *MC, V.*

¢ ▥ **Pirom Guest House 2.** This comfy little inn has incredibly reasonable rates (though no air-conditioning) that only rise during the Elephant Roundup. Owner Kun Pirom is a wealth of information about Surin and its elephants and conducts highly recommended tours of local attractions. The guesthouse's location, down a quiet country tack on the edge of town, makes it a peaceful and restful spot for those who prefer to be surrounded by nature rather than traffic. ✉ *326 Thung Pho Rd., 32000* ☎ *044/515140* ⇌ *6 rooms* ⚐ *No a/c* ⊟ *No credit cards.*

¢ ☒ **Thong Tarin Hotel.** Ask for a corner room at the Surin's most stylish hotel—they're larger and have commanding views of the city. This is a popular choice for those looking for a night on the town as it's only minutes from local watering holes; the hotel's beer garden attracts its own crowd of locals every evening. There's also a nightclub (with ballroom dancing lessons) and the popular Big Bite Restaurant on premise. The rates, which exclude an American breakfast, leap during the Elephant Roundup week. ☒ *60 Sirirat Rd., 32000* ☎ *045/514281* 🖨 *045/511580* 💤 *195 rooms* ♻ *Restaurant, coffee shop, minibars, cable TV, pool, massage, sauna, beer garden, nightclub, laundry service, meeting rooms, travel services* ▭ *AE, DC, MC, V.*

Shopping

About 15 km (10 mi) north of Surin a small road leads to **Khwao Sinarin,** a village famous for its excellent silk. Silver jewelry is now made here as well, and you can find bargains for bracelets and necklaces with a minimal amount of negotiation. You can detour south to **Ban Butom,** 12 km (7 mi) from Surin, where villagers weave the straw baskets sold in Bangkok. They'll be happy to demonstrate their techniques.

Si Saket

❻ *312 km (187 mi) east of Nakhon Ratchasima, 61 km (36 mi) west of Ubon Ratchathani.*

With the exception of a newly constructed temple, **Phrathat Ruang Rong,** which is said to be one of the biggest in the northeastern part of the country, the town of Si Saket is best known for its pickled garlic and onion. But in early March, when the lamduan flower blooms, the town comes alive in a riot of yellows and reds. Locals celebrate with a three-day festival, the **Lamduan Ban Fair,** which centers around the beautiful Somdej Sri Nakharin Park.

Prasat Hin Wat Sra Kamphang Yai, just outside Ban Sa Kamphang, is in better condition than many of the region's other Khmer sanctuaries. It has been carefully restored, even down to the items that have been lost or stolen over the last 900 years. Particularly spectacular are the lintels of the middle stupa, which depict the Hindu god Indra riding his elephant Erawan. The main gate, inscribed with ancient Khom letters, is thought to be from the 10th century, built during the reign of King Suriyaworamann. The temple behind the prasat is a Thai addition, its walls covered with pictures illustrating Thai proverbs. ☒ *40 km (25 mi) south of Si Saket.*

★ The spectacular ruins of **Prasat Khao Phra Vihanalong Viharn** are officially in Cambodia, ever since the World Court resolved that country's bitter territorial dispute with Thailand. Until 1999 the temple was closed to visitors, as thick jungle bars the way from Cambodia. But the lure of tourist dollars led the former rivals to work together. The only practical route to the temple is through Thailand; you have to show your passport at a checkpoint, but no visa is required. The 12th-century compound, a jumble of red laterite, runs for more than 1 km (½ mi). The ruins are spread over four levels, with the access to the first level having the steepest ascent (after this the going gets a little easier). You pass *gopura* gateways and *naga* terraces on your ascent through this compound, which was adapted to suit the landscape, utilizing the natural bedrock of the mountain to form the base of causeways and courtyards. The principal temple structure is on the steepest level, perched on a cliff that plunges into thick rain forest. It's a long climb to the top, but the effort is rewarded by a truly breathtaking view of the jungle beyond. Tour operators in Ubon Ratchathani and Surin offer trips to the ruins, and it's certainly worth the expense. Alternatively, you can take a local bus to Kantharalak, 80 km from the city, and then seek out a songthaew or local van to the border from there. The bus to Kantaralak leaves regularly from Si Saket bus terminal and costs around B30. ☒ *125 km (86 mi) southeast of Si Saket* ☒ *B200 on Thai side of border and an additional B200 on Cambodian side.*

Where to Stay & Eat

$–$$ ✕ **P.S. House.** This family restaurant tries a little harder to impress with its brightly colored decor and detailed menus. It's notable for its wealth of steaks (including saba fish and ostrich meat). ☒ *820/14–16 Si Saket-Ubon Rd.* ☎ *02/208–9335* ☒ *No credit cards.*

¢–$ ✕ **Somkid Restaurant.** Dishes at this Chinese-style eatery are served with a thick rice soup. The plain plastic seating and wooden tables don't do justice to the quality of the food. The restaurant receives regular customers into the wee hours—it's open until 3 AM. ☒ *332/1–3 Ratchagarn Rot Fai Rd.* ☎ *045/614195* ☒ *No credit cards.*

¢ 🏨 **Kessiri Hotel.** This stylish choice gives a nod to the Thai architecture traditions—there's even a *naga* fountain at the entrance to the small lobby area. Local art and fabrics are in abundance here, as is rich ochre-color paneling, which dominates both the lobby and the modest-size rooms. ☒ *1102–05 Khukran Rd.* ☎ *045/614006* 🖷 *045/614008* ⤳ *93 rooms* ♢ *Restaurant, coffee shop, minibars, massage, laundry service* ☒ *No credit cards.*

¢ 🏨 **Phrompiman Hotel.** Near the train station, the night market, and the city's main restaurant and bar district, this hotel is probably the best positioned in the city. The superior air-conditioned rooms are very reasonably priced and are decorated with Thai mural reproductions. However, its sparse lobby area does feel kind of lonely. ☒ *849/1 Lukmuang Rd.* ☎ *045/612677* 🖷 *045/612271* ⤳ *192 rooms* ♢ *Restaurant, coffee shop, minibars, hair salon, massage, laundry service* ☒ *MC, V.*

Ubon Ratchathani

❼ *227 km (141 mi) east of Surin, 167 km (100 mi) south of Mukdahan.*

Eastern Isan's largest city, Ubon Ratchathani is known as the "Royal City of the Lotus." It's the gateway to the so-called "Emerald Triangle, " the verdant region where Thailand, Laos, and Cambodia meet. Here you can see the sun rise over Thailand, sparkling on the surface of the third-largest province's three major rivers, the Mae Khong, Mun, and Chi. The city, which today is simply known as Ubon, was established on the bank of the Mun river in the late 18th century during a time of conflict with the Laos capital, Vientiane. Today the city enjoys good relations with all its neighbors and you can always find a warm welcome here. The city is famous for its political heritage, musical performers, and *moo yor* (processed pork wrapped in a banana leaf), but is best-known for its Candle Procession in late July. Candles are traditionally offered to monks at the start of Buddhist lent, Kao Pansa, and villages throughout the area compete to produce the finest float adorned with huge beeswax sculptures of Buddhist-inspired mythical figures and a towering candle or *tien*. The floats are paraded through the downtown area accompanied by musicians and local dancers, all in traditional costume. The festival is held over two days and is centered at Thung Sri Muang Park.

In the northern reaches of Ubon Ratchathani you can find the Indian-style pagoda **Wat Nong Bua,** a copy of the famous one in India where the Buddha attained enlightenment more than 2,500 years ago. The rectangular white chedi is breathtaking. Another nice temple is **Wat Maha Wanaram,** which houses a revered Buddha image named Phra Chao Yai Impang, believed to have magical powers. Check out the wax float at the rear of the chedi, used in the Candle Procession.

More wax candles, as well as comprehensive and interactive exhibits concerning the history of the province and its make up, can be found at Rajabhat University Ubon's **Culture and Art Centre.** This unique white building houses an interesting museum in its basement where you can find plenty of information in English celebrating the lives of local wax sculptors, as well as musicians and singers who perform in the famous Isan *morlam* style. Morlam is traditional Laotian music with strong rhythms and dynamic vocals. The genre has been augmented with electronic keyboards, helping to keep it alive and as popular, nationally, as ever. ⊠ *Changsanit Rd.* ☜ *Free* ☉ *Mon.–Sat. 8:30–4.*

Where to Eat

Locals love the evening food stalls along Ratchabut Road, beside Thung Sri Muang Park, but another popular spot is Haad Ku Dua, a beach along the banks of the Mun River about 7 km out of town. Here you walk out over wooden gangways to thatched rafts where your food is brought to you as you recline on reed mats and stare out at the thick jungle on the far bank. Try such favorites as *pla chon* (a fish whose name is often translated as "snakehead mullet") or the ubiquitous *gai yang* (roast chicken). Back in town and not far from the downtown area, Supphasit Road also offers a great selection of eateries both day and night.

$ ✕ **Nicha House Garden.** As the name suggests this restaurant is set in a garden, with a Thai-style wooden house to the rear. Recline in a garden chair; choose from local Isan food, seafood, and standard Thai and Chinese dishes. ⊠ *136 Supphasit Rd.* ☏ *045/245990* ☐ *No credit cards.*

¢–$ ✕ **Dee Amnuay Choke.** This bustling, friendly Chinese-style restaurant has an extensive menu and speedy service. This is arguably the most popular restaurant in town for late-evening diners and night prowlers (it's open until 4 AM), and you'll literally be rubbing shoulders with the locals. The decor is very basic, but the food is outstanding and great value for the money. Try the *phad poo pong garee,* a crab curry you can select ready-cooked straight from a massive bowl. ⊠ *377 Supphasit Rd.* ☏ *045/241809* ☐ *No credit cards* ☉ *No lunch.*

¢–$ ✕ **H2O.** As the name suggests, the theme at this restaurant for late-night revelers is water, characterized by a mock waterfall at the end of the garden. The dining areas are varied—you can choose to sit inside in a glass-walled room with live music and air-conditioning, outdoors in the casual garden or under a covered section, which exudes a more sophisticated Thai ambience. The restaurant is a bit far from downtown, but it's a great after-dark experience. It's open until 1 AM. ✉ *488/1 Chayangkul Rd.* ☎ *045/280315* ▭ *No credit cards* ⊘ *No lunch.*

¢–$ ✕ **Indochine.** This long-established restaurant is a favorite for both visitors and locals in search of fine Vietnamese, Chinese, and local dishes. The exquisite wooden entrance leads to a treasure trove of rooms with regional decor and antiques from around Southeast Asia. Upstairs you find the evening restaurant, which is more luxurious than the ground floor, reminiscent of a piano bar. A popular dish is *nem nuang,* minced pork balls on skewers. ✉ *168–170 Supphasit Rd.* ☎ *045/245584* ▭ *MC, V.*

Where to Stay

$ ▣ **Laithong Hotel.** Locally made crafts and colorful textiles make the rooms at this comfortable hotel stand out. This is one of the few places in the area in which you can experience a *phalaeng,* the traditional Isan meal served as you recline on cushions arranged on the floor. You'll be offered a raised bamboo tray with at least half a dozen specialties of the region. If that's too exotic, the Ruen Thong restaurant also serves international dishes. There's also a pub where you can relax with a beer. ✉ *50 Pichit Rangsan Rd.* ☎ *045/264271* ▤ *045/264270* ⤇ *124 rooms* ⚘ *Restaurant, coffee shop, minibars, cable TV, massage, piano bar, pub, nightclub, airport shuttle* ▭ *AE, DC, MC, V.*

$ ▣ **Navada Grand Hotel.** This high-rise hotel is popular with visitors, not only for the standard of its rooms but also for its associated entertainment complex, which includes a movie theater and a nightclub. The grand reception area has a relaxing lobby lounge where you can enjoy a coffee while perusing the daily paper before being sped back to your room in glass elevators. The rooms have dark-wood fittings, local fabrics, their own bars, and fine views of the city. In the evening you may want to visit the hotel's basement nightclub, The Rock, which fills up with the city's young and trendy. ✉ *434 Chayangkul Rd.* ☎ *045/280999* ▤ *045/283424* ⤇ *151 rooms* ⚘ *Restaurant, minibars, cable TV, pool, massage, lobby lounge, laundry service, travel services* ▭ *MC, V.*

¢ ▣ **Sri Isan Hotel.** This is Ubon's closest thing to a chic boutique hotel. The rooms here are modest in size but totally refurbished, and tastefully decorated. The most stunning aspect of the hotel is the central staircase, with mosaic-tile balustrades, winding up the hotel's four floors. The staff are both pleasant and helpful and the hotel is ideally located downtown next to a large covered market beside the Mun River. ✉ *62 Ratchabut Rd.* ☎ *045/261011* ▤ *045/261015* ⊕ *www.sriisanhotel. com* ⤇ *33 rooms* ⚘ *Restaurant, minibars, cable TV, lobby lounge, laundry service* ▭ *MC, V.*

¢ ▣ **Sri Kamol Hotel.** A five-minute walk from the night bazaar, this downtown hotel wins points for its location. The hotel's best feature, however, is the friendliness of its young staff and the warmth of its second-floor restaurant, which overlooks the lobby. ✉ *26 Ubonsak Rd., 34000* ☎ *045/246088* 🖷 *045/243793* 🛏 *82 rooms* ⚇ *Restaurant, refrigerators, cable TV* ▭ *No credit cards.*

Shopping

Chom Mek Border Market, 56 km (35 mi) from the city, is right over the Laos border and is very popular with visitors to the area. The small market, stretching across either side of the road, is interesting in itself, but most people seem to come here to buy wild orchids, which are sold at rock-bottom prices and in such abundance that you can't help but fear for the conservation of the flora of Laos. Other forest products on sale include seasonal wild mushrooms, ant eggs, and young bamboo shoots. You can also come across the usual border market wares such as cheap imitation watches, communist-style binoculars, and the ever tasty Beer Laos. Take a passport just in case you're asked for it, but there are no official checkpoints before the market, no visa requirements, and only a nominal B5 admission fee.

Under your own steam the best way to get the market is to take an hour-long bus ride from Ubon to Phiboon; buses leave every 12 minutes and cost B20. From Phiboon take another bus or songthaew ride to the border. The market is open daily from 8 AM to 4 PM.

NAKHON RATCHASIMA & ENVIRONS A TO Z

AIR TRAVEL

There are Thai Airways and Phuket Airlines flights each day from Bangkok to Buri Ram and Ubon Ratchathani. Due to its distance from town, as well as its limited popularity with travelers, the airport at Nakhon Ratchasima is presently closed. Ubon Ratchathani's airport is close to downtown, but Buri Ram's is 30 km (18 mi) from town.

🛫 Airlines **Thai Airways** ✉ Sofitel Raja Orchid, 9/9 Prachasumran Rd., Khon Kaen ☎ 043/227701 ✉ Manat Rd., Nakhon Ratchasima ☎ 044/255542.

BUS TRAVEL

Most of the towns in Isan are served by buses from Bangkok's Northern Bus Terminal. Nakhon Ratchasima is a major transport hub, with direct bus services to and from Bangkok, Pattaya, Chiang Mai, and Phitsanulok. A bus journey from Bangkok will take roughly four hours and cost B150; from Chiang Mai it will take roughly 11 hours, costing around B350, depending on the standard of the bus.

In general, buses are a bit cheaper than trains. Remember that many towns don't have formal bus terminals, but rather a spot along a main road where most buses stop.

Nakhon Ratchasima has two bus stations—the older terminal in the city center and the newer one north of Mittraphat Road. Buses to and from Bangkok mostly use the old terminal, while buses to other destinations in Isan depart from the newer terminal.

Buses to Ubon Ratchathani take upward of six hours and cost around B200. The best and most established company for this trip is Nakornchai Air (www.nca.co.th), which passes through all the cities in this area, starting from Ubon Ratchathani and going as far as Chiang Mai (overnight). These buses offer, among other things, a steward service, meal stops, movies, safety belts, and inflating massage seats.

Nakhon Ratchasima to Buri Ram by bus takes around two hours, to Surin around three hours, to Si Saket five hours, and to Ubon Ratchathani six hours. Service is regular and information concerning schedules can be obtained from TAT offices and the bus stations themselves. Tickets are best bought at the bus station. Only the bigger companies have a booking service, which it's best to use, unless you wish to risk a long bus journey standing up.

🚌 Bus Stations **Nakhon Ratchasima** ⊠ North of Mittraphat Rd. ☎ 044/242899 ⊠ South of Mittraphat Rd. ☎ 044/245443.

CAR RENTALS
Budget rental cars are available at the airport in Ubon Ratchathani.

In Nakhon Ratchasima, the local agency L.A. Trans Services will deliver a car to your hotel.

🚌 Agencies **Budget** ⊠ Ubon Ratchathani Airport ☎ 045/240507. **L.A. Trans Services** ⊠ Nakhon Ratchasima ☎ 044/267680.

CAR TRAVEL
The region's roads are well maintained, particularly those along the east–west route connecting Phitsanulok and Ubon Ratchathani and the north–south route of Nong Khai and Nakhon Ratchasima. The two routes intersect at Khon Kaen. You should experience no difficulty finding your way around on these roads; if you plan to explore further afield, remember that few road signs are in English.

As with the rest of the country, access to tourist destinations has improved greatly with new asphalt roads and frequent tourist attraction signs in English to help you reach your destination. If you still feel more comfortable being led, hire a car and driver from a tour operator. Costs are around B1,500 per day.

It's advisable to carry your passport, along with your driver's license, with you at all times while driving as police checkpoints are fairly common (though typically a traffic policeman will wave a foreign tourist on).

In the case of motorbikes, make sure your vehicle is visibly taxed and insured and that you wear a helmet at all times. In the past it was common for people not to bother with wearing a helmet in the evenings, but government crackdowns have made it common practice to drive as safely at night as during the day.

EMERGENCIES
🚌 In Nakhon Ratchasima **General Emergencies** ☎ 191. **Police** ☎ 044/242010. **Maharat Hospital** ⊠ Chang Phuak Rd. ☎ 044/254990.
🚌 In Ubon Ratchathani **Police** ☎ 045/254216. **Rom Gao Hospital** ⊠ Auparat Rd. ☎ 045/254053.

MAIL & SHIPPING
Post offices are open weekdays 8–4 and Saturday 8–noon.
🔲 Post Offices **Nakhon Ratchasima** ✉ Mukmontri and Mittraphap Rds. **Ubon Ratchathani** ✉ 17 Srinarong Rd.

MONEY MATTERS
You'll have no difficulty at all finding banks with ATMs in all larger towns. They're easily identifiable by a blue-on-white sign. In smaller towns and villages you might have to seek out the foreign exchange counter of a local bank, though there are increasing numbers of ATMs even in the smallest of towns and it's only in villages that you will experience any difficulties. Banks large and small will exchange foreign currency, particularly dollars, and cash traveler's checks. There's usually a nominal fee.

SAFETY
Many of the major bus companies now fit their seats with safety belts, while the cheaper, local bus companies do not. So, for travel between the cities in this area you may wish to look for Nakornchai Air, or Nakornchai Tour bus companies to take the edge off some of those longer journeys.

Theft is not particularly common in the region, but it's not unheard of, so it's advisable to take the normal precautions like ensuring rental cars are locked and possessions are out of sight. Motorbikes are more prone to theft than cars.

TAXIS & TUK-TUKS
Cities in this part of the country do not have taxis like in Bangkok. The most common means of getting around is by either tuk-tuk, samlor, or motorbike taxi. In all cases, the price is negotiable. Generally speaking fares within city limits range from B30 to B40. The peddle-power samlors (tricycles) are perhaps the more romantic option, but take the longest to reach your destination.

The cheapest means of getting around town, and often between small towns, is by songthaew, where prices can be as low as B5 for a short trip. They may not be as direct, but are certainly a good bargain and fellow passengers will typically help you determine where to get off if you tell them your destination.

TOUR OPERATORS
Tour companies in the area provide one-day tours of the major sights, as well as overnight tours that extend over two or three provinces. The companies in Ubon can also deal with visas and trips to Laos. The companies listed below are reliable, but English-speaking guides are few in number, so don't forget to specify that you require one. Otherwise you may find yourself paying for a driver and pointer only.
🔲 Tour Companies **Greenleaf Travel** ✉ 51/1 Moo 2, Tessaban 15 Rd., Pakchong District, Nakhon Ratchasima ☎ 044/280285. **Nanta Travel** ✉ 334 Suranari Rd., Nakhon Ratchasima ☎ 044/251339. **Pirom Guest House 2** ✉ 326 Thung Pho Rd., Surin ☎ 044/515140. **Saren Travel** ✉ 202/1–4 Tesaban 2 Rd., Surin ☎ 044/520174. **Sakda Travel** ✉ 150/1 Kantalak Rd., Ubon Ratchathani ☎ 045/321937 ⊕ www.sakdatravel.com.

TRAIN TRAVEL

The Northeastern Line runs frequent service from Bangkok to Isan (there are 26 trains a day from Bangkok to Nakhon Ratchasima alone). All trains go via Don Muang airport and Ayutthaya to Kaeng Khoi Junction, where the line splits. One track goes to Nakhon Ratchasima, continuing east to Buri Ram, Surin, and Si Saket before terminating at Ubon Ratchathani; the other line goes north toward Nong Khai.

The train station for Ubon Ratchathani province is not actually in the city itself, but in Warinchamrab, directly across the river. Ubon is a 10-minute songthaew ride from here. Train prices vary according to speed of the train and class of seat. The regular train, with fans and no frills is wildly cheap. For example, a one-hour ride from Buri Ram to Surin costs B9. If you are traveling on a Friday or Sunday evening it's advisable to book in advance.

🚆 Train Stations **Buri Ram** ✉ Niwas Rd. **Nakhon Ratchasima** ✉ Mukhamontri Rd. **Si Saket** ✉ Ratchagarn Rot Fai Rd. **Surin** ✉ Nong Toom Rd. **Ubon Ratchathani** ✉ Sathanee Rd., Warinchamrab District.

VISITOR INFORMATION

The Tourist Authority of Thailand has developed a highly organized network of offices to promote tourism in this long-neglected part of Thailand. There are two main offices responsible for Lower Isan. The TAT office in Nakhon Ratchasima provides information for its own province plus Buri Ram and Surin. The TAT in Ubon Ratchathani takes care of information for Ubon and Si Saket. At both offices you can find English-speaking staff willing to answer queries and provide you with free maps, pamphlets for local guides, and other brochures that should put you on the right track. Office hours are 8:30 to 4:30 daily, though there are typically less staff on duty on a Sunday.

🚆 Tourist Information **Nakhon Ratchasima** ✉ 2102–2104 Mittraphap Rd. ☎ 044/213666. **Ubon Ratchathani** ✉ 264/1 Khuan Thani Rd. ☎ 045/243770.

ALONG THE MAE KHONG

The Mae Khong River, known in Thailand as *Mae Nam Khong*, is Southeast Asia's major waterway, starting in China's Qinghai Province near the border with Tibet. The Mae Khong crosses Yunnan Province, China, and forms the border between Myanmar and Laos as well as the majority of the border between Laos and Thailand, flowing across Cambodia and southern Vietnam into a rich delta before flowing into the South China Sea for a total distance of 4,200 km (2,610 mi).

More than 65 million people live along its banks, the river providing them with 80% of their daily protein intake and 20 million people with their sole source of income. Tides are turning though, with the construction of a series of Chinese hydroelectric/irrigation dams, which are seriously affecting the Mae Khong's flow (in 2004 commercial river-shipping operations had to close when the river was less than 3 feet deep).

In many ways the town of Mukdahan can be seen as symbolic of Thailand's future relationship with the Mae Khong. Plans to build bridges linking it to Laos, and farther afield, Vietnam, will make it more than just the river-reliant oddity it is today by turning it into a major international transit hub.

The small but active riverside community of That Phanom, with its revered Phra That Phanom temple and its dizzying 171-foot pagoda, is the focal point of the region, while Laotian influences—dialect, customs, and architecture—spread out from the provincial capital, Nakhon Phanom.

Mukdahan

❽ *167 km (100 mi) south of Ubon Ratchathani.*

Mukdahan is Thailand's newest (73rd) province, its status being upgraded from that of district in 1982. In 2006 Mukdahan will be permanently linked to its mirror city, Savannakhet in Laos, by the second Laos-Thailand friendship bridge. With increased trade via Route 9 and the Vietnamese port town of Danang, this town is expected to boom. Indeed, Mukdahan's main selling point is its international transit links with Laos's second city and the connection through to the Vietnamese border at Lao Bao.

The town itself is no oil painting, filled as it is with modern white concrete like so many standardized Thai provincial towns. Despite its redeveloped riverside promenade, it doesn't utilize its key geographical element, the Mae Khong. With its tiled walkway and absence of natural shading, this promising waterfront locale seems overly sanitized, offering only a dashed exposure of the majestic river.

The Indochinese market, stretching roadside from the promenade, is the focus of Mukdahan's bustle, with daily trade boats crossing to and from Savannakhet. The majority of goods are standard, cheap Vietnamese, Russian, and Chinese imports, with a profusion of items like car accessories and telescopic lenses. There's also the fabled promise of mudmee silks, but you might need one of those telescopic lenses to hunt out quality fabrics here.

With a Laos visa and B50 in hand for the boatman, you can visit **Savannakhet,** Laos's most populated province. Primarily a transit town, Savannakhet holds very little of interest for tourists, but proves a valuable link for travel farther down the Mae Khong, bus or plane options to Vientiane, as well as providing an opportunity (170 km away) to follow the Ho Chi Minh trail. For those looking for direct access into Vietnam, a cramped 250-km, seven-hour bus trip can get you there.

Where to Stay & Eat

Mukdahan has mostly simple streetside eateries, but there are some good alternatives. Try **BJ Nong Gai Tun** (⊠ Phitak Phanomkhet Rd. ☎ 042/630986) opposite the Palace Hotel for some good noodle soup, such as *nong gai tun yaa cheen* (boiled chicken leg soup with Chinese herbs).

Lang Koo Fat (⊠ Phitak Phanomkhet Rd. ☎ 042/630986) is one of two Vietnamese shopfront restaurants downtown, and the best option for some Vietnamese spring rolls and the ever popular *naem nuang* (processed pork served with transparent rice paper, vegetables, lettuce, and chilis).

Try **Ban Rattiya Jaew Horn 2** (✉ Soi Talat Tesaban 2, Phitak Phanomkhet Rd. ☎ 042/614789) for some Isan hospitality and *laab pla* (spicy minced fish salad) with sticky rice. There's also a night market along Songnang Sanid Road, where you can feast on standard Thai fast food.

¢–$ 🏨 **Mukdahan Grand Hotel.** This modern concrete building provides the town's best lodging. Although the employees speak very little English, they are friendly and try their hardest to be helpful. Rooms are plain, but adequately furnished with twin or king-size beds and a table and chair. The restaurant serves a buffet breakfast that is included in the room rate, as well as Thai and Western dishes for lunch and dinner. ✉ *70 Songnang Sanid Rd., 49000* ☎ *042/612020* 🖷 *042/612021* 📞 *200 rooms* ⚲ *Restaurant, refrigerators, cable TV* ▭ *AE, MC, V.*

That Phanom

🟢 *40 km (24 mi) north of Mukdahan, 50 km (31 mi) south of Nakhon Phanom.*

North of Mukdahan is the village of That Phanom, site of northeast Thailand's most revered shrine. No one knows just when **Phra That Phanom** was built, though archaeologists believe its foundations were in place by the 5th century. The temple has been rebuilt several times—its chedi now stands 171 feet high, with a decorative tip of gold that weighs more than 20 pounds. A small museum houses the shrine's ancient bells and artifacts. Droves of devotees attend an annual festival, usually held in February. The normally sleepy town comes to life as thousands fill the narrow streets.

Where to Stay & Eat

Despite having cheap eating options along Phanom Panarak Road, That Phanom is notable for its uniquely designed riverside restaurants. *Pla pow* (barbecued fish) is the main dish on offer, served with chili dips and sticky rice. There are six of these restaurants, with **Gung Haeng** probably the best pick for some *som tam* (spicy papaya salad) and songs. **Urng Kum Pla Pow** is another reliable option, but if you feel like some more solid seating, then try the two-level **Ngarm Da Song Fang Khong** on the roadside. Its menu has English translations; try *pad cha pla* (fried fish in spicy sauce), with some *laab pla* (spicy minced fish salad) to pep it up.

That Phanom is not as luxurious as Nakhon Phanom, but it's certainly more of a welcoming stay. Most of its accommodation takes the form of small concrete bungalow-style blocks placed near the Mae Khong River with a couple of uninspiring Chinese hotels standing near the bus pick up point for Bangkok. Two more interesting options are the rather eccentric Niryana Guesthouse and the Kritsada Rimkhong Resort, which offers the only real river views.

¢ 🏨 **Kritsada Rimkhong Resort.** This expanding bungalow complex is by no means a resort, but with the addition of two air-conditioned two-room wooden bungalows on stilts, it edges ahead of the competition. Cool tile flooring and dark varnished furniture in the rooms are pleasant; there are views of the Mae Khong River from balconies. The

CloseUp

THAILAND'S PARTYING PROVINCES

IN A NATION THAT LOVES TO HAVE A GOOD TIME, Isan bangs the drum the loudest and puts so much into its festivals that you soon forget this is Thailand's poorest region. Isan treats national celebrations and ceremonies with such gusto and enthusiasm that people flock from around the country to experience them. From the rice paddies to the bustling cities, the region rocks during its festivals, which are often begun as reverent affairs of Buddhist worship, but are more often than not fueled by a simple passion for living and copious amounts of sato (rice whiskey).

Singing and dancing are always major components of any Isan festival. Brass bands often boom in processions and troops of young students in traditional costumes dance in elegant smiling lines, defying the blazing sun. Then come the good ole boys and their traditional Isan instruments: the kahn and wuud bamboo organs, the pin guitars and pong larng xylophones, followed by the dit hai performers, traditionally garbed young women who dance fervently as their fingers effortlessly rise and fall to pluck notes from stringed fish pots.

There's a festival in Thailand every month of the year, often called Heet Sib Song (the 12 customs), and associated with various forms of Buddhist merit-making or ceremony. Of particular note are the third month's Boon Khao Jee in Roi Et, which features unique roasted rice-and-egg offerings; the sixth month's Boon Bung Fai, a rocket festival best known in Yasathon; and Boon Khao Pansa, the start of Buddhist lent, marked with the incomparable Candle Procession in Ubon Ratchathani. But what also makes the region stand out are some of the more unique parties found here. These include the Elephant Roundup of Surin on the third weekend in October for its shows and spectacle and the Phi Ta Korn ghost festival of Dan Sai district in Loei, which is held at the end of June or early July. This festival includes a procession of dancers dressed in colorful masks, holding elongated wooden phalluses that they light-heartedly poke at the giggling onlookers. Their antics follow the awakening of the spirit of a monk, Pra Ub Pa Kud, which resides in a stream in the form of white marble. Once his spirit is led back to the local temple it's believed he'll protect the village from harm for another year.

But the pièce de résistance has to be the Bon Fai Naak festival in Nong Kai in late October. Here, thousands of onlookers crowd the banks of the mighty Mae Khong in anticipation of the supernatural conflagrations of the mythical (or not so mythical) nagas, water serpents that appear in so much Buddhist folklore. All eyes are focused on the waters of this famous river, only turning to thank a joyful neighbor as the drinks are passed round. Anticipation rises and then the whoops and cheers erupt as into the night sky from the very depths of the waters ascend multicolor balls of fire and light. The nagas have not disappointed and have breathed their mysterious life into another moon-drenched night. The authenticity and nature of these annual, unearthly fireballs has been the matter of much speculation, but that fails to stop the throngs who come for the wonder and pure fun of it. This is Isan—suspend your disbelief and have a thumping good time.

—Ivan Benedict New

ground-level concrete bungalows are spacious; some only have fans, so be sure to request air-conditioning if you need it. ✉ *90–93 Rimkhong Rd., 48000* ☎ *042/525439, 01/0563449, or 01/2624111* ⊕ *www. geocities.com/ksdresort* ➟ *10 rooms* ⌂ *Refrigerators, cable TV; no a/c in some rooms* ⊟ *No credit cards.*

¢ 🏠**Niryana Guesthouse.** That Phanom's only true guesthouse, the Niryana's slightly weather-beaten look belies the value to be found within. The owner is a real character, and she will be happy to provide you with local maps and make suggestions for cycling tours to take in the surroundings. The small corridors are filled with oil and acrylic artwork done by the owner herself; rooms are replete with woven bamboo bedsteads and antique wooden furniture. During high season (November through February), breakfasts of French baguettes and Laotian coffee are on offer to set you up for the day ahead. Thai lessons are also available. ✉ *110 Moo 14, Rimkhong Rd., 48000* ☎ *042/540088* ➟ *6 rooms* ⌂ *Travel services; no a/c* ⊟ *No credit cards.*

Nakhon Phanom

🔟 *50 km (31 mi) north of That Phanom, 252 km (156 mi) east of Udon Thani.*

Nakhon Phanom translates from Sanskrit as the "City of Mountains, " and although this sleepy town boasts no actual mountain views to savor, it does represent the last chance for you to enjoy the spectacular sunrise over the Mae Khong from a top-story hotel room. The long, well-kept river promenade provides pleasant strolls and panoramic views from under tree canopies, with opportunities for quick forays into local temples.

The town also hosts a small but uneventful Indochinese market, opposite the immigration office, for some basic shopping, and with a Laos visa and B30 for the ferry crossing, you can propel yourself away from the nearby harbor and into the Laotian town of **Tha Khaek.** It's not the most obvious crossing point, as you have to travel either farther down the Mae Khong to Savannakhet or up to the capital Vientiane (both of which have more convenient transport links with Mukdahan and Nong Khai). The town is typical of Laotian border ports with some surviving French colonial architecture mixed up with newer facilities. To this end, Tha Khaek proves to be little more than a stepping stone.

Renu Nakhon, a small village 50 km (31 mi) south of Nakhon Phanom, represents one of the province's more interesting side trips. Based around the temple of **Wat Phra That Renu Nakhon,** this small, tourist-orientated fabric center is focused on the production and sale of predominantly mudmee silks and cottons. The shophouses at the temple's entrance make shopping easy, with dozens of local designs, fabrics, and ready-to-wear shirts and jackets on sale. Saturday is market day and village weavers from surrounding households set up shop offering homespun fabrics along with some unessential tourist treats and the chance for a good haggle. If it all seems a bit much then take a short walk behind the temple grounds where you can find calmer climes and can watch firsthand the households busily weaving for next week.

Where to Stay & Eat

¢–$ ✕ **View Khong.** The most noticeable riverside restaurant in Nakhon Phanom is attached to and owned by the Maenamkhong Grand View hotel. There's no real attention to decor here, with a simple windowed, air-conditioned dining room, cushioned seating on street level, and a row of tables and plastic chairs lower down on the waterfront. However, there's a good menu with an emphasis on river fish and some Western options. Moreover, a cool evening breeze and a gaze at the shimmering lights across the water in Laos make for a relaxing meal. *Pla neua orn samunpai* is a recommended fish dish with *yam huapee* (spicy banana flower salad) providing a tasty, tingling contrast. ⊠ *527 Soonthornvijit Rd.* ☎ *042/513564 up to 70* ▤ *MC, V.*

$–$$$ ▥ **Nakhonphanom River View Hotel.** This is Nakhon Phanom's only five-star hotel, with a spread of rooms from Standard to Presidential. The rooms are clean and airy, though the views aren't as panoramic as you might hope from this riverside location. If you're willing to spend more, you can get one of the Riverview rooms, which really do have splendid vistas. There's a beautiful waterfront pool where you can pamper yourself with a massage right on the edge of the legendary river. ⊠ *9 Nakhonphanom-That-phanom Rd.* ☎ *042/522333 up to 40* 📠 *042/522777 or 042/522780* ⊕ *www.northeast-hotel.com* ➥ *122 rooms* ⌂ *Restaurant, minibars, cable TV, pool, massage, lobby lounge, convention center* ▤ *MC, V.*

¢–$$ ▥ **Mae Nam Khong Grand View.** If you're looking for reasonably priced views over the Mae Khong River, then this is the place. This friendly, clean, and comfortable five-story hotel can be a rewarding stay if you snag an east-facing corner room—big windows give you a magnificent view of the Mae Khong. The hotel also has the only real riverside dining option here, which serves Thai and Western dishes. ⊠ *527 Soonthornvijit Rd.* ☎ *042/513564* 📠 *042/511037* ➥ *116 rooms* ⌂ *Restaurant, minibars, cable TV, bar* ▤ *AE, MC, V.*

ALONG THE MAE KHONG A TO Z

AIR TRAVEL

Thai Airways and PB Air both have one flight daily between Bangkok and Nakhon Phanom.

📋 **Airlines PB Air** ⊠ Fuangnakhon Rd., Nakhon Phanom ☎ 042/587207. **Thai Airways** ⊠ Nittayo Rd., Nakhon Phanom ☎ 042/513014.

BUS TRAVEL

Direct service from Bangkok to Nakhon Phanom leaves from Bangkok's Northern Bus Terminal every half hour from 7 PM to 8:30 PM; the trip takes 11 hours. Buses back to Bangkok leave from Nakhon Phanom's bus station, on Highway 22, as well as from Nakorn Pranarak Road next to the market. Buses depart every 15 minutes from 5:30 PM to 6:30 PM. Costs both ways are B635 for VIP buses and B410 for first-class air-conditioned buses.

Air-conditioned bus connections from Nakhon Phanom to Udon Thani (5 hours) and Nong Khai (7 hours) leave from 5:30 AM to 3 PM, with Nong Khai buses stopping services at 11 AM. Both cost B122 one-way.

Buses from Nakhon Phanom to That Phanom (one hour) and Mukdahan (3 hours) take the same route starting at 6 AM, running every 40 minutes until 5 PM. Costs are B17 (fan) or B40 (air-conditioning) to That Phanom and B40 (fan) or B56 (air-conditioning) to Mukdahan. Khon Kaen (5 hours) can also be reached, with buses leaving Nakhon Phanom roughly every two hours from 6:10 AM to 4 PM; the fare is B97 (fan) or B175 (first-class with air-conditioning). Buses to Ubon Ratchathani (4 hours) cost B97 (fan) or B164 (first-class with air-conditioning).

That Phanom district has two private companies operating nightly buses to Bangkok found on Chaiyangun Road, while Mukdahan's bus terminal on Highway 212 has fan buses leaving every half hour to Ubon Ratchathani (3 hours; B51) between 6:30 AM and 5 PM. Buses to Bangkok (11 hours) are also available here between 8 AM and 6 PM at a cost of B336 for first-class air-conditioned buses and B575 for 24-seat VIP buses.

🚌 Bus Stations **Mukdahan** ✉ Highway 212 Rd. ☎ 042/611421. **Nakhon Phanom** ✉ Klang Muang Rd. ☎ 042/513444. **That Phanom** ✉ Thai Sangaon Tour, Chaiyangun Rd. ☎ 042/541757 or 09/8631243. ✉ Cherd Chai Tour, Chaiyangun Rd. ☎ 042/541375 or 01/7683559.

CAR RENTALS

Mukdahan is the Mae Khong route's only rental prospect, with passport copies and international driver's license required.

🚌 Agencies **Mae Khong World Holiday** ☎ 2820 Thamrongprasit Rd. ☎ 042/515775. **S.P.B.R. Tour** ✉ 165/2 Thamrongprasit Rd. ☎ 042/512384 or 01/8737495.

CAR TRAVEL

Roads from Udon Thani (via Sakhon Nakhon) to Nakhon Phanom, That Phanom, and Mukdahan, and trailing the 212 Mae Khong River road down to Ubon Ratchathani, are in reasonable condition, but they're narrow, two-lane squeezes.

Nakhon Phanom and That Phanom can also be reached from Khon Kaen. Mukdahan to Khon Kaen requires some cross-country drives following the good 212 and 2136 roads to the town of Phon Thong, then the 2116 road skirting Roi Et, which becomes a minefield of pots holes until Yang Talat town when it improves, taking you on to the 209 and into Khon Kaen.

Driving from Bangkok to the Mae Khong towns you should use the faster Highway 2 until Khon Kaen and then backtrack the route described above.

EMERGENCIES

🚌 In Mukdahan **Police** ☎ 042/611333. **Mukdahan International Hospital** ✉ Chatu Phadung Rd. ☎ 043/236005.
🚌 In Nakhon Phanom **Police** ☎ 042/511266. **Nakhon Phanom Hospital** ✉ Apibanbuncha Rd. ☎ 042/511422.
🚌 In That Phanom **Police** ☎ 042/515554. **That Phanom Hospital** ✉ Highway 212 Rd. ☎ 042/541735.

HEALTH

Urban areas are free of malaria, but if you're traveling along the Mae Khong or in the national parks during the rainy season, you're well advised to pack sprays and creams and sleep under mosquito nets.

MAIL & SHIPPING

Post offices are open weekdays 8:30 to 4:30 and Saturday 9 to noon.

🏠 Post Offices **Mukdahan** ✉ Ratchaphant Pracha Rd. **Nakhon Phanom** ✉ Sunthonvijit Rd. **That Phanom** ✉ Chayangun Rd.

MONEY MATTERS

You'll have no difficulty finding banks with ATMs in all larger towns. They're easily identifiable by a blue-on-white sign. In smaller towns and villages you might have to seek out the foreign exchange counter of a local bank.

SAFETY

The Mae Khong towns pose little trouble for travelers, with the strong currents of the river itself being their only real danger. Swimming, diving, or kayaking is not recommended.

TAXIS & TUK-TUKS

Tuk-tuks and car taxis aren't really an option along the Mae Khong; songthaews are the most common means of public transport. Motorbike taxis and the ever-present pedal-powered samlors are available, but with these towns being so manageable in size, walking is the more enjoyable option.

TOUR OPERATORS

North by North East Tour, based in Nakhon Phanom, organizes the most comprehensive packages for seeing the Mae Khong stretch. This tour company has some good four-day/three-night programs for this area, including visits to ethnic-Lao and traditional Isan villages, the Laotian towns of Savannakhet and Tha Khaek, Ho Chi Minh's residence, Wat Phra That Phanom, and Indochinese markets, as well as Pha Taem National Park, Mukdahan National Park, and Khao Phra Viharn's temple complex on the Cambodian border. Prices are good and online booking is available on their informative Web site.

🏠 Tour Companies **North by North East Tours** ✉ 746/1 Sunthornvichit Rd., Nakhon Phanom ☎ 042/513572 or 042/513573 ⊕ www.thaitourism.com/ISAN/default.asp.

TRAIN TRAVEL

There are no direct train links with Nakhon Phanom or Mukdahan, however the Northeastern Line does make stops in Ubon Ratchathani to the east and Khon Kaen, Udonthani, and Nong Khai to the northeast. Trains bound for Ubon leave from Hualamphong station in Bangkok 5:45 AM, 6:40 AM, 6:45 PM, 9 PM, and 11:40 PM, taking approximately 11 hours and costing between B175 for third-class seats up to B1,080 for a first-class sleeper. Khon Kaen trains leave at 8:20 AM, 8 PM, and 8:45 PM, taking around eight hours and costing between B157 and B978. Udon Thani and Nong Khai trains leave at the same time as Khon Kaen's adding an extra two and three hours respectively, costing B175 to B1,077 and B183 to B1,117.

VISITOR INFORMATION

The Tourist Authority of Thailand has only one office in this area, responsible for Nakhon Phanom, That Phanom, and Mukdahan. It stocks good maps of all the towns, but lacks English information for its host province. There is, however, an essential booklet in English for Mukdahan, with all its attractions covered.

Tourist Information **Tourist Authority of Thailand** ✉ 184/1 Soontornvit Rd., Nakhon Phanom ☎ 042/513490.

UDON THANI & ENVIRONS

Prehistory, geography, myth, superstition, and Vietnam War–era boom towns make this area of Northern Isan one of the richest and most varied destinations in Thailand. Its geography, spreading east from the mountain ranges of Petchabun, through to the rich depths of the Mae Khong River, give this region one of the most varied terrains in the country.

Thailand's largest fossilized remains have been unearthed in Isan's plateau, along with proof of Southeast Asia's oldest Bronze Age civilization. Although its soils have proven to be of archaeological value, the vast waters of the Mae Khong have been held in even greater value. During the Ayutthaya period (1350–1758) these small riverside communities saw strategic garrison towns spring up, heralding drawn-out territorial disputes between Laos and Siam that continued until 1907 and the Siamese-French treaties.

The French colonization of Laos from 1893 to 1953 and its gaining of all territories east of the Mae Khong River left a strong influence on these bordering towns in the form of architecture and a diversity in culture and surroundings that can be found in few other places in Thailand. The start of the Vietnam War, however, brought this area into the 20th-century with a bang. Thailand's major alliance with the United States during the war helped bring money into this whole region, causing its greatest economic thrust and spawning overnight boomtowns that today stabilize Thailand's poorest reaches.

Most travelers making their way into Laos find themselves spending some time in Nong Khai, the main crossing point into the country. Although Nong Khai has little to offer other than temple tours and the annual, mysterious spectacle of balls of fire rising from the Mae Khong during the *Bon Fai Naak* festival, it does offer a wide range of accommodation and might be your last chance to immerse yourself in Thailand before you venture into the tropics of Laos.

Udon Thani serves as the best stopover point for this region, with transit links on the way to the lower reaches of the Isan plain, as well as into Laos. Those looking for a bit of Bangkok sophistication (without the grime) will enjoy the city with its mix of foreign foods and tongues and the pumping bars and clubs that make for a memorable night out.

Loei is the prime natural attraction for this region, containing the last mountainous ranges of northern Thailand, culminating in the evergreen heights of its deservedly famous Phukradung National Park. With the Laotian-influenced festival of Phi Ta Khon and the strong French colonial styles of architecture in Chiang Khan, the region is as rich culturally as it is naturally.

Khon Kaen, aside from its cretaceous bones and wartime legacy, is the quintessential Isan city. It holds the key to Isan's heart with its generous hospitality, wild foods, and royal fabrics. Whether on excursions out to rural Isan communities or scooting around its Bangkok-style pubs and clubs, you're guaranteed a true slice of Isan life.

Udon Thani

⑪ *564 km (350 mi) northeast of Bangkok, 401 km (250 mi) northwest of Ubon Ratchathani.*

As the site of a major U.S. Air Force base during the Vietnam War, Udon Thani quickly grew in size and importance. There are still traces of the massive U.S. presence in its hostess bars, hamburger joints, and shopping malls, but the independent Thais have managed to keep their hold on the city.

The **Udon Thani Provincial Museum** opened in January 2004 and showcases most of the province's sights. The museum occupies the impressive Rachinuthit building, which was built during Rama VI's reign and was originally used as a girls' school. Divided into two floors and seven sections, the museum takes you through the history, geology, archaeology, anthropology, and urban development of the city. Sliding across the buffed golden teak floorboards from one room to the next you pass models of ethnic groups and miniatures of attractions, as well as ethnic artwork. ⊠ *Phosi Rd.* 🎫 *Free* ⏱ *Daily 9–4.*

The chief attraction near Udon Thani is **Ban Chiang**, about 60 km (36 mi) east of the city. At this Bronze Age settlement, archaeologists have found evidence to suggest a civilization thrived here more than 7,000 years ago. The United Nations declared it a World Heritage Site in 1992. The peculiar pottery—red-on-cream with swirling geometric spirals—indicates that this civilization was ahead of its time in cultural development. Even more intriguing are the copper bells and glass beads found here, many of which are similar to some found in North and Central America. This poses the question: did Asians trade with Americans 7,000 years ago, or even migrate halfway around the world? You can reach Ban Chiang from Udon Thani on the local bus, or take a car and driver for about B600.

off the beaten path

BAN PHUE – One hour by bus northwest of Udon Thani is a 1,200-acre mountainside retreat near the village of Ban Phue. It's littered with rocks of all sizes, some in shapes that the faithful say resemble Buddhist and Hindu images. Wat Phra Buddha Baht Bua Bok, at the peak, is named after the replica of the Buddha's footprint at its base. The 131-foot pagoda is in the style of the revered Wat That Phanom, farther to the east. Take the path to the right of the temple and you'll reach a cave with a series of silhouette paintings thought to be 4,000 years old.

Where to Stay & Eat

Udon Thani is famous for its version of *gai yang,* or roast chicken, which you can try at stalls on virtually every street.

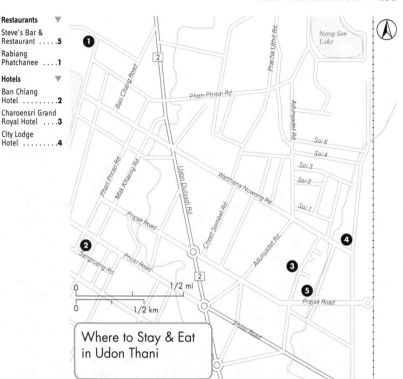

Where to Stay & Eat
in Udon Thani

$ ✕ **Steve's Bar and Restaurant.** Steve, an ex-fireman from England, and his Thai wife serve up traditional pub classics at this long-standing expat haunt in the center of town. An indoor air-conditioned dining room fills up with those craving authentic steak-and-kidney pies and fish-and-chips. Portions are large and it's a good spot to catch sports on the big screen. ⊠ *254/26 Prajaksilapakom Rd.* ☎ *042/244523* ⊕ *www. stevesbarudon.com* ⊟ *No credit cards.*

¢ ✕ **Rabiang Phatchanee.** On the edge of the lake at Nong Prajak Park you find this pleasant, traditional Thai restaurant. An extensive menu features standard favorites alongside some interesting variations. *Pla deuk fu phat phet* (fried crispy catfish with a chili sauce) is fiery but ever so tasty, while *som pla choh tot* (sour soup with water mimosa and serpent head fish) is authentic Isan food (though quite sharp). Live music plays in the background. ⊠ *53/1 Bannon Rd.* ☎ *042/241515, 042/ 244015, or 042/325890* ⊟ *MC, V.*

$–$$ ⊞ **Charoensri Grand Royal.** Just to make sure you get the message, the city's top hotel calls itself both grand and royal. It's certainly luxurious, with softly carpeted rooms furnished in pale woods and decorated in restful pastels. The two restaurants serve Thai, Chinese, and Western food, and there's a variety of beers on tap in the pleasant beer garden. ⊠ *277/1 Prajaksilapakom Rd., 41000* ☎ *042/343555* 📠 *042/343550*

      260 rooms ☆ 2 restaurants, room service, minibars, cable TV, pool, gym, health club, sauna, bar, beer garden, piano, convention center, meeting rooms, car rental, travel services ⊟ AE, DC, MC, V.

$ ▦ **Ban Chiang Hotel.** Ban Chiang is a nicely furnished hotel, tastefully decorated with local paintings. The rates make it quite a bargain, and you'll be tempted to spend your savings on pampering yourself at the hotel spa. ⊠ *5 Phosi Rd., 41000* ☎ *042/2327911* 🖷 *042/223200* *149 rooms ☆ Restaurant, minibars, cable TV, pool, gym, spa, Internet, convention center, meeting rooms, airport shuttle* ⊟ *AE, DC, MC, V.*

¢ ▦ **City Lodge Hotel.** The name is uninspiring, but City Lodge is actually an excellent English-owned boutique hotel. It's tastefully designed with a decidedly modern bent: heavy on pastel shades and chrome fittings, with contemporary furnishings and arresting local art. The hearty complimentary breakfast and well-stocked bar make this place particularly good value. ⊠ *83/14–15 Wottananuvong Rd., 41000* ☎ *042/224439 or 07/9520632* *10 rooms ☆ Restaurant, minibars, cable TV, laundry facilities* ⊟ *No credit cards.*

Shopping

If you're here for textiles, there's a busy community of silk weavers at the village of **Ban Na Kha,** about 14 km (8 mi) north on the Nong Khai Road. This working village produces geometric *khit* fabric, which you can buy in local village shops, or, if you can't make the trip, in Udon city. **Udon Bo-Pin Trachoo** (⊠ 129 Udon-Nong Sam Rd. ☎ 042/245618), and the smaller **Mae Lamun** (⊠ 123/1 Prajak Rd. ☎ 042/242498), found on the second floor of a Buddhist paraphernalia store, are both well-stocked tourist-oriented centers that deal in khit, as well as other Isan fabrics. The annual khit fabric fair, held at Thung Sri Muang Park in December, is also a good opportunity to pick up some bargains.

Khon Kaen

⑫ *190 km (118 mi) northeast of Nakhon Ratchasima, 115 km (69 mi) south of Udon Thani.*

Thailand's third-largest city, Khon Kaen has seen rapid growth due to the government's efforts to bolster the economy of the northeastern region. Khon Kaen has long been renowned for its mudmee silk, celebrated each December with a huge festival. At **Chonnabot,** 50 km (30 mi) to the south, you can see the silk being processed, from its cocoon stage through its spinning and dying to its weaving on hand looms.

About 50 km (30 mi) north of Khon Kaen is a small village called **Ban Kok Sa-Nga,** where virtually every household raises king cobras. The practice was started by a local medicine man some 50 years ago, but is now under the strict control of the Thai Tourism Authority. An official king cobra breeding center has been established on the grounds of the local temple. The village's main income derives, as does most of the region's, from farming and silk weaving. During the Songkran water festival in April and New Year's celebration in December, this small rural community comes alive as the cobras are brought out to take part in snake fights. You can visit the village at any other time, of course, but the spectacle is not quite the same, as you have to negotiate payment with specific households in order to see the two-minute, two-round fights. The village can be reached by taking bus number 501, which runs every half hour from Khon Kaen bus station to Ban Kok Sa-Nga.

About 80 km (50 mi) west of Khon Kaen is **Phuwiang National Park,** where the world's oldest fossils of carnivorous dinosaurs, the Siam Mityrennous Esannensil, were discovered. There are dinosaur museums at the park entrance, at Phu Pratu Teema, as well as in the nearby village of Kok Sanambin.

Where to Stay & Eat

Khon Kaen has a wealth of restaurants and cheap foodstalls on Klangmuang Road, and options along this stretch are as varied as Vietnamese, homemade pizza, and local Isan cuisine. A good late-night food stop is the night market off Namuang Road, which is open until the wee hours. Afternoon and early-evening snackers head to Bung Kaen Nakorn Lake, about five minutes south from the city center. Here you can find a dozen well-priced seafood restaurants, with Mae Khong River fish restaurants serving up some true local touches.

¢–$ ✕ **Bua Luang.** This open-plan lakeside restaurant is perched on the northern end of Bung Kaen Nakhon. One specialty worth trying is the *tom yam mapow orn* (prawns with coconut palm heart in spicy hot-and-sour soup). ✉ *105 Phiphatmongkol Rd.* ☎ *043/222504 or 043/320202* 🖃 *MC, V.*

¢–$ ✕ **Mr Chai.** This colorful spot is a cross between a pub and a restaurant, making it a great spot for an early-evening meal and a few drinks. A DJ plays Thai pop songs while you tuck into *pla duk foo* (crispy catfish salad) and *tom yam gai barn* (spicy hot-and-sour free-range chicken soup with lemongrass) and sip on some draft beer pumped from the back of a New York taxi. ✉ *Srichan Rd.* ☎ *043/246880* 🖃 *No credit cards.*

¢ ✕ **Khom Hom.** This pleasant open-air restaurant is a good option for those wanting to sample some of Northeastern Thailand's best-known delicacies. Not solely an Isan restaurant, as the sign may suggest, there are plenty of standard dishes on offer. The restaurant also has an insightful two-hour performance, from 7 PM to 9 PM, of traditional Northeastern music and dance. ✉ *Klangmuang Rd.* ☎ *043/243252 or 01/5440828* 🖃 *No credit cards.*

$$ ▦ **Bungalow Thongwong.** For home comforts and informative tours of Ban Chiang and other places of local interest, you couldn't do better than stay with the hospitable couple that runs this bungalow halfway between Udon Thani and Khon Kaen. The proprietors are a wealth of information about the region, and can introduce you to all aspects of local life and culture. The newly built bungalow has two separate units, with individual sitting rooms and kitchens. Guests can also enjoy marvelous Thai home cooking at the family's table. The daily room rate includes all meals, airport transfers, and a car and driver to Ban Chiang, Khon Kaen, Udon Thani, and other points of interest. ✉ *214 Moo 2, Non Sa-At, 41240* ☎ *042/391205* ⊕ *www.thaihomestay.co.uk* ⤲ *2 suites* △ *Kitchens* 🖃 *No credit cards.*

$ ▦ **Sofitel Raja Orchid.** Khon Kaen's skyline is dominated by the gleaming 25-story facade of the Sofitel Raja Orchid, one of Isan's most luxurious hotels. Everything about it is first-rate—the rooms are elegant, furnished with native woods and handwoven silks. If you're looking to splurge, there's always the 6,500-square-foot royal suite, which has its own helipad. The hotel is the center of Khon Kaen's nightlife, with Isan's largest karaoke bar, Studio 1, and a disco, the Funhouse, that really lives up to its name. German visitors marvel at Thailand's first microbrewery, the Kronen Brauhaus, where you can even order bratwurst. ⊠ *9/9 Prachasumran Rd., 44000* ☎ *043/322155, 800/221–4542 in U.S.* 🖷 *043/322150* ⊕ *www.sofitel.com* ⇌ *293 rooms* ♨ *5 restaurants, café, room service, minibars, cable TV, pool, fitness classes, gym, health club, sauna, 3 bars, nightclub, dry cleaning, laundry service, concierge, business services, meeting rooms, car rental, helipad, travel services* ☰ *AE, DC, MC, V.*

¢ 🏨 **Kaen Inn.** This extremely popular hotel is one of Khon Kaen's better value choices. The earth-color rooms are slightly dated, but clean and well furnished, mixing light wood trim and comfortable bamboo furniture. It's close to bars and restaurants. ⊠ *56 Klangmuang Rd.* ☎ *043/245420* 🖷 *043/239457* ⇌ *160 rooms* ♨ *Restaurant, coffee shop, minibars, in-room safes, bar, billiards* ☰ *MC, V.*

¢ 🏨 **Roma Hotel.** An inexpensive lodging near the bus station, Roma Hotel has large, sparsely furnished rooms and baths with plenty of hot water. Air-conditioned rooms are better maintained than the fan-cooled ones. The staff is friendly. ⊠ *50/2 Klangmuang Rd., 40000* ☎ *043/236276, 043/237206, or 043/237177* 🖷 *043/243458* ⇌ *46 rooms* ♨ *Restaurant, coffee shop* ☰ *MC, V.*

Shopping

Khon Kaen is littered with local souvenir shops. Locally made woven bamboo products can be found at **Moradok Thai** (⊠ 26–27 Ammat Rd. ☎ 043/243827). Silver trinkets are on sale at the centrally located **Mae Ying** (⊠ 227/7 Klangmuang Rd. ☎ 043/2321427). A smaller collection of ceramics can be found at the **Sunhatthakarn Si Phak Handicraft Centre** (⊠ 277 Mu 3 Mittraphap Rd. ☎ 043/228147). Most notable, however, is the province's famed mudmee silks and cottons. If you don't have time to make it to the source at the nearby villages of Chonnabot, Ban Muang Pha, i or Phu, then pay a visit to **Rin Thai Silk** (⊠ 412 Namuang Rd. ☎ 043/220705 or 043/221042). This small but well-stocked shop carries numerous mudmee and plaid patterned silks and cottons from all over the province.

Loei

🔟 *152 km (90 mi) west of Udon Thani, 43 km (26 mi) south of Chiang Khan.*

Loei, one of Thailand's most sparsely populated provinces, is a fertile basin fed by the Loei and Man rivers, tributaries of the Mae Khong, making it one of the country's most geographically scenic regions. Its unique topography, bordered by the Eastern and Western Phetchabun mountain ranges and its susceptibility to China's winter winds, result in Loei bearing some of the most dramatic temperatures in the country. Summers can reach 104° F, while winter nights can drop to freezing.

Once the site of a prehistoric Bronze Age mining settlement, Loei started life in the 15th century when the kingdoms of Ayutthaya and Lan Xang, in Laos, built Phra That Si Song Rak temple in what is now Dan Sai district. The temple's name literally translates as the "Sublime Love of Two" and served as a sign of beneficial relations between the two kingdoms at a time when Myanmar was infringing on domains based on the Mae Khong. 1853 saw King Rama IV bestow Muang Loei Thai with town status and present day Loei achieved its independent provincial status in 1933.

The province sees a rare blend of culture and language between its northern Thai neighbors, Laotian migrations, and northeastern affection. The result is a warm, traditional lifestyle and the unique Thai Loei language. Dan Sai district has its animated Phi Ta Khon festival in June, which is reminiscent of the Puyoe Yayoe festival in Muang Kaen Tao, Laos.

Despite its rich, embracing nature, the town itself is rather drab, with predictable concrete blocks and shophouses lining the streets. As a short stopover, Loei can be useful as a place to gather information, but the places worth exploring lie out of town. Phu Kra Dueng National Park is Loei's most visited station for its evergreen plateau, and Chiang Khan with its Laotian roots and colonial architecture is the heart of the province.

Where to Stay

$$ ☒ **Phu Pha Nam Resort.** With the exception of the rustic tiled floors of its pavilion-style restaurant and the stone walls in the billiards room, this entire hotel seems to be constructed of richly colored teak. You sleep on carved teak beds in teak-floor rooms, all of which have sitting areas with windows framing views of the nearby hills. The resort is on a 52-acre estate about 70 km (42 mi) south of Loei. ☒ *252 Moo 1, Koakngam Amphur Dansai, 42120* ☎ *042/892055* ☐ *042/ 892057* ⊕ *www.phuphanamresort.com* ⇌ *49 rooms* ⚬ *Restaurant, minibars, cable TV, massage, fishing, mountain bikes, billiards* ☐ *AE, DC, MC, V.*

$–$$ ☒ **Loei Palace.** The sinuous white facade of the massive Loei Palace dominates the city's skyline. Surrounded by well-tended gardens, the pool is a welcome sight after a day exploring the mountains. The excellent restaurant, serving Thai, Chinese, and other dishes, reassures you that sophisticated cuisine is still to be found in this remote region. An interesting outing is to the Chateau de Loei, Thailand's top vineyard. ☒ *Loei-Naduang Rd., 42000* ☎ *042/815668* ☐ *042/815675* ⊕ *www.amari.com* ⇌ *161 rooms* ⚬ *2 restaurants, café, minibars, cable TV, pool, gym, massage, bar, laundry service, business services, meeting rooms, travel services* ☐ *AE, DC, MC, V.*

¢–$ ☒ **Kings Hotel.** This central hotel represents Loei's best value. An unassuming entrance leads into a modest five-floor atrium-style complex, with a small square garden at its base. The rooms are clean and white with functional wood furnishings; cheaper fan-cooled rooms are also available by way of a thigh-burning hike up to the fifth floor. Prices and cleanliness undercut the competition, making it a good deal downtown.

✉ *11/9–12 Chumsai Rd., 42000* ☎ *042/811701, 042/811783, or 042/811225* 🖷 *042/811235* ⇨ *50 rooms* ⌂ *Restaurant, cable TV, laundry service* 🖃 *MC, V.*

¢ 🖼 **Sugar Guesthouse.** This is the one and only guesthouse in Loei. Rooms are basic but clean, ranging from cheap fan rooms with steel frame beds to bigger fan and air-conditioned rooms with teak beds, chairs, and wardrobes. The owner speaks English and has set up the place for travelers' needs with motorbike and bicycle rental, a good breakfast menu to get the day rolling, and tour services to tourist destinations in the province. If you're looking for a home away from home, this could be it. ✉ *4/1 Wisuttitep Soi 2 Rd., 42000* ☎ *042/812982 or 09/7111975* 🖷 *042/830129* ⇨ *8 rooms* ⌂ *Cable TV, laundry service, car rental, travel services* 🖃 *No credit cards.*

Phu Kra Dueng National Park

⑭ *70 km (42 mi) south of Loei.*

FodorsChoice
★

This was supposed to be Thailand's first national park, but lack of funding prevented that from happening. It wasn't until 1949 that government funds were finally allocated, and it took another 10 years before Phu Kra Dueng was finally granted national park status, becoming Thailand's second (after Nakhon Ratchasima's Khao Yai). Regardless of the slow start, it's become one of Thailand's most visited destinations.

The park consists of a lone, steep-sided mountain, which rises out of a flat plain that sprawls over 348 square km (134 square mi), and is crowned by a 60-square-km (23-square-mi) plateau. It takes a tiring four hours to hike and climb the 5 km (3 mi) to the top, but there's a spectacular and altogether gratifying panorama at 4,265 feet above sea level waiting for you once you've conquered it.

The mountain top is usually covered in mist from October to February, when the temperature can drop as low as freezing. The summit, full of rich flora year-round, is mostly a combination of dense evergreen forest and equally dense pine forest, but from February onward color begins to saturate the park. Summer brings out the mountain's famed red-and-white rhododendrons and flowering grasses such as Pro Phu and Ya Khao Kam. In winter the park is ablaze with lush green mosses and fern, set against the reddening of maple tree leaves. More than 276 animal species have been identified here, such as serows (a type of Asian goat), Asiatic elephants, tigers, bears, and boars, plus 171 species of birds including silver pheasants, black hawks, and red jungle fowl.

Main tourist attractions are well signposted. Trails take you through forest vegetation and vast grasslands, and along streams to waterfalls, caves, and overhanging cliffs (perfect for taking in a sunrise or sunset). There's plenty to do, and the park is equally good for a day-trip or extended exploration. The park headquarters at the base of the mountain has a good map and plenty of information for you to plan your wanderings.

Accommodation, food, and conveniences are readily available from top to bottom. Most people bring their own tents (there's a B20 pitching fee), but small corrugated steel A-frame huts are abundant for B100, and there are also larger, more expensive bungalow rooms from B900 to B3,600. The park is open from late September to early June, but the crowds will come out in force from late October through mid-January, so unless you're bringing you own tent, be sure to contact the park headquarters to reserve accommodation as soon as possible.

Note that they stop letting visitors into the park at 2 PM—the climb to the top takes a long time and they don't want people tackling it in the dark. If you are already inside the park, however, you don't need to be worried about being ushered out.

You can reach the park by bus from Loei's bus terminal; orange fan-cooled buses cost B26 and second-class air-conditioned buses cost B40. You have to get off at Pha Nok Khao junction and continue to the park by songthaew for another 20 km (12 mi); a songthaew generally costs B300 for up to six people. ⊠ *Hwy. 201, Loei-Phu Kra Dueng Rd.* ⊕ *www.dnp.go.th/National_park.asp* ⊠ *B200* ⊙ *Late-Sept.–early June, daily 7–2.*

Chiang Khan

⑮ *235 km (146 mi) east of Nong Khai, 43 km (26 mi) north of Loei.*

Travel north of Loei and soon you come to Chiang Khan, a village on the banks of the Mae Khong. Because of the old wooden houses along the river, the community retains much of its rural charm. On the eastern edge of town are scores of restaurants with seating areas facing the river and Laos. Downriver, a series of rapids tests the skills of the boatmen. From Chiang Khan the road turns south to Loei, the provincial capital, a major stop on bus routes in all directions.

Where to Stay

★ ¢–$$ ⊞ **Chiang Khan Hill Resort.** On the banks of the Mae Khong, this resort commands a marvelous view of a series of rapids. You can also see across to the Laotian countryside, making this resort worth a trip in its own right. Rooms are in octagonal bungalows; the best are the ones overlooking the water. There's an excellent open-air restaurant where the deep-fried shrimp cakes are crispy and delicious and the *somtan* (relish) tingles with lime. The chicken dishes are made from free-range birds. ⊠ *Kaeng Khut Khu, 28/2 Mu 4* ☎ *042/821285 or 042/821414* ⊟ *042/821414* 🛏 *50 rooms* ⬧ *Restaurant, refrigerators, cable TV, pool* ⊟ *MC, V.*

¢ ⊞ **Loogmai Guesthouse.** A small French colonial port house is the setting for this elegant guesthouse. Stylish, minimalist studios have well-chosen, untreated, antique wooden furnishings. The owner, Somboon, is a local artist who exhibited his work in Germany for 25 years, and his influence is plain to see. The upstairs fan-cooled room with private bathroom and a view over the Mae Khong is the one to aim for and well-worth booking in advance. ⊠ *112 Mu 1, Soi 5, Chaikong Rd.* ☎ *09/ 2100447* ✉ *loogmaiguest@thaimail.com* 🛏 *5 rooms* ⬧ *Laundry facilities* ⊟ *No credit cards.*

¢ ⊞ **Rimkong Pub & Guesthouse.** This is the most sociable and informative place in Chiang Khan. A converted 35-year-old wooden shophouse,

Rimkong has simple, mattress-on-the-floor fan-cooled rooms next to the Mae Khong. The owner, Pascal from France, is the man to speak to for maps, information on sights of interest, and timetables for public transportation—ask to see the folder at the bar. ✉ 294, Soi 5, Chaikong Rd. ☎ 042/821125 ⊕ http://rimkhong.free.fr ⇆ 6 rooms ⚫ Restaurant, laundry facilities ⊟ No credit cards.

Nong Khai

🄰 51 km (32 mi) north of Udon Thani, 60 km (36 mi) east of Chiang Khan.

Nong Khai is literally the end of the line—it's the country's northernmost railhead and bus terminus. To the east and west the mighty Mae Khong meanders through largely uncharted territory, while across the river to the north lies Laos. The French influence that is still evident in the Laotian capital of Vientiane can also be seen in Nong Khai. The architecture of the town has noticeable Gallic touches, particularly the governor's residence on Meechai Road. Running parallel to Meechai Road is Rim Khong Road, lined by small guesthouses and restaurants. Laotian goods, mostly textiles, are cheap and plentiful at Nong Khai's lively night market.

One of the main draws to Nong Khai is access to Laos via the **Friendship Bridge**. The ½-mi-long bridge, which opened in 1992, has brought Nong Khai and its province a boost in tourist traffic, which means you can find accommodations here that rival those of bigger towns. To cross into Laos, you must buy a visa for $30. From the Laotian side it's a 25-km (15-mi) samlor ride to the immensely charming capital city of Laos, sleepy little Vientiane.

Wat Pho Chai is Nong Khai's best-known and most attractive temple, easily accessible by way of Prajak Road. It houses a revered gold Buddha image, Luang Pho Phra Sai, which was lost for many centuries after capsizing in a storm and falling to the muddy bottom of the Mae Khong. Its rediscovery, part of the local lore, is displayed in a number of beautiful murals seen spread over the *ubosot* (ordination hall) walls. 🖾 Free ☉ Daily 6–6.

Thailand's strangest temple grounds are 5 km (3 mi) west of town on the Nong Khai–Phon Pisai Road at **Wat Khaek** (also called Sala Kaew Koo). The temple's gardens, created by an ecumenically minded monk, have an extraordinary collection of immense (and immensely bizarre) statues representing gods, goddesses, demons, and devils from many of the world's faiths, though the emphasis is on Hindu gods. 🖾 B100 ☉ Daily 6–6.

Wat Noen Pranao is in a shaded forest, and makes for an interesting excursion. The central ubosot is the dominating structure, with its rich motifs and gold stenciling, but the aging wooden hall to its east and the small courtyard bungalows are also worth investigating. This is Nong Khai's leading meditative retreat and is serious business for those involved, who practice meditation and abstinence to heal their troubled souls. It's free to stay, including daily courses and meals, but donations are greatly appreciated. You can reach the center on the Nong Khai–Phon Pisai Road by songthaew, which costs around B50.

Where to Stay

$–$$ ☒ **Mae Khong Royal.** The main attraction of this Western-style lodging is its large pool, which is a godsend in the hot summer season. The nearby terrace, cooled by breezes off the Mae Khong River, is also pleasant. Rooms have great views of the Friendship Bridge and Laos. The hotel's only disadvantage is its isolated location about 2 km (1 mi) outside the town. ☒ *222 Jommanee Beach, 43000* ☎ *042/411022, 02/272–0087 in Bangkok* 🖷 *042/421280, 02/272–0090 in Bangkok* 🛏 *177 rooms* ☖ *Restaurant, coffee shop, room service, minibars, cable TV, miniature golf, 2 tennis courts, pool, billiards, bar, beer garden, dance club, shop, laundry service, meeting rooms, travel services* 🖃 *AE, DC, MC, V.*

¢ ☒ **Maekhong Guest House.** At this rambling collection of Thai-style buildings, meals are served on a wooden terrace perched on the banks of the river. One of the pleasures of an evening here is to sit at the balustrade and watch the fishermen haul in their nets. Most of the rooms are spartan, but a quartet of "VIP" rooms in a wooden annex overlooking the river is much nicer. There's also a reasonably priced Internet café. ☒ *519 Rimkhong Rd., 43000* ☎ *042/460689* ⊕ *www.maekhongguesthouse.com* 🛏 *40 rooms* ☖ *Restaurant, Internet, travel services* 🖃 *No credit cards.*

¢ ☒ **Mut Mee Guesthouse.** A wonderful little oasis of charm and friendliness right on the bank of the Mae Khong River, this great find seems to be the heart of a seasonal community that includes artists; qualified yoga, fitness, and reiki instructors; and many others. Rooms are scattered around a tropical garden and are stylishly decorated with terra-cotta tiles, stone-slab bathrooms, and antique four-poster beds. Steel-welded Buddha images add a nice touch to the window grates and local artwork hangs on the walls. The small pavilion restaurant and lounge serve up healthy dishes and juices. ☒ *1111/4 Kaeworawut Rd., 43000* ☎ *042/460717, 01/2612646* 🖷 *042/460717* ⊕ *www.mutmee.net* 🛏 *27 rooms* ☖ *Restaurant, laundry service, travel services* 🖃 *No credit cards.*

Fodor'sChoice ★

¢ ☒ **Pantawee Resort.** It's not really a resort, but this spacious complex on the banks of the Mae Khong River is certainly comfortable. It's also ideally located just west of the Friendship Bridge. Many of the inexpensive rooms have sweeping views of the river—ask for Number 5, which has a private terrace with access to the waterside restaurant and café. The resort is a 15-minute bus ride from town. ☒ *210 Khaewworawut Rd., 43000* ☎ *042/411008* 🖷 *042/420059* 🛏 *36 rooms* ☖ *2 restaurants, café, refrigerators, cable TV, Internet, travel services* 🖃 *AE, DC, MC, V.*

¢ ☒ **Ruan Thai Guesthouse.** An ornate wooden house set in lush green gardens makes this one of the more attractive guesthouses along Rimkhong Road. The original house and additional two-story wooden chalets mean plenty of rooms and a range of prices. Rooms are comfortable, with cozy plaid bedding and chunky wooden furniture. Even though there are no views of the Mae Khong River, it's only a few feet away. ☒ *1126/2 Rimkhong Rd., 43000* ☎ *042/415219 or 042/461246* ⊕ *www.ruanthaihouse.com* 🛏 *17 rooms* ☖ *Laundry services, travel services* 🖃 *No credit cards.*

Shopping

Village Weaver Handicrafts (✉ 1020 Prajak Rd. ☎ 042/422651 up to 3) is an inviting converted shophouse rich with woodwork and vibrant fabrics. It was established as an outlet for the Village Weaver Handicrafts Self-Help Project, which supports local women villagers in a network of about 50 villages, helping them earn personal income to counter the constant threat of poverty. The store has a small workshop at its rear where skilled seamstresses weave high-quality mudmee fabric. The center is open from 9 AM to 7 PM.

> **en route**
>
> You can take a marvelous scenic trip on the old dirt road west along the Mae Khong. Take your own wheels or travel by bus to **Si Chiang Mai,** 50 km (31 mi) from Nong Khai. This sleepy backwater is famous for producing spring-roll wrappers—you can see the white translucent rice flour everywhere, spread out on mats to dry. Just out of Si Chiang Mai at road marker 83 you come to Wat Hin Maak Peng, a meditation temple run by *mae chee* (Buddhist nuns).

UDON THANI & ENVIRONS A TO Z

AIR TRAVEL

There are two major airports in this region, at Udon Thani and Khon Kaen, and both have several daily flights from Bangkok. The major carrier is Thai Airways, but a number of budget airlines, such as Air Asia, Nok Air, and Phuket Airways, also service these routes and have offices at Udon Thani International Airport. Phuket Airways also has a link between Chiang Mai and Udon Thani, with one flight per day on Sunday, Monday, Wednesday, and Friday.

✈ Airlines **Air Asia** ☎ 042/224313 up to 5 in Udon Thani. **Nok Air** ☎ 042/348771, 042/348772 in Udon Thani. **Phuket Airways** ☎ 042/224161, 042/224162 in Udon Thani. **Thai Airways** ✉ Sofitel Raja Orchid, 9/9 Prachasumran Rd., Khon Kaen ☎ 043/227701 ✉ Mak Khaeng Rd., Udon Thani ☎ 042/243222.

BUS TRAVEL

There are regular buses connecting Udon Thani to Khon Kaen, Nong Khai, Nakhon Phanom and Loei, as well as far off Bangkok and Nakhon Ratchasima. Bangkok-bound buses, via Nakhon Ratchasima, are nine-hour trips departing every night at 8 and 8:20. Fares are B330 for first-class air-conditioned buses or B490 for VIP buses. Further hourly connections to Khon Kaen from Udon Thani depart between 6 AM and 5 PM and cost B85 for first-class air-conditioned buses.

From Udon Thani, first-class air-conditioned buses run every half-hour to Nong Khai (1½ hours) from Udon's bus terminals on Udon Dutsadi Road or at the more accessible station off Prajak Road. Buses cost B30, running throughout the day from 5:45 AM to 6 PM. Udon also has buses heading east to Nakhon Phanom and further along the Mae Khong. It's five hours to Nakhon Phanom; buses leave between 5:30 AM and 11 AM, costing B122.

Getting to Loei from Nong Khai (4 hours) means taking a fan-cooled bus. Buses depart daily from 5:40 AM to 10 AM and cost around B84.

You can also connect to Phitsanulok from Loei, with buses running from 6 AM to 4 PM and costing B79 for fan-cooled or B161 for air-conditioning.

🚌 Bus Stations **Khon Kaen** ✉ Prachasamosorn Rd. (fan) and Ammart Rd. (a/c) ☎ 042/611421. **Loei** ✉ Maliwan Rd. ☎ 042/833586. **Nong Khai** ✉ Prajak Rd. ☎ 042/411612. **Udon Thani** ✉ Prajak Rd. ☎ 042/221489.

CAR RENTALS

Avis and Budget have branches at the Udon Thani airport. OK Mom Travel and Narujee Car Rental are reliable local agencies.

🚌 Agencies **Avis** ✉ Udon Thani Airport ☎ 042/244770. **Budget** ✉ Udon Thani Airport ☎ 042/246805. **Narujee Car Rent** ✉ Kosa Rd., Khon Kaen ☎ 043/224220. **OK Mom Travel** ✉ 345/9 Phosi Rd., Udon Thani ☎ 042/346673.

CAR TRAVEL

Roads are generally in good condition around Udon Thani. The fast four-lane Highway 2 links Udon to Bangkok, making travel to Khon Kaen and Nong Khai also easy. Highway 22 through Sakhon Nakhon also provides links to Nakhon Phanom and the Mae Khong River towns, but narrow two-lane roads can be slow going. Loei's spacious 210 road offers easy access to and from Udon with the optional 211 road being smaller but more scenic as it follows the Mae Khong River route, swinging through Chiang Khan to Nong Khai. The 212 follows the Mae Khong, connecting Nong Khai to Nakhon Phanom and Mukdahan.

EMERGENCIES

🚑 In Nong Khai **Police** ☎ 042/411020. **Nong Khai Provincial Hospital** ✉ Meechai Rd. ☎ 042/411504.

🚑 In Udon Thani **Police** ☎ 042/611333. **Wattana Hospital** ✉ Pho Niyom Rd. ☎ 042/465201 up to 8.

MAIL & SHIPPING

Post offices are open weekdays 8:30 to 4:30 and Saturday 9 to noon.

📮 Post Offices **Loei** ✉ 137 Charoenrat Rd. **Nong Khai** ✉ 1167/23 Meechai Rd. **Udon Thani** ✉ Mukmontri and Wattana Rds.

MONEY MATTERS

You'll have no difficulty finding banks with ATMs in all larger towns. Udon Thani is littered with banks, mainly found on Prajak Road. In Khon Kaen, you can find a glut on Srichan Road, and in Nong Khai on Meechai Road. Loei banks are clustered around Charoenrat Road.

SAMLORS & SONGTHAEWS

Motorized samlors and songthaews are the most common means of public transportation in the region, with the exception of Khon Kaen and Udon Thani, which have good public bus routes. Motorbike taxis and pedal samlors are widespread and available late into the evening.

TOUR OPERATORS

Central and eastern Isan are well covered by Kannika Tours, Prayoon Transport Tours, and Thorsaeng Travel in Udon Thani.

🚌 Tour Companies **Kannika Tours** ✉ 36/9 Sisutha Rd., Udon Thani ☎ 042/240443. **Prayoon Transport Tours** ✉ 546/1 Phosi Rd., Udon Thani ☎ 042/221048. **Thorsaeng Travel** ✉ 546/1 Phosi Rd., Udon Thani ☎ 042/221048.

TRAIN TRAVEL

Trains run three times daily from Bangkok's Hua Lamphong train station to Khon Kaen, Udon Thani, and Nong Khai, departing at 8:20 AM, 8 PM, and 8:45 PM. Travel times are eight hours to Khon Kaen, 12 hours to Udon, and 13 hours to Nong Khai. Fares to Khon Kaen run from B157 for third class (fans) up to B978 for a first-class sleeper. The range for travel to Udon Thani is B175 to B1,077, and to Nong Khai, B183 to B1,117.

The Nong Khai sleeper departs from Bangkok at 7 PM to arrive at 7:10 AM and on the return trip leaves Nong Khai at 6:35 PM to be back in Bangkok at 6:10 AM.

VISITOR INFORMATION

🛈 Tourist Authority of Thailand **Khon Kaen** ✉ 15/5 Prachasamosorn Rd. ☎ 043/244498 or 043/244499. **Nong Khai** ✉ Thai-Laos Friendship Bridge Rd. ☎ 042/467844. **Loei Tourism Coordination Center** ✉ Charoenrat Rd. ☎ 042/812812. **Udon Thani** ✉ 16/5 Mukmontri Rd. ☎ 042/325406.

THE SOUTHERN
BEACHES

6

Updated by
Karen Coates,
Mick Elmore,
Natawee
Kiatwerakul,
and Trevor
Ranges

IN THE MILES OF SANDY BEACHES in Southern Thailand there is pretty much something for everyone, from secluded beaches in the marine national parks, to the loud and gaudy resort towns, where the bars are a bigger draw than the beaches. Accommodations range from superlative world-class resorts to open-air bungalows charging little more than pocket change. Water sports abound, ranging from sea-kayaking around otherworldly rock formations to snorkeling the waters of crystal-clear bays. And the food may be the best thing of all—you'll have exotic fruits for breakfast and amazing seafood for dinner.

Thailand has two shores: the eastern shore faces the Gulf of Thailand and includes the well-known destinations of Pattaya, Ko Chang, and Ko Samui, among others; the western shore fronts the Andaman Sea, where you'll find the islands of Phuket, Ko Phi Phi, Koh Lanta, and various marine parks. Both shores had been experiencing a tourism boom for years—with many places facing the consequences of overdevelopment—when the tsunami hit the Andaman Coast on December 26, 2004. Several beaches on Phuket, the beach area of Khao Lak, and much of Ko Phi Phi were devastated by the waves, and although many areas on the Andaman Coast were unaffected by the tsunami, tourism on that shore came to a near standstill in the months following the disaster. At this writing, things were starting to look up, with many properties having completed repairs, poised for tourists to return for the 2005–2006 high season (December through February). The eastern shore was completely unaffected by the tsunami, as a strip of land separates it from the Andaman Sea, and many tourists diverted their vacations there after the disaster. The Gulf resorts may continue to see increased visitors if people remain wary of vacationing along the Andaman Coast, though it's hard to say just how much of an increase there will actually be, since some visitors have forgone the beaches region altogether, heading north from Bangkok instead, and may continue to do so.

No matter how things play out over the next couple of years, the issue of overdevelopment will remain in the spotlight. Once adventurous travelers find a new, secluded, undeveloped beach and start talking about it, rapid development has followed at a frightening pace. In many spots this development hasn't been regulated or monitored properly and the country is now pulling in the tourist dollar at the expense of the environment. It's a cycle that's hard to stop. Two prime ministers in the 1990s said Pattaya was a polluted mess, much to the consternation of the local tourism industry. During the fast-paced development of Phuket, a common cry was not to make the same mistakes as were made in Pattaya. During the more recent development of Ko Chang, the word has been not to make the same mistakes that were made at Phuket. Whether any lessons have finally been learned will only be evident when the areas destroyed by the tsunami are rebuilt.

Fortunately, Thailand's coastal region is so vast that many areas remain pristine, and mistakes are being slowly corrected in the most abused beach resorts. Much of Thailand's coast is mangrove forest, but there are ample white sandy beaches and islands, too. Different regions offer different advantages. If you want high-powered water sports and wild nights,

It's unlikely that any traveler, however intrepid, would wander down the peninsula exploring the towns along the coast. Visitors usually settle in at one resort for as many days as they have set aside. Should you wish to cover both coasts, there is a six-hour land/boat service between Phuket and Ko Samui, and both Thai Airways and Bangkok Airways have daily direct flights between the islands. You can travel from Bangkok to the beaches along the northern part of the Gulf of Thailand in a few hours. Getting to the southernmost resorts takes time. By land, count on a good 12 to 14 hours (usually through the night), or by air (including airport transfers), half a day.

6

If you have 2 days

Drive south of Bangkok to ▣ **Hua Hin** ⑦ on the western edge of the Gulf of Thailand. Spend two days soaking up the rays. If you're more in the mood for a party, the resort town of ▣ **Pattaya** ① is on the gulf's eastern shore.

If you have 5 days

Fly from Bangkok to **Ko Samui** ⑪–⑰. A tour of the little island can easily be accomplished in less than a day. For those who are restless lying on beaches, spend an afternoon scuba diving to the Angthong Marine National Park. More adventurous types can take a long-tail boat to ▣ **Ko Pha Ngan** ⑱ for a night or two, then proceed to **Ko Tao** ⑲. From Ko Tao, take the ferry over to **Chumphon** ⑨ on the mainland and pick up the train for Bangkok.

If you have 7 days

Take an overnight train down to **Surat Thani** ⑩. When you arrive the next day you can head to ▣ **Phang Nga Bay** ㉟. Here you can see the limestone rocks that tower out of the sea. Look familiar? It's where they filmed the James Bond movie *The Man with the Golden Gun*. On your fourth day head south to ▣ **Phuket** ⑳–㉞, an island that can be reached via a causeway. You can see most of the sights of Phuket in a day, but if you want to see every beach you'd need considerably more time. On your sixth day head to **Ko Phi Phi** ㊵ for some snorkeling. On your last day relax on the beach, then fly back to Bangkok.

---

head toward Pattaya. Patong Beach on Phuket was similar, but it suffered much destruction from the tsunami, so it may be toned down for a while. All-inclusive resorts are popular on Phuket and Ko Samui (Samui also has more than 20 spas). The big resorts offer seclusion and privacy at a price, but that can be found in more modest accommodation on less developed islands, too. Ko Samet and Ko Chang southeast of Bangkok, and Cha-am and Hua Hin on the coast to the southwest, are popular weekend getaways for people in the capital.

Wherever you end up, you'll never be anything less than amazed by the beauty of the region. You could spend your holidays in Thailand for 25 years and not return to the same spot, yet many travelers come back to the same beach and the same resort year after year. And that is probably the best recommendation one can give for the Southern Beaches.

Exploring the Southern Beaches

You don't have to travel far from Bangkok to find exhilarating beaches. The Eastern Gulf offers several close enough for a weekend away from Bangkok. Gaudy Pattaya is a wild and crazy place, but now also has a few resorts secluded from the main town, as well as some places for families. Further south along the coast that runs west to east all the way to the Cambodian border are some nice beach resorts and even better islands, including long-time escape from Bangkok favorite Ko Samet, and Ko Chang. Ko Chang, which is Thailand's second largest island, has seen considerable growth in the past couple of years, with classy resorts popping up among the more modest budget bungalows.

Back over on the west coast south of Bangkok you first come to Cha-am and Hua Hin on the Gulf of Thailand, the former with bigger and more stand-alone resorts, and the latter with both world-class resorts and medium-range accommodation. These cities, like the beaches to the southeast, can fill up with Bangkok escapees on weekends and holidays, but are less busy during the week. The beaches only get better as you head south, with scores worth exploring along the narrow peninsula that stretches all the way to the Malaysian border, all reachable from the town of Surat Thani, about 11 hours by train or a one-hour flight south of Bangkok. The island of Ko Samui is also along this strip—it's very developed, but perenially popular, in part because daily flights from Bangkok make it so easy to reach.

Phuket is the hub of the western coast, with daily flights from Bangkok landing in its airport and ferries to Ko Phi Phi, Krabi, and the Similan and Surin Islands departing daily from its docks. Though it's got its share of overdevelopment issues, Phuket has many beautiful beaches and a lot of variety in restaurants, hotels, activities, and nightlife. Once you leave Phuket, though, the attractions become even more spectacular. Krabi has beautiful limestone cliffs shooting straight up out of the water that have become popular with rock climbers. Ko Phi Phi suffered severe damage from the tsunami, but one side of the island remained unscathed, and it will once again be a prime destination for snorkeling and diving.

A note of caution: within a few months of the deadly tsunami, two southern Thailand ferry accidents killed nearly two dozen tourists. In both cases, the boats were ill-equipped and foolishly overloaded (more than 60 people in a boat made for 22, for example). Don't take the chance of getting on rickety or overcrowded boats; speed boats can often be hired to travel the ferry routes.

About the Restaurants

Restaurants of all sorts are available in the beach regions, from exclusive (and expensive) resort restaurants to wooden shacks that seem like they're about to fall over. On Ko Chang and Ko Samet "dining rooms" are set up each night on the beach, where in the daytime there is only sand and sunbathers. Phuket has the widest range of restaurants, from the fast-food giants of America to beach huts to five-star Western-style restaurants.

Beaches The curving beaches on the island of Phuket, some small and intimate, some large and sweeping, are made for sun-soaked idleness. If the crowds are too intense, across the bay you'll find the less traveled beaches of Krabi, many overhung by dramatic limestone cliffs. Along the Gulf of Thailand, beaches come in all shapes and sizes. You can relax by the shore in genteel surroundings at Cha-Am and Hua Hin. If you seek idyllic beaches, go south of Hua Hin or Ko Samet.

Scuba & Snorkeling The Similan Islands in the Andaman Sea and the Angthong National Park in the Gulf of Thailand, each protected by the government, are superb dive sites where visibility ranges from 60 to 120 ft. Ask at your hotel about taking an overnight dive trip, or investigate a three- to four-day live-aboard cruise. Be sure to wear something to protect your feet when swimming or wading among coral reefs. Better still, don't touch coral at all. Irreparable damage is being caused to Thailand's coral reefs by inconsiderate divers and swimmers.

6

As with Thai restaurants in Bangkok, the appearance of the establishment doesn't necessarily determine the quality of the food (for example, on Ko Si Chang locals swear by a place no one in their right mind would pick based on appearance). Note that many restaurants are seasonal—if you're traveling off-season and find a lot of closed doors, your best bet is to ask the locals for a recommendation.

Around the beach resorts seafood is king, usually lightly sautéed in oil and garlic or spiced up with chilies. Grilled king prawns melt in your mouth. A dish like *her thalee kanom khrok*, seafood cooked in coconut milk to which spices, including lemongrass, are added, is one of the joys of visiting the south. Crabs are a real treat on Phuket. Around Surat Thani the oysters are famous; they are farmed on bamboo poles in river estuaries. Another east coast specialty is salted eggs, coated in a mixture of salt and earth from anthills and rolled in the ashes of rice husks. In August, head to Surat Thani to sample the luscious rambutan, a local fruit in season.

In the Gulf of Thailand squid and shrimp are common, often lightly grilled with garlic, or in tom yum (hot and sour) soups with other seafood. Many of the beach area restaurants have chefs from the northeastern province of Isan, so they cook in that style, which often means spicy. The southeast provinces Rayong, Chanthaburi, and Trat are considered fruit baskets of Thailand and during May and June there are tropical fruits in overabundance.

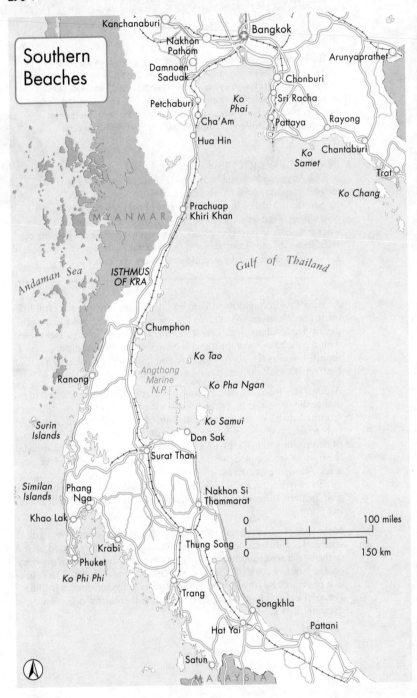

Southern Beaches

Kanchanaburi

Nakhon Pathom

Bangkok

Arunyaprathet

Damnoen Saduak

Chonburi

Sri Racha

Petchaburi

Ko Phai

Cha'Am

Pattaya

Rayong

Hua Hin

Chantaburi

Ko Samet

Trat

Ko Chang

Prachuap Khiri Khan

MYANMAR

Andaman Sea

ISTHMUS OF KRA

Gulf of Thailand

Chumphon

Ko Tao

Angthong Marine N.P.

Ranong

Ko Pha Ngan

Surin Islands

Ko Samui

Don Sak

Surat Thani

Similan Islands

Phang Nga

Nakhon Si Thammarat

Khao Lak

0   100 miles

Krabi

Thung Song

0   150 km

Phuket

Ko Phi Phi

Trang

Songkhla

Hat Yai

Pattani

Satun

MALAYSIA

In the far south of Thailand, the food can get very spicy; they say the hottest curries come from the country's southernmost region. Most of the time Thais are very good about toning down the heat for Westerners, but you might want to ask. The magic words are *mai phet* (pronounced "my pet"), meaning "not spicy."

The vast majority of restaurants are on the up-and-up, but if prices are not listed, it's wise to ask or you might get an unpleasant surprise when they hand you the bill. Such experiences are the exception, but they happen.

About the Hotels

There's something for every budget in this region, whether you're looking for the height of luxury or a simple thatch hut on the beach. Many places combine the two experiences by offering pricey, luxury bungalows.

Thailand's tourism industry has grown at a phenomenal rate since the early 1990s. The development first took off in Phuket, which will probably remain the most popular resort island in the region despite the tsunami, then expanded to Krabi and Ko Phi Phi. The big resorts in Krabi and on Phuket were already rebuilding and bouncing back by February of 2005, but Ko Phi Phi has only a smattering of resorts left. The future of Phi Phi is still a question mark: it will be rebuilt, but in what way is not known.

Development has spread up the coast of the mainland, and Ko Samui—and to a lesser extent, neighboring Ko Pha Ngan—and Ko Tao in the Gulf of Thailand have experienced similar growth to Krabi and Phuket. Samui, which has introduced direct flights from Bangkok, has gained many top-rate resorts, and is now in heated competition with Phuket for the region's wealthy tourists. Rates fluctuate widely—in holiday periods they can more than double. Always double-check your rate when you book.

	WHAT IT COSTS In Baht				
	$$$$	**$$$**	**$$**	**$**	**¢**
RESTAURANTS	over B400	B300–B400	B200–B300	B100–B200	under B100
HOTELS	over B6,000	B4,000–B6,000	B2,000–B4,000	B1,000–B2,000	under B1,000

Restaurant prices are per person, for a main course at dinner. Hotel prices are for a standard double room, excluding tax.

Timing

In the Eastern Gulf, December to March is the best time to visit, when the seas are mostly calm and the skies mostly clear. Pattaya is a 24-7 place all year, and Ko Samet also stays open year-round. But many places on Ko Chang and the other islands in the archipelago literally close down during rainy season because the seas are rough, making boat travel difficult, and the hot, humid, and rainy weather keeps visitors to a minimum. But the big car ferries continue to run on a limited schedule, and the larger, more expensive resorts and many of the medium-range hotels stay open, offering cheaper rates.

Cha-Am and Hua Hin are year-round locations, too, particularly Hua Hin, which is a developed historical city that has more to offer than just the beach.

As you head further south, the peak season depends on which side of Thailand you visit. In the Western Gulf (including Ko Samui, Ko Pha Ngan and Ko Tao) the monsoon season runs from late October through December—with the exception of the week from Christmas to New Year's, prices can be halved during this period—and peak season runs from January through early July. But even during the off season flying to Ko Samui is still convenient, making it a year-round location. The peak season on the west coast along the Andaman Sea is November through April. The monsoon season is May through October, during which high seas can make beaches unsafe for swimming, but hotel prices are considerably lower.

THE EASTERN GULF

The Eastern Gulf has long been a favorite escape from the heat and humidity of Bangkok. Its proximity to the capital means that weekend trips are possible, which in turn means that the area is overrun with sunseekers during long or holiday weekends. As the capital becomes more and more congested and the residents more affluent with disposable income, the region is growing rapidly. Some of the closer beaches have become so crowded that people now continue down the coast to quieter shores.

Many people go no farther than the coastal city of Pattaya, less than two hours south of Bangkok. It's the most highly developed area of the Eastern Gulf—too much so, it seems, as two consecutive prime ministers have criticized the area as a good example of the evils of unchecked development. For 10 years now the city has been cleaning up its beaches and its act, but it remains an eyesore to many people. But if you're looking for raucous entertainment, this is the spot.

Head farther south and east for more tranquil environs. Ko Chang, Thailand's second largest island after Phuket, has started to experience the tourism onslaught and the pressures to overbuild are strong, but at this writing, it remains a charming and beautiful island.

Pattaya

❶ *147 km (88 mi) southeast of Bangkok.*

Many make the trip from Bangkok wanting to trade the chaos of one city for the chaos of another—but one with a beach and water sports. Pattaya gets its fare share of criticism, and it deserves much of it, but it has made great strides to clean up at least some parts of itself. Water quality in the bay is improving, with the introduction of modern water- and sewage-treatment plants. It's still dirty compared to most places in the region, though.

Pattaya has its raunchy side for sure. The sex trade is a big part of the city—arguably its biggest money earner—and go-go bars, hostess bars, short-time hotels, and massage parlors are common and busy. But

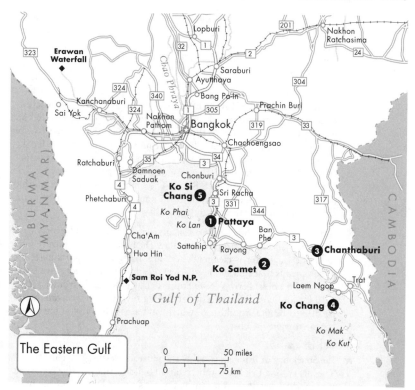

The Eastern Gulf

there's much else to the dynamic city (the food is as good as in Bangkok), and it's possible to escape the seedy side, especially if you stay at a resort a bit out of town. There are pleasant, self-contained resorts, some of which are on a secluded island. Pattaya has a big water-sports industry with Pattaya beach full of Jet Skis, paragliders, and even water-skiers.

Until the end of the 1950s, Pattaya was a fishing village sitting on an unspoiled natural harbor. Even after it was discovered by affluent Bangkok residents, it remained rather small and tranquil. Then came the Vietnam War, with thousands of American soldiers stationed at nearby air and naval bases. They piled into Pattaya, and the resort grew with the unrestrained fervor of any boomtown. But the boom eventually went bust. It would have been pretty much abandoned, but it's just too close to Bangkok and the natural harbor is too nice to ignore. So in the late 1990s, after much talk and government planning, Pattaya started regaining popularity. Two expressways were finished, making the trip from Bangkok even easier. When Bangkok's new international airport opens in 2005 or 2006 on the southeast side of the capital, it will be even more convenient to visit Pattaya, so the numbers may yet increase.

The curving bay of Pattaya, along which runs Beach Road, lined with palm trees on the beach side and modern resort hotels on the other is the central part of the city. By the old pier are pedestrian streets where bars, clubs, and open-air cafés proliferate. South of this area is Jomtien, a beach that is kind of overdeveloped but still pleasant enough. The northern part of the bay, over steep hills, is the quietest, most easygoing section of Pattaya.

Beaches

Some resorts, like the Royal Cliff Beach Hotel, have their own beaches—rocky outcroppings around the resorts make them more secluded and more private. In addition to those smaller beaches, Pattaya has two big ones: **Pattaya Beach** on Pattaya Bay is the more active beach with Jet Skis, paragliders, and other water sports on offer all day. The bay is usually crowded with small boats. There's a nice landscaped walkway between the beach and Pattaya Beach Road. The other beach, of a bit south of the city proper, is **Jomtien Beach.** It's a long, narrow beach with grainy sand, and is quieter than Pattaya.

A third and better option is **Ko Lan**, an island 45 minutes by ferry or 15 minutes by speedboat from Pattaya Bay. The beaches here have nice white sand and the water is cleaner. There are many water sports here, too, which means that this is not where you can find that quiet place to sun and read a book. Ferries leave South Pattaya Pier daily from 10 AM to 6:30 PM and cost B20. Speedboats on Pattaya Beach are available for B1,500 to B2,000 round-trip, which isn't a bad deal if you have a few people to split the cost.

What to See

★ **The Sanctuary of Truth** is probably the most interesting place in Pattaya. The late tycoon Lek Wiriyaphen started building this massive teak structure in 1981—it's still not finished but it's open. The aim of the building, which looks like an intricate collection of carvings, was to make a statement about the balance of different cultures, mixing modern and traditional arts. The setting right next to the water north of Pattaya is pleasant, too. ⊠ *206/2 Moo 5, Naklua 12, Naklua Rd., Banglamung* ☎ *038/225–407* ⊕ *www.sanctuaryoftruth.com* 🎫 *B500* 🕙 *Daily 9–6.*

Though it's more famous for its nightlife, Pattaya also has quite a few activities designed for families. Children love the **Elephant Kraal,** where a few dozen pachyderms display their skills in a two-hour show. There are demonstrations of everything from their part in ceremonial rites to their usefulness in construction. Everything is staged, but it's always fun to see elephants at work and at play. Although it's a bit unsettling to see these gentle giants languishing in the city, the Elephant Kraal has a good reputation as one of the few places that doesn't mistreat the animals. One-hour elephant rides are available for an extra B700 between 8 and 5. For tickets, go to the Tropicana Hotel on Pattaya 2 Road. ⊠ *5 km (3 mi) from Pattaya* ☎ *038/249–145 up to 7* ⊕ *www.elephant-village-pattaya.com* 🎫 *B400* 🕙 *Daily shows at 2:30 PM.*

Also popular with kids is the **Pattaya Monkey Training Center.** The pig-tailed monkeys, who live about 40 years, are adept at harvesting coconuts, a skill they are taught over the course of a year. This training is not just for show, and once schooled in coconut collecting, the monkeys are worth several thousand dollars to resorts that want their coconut trees harvested. But at this training center they are also taught a few other entertaining tricks that bring a smile to the face of even the most jaded traveler. ☒ *Km 151, Soi Chaiyapruk, Sukhumvit Rd.* ☎ *038/756–367 or 038/756–570* 💲 *B250* ⊘ *Daily shows at 9, 11, noon, 1, 2, and 5.*

If you want to see elephants and monkeys in one trip, **Nong Nooch Village** has a small zoo. Two restaurants serve refreshments that you can enjoy beneath a coconut tree. Despite its touristy nature—the elephants do silly tricks like drive big scooters made for them—the village is a pleasant place to kick back, particularly if you're traveling with children. Hotels will arrange transportation for morning and afternoon visits, as it's 15 km (9 mi) south of Pattaya. ☒ *163 Sukhumvit Hwy., Bang Saray* ☎ *038/709358* 💲 *B550* ⊘ *Daily 9–5:30; folklore show daily 9:45, 10:30, and 3.*

The **Million Years Stone Park and Crocodile Farm** has grounds landscaped with rock gardens and flowers but its main attraction is hundreds of crocodiles. There are six hour-long crocodile shows daily. ☒ *22/1 Mu, Nongplalai, Banglamung* ☎ *038/249–347* ⊕ *www.thaistonepark.com* 💲 *B300* ⊘ *Daily 11–5.*

The **Bottle Museum** is certainly unique. Dutchman Pieter Beg de Leif created more than 300 miniatures—tiny replicas of famous buildings and ships—in bottles. ☒ *79/15 Moo 9, Sukhumvit Rd.* ☎ *038/422957* 💲 *B150* ⊘ *Daily 8:30–8.*

The **Ripley's Believe It or Not** is the same one you can find in America with its collection of curiosities from all corners of the world. Many are actual items, others are replicas. There's an extensive collection here in 250 categories from peculiar lifestyles to optical illusions. ☒ *3rd fl., Royal Garden Plaza, 218 Moo 10 Beach Rd.* ☎ *038/710–294 up to 8* ⊕ *www.ripleysthailand.com* 💲 *B380* ⊘ *Daily 11–11.*

Where to Eat

Much of Pattaya feels like little America. For example, in the Royal Garden Plaza, a little mall right on Pattaya Beach Road, there's a McDonald's, a Burger King, *and* a Kentucky Fried Chicken all next to one another. But Pattaya is also near Thailand's major fruit-producing provinces, as well as many fishing grounds in the Gulf of Thailand, ensuring both produce and seafood are fresh. There are plenty of fancier full-scale restaurants here, a necessity because Pattaya's noise and crowds seriously detract from the simple places on the beach.

$$$$ ✕ **Casa Pascal.** This is one of Pattaya's priciest options, but the extra cost is worth it for great Italian food in a pleasant setting. The gourmet set menu, which they change every two weeks, costs B1,050, and is a six-course extravaganza with sherbet halfway through to prepare your palate for the main course. There's a Sunday champagne brunch (buffet style) for B500. ☒ *485/4 Moo 10, 2nd Rd., opposite Marriott* ☎ *038/723–660* 🖃 *AE, DC, MC, V.*

$$ ✕ **Bruno's.** This restaurant and wine bar has built up a good reputation among the local expat community since it opened in 1986. The lunchtime set menus for B370 are a real bargain, and the set dinner menu is pop-

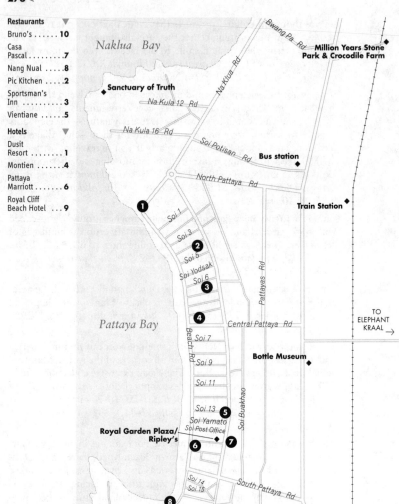

Naklua Bay

Bwang Pa Rd

◆ **Million Years Stone
Park & Crocodile Farm**

Na Klua Rd

◆ **Sanctuary of Truth**

Na Kula 12 Rd

Na Kula 16 Rd

Soi Potisan Rd

Bus station ◆

North Pattaya Rd

Train Station ◆

❶

Soi 1

Soi 3

❷

Soi 5

Soi Yodsak

Soi 6

❸

❹

Central Pattaya Rd

Pattaya3 Rd

Pattaya Bay

Beach Rd

Soi 7

Soi 9

TO
ELEPHANT
KRAAL →

Bottle Museum ◆

Soi 11

Soi Buakhao

Soi 13

❺

Soi Yamato

Soi Post Office

**Royal Garden Plaza/
Ripley's**

❻

◆ **❼**

Soi 14

Soi 15

South Pattaya Rd

❽

❾

❿

Thepprasitz Rd.

TO
MONKEY TRAINING CENTER
AND NANG NOOCH VILLAGE
↓

Where to Stay
& Eat in Pattaya

ular, too. The international cuisine here leans toward Swiss recipes, but you can also find a wide range of American staples. The wine list is extensive. ⊠ *Chateau Dale Plaza, Thappraya Rd.* ☎ *038/364–600 and 1* ▭ *AE, DC, MC, V.*

$$ ✕ **Pic Kichen.** This restaurant is actually a series of classic teak pavilions. You can dine inside or outside and you can choose from table seating, floor seating or sofas in Pic's jazz pit. The Thai dishes are consistently good, especially the deep-fried crab claws and spicy eggplant salad. All food can be made mild or spicy, but if you're really adverse to chilies, you should try the ginger-scented white snapper. ⊠ *255 Soi 5 Pattaya 2 Rd.* ☎ *038/428374* ▭ *AE, DC, MC, V.*

$ ✕ **Nang Nual.** At the southern end of Pattaya Beach Road amid the bar scene is one of the city's best places for seafood. A huge array of freshly caught fish is laid out on blocks of ice at the entrance. Point to what you want and explain how you'd like it cooked (most people ask for it to be grilled). A menu filled with photographs of the entrées overcomes the language barrier, and they will understand the type of cooking, if you don't make it too complicated. For meat-lovers, the huge steaks are an expensive treat. There's a dining room upstairs, but ask for a table on the terrace overlooking the ocean. A newer branch is across from Jomtien Beach, near the Sigma Resort. ⊠ *214–10 S. Pattaya Beach Rd.* ☎ *038/428–708* ✉ *1 25/24-26 Moo 1 2 Jomtien Beach Rd.* ☎ *038/ 231548* ▭ *AE, MC, V.*

$ ✕ **Sportsman's Inn.** It's the best spot in Pattaya for well-prepared British pub grub (steak-and-kidney pie, bangers and mash, and fish-and-chips), as testified to by the many expats who get their daily sustenance here. There are good British versions of American staples like burgers and fries, too. Note that there's also a Sportsman on Soi 13, but they are not affiliated. ⊠ *Soi Yod Sak, Soi 8* ☎ *038/361548* ▭ *No credit cards.*

$ ✕ **Vientiane Restaurant.** This restaurant, named after the capital of Laos, serves Laotian and Thai cuisine. The dishes from Thailand's northeastern province of Isan include arguably the best *som tam* (spicy papaya salad) in Pattaya. For something less spicy try the *gai yang* (roast chicken) with sticky rice. Laotian food is very spicy, so be sure to specify if you want those dishes mild. If it's a pleasant evening, ask for a table outside on the terrace. There's an air-conditioned dining room if it's too hot out for comfort. The restaurant is near the Marriott Resort. ⊠ *485/18 2nd Rd.* ☎ *038/411–298* ▭ *MC, V.*

Where to Stay

Pattaya is second only to Bangkok in the number of hotel rooms in Thailand. Many cater mostly to the weekend crowd, others to the sex trade, and still more to group tours who have Pattaya thrown into their Thailand package.

For seclusion, you have to do some spending, but there are some excellent places to stay, like the Dusit Resort, the Royal Cliff Beach Hotel, and the Pattaya Marriott Resort & Spa. Booking rooms in the better hotels is a wise idea. Be sure to ask about packages and discounts, as they'll save you a chunk of change.

$$$$ 🏨 **Royal Cliff Beach Hotel.** This hotel is now an institution in Thailand, known for its size and its setting, perched high on a bluff jutting into the gulf. This self-contained resort is actually a cluster of four well-kept hotels. Most rooms gaze down at the shore. The lavish suites in the Royal Wing (about double the price of standard rooms) have extras like butler service and breakfast served in your room. The Royal Cliff Terrace has two-bedroom suites perfect for families. The standard rooms are roomy and well furnished, too. There are several swimming pools, each with a view. The beach is nice, but it's a bit of a hike down some stairs. The resort is about 1½ km (1 mi) south of town. ⊠ *Jomtien Beach* ☎ *038/ 250421, 02/282–0999 in Bangkok* 🖷 *038/250141* ⊕ *www.royalcliff. com* 🛏 *952 rooms, 162 suites* ⚒ *4 restaurants, miniature golf, 2 tennis courts, 3 pools, sauna, 2 beaches, windsurfing, boating, squash, bar, shops* ▭ *AE, DC, MC, V.*

★ **$$$** 🏨 **Dusit Resort.** At the northern end of Pattaya Beach, this large hotel has superb views. The beautifully kept grounds, with a lap pool and a free-form pool with a swim-up bar, are on the tip of a promontory pushing into the ocean. The rooms have comfortable sitting areas and private balconies. For a bit more you can book one of the larger "Landmark" rooms. The Empress, which serves sophisticated Cantonese fare, has views of Pattaya Bay. This retreat is only a short songthaew ride from Pattaya attractions. It's the service that sets it apart though, and it's self-contained, so you don't have to venture into town if you don't want to. ⊠ *240/2 Pattaya Beach Rd., 20260* ☎ *038/425611, 02/236–0450 in Bangkok* 🖷 *038/428239* ⊕ *http://pattaya.dusit.com* 🛏 *500 rooms, 28 suites* ⚒ *4 restaurants, 3 tennis courts, 2 pools, health club, massage, sauna, windsurfing, boating, Ping-Pong, squash, bar, shops* ▭ *AE, DC, MC, V.*

$$$ 🏨 **Pattaya Marriott Resort & Spa.** This traditional-style hotel is a block from the beach. It has a large lobby that opens out onto a tropical garden and towering trees line the path to the shimmering pool. The rooms are good sized and have private balconies with ocean views. Next door is the Royal Garden Plaza, so you're steps away from some of the town's best shopping, some good restaurants, and movie theaters. ⊠ *218 Beach Rd., Chonburi 20260* ☎ *038/412120, 02/477–0767 in Bangkok* 🖷 *038/429926* ⊕ *www.marriotthotels.com* 🛏 *300 rooms* ⚒ *2 restaurants, 4 tennis courts, pool, health club, hair salon, bar, business services, meeting rooms, travel services* ▭ *AE, DC, MC, V.*

$$ 🏨 **Montien.** Although it couldn't be described as plush, this centrally located hotel has a laid-back atmosphere that many people prefer. With its generous off-season discounts, the Montien is one of the best values in town. It's across from the beach, with a breeze cooling the hotel. The Garden Restaurant has a dance floor and stage for entertainment. It's associated with the Montien in Bangkok, and tends to get tour groups, but it's not overrun by them. ⊠ *Pattaya Beach Rd., Chonburi 20260* ☎ *038/428–155, 02/233–7060 in Bangkok* 🖷 *038/423155* ⊕ *www. montien.com* 🛏 *320 rooms* ⚒ *2 restaurants, coffee shop, snack bar, 2 tennis courts, pool, bar, meeting rooms* ▭ *AE, DC, MC, V.*

Nightlife

Nightlife is one of Pattaya's main draws. Scattered throughout town are hundreds of beer bars, which are low-key places where the girls merely want to keep you buying drinks. The raunchy go-go bars are mostly found on the southern end of town. Gay bars are in the sois between Pattaya Beach Road and Pattaya 2 Road called Pattayaland.

In the Pattaya Marriott Resort & Spa, **Shenanigans** (⊠ 218 Beach Rd. ☎ 038/710641) tries hard to conjure up an Irish pub by serving favorite brews like Guinness. A large-screen TV makes this popular with sports fans. For live music, try **Tony's** in the heart of the nightlife district (⊠ Walking Street Rd., South Pattaya ☎ 038/425795). Grab a beer and head to the outdoor terrace.

Sports & the Outdoors

BUNGEE JUMPING If you like a thrill, try **Jungle Bungee Jump** (⊠ At the Jomtien Fishing Park off main road to Jomtien Beach ☎ 06/378–3880 ⊕ www.thaibungy. com). They are overseen by the Standards Association of New Zealand.

GOLF The **Laem Chabang International Country Club** (⊠ 106/8 Moo 4 Beung, Srirach, Chonburi ☎ 038/372273) has lovingly maintained links near Pattaya. The greens fee is B1,500, plus B200 for a caddie. Thailand's longest fairway is at the **Royal Thai Navy Course** (⊠ Phiu Ta Luang Golf Course, Sattahip, Chonburi ☎ 02/466–1180). It's about 30 km (18 mi) from Pattaya. Bordered by dense vegetation, it's considered one of the country's most difficult courses. The **Siam Country Club** (⊠ 50 Moo 9 T. Poeng A., Banglamung, Chonburi ☎ 038/418002), close to Pattaya, offers a challenging course with wide fairways lined by wooded hills.

WATER SPORTS Pattaya Beach is action center for water sports. Just go to the beach and you don't have to ask, they will ask you. Jet skiing is generally B600 for 30 minutes, parasailing B500 for 15 minutes, and waterskiing starts at B1,000 for 30 minutes. All activities are available from 7 AM to 4 PM. Big inflatable bananas that hold five people and are towed behind a speed boat are also a part of Pattaya Beach, yet another thing to dodge, but riders have a screaming good time on them. They cost B1,000 or more for 30 minutes. For windsurfing, it's best to try Jomtien Beach, where you won't have to deal with all the motorized activities on Pattaya Beach.

Pattaya offers scuba diving, too, but there are many other places in the region that are much better for diving.

Ko Samet

❷ *30 min by passenger ferry from Ban Phe, which is 223 km (139 mi) southeast of Bangkok.*

East of Pattaya is the small village of Ban Phe, which is the jumping-off point to 6 km (3 mi)-long Ko Samet and its beautiful beaches. Two passenger ferries make the crossing, one going to Na Duan on the north shore, the other to An Vong Duan halfway down the eastern shore. You can ride a songthaew from Na Duan down the center of the narrow island, but all the island's beaches are an easy walk from either of these villages. Indeed, from the southern tip to the north is a comfortable three-hour walk.

Along with several neighboring islands, Ko Samet was made a Marine National Park in 1981, so there's a B200 entrance fee. The government has been unable (or unwilling) to control development on the island, and although Jet Skis are prohibited in national parks, some find their way to Samet. But there are no high-rises and just one rutted road for songthaews. Most goods are brought straight to the resorts by boat.

Ko Samet is popular with Thais and Bangkok expats, especially on weekends. Many people thought that the development of Ko Chang, a couple of hours east, would pull business away from Ko Samet, but that has yet to happen. People are not giving up on Samet just yet and it remains popular, mostly with people looking for a bit of peace and quiet and clean air. It's for the laid-back traveler who just wants to sunbathe and read on the beach.

Beaches

Ko Samet is known for its sugary beaches. The island's other name is Ko Kaeo Phitsadan (Island with Sand Like Crushed Crystal), so it isn't surprising that its fine sand is in great demand by glassmakers. The smooth water is another attraction. The beaches are a series of little bays, with more than 10 of them running along the east side of the island. The west side is mostly rocky and offers fewer accommodations.

The beaches are busier on the northern tip near Na Duan and become less so as you go south, with the exception of a congregation of bungalows near An Vong Duan, the second ferry stop.

All the beaches have licensed massage ladies walking around offering one- and two-hour Thai massages, which generally cost B50 an hour (not including tip).

Much of the north shore of the island, before the series of little bays down the east side, is rocky, but **Nanai Beach** is a nice little sandy stretch. The view is toward the mainland. The Samed Cliff resort is just above this beach.

Fodor'sChoice ★ **Ao Vong Duan** is a beautiful half-moon bay, but its beach is packed with bungalows, and it's the place where you can find many jet skiers, sail boats, and windsurfers. It also has many restaurants. For a little more seclusion, two beaches—Ao Cho to the north and Ao Thian to the south—flank Ao Vong Duan. They're both a pleasant five-minute walk away.

Ao Kiu, near the southern end of the island, is beautiful and even more secluded. From here it's an easy walk around the southern end of the island, where you can watch the sunset. The Ao Kiu Coral Beach Resort is on this beach.

Where to Stay & Eat

The island has many bungalows and cottages, with and without electricity. Make sure that yours at least has mosquito netting: come dusk, Ko Samet's mosquitoes take a fancy to tourists. Restaurants set up along the beach in the late afternoon; seafood is the logical choice, but there's something for everyone. While you dine the sounds of the surf are soothing, and sometimes waves splash your feet. All three resorts below have good restaurants, but it's worth it to spend one night strolling the beaches around Ao Vong Duan and trying one of the beach restaurants. After you do, chances are you'll return.

$–$$ 🏠 **Vong Deuan Resort.** This resort offers the best bungalows on Ao Vong Duan beach and is near much of the island's activity. The best rooms are the superior ones with air-conditioning (B2,500); the other bungalows are smaller, but otherwise offer the same amenities. ⊠ *Ao Vong Duan* ☎ *01/446–1944, 038/651777 in Ban Phe* ⊕ *www.vongdeuan.com* 🛏 *45 bungalows* 🍴 *Restaurant* ☰ *MC, V.*

$ 🏠 **Samed Cliff Resort.** This little cluster of bungalows has all the amenities you need—air-conditioning, hot water, even TVs and small minibars. The rooms are simply furnished, but clean and comfortable. Out front is a small beach with white sand and calm surf. The restaurant serves Thai food, as well as a few other dishes. For dinner venture out to one of the grills set up on the beach. This place is popular, so make reservations in advance. They offer all-inclusive packages, too. ⊠ *Nanai Beach* ☎ *016/457115, 02/635–0800 in Bangkok* ⊕ *www.samedcliff. com* 🛏 *30 bungalows* 🍴 *Restaurant, pool* ☰ *MC, V.*

¢ 🏠 **Ao Kiu Coral Beach Resort.** The beach here is tops, and more secluded than others. The most basic of the concrete bungalows are fan rooms for B600, but there are other options, including comfortable two-bedroom bungalows with living rooms for B3,000. Note that this place can be difficult to get ahold of though, and they change their phone number from time to time. ⊠ *76 Moo 4, Rayong* ☎ *01/218–6231* 🛏 *30 bungalows* 🍴 *Restaurant* ☰ *No credit cards.*

Chanthaburi

❸ *100 km (62 mi) east of Rayong, 180 km (108 mi) east of Pattaya.*

Buses from Rayong and Ban Phe make the 90-minute journey to the pleasant provincial town of Chanthaburi, which is on the way to Ko Chang. (You can also take a four- to five-hour bus journey from Bangkok's Eastern Bus Terminal.) Unless you're going for the gems, or the fruit in May and June, it's best to keep your visit short and continue on to Ko Chang.

The gem mines are mostly closed, but Chanthaburi is still renowned as a center for gems. Rubies and sapphires still rule, but stones from all corners of the world are found in the town's shops. On Gem Street, in the center of town, you can see traders sorting through gems and making deals worth hundreds of thousands of baht. The street becomes a gem market on Friday and Saturday.

Chanthaburi has played a big role in Thai history. It was here that the man who would become King Taksin gathered and prepared his troops to retake Ayutthaya from the Burmese after they sacked the capital of Siam in 1767. The King Taksin Shrine, shaped like a house-size helmet from that era, is on the north end of town and it's where locals hold a celebration in his honor from December 28 to early January.

The French occupied the city from 1893 to 1905 and some architecture from that time is still evident, particularly along the river where the city was concentrated during those years. The French influence is also evident in Thailand's largest Catholic church, the Cathedral of Immaculate Conception, which is across the river from the center of town and an easy stroll from Gem Street. A footbridge to the cathedral was washed away by a flood in 2002, but there's talk of rebuilding it. The walk to the next bridge is a bit farther now, or an easy motorcycle taxi ride away. First built in 1711 by Christian Vietnamese who migrated to the area, the cathedral has been rebuilt four times since and the present building was completed in the early 1900s when the city was under French control. The best time to visit is during the morning market on the grounds when local foods, fruits, and desserts are sold. But it's good for peaceful solitude anytime.

The province of Chanthaburi has few beach resorts of note, and those cater mostly to Thais. Laem Sadet, 18 km (11 mi) from Chanthaburi, is the most popular, and its accommodations range from small bungalows to low-rise hotels. Chanthaburi is once again becoming a gateway to western Cambodia as Thailand's neighbor opens its borders.

Ko Chang

★ ❹   *1 hr by ferry from Laem Ngop, which is 15 km (9 mi) southwest of Trat; Trat is 400 km (250 mi) southeast of Bangkok.*

Ko Chang, or Elephant Island, is the largest and most developed of the 52-island archipelago that was made into Mu Ko Chang National Park in 1982 (many of these islands are not much more than sandbars). Most of Ko Chang is mountainous and it has only a few small beaches. The 30-km (18-mi) long island has only nine villages and 24 km (15 mi) of road linking them, with a few villages accessible only by boat. But this little paradise has been the focus of rapid development in the past few years—there has been a big jump from just 28 resorts in 2001 to more than 100 at the beginning of 2005.

Thailand's media has spilled a lot of ink on stories about the development of Ko Chang, especially in wake of Prime Minister Thaksin Shinawatra's 2002 comment that the government plans to turn it into "a second Phuket." Forestry Chief Plodprasop Suraswadi, the chairman of the committee drafting Ko Chang's master tourism plan, went one step further by suggesting the island be developed solely with wealthy travelers in mind. He stated that the country should limit the number of visitors to the island and that backpackers would not be welcome on it.

The island is certainly in for more development. The Tourism Authority of Thailand (TAT) said 400,000 tourists visited in 2002 and they aim to double that within 20 years. Exactly how this will all play out is unknown, but the tsunami may indeed speed up the development if travelers shun Phuket and the Andaman Coast out of fear or if they have to find alternatives to the heavily damaged areas there. Already it seems like every beach has something being built or renovated, and those construction sites can certainly ruin your serenity as crews blast electric drills and saws early and late in the day. You'll want to be sure that there's no construction project near your hotel. The places listed below are well-established, and minor changes aside, they should remain pretty much the same.

To get to Ko Chang you first have to get to Trat in the east of Thailand. The easiest way is on one of Bangkok Airway's daily flights. There are also air-conditioned buses from Bangkok's Eastern and Northern bus terminals; the trip takes a little over five hours. Another option is to have a hotel or tourist office in Bangkok arrange a car or shared taxi, which is much quicker and reasonably priced.

At the same time that the government claims it will restrict cars to Ko Chang—one minister claimed the island would be off-limits to vehicles from the mainland by 2007—a proliferation of new piers for car ferries have appeared along the coast south of Trat. They all accept walk-on passengers and will drop you at one of two piers on Ko Chang. Some resorts will arrange transportation from the airport; if you have to make it here on your own, take a songthaew to the pier, get the ferry to Ko Chang, and then take another songthaew to your hotel.

Songthaews are the easiest way to get around the island; just flag one down on the road. They cost between B30 and B50, or more if you venture toward the eastern part of the island.

If you plan to go many places in a day small 100cc motorcycles are readily available for B200 a day, but drive them with care. Bicycles are harder to find for rent, but some resorts have them.

Beaches

Ko Chang's best beaches are found on the western shore. Haad Sai Khao (White Sand Beach) is the farthest north and the most developed. A few miles south is the more serene Haad Khlong Phrao, a long, curving beach of pale golden sand. Nearby Haad Kai Bae is a mix of sand and pebbles. It has a gentle drop-off, making it safe for weak swimmers. Still farther south is Haad Ta Nam (Lonely Beach), which is perhaps the most picturesque beach. But it's also the smallest one and therefore more crowded. Farther along on the southwest corner of the island is the fishing village Bang Bao, which is also experiencing development with restaurants, dive shops, and cheap bungalows popping up.

Though the east coast is beautiful, it's mostly rugged rain forest and beaches are in short supply.

Troops of masseurs walk the beaches—they wear uniforms and are licensed. The general price for Thai massage is B250 an hour.

Where to Stay & Eat

Despite the government's interest in turning Ko Chang into an exclusive luxury destination, mid-level and budget travelers still have plenty of options. In fact, as the tourism industry grows on the island, mid-level resorts are becoming more common than expensive upscale establishments.

Resorts are being built on some of the other islands in the marine park, including Ko Mak, which is the third-largest island in archipelago. You can find a few bungalows for rent there, along with the Koh Mak Panorama Resort, listed below.

If the other islands interest you, the Tourism Authority of Thailand's Trat office (039/597255 and 039/597259) has information. It's near the pier at Laem Ngop, one place to catch the ferry to Ko Chang and the other islands. There's a daily ferry to Ko Mak and Ko Kharn that leaves

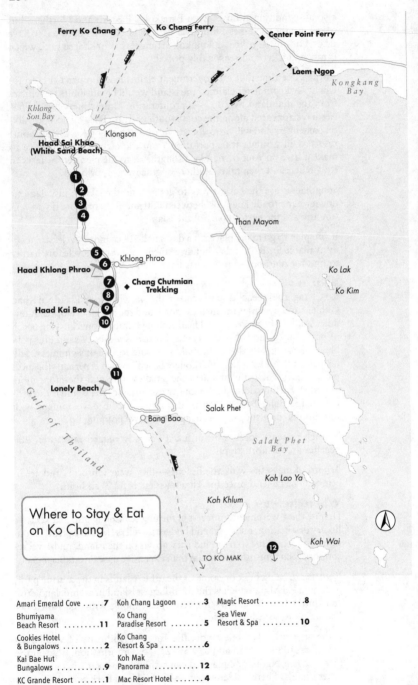

Where to Stay & Eat
on Ko Chang

from here, at this writing, at 3 PM. It's a three-hour journey to Ko Mak on the passenger ferry.

FodorsChoice For seafood and skewers of chicken, pork, or beef, the neighboring Mac
★ Resort Hotel and Koh Chang Lagoon Resort, on White Sand Beach, excel. Both set up BBQs on the beach just before sunset. Koh Chang Lagoon Resort also offers a reasonable vegetarian selection. The only real problem is deciding which one, but you can't miss with either.

¢ ✕ **Magic Resort.** The restaurant at this resort is a rather worn wooden structure that sits over the water. A pleasant breeze usually cools the open-air dining area and there are good views of the coastline and Ko Chang's high hills. The Thai seafood is very good—try the crab if you want something spicy. There's also a reasonable Western menu. Breakfast is available all day. ✉ *34 Moo 4, Haad Khlong Phrao Beach, Ko Chang 23170* ☎ *039/551064* 🟰 *MC, V.*

$ ✕🏨 **Cookies Hotel & Bungalows.** The best part of Cookies is its beachfront restaurant. The Thai food is consistently good and inexpensive and the Western backpacker fare is okay, too. The *tom yum talay* (hot-and-sour seafood soup) is a bit hot but definitely a standout; the banana shakes and the banana pancakes alone are worth a visit. As for the concrete bungalows, they're somewhat worn and basic, but they're close to the beach and prices are reasonable, even during high season. The adjacent three-story hotel is more comfortable, but although all the rooms have ocean views, the building is across the street from the beach and restaurant, so you're more likely to hear the traffic than the surf. ✉ *7/2 Moo 4, Band Haad Sai Khao, White Sand Beach, Ko Chang 23120* ☎ *039/ 551105 or 039/551106* 🖷 *039/551107* 🌐 *www.kohchangcookies.com* 🛏 *26 bungalows, 33 rooms* ♢ *Restaurant* 🟰 *MC, V.*

★ $$$$ 🏨 **Amari Emerald Cove Resort.** This is currently the island's top hotel and lives up to its five-star standards with spacious and tastefully decorated rooms. The well-kept grounds include a 50-meter lap pool and numerous fountains, plants, and trees. With a 200-plus staff, service is exemplary, too. The beach is rather small and can get crowded, though. ✉ *88/8 Moo 4, Haad Khlong Phrao, Ko Chang 23170* ☎ *039/551195, 02/255–3960 in Bangkok* 🖷 *039/511196* 🌐 *www.amari.com* 🛏 *158 rooms, 7 suites* ♢ *3 restaurants, 2 bars, 2 pools, spa, fitness room, meeting rooms, tourist center* 🟰 *AE, MC, V.*

★ $$-$$$ 🏨 **KC Grande Resort.** The bungalows here vary greatly, from spacious multiroom air-conditioned ones with all the amenities, to small one-room fan-cooled huts (though these also have a minibar and TV). This is the first property you see on the west side of the island as you drive in from the piers, and its location between a nice beach and a steep jungle-covered hill is certainly a plus. You can get a bungalow right on the beach or a row or two back. ✉ *1/1 Moo 4, Band Haad Sai Khao, White Sand Beach, Ko Chang 23120* ☎ *039/551199, 02/539–5424 in Bangkok* 🖷 *039/551198* 🌐 *www.kcresortkohchang.com* 🛏 *64 bungalows* ♢ *Restaurant, pool, dive shop* 🟰 *No credit cards.*

$$-$$$ 🏨 **Mac Resort Hotel.** A deluxe room with Jacuzzi and a balcony overlooking the beach or one of the bungalows clustered around the big, beachfront pool are the way to go at the Mac. It's a friendly place, with a nightly barbecue on the beach. ✉ *7/3 Moo 4, Haad Sai Khao, White*

Sand Beach, Ko Chang 23120 ☎ *039/551124* 🖷 *039/551125* 🛏 *25 rooms* ⚭ *Restaurant, pool* ▭ *MC, V.*

★ **$$** 🏨 **Bhumiyama Beach Resort.** The two-story bungalows here are modern and classy, with white walls and a lot of polished wood. The resort has two pools, one spilling into the one below, and landscaped grounds with several fountains and sculpture. It's next to Lonely Beach, which is beautiful, but rather small and often crowded. ⊠ *Haad Tah Nam, Lonely Beach, Ko Chang 23170* ☎ *039/558068 and 039/558069, 02/ 266–4388 in Bangkok* 🖷 *039/558070* 🛏 *46 rooms* ⚭ *Restaurants, bar, 2 pools* ▭ *MC, V.*

$$ 🏨 **Kai Bae Hut Bungalows.** There are many sets of bungalows on Kai Bae Beach, which has been backpacker central on Ko Chang for awhile, but this property is the most established and reliable. One-room bungalows have fans or air-conditioning. There are a few air-conditioned hotel rooms in an adjacent building, but the bungalows are closer to the beach, and with so many other resorts around, you can easily wander over to nearby restaurants for a meal. ⊠ *10/3 Moo 4, Kai Bae Beach, Ko Chang 23120* ☎ *09/936–1149* 🛏 *38 bungalows, 20 hotel rooms* ⚭ *Dive shop* ▭ *No credit cards.*

$$ 🏨 **Ko Chang Paradise Resort.** The bungalows here are spacious and include porches and all the amenities expected in a big city hotel. They're simply furnished with a few wood accents offsetting white walls and fabrics. The pool is beachside and some trees along the beach have swings attached to them—during high tide, you can swing out over the surf. The resort is close to Ko Chang Plaza, which has an ever-growing number of stores. ⊠ *39/4 Moo 4, Haad Khlong Phrao, Ko Chang 23120* ☎ *039/551-100 and 1* 🖷 *039/551–212* ⊕ *www.kohchangparadise. com* 🛏 *50 bungalows* ⚭ *Restaurant, pool* ▭ *MC, V.*

$$ 🏨 **Ko Chang Resort & Spa.** This self-contained complex on the edge of the bay has a long history—it was one of the first major lodgings built on Ko Chang in the late 1980s. Rustic bungalows line the beach and the hillside, and a newer hotel building sits between the bungalows and Ko Chang's one road. The bungalows closest to the beach are nice, but they're more expensive and get more foot-traffic than the hillside ones as other guests pass by to get to the beach. There's a spa offering treatments from traditional Thai massage (B300 an hour) to two-hour packages with sauna and body scrubs (B2,000). The spa is open to nonguests—there are free transfers from any Ko Chang resort. ⊠ *Klong Prao Beach, Ko Chang 23170* ☎ *039/551–082, 02/692–0094 in Bangkok* ⊕ *www.kohchangresortandspa.com* 🛏 *145 rooms* ⚭ *2 restaurants, pool, spa* ▭ *AE, MC, V.*

$$ 🏨 **Sea View Resort & Spa Koh Chang.** This resort is at the far end of Kai Bae Beach, which means it's quieter than most. Choose between bungalows just beyond the sands of Kai Bae Beach or rooms in the hotel section back and above the beach. The grounds include a big beachside pool and an attractive terrace restaurant. A spa offers everything from haircuts to three-day B14,600 packages. ⊠ *10/2 Moo 4, Kai Bae Beach, Ko Chang 23170* ☎ *039/529–022* 🖷 *039/551–153* ⊕ *www. seaviewkohchang.com* 🛏 *74 rooms, 2 suites* ⚭ *2 restaurants, bar, pool, spa, exercise room* ▭ *MC, V.*

★ $ ☒ **Koh Mak Panorama Resort.** If the bungalows here look more like something you'd find on safari in Africa, it's thanks to owner Khun Luang, a Chanthaburi gem dealer who spent many years on the continent searching for rough stones. Most of the bungalows are clustered in a coconut grove above a slope that leads down to a manmade river. Bungalows have many amenities—cable TV, phone, hot water—but no air-conditioning. A few two-room bungalows on stilts right on the shoreline are a better option, but pricey at B12,000. Most of the coastline is rocky, but there's a small sandy beach near the bungalows. The sprawling open-air restaurant serves wonderful Thai food (a good thing since there's no other place to eat in the immediate vicinity). Ko Mak is a small island south of Ko Chang—the resort will arrange transportation via speed boat from the pier at Laem Ngop. ☒ *44 Moo 1, Ko Mak 23000* ☎ *02/630–5768 up to 9 in Bangkok, 01/875–3267 mobile* ⊕ *www.koh-chang.com/kohmakpanorama* ↪ *114 bungalows* ⌂ *Restaurants, bar, Internet* ⊟ *MC, V.*

Sports & the Outdoors

ELEPHANT TREKS   **Ban Kwan Chang** (☎ 01/919–3995, 09/815–9566, or 06/334–2880) in Klongson Village on the north end of the island offers a trekking program supported by the Asian Elephant Foundation. Half-day tours (from 8:30 AM until around noon) include a bathing and feeding session and a 90-minute trek into the jungle. The cost is B900 per person, which includes transportation from your hotel. There are shorter treks, as well. Most hotels can arrange trips for you, if you don't want to call yourself.

Chang Chutiman Trekking (☎ 09/939–6676 or 07/135–7424), just off Haad Khlong Phrao, offers one-hour treks for B500 and two-hour treks for B900.

HIKING   Hiking trips, particularly to some of the island's waterfalls, are still a new endeavor, but are starting to crop up. It's a good idea to hire a guide if you plan to venture farther than one of the well-traveled routes, as good maps of the mostly jungle terrain are unheard of. At this writing, guided trips were starting to spring up. **Jungle Way** (☎ 09/223–4795) is based in the northern village of Klongson.

SCUBA DIVING &   Scuba diving, including PADI courses, are readily available. Divers say
SNORKELING   that the fish are smaller—no sharks for one—than in other parts of Thailand, but the coral is better and most of the dives are less than 18 meters (54 feet). Prices generally run from B3,200 for a two-day PADI introductory course to more than B20,000 for dive master certification.

Ploy Scuba Diving (☎ 06/155–1331 ⊕ www.ployscuba.com) offers a full range of dives and internationally recognized PADI courses, from beginner to dive master. Their main office is on Bang Pao Pier on the south of the island. There are offices on many of the beaches around the island, too.

OK Diving (☎ 09/936–7080 ⊕ www.okdiver.com), which has offices on White Sand Beach and Haad Khlong Phrao, and **Water World Diving** (☒ Koh Chang Plaza, Khlong Phrao Beach ☎ 09/224–1031 ⊕ www.waterworldkohchang.com) both offer day dives and PADI courses, as well as snorkeling excursions.

Snorkeling off a boat costs as little as B500 a day. Snorkelers usually just tag along on dive boats, but boat excursions that feature snorkeling are available. **Thai Fon** (☎ 06/141–7498) leaves White Sand Beach each morning for a 10-hour, 15-island tour of the marine park. The trip includes stops at two or more islands (skirting the shores of the others), a buffet lunch, and two snorkeling stops. The cost is around B800. It's a good way to see some of the archipelago, including uninhabited islands, but it's a long day.

Ko Si Chang

⑤ *40 min by ferry from Sri Racha, which is 100 km (62 mi) southeast of Bangkok.*

Ko Si Chang is not known for its beaches—most of the coast is rocky—but it's off the main tourist routes, so it has an easy-going pace that makes it a real escape. It's still relatively close to Bangkok, so Thais flood the island on weekends. During the week, however, it's peaceful. Foreign visitors have increased (they're now counted by the day, not by the week), but the development mania that has taken hold of Ko Chang has not found its way here yet. This is a great island for people who want to fill their days with nothing more complicated than a long stroll. All the sights on the island are within pleasant walks of each other and there are few cars around to be a danger to pedestrians.

For centuries Ko Si Chang was considered a gateway to Thailand—for nearly 200 years it was the spot where large ships stopped and loaded their goods onto smaller barges that then carried the goods the rest of the way to Bangkok and Ayutthaya. This practice still occurs and ships and barges are anchored between the island the mainland. Most locals are fishermen and business folk who support fishing. Rubbish from the shipping and fishing industries lining the coast is a bit of a blight, but it's a clean island otherwise.

Ko Si Chang has been a popular retreat for three generations of royalty. In the 1800s King Rama IV noted that people on this island lived longer than most Thais (to 70 and 80 years). He concluded that this phenomenon had something to do with the island's climate and he started to spend time here. His son, King Rama V, went one step further and built a summer palace on the island, and King Rama VI would spend up to eight or nine months a year here.

To get to Ko Si Chang, you need to get on a ferry at Sri Racha, which can be reached by bus from Bangkok; ferries depart from the pier at the end of Soi 14 and run every hour from 9 AM to 6 PM. It's B40 each way. Transportation around the island is limited to motorcycle taxis, which will take you to most places for B20, and the island's unique "stretch tuk-tuks," which cost about B50 to most spots. Bicycles are not widely available yet.

What to See
Most people visit Ko Si Chang to relax in a friendly, nontourist-oriented community, but there are a few places worth visiting, too.

After his father King Mongkut (Rama IV) first noted people on the island lived longer here than anywhere else in Thailand, King Chulalongkorn (Rama V) built **Chudhadhuj Palace** (named after Prince Chudhadhuj who was born on the island on July 5, 1893). The palace was abandoned in 1894 when France blockaded the Gulf of Thailand during a political crisis. Few buildings remain today, but the palace gardens are great for strolling around in, and the grounds are only about a mile south of town. Vimanmek Mansion was originally started here before being moved to Bangkok in 1901, and its beachside foundation remains. Nearby, an old wooden pier has been restored to its former glory.

On the north side of town is **Khao Yai Temple,** which attracts hordes of weekend visitors from Bangkok. The temple is actually a real hodge-podge of shrines and stupas that line a 400-step walkway up a steep hillside. It's an arduous climb to the main temple building, but the view of the northern half of the island, the mainland, and the rows of barges and ships, is worth the effort. (You can see from the top that Ko Si Chang has no natural water sources, and the reservoir just below the temple can't seem to hold water even with a plastic lining. Nearly every roof on the island has a big water collection jar underneath.)

Wat Yai Prik, just west of town, can't be missed as you near the island by boat—it's on the top of a hill and has eight 40-foot reservoirs, and many smaller ones. Much of the land around the wat is covered in concrete so the rain runoff can be collected. Seems everywhere you turn you see pipes from the roof collection funnels to the concrete reservoirs. The wat often donates drinking water to villagers when they need it. But Yai Prik is equally dedicated to the spiritual as it is to the practical. For 26 years this was a meditation center, until its status changed in 1999—to a wat that includes meditation. Meditation courses are available; signs throughout the grounds explain Buddhist principles. It's worth a look for folks interested in the many conservation practices the residents (22 monks, one novice, and 22 nuns) employ, as well as to see a wat where simplicity rules—though donations are accepted, they don't collect wealth to build ornate temples.

Where to Stay & Eat

The island caters to mostly Thai weekend visitors, and therefore has a limited selection of guesthouses and hotels. You need to book ahead for a weekend stay, but getting a room during the week is no problem.

$ ✕ **Pan & David.** Pan and David are a Thai-American couple, and not surprisingly, their eatery offers a good mix of both Thai and Western food, as well as some inventive combinations of the two. The spaghetti with a spicy seafood sauce is tops. The open-air dining area is cooled by ocean breezes. ⊠ *167 Moo 3, Mekhaamthaew Rd.* ☎ *038/216629* ▤ *No credit cards.*

¢ ✕ **Lek Noi.** Lek Noi doesn't look like much—it's little more than a shack with plastic chairs and simple wooden tables—but many locals cite this as the best place for seafood on the island. It's a little more than a half-mile out of town on the way to Chudhadhuj Palace. ⊠ *Makhaamthaew Rd.* ☎ *No phone* ▤ *No credit cards.*

\$ ⛵ **Rim Talay Resort.** For something a little different, stay in one of three boats that have been converted into bungalows. They're air-conditioned and sit on the beach, overlooking the rocky coast. The resort also has a hotel building, but it's rather barebones and the converted boats are much more comfortable. Pan & David is next door. ✉ *130 Moo 3, Mekhaamthaew Rd.* ☎ *038/216237* 📞 *3 bungalows* ▭ *No credit cards.*

¢ ⛵ **Sichang Palace Hotel.** This is the island's biggest hotel. There's nothing particularly special about it, but it's comfortable enough and centrally located. It's often full on weekends, but nearly empty during the week. The pool is great for an afternoon dip after walking around the island. ✉ *81 Atsadang Rd.* ☎ *038/216276 up to 9* 📞 *56 rooms* ⚙ *Restaurant, pool* ▭ *No credit cards.*

EASTERN GULF A TO Z

AIR TRAVEL
Because this region is so close to Bangkok, it's unlikely that you'll need to fly to get here. However, Bangkok Air does have daily flights from Bangkok to Trat.

🛫 **Trat Airport** ✉ 99 Mu 3 Tasom, Trat 23150 ☎ 039/525-777 ⊕ www.bangkokair.com.

BUS TRAVEL
The bus is probably the best way to travel to the Eastern Gulf. Buses to Pattaya, Ban Phe (where you catch boats bound for Ko Samet), Chanthaburi, Trat (where ferries to Ko Chang depart), and Sri Racha (where ferries to Ko Si Chang depart) leave from Bangkok's Eastern Bus Terminal at least every hour daily.

The same buses stop in the major towns, so you can also travel between towns easily.

CAR TRAVEL
The resorts along the Eastern Gulf are fairly close to Bangkok, making a car trip here more reasonable. The drive to Pattaya takes between two and three hours. To Ban Phe it's another 90 minutes. Chanthaburi is less than four hours from Bangkok on good roads. Often the most difficult part of a drive to the region is getting out of Bangkok, which is no mean feat.

EMERGENCIES
It's best to try the Tourist Police first in an emergency. Their general number is 1155.

🚑 **Hospitals Chanthaburi** ✉ Taksin Chanthaburi Hospital, 25/14 Taluang Rd., Chanthaburi ☎ 039/351467. **Ko Chang** ✉ Ko Chang International Clinic, 9/14 M 4 White Sand Beach, Ko Chang ☎ 039/551151, 01/863-3609 24 hours ⊕ www.kohchanginterclinic.com. **Ko Si Chang (Sri Racha)** ✉ Samitivej Hospital, 8 Soi Laemket, Choemchompon Rd., Sri Racha ☎ 038/324100. **Pattaya** ✉ Bangkok Pattaya Hospital, 301 Moo 6, Sukhumvit Rd. Km 143, Banglamung, Chonburi ☎ 038/259911 emergency, 66/3825-9999.

HEALTH
Health authorities have done a great job controlling mosquitoes around the southern resorts, but you'll still need a good supply of repellent.

Malaria is very rare, but not unheard of in Thailand's southeast, so if you develop flulike symptoms between a week and three weeks after visiting the region, be sure to ask your doctor to test you for it.

AIDS remains a big problem in much of Thailand, and those who claim that the Pattaya sex scene is safe from the epidemic are kidding themselves.

MAIL & SHIPPING
The reception desk at your hotel will post your cards and letters, a much easier option than hunting down the nearest post office.

🏢 Post Offices **Pattaya** ✉ Soi Post Office.

MONEY MATTERS
Banks with ATMs are easy to locate in Pattaya, Chanthaburi, Trat, Ko Chang, and Sri Racha. Though hotels and resorts can also exchange currency, remember that the more remote the hotel, the less you'll get for your dollar.

TRAIN TRAVEL
One train per day makes the round-trip journey down the eastern coast. Unfortunately, it's a third-class hard seat train that is excruciatingly slow, and the view on the way down is uninspiring, a mix of flat agricultural land and industrial estates. But if you like trains or have a good book to finish, it's a cheap option at B31. It departs Bangkok's central Hua Lamphong Station at 6:55 AM and arrives in Sri Racha (where you disembark if you're going to Ko Si Chang) at 9:55 AM and Pattaya at 10:19 AM. The return train departs Pattaya at 2:50 PM, and Sri Racha at 3:13 PM, arriving in Bangkok at 6:10 PM. Note that this schedule is subject to change; updates are available from the 24-hour information hotline 02/220-4334. (It's also best to call this Bangkok number from Pattaya or Sri Racha.)

VISITOR INFORMATION
🏢 Tourist Information **Tourism Authority of Thailand (Pattaya Office)** ✉ 382/1 Moo 10, Chaihat Rd. ☎ 038/427667, 038/428750. **Tourism Authority of Thailand (Trat office)** ✉ 100 Moo 1, Trat-Laem Ngop Rd. ☎ 039/597255, 039/597259, or 039/597260 🖷 039/597255.

THE WESTERN GULF

South of Bangkok lies the Western Gulf coast, hundreds of miles of shoreline where resort towns are the exception, rather than the rule. Most towns along the gulf are either sleepy fishing villages or culturally and historically significant towns, such as Surat Thani. Some touristy areas have grown up out of the smaller villages, but they are considerably less developed than some of their counterparts in the other coastal areas. Thus, the allure of the Western Gulf is its charming towns, spectacular beaches, and developed—but not overgrown—tourist destinations.

About three hours south of Bangkok are the laid-back beaches of Cha-am and Hua Hin. Popular with families and weekend warriors escaping from the bustling capital, these nearby towns offer visitors quiet beaches and lots of great seafood restaurants. Bangkokians have traveled to Hua Hin since the 1920s, when King Rama VII built a palace here. Where

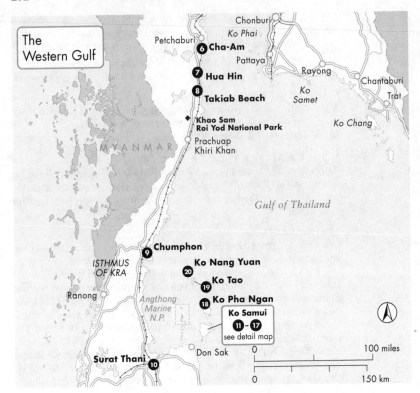

royalty goes, high society inevitably follows, but despite the attention the city received, Hua Hin was spared the pitfalls of rapid development thanks to Pattaya's explosion onto the tourism scene. The Eastern Gulf city received most of the development dollars, as well as most of the woes of overdevelopment, while Hua Hin retained its tranquil beauty.

Another 300 mi south is Surat Thani, the former capital of an ancient Siamese kingdom. As the center of its own civilization, Surat Thani developed its own artistic and architectural style. In modern times it has remained an important commercial and historic Thai city, and the province is home to one of the most pristine tropical forests in Thailand, Khao Sok National Park. However, most travelers know Surat Thani only as a departure point for the islands off its coast, primarily Koh Samui.

Koh Samui is the most popular tourist destination on the Western Gulf coast, which isn't surprising, considering Samui's gorgeous beaches, perfect weather, and sparkling blue water. Samui has been developed quite rapidly since the mid 1990s, but there's still a good variety of experiences to choose from. Here, you can find beaches in all stages of development. If you can't find what you want on Samui, there are boats departing regularly to Ko Pha-ngan, a more natural island that draws backpackers and New Age–hippies, and to Ko Tao, a hot spot for scuba divers.

Cha-am

❻ *163 km (101 mi) south of Bangkok, 40 km (25 mi) from Petchaburi town.*

It may not be the cleanest or most picturesque seaside town, but Cha-am does offer an authentic Thai-style beach experience. The small, quiet town is centered around the main pier; its main street, full of restaurants, bars, guesthouses, and hotels, lies along a tree-lined strip of beach. You can often see Bangkok families here—gathered at large, umbrella-covered tables for all-day meals, stocking up on fresh seafood and beer from wandering vendors.

Around the pier there are beach chairs, Jet Skis, Windsurfers, and banana-boat rides for hire, but the beach here has fairly dirty sand. Most visitors head to one of the many all-inclusive resorts farther from the town beach, where the sand is generally nicer and the water is better for swimming. Other than during occasional festivals, such as the seafood festival in September, there isn't a whole lot going on in Cha-am town.

Where to Stay & Eat

Fresh seafood is available at small cafés along Ruamjit (Beach) Road, where there are also stalls selling trays of deep-fried squid, shrimp, and tiny crab (for around B25). A steadily improving mix of small hotels and guesthouses for all budgets lines this road, while a string of luxury hotels and resorts runs along the main highway south of town to Hua Hin.

$–$$$ ✕ **Poom Restaurant.** The seafood here is perhaps the best in town, evidenced by a steady stream of locals. Try the charcoal-barbecue whole fish, large prawns, crab, and squid—all fresh and accompanied by delicious chili sauce dip. The decor is nothing special—of the metal-table-and-plastic-chair variety—but there's some outside seating under the trees. The restaurant next door (owned by the same people) has an air-conditioned dining area, if you really can't take the heat. ✉ *274/1 Ruamchit, Cha-am* ☎ *032/471–036* ▭ *No credit cards.*

¢ ✕▦ **Jolly and Jumper.** This eclectic spot is made up of basic rooms (singles and doubles) and one large "family room" (two double beds) overlooking the beach. The crowd is mainly backpackers, but the place is sedate enough for it to appeal to all budget travelers. Friendly, animal-loving Dutch owner Mariska (aka Jolly) has mynah birds left behind by tourists; she once even rescued an elephant from the streets of Cha-am and arranged accommodation for it in Chiang Mai. Fresh Dutch coffee and Western-style breakfasts, soups, steaks, and burgers are served on red-and-white-check table cloths ($). ✉ *274/3 Ruamchit Rd., Cha-am* ☎ *032/433–887* ➷ *12 rooms* ♨ *Restaurant; no a/c in some rooms, no TVs in some rooms* ▭ *No credit cards.*

$$$$ ▦ **Dusit Resort and Polo Club.** The spacious lobby serves as a lounge for afternoon tea and evening cocktails, sipped to the soft tunes of traditional Thai music. Just past an ornamental lily pond is the swimming pool, complete with bubbling fountains, beyond which is the beach. All rooms have private balconies with ocean views. There's a shuttle service to Hua Hin and car service to Bangkok. ✉ *1349 Petchkasem Rd., Cha-am 76120* ☎ *032/520009, 02/6363333 in Bangkok* ▱ *032/520296*

⊕ *www.dusit.com* ↩ *291 rooms, 9 suites ⌂ 4 restaurants, room service, cable TV, in-room safes, 5 tennis courts, 2 pools, gym, steam room, boating, parasailing, waterskiing, squash, horseback riding, 2 bars, business services, meeting rooms, travel services* ▤ *AE, DC, MC, V.*

$$$–$$$$ ▦ **Regent Cha-am.** Taking a swim couldn't be easier than at the Regent Cha-am, which has a quartet of pools spread among the dozens of bungalows that face the beach. The Lom Fang restaurant, overlooking a lake, grills up excellent fish accompanied by a spiced curry-and-lime sauce. The more formal restaurant, the Tapien Thong Grill Room, serves seafood and steak. In the evening live musicians sing your favorite pop songs in Thai. The hotel has its own car service from Bangkok. ✉ *849/ 21 Cha-am Beach, Cha-am 76120* ☎ *032/451240–9, 02/2510305 in Bangkok* 🖷 *32/471491–2, 02/253–5143 in Bangkok* ⊕ *www.regent-chaam.com* ↩ *630 rooms, 30 suites ⌂ 7 restaurants, coffee shop, cable TV, minibars, IDD telephones, 3 pools, hot tub, gym, tennis court, squash, snorkeling, boating, massage, spa, meeting rooms, travel services, shuttle service to Bangkok, shops, pub* ▤ *AE, DC, MC, V.*

$ ▦ **Kaenchan Beach Hotel.** Chinese box lanterns and Thai teak benches with silk cushions fill this boutique hotel's modern entrance hall and open-fronted bar and lounge. Some rooms have ocean views, and garden bungalows are also available. The price drops by 25% during the week. The Thai and international restaurant specializes in seafood. ✉ *241/4 Ruamchit Rd., Cha-am* ☎ *032/470–777* 🖷 *032/470–780* ⊕ *www.kaenchanbeachhotel.com* ↩ *54 rooms ⌂ Restaurant, pool, bar, meeting room* ▤ *MC, V.*

★ $ ▦ **Sabaya Jungle Resort.** Whether you're relaxing in your room or chilling out in the common area, you can feel at home at this cute, personable resort. Bungalows are small but cozy, with comfortable mattresses on carpeted floors, and stylish bathrooms with bamboo walls and fragrant toiletries. The common area has DVDs to watch and comfortable chairs to relax in and have coffee or tea. Sabaya also has a competent spa staff to ensure that you know you're on holiday, and pool room if you are up for a game. The resort is not on the beach, but it's only about a block away. The water there is swimmable and water sports can be found a short walk down the beach toward town. ✉ *304/7 Nong Chaeng Rd., Cha-am 76120* ☎ *032/470716–7* ⊕ *www.sabaya.co.th* ↩ *7 bungalows ⌂ Restaurant, cable TV, minibars, spa, massage, billiards, laundry service* ▤ *No credit cards.*

Hua Hin

❼ *66 km (41 mi) from Cha-am, 189 km (118 mi) south of Bangkok.*

Before the introduction of low-cost air carriers in 2003, Bangkokians had few choices for weekend getaways. One of the preferred destinations has been the golden sand near the small seaside city of Hua Hin, and Bangkok's rich and famous are frequent visitors here. The most renowned visitors are the King and Queen of Thailand who now use the Klai Kangwol Palace north of Hua Hin town as their primary residence. The palace was completed in 1928 by King Rama VII, who gave it the name Klai Kangwol, which means "Far From Worries."

Hua Hin's beach is the nicest of those along this part of the coast, but it's also the most popular. The sand is soft enough for sunbathing, though wandering hawkers will frequently disrupt your solace with silk cloth and fresh fruit for sale. You can get away from them figuratively by booking a relaxing beach massage or literally by taking a horseback ride to less populated parts of the beach. Jet Skis, kayaks, Windsurfers, and all other water sports can be arranged at various areas along the beach or through any tour agent.

Hua Hin town, which has many hotels and guesthouses, is also a great place to try fresh Thai seafood dishes. Many of these restaurants are on wooden piers, allowing you to dine above the sea. (It should be noted that the piers have been under constant threat of demolition by the government. Although this threat has been in effect for many years, the restaurants and guesthouses residing on them may be destroyed without much notice.)

The town also has a vibrant night market where souvenirs and local foods are available in abundance. The **Chatchai Street Market** is fun to explore. In the morning vendors sell meats and vegetables. From 5 PM to 11 PM daily, stalls are erected along Dechanuchit Street. You can practice your haggling skills over goods as diverse as jewelry, clothes, vases, lamps, toys, and art. You can also sample a variety of Thai delicacies, exotic fruits, desserts, pancakes, barbecue chicken, and just about anything that can be skewered on a stick, including the local favorite, squid.

When the upper classes from the capital followed the royal family to Hua Hin, they needed somewhere to stay. The Royal Hua Hin Railway Hotel was constructed to give these weary travelers somewhere to rest their heads. Near the intersection of Damnernkasem and Naresdamri roads you can still see the hotel, now called the **Sofitel Central Hua Hin Resort.** The magnificent Victorian-style colonial building was a stand-in for the hotel in Phnom Penh in the film *The Killing Fields.* Be sure to wander through its well-tended gardens and along the lovely verandas.

off the beaten path

KHAO SAM ROI YOD NATIONAL PARK – You pass rice fields, sugar palms, pineapple plantations, and crab farms as you make your way to this park, about 63 km (39 mi) south of Hua Hin. The park has two main trails and is a great place to spot wildlife, especially monitor lizards and barking deer. With a little luck you can see the dusky langur, a type of monkey also known as the spectacled langur because of the white circles around its eyes. About a half-mile from the park's headquarters is Khao Daeng Hill, which is worth a hike up to the view point, especially at sunrise. Another 16 km (10 mi) from the headquarters is Haad Laem Sala, a nice white-sand beach—you can pitch a tent here or stay in a guesthouse. Near the beach is Phraya Nakhon Cave, once visited by King Rama V. The cave has an opening in its roof where sunlight shines through for a beautiful effect. If you don't have a car (or haven't hired one), you'll have to take a bus to the Pranburi district in Prachuab Kiri Khan Province. From here, you'll be able to get a songthaew to take you to the park. ☏ 066/3261–9078 ⊕ *www.dnp.go.th.*

Where to Stay & Eat

$$–$$$ ✕ **Fisherman's Wharf.** East meets West at this surf-and-turf restaurant that uses the best of Thailand's fresh produce and seafood in some well-known Western entrees. Try the beer-batter fish-and-chips served in traditional newspaper wrapping. You can start your day with the best eggs Benedict in town or wrap it up with the daily B30 draft-beer happy hour. The Sunday roast gives you a chance to mingle with the expat community. ⌧ *8 Chomsin Rd., Hua Hin* ☎ *06/603–5335* ▭ *MC, V.*

$–$$ ✕ **Monsoon Restaurant & Bar.** Monsoon serves tasty tapas, afternoon tea (3 PM–7 PM), and a full menu of Thai and Vietnamese cuisine, including vegetarian entrees and a daily set menu. To wash down dishes such as *luc lac* (sauteed beef) and *tom yam goong* (spicy shrimp soup), Monsoon serves up creative cocktails like the Tonkin Wave (Midori, Creme de Banana, and pineapple juice). The restaurant is in a two-story colonial-style building, which has an elegant open-air dining room and garden terrace. ⌧ *62 Naresdamri Rd., Hua Hin* ☎ *032/531062* ⌳ *Reservations essential* ▭ *MC, V.*

$–$$ ✕ **Sang Thai.** Ignore the ramshackle surroundings and floating debris in the water—for interesting seafood dishes from grilled prawns with bean noodles to fried grouper with chili and tamarind juice, this open-air restaurant down by the wharf can't be beat. It's popular with Thais, which is always a good sign. Don't miss the *kang* (mantis prawns). ⌧ *Naresdamri Rd.* ☎ *032/512144* ▭ *AE, DC, MC, V.*

¢–$$ ✕ **Hua Hin Restaurant (KOTI).** A longtime local favorite for Thai-style seafood, Koti has a no-nonsense decor and typically full tables that attest to its primary focus: good food. A large menu (in English) includes fried fish with garlic and pepper and *hor mok talay* (steamed seafood curry). ⌧ *61/1 Petchkasem Rd., Hua Hin* ☎ *032/511252* ▭ *No credit cards.*

★ **$$$$** ▦ **Chiva-Som.** Even with the proliferation of spas in Hua Hin, Chiva-Som has not been toppled from its lofty position as the region's best health resort. The resort focuses on holistic healing and a wholesome diet, but the setting on the beach will do you a world of good, too. The tasteful and comfortable rooms have lots of natural woods and private terraces that overlook the ocean. Rates include all meals, a medical checkup, and a daily massage. ⌧ *73/4 Petchkasem Rd., Hua Hin 77110* ☎ *032/536536, 02/387116905–10 in Bangkok* 🖷 *032/381154* ⊕ *www.chivasom.com* ↝ *57 rooms* ⌳ *Restaurant, cable TV, in-room DVD players, pool, massage, spa* ▭ *AE, DC, MC, V.*

$$$$ ▦ **Hilton Hua Hin Resort & Spa.** At the start of the main beach, in the liveliest part of town, the Hilton is perfect for beach enthusiasts who want to be close to the action. Towering over Hua Hin, this 17-story hotel is especially popular with European tour groups. Its rooms are spacious, modern, and functional. The lagoonlike pool dominates the garden. The beach in front of the resort is next to the public accessway, thus it's popular with vendors and tourists from other hotels. On the streetside of the hotel is the Hua-Hin Brewing Company, a popular bar, restaurant, and people-watching venue. ⌧ *33 Naresdamri Rd., Hua Hin 77110* ☎ *032/512888* 🖷 *032/511135* ⊕ *www.hilton.com* ↝ *255 rooms, 41 suites* ⌳ *3 restaurants, room service, cable TV, telephone, minibars, in-room safes, in-room hot tubs, 2 tennis courts, pool, health* *club, squash, playground, café, pub, bar, babysitting, children's programs, business services, meeting rooms, travel services* ☰ *AE, DC, MC, V.*

$$$$ ⊞ **Hua Hin Marriott Resort & Spa.** Adjacent to the Sofitel Hua Hin Resort, this hotel has accommodations and service equal to those of its neighbor. But the modern facility doesn't have the colonial ambience, so the rates are a few hundred baht less. Rooms are comfortable, if uninspired. Among the four restaurants is the Salathai, which is less elegant than the similarly named restaurant at the Sofitel, but serves better food. ⊠ *107/1 Phetkasem Rd., Hua Hin 77110* ☎ *032/511881, 02/476–0021 in Bangkok* 📠 *032/512422* ⊕ *www.marriotthotels.com/hhqmc* 🛏 *209 rooms, 7 suites* ⚬ *3 restaurants, café, cable TV, minibars, in-room VCRs, in-room safes, Internet, tennis court, pool, hot tub, health club, massage, spa, jetskiing, kayaking, sailing, snorkeling, Ping-Pong, boating, volleyball, waterskiing, bar, playground, meeting rooms* ☰ *AE, DC, MC, V.*

★ **$$$$** ⊞ **Sofitel Central Hua Hin Resort.** Even if you don't stay at this local landmark, its old-world charm makes it worth a visit. Wide verandas open onto splendid gardens that lead down to the beach. More than two-dozen gardeners take their work very seriously, caring for the topiaries that look like shadows at night. The lounges on either side of the reception area are open to let in sea breezes. The best rooms are those on the second floor—they have unforgettable views of the ocean. Come during the low season, when rates are almost half of what they are the rest of the year. ⊠ *1 Damnernkasem Rd., Hua Hin 77110* ☎ *032/512021, 02/541–0123 in Bangkok* 📠 *032/511014* ⊕ *www.sofitel.com* 🛏 *117 rooms, 30 suites* ⚬ *2 restaurants, cable TV, in-room safes, 4 tennis courts, 6 pools, massage, spa, health club, snorkeling, boating, bar, nightclub, meeting rooms, Wi-Fi, children's programs, playground* ☰ *AE, DC, MC, V.*

$ ⊞ **Jed Pee Nong.** This complex of bungalows and a small high-rise building is on one of the main streets leading down to the public entrance to the beach. The bungalows are clustered around a swimming pool, but most rooms are in the hotel building. Rooms have huge beds and not much else, but the price couldn't be better. The terrace restaurant facing the street stays open late. ⊠ *17 Damnernkasem Rd. Hua Hin, 77110* ☎ *032/512381* 🛏 *44 rooms* ⚬ *Restaurant, coffee shop, cable TV, in-room safes, pool* ☰ *MC, V.*

$ ⊞ **Sirin.** This hotel about a block from the beach has huge, comfortable rooms with extra-large beds and plenty of light streaming in through the wide windows. There's a dining room, which doubles as a lounge, but there are plenty of other restaurants nearby. ⊠ *18 Damnernkasem Rd., Hua Hin 77110* ☎ *032/511150 or 032/512045* 📠 *032/513571* 🛏 *35 rooms* ⚬ *Restaurant* ☰ *AE, DC, MC, V.*

★ **¢–$** ⊞ **Fulay Guesthouse.** This unique guesthouse is built upon a pier that juts out over the gulf. The Cape Cod–blue planks of the pier match the color of the trim around the white-washed walls; rooms have kitschy effects like seashell-framed mirrors and sand-encrusted lamps. Two large, private houses claim prime real estate toward the end of the pier with private wooden decks ideal for sipping afternoon drinks or watching early morning sunrises. If you prefer not to sleep to the sound of the sea beneath your bed, opt for the more modern but reasonably priced Fulay Hotel across the street. ⊠ *110/1 Naresdamri Rd., Hua Hin 77110*

☎ *032/513670* 🖨 *032/530320* ⊕ *www.fulay-huahin.com* ⌂ *Restaurant, massage, laundry service, bar; no a/c in some rooms, no TV in some rooms* ⊟ *MC, V.*

¢ 🖼 **Pattana Guesthouse.** Two beautiful teakwood houses are hidden down a small alley in the heart of Hua Hin. The main house used to be a fisherman's residence and now holds a variety of clean, simple rooms facing a small garden bar and café. Rooms are available with air-conditioning or fans, and with private or shared bathrooms. ⊠ *52 Naresdamri Rd., Hua Hin 77110* ☎ *032/513393* ⤴ *13 rooms* ⌂ *Fans, café, bar, laundry service; no a/c in some rooms* ⊟ *No credit cards.*

Sports & the Outdoors

Hua Hin Golf Tours (☎ 032/530119 ⊕ www.huahingolf.com), in central Hua Hin town, can arrange for you to play at any of the 10 or so courses in the area. There's no surcharge to the greens fees and free transportation is provided. Rental clubs are available from the pro shop. If you feel like doing it on your own, across the tracks from the quaint wooden railway station is the well-respected **Royal Hua Hin Golf Course** (⊠ Damnernkasem Rd., Hua Hin ☎ 032/512475). You can play for B800, plus B200 for a caddie. There's a lounge for refreshments.

Nightlife

There aren't many options for nightlife in Hua Hin. Your best bet is **Hua Hin Brewing Company** (⊠ 33 Naresdamri Rd. ☎ 032/512888), on the street side of the Hilton Hotel, across from one of Hua Hin's seedier beer-bar sois (Soi Bindhabatr). Local bands energetically perform Thai and Western pop-rock music nightly. Although this isn't a true brewpub (the beers are made in Bangkok), the selection is good, and you can try a sampler of their three tasty beers. The outdoor patio offers a full menu, as well as a prime spot to people-watch.

Takiab Beach

❽ *4 km (2½ mi) south of Hua Hin.*

Khao Takiab, the beach directly to the south of Hua Hin, is a good alternative for people who wish to avoid Hua Hin's busier scene; tourists who stay in Takiab are mostly well-off Thais who prefer Takiab's exclusivity to Hua Hin's touristy atmosphere, and you can find many upscale condos and small luxury hotels. The beach itself is wide and long, though the water is quite murky and shallow, and not very suitable for swimming. Sunbathing is the ideal activity here, especially during the low tide when Takiab's golden, sandy beach is flat and dry. To get to Takiab, flag down a songthaew (B10) on Petchkasem Road in Hua Hin. Alternatively, you can take a horseback ride from the beach in Hua Hin and trot along the coast to Takiab (horses are also available from Takiab). The usual water activities like jet skiing and banana-boating are available here, and are more enjoyable than in Hua Hin as the beach and water are less crowded. The southern part of the beach ends at a big cliff, which has a tall, standing image of the Buddha. You can hike to the top of the hill, where you find a small Buddhist monastery and several restaurants with excellent views.

Where to Stay & Eat

$–$$ ✕ **Supatra-by-the-sea.** The outdoor seating at this restaurant on the southern end of the beach allows you to dine beneath the tranquil gaze of the standing Buddha on the adjacent hillside. The dining room is exquisitely designed in Lanna-style and has water-lily ponds beside several tables. Entrées are mainly seafood-based, such as prawn sour soup with deep-fried green omelet, although other Thai dishes and vegetarian dishes are included on the extensive menu. The full bar serves inventive cocktails, which may be enjoyed beside the beach. ⊠ *122/63 Takiab Beach* ☎ *032/536561* ▤ *AE, MC, V.*

$$$–$$$$ ▥ **Smor Spa Village & Resort.** Smor's accommodations are nearly identical in design to neighboring Kaban Tamor Resort—spacious, single-story, mushroomlike bungalows—but the rooms at Smor have private, outdoor Jacuzzis. The spa has several treatment rooms, saunas, and steam rooms. Sun beds are available on the lawn adjacent to the beach, which is convenient when all of the sand is submerged during high tide. ⊠ *122/ 64 Takiab Beach, 77110* ☎ *032/536800* 🖷 *032/536464* ⊕ *www. smorspahuahin.com* ⚲ *6 rooms* ♨ *Cable TV, minibars, IDD phones, massage, spa, laundry service* ▤ *MC, V.*

$$$ ▥ **Kaban Tamor Resort.** Rooms at this stylish resort are inside two-story structures that were designed after seashells, but look more like mushrooms. The spacious, round rooms have white walls and pale wooden floors and are filled with plenty of natural light. A small pool and soft grass are alongside the beach and the open-air restaurant serves tasty Thai food. Guests at Kaban Tamor get a 20% discount at Smor spa next to the resort. ⊠ *122/ 43–57 Takiab Beach, 77110* ☎ *032/521011–3* 🖷 *032/521014* ⊕ *www. kabantamor.com* ⚲ *18 rooms* ♨ *Restaurant, room service, cable TV, minibars, IDD phones, pool, bar, laundry service* ▤ *AE, MC, V.*

Chumphon

❾ *400 km (240 mi) south of Bangkok, 211 km (131 mi) south of Hua Hin.*

Chumphon is regarded as the gateway to the south, since trains and buses connect it to Bangkok in the north, to Surat Thani and Phuket to the south, and to Ranong to the southwest. Ferries to Ko Tao dock at Pak Nam at the mouth of the Chumphon River, 11 km (7 mi) southeast of town. Most of the city's boat services run a free shuttle to the docks.

If you're overnighting here or have a couple of hours to spare before catching a bus, visit the night market. If you have more time, just north of Chumphon there's an excellent beach, **Ao Thong Wua Laen.** You can catch a songthaew on the street across from the bus station. The curving beach is 3 km (2 mi) of white-yellow sand with a horizon dotted by small islands that make up one of the world's strangest bird sanctuaries. Vast flocks of swifts breed here, and their nests are harvested for the bird's nest soup served up in the best Chinese restaurants of Southeast Asia. It's such a lucrative business that the concessionaires patrol their properties with armed guards.

Where to Stay

$–$$ ▥ **Chumphon Cabana Beach Resort.** This friendly resort at the south end of Chumphon's Thong Wua Beach is a great place to stay if you want to make brief visits to Ko Samui and other nearby islands. The hotel wins top marks for its ecology-friendly program, designed to save water and power and keep the beach free of the litter that too often disfigures Thai resorts. Accommodations are in bamboo-wall bungalows hidden in the lush foliage and rooms with private balconies in several low-rise buildings. Furnishings are simple but tasteful. ⊠ *69 Thung Wua Laen Beach, 86230* ☎ *077/560245 up to 9* 🖶 *077/560247* ⊕ *www.cabana.co.th* 🛏 *108 rooms, 25 bungalows* ⚑ *Restaurant, cable TV, minibars, dive shop, bar, meeting rooms, laundry service, travel services* 🖃 *MC, V.*

¢ 🖫 **Marokot Hotel.** This is not the most luxurious hotel in Chumphon, but the rooms are comfortable and the baths have plenty of hot water. The hotel is a short walk from the night market. Best of all, the rates are among the lowest in town. ⊠ *102/112 Taweesinka Rd., 86000* 🖶 *077/503628 up to 32* 🖶 *077/570196* 🛏 *12 rooms* 🖃 *No credit cards.*

Surat Thani

🔟 *193 km (120 mi) south of Chumphon, 685 km (425 mi) south of Bangkok.*

Surat Thani is the main embarkation point for boats bound for Ko Samui. Although it's not a particularly attractive city, don't despair if you have to stay overnight while waiting for your ferry. There are some good restaurants and a handsome hotel. In addition, at every nightfall sleepy downtown Surat Thani turns into an electrifying street fair centered around the **San Chao Night Market,** which is illuminated by the lights of numerous food stalls and shop carts. The market is quite popular with Surat locals, as well as the few tourists in town. If there are too many choices, "Paad Thai Seafood" is the best solution—it's safe and consistently good. Looking for a tasty dessert? Across the street from the market, you can find Tavorn Roti, which serves delicious traditional roti.

There's also the possibility of an entertaining excursion to one of Thailand's most unusual educational establishments, the **Monkey Training College** (⊠ Km 91, Hwy. 401 ☎ 077/273378). Here, under almost scholastic conditions, monkeys are trained to climb high palms and collect the coconuts that are still an important part of the local economy. And for those who can't get enough of Thailand's cultural sites, the 1,000-year-old **Wat Phra Barommathat** in the ancient city of Chaiya is the most intriguing one in the area. The simian school and Chaiya are only a short songthaew ride from Surat Thani.

off the
beaten
path

KHAO SOK NATIONAL PARK – After a few hours by bus south of Surat Thani town, you can find yourself traveling through a different landscape of tall mountain ranges covered with lush greenery and small streams. Soon you reach Ratchabhrapa (Chiew Lan) Dam and Khao Sok National Park, which contains 161,000 acres of the most beautiful forest in Thailand. The park is home to such diverse and rare wildlife as the gaur, banteng, sambar deer, bear, Malayan tapir, macaque, gibbon, serow, mouse deer, and porcupine. It's also one of the few places to see a Raffesia, the world's largest flower, and rare bird species like hornbills. Hiking, boat rides, and night safaris are some of the activities in the park. Rain is inevitable in Khao Sok as the weather is influenced by monsoon winds from both the northeast and west year-round—the best time to visit the Khao Sok is December to April. Both the national park and some private resorts offer various types of lodging, but don't expect too much. Only very basic accommodation can be found in the park. A privately run, funky shaped tree house accommodation is 1 km (½ mi) before the park's entrance.

Where to Stay & Eat

$$ ✕🏨 **Wang Tai Hotel.** If you find yourself searching for a place to stay in Surat Thani, this modern high-rise offers everything to prepare you for the onward journey. Rooms here overlook the Tapi River. The local tourist office is a few blocks away. The hotel's restaurant is among the best in Surat Thani, with a predominantly Thai and Chinese menu. The dim sum is excellent. ⊠ *1 Talad Mai Rd., 84000* ☎ *077/283020, 02/253–7947 in Bangkok* 🖷 *077/281007* ➷ *230 rooms* ⟁ *Restaurant, coffee shop, room service, minibars, cable TV, pool, health club, lounge, laundry service, travel services, meeting rooms* ▭ *AE, MC, V.*

Ko Samui

20 km (12 mi) by boat east of Don Sak.

Ko Samui is half the size of Phuket, so you could easily drive around it in a day. But Samui is best appreciated by those who take a slower, more casual approach. Most people come for the sun and sea, so they head straight to their hotel and rarely venture beyond the beach where they are staying. However, every beach has its own unique character and with a little exploration, you may find the one most suitable for you.

On the east coast of Samui lies Chawaeng beach, the primary destination of travelers to Ko Samui. Chawaeng has the best beach; the greatest variety and number of hotels, restaurants, and bars; and consequently, the largest crowds. During the day, the beaches are packed with tourists; the ocean buzzes with Jet Skis, parasailers, and banana boats. At night, the street comes alive as shops, bars, and restaurants vie for your vacation allowance.

Lamai beach, to the south of Chawaeng, is just as long as Chawaeng beach and nearly as nice. The water is deeper and so it is less suitable for young children, but water sports are readily available and the beach itself is much less congested. The accommodation here ranges from a few swanky resorts, far from the center of town, to a large selection of budget guesthouses and bungalows. Lamai's nightlife might be slightly more subdued than Chawaeng's but it's also a bit more sordid, with many beer-bars blasting Thai pop music and employing numerous young Thai hostesses.

On the northern coast are the less-developed beaches of Maenam and Bophut. Maenam town is a relatively busy, local business district with commercial businesses along the road from Chawaeng to Nathorn. However, Maenam beach is one of the least developed and most natural beaches on the island. There's little nightlife and few distractions there.

Bophut beach has both high- and low-end accommodation and a small romantic fishermen's village with several nice seaside restaurants, bars, and boutique shops.

Nathorn Town, on the west coast of Samui, is the primary port on the island, where ferries and transport ships arrive from and depart to the mainland. Nathorn is the location of the governmental offices, including the Tourism Authority of Thailand. There are banks, foreign exchange booths, shops, travel agents, restaurants, and cafés by the ferry pier. There are even a few places to rent rooms, although there would be little reason to stay in Nathorn as nicer accommodation can be found a short songthaew ride away.

The high-class resorts of Choengmon beach, on the northeastern cape, provide luxury accommodation and service on small, often private beaches. Several other high-end resorts and alternative health retreats are on various beaches around the rest of the island. These include many international chains, designer-boutique resorts, and top-tier spas.

off the beaten path

MU KO ANGTHONG NATIONAL MARINE PARK – Although some visitors prefer to enjoy sunbathing on the white sand and swimming in the blue sea of Samui Island, many choose a trip to Angthong National Marine Park. Angthong is an archipelago of 42 islands, which cover some 250 square km (90 square mi), and lie 35 km northwest of Samui. The seven main islands are Wua Ta Lap Island, which houses the National Park's headquarters, Phaluai Island, Mae Ko Island, Sam Sao Island, Hin Dap Island, Nai Phut Island, and Phai Luak Island. The islands feature limestone mountains, strangely shaped caves, and emerald green water. Most tourists do a one-day trip, which can be arranged by most travel agents on Samui. Prices vary from agent to agent since they all offer different tours (i.e., some offer kayaking around several islands, while others take you out on small speed boats to do snorkeling or more comprehensive tours of the numerous caves and white sand beaches). If you're interested in more than a one-day tour, you can hire a taxiboat to take you out to the National park's headquarters on Wua Talap Island where there are five huts for rent and a campsite. If you stay overnight you should also have time to hike up to the viewpoint at the top of Wua Talap. The park is open year-round, although the seas can be rough and the waters less clear during the monsoon season (October through December). ☎ *077/286025 or 077/420225* ⊕ *www.dnp.go.th.*

Sports & the Outdoors

Although many people come to Samui to chill out on the beach, there are dozens of activities, certainly more than one vacation's worth. In addition to the activities listed below, you can arrange paintball, go-karting, shooting, and bungee jumping through most hotels and tour agents on the island.

You can go up into the mountains and explore the jungle and some of the waterfalls by car. If you're more adventurous, you can get a different view of the jungle by sailing through the air on a zipline. **Canopy Adventures** (☎ 077/414150) will have you zipping between six tree houses on 300 meters of wire strung across the tree canopies. If you prefer to stay on the ground you can arrange a ride at the **Sundowner Horseranch** (☎ 077/424719) in Ban Thale. Elephant treks are available through **Samui Namuang Travel & Tour** (☎ 077/418680). The interior of the island can also be explored on mountain bikes from **Red Bicycle** (☎ 077/232136).

Although no one has figured out how to fit an actual golf course on the island, one enterprising company, **Extra Golf Club** (☎ 077/422255), has built a 3-hole course. If you want 18 holes, you'll have to take up Frisbee golf instead (same idea as regular golf, but Frisbees are tossed from the putting area to the "holes," which are actually baskets). Head to **Frisbee Golf** (☎ 01/8942105), near Bophut, laugh your way through a round of "golf," and grab an ice-cold beer at the end.

★ The ultimate spa experience on the island is at **Tamarind Springs** (✉ 205/7 Thong Takian, Lamai Beach ☎ 077/230571 or 077/424436 🖷 077/424311 ⊕ www.tamarindretreat.com). Leave your cell phone at the door, put the camera away, and, oh yeah, forget about all that stress and tension, too—you've arrived at the ultimate cure for the outside world. In a beautiful green valley, Tamarind Springs truly is a quiet and peaceful oasis for the body and soul. Start your experience in the steam room, built between two enormous boulders that make up two of the room's walls; alternate between that and the cool spring bath, in the shade of the larger boulder's back side. Then take a journey across a grassy clearing, up some stone steps, and enter the massage area. There are many different massage options available from Thai massage to herbal relaxation to the "Over the Top" massage package, which lasts 2½ hours. If you want to stay here, there are eight individually designed hippie-chic houses available for rent, each with boulders coming through the walls and open-air living rooms. However, houses are generally reserved for those looking for the Tamarind experience, that is to say, individuals who are looking for regular massage treatment, perhaps a yoga class or two, and real relaxation, not just idealized "luxury."

Mae Nam

⑪ *10 km (6 mi) northeast of Na Thon.*

Mae Nam lies on the northern coast of Samui. Its long and narrow curving beach has coarse golden sand shaded by tall coconut trees. It's a very quiet beach, both day and night, with little nightlife and few restaurants. The gentle waters are great for swimming, but water sports are limited to what your hotel can provide. Several inexpensive guesthouses and a few luxurious resorts share the 5-km (3-mi) stretch of sand. Mae Nam is certainly the most "un-Samui" of Samui's beaches; a place for those who want simple relaxation on an otherwise highly developed island.

Mae Nam is also the departure point for speedboats leaving Samui for Phang Ngan and Ko Tao. Transport on these boats can be arranged from anywhere on the island.

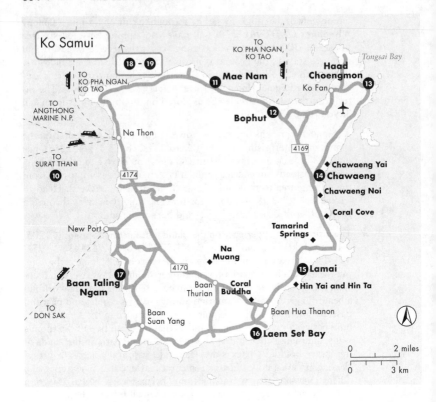

Ko Samui

18 - 19

TO
KO PHA NGAN,
KO TAO

TO
KO PHA NGAN,
KO TAO

11 Mae Nam

TO
KO PHA NGAN,
KO TAO

Tongsai Bay

Haad
Choengmon

Ko Fan

13

TO
ANGTHONG
MARINE N.P.

Na Thon

12 Bophut

4169

TO
SURAT THANI

10

4174

Chawaeng Yai

14 Chawaeng

Chawaeng Noi

Coral Cove

New Port

Tamarind
Springs

Na
Muang

4170

Baan
Thurian

Coral
Buddha

15 Lamai

17

Baan Taling
Ngam

Hin Yai and Hin Ta

TO
DON SAK

Baan
Suan Yang

Baan Hua Thanon

16 Laem Set Bay

0   2 miles

0   3 km

WHERE TO
STAY & EAT
$–$$$

✕ **Koseng.** This two-story seafood restaurant has been feeding Mae Nam locals for decades. Although the interior is quite simple, the big sign in front of the restaurant shows off the stars it has earned along with a few suggested dishes from Khun Muek Daeng, Thailand's renowned food critic. Once inside, do not be intimidated by the local crowd—menus are in both Thai and English and staff speak English. The most famous dish, stir-fried crab with black pepper, is highly recommended. ✉ *95 Soi Koseng, Mae Nam Beach* ☎ *077/425365* ✍ *Reservations essential* ▭ *No credit cards.*

¢–$ ✕ **Angela's Bakery & Café.** Angela's, on the main road running through Mae Nam, serves salads and sandwiches, both traditional and inventive. The "Hot Bandana" is a tasty vegetarian sandwich baked inside a breadbowl and wrapped in a bandana. Entrées represent Samui's British influence: bangers and mash, fish-and-chips, and the like. In addition, Angela's sells 20 types of bread, more than 40 desserts, a variety of imported meats and cheeses, and several types of muffins, just in case you were looking for some picnic goodies. ✉ *64/29 Samui Ring Rd., Mae Nam Beach* ☎ *077/427396* ⊕ *www.angelasbakery.com* ▭ *No credit cards.*

¢–$ ✕ **Twin Restaurant.** Run by two friendly twin sisters, Twin Restaurant serves both Thai and Western food from breakfast to dinner. Located on the main road, it's very easy to find. The open-air restaurant is small, with only nine tables. You can peek into the restaurant's very clean kitchen where they prepare tasty, inexpensive dishes, such as curry soup, and more extravagant fare, like steaks. ⊠ *237 Samui Ring Rd., Mae Nam Beach* ▭ *No credit cards.*

$$–$$$$ 🏨 **Amarin Victoria Hotel.** For those who want more urbane lodging, Amarin Victoria is a "city hotel" near the sea. The decor is hip and trendy; polished concrete walls lead to comfortable, yet stylish rooms. Black and white are the predominant colors here, and most rooms have multiple, pivoting doors that allow the various sections to open to each other. The rooftop pool and lounge area compensate for the hotel's short distance from the beach. ⊠ *12/71 Samui Ring Rd., Mae Nam Beach, Ko Samui 84330* ☎ *077/425611–15* 🖷 *077/427552* ⊕ *www.amarinsamuiresort. com* ⌂ *46 rooms, 14 suites* ⚲ *Restaurant, room service, minibars, in-room safes, cable TV, in-room DVD players, pool, massage, spa, hair salon, lounge, library, laundry service, Internet, meeting rooms* ▭ *AE, DC, MC, V.*

★ $$$–$$$$ 🏨 **Santiburi.** The villas on this beachfront estate make you feel as if you're staying at a billionaire's holiday hideaway. The carefully chosen furnishings in the teak-floor rooms are casual, yet elegant. The "less is more" philosophy extends to the huge bathrooms, which have shiny black tiles. Floor-to-ceiling French windows flood the living rooms with light. The main building, a classic Thai pavilion overlooking the oval swimming pool, has European and Thai restaurants. The private beach is ideal for water sports and has a jetty for the hotel's own cruise ship, a 60-year-old junk. ⊠ *12/12 Samui Ring Rd., Mae Nam Beach, Ko Samui 84330* ☎ *077/ 425031–38, 02/636–3333 in Bangkok, 800/223–5652 in U.S.* 🖷 *077/ 425040* ⊕ *www.santiburi.com* ⌂ *71 villas and suites* ⚲ *3 restaurants, snack bar, room service, in-room safes, minibars, cable TV, in-room DVD players, 2 tennis courts, pool, health club, hair salon, massage, spa, beach, windsurfing, boating, squash, 2 bars, shop, babysitting, dry cleaning, laundry service, Internet, car rental, travel services* ▭ *AE, DC, MC, V.*

¢–$$ 🏨 **The Florist.** This guesthouse is quite small and you're likely to feel that you are sharing rooms in someone's home. All rooms have balconies with partial sea view, but the huge seafront room has a full-on view of Phang Ngan from its large deck, outdoor tub, and huge sun bed. Although the rooms have aging furniture and a slightly musty smell, they are private enough to keep doors open at night to allow the breeze to blow through. There's a small pool and beachside deck. From the public accessway to Maenam beach, walk a short distance down the beach to your left. ⊠ *190 Mae Nam Beach, 84330* ☎ *077/425671–2* ⌂ *7 rooms, 1 suite* ⚲ *Restaurant, minibars, pool, laundry service; no TV in some rooms* ▭ *AE, DC, MC, V.*

Bophut

⑫ *11 km (7 mi) east of Na Thon.*

A small headland separates Maenam from the North shore's other low-key community, Bophut. The beach here is quite narrow, but more than wide enough for sunbathing. During the rainy season the runoff waters make the sea slightly muddy. Otherwise, the water is like glass, good for swimming (though it's deep enough to be unsuitable for young children). Lodgings here range from backpacker hangouts to upscale resorts. Unlike ultraquiet Maenam, Bophut has a bit more nightlife—Central Bophut, referred to as the fishermen's village, has a beachside strip of old two-story Chinese shophouses that have been converted into restaurants, bars, and boutiques. Although the scene is small, there's ample variety, including Italian and French cuisine, English and Australian pubs, and even a few clubs with DJs. Bophut, quaint and romantic, has a devoted following of return visitors who enjoy its compact and quiet environment.

WHERE TO STAY
& EAT
$$–$$$

✗ **La Sirene.** For elegant French cooking, try this small bistro on the waterfront. A four-course tasting menu begins with homemade pâté followed by medallions of beef or pork in a mustard sauce, then a salad, and then dessert—all for less than B500. À la carte dishes, including Thai selections, are also served up by the owner, who moved here from Nice. A few tables are in the dining room, but the real delight is to sit on the deck overlooking the boats moored a few yards offshore. ⊠ 65/1 Bophut Beach ☎ 077/425301 ☰ MC, V.

¢–$ ✗ **Happy Elephant.** Owner Khun Sasothon displays the day's freshest seafood on ice in front of his restaurant. Choose your favorite and specify how you'd like it cooked. After a drink at the bar, sit outside on the deck perched above the beach and dine under the stars. You can spot the twinkling lights of Ko Pha Ngan across the ocean. Other dishes are also delicious—the *tom yam pla nam sai* (spicy soup with fish) is strongly recommended. ⊠ 79/1 Moo 1 ☎ 077/427222 ☰ AE, MC, V.

¢–$ ✗ **Eddy's Restaurant.** Owner-and-chef Eddy creates food with character. This is not surprising, as Eddy will excitedly tell you, he "just loves to cook." However, he'll also be the first to admit that his flair for creativity may not suit every person's palate. Roast pumpkin and crispy bacon salad with yogurt dressing and toasted coconut is just one of many unique creations. Fortunately, he serves a lunch sampler that allows you to mix and match three selections from the menu. He also claims to make Samui's best burger—it's undoubtedly Samui's largest and most creative. Eddy's prices are extremely reasonable. ⊠ 3/3 Samui Ring Rd., Bophut Beach ☎ 077/245127or 077/245224 ☰ No credit cards ☉ Closed weekends.

★ $$$$ ✗▣ **Anantara Resort and Spa Koh Samui.** Anantara captures the essence of Samui: coconut trees dot the grounds, monkey statues and sculptures decorate the entire resort, and, of course, there is a beautiful beach. All rooms have ocean views from their large patios and are designed in a modern Lanna style. Each room also has a tank with several colorful Thai fighting fish. You'll feel like a rock star, performing on stage when dining at the Full Moon Italian Restaurant whose dining room is a large open platform beside the swimming pool. The High-Tide Thai restaurant allows you to interact with your chef, who is working near your table, and will alter any dish to your exact specifications. Booking a treatment at the stylish spa is a must. ⊠ 101/3 Samui Ring Rd., Bophut Beach, 84320 ☎ 02/8775803 🖷 02/8777497 ⊕ www.anantara.com ⤴ 82 room, 24 suites ⚙ 2 restaurants, room service, minibars, in-room safes, cable TV, in-room DVD players, pool, hot tub, massage, spa, mountain bikes, snorkeling, boating, kayaking, fishing, library, bar, Internet, laundry service, babysitting ☰ AE, DC, MC, V.

$$–$$$ 🏨 **Peace Resort.** Formerly the budget accommodation Peace Bungalow, Peace Resort was renovated in 2001 and is now a vibrant mid-range resort. Clusters of cottages have bright yellow rooms, with green-and-blue trim and lots of natural lighting. Superior rooms have big beds and tile floors; deluxe rooms also have separate living rooms. Bathrooms in both have mini indoor gardens. The staff is very friendly and helpful. ⊠ *178 Samui Ring Rd., Bophut Beach, 84320* ☎ *077/425357 or 077/427063* 🖷 *077/425343* ⊕ *www.peaceresort.com* ⇨ *102 rooms* ⟺ *Restaurant, room service, minibars, in-room safes, cable TV, pool, hot tub, massage, spa, bar, library, laundry service, Internet, travel services* ⊟ *MC, V.*

$ 🏨 **The Lodge.** The Lodge is small, elegant two-story building, a renovated Chinese shophouse in the center of the fishermen's village. The building has one terrace facing the street, perfect for people-watching, and the other terrace overlooks the ocean and distant Koh Pha Ngan. The rooms have warm and romantic lighting and the location, on the beach in central Bophut, can't be beat. ⊠ *91/1 Fisherman's Village, Bophut Beach, 84320* ☎ *077/425337* 🖷 *077/427565* ⊕ *www.apartmentsamui.com* ⇨ *8 rooms, 2 penthouses* ⟺ *Minibars, in-room safes, cable TV, bar, laundry service* ⊟ *MC, V.*

¢–$ 🏨 **Cactus Bungalows.** Colorful, funky huts set in an unmanicured, natural environment give Cactus Bungalows a real laid-back vibe. Instead of clunky bedsteads, mattresses rest on rounded platforms, giving rooms an organic feel. The bar and restaurant by the beach is pretty basic, but it does have a pool table. ⊠ *Bophut Beach, 84320* ☎ *077/245565* ⇨ *13 bungalows, 1 suite* ⟺ *Restaurant, cable TV, laundry service; no a/c in some rooms* ⊟ *No credit cards.*

NIGHTLIFE Down in the fishermen's village, there are a variety of nightlife venues to choose from, including a couple of pubs like Billabong and Frog-and-Gecko. **L'Orienteek** is a stylish chill-out lounge in an old teak house. Down the beach, a short walk from the beach road, is the **Gecko Beach Bar,** which throws Sunday beach parties featuring international guest DJs and rooms to crash in if you get too partied out.

Haad Choengmon
⑬ *20 km (12½ mi) east of Na Thon.*

On the northeast coast of Samui lies Haad Choengmon. Choengmon is one of several small beaches that line the northeastern cape. A few guesthouses, a handful of resorts, and some restaurants are scattered along the shore of this laid-back beach. The sand is firm and strewn with pebbles and shells, but adequate for sunbathing. For a little adventure, walk east to the bend in the beach and wade through the water to **Ko Fan Noi,** the small island 30 yards offshore. The water all along the beach is swimmable, with a shallow shelf, and there are all varieties of water sports to choose from, including catamarans, Sunfish, Windsurfers, and kayaks.

Off the western shore of the northeastern tip of Ko Samui is **Ko Fan** (not to be confused with Ko Fan Noi), a little island with a huge seated Buddha image covered in moss. Try to visit at sunset, when the light off the water shows the statue at its best.

✕🏨 **Sila Evason Hideaway & Spa.** From the moment you're greeted by the management and introduced to your private butler, you realize that this is not just another high-end resort—and you're about to embark on an amazing experience. Your butler will escort you via electric car to your private villa. The rooms have plush bedding, tubs with ocean views, separate outdoor showers, and a variety of lighting options. The 30-meter pool on the cliff matches the color of the ocean and the infinity edge is level with the horizon so you feel like you could swim off into the sea. Dining on the Hill serves an exquisite and comprehensive breakfast buffet, and Dining on the Rocks has a romantic private terrace perfect for indulging in innovative and exotic cuisine. The resort even employs its own consultants to make sure the resort is environmentally friendly. If you think the place is beyond your budget, you should set aside a dollar a day for a few years and go for the weekend. It won't be your last visit. ✉ *9/10 Bay View Bay, 84320* ☎ *077/245678* 🖷 *077/ 245671* 🌐 *www.sixsenses.com* 🛏 *66 villas* ♨ *2 restaurants, room service, minibars, in-room safes, cable TV, in-room DVD players, pool, massage, spa, gym, beach, 2 bars, library, shop, laundry service, Internet, meeting rooms, travel services* 🖃 *AE, DC, MC, V.*

✕🏨 **Tongsai Bay.** The owners of this splendid all-suite resort managed to build it without sacrificing even one of the tropical trees that give the place a refreshing and natural sense of utter seclusion. The suites, contained in luxurious wooden bungalows, have large private terraces. The suites also have outdoor bathtubs and some have beds outside the rooms, protected by mosquito nets. Furnishings are nothing short of stunning, with individual touches such as fresh flowers. The resort is perfect for honeymooners, as the entire resort exudes a "love at first sight" vibe. It's on a private beach just to the north of Choengmon that is suitable for sunbathing. The water is okay for cooling off in, but better for water sports, like windsurfing, which are available from the resort. ✉ *84 Tong Sai Bay, 84320* ☎ *077/425480 or 077/425544* 🖷 *077/ 425462 or 077/425620* 🌐 *www.tongsaibay.co.th* 🛏 *83 suites* ♨ *3 restaurants, minibars, room service, cable TV, in-room DVD players, IDD telephones, in-room safes, 2 tennis courts, 2 pools, gym, massage, spa, beach, bar, library, Internet, laundry service, meeting rooms* 🖃 *AE, DC, MC, V.*

🏨 **Imperial Boathouse.** A fleet of 34 converted rice barges provides the accommodation at this extraordinary resort. The big boats are beached like a school of hapless whales looking out onto the sea. Boat lovers will particularly enjoy these rustic rooms, which are far from modern, but capture the essence of the sea, replete with shell decorations, nautical rope, and plenty of wood. On the upper deck there's a living room with a bar and an outdoor sundeck. Below you'll find a sitting area, bedroom, and large bath with a grand oval tub. Landlubbers can elect to stay in conventional hotel rooms. These rooms are less expensive, and have no sea view, but have contemporary design and decoration. ✉ *83 Choeng Mon Beach, 84140* ☎ *077/425460, 02/2540023 in Bangkok* 🖷 *077/ 421462* 🛏 *34 boat suites, 8 honeymoon suites, 168 rooms* ♨ *2 restaurants, room service, in-room safes, minibars, cable TV, 2 pools, dive shop, windsurfing, boating, gym, massage, spa, game room, 2 bars, shops, laundry service, Internet, travel services* 🖃 *AE, DC, MC, V.*

$$$–$$$$ ⊡ **Hotel The White House.** Step back in time as you enter the classic lobby, which is filled with giant Chinese vases, Persian carpets, and classic Lanna art. Beyond the lobby, lush gardens with tall palms, fragrant flowers, and vines provide the surroundings for a row of two-story concrete buildings with nearly 9-foot-tall wooden doors and Ayutthaya-style roofs. The decoration in the rooms contributes to the old-world feeling of opulent style, with silk comforters and throw pillows covering the beds and separate sitting rooms in ground floor rooms. The pool is surrounded by Thai sandstone art. ⊠ *59/3 Choeng Mon Beach, 84320* ☎ *077/245315–7 or 077/425233* ⊟ *077/245318* ⊕ *www.samuidreamholiday.com* ⌁ *32 rooms, 8 junior suites, 2 Thai suites* ⌂ *2 restaurants, cable TV, IDD telephones, minibars, pool, massage, spa, hot tub, travel services* ⊟ *AE, DC, MC, V.*

$$–$$$ ⊡ **Samui Honey Cottages.** The cottages at this small, cozy resort on one of Samui's quieter beaches have glass sliding doors and peaked ceilings. Bathrooms have showers with glass ceilings. Dine alfresco under hanging gardens, or walk down the beach and have fresh seafood at the beachside restaurant across the channel from Koh Fan Lek. ⊠ *24/34 Choeng Mon Beach, 84320* ☎ *077/245032 or 077/279093* ⊟ *077/427094 or 077425081* ⊕ *www.samuihoney.com* ⌁ *18 bungalows, 1 suite* ⌂ *Restaurant, cable TV, in-room safes, minibars, laundry service* ⊟ *MC, V.*

¢ ⊡ **Island View II.** The bungalows here are so small they have room for the beds and little else. But there are few reasons to stay indoors, and the bungalows do have their own decks with tables and chairs. Two rooms still have fans for travelers on a tight budget. A small beach bar and restaurant sits just 10 yards from the water and beachside massage is available next door. ⊠ *Choeng Mon Beach, 84320* ⌁ *9 rooms* ⌂ *Restaurant, minibars, massage, bar, travel services, laundry service; no a/c in some rooms* ⊟ *No credit cards.*

Chawaeng
⓮ *20 km (12.5 mi) east of Na Thon.*

Ko Samui's most popular beach is Chawaeng, a fine stretch of glistening white sand, divided into two main sections—Chawaeng Yai (yai means "big") and Chawaeng Noi (noi means "little"). Travelers in search of sun and fun flock here, especially during high season. But despite the crowds, Chawaeng is no Pattaya or Patong—the mood is very laid-back.

Chawaeng Yai is divided by a coral reef into two sections: the secluded northern half is popular with backpackers, while the noisy southern half is packed with tourists that flock to the big resorts. Many of the women, young and old, wear little to the beach at Chawaeng Yai (note that locals find this display of skin offensive, although they usually say nothing). Chawaeng Noi is not as developed. The salt air has yet to be permanently tainted by the odor of suntan oil, but there are already hotels here, and more are on the way.

South of Chawaeng is **Coral Cove,** popular with scuba divers. It's not as idyllic as it once was, because unthinking travelers have trampled the beautiful coral while wading through the water (and worse, many have broken off pieces to take home as souvenirs). To see the lovely formations that still exist a little farther from shore, get a snorkel and swim over the reef—just be careful not to inflict further damage by stepping on it.

$$$$ ✕ **Zico's.** That disc on your table isn't a coaster! Flip it over to signal that you need a break from the never ending parade of food that the waitstaff courteously deliver. Hungry again? Flip back to sample more of the all-you-can-eat barbecue consisting of 15 different skewers of beef, fish, lamb, and shrimp, as well as an ample salad bar. Brazilian samba music sets the scene, but authentic Brazilian dancers steal the show, performing nightly, shaking up the room in skimpy outfits and posing for photos with awestruck diners. ⊠ *38/2 Samui Ring Rd., Chawaeng Beach* ☎ *077/232560 up to 3* ⚐ *Reservations essential* ▭ *AE, DC, MC, V.*

$$–$$$ ✕ **Betelnut.** Owner and internationally experienced chef Jeffrey Lord oversees both the dining room and the kitchen, greeting guests and explaining the menu before rushing back to the kitchen to assist with his creative concoctions. The style is a unique Californian-Asian fusion cuisine. Try "The Buddha jumped over the wall" as a starter, or blackened tuna with Samui salsa for an entrée. Also excellent is the summer roll with prawns and scallops, covered with sesame sauce. For dessert, try one of the interesting ice cream flavors, like red chili, a great mix of sweet and tingly. ⊠ *Samui Ring Rd., South Chawaeng Beach* ☎ *077/413370 or 077/414042* ⊕ *www.betelnutsamui.com* ▭ *MC, V.*

¢–$ ✕ **Ninja.** Don't let the tattered menus turn you off, they're well-worn for a reason. This no-frills dining room is authentic Thai and therefore very popular with locals and foreigners alike. The menu has pictures to make ordering easy. The Thai curries like *massaman* (peanut-based) or *panaeng* (chili paste and coconut milk) are solid choices, but you really can't go wrong here. Save room for classic Thai desserts, such as *khao niew mamuang* (mango and sticky rice). ⊠ *Samui Ring Rd., Chawaeng Beach* ☎ *No phone* ▭ *No credit cards.*

$$$$ ▦ **Amari Palm Reef Resort.** This luxurious resort at the north end of Chawaeng is on a beach that's too shallow for swimming, which can be somewhat of an advantage, as it keeps the crowds away. The bungalows all have gleaming wood floors and teak furnishings. The huge beds are raised on platforms that make you feel like royalty. The dining room, which serves mostly Western fare, is one floor up to take advantage of the view. A Thai restaurant is in a wood-panel room in the rear. ⊠ *Samui Ring Rd., Chawaeng Beach, 84320* ☎ *077/422015, 02/255–4588 in Bangkok* 🖷 *077/422394* ⊕ *www.amari.com* ⇴ *179 rooms, 8 suites* ♻ *2 restaurants, room service, cable TV, minibars, in-room safe, 2 pools, dive shop, squash, massage, spa, hot tub, bar, laundry service, babysitting, travel services* ▭ *AE, DC, MC, V.*

$$$$ ▦ **Chawaeng Regent Beach Resort.** Some of the suites in this resort hotel are duplexes, with fine views from upper terraces. The bungalows are scattered throughout the tropical gardens, connected to the reception area by elevated walkways. Rooms have teak and marble floors and are furnished with stylish cane furniture. One of the two restaurants, the Red Snapper, serves interesting Thai-Italian fusion. ⊠ *155/4 Samui Ring Rd., Chawaeng Beach, 84320* ☎ *077/422389–90* 🖷 *077/422222 or 077/422231* ⊕ *www.chawaengregent.com* ⇴ *138 rooms, 6 suites*

♨ *3 restaurants, room service, IDD telephones, in-room safes, minibars, cable TV, in-room DVD players in some rooms, 2 pools, health club, massage, spa, hair salon, dive shop, game room, Ping-Pong, billiards, beach, bar, babysitting, shops, laundry service* ☰ *AE, DC, MC, V.*

$$$$ 🏨 **Imperial Samui.** A landscaped terrace leads directly down to a private beach at this resort on the less-crowded southern end of Chawaeng Noi. If you want to do more than sunbathe, this is the place for you—the Imperial offers every kind of beach activity imaginable. In addition, one of the two pools is filled with salt water, a rare luxury on Ko Samui. The elegant Jamjuree restaurant serves elaborate royal Thai dishes. A second restaurant, the less formal Tara, opens onto the beach. The rooms, some of them on two levels, have polished teak floors and are richly furnished with dark woods and shimmering fabrics. ✉ *Chawaeng Noi Beach, 84320* ☎ *077/422020–36* 🖷 *077/422396* ⊕ *www.imperialhotels.com* ⇆ *120 rooms, 13 junior suites, 11 lavish suites* ♨ *2 restaurants, room service, in-room safes, minibars, IDD telephones, cable TV, tennis court, 2 pools, massage, spa, beach, windsurfing, boating, basketball, billiards, Ping-Pong, dive shop, bar, babysitting, meeting rooms, laundry service, travel services* ☰ *AE, DC, MC, V.*

★ $$$$ 🏨 **Poppies.** More than 80 competent and friendly employees are on hand to pamper guests at this romantic beachfront resort on the quieter southern end of Chawaeng. A large number of them are employed by the restaurant, which is as popular (and remarkable) as the resort itself and serves Thai and seafood under the stars or in the dining room. Cottages have living rooms with sofa beds, making them suitable for families or larger groups. The floors and trim are of handsome teak, and silk upholstery gives the place a decadent feel. Baths have sunken tubs and showers made of marble. Because of the friendly staff, southern location, and first-rate restaurant the majority of guests are repeat visitors or word-of-mouth referrals. ✉ *Samui Ring Rd., South Chawaeng Beach, 84320* ☎ *077/422419* 🖷 *077/422420* ⊕ *www.poppiessamui.com* ⇆ *24 rooms* ♨ *Restaurant, room service, minibars, IDD phones, pool, hot tub, massage, spa, Internet, library, laundry service, shop, travel services* ☰ *AE, DC, MC, V.*

$$$–$$$$ 🏨 **Central Samui Beach Resort.** This spacious resort has larger grounds and more amenities than any other resort on Chawaeng Beach. The main building, which has the rooms, is set back behind a large field separating it from the beach. Badminton, basketball (hung from a coconut tree), and Ping-Pong cover one side of the field; a sunbathing area, which runs from the grass to the pool, occupies the other. Multiple happy hours run different hours at the indoor, pool, and beach bars. Dining possibilities include an excellent Japanese restaurant, as well as two others serving Thai and Chinese dishes. The beach has a large cordoned-off swimming area to protect swimmers from Jet Skis. Rooms have hardwood floors and bathtubs with doors that open into the main body of the room. ✉ *38/2 Samui Ring Rd., South Chawaeng Beach, 84320* ☎ *077/230500* 🖷 *077/422385* ⊕ *www.centralhotelsresorts.com* ⇆ *199 rooms, 9 suites* ♨ *4 restaurants, room service, cable TV, minibars, IDD phones, in-room safes, 3 pools, hot tub, health club, sauna, tennis courts, sailing, windsurfing, volleyball, dive shop, playground, 3 bars, business services, meeting room, laundry service, shops* ☰ *AE, DC, MC, V.*

$$$–$$$$ ✕▦ **Muang Kulaypan Hotel.** This hotel puts a little more emphasis on design. Instead of the teak, antiques, and flowing fabrics you'll find at most resorts going for a "classic Thai" look, here you'll get simple lines, minimal furnishings, and sharp contrasts. There's a sort of subtle Javanese-Thai theme throughout, reflected in the artwork selected for the rooms. The VIP Inao suite allows you to sleep in a bed once used by King Rama IV. Bussaba Thai restaurant serves uncommon, but authentic Thai food. Note that rooms on the wings, farther from the main road, are considerably quieter. Standard rooms are the only rooms that don't have an ocean view. ⊠ *100 Samui Ring Rd., North Chawaeng Beach, 84320* ☎ *077/230849–50* 🖷 *077/230031* ⊕ *www.kulaypan.com* 🛏 *41 rooms, 1 Inao Suite* ⚭ *Restaurant, room service, minibars, in-room safes, IDD telephones, cable TV, pool, gym, Ping-Pong, laundry service, shop, bar* ▭ *AE, DC, MC, V.*

$$$ ▦ **Princess Village.** Princess Village does the classic Thai thing better than any other resort on Samui. Rooms here are in old, authentic teak houses that were transported from Ayutthaya and placed around a spacious field beside the beach. They're all gorgeously decorated with Thai furniture. Afternoon tea is served to each house on it's outdoor deck and there's a lovely sala on stilts above a lily pond to chill out on anytime. ⊠ *Central Chawaeng Beach, 84320* ☎ *077/422216 or 077/230292* 🖷 *077/ 422382* ⊕ *www.samuidreamholiday.com* 🛏 *12 villas, 2 suites* ⚭ *Restaurant, IDD phones, cable TV, in-room safes, minibars, beach, library, massage* ▭ *AE, DC, MC, V.*

$$–$$$ ▦ **Baan Talay Resort.** This resort has two-dozen bungalows huddled around a shimmering pool. The huts are just a stone's throw from the beach. The open-front restaurant and bar, both facing the surf, are great places to unwind after a day of water sports. ⊠ *Chawaeng Beach Rd., 84140* ☎ *077/413555* 🖷 *077/413371* ⊕ *www.baantalay.com* 🛏 *24 rooms* ⚭ *Restaurant, minibars, cable TV, pool* ▭ *AE, MC, V.*

$$ ▦ **Montien House.** Two rows of charming bungalows line the path leading to the beach at this comfortable little resort. Each modest bungalow has a private patio surrounded by tropical foliage. Rooms are furnished in a spare style, which is nonetheless quite cozy. Penthouses in an adjacent building provide more luxurious accommodation, with separate living and dining rooms. The management is attentive and helpful. ⊠ *Central Chawaeng Beach, 84320* ☎ *077/422169* 🖷 *077/422145* ⊕ *www.montienhouse.com* 🛏 *57 rooms, 3 suites* ⚭ *Restaurant, minibars, cable TV, pool, massage, bar, laundry service, travel services* ▭ *MC, V.*

¢–$$ ▦ **The Island.** Modern white wooden bungalows with thatch roofs contain two to three spacious rooms each. The resort has a quintessential island vibe, and the huts are clean, comfortable, and reasonably priced. Both fan-cooled and air-conditioned rooms are available. The beach is nice for sunbathing, but the shoreline is rather rocky. But it's not a far walk to a beach with better swimming and water sports options. ⊠ *162/ 21 North Chawaeng Beach, 84320* ☎ *077/230151–3* 🖷 *077/230942* ⊕ *www.rft.co.th* 🛏 *64 rooms* ⚭ *Restaurant, minibars, cable TV, travel services, laundry service* ▭ *MC, V.*

★ **$**   ▦ **Al's Hut.** A row of white huts follows a path beneath towering tamarind trees from the entrance of the resort, straight down to the beach.

The trees provide a shady, beautiful setting and the huts are set far enough apart to make the resort feel less crowded than many. Doors to the huts have multicolor glass, but the rooms are otherwise simple and cozy. Al's is centrally located, on the nicest section of beach, and close to all the action. It's a great value. ⊠ *159/86 Central Chawaeng Beach, 84320* ☎ *077/231650* 🖷 *077/230753* ⊕ *www.rft.co.th* 🛏 *32 rooms* ♿ *Restaurant, cable TV, minibars, travel services* ▤ *MC, V.*

¢ 📷 **Charlie's Hut.** Charlie's Hut is one of the last true backpacker lodgings on Chawaeng Beach. The huts are really small, but very cool looking (think Hobbits on Gilligan's Island) and come with either shared or attached bathroom. Some huts with attached bath have a small patio and air-conditioning. Make sure you ask for one with a patio or air-conditioning if you want one. The location is prime, in the center of town where all the nightlife is a short walk in either direction and the beach is pristine. This is also *the* place to find other backpackers to swap stories and party with. The one drawback: the staff is extremely rude, perhaps jaded from years of dealing with scores of travelers. Also, the place is frequently full and they don't accept reservations. ⊠ *Samui Ring Rd., Chawaeng Beach, 84320* 🛏 *50 rooms* ♿ *Restaurant, beach, Internet, travel services; no a/c in some rooms.*

NIGHTLIFE There are plenty of places to go in the evening in Chawaeng. Soi Green Mango is a looping street chockablock with beer bars and nightclubs large and small, including the enormous **Green Mango,** and trendy DJ club **Mint Bar.** At the corner of Beach Road and Soi Green Mango is the multilevel, open-air, chill-out bar called **The Deck.**

Ark Bar is one of Samui's original nightlife venues on the beach. They throw a party with free barbecue every Wednesday, starting at 2 PM. Farther south, across from Central Samui Beach resort, is the relaxing **Barefoot Bar,** and down Soi Coliburi (which looks like an unnamed street) there are several clubs, the most popular and stylish of which is **POD.**

The popular **Reggae Pub** (☎ 077/422331), on the far side of the lagoon opposite Chawaeng's main strip, is a longtime favorite. It has several bars and dance floors. **Coco Blues Company** (☎ 077/414354 ⊕ www. cocobluescompany.com), on the northern side of town, has live blues music nightly from their house band and visiting blues artists. **The Islander Pub & Restaurant** (⊠ Central Chaweng, near Soi Green Mango ☎ 077/ 230836) has 11 televisions channelling Thai, Australian, and Malaysian satellites and holds in-house pool competitions and a quiz night.

Lamai
❶⓯ *18 km (11 mi) southeast of Na Thon.*

A rocky headland separates Chawaeng from Ko Samui's second-most-popular beach, Lamai. It lacks the glistening white sand of Chawaeng, but its clear water and long stretch of sand made it the first area to be developed on the island. Lamai does have more of a steeply shelving shoreline than Chawaeng, which makes the swimming a bit better. It's not as congested as Chawaeng, though there are plenty of restaurants and bars, many of which are geared to a younger party-oriented crowd and those (to put it gently) who are looking for Thai companions. Chawaeng Beach

Road's rampant commercialization, hawking souvenir goods, is quite a bit more family-friendly than Lamai's semi-sordid strip. However, if you are young and looking for fun, there are more budget accommodations available here than in Chawaeng, and there are quite a few happening clubs. Nonetheless, the farther from central Lamai you wander, the more likely you are to discover a nice resort with a beautiful beach and a quieter scene than you will find in Chawaeng.

Every visitor to Ko Samui makes a pilgrimage to Lamai for yet another reason: at the point marking the end of Lamai beach stand two rocks, named **Hin Yai** (Grandmother Rock) and **Hin Ta** (Grandfather Rock). Erosion has shaped the rocks to resemble weathered and wrinkled private parts. It's nature at its most whimsical.

About 4 km (2½ mi) from Lamai, at the small Chinese fishing village of Baan Hua Thanon, the road that forks inland toward Na Thon leads to the **Coral Buddha,** a natural formation carved by years of erosion. Beyond the Coral Buddha, toward Na Thon, lies the village of Baan Thurian (famous for its durian trees), where a track to the right climbs up into jungle-clad hills to the island's best waterfall, **Na Muang.** The 105-foot falls are spectacular—especially just after the rainy season—as they tumble from a limestone cliff into a small pool. You are cooled by the spray and warmed by the sun. For a thrill, swim through the curtain of falling water; you can sit on a ledge at the back to catch your breath.

WHERE TO STAY
& EAT
$$–$$$

✕ **The Cliff.** Halfway along the road from Chawaeng to Lamai is the Cliff, which is actually perched on a big boulder overlooking the sea. You can have lunch or dinner either inside the spartan dining room or out on the scenic deck. The lunch menu includes sandwiches and hamburgers; dinner features steaks and Mediterranean grill. The prices are a bit high for the small servings, and the service isn't great, but the Cliff is a nice place to stop to have a drink and check out the view. In the evening, cooler-than-thou staff serve cocktails in the enclosed, air-conditioned club. ✉ 124/2 Samui Ring Rd., Lamai Beach ☎ 077/414266 ⊕ www.thecliffsamui.com ⌨ Reservations essential ☰ AE, MC, V.

¢–$

✕ **Mr. Pown Seafood Restaurant.** This place is nothing fancy, but it serves up reliable Thai dishes and seafood, as well as some German and English fare. Try the red curry in young coconut (a moderately spicy, not quite "red" curry with cauliflower and string beans served inside a coconut) or the catch of the day. The staff is courteous. ✉ Central Lamai Beach ☰ No credit cards.

$$$$

▦ **Buriraya Resort & Spa.** At the far northern end of Lamai, Buriraya is technically on its own secluded, private beach (two small beaches to be exact). The name translates to "city of celebration" and you will certainly feel like celebrating your discovery of this gorgeous retreat. Most rooms are in multistory buildings connected by elevated walkways that pass through tropical gardens. All have outdoor Jacuzzis on terraces with ocean views, opulent decoration, and floor-to-ceiling glass doors leading from the bedroom to the deck. Separate villas have jumbo Jacuzzis, daybeds, fishponds, gardens, and even miniature waterfalls within their private, gated compounds. Shuttle service is available to Chawaeng beach, where guests are free to use the facilities at the Princess Resort. ✉ *208/1 North Lamai Beach, 84320* ☎ *077/429300* 🖶 *077/429333* ⊕ *www.buriraya.com* 🛏 *45 rooms, 33 suites* ⌂ *2 restaurants, room service, minibars, in-room safes, cable TV, DVD players in some rooms, 2 pools, in-room hot tubs, massage, spa, gym, beach, kayaking, mountain bikes, bar, laundry service, Internet, meeting rooms* ▭ *AE, DC, MC, V.*

$$$$ 🏨 **Pavilion.** Just far enough from central Lamai, the Pavilion offers a little respite from the downtown hustle and bustle. Rooms in the main building are more modern and more expensive than the stand-alone thatched bungalows, but are not necessarily better. Although Junior Suites have large outdoor daybeds and jacuzzis, bungalows are considerably larger and are closer to the pool, sundeck, and beach. If the bungalows are full, rooms 201 to 208 are the best of the rest. The stylish restaurant serves tasty Thai and Italian, as well as fresh seafood. The beachside pool is a refreshing alternative to the often overcrowded sands. ✉ *124/24 Lamai Beach, 84320* ☎ *077/232083–7 or 077/233108–10* 🖶 *077/424029* ⊕ *www.pavilionsamui.com* 🛏 *50 rooms, 8 suites* ⌂ *Restaurant, room service, minibars, in-room safes, cable TV, pool, hot tub, massage, spa, 2 bars, library, laundry service, Internet, meeting rooms, travel services* ▭ *AE, DC, MC, V.*

$$ 🏨 **Aloha Resort.** Ask for a room with a view of the ocean at this beachfront resort—many overlook the parking lot. However, all rooms have private terraces or balconies that do face in the general direction of the beach. The rooms are divided between those in the main building and those in attractive, but aging bungalows. The rooms have carpets, furniture, and bedding that appear to have not been replaced since the resort first opened 20 years ago, but Aloha is one of the only family-style accommodations you'll find in Lamai. The popular restaurant, Mai Thai, serves Thai, Chinese, and European food, while the more casual Captain's Kitchen has a nightly barbecue. ✉ *128 Moo 3, 84130* ☎ *077/424014* 🖶 *077/424419* ⊕ *www.samui-hotels.com* 🛏 *80 rooms* ⌂ *2 restaurants, room service, minibars, cable TV, pool, beach, bar, babysitting, laundry service, airport shuttle* ▭ *AE, MC, V.*

¢–$ 🏨 **Lamai-Wanta.** Incredibly spartan rooms are kept immaculately clean, which is not surprising considering the owners–managers are a nurse and doctor couple. The two beachfront villas are their private residences, the other 10 bungalows and 40 attached rooms are for guests. Rooms have king-size beds and many tall, thin windows with interior shutters. Another highlight is an infinity-edge swimming pool directly on the beach surrounded by beach chairs, a beach bar, and restaurant. If you have come to Lamai to relax and enjoy the beach, Lamai-Wanta has all that you need, plus a small on-site clinic (in case you crash your motorbike). ✉ *Central Lamai Beach, 84320* ☎ *077/424550* 🖶 *077/424218* ⊕ *www.lamaiwanta.com* 🛏 *40 rooms, 10 bungalows* ⌂ *Restaurant, cable TV, in-room safes, minibars, pool, bar* ▭ *AE, MC, V.*

NIGHTLIFE Central Lamai is where all the action is. The one-stop, sprawling party spot **Bauhaus** has foam parties on Monday and Friday nights. In the dead-center of town there's a muay thai boxing ring that features women boxers on weekends and muay thai fights (exhibitions more than actual fights) staged regularly during high season. The boxing ring is surrounded by beer bars with highly skilled connect four players and across the street is the heart of Lamai's club scene: **Fusion,** a dark, chilled-out open-air club spinning hip-hop and progressive house; **SUB,** a huge indoor dance club that also has an outdoor party area with enormous projection TV screen; and **Club Mix,** another megasized club featuring international and local DJs.

Laem Set Bay

⑯ *17½ km (11 mi) south of Na Thon.*

This small rocky cape on the southeastern tip of the island is far from the crowds. It's a good 3 km (2 mi) off the main road, so without your own transport it's hard to reach. You may want to visit the nearby **Samui Butterfly Garden,** 2 acres of meandering walks enclosed by nets that take you through kaleidoscopic clouds of butterflies. It's open daily 10 to 4.

WHERE TO STAY
& EAT
★ $–$$$

✕🏨 **Laem Set Inn.** This rustic retreat on Laem Set Bay is made up of a cluster of restored traditional houses. The top-price Kho-Tan suite is an old rosewood house overlooking the sea and sleeps up to 10 guests, many in a cozy upstairs attic that would suit the Brady Bunch well. To ensure your complete privacy, it has its own pool. Another suite was made from an old post office in Ko Samui, while the restaurant was fashioned out of four teak houses. Cheaper accommodations are in small, thatched beachfront cottages with woven bamboo walls. There are cozy bunkbeds for children. The small coral-sand beach is very rocky, and unsuitable for swimming, but okay for cooling off in. ✉ *110 Laem Set, 84310* 🕿 *077/424393 or 077/233299* 🖷 *077/424394* ⊕ *www.laemset.com* ⤶ *4 rooms, 3 suites, 9 cottages* ⚖ *Restaurant, in-room safes, minibars, pool, beach, snorkeling, boating, bicycles, fitness classes, Internet* ▭ *MC, V.*

Baan Taling Ngam

⑰ *3 km (2 mi) south of Na Thon.*

The southern and western coasts are less developed, and with good reason—their beaches are not so golden, the water not so clear, and the breezes not so fresh. But there's one very good reason for coming here: a luxury hotel on a pretty stretch of shore with magnificent views of nearby islands and even the mountainous mainland.

WHERE TO STAY
& EAT
$$$$

✕🏨 **Le Royal Meridien Baan Taling Ngam.** Its name means "home on a beautiful bank," but that doesn't come close to summing up the stunning location of this luxurious hotel. Most of the rooms are built into the 200-foot cliff, but the beachside villas are even better. The swimming pool is a magnificent trompe l'oeil, looking as if it's part of the ocean far below. There's a second pool by the beach where you can find an activities center. The beach is extremely narrow, so sunbathing is not feasible at high tide, but you can swim here. The southeast corner of the island is also closest to Ang Thong National Marine Park, making it the best resort from which to explore that island chain. You can dine on Thai and European fare at the Lom Talay; seafood is served at the more casual Promenade. ✉ *295 Taling Ngam Beach, 84140* 🕿 *077/423100, 02/6532201–7 in Bangkok* 🖷 *077/423220* ⊕ *www.lemeridien.*

com 🔁 *40 rooms, 30 villas ♨ 2 restaurants, room service, minibars, IDD telephones, cable TV, DVD players, Internet, tennis court, 7 pools, health club, spa, massage, snorkeling, sailing, kayaking, windsurfing, Ping-Pong, mountain bikes, driving range, babysitting, library, hair salon, shop, bar, travel services* 🖃 *AE, DC, MC, V.*

Ko Pha-ngan

⑱ *12 km (7 mi) by boat north of Ko Samui.*

Since Ko Samui is now an international tourist hot-spot, travelers looking for a cheaper and/or more laid-back scene now head for Ko Pha-ngan. Decades ago, the few wanderers who arrived here stayed in fishermen's houses or slung hammocks on the beach. Today, simple bungalow colonies have sprung up on even the most remote beaches, and investors are buying up beach property with plans for sprawling resorts. For now, though, Pha-ngan remains a destination for backpackers looking for budget accommodation and hippies (old-school and nouveau) searching for chilled out beaches and alternative retreats.

Since the island's unpaved roads twist and turn, it's easier to beach-hop via boat. If you want to find the beach that most appeals to you, take a longtail boat around the island—the trip takes a full day and stops in many places along the way. The southeast tip of the island is divided by a long promontory into **Haad Rin West** and **Haad Rin East.**

★ If Haad Rin is too crowded, take a boat up the east coast to **Haad Tong Nai Pan,** a horseshoe bay divided by a small promontory. The most beautiful, and most remote beach, accessible only by boat, is **Haad Kuat (Bottle Beach),** which has gorgeous white sand and only four simple accommodations.

Haad Rin East & West

Haad Rin Town has many good restaurants, shops, and bars. It's densely built-up, and not very quiet, but full of fun. The town is sandwiched between Haad Rin West and East. The west side is where the main pier of the island is located and where literally boatloads of visitors disembark, most of whom stay in Haad Rin town.

Haad Rin West has swimmable water, but you needn't settle for this beach when Haad Rin East is only a short walk away. Haad Rin East is a beautiful beach lined with bungalows and bars. Once a month Haad Rin East gets seriously crowded when throngs of young people gather on the beach for an all-night "Full Moon" party. Check your calendar before heading to Pha-ngan as the island starts to fill up at least a week prior to the big event. Boats from Thong Sala, the major town, take about 40 minutes to reach Haad Rin East. Nearby are the beaches of Haad Leela and Srikantang if you want to stay away from the crowds, but still want to party.

✕ **Lucky Crab Restaurant.** The extensive menu includes entrées from all around the world, which is appropriate on a beach that hosts visitors from virtually everywhere. Despite the hundreds of selections on the menu, the specialty at the Lucky Crab is barbecue seafood, served with one of 12 different sauces. Select your fish, select your sauce, then enjoy the breeze from the ceiling fans while you await your tasty food at this fun and friendly eatery. Also worth trying is the sizzling seafood in a hot pan. ✉ *94/18 Haad Rin W, Ko Pha-ngan* ☎ *077/375125 or 077/375498* ▭ *No credit cards.*

¢–$

¢–$ ✕ **Nira's Bakery and Restaurant.** Walking into the restaurant, you'll be bombarded by the mouth-watering smell of fresh baked goods. The scent will make you feel that you're no longer on a remote Thai island. The owner picked up his baking skills while living and working in Germany, and then opened this funky bakery in the mid-1980s, before the island even had electricity. Traditional homemade lasagna, fresh fruit juices, and gourmet sandwiches are a few of the specialties available at the juice bar, sandwich bar, and air-conditioned bakery. ✉ *130 Central Haad Rin Ko Pha-ngan* ▭ *No credit cards.*

$$–$$$ ▦ **Drop In Club Resort and Spa.** This is the only hotel-style lodging on Ko Pha-ngan. Air-conditioned rooms in two- and four-story buildings are done in a classic Thai style, with peaked roofs. Only rooms on the higher levels have a view. Located in central Haad Rin, most guests spend their days at the beach, a short walk from the resort, and their nights on the town. ✉ *154/1–10 Haad Rin, Ko Pha-ngan 84280* ☎ *077/375444–5* 🖷 *077/375446* ⊕ *www.dropinclub.com* ⤵ *46 rooms* ♨ *Restaurant, room service, IDD phones, minibars, cable TVs, pool, Jacuzzi, massage, spa, travel services, laundry service, bar* ▭ *AE, MC, V.*

$–$$ ▦ **Phangan Bayshore Resort.** This resort is near the action, but away from the crowd. It's one of the island's original resorts, opened in 1976, so the layout is spacious rather than cramped. The best huts are lined up neatly and angled toward the sea. Beachside rooms are old-school basic huts with mosquito nets, fans, and not much else. Concrete huts on the far side of the road have air-conditioning, parquet floors, and modern baths, but aren't as fun as the beachside ones. It's only a short walk to the party part of town, but the resort is far enough away to be secluded from the late-night noise. ✉ *Haad Rin E Ko Pha-ngan, 84280* ☎ *077/375227* 🖷 *077/375226* ⊕ *www.phanganbayshore.com* ⤵ *60 rooms* ♨ *Restaurant, minibars, cable TV, in-room safes, laundry service* ▭ *MC, V.*

★ ¢–$$$ ▦ **Coco Hut Resort.** Coco Hut Resort is on Leela beach, a five-minute walk from Haad Rin West. Although Leela beach is not as beautiful as Haad Rin, it's quieter and much more relaxing. Rooms range from backpacker rooms with shared bath in a large wood and concrete building to cute clapboard huts on the beachfront and hill. Rooms on the beach are either air-conditioned or fan-cooled, so that even budget travelers can afford the nicest huts. Rooms away from the beach are connected via boardwalk and have ladders leading up to tiny little lofts. The resort provides a slew of services and amenities. Beach volleyball, rafts, and kayaks to keep you busy during low tide, when the water is too shallow to swim in. ✉ *130/20 Leela Beach, Ko Pha-ngan 84280*

🖥📠 077/375368 ⊕ *www.cocohut.com* ⇝ *63 bungalows, 24 rooms*
⌂ *Restaurant, cable TV, minibars, pool, massage, volleyball, billiards,*
Internet, bar, travel services; no a/c in some rooms ▤ *MC, V.*

¢–$$ 🖥 **Sarikantang.** This small resort, with both wooden and concrete huts
on Leela beach, is a short walk from Haad Rin. All the concrete huts
have outdoor showers and baths, hot water and air-conditioning, while
some of the wooden huts have only cold water and fans. The huts are
behind the pool; none of the rooms are beachfront. This is a family-run
resort that genuinely tries to help you enjoy your stay, much unlike some
of the profit-oriented resorts nearby. ⊠ *129/3 Leela Beach, Ko Pha-ngan*
84280 🖥 *077/375055–56* 🖨 *077/375057* ⊕ *www.sarikantang.com*
⇝ *48 rooms* ⌂ *Restaurant, cable TV, some in-room DVD players,*
minibars, in-room safes, pool, massage, spa, gym, kayaking, volleyball,
Internet, laundry service; no a/c in some rooms ▤ *MC, V.*

NIGHTLIFE   Haad Rin East is lined with bars and clubs, pumping music, and pour-
ing drinks from dusk until dawn, 7 days a week, 365 days a year. All
this culminates in a huge beach party with tens of thousands of revel-
ers every full moon (or the night after, if the full moon lands on a major
Buddhist holiday). Check out ⊕ www.fullmoonparty.com for details.
If you're only here for a night, check out **Cactus** and **Drop In Club**, two
of the most popular nightspots.

Haad Thong Nai Pan

Fodor'sChoice   If Haad Rin is too crowded, take a boat up the east coast to Haad Tong
★   Nai Pan, a horseshoe bay divided by a small promontory. On the beach
of the southern half are several guesthouses and restaurants. The north-
ern part of the bay is called Tong Nai Pan Noi, where a glistening cres-
cent of sand curves around the turquoise waters. Coconut trees behind
the beach hide the homes of the villagers. The best time to visit this long
stretch of white sand beach is from December to August, as the area
can be hard to reach by boat during the monsoon months (Septem-
ber–November). However, a bumpy road can be your alternative dur-
ing those months.

WHERE TO   ✕🖥 **Panviman Resort.** The big attraction at this friendly resort is its two
STAY & EAT   restaurants, the best of which is a circular Thai-style dining area that is
★ $$–$$$ open to the ocean breezes. It serves excellent Thai food. The no-frills ac-
commodations are in the thatched cottages, stone-and-stucco bungalows,
and some more upscale family cottages. ⊠ *22/1 Thong Nai Pan Noi Bay,*
84280 🖥 *077/445101 up to 9, 077/445220 up to 4* 🖨 *077/445100*
⊕ *www.panviman.com* ⇝ *24 rooms, 14 cottages, 18 deluxe cottages* ⌂ *2*
restaurants, cable TV, pool, massage, game room, library, beach, travel
services, laundry service, bar; no a/c in some rooms ▤ *MC, V.*

Haad Thien

Haad Thien is geographically close to Haad Rin, but the best way to
get there is by boat—the alternative is a one- to two-hour trek. Haad
Thien doesn't have the white sand of Haad Rin, but is good for swim-
ming. This is a real chilled-out spot suitable for people who like their
holidays very quiet (which seems, in Haad Thien's case, to mean hip-
pies, young and old).

✕🖾 **The Sanctuary.** The Sanctuary is two resorts in one: a health and wellness center for those who are interested in fasting for physical purification and a health-conscious retreat for those interested in a little alternative health and therapy (like yoga) along with a secluded beach. Beds are available in a 12-person dorm; in small bungalows on the hillside that have large patios, ocean views, and private baths; or in large funky villas equipped with hammocks and kitchenettes, but without proper windows or doors. The resort is a real hideaway, a private paradise for down-to-earth people. The food, all vegetarian, is prepared only with natural ingredients. The beach is a bit rocky, but you can swim here and there are kayaks available for free. ⊠ *Haad Thien, Ko Pha-ngan 84280* ☎ *01/2713614* ⊕ *www.thesanctuary-kpg.com* ⋑ *12 dorm beds, 14 bungalows* ⚐ *Restaurant, room TVs some in-room DVD players, massage, spa, kayaking, beach, library, bar* ▤ No credit cards.

Haad Kuat (Bottle Beach)

Haad Kuat is one of the most remote beaches on Ko Pha-ngan. The only way to get there is via boat from Chalok Lam, a 20-minute songthaew ride from Thong Sala pier. It might be more difficult to get to than any other beach, but it's definitely worth the hassle. The beach itself is about a quarter-mile-long stretch of fine, white sand. The water is a beautiful sparkling blue, perfect for swimming, especially on the western end of the beach. There are only four resorts on Haad Kuat, so the beach isn't too crowded in the morning or late in the afternoon (though it does receive many day-trippers from the rest of the island mid-day). The scene is young and fun: each guesthouse blares the latest Western hits in the restaurant-common areas for travelers chilling out on triangular pillows. If you prefer peace and quiet, stick to the beach or string a hammock up in front of your hut. If you get tired of lounging around, follow the steep trail up to the viewpoint above the western end of the beach.

✕🖾 **Smile Bungalows.** There are only four guesthouses on Haad Kuat, and Smile Bungalow, on the far western end of the beach, is the best of the bunch. The restaurant has the most comfortable seating area, with both standard wooden tables, and foot-high tables surrounded by triangular pillows. The huts are built on the hillside overlooking the beach, and have large wooden decks and bright bathrooms decorated with shells. The bungalows higher up on the hill are duplexes and have great ocean views. The staff at Smile Bungalow is friendly and fun, and frequently hang out with the guests in the evening when the music gets turned up, the lights turned down, and playing cards and beer bottles cover all the tables. The beach in front of Smile Bungalows is also the best spot for swimming. The one small drawback is that the bungalows only have electricity from 6 PM to 6 AM. ⊠ *Haad Kuat* ☎ *01/780–2881* ⋑ *25 rooms* ⚐ *Restaurant, laundry service* ▤ No credit cards ☉ Closed Oct.–May.

Ko Tao

⓳ *47 km (29 mi) by boat north of Ko Pha-ngan.*

Only a few years ago, the tiny island of Ko Tao could be compared to the one inhabited by Robinson Crusoe: no electricity, no running water, no modern amenities of any kind. Today it's built up with air-conditioned huts with cable TV, tattoo parlors, discos, and a few 7–11s. Dozens of small bungalow colonies offer every level of accommodation, from ultrabasic to modern luxury. The peace and quiet has disappeared from the main beaches, but the primary reason to come here is still the underwater world. Ko Tao is an excellent place to get your scuba certification, as most operators don't have pools and so the initial dives must be done in the shallow, crystal clear ocean water. Advanced divers will appreciate the great visibility, decent amount of coral, and exotic and plentiful marine life.

Sairee Beach is the nicest beach on the island and one of the most popular. The beach is west-facing and therefore great for watching the sun set and kayaking to Koh Nang Yuan. Chalok Baan Kao Beach, on the southern shore, is another nice beach, which is popular with travelers of all stripes. Numerous other small beaches dot the shores of Ko Tao; they generally have only a few guesthouses each, a more laid-back scene, and nice snorkeling conditions directly off the beach.

Getting to Ko Tao is easy—it's on the scheduled ferry routes out of Ko Pha-ngan and Ko Samui, and two boats a day make the two-hour (express service) or six-hour (regular service) run from Chumphon on the mainland. If you want to check out Ko Tao, but want to stay in the extravagant hotels only available on Ko Samui, speedboats leave at 8:30 AM from Bophut pier, taking snorkelers on day trips to the island and its neighbor, Ko Nang Yuan.

Where to Stay

$$–$$$ 🏠 **Ko Tao Resort.** Of all the bungalow colonies on Ko Tao, this cluster of thatched cottages overlooking the sea at Chalok Kao, is one of the best. It's also one of the few resorts around that provides 24-hour electricity. The simply but adequately furnished rooms (with air-conditioning or fans) all have small private terraces, some with ocean views, some with mountain views. The open-sided restaurant overlooks the beach, and serves Thai, Chinese and Western food. Dive instructors are PADI-certified, and offer all levels of instruction, in addition to daily dive trips around the island. ✉ *19/1 Moo 3, Chalok Baan Kao, 84280* ☎ *077/456133 or 077/456198* 🖷 *077/456419* ⊕ *www.kotaocottage. com* 🛏 *40 rooms* ⚒ *Restaurant, minibars, cable TV, laundry service, dive shop; no a/c in some rooms* ▭ *No credit cards.*

¢–$ 🏠 **Black Tip Dive Resort.** Black Tip Dive Resort is on Tanote Bay, on the eastern shore of Ko Tao. Accommodation ranges from simple fan huts with shared bath to larger deluxe family bungalows with air-conditioning. The beachside huts are the nicest—they have prime real estate in the center of this small, secluded beach. The dive shop has quality equipment and offers full-day diving trips around the island. If you're only interested in snorkeling, this bay is a great one for seeing colorful coral, large fish (the water drops off steeply around the large boulders in the center of the bay), and even small black tip reef sharks that cruise the northern side of the bay around sunset. ✉ *40/6 Tanote Bay, 84280* ☎ *077/ 456488* ⚒ *Dive shop, snorkeling, waterskiing; no a/c in some rooms* ▭ *MC, V.*

Ko Nang Yuan

15 min by boat north of Ko Tao.

At high tide these three small islands sit beside each other in an obtuse, triangular pattern, separated by shallow translucent water. At low tide the receding water exposes two narrow sandbars connecting the outer islands, where the bungalows are, to the central island housing a lodge, restaurant, and beach bar. The islands are privately owned by the Ko Nang Yuan Dive Resort, and all visitors who wish to set foot on the island must shell out a B100 fee. While many visitors opt to pay, many others simply dock off shore to snorkel and dive the gorgeous waters surrounding the islands. The islands are quite close to Ko Tao; you can kayak from Sairee beach, or hire a longtail to ferry you here. The islands are quite busy throughout the day, less so very early in the morning or very late in the afternoon. The best option for enjoying the island's peaceful hours is getting a super-early start, or spending a night at the resort. While you are visiting, take a trip up to the viewpoint on the southern island for some photos to make your friends at home jealous.

Where to Stay & Eat

★ **$–$$** ✕🖼 **Ko Nang Yuan Dive Resort.** The rooms are perched on the hills of the two opposite facing islands. Rooms on the northern island are older and more basic, with fans, while rooms on the southern island are more stylish, with family rooms, minibars, and air-conditioning. All rooms have unbelievably awesome views. The restaurant, beach bar, and other facilities, are located on the larger, central island. Although at high tide it's not difficult to wade across the submerged sandbar, exercise caution at night, especially while swimming, as there's sharp coral in the water and the nearest clinic is back on Ko Tao. There's also a certified dive shop on the island for guests who wish to dive the sites around Ko Nang Yuan or Ko Tao. ✉ *Ko Nang Yuan, 84280* ☎ *01/2295085* 🖶 *01/2295212* 🛏 *12 rooms* △ *Restaurant, minibars, dive shop, bar* ▭ *MC, V.*

WESTERN GULF A TO Z

AIR TRAVEL

Thai Airways and One-Two-Go fly to Surat Thani daily. Bangkok Airways, the sole airline with direct service to Ko Samui, offers 23 flights a day from Bangkok. Direct flights from Krabi, Phuket, and Chiang Mai to Samui are also available from Bangkok Airways.

Compared to other flights around Thailand, flights to Ko Samui are quite expensive. Following the introduction of low-cost airlines in 2003, flights to neighboring countries are often cheaper than flights to Ko Samui. However, some discount fares are available from the Bangkok Airways Web site—the first and last flights of the day are less than half the cost of the other flights. Also, most flights are on propeller planes, which take about 30 minutes longer, so when booking, check for flights on the few 717s, which are less frequent but more spacious and a bit faster. Reservations are essential during holiday seasons.

⁊ Carriers **Bangkok Airways** ☎ 17711 ⊕ www.bangkokairways.com. **One-Two-Go** ☎ 1126 ⊕ www.onetwo-go.com. **Thai Airways** ☎ 02/6282000 ⊕ www.thaiairways.com.

AIRPORTS & TRANSFERS

There are two airports in the Western Gulf, at Surat Thani and Samui (there used to be airports at Chumphon and Hua Hin, but they are no longer in service for commercial flights). Samui Airport, privately owned by Bangkok Airways, levies a B400 airport tax from every passenger for each domestic departure.

For those who would like to go straight from Surat Thani Airport to Ko Samui or Ko Pha-ngan, Seatran Ferry provides free daily transfers to Donsak pier that leave the airport at noon. Samui Airport has a mini-van shuttle service to anywhere on the island for B100 to B200, depending on your destination.

⁊ Airport Information **Ko Samui** ☎ 077/425011-2. **Surat Thani** ☎ 077/441230-2.

BOAT & FERRY TRAVEL

Every day the Seatran Ferry departs hourly to make the two-hour journey between Surat Thani's Donsak Pier and Ko Samui's Na Thon Pier. The cost is B150, which includes free shuttle service to and from Surat Thani's airport, train station, or bus terminal. The same company also offers speed boat service from Donsak pier to Na Thon Pier and from Na Thon Pier to Ko Pha-ngan's Thong Sala Pier for less than B200 baht, including the same shuttle service deal.

Songserm, although it offers a smaller, slower boat, provides more comprehensive routes. Slow boats depart from Surat Thani for Ko Pha-ngan's Thong Sala Pier once a day at 8 AM and return at noon, stopping along the way at Na Thon Pier in Ko Samui. The journey in either direction takes almost four hours. Faster boats leave from Ko Samui to go to Ko Pha-ngan three times a day, starting at 9 AM. The journey takes 40 minutes. From Chumphon, one express ferry travels daily to Ko Tao. It takes two hours.

For visitors who wish to go straight from Bangkok or Hua Hin to Ko Tao and Ko Nang Yuan, Lomprayah Travel makes it easy and affordable. They offer joint tickets that include a VIP bus ride leaving from Bangkok's famous Khaosan Road to Chumphon's Catamaran Pier and ferry service aboard a massive, high-speed catamaran. The catamaran takes passengers to Ko Tao's Mae Haad pier within two hours; it departs twice a day and costs B650 from Hua Hin, B850 from Khaosan Road, and 550 from Chumphon. The same boat continues its journey to Ko Pha-ngan and Ko Samui respectively. Lomprayah Travel also provides service from Ko Samui's Mae Nam Pier, twice daily. It reaches Ko Pha-ngan in 30 minutes and then continues its journey to Ko Tao (two hours).

From Ko Samui to Ko Pha-ngan, most ferry companies will drop you off at Pha-ngan's Thong Sala Pier. However, if you wish to go straight to Haad Rin, the full moon party beach, Haad Rin Queen ferry line takes you directly from Samui's Big Buddha Pier (Bangrak) to Haad Rin West five times daily for B100.

Getting to Ko Nang Yuan from Ko Tao can be done easily by hiring a longtail boat from Sairee Beach. The journey takes about 15 minutes and costs B50 per person.

Ferry schedules can be altered during the monsoon season, so call ahead. 🚢 Boat & Ferry Lines **Lomprayah** ☎ 02/6292569–71 in Bangkok ⊕ www.lomprayah. com. **Seatran Ferry & Express** ☎ 077/275060 up to 2 Surat Thani, 077/471174 up to 7 Donsak Pier, 077/426000 up to 2 Ko Samui, 077/238129 Ko Pha-ngan ⊕ www.seatranferry. com. **Songserm** ☎ 077/287124 Tha Thong Pier in Surat Thani, 077/420157 Ko Samui.

BUS TRAVEL
Buses to Cha-am, Hua Hin, Chumphon, and Surat Thani (the latter two departure points for Ko Samui and other islands) leave from Bangkok's Southern Bus Terminal. Buses to Cha-am (2½ hours, B113) leave every 30 minutes from 6:30 AM to 7 PM; buses to Hua Hin (three hours, B130) leave hourly. Expect a long bus ride to Chumphon and Surat Thani; the outbound journey could take six to nine hours. Buses usually leave at night and arrive at your destination in the morning. Costs are around B300–B590.

Buses can also transport you between destinations within the south. A daily bus travels from Phuket to Surat Thani, arriving in time for the ferry to Ko Samui. Check with the bus station a day prior to departure for exact time and to assure yourself a seat.
🚌 Bus Stations **Bangkok** ⊠ Southern Bus Terminal, Baromratchchonnani Rd. ☎ 02/ 4347192 or 02/4351200. **Cha-am** ⊠ Cha-am Beach ☎ 032/471654 or 032/433288. **Chumphon** ⊠ Tha Tapao Rd. **Hua Hin** ⊠ Dechanuchit Rd. **Surat Thani** ⊠ Taladmai Rd.

CAR RENTALS
Budget and Hertz have counters at the Ko Samui airport, and National has its counter in Samui town. TA Car Rental is a local reputable company based on Samui. Otherwise, car rentals can be arranged from your hotel or any tour operator, as there are numerous authorized Budget agents and many smaller rental companies, which offer cheaper rates than the major car-rental agencies, but with perhaps less-professional assistance in the event you have an accident. Remember that although Thai's are legally required to drive on the left side of the road they frequently drive on the wrong side too (that is the "right" side). In addition, roads on Samui are very narrow, and traffic laws are not strictly enforced. Also, although Thai people are generally very friendly and helpful, in the event of an accident, there's often an automatic assumption that it's your fault simply because you're a visitor (and have more money). Remember to remain calm, and realize that what is the just solution may not always be the ultimate outcome.

Motorbikes can also be rented on Ko Samui. They're cheap and convenient, and therefore, especially popular modes of transportation for many visitors. Remember that helmets are required by law, and covered shoes recommended by common sense. Although there are several decent hospitals on the islands, they are frequently filled with Western tourists sometimes seriously injured by motorbike crashes. Drive carefully.

In many tourist areas there's often car service available for hire. This can be a better option than renting a car. Many of the major car-rental agencies charge fares comparable to or greater than fares in Western cities. In comparison, it may be cheaper and more convenient to hire a car with a driver that knows his way around and is liable for accidents. Hiring a car for a day is usually much cheaper than taxis as well, and multiple days are usually cheaper per day than several single day trips.

Agencies Budget ⊠ Ko Samui Airport ☎ 077/427188. **Hertz** ⊠ Ko Samui Airport ☎ 077/245609. **National** ⊠ Tesco Lotus, Chawaeng Beach ☎ 077/245391. **TA Car Rental** ⊠ Choengmon Beach, Ko Samui ☎ 077/245129.

CAR TRAVEL

Driving to Cha-am and Hua Hin is rather easy because the journey is short. But to Chumphon and Surat Thani, it's a long drive from Bangkok, and can be tiresome and boring. There's only one highway (Petchakasem Road) as far south as Chumphon, where it divides into one road following the Andaman Sea coast to Phuket and another snaking along the Gulf of Thailand to Surat Thani, where the ferries cross to Ko Samui. The highway narrows to a one-lane road once you leave the greater Bangkok sprawl. The road is heavily trafficked by long-haul transport trucks, and driving without familiarity of Thai driving habits can be unsettling, especially at night.

EMERGENCIES

If you're on the mainland, Surat Thani Hospital has a good reputation. The new Bangkok-Samui Hospital near Chawaeng is your best bet on the islands. For any emergencies, call tourist police at 1699, 24-hour service.

Hospitals Samui International Hospital ⊠ Chawaeng Beach, Ko Samui ☎ 077/421230. **Surat Thani Hospital** ⊠ Surat-Phun Phin Rd., Surat Thani ☎ 077/272231.

HEALTH

There are no health risks particular to the Western Gulf beyond the ones that apply to the whole Southern Beaches region. Though there isn't a strong risk of malaria, mosquitoes can be a nuisance, so make sure you have repellent. All accommodations, from luxury resorts to humble bungalows, either have screens on all windows and doors or at least mosquito netting over the beds.

Be careful at the beach, as the sun can be stronger than you think. Wear a hat and bring along plenty of sunscreen. Protective clothing while diving or snorkeling is a good idea, as accidentally brushing against or stepping on coral can be painful. Keep an eye out for dangerous creatures, especially jellyfish and sea urchins. If you're stung, seek medical attention immediately.

MAIL & SHIPPING

The reception desk at your hotel will post your cards and letters, a much easier option than hunting down the nearest post office.

Post Offices Hua Hin ⊠ Phetkasem Rd. **Surat Thani** ⊠ Taladmai Rd.

MONEY MATTERS

Banks are easy to locate in all mainland towns and on Ko Samui (in Chawaeng, Lamai, and Mae Nam). All banks will exchange foreign currency and most have ATMs. Remember that hotel exchange rates differ significantly from those at banks or currency exchange houses. Remote islands like Ko Pha-ngan and Ko Tao do not widely accept credit cards, but have many eager currency exchangers. Some places will add a small service charge when you pay with a credit card.

TAXIS, TUK-TUKS & SONGTHAEWS

Many parts of Thailand do not have regular auto taxis as we commonly know them. Most areas have a variety of different motorized taxi services from bicycle-drawn carriages (samlors) and motorized tricycles (tuk-tuks) to big and small trucks with benches in the back (songthaews, which means two rows of seats). Traveling around Cha-am is easiest by flagging down a motorbike taxi, which can be found on any street corner. Don't forget to wear your helmet. Hua Hin has more transportation options, including motorbike taxis, samlors, and tuk-tuks at negotiable prices. Surat Thani, a bigger town, has songthaews and regular bus services throughout the day. Samui has many songthaews that circle Samui Ring road and cost B20–B50 during the day. At night these songthaews become chartered taxis for negotiable prices. "Metered" taxis can be found in the larger towns and on Samui. They don't actually run their meters, however, and are unscrupulous bargainers. Taxis do not normally meet incoming flights at the airport in Ko Samui. If you're likely to be needing a taxi throughout your stay on Samui, ask your driver for his card and you can negotiate lower, multiday rates.

TOUR OPERATORS

Dive Deep runs trips from Ko Samui to Angthong National Marine Park and other destinations.

🚹 Tour Operators **Dive Deep** ☒ Chawaeng Beach Resort, Ko Samui ☎ 077/230155.

TRAIN TRAVEL

The *Southern Line* train from Bangkok's Hualamphong Station leaves throughout the day, beginning at 7:45 AM and running until 10:50 PM. Trains going south along the Western Gulf stop at Hua Hin, Chumphon, and Surat Thani. The 10 daily trips from Bangkok to Hua Hin take four hours. The journey to Chumphon takes seven hours. The best option to Chumphon is the first train at 7:45 AM or the last train at 7:15 PM. On the first you arrive fairly early so that you can still enjoy your day, and the latter is an overnight sleeper train.

Many express trains from Bangkok's Hualamphong railway station stop at Surat Thani on their way south. The journey takes just less than 12 hours, and the best trains are the overnighters that leave Bangkok at 6:30 PM and 7:20 PM, arriving in Surat Thani a little after 6 AM. First-class sleeping cabins are available only on the 7:20 PM train. There are later trains departing from Bangkok, but there are no sleeping beds available on them.

Surat Thani is the closest train station to Phuket. A bus service links the two cities. The State Railway of Thailand, in conjunction with Songserm Travel, issues a combined train and bus ticket to Phuket for B670. The bus ride takes about five hours. There's a similar deal for passengers headed to Ko Samui.

🖪 **State Railway of Thailand** ☎ 1690 ⊕ www.railway.co.th

VISITOR INFORMATION

The Tourism Authority of Thailand has offices in several resorts in southern Thailand. You can drop by for maps and brochures, as well as information about local excursions.

🖪 Tourist Information **TAT Central Region Office 2** ⊠ Petchakasem Rd., Cha-am, Petchaburi ☎ 032/471005 or 032/471502 ⊕ www.tourismthailand.org. **Petchaburi Town** ⊠ Radvitee Rd. ☎ 032/402220. **Hua Hin** ⊠ Petchakasem Rd. ☎ 032/511367. **Ko Samui** ⊠ Na Thon ☎ 077/421281. **Surat Thani** ⊠ 5 Talat Mai Rd. ☎ 077/281828.

KO PHUKET

Phuket was one of the region's economic powerhouses—millions of tourists visited the island every year and many beaches were exhibiting the rampant overbuilding that turned Pattaya from peaceful getaway to eyesore. However, the tsunami changed all that. Although only a few of the island's many beaches were directly affected (the worst damage actually occurred north of the island along the Andaman Coast), the beaches that were hit, were hit really hard and the island suffered its share of destruction and casualties. It may take years for this prime tourist destination to fully recover—weeks and months after the waves hit, airplanes landed in Phuket nearly empty, the beaches were barren, and businesses cried for help—but it's important to note that most of the island wasn't hit at all, and the affected areas have, at this writing, already made great progress in rebuilding. In fact, if you're considering a Phuket vacation, this might be the time to go. Hotels, restaurants, and airlines are offering unbeatable deals (some lasting through 2005), and you just might experience something that Phuket hasn't seen in a very, very long time: solitude.

Ko Phuket is linked to the mainland by a causeway, and the rest of the world by an international airport. Its indented coastline and hilly interior make the island seem larger than its 48-km (30-mi) length and 21-km (13-mi) breadth. Before tourism, Ko Phuket was already making fortunes out of tin mining and rubber plantations. Backpackers discovered Ko Phuket in the early 1970s. Word quickly spread about its white, sandy beaches and cliff-sheltered coves, its plunging waterfalls and impressive mountains, its cloudless days and fiery sunsets.

This love of Phuket has brought serious problems. Entrepreneurs built massive resorts, first at Patong, then spreading out around the island. Before the tsunami, there was no easy way to navigate the island, which was plagued by horrendous traffic and overdevelopment. Some would say Phuket was being loved to death. Now, many hope the tsunami's silver lining will be a bit of thought and reflection before rebuilding.

Even though it may seem like every other business here is a tour operator or dive shop or tailor or jeep rental or pub, there's still a lot to love about the island. The beaches are beautiful and this is a top destination for snorkeling and diving (with more than 180 registered dive shops). The island offers some of the most exclusive resorts and spas in the world yet the food, drink, and accommodations are cheap compared to most visitors' home countries (though Phuket is quite expensive by Thai standards). And direct flights to the island make this a very convenient getaway.

When planning your trip, keep in mind that the monsoon season runs from May to October, and swimming on the west side of the coast is not advisable during this time as the current can be dangerous.

This section starts with Phuket Town, the hub of the island, and is organized counter-clockwise from there. It's best to pick one or two choice spots and stick with them. The frazzling travel between destinations can very well undo any relaxation you enjoyed the previous day.

Numbers in the text correspond to numbers in the margin and on the Ko Phuket map.

Phuket Town

20 *862 km (539 mi) south of Bangkok.*

Though very few tourists linger here, Phuket Town, the provincial capital, is one of the more interesting places on the island. About one-third of the island's population lives here, and the town is an intriguing mix of old Sino-Portuguese architecture and the influences of the Chinese, Muslims, and Thais that inhabit it. The old Chinese quarter along Talang Street is especially good for a stroll, as its history has not yet been replaced by modern concrete and tile. And this same area also has a variety of antiques shops, art studios, and funky cafés.

The other major thoroughfares in town are Ratsada, Phuket, and Ranong roads. Ratsada connects Phuket Road, where you can find the Tourism Authority of Thailand (TAT) office, to Ranong Road, where there's an aromatic local market filled with fruits, vegetables, spices, and meats. Ranong Road also has a songthaew terminal, where minibuses depart for the most popular beaches every half hour. The fare is B15–B30.

If you want to get your bearings, there's a fine view of Phuket Town and the island's interior from the top of **Khao Rang,** a hill northwest of town. It can be a tricky drive—you'll need to watch carefully for street signs, as many aren't marked or are covered by foliage. From the town's center, take either Ranong or Thalang Road west and turn north on Kho Sim Bi Road. Follow the winding, forested road up to the top.

About 5 km (3 mi) north of Phuket Town is the **Phuket Orchid Garden & Thai Village,** offering gardens and cultural shows. A 500-seat amphitheater presents various aspects of southern culture. Here you can see classical dance, shadow puppet shows, Thai boxing exhibitions, sword fighting, and an "elephants-at-work" show. ⊠ *Thepkasati Rd.* ☎ *076/*

214860 or 076/214861 ⊠ *B400 entry; B600 for show and lunch or dinner* ☉ *Shows at 11 AM and 5:30 PM.*

Several miles north of Phuket Town, dominating a major crossroads, is the **Heroines Monument,** a tribute to a pair of women who rallied the locals and repelled Burmese invaders in 1785. At the time, Phuket was without a leader after the governor's death and the Burmese tried to capitalize on this moment of weakness. The governor's wife and her sister persuaded all the town women to dress as men and pretend to bear arms against the Burmese. They didn't really fight, but the Burmese believed them to be a powerful army, so they retreated. The people of Phuket hold these two women in great esteem. Some stories, however, differ, having the two women actually fighting. ⊠ *12 km (7 mi) north of Phuket Town.*

The **National Museum,** opposite the Heroines Monument, has an interesting exhibition of the island's culture and history, including its encounter with the Burmese and their defeat by the island's two heroines. ⊠ *12 km (7 mi) north of Phuket Town* ☎ *076/311426* ⊠ *B30* ☉ *Daily 9–4.*

Just north of the National Museum, you can take a scenic drive along **Highway 4027.** This highway drive offers access to a quieter part of the island where local village life still exists. Heading north on the highway, there are a number of small roads heading off eastward. Watch for Yabu Soi, just before Km 15. Turn east, then east again when you come to a Y junction. This will take you to Yabu Cape, a small beach surrounded by Muslim fishermen's houses. You can see Phuket Town in the distance.

Where to Eat

$$ ✕ **Khanasutra, A Taste of India.** This restaurant's name is not making false promises—the Sikh owner and Indian chef turn out flavorful, authentic Indian cuisine. The fish tikka is recommended. Part of the unique decor is a bedouin-style tent, where you can have a few cocktails after dinner. ⊠ *18–20 Takua Pa Rd., Phuket Town* ☎ *01/894–0794* ▤ *No credit cards* ☉ *No lunch Sun.*

$ ✕ **Nai Yao Restaurant.** This popular local seafood spot is a Honda shop by day, but transforms into a simple, enjoyable sidewalk restaurant at night. Fresh fish, crab, mussels, and prawns are the staples, but chicken, pork, beef, and vegetable dishes are available, too. ⊠ *On Phuket Rd., opposite TAT office* ☎ *No phone* ▤ *No credit cards* ☎ *No lunch.*

¢ ✕ **Kopi de Phuket.** For a good cup of coffee, try this artistically designed shop, which also serves snacks, sandwiches, breads, and shakes. It's across from the Honda Shop/Nai Yao Restaurant. It opens daily at 9:30 AM. ⊠ *Phuket Rd.* ☎ *No phone* ▤ *No credit cards.*

¢ ✕ **RuamJai Vegetarian Restaurant.** Along with vegetable dishes and curries, this popular restaurant serves up all manner of faux fried chicken, hot dogs, and burgers made from vegetable protein and tofu, shaped and prepared to look and taste (almost) like the real thing. ⊠ *On Ranong Rd., near market.* ☎ *No phone* ▤ *No credit cards.*

¢ ✕ **Wilai.** Thai fast food is served from big vats at this little shop in the heart of the old Sino-Portuguese district. The owner makes different dishes every day to keep her regular customers interested. She focuses on curries, vegetables, fish, and soups, and she'll warn hapless foreigners away

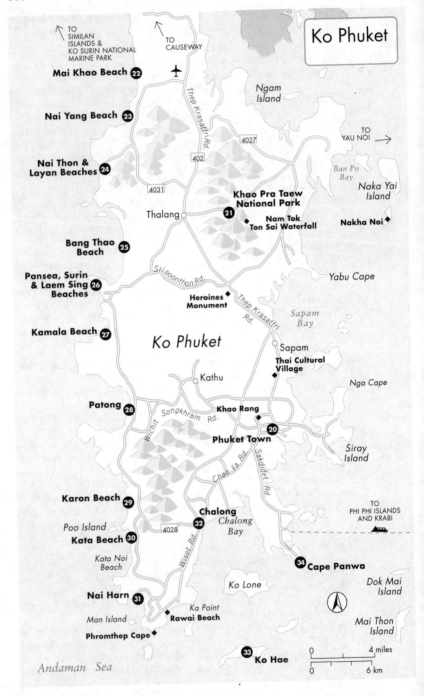

Ko Phuket

TO SIMILAN ISLANDS & KO SURIN NATIONAL MARINE PARK

TO CAUSEWAY

Mai Khao Beach 22

Ngam Island

Nai Yang Beach 23

TO YAU NOI

4027

Nai Thon & Layan Beaches 24

Ban Po Bay

Naka Yai Island

402

4031

Khao Pra Taew National Park 21

Nakha Noi

Thalang

Nam Tok Ton Sai Waterfall

Bang Thao Beach 25

Srisoonthon Rd.

Yabu Cape

Pansea, Surin & Laem Sing Beaches 26

Thep Krasattri Rd.

Heroines Monument

Sapam Bay

Kamala Beach 27

Ko Phuket

Sapam

Thai Cultural Village

Kathu

Nga Cape

Patong 28

Wichit Songkhram Rd.

Khao Rang

20

Phuket Town

Siray Island

Karon Beach 29

Chao Fa Rd.

Sakdidet Rd.

TO PHI PHI ISLANDS AND KRABI

Poo Island

Chalong 32

Chalong Bay

Kata Beach 30

4028

Wiset Rd.

Kata Noi Beach

Cape Panwa 34

Dok Mai Island

Ko Lone

Nai Harn 31

Ka Point

Man Island

Rawai Beach

Mai Thon Island

Phromthep Cape

Ko Hae 33

Andaman Sea

0   4 miles
0   6 km

from the spicy ones. Try a traditional cup of coffee, made with a cloth bag. Ask her about the temple in her backyard. The restaurant closes at 4 PM. ⊠ *14 Talang Rd.* ☏ *076/222875* ▤ *No credit cards* ⊗ *No dinner.*

Where to Stay

$$ 🏨 **Metropole.** The grand old Metropole—the town's first luxury hotel—has a shuttle service to the closest beaches, so you can stay in town and commute to the sea. The advantages are not only cheaper accommodation, but the opportunity to visit more than just one beach. Rooms are bright, with picture windows that let in a lot of sun. A spacious lounge is a cool retreat during the day, and the karaoke bar is fun at night. The hotel's handsome Chinese restaurant serves great dim-sum; for Western food, try the Metropole Café. ⊠ *1 Montri Rd., 83000* ☏ *076/215050 or 076/214020* 🖷 *076/215990* ⊕ *www.metropolephuket.com/* ➽ *248 rooms, 20 suites* ♨ *2 restaurants, minibars, cable TV, pool, gym, health club, hair salon, massage, laundry service, business services, meeting rooms, airport shuttle, car rental, travel services* ▤ *AE, DC, MC, V* ⊚ *EP.*

$$ 🏨 **Royal Phuket City Hotel.** This is arguably Phuket Town's best address (it's where Thai Prime Minister Thaksin Shinawatra stayed when he was in town for a 2003 conference). Rooms are spacious and contemporary, but don't have great views. The large Club Asia health club is popular with locals. The top-floor Thai Thai Room has outdoor seating and great views; the Cappuccino 154 deli on the ground floor caters its baked goods to other coffee shops around town. ⊠ *154 Phang Nga Rd., Phuket 83000* ☏ *076/233333* 🖷 *076/233335* ⊕ *www.royalphuketcity.com* ➽ *251 rooms* ♨ *4 restaurants, lounge, health club, spa, massage, pool, cable TV, minibars, in-room safes, Internet, travel services, babysitting, laundry services* ⊚ *EP* ▤ *AE, DC, MC, V.*

$ ✕ **China Inn Cafe.** At this writing, this B&B was still undergoing renovations (three years and counting), but it's definitely one to inquire about. In an old building in the Chinese district, there are so many Chinese antiques here it could be a museum. Currently, there are just two rooms: a massive air-conditioned room on the second floor with patio overlooking the busy street, and a smaller (but not small) fan room facing the rear, with a patio that overlooks a garden café. ⊠ *20 Talang Rd., Phuket 83000* ☏ *076/356239 or 01/979–8258.*

$ 🏨 **Pearl Hotel.** For a less-expensive option, this is a comfortable, convenient hotel in the center of Phuket Town, though it's a little tired around the edges. However, the hotel does offer twice-daily shuttle service to its beach counterpart, the Pearl Village, which is a beautiful resort, so you get the best of both worlds here. The top-floor Chinese restaurant has lovely views. The ground-floor café doubles as a nightclub with live music. There's also live music—anything from old waltzes to contemporary country tunes—in the funky cocktail lounge. ⊠ *42 Montri Rd., 83000* ☏ *076/211044* 🖷 *076/212911* ➽ *212 rooms* ♨ *3 restaurants, minibars, cable TV, pool, massage, laundry service, airport shuttle, car rental, travel services* ▤ *AE, MC, V* ⊚ *EP.*

¢ 🏨 **Talang Guesthouse.** This inexpensive hotel is becoming ever-more popular with backpackers, offering basic fan and some air-conditioned rooms in an old building. Two rooms on the roof are spacious and, naturally, have the best sunset views. Rooms toward the front overlook the

street, so they're not as quiet. ✉ *37 Talangs Rd., 83000* ☎ *076/214225*
🛏 *14 rooms* ⚲ *Travel services; no a/c in some rooms, no room TVs*
▭ *No credit cards* ⼁◯⼁ *BP.*

¢ ▦ **XVI (The 16).** For a slightly more expensive, but still budget option,
try this small guesthouse. A pair of old shophouses were gutted and renovated by local Thai architect Khun Malida in a chic style that would-
n't be out of place in London or New York. The four uniquely decorated
rooms feature spartan but stylish open layouts finished in wood, steel,
and glass. The downstairs bar features house music until the wee hours.
✉ *16 Rassada Rd., 83000* ☎ *076/222812* 🖷 *076/369067*
✉ *thexvi@yahoo.com* 🛏 *4 rooms* ⚲ *Restaurant, bar* ▭ *MC, V* ⼁◯⼁ *EP.*

Nightlife

You can watch muay thai in town on weekends, but ticket prices are
higher (B700–B1,000) than in other parts of Thailand. Travel agents often
seem desperate to arrange tickets for you.

O'Malleys Irish Pub & Restaurant (✉ 2/20–21 Montri Rd. ☎ 076/220170
⊕ www.phuket-town.com/omalleys) is a good "Irish" pub run by a Swede,
where you can get German beer and American bar food.

Khao Pra Taew National Park

❷❶ *19 km (12 mi) north of Phuket Town.*

Thailand's islands have several national parks, and this one is home to
Phuket's last remaining virgin forest and populations of endangered animals. The park boasts two easily accessible waterfalls. From Highway
4027, watch the signs and turn west toward Bang Pae Waterfall and the
Gibbon Rehabilitation Center. You'll have to pay the standard foreigner's fee to the park: B200 (Thais pay B20). The park advertises the
good deeds of the Gibbon Center, and indeed it's a worthy cause. (What
they don't tell you is that the center, which sits near the parking lot at
Bang Pae, receives none of your entrance fee.) After visiting the center,
follow the paved trail along the waterfall. It's a relatively easy hike, quite
lush in the rainy season.

To access **Tonsai Waterfall** on the other side of the park, follow the signs
and turn east off Highway 402. Here, you can find two trails (600 meters and 2 km), through rich tropical evergreen forest. Expect buckets
of rain in the monsoon season. Gibbons, civets, macaques, mouse deer,
wild boar, lemurs and loris live in the park, but spotting one would be
a rare and impressive feat.

Both park entrances have bathrooms, parking lots, and food stalls. If
you plan to visit both waterfalls, make sure you get entrance tickets at
your first stop—they're good for both sites.

Nakha Noi, Yao Noi

26 km (16 mi) northeast of Phuket Town.

Continuing northwest on Highway 4027, watch for signs for Naka (or
Nakha) Island and Po Bay, pointing east down a newly paved road. At

THE GIBBON REHABILITATION PROJECT

JUST INSIDE KHAO PRA TAEW NATIONAL **PARK,** between a jungled hillside and a gurgling stream, dozens of gibbons swing from branch to branch, filling the forest with boisterous hooting.

It seems like a happy sign of jungle life, but something is wrong with this picture. These animals are roaming around free; instead they live in cages near the park entrance as part of the Gibbon Rehabilitation Project. Most of these small apes were poached from jungles around Thailand and kept as pets or zoo and bar amusements. They were forced to perform shows, do tricks, drink beer or get their pictures taken with tourists before they were rescued by this project. As a branch of the Wild Animal Rescue Foundation of Thailand, the center aims to rehabilitate the gibbons in their natural habitat, with the intention of releasing the animals into the wild (though some animals that were abused will never be able to live freely again).

The center holds more than 60 gibbons. They're kept in large cages, away from visitors. The idea is to purge them of their familiarity with people, although visitors can hear them in the distance and glimpse their playful leaps through the trees. All gibbons are named, and their life stories are posted at the center for tourists to read: Lamut and Pai Mei were working as tourist attractions at Patong Beach before their rescue. A baby, called Bam-Bam, was found in a cardboard box at a roadside. Saul, a young blonde male, is missing a patch of fur, which researchers think could be the result of bullets that grazed him when his mother was shot.

When new gibbons arrive at the center, they get a complete medical check-up, including tests for HIV, hepatitis, and tuberculosis. It costs $700 a year to treat, feed, and house each animal, and although the center sits within the national park, it receives none of the $5 entrance fee. In fact, the center receives no funding from the Thai government—it survives on donations alone. For B1,500, the price of a good night out in Patong, visitors can "adopt" a gibbon for a year. If you're unable to make it out to the center, the web site of The Wildlife Friends of Thailand (www.wfft.org), has information on how to adopt a gibbon or make a donation.

— Karen Coates

its end, you can charter a private longtail fishing boat to neighboring Naka Noi island for B700 per person; the trip takes a half-hour. Naka Noi is home to a private company that runs a pearl farm for which most tour agents in Phuket Town can arrange a tour.

For a cheaper island trip, head east from Highway 4027 on the unmarked road just south of the Naka Island turnoff. This road will bring you to Bang Rong Pier, where two boats a day (around 8 AM and noon) head to Yao Noi for B50 per person. Cheap bungalows and food await travelers, and you can also snorkel and explore the small local villages, beaches, and caves. From Yao Noi there's also ferry service onward to Krabi, on the mainland.

Mai Khao Beach

㉒ *37 km (23 mi) northwest of Phuket Town.*

This is Phuket's northernmost beach, still a haven for leatherback turtles that lay their eggs here between November and February. It's an increasingly rare event, but one new nest was found less than two weeks after the tsunami hit. The beach here sustained only minor tsunami damage and some speculate the waves cleared the way for the turtles, as there are now fewer fishing boats in their path and fewer tourists on the beach to endanger the nests.

The Marriott Resort and next-door Sirinath Marine National Park (established to protect the turtles) are the only things to occupy this beach, which connects with Nai Yang Beach, to form Phuket's longest stretch of sand. It's great for running, sunbathing, and swimming (in the hot season, although dangerous during the monsoons).

Where to Stay

$$$$ ✕⛨ **J. W. Marriott Resort & Spa.** Wow. This secluded resort offers the longest
Fodor'sChoice   stretch of sand on the island. It has luxurious rooms with impeccable clas-
★   sic Thai design and an unbeatable spa with amenities that meet or exceed those in the guest rooms. And did we mention it was named one of Asia's top 25 hotels in 2004 by *Travel and Leisure*? The Marriott is the only thing on this beach, but it has everything you need, and then some. ✉ *231 Moo 3, Mai Khao, 83110* ☎ *076/338000* ⎙ *076/348348* ⊕ *www. marriott.com/HKTJW* ⇆ *265 rooms* ♻ *5 restaurants, 2 bars, room service, minibars, in-room safes, cable TV, in-room DVD players, Internet, babysitting, business services, meeting rooms, health club, 2 tennis courts, golf privileges, 2 pools, shops* ▤ *AE, MC, V* ⊙ *EP.*

Nai Yang Beach

㉓ *34 km (20 mi) northwest of Phuket Town.*

Nai Yang did suffer some damage from the tsunami, but its businesses were fully operational by March 2005.

Nai Yang Beach is really a continuation south of Mai Khao, making a long stretch of sand good for running or swimming in the dry season. Casuarina trees line the gently curving shore. The Pearl Village Resort is the biggest establishment on the beach, but it's hidden behind a screen of trees and a small string of beachside restaurants and bars, tour guides, tailors and shops. It's a far quieter beach than most, and fishing boats anchor nearby, making for picture-perfect sunrises and sunsets.

Where to Stay & Eat

¢–$ ✕ **Bank Restaurant.** Nai Yang Beach has a number of seafood restaurants with tables in the sand, but this is definitely one to try. It's run by a woman whose husband goes out fishing each night and returns by morning with the day's catch. Red tablecloths and lights hanging from the trees give this beachside spot a romantic air. It's just south of Pearl Village. ⊠ *Nai Yang Beach* ☎ *01/978–5728* ▭ *No credit cards.*

★ $$$$ ✕⊡ **Pearl Village Resort.** Set on 35 acres of landscaped gardens next to a national park, this resort is a relaxing, quiet place. It offers the amenities of an exclusive resort, but lies close enough to local beach life so that you don't feel totally isolated. It's just a short walk from the beach, across a small road lined with vendors. As you stroll around the grounds, you can encounter streams, ponds, and a vast swimming pool with an island and waterfall. If that's not enough nature for you, you can also hike or bike through the nearby park. Rooms are large and airy, furnished with light woods and bamboo. All have views of the gardens and/or pool. The Pae Thip Restaurant sits on stilts over water and serves traditional Thai food at very reasonable rates. ⊠ *Nai Yang Beach & National Park, 83110* ☎ *076/327006 or 076/327015* ⊟ *076/327338* ⊕ *www.phuket.com/pearlvillage* ⇱ *226 rooms* ♧ *5 restaurants, room service, minibars, cable TV, laundry service, driving range, 2 tennis courts, pool, spa, massage, dive shop, snorkeling, business services, meeting rooms, bicycles, travel services* ▭ *AE, MC, V* ⦿ *EP.*

$$ ⊡ **Crown Nai Yang Suite Hotel.** This all-suites hotel is closer to the sand than the Pearl Village, and offers spartan accommodations at slightly lower prices. Though it lacks the gardens and ambience of its neighboring resort, a full range of sports facilities is available. ⊠ *117 Moo 1, National Park Rd.,,, Saku Village 83110* ☎*076/327420 up to 9* ⊟*076/327322* ⊕ *www.crownnaiyang.com* ⇱ *96 suites* ♧ *2 restaurants, minibars, cable TV, pool, meeting rooms, travel services* ▭ *AE, MC, V* ⦿ *EP.*

¢–$ ⊡ **Nai Yang Beach Resort.** These basic bungalows are a short walk from the beach. They surround a small fish pond and come with a variety of amenities—choose between fans or air-conditioning, and with or without TVs and minibars. The higher the price, the better the view, although none of the rooms overlook the sea. ⊠ *65/23–24 Nai Yang Beach Rd., Moo 5, T. Sakhu, Thalang, Phuket, 83140* ☎ *076/328300* ⊟ *076/328333* ⊕ *www.naiyangbeachresort.com* ⇱ *35 rooms* ♧ *Restaurant* ⦿ *EP.*

Nai Thon & Layan beaches

㉔ *30 km (18.6 mi) northwest of Phuket Town.*

Just a few miles north of Bang Thao Bay, follow a smaller highway off the main routes (4030 and 4031) along a scenic coastline reminiscent of California's Pacific Coast Highway. These beaches are good for swimming in the dry season. There's more development on the way, but for now they're two of the island's quiet gems—even quieter since the tsunami has slowed tourism to the island in general.

Where to Stay

★ $$$–$$$$ 🏨 **Andaman White Beach Resort.** With a small, private stretch of sand, bordered by rocks on the north and south ends, this resort offers some of the most spectacular views of the Andaman Sea. Villas are lovely—a few saffron-and-yellow accents add some color to cream walls and linens and shiny wood floors. ⊠ *28/8 Moo 4, Tambon Sakoo, Amphur Thalang, 83110* ☎ *076/316300* 🖷 *076/316399* ⊕ *www.andamanwhitebeach. com* ⇆ *30 rooms and suites* ⚒ *Restaurant, pool, spa, bar, snorkeling, dive shop, travel services* ▭ *AE, MC, V* ¶⊙¶ *EP.*

★ $$–$$$$ 🏨 **Layan Beach Resort & Spa Village.** The spa is the focus of this resort, which is tucked away on a hillside overlooking the sea, a small beach, and nearby island. In fact, the spa looks like it's own exclusive set of villas. You won't find much else around here, for now. The standard rooms aren't terribly exciting, but they're spacious and bright. ⊠ *62 Moo 6, Layan Village, 83110* ☎ *076/313412–4* 🖷 *076/313415* ⊕ *www. layanphuket.com* ⇆ *52 rooms and villas* ⚒ *2 restaurants, spa, massage, pool, gym, bicycles* ▭ *AE, MC, V* ¶⊙¶ *EP.*

Bang Thao Beach

㉕ *22 km (14 mi) northwest of Phuket Town.*

Once the site of a tin mine, Bang Thao Beach (a resort area collectively called Laguna Phuket) now glistens with the more precious metals worn by its affluent visitors. Due to the ingenuity of Ho Kwon Ping and his family, this area was built nearly 20 years ago in a spot so damaged from mining, most thought it beyond repair. Now it's recovered enough to support an array of accommodation, eateries, and golf courses set around the lagoons. The beach itself is a long stretch of white sand with vendors offering a variety of sports equipment rental, inexpensive seafood, beach massages and cocktails. The beach is good for swimming in the hot season; the lagoon for kayaking anytime. This area was spared much of the tsunami's effects, saved by headlands to the south.

The once quiet bay was one of the island's major destinations, though it's been quieter since the tsunami. A free shuttle service brings visitors between the five resorts that line the shore. Of the Laguna quintet, the odd man out is the Dusit, which doesn't match up to the other four. None are cheap. As anywhere on the island, some of the older resorts are showing signs of age and tropical weather damage, despite frequent renovations.

Where to Stay & Eat

$$–$$$ ✕ **Lakeside Tropical Restaurant.** Outside of the resort complex, this Thai–European restaurant offers open-air seating on a lagoon. Traditional curries, soups, steak, and seafood are complemented by a decent wine list. Note that it's a long walk from the resorts. ⊠ *On main road heading to Laguna Phuket* ☎ *076/271384* ▭ *MC, V.*

¢ ✕ **Seafood.** The friendly women at this popular streetside shanty serve made-to-order seafood, noodles, and stir-fry. Every meal comes with a bowl of aromatic cardamom soup. It's safe for foreign bellies, but if you're wary of street food or spicy food, you probably won't be comfortable here. It's about 5 km from the resorts, heading east. Look for a small sign on the left side of the road that says SEAFOOD—if you reach the mosque, you've gone too far. ☎ *No phone* ▤ *No credit cards.*

$$$$ 🏨 **Banyan Tree Phuket.** Of the quintet of resorts on Laguna Beach, this is the most exclusive—and expensive. Your secluded villa has a bathroom as big as the bedroom; an outdoor shower for rinsing off after a swim is a nice addition. Teak floors and locally woven fabrics remind you that you are in Thailand. The king-size bed is on a raised platform so that you can gaze out onto your garden. The most expensive villas have their own private pools. Rejuvenating treatments in the spa include herbal massages. ⊠ *33 Moo 4 Srisoonthorn Rd., Cherngtalay, Amphur Talang, 83110* ☎ *076/324374* ⊟ *076/324375* ⊕ *www.banyantree. com* ➔ *104 villas* ⏦ *2 restaurants, café, minibars, cable TV, in-house movies, in-room DVD players, pool, hot tub, 18-hole golf course, 5 tennis courts, pro shop, aerobics, gym, hair salon, massage, beach, windsurfing, boating, bicycles, billiards, squash, 2 bars, shops, babysitting, children's programs, dry cleaning, laundry service, business services, airport shuttle, car rental, travel services* ▤ *AE, MC, V* ⦿| *EP.*

$$$$ 🏨 **Laguna Beach Resort.** This is another in the Sheraton's league, with traditional Thai and Angkor details, including a vast, meandering pool with replica Angkor Wat wall carvings. This resort has less of an amusement park feel than its neighbor, but still has plenty of kids activities. ⊠ *Bang Tao Bay, Phuket, 83110* ☎ *076/324352* ⊟ *076/324353* ⊕ *www.lagunabeach-resort.com* ➔ *254 rooms* ⏦ *5 restaurants, cable TV, minibars, sailing, kayaking, dive shop, windsurfing, snorkeling, tennis, golf* ▤ *AE, MC, V* ⦿| *EP.*

$$$$ 🏨 **Sheraton Grande Laguna.** Everything about this resort is grand—even the swimming pool, which is 323 meters long. Some rooms offer patios, from which you can jump directly into the pool. If you like Walt Disney World, you want this resort, an island within an island, surrounded by a lovely lagoon. It's a big spread and a long walk from one end to the other. Seafarers can choose a villa with private boat dock. Life-size chess is just one of many activities catering to kids. ⊠ *Bang Thao Bay, 83110* ☎ *076/324101–7* ⊟ *076/324108* ⊕ *www.lagunaphuket.com* ➔ *365 rooms,* ⏦ *10 restaurants, cable TV, Internet, minibars, in-room safes, golf, spa, boating, dive shop, snorkeling, windsurfing, meeting rooms, travel services* ▤ *AE, DC, MC, V* ⦿| *EP.*

$$$–$$$$ 🏨 **Allamanda Laguna Phuket.** This all-suites resort sits on the lagoon, but not the beach (unlike the other four) and therefore offers lower rates. You definitely get more bang for your buck here than at the other four resorts in this complex. Suites come in various configurations (one or two bedrooms), but all have kitchenettes. ⊠ *29 Moo 4 Srisoonthorn Rd., Cherngtalay 83110* ☎ *076/324359* ⊟ *076/324360* ⊕ *www. allamanda.com* ➔ *235 suites* ⏦ *2 restaurants, cable TV, minibars, in-room safes, 3 pools, hot tub, spa, boating, snorkeling, windsurfing, horseback riding, volleyball, library, babysitting, business services, meeting rooms, laundry service, travel services* ▤ *AE, MC, V* ⦿| *EP.*

$$–$$$ 🏨 **Bang Tao Beach Resort & Spa.** On the southern edge of Bang Tao Beach— and not part of the Laguna complex—this Best Western facility offers

cheaper accommodation that's right on the beach. You can get very nice sea views and the basic, decent rooms you expect of Best Western, for one-half to two-thirds the price of the other resorts. The place can be a little difficult to find, though, as it's on a small, twisty road connecting Bang Thao and Surin Beach. ⊠ *124/29 Moo #3, Tumbon Cheung Thalay, 83110* ☎ *076/270680 up to 5* 🖷 *076/270679 or 076/270686* ⊕ *www.bangtaobeach.com* ⇨ *235 rooms* ♢ *2 restaurants, cable TV, minibars, in-room safes, 3 pools, gym, hot tub, sauna, massage, beach, bar, meeting rooms, laundry service, Internet* ▤ *AE, MC, V* ⊧ *EP.*

Pansea, Surin & Laem Sing beaches

❷ *21 km (12 mi) northwest of Phuket Town.*

South of Bang Thao you can find a jagged shoreline with little inlets. Once secluded, these areas are developing quickly with villas, restaurants, high-end resorts, cheap backpacker hotels and what is becoming the usual Phuket beach slurb. Surin Beach is about 500 meters of sand where you can get a beer and pretty much anything else that you want. There's a public parking lot above the beach, literally a garbage dump in the off season. Dozens of sites are under construction between here and Laem Sing. So many little restaurants, with Thai and Western food for a few dollars, have popped up, it's nearly impossible to recommend one over another.

Head north a bit and things change. On the spit of land separating these beaches from Bang Tao sit two of the island's most luxurious resorts, though you may never find them without careful sleuthing. An overgrown sign points the way up a small road to the Chedi; no sign marks the Amanpuri beyond that. Tsunami damage in this area was contained to the beach, and both resorts have been operational throughout. The Chedi is still making repairs to its beachfront rooms and facilities, which should be completed by October 2005.

Where to Stay

★ **$$$$**   🏨 **Amanpuri Resort.** You'd be hard-pressed to find a more elegant hotel in Thailand—nor one quite as expensive (the nightly rate for the largest of the villas is more than $7,000!). The reception area, with beautifully polished teak floors, is completely open in the dry season so that you can enjoy the breezes off the ocean. Here you can find two palm-shaded restaurants overlooking the blue-tile swimming pool. Choose between rooms in secluded hillside pavilions or immense villas with private swimming pools. Pavilion prices differ according to view, and villas offer between two and six bedrooms. There's no TV in the rooms. From the split-level bar you have stunning sunset views. ⊠ *Pansea Beach, Phuket 83000* ☎ *076/324333* 🖷 *076/324100* ⊕ *www.amanpuri.com* ⇨ *40 pavilions, 30 villas* ♢ *2 restaurants, bar, pool, 6 tennis courts, gym, spa, dive shop, library, travel services* ▤ *AE, MC, V* ⊧ *EP.*

★ **$$$$**   🏨 **Chedi.** Almost completely hidden by a grove of coconut palms, this resort has more than 100 thatch-roof cottages overlooking a quiet beach. You know this place is special when you walk into the lobby, which has a sweeping view of the Andaman Sea. The decor is sleek and geometric. An octagonal pool is set amid the tropical flora. Each of the cottages has its own sundeck. The interiors, done in wood and stone, with high, pointed ceilings, are simple but elegant. ⊠ *118 Moo 3, Cherngtalay, Phuket 83110* ☏ *076/324017* 🖶 *076/324252* ⊕ *www. ghmhotels.com/thechediphuket/index.asp* ⤳ *108 chalets* ⌂ *3 restaurants, cable TV, minibars, in-room safes, 2 tennis courts, pool, spa, boating, snorkeling, windsurfing, bar, library shop, babysitting, children's programs, travel services* ▭ *AE, MC, V* ⚊◯⚊ *EP.*

¢–$ 🖼 **Surin Bay Inn.** For cheaper accommodation near Surin Beach (only a few minutes' walk away), try this small hotel. Some rooms have balconies overlooking the street along the beach. This is one of the cleanest, nicest budget options in the area. ⊠ *106/11 Surin Beach, 83110* ☏ *076/271601* 🖶 *076/271599* ⊕ *www.surinbayinn.com* ⤳ *12 rooms* ⌂ *Restaurant, minibars, in-room safes, bar, laundry service, Internet, airport shuttle* ▭ *MC, V* ⚊◯⚊ *BP.*

Kamala Beach

㉗ *18 km (11 mi) west of Phuket Town.*

South of Bang Thao you reach Kamala Beach, a curving strip of coral sand backed by coconut palms. Before the tsunami, Kamala town was quickly turning into a beach strip of shops and restaurants, like so many others. But unlike the more upscale enclaves to the north, Kamala Beach had some reasonably priced accommodations, set apart from the development. All of that changed on December 26. Kamala Beach suffered some of the worst destruction on Phuket. The waves washed inland several hundred meters, pulverizing most everything in the way. As of this writing, many places were closed, with no definitive plans for reopening.

However, one Kamala attraction is trying hard to attract the old crowds: the island has its own theme park, **Phuket FantaSea,** where the kids can ride the elephants while you poke among the shops. In the evening there's a Las Vegas–type extravaganza with dozens of dancers performing modern and classical routines, 30 elephants going through their paces, magicians doing tricks, acrobats spinning above the crowd—well, you get the picture. The night ends with a fireworks display. The park's Golden Kinaree restaurant boasts the island's biggest buffet. FantaSea lost a bundle when tourists stopped showing up post-tsunami, but thanks to a hefty government loan, the shows will go on. ⊠ *99 Moo 3 Kamala Beach, Kathu, Phuket 83120* ☏ *076/385111* 🖶 *076/385222* ⊕ *www.phuket-fantasea.com* 🎟 *Admission* ◷ *Fri.–Wed. 5:30–11:30* PM.

Patong

㉘ *13 km (8 mi) west of Phuket Town.*

You'd hardly believe it today, but Patong was once the island's most remote beach, completely cut off by the surrounding mountains. A boat was the only way to reach Phuket Town. In 1959 a highway linked the two towns, and the tranquil beachfront was bought up by developers who knew the beautiful beach wouldn't stay a secret for long. Today

Patong is virtually indistinguishable from Pattaya, Patpong, and other dubious tourist destinations.

When it comes to Patong, you either love it or hate it. "It's nothing but hookers," said one astonished tourist from Milwaukee. That's not entirely true, but it's not difficult to think so. There are a few luxury hotels, upscale restaurants, and even some smart nightspots, but Patong is mostly a crowded, noisy destination with little local culture. If you want nothing more than American burgers, English fish-and-chips, German beers, and Thai ladies of the evening, then this is your scene.

Patong has its fair share of environmental problems. According to the Phuket *Gazette*, the town's waste facilities were not equipped for the hordes of people who showed up. Hence, a slimy green film regularly covered the beach. And as developers use every inch of space along the beach, they've moved farther inland, cutting into hillsides that erode and turn into mudslides in the rainy season. When it rains a lot—as it does each year during the monsoons—flooded roads sometimes make Patong impassable. In 2004, a 19-year-old Canadian tourist made tragic front-page news: he died when a power line came down and zapped him as he stood in a flooded street. Furthermore, the traffic getting in and out of Patong is truly dangerous, no matter who's driving.

The beach was hit hard by the tsunami, and anything down low on the water was destroyed. Much within two blocks of the beach was damaged. Most establishments have reopened, but a few are closed for the foreseeable future. Everything else in Patong remains as it was—lots of lights and lots of action, but far fewer people than pre-tsunami times. Here, business owners are pleading for tourists to book a trip and drop their dollars into the well-drained Patong coffers.

Where to Stay & Eat

It's hard (and some would argue irresponsible) to recommend Patong at all, for taste, safety, and environmental reasons. However, if you find yourself at this beach, here's the good news: the north end of Patong boasts three internationally acclaimed restaurants, all in a row, set on the cliffside overlooking the beach, and there are a few pricy resorts on quieter sands that are far enough away from the center of the action that you can ignore it.

$$–$$$$ ✕ **Baan Rim Pa.** If you suffer from vertigo, take a pass on this restaurant. You dine on a terrace that clings to a cliff at the north end of Patong Beach. There are tables set back from the edge, but you'll then miss the gorgeous ocean views. The food is among the best Phuket has to offer. Well-thought-out set menus make ordering simpler for those unfamiliar with Thai food. They've turned down the heat on many favorites, so you may be disappointed if you like spicier fare. The restaurant has a piano bar open Tuesday through Sunday to offer a tamer side of Patong's nightlife. ✉ *Prabaramee Rd., Kalim Beach, Patong, Phuket* ☎ *076/340789* ⚑ *Reservations essential* ▭ *AE, MC, V.*

FodorsChoice ★

$$$$ ✕ **Da Maurizio.** An Italian bar–ristorante is the last in the trio of Patong's cliff restaurants. Dining is just above a secluded beach. Try pizza, fettuccine, ravioli and other Italian traditions, or opt for fresh seafood baked in a wood-burning oven. ✉ *223/2 Kalim Rd., Patong* ☎ *076/344079* 🖷 *076/342460* ⚏ *Reservations essential* ▤ *AE, MC, V.*

$$$$ ✕**Otowa.** This Japanese-French fusion restaurant sits between its two other clifftop neighbors, offering the same spectacular views. The chef has cooked in Tokyo and Monaco before settling in Thailand. Menu items include foie-gras sushi, goose liver, and Kobe beef, and abolone cooked in burgundy butter. ✉*223 Prabaramee Rd., Kalim Beach, Patong* ☎*076/344254* ⊕ *www.otowa.com* ⚏ *Reservations essential* ▤ *AE, MC, V.*

$$–$$$ 🏨 **Impiana Phuket Cabana.** This hotel's chief attraction is its unbeatable location, right in the middle of the city facing the beach. Unfortunately, this means it was directly in the tsunami's path. At this writing, the hotel was planning to reopen in October 2005, but it's imperative that you double-check with them. Modest rooms are in chalet-type bungalows furnished with rattan furniture. The Impiana has a trio of good points: good travel services, a reputable dive shop, and a festive cigar bar, La Salsa, with pictures of Che smoking stogies and Fidel hamming it up with Hemingway. At this writing, we haven't gotten word of any of these things disappearing or changing, but if they're important to you, you should inquire about them when booking. ✉ *41 Taweewong Rd., 83150* ☎ *076/340138* 🖷 *076/340178* ⊕ *www.impiana.com* 📞 *80 rooms* ⚏ *Restaurant, minibars, pool, dive shop, airport shuttle, travel services* ▤ *AE, MC, V* ⏏◯| *EP.*

$$$–$$$$ 🏨 **Avantika.** The south end of Patong is a little quieter than the rest, and several "boutique" hotels have sprung up in the past year. Try this one, just across the road from the beach. Rooms are very elegant, with four-poster beds, dark woods, and white linens. Rooms on the fourth floor have the best sea views. ✉ *4/1 Thaweewong Rd., Patong* ☎ *076/ 292802 up to 7* 🖷 *076/292808 up to 9* ⊕ *www.avantika-phuket.com* 📞 *31 rooms* ⚏ *Cable TV, minibars, Internet, spa, restaurant, pool* ▤ *AE, D, MC, V.*

Karon Beach

㉙ *20 km (12 mi) southwest of Phuket Town.*

Just south of Patong lie Karon Beach and its smaller northern counterpart, Karon Noi. Bunches of hotels, restaurants, tailors, dive and gift shops have sprung up along the main Karon beach to accommodate the tourists tempted by this long stretch of white sand and good dry-season swimming (it's good for running year-round). A sprawling Meridien resort is wedged into Karon Noi. If none of the following options tickle your fancy, there are literally dozens upon dozens of others. Best to call hotels individually, as some were still under repair as of this writing. Most businesses, however, are back to normal.

Where to Stay & Eat

$–$$ ✕ **On the Rock.** Built, you guessed it, on a rock overlooking Karon Beach, this restaurant has great views of the water. Seafood is the specialty, but Italian and traditional Thai dishes are on the menu, too. This restaurant is part of the Marina Cottage hotel. ✉ *South end of Karon Beach* ☎ *076/330625* ▤ *AE, MC, V.*

$$$$ ⌂ **Le Meridien.** Between Patong and Karon Beach sits this sprawling resort. There are more bars, cafés, and restaurants in this hotel than in many small towns. Its range of outdoor diversions—everything from tennis to waterskiing—means you never have to leave the property. There are hundreds of guests at any given time, yet the resort never feels too crowded, thanks to its thoughtful design. Two huge wings are where you'll find the sumptuous rooms, which are furnished in teak and rattan. Most have sea views, others overlook the pair of pools. At this writing, the Meridien was set to reopen in June 2005, but it's best to call to confirm that repairs haven't taken longer than anticipated. ⌂ *8/5 Moo 1, Karon, Muang, Phuket 83100* ☎ *076/340480* 🖷 *076/340479* ⊕ *www. lemeridien-phuket.com* 🛏 *470 rooms* 🍴 *7 restaurants, room service, minibars, cable TV, driving range, miniature golf, 4 tennis courts, 2 pools, gym, health club, spa, massage, dive shop, boating, squash, volleyball, archery, 3 bars, babysitting, children's programs, laundry service, meeting rooms, travel services* ☰ *AE, DC, MC, V* ⧉ *EP.*

$$–$$$ ⌂ **Diamond Cottage Resort and Spa.** Although not on the beach, this nice spread is perched on the ridge separating Karon and Kata, making it a short walk to either beach. Nicely appointed bright red-and-yellow rooms with patios overlook the pool or gardens. The cottages are slightly bigger and more secluded than basic rooms. ⌂ *6 Karon Rd., A., Muang, Phuket 83100* ☎ *076/286446 up to 50* 🖷 *076/286451* ⊕ *www.diamondcottage.com* 🛏 *67 rooms and villas* 🍴 *Restaurant, cable TV, minibars, in-room safes, 2 pools, fitness center, sauna, spa, travel services* ☰ *AE, MC, V* ⧉ *EP.*

★ $$–$$$ ⌂ **Marina Cottage.** This surprisingly quiet option has its cottages spread out over a lush hillside separating Karon from Kata Beach. Those cottages higher on the hill are quiet. A wonderful pool and second restaurant (the other is On the Rock, listed above) are surrounded by more trees and plants. Best of all, Marina Cottage has its own beach access, keeping the hordes at bay. The rooms do not have TVs. Did we say this place is quiet? ⌂ *47 Karon Rd., 83100* ☎ *076/330493 or 076/330625* 🖷 *076/330516* ⊕ *www.marinaphuket.com* 🛏 *104 rooms* 🍴 *2 restaurants, minibars, pool, dive shop, car rental, travel services* ☰ *MC, V* ⧉ *EP.*

$$ ⌂ **Phuket Orchid Resort.** This resort is slightly inland, but the beach is just a short walk away. The lack of a beachfront brings the rates down considerably, but the lower rates make it very popular. A hodge-podge of Thai, Khmer, and Chinese architectural and design flourishes are everywhere, even in the sprawling pool and surrounding patios. And yes, lots of orchids are sprinkled about the main lobby. Some rooms have direct pool access. If you want a no-smoking room, be sure to demand it when booking. ⌂ *34 Luang Pohchuan Rd., Karon Muang, Phuket 83100* ☎ *076/396519* 🖷 *076/396526* ⊕ *www.katagroup.com* 🛏 *525 rooms* 🍴 *3 restaurants, cable TV, minibars, in-room safes, 2 pools, spa, bar, shops, babysitting, laundry service, meeting rooms, car rental, travel services* ☰ *AE, MC, V* ⧉ *EP.*

$–$$ ⌂ **In On The Beach.** This new place way at the north end of Karon is truly on the beach. Many of the rooms have good sea views. It's a quick walk from here to the rest of the sprawl of Karon Beach. ⌂ *Moo 1, Patak Rd., Karon Beach, Phuket 83100* ☎ *076/398–220* 🖷 *076/398–225* ⊕ *www.*

karon-inonthebeach.com 📞 *30 rooms* ⌂ *Restaurant, cable TV, minibars, laundry service, Internet, travel services* ▭ *AE, DC, MC, V* 🍴 *CP.*

Kata Beach

30 *22 km (13 mi) southwest of Phuket Town.*

Of the three most popular beaches on the west coast of Phuket, this is the calmest of the lot. A shady sidewalk runs the length of the beach. Club Med dominates a large hunk of the beachfront, keeping the development frenzy to the southern end. There's also a committed group of regulars here who surf the small local breaks. To the south, Kata Noi is almost exclusively taken up with the very long and expensive Katathani Resort & Spa. This is a public beach (as all beaches in Thailand are), so be sure to exercise your beach rights and soak up some sun on delightfully quiet Kata Noi if you're in the area. It's just as exquisite now as it was before the tsunami.

Where to Stay & Eat

$$$$ 🏨 **Kata Thani Resort & Spa.** This long, sprawling lodge fronts most of the Kata Noi beach. This seems to intimidate day-trippers, whose general absence keeps nearly 1 km of smooth sand delightfully calm. Glass-walled suites here have some of the best ocean views on the island. You can shower and watch the sunset at the same time through huge bathroom windows. Regular rooms (if you can call them that) are very tastefully furnished, with all the bells and whistles you'd expect in this price range. ✉ *14 Kata Noi Rd., Karon, Muang, Phuket 83100* ☎ *076/330124* 📠 *076/330127* ⊕ *www.katathani.com* 📞 *226 rooms* ⌂ *6 restaurants, 2 tennis courts, 3 pools, massage, health club, library, shops, babysitting, children's programs, laundry service, Internet, travel services* ▭ *AE, MC, V* 🍴 *EP.*

$$$–$$$$ ✕🏨 **Mom Tri's Boathouse.** A classic address on the south end of Kata, if no longer the snazziest. But it's right on the beach. The main lobby has a nautical flair, befitting the name. Plus, the Boathouse Wine & Grill has more than 400 labels in its cellar. ✉ *Kata Beach, Phuket 83100* ☎ *076/330015* 📠 *076/330561* ⊕ *www.boathousephuket.com* 📞 *33 rooms, 6 villas* ⌂ *Restaurant, minibars, cable TV, Internet, bar, travel services* ▭ *AE, D, MC, V* 🍴 *EP.*

$$$ 🏨 **Kata Beach Resort.** You can't miss this newly refurbished beacon on the beach. It's really big, really busy, and it's pink. The rooms are a little basic for the price, but sport nice Thai trimmings. ✉ *1 Pakbang Rd., Tambon Karon, 83100* ☎ *076/330530 up to 4* 📠 *076/330128* ⊕ *www.katagroup.com* 📞 *267 rooms* ⌂ *5 restaurants, in-room safes, minibars, 3 pools, health club, massage, hair salon, bar, meeting rooms, travel services* ▭ *AE, MC, V* 🍴 *EP.*

¢ 🏨 **Da Bungalows.** Across the street from the Boathouse sits a set of snug, white bungalows high on the hill with views of the beach and ocean. Some of the rooms are surprisingly spacious; all come with pleasant balconies. The friendly owner Da also runs the local surf shop, which doubles as the hotel office. The place is small and popular with the international surfer crowd, so it's best to call in advance about rooms.

CloseUp

A FESTIVAL FOR HEALTH AND PURITY

PHUKET'S MOST IMPORTANT FESTIVAL is its annual *Vegetarian Festival*, held in late September or early October. Though no one knows the precise details of the event's origins, the most common story is that it started in 1825, when a traveling Chinese opera group fell ill. The Taoist group feared that their illnesses were the result of their failure to pay proper respects to the nine Emperor Gods. After sticking to a strict vegetarian diet to honor these gods, they quickly recovered. This made quite an impression on the local villagers, and the island has celebrated a nine-day festival for good health ever since. Devotees, who wear white, abstain from eating meat, drinking alcohol, and having sex. Along with detoxing the body, the festival is meant to renew the soul—not killing animals for food is supposed to calm and purify the spirit.

The festival involves numerous temple ceremonies, parades, and fireworks. But what most fascinates visitors are the grisly body-piercing rituals. Some devotees become mediums for warrior spirits, going into trances and mutilating their bodies to ward off demons and bring the whole community good luck. These mediums pierce their bodies (tongues and cheeks are popular choices) with all sorts of things from spears to sharpened branches to florescent light bulbs. Supposedly, the presence of the spirits within them keeps them from feeling any pain.

The events are centered around the island's five Chinese temples. Processions are daily from morning until mid-afternoon. The Tourism Authority of Thailand office in Phuket Town can provide a list of all activities and their locations. Note that you might want to invest in earplugs—it's believed that the louder the fireworks, the more evil spirits they'll scare away.

✉ 235/1 Koktanode Rd., A., Muang, Phuket 83100 ☎ 076/333055 🛏 5 rooms � No a/c in some rooms ☐ No credit cards ○ EP.

¢–$ 🏨 **Katanoi Bay Inn.** If you want to enjoy the serenity of Kata Noi without draining your wallet, here's the spot. Simple, clean rooms, most with air-conditioning, all with small balconies. Most rooms overlook the Katathani across the road, but some manage to squeeze in a small view of the beach. ✉ 4/16 Moo 2, Patak Rd., Katanoi Beach, Phuket 83100 ☎ 076/333308 up to 9 🛏 22 rooms ⚞ Restaurant, minibars; no a/c in some rooms, no room TVs ☐ MC, V ○ EP.

Nai Harn

㉛ *18 km (11 mi) southwest of Phuket Town.*

South of Kata Beach the road cuts inland across the hills before it drops into yet another beautiful bay, Nai Harn. On the north side of the bay is the gleaming white Royal Meridien Phuket Yacht Club. On the south side is a nice little beach, removed for now from the tailors and cheap restaurants that have sprung up at the entrance to the Royal Meridien. Perhaps the drive will be even more enjoyable, in the post-tsunami lull.

From the top of the cliff at **Phromthep Cape,** the southernmost point on Ko Phuket, you're treated to a fantastic, panoramic view of Nai Harn Bay, the coastline and a few outlying islands. At sunset, you can share the view with swarms of others who pour forth from tour buses to view the same sight. If you're driving, arrive early if you want a parking spot. There's a lighthouse atop the point.

Not far from Chalong is **Rawai Beach,** where you can find a slurb on the water and over-price boat service to wherever you want to go. At the southern end of Rawai Beach lies the village of **Chao Le,** whose inhabitants are called *chao nam,* (water people) or more commonly in English, sea gypsies. You can visit them if you want: they are used to tourists.

Where to Stay & Eat

$–$$ ✕ **Phromthep Cape Restaurant.** Although it doesn't look like much from the Phromthep Cape parking lot, views from the tables out back are hard to beat. Just slightly down the hilltop from the lighthouse, you get unobstructed sights of the cape and coastline. Plus, you get lower prices and better views than most places on the island that boast of their panoramas. The restaurant serves Thai food and some Western fare. ⊠ *94/6 Moo 6, Rawai Beach, 83130* ☎ *076/288656* ⊕ *www.phuketdir.com/phromthepcaperest* ☰ *AE, MC, V.*

$$$$ ✕🏨 **Royal Meridien Phuket Yacht Club.** This place used to be home to the annual King's Cup Regatta—now the only yachts here are decorative carvings on the walls. But the place is still every inch a luxury destination, and was recently renovated. Beautifully appointed rooms in a modern Thai style all have balconies overlooking the sea with views of Promthep Cape in the distance. The building's layout has balconies staggered up the hillside. Some would say this is to afford each room a perfect view of the sea. Others would say it allows you to look down and see your sun-tanning neighbors. ⊠ *Nai Harn Beach, Phuket 83130* ☎ *076/380200* 📠 *076/380280* ⊕ *www.lemeridien-yachtclub.com* ⇨ *110 rooms and suites* ⚒ *6 restaurants, room service, minibars, in-room safes, 2 tennis courts, pool, health club, hair salon, massage, spa, beach, snorkeling, windsurfing, boating, laundry service, business services, car rental, travel services* ☰ *AE, DC, MC, V* ⦿ *EP.*

Chalong

32 *11 km (7 mi) south of Phuket Town.*

The waters in horseshoe-shape Chalong Bay are usually calm, as the entrance is guarded by Ko Lone and Ko Hae. It's not a scenic stop in itself, as it's more of a working port than a beach. From the jetty you can charter boats or book one-day or half-day trips to Ko Hae, Ko Lone, and other nearby islands for snorkeling, diving, parasailing, and other activities (B650–B1,200). Waterfront businesses survived the tsunami just fine.

Not far from Chalong Bay you can find **Wat Chalong,** the largest and most famous of Phuket's Buddhist temples. It enshrines gilt statues of two revered monks who helped quell an 1876 Chinese rebellion. They're wrapped in brilliant saffron robes. Wats are generally open during daylight hours, and you can show up at 5 PM to see the resident monks pray.

Where to Eat

$–$$ ✕ **Jimmy's Lighthouse Bar & Grill.** This very popular restaurant is still a hangout for sailors, though many of the old salts now go next door to the marina. The remaining crowd is largely tourists. The place is good both for lunch and dinner. ✉ *45/33 Chao Fa Rd.* ☎ *076/381709* ▭ *No credit cards.*

★ **$** ✕ **Kan Eang.** Grab a palm-shaded table next to the seawall and order some delicious grilled fish. Be sure that your waiter understands whether you want yours served *phet* (spicy hot) or *mai phet* (not spicy). Succulent and sweet crabs should be a part of any meal here. It's right on the waterfront to the south of the pier. ✉ *44/1 Viset Rd.* ☎ *076/381212* ▭ *AE, MC, V.*

Ko Hae (Coral Island)

㉝ *10 km (7mi) from Chalong Bay.*

Although this was once a quiet island, it's now a playground for (primarily) Asian tour groups. Before the tsunami slowed tourism down, as many as 1,000 day-trippers would race to the island each morning in an armada of speedboats that dropped them on shore. But after lunch the crowds leave and a quiet island remains. That's the time to be at Ko Hae. After a few repairs, the Coral Island Resort resort has returned to normal operations.

Where to Stay

$$ ✕▥ **Coral Island Resort.** This nice set of beachfront cottages works hard to keep a stiff upper lip in the face of the daily hordes that descend upon the rest of the beach. It's the only place to stay. Signs keep most of the nonguests at bay, leaving a quieter oasis around the resort. All the boat traffic stirs up the water, but also chases the fish to this end of the beach, making for decent snorkeling right in front of your room. Plus, the very friendly staff spends most of their mornings cleaning up the day-tripper's garbage, making this the cleanest stretch of beach. Several magnificent hornbills chatter at the guests here in the evenings, and you can sleep with your windows open and drift off to the sound of waves lapping at the beach. ✉ *48/11 Chaofa Rd., Chalong Bay, Phuket 83130* ☎ *076/281060* 🖶 *076/381957* ⊕ *www.coralislandresort.com* ⇥ *64 rooms* ⌂ *Restaurant, bar, pool, dive shop, billiards* ▭ *AE, MC, V* ⟋⟍ *EP.*

Cape Panwa

㉞ *10 km (6 mi) south of Phuket Town.*

Heading south out of Phuket Town (or northeast from Chalong Bay), follow the signs for Makham Bay, but don't stop there. This route will take you past the PTT petroleum dump, Phuket deep-sea port, and a Thai Navy base. At the end of the road is the Phuket Aquarium. Just a little farther on is Cape Panwa, where you can find several public spots to pull over and gaze over the ocean and outlying islands. The area was not damaged by the tsunami.

Where to Stay

★ **$$–$$$** ✕🏨 **Cape Panwa Hotel.** It could be argued that Sheraton made a mistake when it pulled out of this lovely place for its massive joint on Laguna Beach. Set in a hillside coconut grove with a secluded beach, this resort is the only thing here. And what a wonderful thing it is. Basic rooms are, well, basic yet tastefully appointed, and have wonderful sea views. The several villas on the property are very nice and come with every convenience. The Panwa House Restaurant is in an antiques-filled plantation house right off the beach. And the beach, though small, is perfectly secluded, accessible only from the resort or by boat. You can snorkel right in the bay. Furthermore, you won't go hungry here with eight bars and restaurants to choose from. The resort also features its own boat jetty and a tram to take you from the beach up the hill to your room. At this writing, it didn't yet contain the ubiquitous Phuket spa, but one is planned for late 2005. ✉ *27 Moo 8, Sakdidej Rd., Cape Panwa, Phuket 83000* ☎ *076/391123 up to 5* 🖷 *076/391177* ⊕ *www.capepanwa. com* 🛏 *246 rooms, 6 villas* ᗕ *2 pools, cable TV, in-room DVD players, Internet, gym, minibars, tennis courts, volleyball, water sports, meeting rooms, travel services* ▭ *AE, MC, V* ⦿| *EP.*

KO PHUKET A TO Z

AIR TRAVEL

Although flights to Phuket used to be quite expensive, the emergence of discount airlines has dropped prices dramatically. A flight now costs around B1,000–B1,500, little more than taking the train and a bus from Bangkok—but the trip takes just over an hour, rather than a full day.

Thai Airways flies between Bangkok and Ko Phuket six to eight daily. Bangkok Airways has four flights daily between Phuket and Bangkok and Phuket Air offers one flight a day between Bangkok and Phuket.

New, low-cost airlines include Air Asia and Orient Thai, both of which offer two to three flights per day. With Air Asia book and buy your tickets all online for the best fares. With Orient-Thai, you can book online for an added fee or just go to the airport to buy a ticket for the best price. Keep in mind that as tourism creeps back up to pre-tsunami levels, planes will fill up fast during high season.

🖪**Air Asia** ⊕ www.airasia.com. **Bangkok Airways** ☎ 076/351235 ⊕ www.bangkokair. com. **Orient Thai** ☎ 076/328620 ⊕ www.orient-thai.com. **Phuket Air** ☎ 076/351337 ⊕ www.phuketairlines.com. **Thai Airways** ☎ 076/211195 ⊕ www.thaiairways.com.

AIRPORTS & TRANSFERS

Phuket's airport is at the northern end of the island. All hotels are to the south. Be sure to check whether yours offers a free shuttle. Taxis meet all incoming flights. Fares are higher than in Bangkok; expect to pay B700 to Patong, Kata or Karon, or B400 to Phuket town. On your way back to the airport, you have to book a taxi for a minimum of B400. Many hotels charge B350–B400 per person.

There are also frequent minibus and van services to Phuket Town, Patong, Kata, and Karon that costs between B80 and B120. However, it might be worth springing for a cab as not all van drivers are reputable and might try to take you on an extended detour to a friend's shop or restaurant.

BUS TRAVEL

Numerous buses in various classes leave from Bangkok's Southern Bus Terminal, generally in the late afternoon and evening. The trip takes from 13 to 16 hours, depending on the bus and road conditions. You need to go to either a travel agent or to the bus station to check exact times and purchase tickets in advance, especially for VIP buses. Costs run from B278 for a non-air-conditioned bus to B755 for an air-conditioned VIP bus. VIP buses with ample leg room, padded foot rests and comfortable seats are well worth the added price. Be sure to have a long-sleeve shirt or sweater handy to combat the powerful air-conditioning. There will be stops along the way for food, drinks and bathroom breaks.

Most long-haul VIP buses are overnight, but you can leave Phuket on the 7 AM bus and arrive in Bangkok that evening. Day trips are recommended as Thailand's highways grow even more dangerous at night.

There are buses from Phuket to pretty much every major destination in southern Thailand. This includes, but is not limited to: Surat Thani, Krabi, Trang, Hat Yai, Satun, Phang Nga, and the ferry crossing to Ko Samui. You can check departure times at your hotel or the centrally located bus station just east of Montri Road, two blocks north of Phang Nga Road in Phuket Town.

CAR RENTALS

Residents of Phuket readily admit that their traffic is insane. Roads are badly congested and badly marked. That said, Phuket is the only island where you might want a car to get around. (Though it should be noted that even the Tourism Authority of Thailand recommends tourists avoid motorbikes here, either as taxis or rentals). All hotels can arrange for car rentals, and many have booking offices on the premises. Look for Avis, Budget, and Hertz at the airport. In town you can find rental cars at various private shops near the Pearl and Metropole hotels, as well as shops along all the major beaches. Prices will be a little lower than those at the airport, but not a lot.

You can rent a Suzuki Caribian (called a jeep) for as little as B700 per day in the off season. It's clunky but reliable transportation, though they tend to leak in heavy rains. Add another B500 for a Thai driver to deal with the nutty traffic. Small Toyota sedans start at B1,500 in the low season and can double in the high. The above prices do not include fuel, but do include a basic insurance plan.

🛈 **Agencies Avis** ✉ Phuket Airport ☎ 076/351244. **Budget** ✉ Phuket Airport ☎ 076/205396.

CAR TRAVEL

Here's a neat trick for the long-distance drivers in the crowd. You can take Highway 4 from Thonburi in Bangkok all the way to the Causeway at the north end of Phuket island, where it turns into Highway 402. It's a long drive, but once you're out of the capital all you have to do is follow the compass due south. Follow Highway 4 to Chumphon, where it jogs west and south and follows the Andaman Sea coast to Phuket Island. Phuket Town is 862 km (517 mi) from Bangkok; bus companies make the trip in 13–15 hours. Your results may vary.

Phuket isn't an island on which to take a leisurely Sunday drive. If you are driving, make sure you pick up at least two or three tourist maps (available at the airport, travel agencies and most any tourism-related office), as they differ in details. Streets are poorly marked, and you'll need all the help you can get.

EMERGENCIES
Emergency Numbers Fire ☎ 199. **Marine Police** ☎ 076/211–883. **Police** ☎ 191. **Tourist Police** ☎ 1699 or 076/219878 in Phuket.
Hospitals Bangkok Phuket Hospital ✉ 2/1 Hongyok Rd., Phuket Town ☎ 076/254424–30. **Phuket International Hospital** ☎ 076/249–400.

HEALTH
Fears of water contamination or disease outbreaks from the tsunami have so far been unfounded, but you might want to check with the CDC (www.cdc.gov) and the World Health Organization (www.who.int/en/) for the latest assessment before traveling here.

Though Phuket does not have as many dogs as other parts of Thailand, be extremely cautious around dogs you don't know. Furthermore, rabies is common in Thailand. If you're bitten, find a hospital quickly. Thai hospitals are used to treating dog bite patients (that should tell you something) and they use the same rabies treatment used in the United States. Don't be lax on this: once rabies symptoms start, there's nothing you can do.

MAIL
The reception desk at your hotel will post your cards and letters, a much easier option than hunting down the nearest post office.
Post Offices Phuket ✉ Montri Rd. and also on Phuket Rd., south of the roundabout **Patong** ✉ Thaweewong Rd. and also on Rat-u-Thit Rd. **Karon/Kata** ✉ Patak Rd.

MONEY MATTERS
Banks are easy to locate in Phuket Town, Patong, Karon Beach, and Kata Beach. All banks will exchange foreign currency and most have ATMs. Remember that hotel exchange rates are never as good as those at banks or currency exchange houses. The more remote the hotel, the less you'll get for your dollar.

SAFETY
Driving on Phuket is dangerous. Driving a motorcycle here is very dangerous. Hundreds of foreigners are injured here every year in motorcycle accidents. Furthermore, remember that a small wreck on a motorcycle is made much worse if you're only wearing shorts and flip-flops.

Every year a few foreigners drown in Phuket. Be very careful when swimming during the monsoon season, as strong undertows often develop, especially along the west coast. Pay close attention to posted warnings and listen if locals tell you not to swim in a certain place. Also watch out for jellyfish.

TAXIS & SONGTHAEWS

You'll never have a problem finding transportation in Phuket. There are no fleets of taxis here—what you'll find are the ubiquitous little red trucks known as tuk-tuks. And if you don't find one, don't worry; they'll find you. And they will be happy to take you to your destination for an absurd price. Be ready to bargain hard or simply walk away. Fares within any one town shouldn't be much more than B20 per trip, but they will often demand a flat B100. Keep in mind you can catch a minivan from the airport to Phuket town for B100, a distance of 30 km (19 mi).

There's supposedly a bus service in Phuket Town, but good luck finding one or a route map. The best and cheapest way of getting between beaches on the island is by the ubiquitous songthaews. You catch them in front of the market on Ranong Road or at the bus stops in the beach towns. These are marked on most maps and locals can help you find them. Prices run from B15 to B30 per trip depending on the beach you're visiting. They run every half-hour from 7 AM to 5 PM. If you miss that last songthaew, you may well spend B400 on a tuk-tuk for a ride that costs you only B15 earlier in the day. Hint: if you just missed that last songthaew, you can sometimes arrange a cut-rate ride on the sly with a hotel taxi driver who wants to go home or to a different beach town for dinner. If he drives alone, he makes no money. If he takes you for, say, half the normal hotel fare, he gets to keep that, which will probably pay for his dinner.

TOUR OPERATORS

As the saying goes, you can't throw a stone at a dog in Phuket without hitting a tour operator. Nearly all of them are selling the same package tours and renting the same cars and motorcycles, so feel free to comparison shop and haggle over prices. Common half-day sightseeing tours include visits to Wat Chalong, Rawai Beach, Phromthep Cape, and Khao Rang. Other half-day tours take in the Thai Cultural Village and the cultured-pearl farm on Nakha Noi Island.

It's not unreasonable to pay the extra money to book a trip or rental through your hotel: it's more convenient, you may be less likely to get ripped off, and it will give you an extra venue to complain to should something go wrong. In general, be wary of what tour operators tell you; they are in business to sell you a trip to the beach, not to tell you how to get there on your own. If you feel you have been ripped off or cheated, note the offender's name and other info and be sure to report him to the local Tourism Authority of Thailand office. Also let the manager at your hotel know, so he or she can steer other tourists clear.

That said, try Santana for diving and canoeing. They were Patong's first operator for such things, and are still in business. Also, they will pick you up so you don't have to go to Patong, which is a different sort of dive.

Dive Asia, in Kata Beach, is a certified PADI instructor and operator, in business since 1988.

John Gray's Sea Canoe is known internationally for ecotourism trips, including canoe trips through Phang Nga Bay. You can pick up a descriptive flyer at one of the ubiquitous travel shops, then book a tour directly from the company.

Elephant shows: Throughout the island, there are opportunities to ride or view elephants at work. Many were former logging elephants, whose jobs are now to entertain tourists. It's best to research the establishment a bit first; examine how the animals are kept and treated (Is it clean? Are they beaten?), and whether they show signs of abuse (such as sores on the legs from chains or other wounds). In Thailand, even some of the most well-known and respected facilities have been accused of abusing elephants. Be a conscientious traveler and do a little research, as conditions and reputations change quickly. And don't be afraid to make a statement. If you think chaining an elephant to a concrete slab in a park, or putting him on stage in a show, is not the best way to treat an elephant, then don't pay to see or ride him. Better yet, write a letter to the establishment and the Tourism Authority of Thailand.

🔏 **Dive Asia** ☎076/330598 ⊕www.diveasia.com. **John Gray's Sea Canoe** ☎076/254505 ⊕www.johngray-seacanoe.com. **Santana** ☎076/294220 ⊕www.santanaphuket.com.

TRAIN TRAVEL

Surat Thani is the closest train station to Phuket. A bus service links the two cities. Express trains from Bangkok's Hualamphong railway station stop at Surat Thani on their way south. The journey takes 12 hours or so. Note that if you leave Bangkok at 3 PM, you'll arrive to a dark train station in Surat Thani at around 3 AM. Sleepers are not available on all trains, so check first at a train station or with a travel agent. Prices vary depending on type of seat and speed of train. You can travel for as little as B400 in a hard, hot seat. These days, it's cheaper to fly a budget airline than to take a first-class sleeper that only gets you to Surat Thani.

VISITOR INFORMATION

The Tourism Authority of Thailand has offices in several resorts in southern Thailand. You can drop by for maps and brochures, as well as information about local excursions.

🔏 **Tourism Authority of Thailand** ✉ 73–75 Phuket Rd. ☎ 076/212213 ⊕ www.phukettourism.org.

THE ANDAMAN COAST

The Andaman Coast stretches from Ranong Province, bordering Myanmar to the north, to Satun Province, flanking Malaysia to the south. Along this shore are hundreds of islands and thousands of beaches. Because of their proximity to Phuket, Phang Nga and Krabi provinces are the two most popular destinations on the Andaman Coast.

The effects from the tsunami varied greatly around the region. Generally speaking, west-facing coasts were hardest hit, followed by south-

and north-facing shores. East-facing beaches and areas shielded to the west by other bodies of land were less harmed.

Cleanup was undertaken almost immediately, and considering the popularity of this region and the inherent economic value of these beautiful beaches and islands, reconstruction has and will continue to proceed rapidly. In some instances, Khao Lak, for example, resorts built in the year preceding the tsunami have already begun to be rebuilt exactly as they had been the year before, with reopenings occurring regularly. The impact on the beaches and underwater marine life was harmful in some regard and beneficial in others. Certain shallow coral reefs have been closed to the public pending further study. However, most beaches were not adversely affected by the waves; many areas were actually cleansed by the deep ocean water and are more beautiful than they have been in many years.

Phang Nga Bay National Park is Phang Nga's most heralded attraction, drawing thousands of day-trippers from Phuket. There are dozens of little islands to explore, as well as offshore caves and startling karst formations rising out of the sea. Most visitors make an obligatory stop at Phing Kan Island, made famous by the James Bond movie *The Man with the Golden Gun.*

The Similan and Surin Islands National Parks are well-known to scuba divers for their crystalline waters and abundant marine life. You can camp on either of the islands, as no commercial lodging is available in either park. Many divers opt to stay on live-aboard ships departing from Phuket or Khao Lak.

Prior to the tsunami, Khao Lak, the departure point for boats to the Similans, was an up-and-coming beach "town" in its own right. Khao Lak Lamru National park attracted nature lovers, while the beaches along this coast drew beachgoers who wanted a more tranquil vibe than Phuket has to offer. Although most resorts were destroyed, the "town" was spared and Khao Lak should once again be catering to solitude-seeking travelers by late 2006. Travelers looking for even greater seclusion head to the Ko Yao Islands, which has cultural tours and home stays that provide insight on southern Thai lifestyles.

Krabi Province lies to the east of Phuket. Its capital, Krabi Town, sits on the northeastern shore of Phuket Bay. Once a favorite harbor for smugglers bringing in alcohol and tobacco from Malaysia, the town has been transformed into a gateway to the nearby islands. Ao Nang, a short distance from Krabi Town, has evolved into a quaint beach town. Ao Nang, and nearby Noppharat Thara, exist simply to cater to tourists, and restaurants and shopping abound. With its coast lined with long-tail boats, Ao Nang is a more convenient base of operations for exploring nearby islands and beaches than Krabi Town is. Longtail boats and ferries depart Ao Nang to Ko Phi Phi, Ko Lanta, Nang Cape, and the multitude of smaller islands in eastern Phang Nga bay.

The islands of Ko Phi Phi were once idyllic retreats, with secret silver-sand coves, unspoiled stretches of shoreline, and limestone cliffs dropping precipitously into the sea. But then the islands were portrayed in

Andaman Coast

The Beach (2000). By the time the film had been released on DVD, Phi Phi was a hot property. Sadly, Ko Phi Phi was also hit hard by the tsunami, which destroyed many resorts, restaurants, bars, and shops along all but the east-facing beaches. The untouched beaches are certainly still beautiful and the affected areas were quickly cleaned up. As of spring 2005, many businesses were resuming normal operations.

Farther south, more adventurous travelers are discovering the relative serenity of Krabi's "hidden" gem, Ko Lanta. Ko Lanta, one of the largest islands in Thailand, has many beautiful beaches, accommodation to please both budget and spendthrifty travelers, and a few activities such as elephant trekking in the jungle.

Numbers in the text correspond to numbers in the margin and on the Andaman Coast map.

Phang Nga Bay National Marine Park

㉟ *100 km (62 mi) north of Phuket, 93 km (56 mi) northwest of Krabi.*

FodorśChoice
★

The best way—actually, the only way—to visit Phang Nga Bay is by boat. Talk with one of the travel agencies on Phuket that offers half-day tours of the area, or you can hire your own boat and spend as long as you want. There are two inlets, just before you reach the town of Phang Nga, where you can arrange for longtail boats. Most tour buses go to the western inlet, where you can rent a boat for about B1,300 for two hours. The second inlet sees fewer foreign tourists, so the prices are better—about B800 for three hours. The bay can be explored via tour boat, speed boat, or sea canoe. Most tourists don't arrive from Phuket until 11 AM, so if you get into the bay earlier you can explore it in solitude. To get an early start, you may want to stay overnight in the area. Be sure to take time to appreciate the sunsets, which are particularly beautiful on the island of **Ko Mak.**

There are several key sights around Phang Nga Bay. The island of **Ko Panyi** has a Muslim fishing village consisting of houses built on stilts. Restaurants are no bargain, tripling their prices for tourists. Beautiful **Ko Phing Kan**, now known locally as James Bond Island, is well worth a visit. The island of **Ko Tapu** resembles a nail driven into the sea. **Kao Kien** has overhanging cliffs covered with primitive paintings of elephants, fish, and crabs. Many are thought to be at least 3,500 years old. **Tham Lot** is a stalactite-studded cave that has an opening large enough for boats to pass through.

The tsunami had minimal effect on the islands of Phang Nga Bay. Rising tides from the tsunami wrap caused water damage to some coastal areas, but the impact was relatively minor and damage was repaired in early 2005.

Where to Stay & Eat

$-$$ ✕🏨 **Phang Nga Bay Resort Hotel.** Each of the comfortable rooms at this modern resort have private terraces overlooking a jungle-ringed estuary. The four levels are set back to ensure picture-perfect views from everywhere. The nearest beaches are more than 1 km (½ mi) away, but the hotel operates a boat that brings you there. Rooms are conventionally but comfortably furnished, with all modern amenities. The restaurant, which has a terrace overlooking the water, serves Thai, Chinese, and Western dishes. ⊠ *20 Thaddan Panyee, 82000* 🕾 *076/411067 or 01/917–4147* 🖷 *076/412057* 🛏 *88 rooms* ♨ *Restaurant, coffee shop, minibars, cable TV, 2 tennis courts, pool, billiards, dance club* 🗏 *AE, MC, V.*

¢ 🏨 **Ao Phang Nga National Park.** In addition to the camping grounds (where you can rent tents), the park has a few well-built bungalows within its grounds. The bungalows have one to three bedrooms (sleeps up to 10), and are either simple fan-cooled affairs or plusher with air-conditioning, TV, and minibars. Near the bungalows and visitor center are three piers for hiring boats to explore the park. Rates vary based on the number of individuals in your party. ⊠ *80 Ban Tha Dan Koh Panyi, 82000* 🕾 *076/522236, 02/5620760 for reservations* 🖷 *076/412188* ⊕ *www.dnp.go.th* 🛏 *8 bungalows* ♨ *Restaurant, travel services; no a/c in some rooms, no TVs in some rooms* 🗏 *No credit cards.*

¢ 🏨 **Sayan Guesthouse.** Operated by Sayan Tour out of Phang Nga town, Sayan Guesthouse gives you the opportunity to live in a Muslim fishing village on Ko Panyi. It's actually more of a tourist attraction than a true working fishing village, but it's both realistic and interesting. If you want to spend a night out in the bay, this is the only place to stay. If your stay is part of an overnight tour, your room price includes transfer via longtail boat from the mainland, a seafood dinner, and visits at all the interesting islands and caves in Phang Nga National Park. Huts are simple rattan structures with fans and mosquito nets. ⊠ *Ko Panyi, Phang Nga Bay, 82000* ☎ *076/430348* ⊕ *www.sayantour.com* ⋑ *9 rooms* ♨ *Fans, tour services* ▤ *MC, V.*

Ko Yao (Yao Island)

㊱ *45 min by boat from Bangrong Pier, Phuket or 45 min by boat from Chaofa Pier, Krabi*

Ko Yao Yai and Ko Yao Noi are the two large islands in the center of Phang Nga Bay. Both are quiet, peaceful places, fringed with sandy beaches and clear water. Most inhabitants still make their living through traditional means such as fishing, rubber tapping, and batik-painting. Considering their size and proximity to Phuket and Krabi, it's surprising how little development these islands have seen. During the 1990s many tourists began to discover the islands and the impact was, unsurprisingly, negative. So, to reduce the impact on the land and their culture the villagers residing on Ko Yao organized the "Ko Yao Noi Ecotourism Club" to regulate growth on the islands. They've certainly been successful—they even picked up a 2003 award for tourism development sponsored by Conservation International and *National Geographic Traveler.*

A visit to Ko Yao will allow you to experience the local culture and customs while exploring the beauty of the islands (kayak and mountain bike are popular transportation options). The Ecotourism Club provides homestays if you really want the full experience of the islands; otherwise, most resorts provide day tours or information for self-guided exploration.

Where to Stay & Eat

$$$–$$$$ ✕▥ **Koyao Island Resort.** Koyao Island Resort has arguably the best view
Fodor'sChoice of any beach resort in Thailand. From east-facing Haad Pa Sai you have
★ a panoramic vista of a string of magnificent islands. The bungalows are almost entirely open-air so you not only admire the surroundings, you're part of them—you can even throw open the doors and watch the sunrise from your bed! An ideal romantic hideaway, Koyao Island Resort even arranges private beach barbecues. Although the beach is not great for swimming or sunbathing, there are beach chairs on the grass beside the sea, and kayaks and mountain bikes available for use around the island. Boats can be hired to visit nearby islands for diving or snorkeling, and day trips, including cultural tours to batik and Muslim fisherman villages, can be arranged. The restaurant serves great fresh seafood; you can select your meal from their saltwater pond. ⊠ *24/2 Koh Yao Noi, Phang Nga, 82160* ☎ *076/597474* 🖷 *076/597477* ⊕ *www.koyao.com* ⋑ *15 villas* ♨ *Restaurant, fans, cable TVs, minibars, IDD phones, in-room safes, Internet, library, massage, boating, babysitting, airport shuttle* ▤ *AE, MC, V.*

CloseUp

KHAO LAK

BEFORE THE TSUNAMI, the coastal area collectively known as Khao Lak was one of Thailand's hottest new resort destinations. Originally used as just a launching point for boat trips to the idyllic Similan Islands, Khao Lak quickly blossomed into a tourist destination in its own right.

Unfortunately, Khao Lak bore the full brunt of the tsunami and it devastated most of the resorts along the coast, killing thousands of Thais and international tourists. Very few resorts were not completely destroyed. And though the area's shops, restaurants, and bars lie on the road that runs along a hill (far beyond the high water mark), the destruction of the resorts and the devastating death toll halted all tourist arrivals, causing undamaged businesses to shut down.

Directly after the disaster, the Thai government made some very optimistic claims that Khao Lak would recover within a year. Although some damaged properties were giving fall 2005 reopening dates, most tour operators are skeptical, and believe a two-year target is more realistic. It's anyone's guess how quickly the area will be revived, but it won't be surprising if Khao Lak is welcoming tourists once again in early 2006.

Khao Lak-Lamru National Marine Park (☎ 076/720023, 02/5790529 for National Park Division in Bangkok ⊕ www.dnp.go.th) is still one of the area's primary attractions. The park grounds cover more than 125 square mi from the sea to the mountains, including a secluded sandy beach and several waterfalls, and preserves some pristine tropical evergreen forest. Three rudimentary cabins are available for rent, as are tents. The park headquarters is on the road from Khao Lak beach to Khao Lak town.

If you're in the Khao Lak area, check out two local businesses that were not affected by the tsunami and will be open by fall 2005. **Jai Restaurant** (⊠ 5/1 Moo 7 ☎ 09/7287250 or 076/420390 ▤ No credit cards) is popular with the locals, which is always a good sign. Choose your own fish or jumbo prawns from the display boat out front and then select a cooking style. We suggest deep-fried snapper with chili sauce (not spicy). The **Happy Snapper Bar** (☎ 076/423540 ⊕ www. happysnapperbar.com) is owned by a renowned Thai rock musician and is known for having live music five nights a week. Although this hip venue would hold its own in Bangkok, it's perfectly in sync with the area and the staff is very friendly.

Only a handful of resorts survived the tsunami. **La Flora** (⊠ 59/1 Bang Niang Beach, 882190 ☎ 076/428000 ⊟ 076/423499 ⊕ www.sanctuaryresorts. com ▤ AE, MC, V), a boutique resort, was one of the area's best lodging options. It was hit hard by the tsunami shortly after its grand opening, but it quickly set upon rebuilding and is scheduled to reopen in late 2005 or early 2006. When it's restored to its former glory, it will have a spa and three upscale restaurants.

Another beautiful resort, **Baan Krating** (⊠ 28 Khao Lak, 82190 ☎ 076/423088 ⊟ 076/423087 ⊕ www.baankrating. com), has a fortunate location, on a cliff above a rocky beach—it was not damaged by the tsunami at all. The beautiful view here and a path to the beach that travels within Khao Lak Lamru National park will help ensure that the resort will survive.

The best budget option in the area is **Khao Lak Nature Resort** (⊠ 26/10 Khao Lak), near the Khao Lak Lamru National Park. Basic wooden huts have rattan walls and many windows that look out into the surrounding forest. Note that some huts don't have air-conditioning.

¢ ▦ **Koh Yao Homestay.** Koh Yao Homestay is organized by a community of Koh Yao residents who welcome tourists to share their way of life. The community provides visitors with lodging in their own homes, meals (consisting primarily of fish caught by village fishermen), and knowledge about their local customs. Visitors learn about rubbertapping, batik-dying, fishing, rice-farming, coconut-harvesting and other traditional trades from the people who have practiced them for centuries. More environmentally friendly and less invasive on the island's indigenous people than resort development, the homestay program is a unique way to learn about local people while helping to preserve their way of life. ✉ *Baan Laem Sai, Koh Yao Noi, Phang Nga, 82160* ☎ *076/597428* ⊕ *www.kohyaohomestay.com* ▭ *No credit cards.*

Mu Ko Similan National Marine Park

★ *70km (45 mi) 1.5 hrs by boat from Thaplamu Pier*

The Similan Islands National Park consists of the nine Similan Islands, as well as Ko Tachai and Ko Bon, which are located farther north. Before the tsuanmi, the diving around the Similan Islands was world class, with visibility of up to 120 feet; abundant blue, green, and purple coral; and rare marine life, such as whale shark, the world's largest fish. The tsunami had a considerable effect on the islands. Shallow reefs were particularly hard hit, and as of this writing islands 1, 2, and 3 were indefinitely closed to divers, snorkelers, and visitors. In addition, the popular dive sites Christmas Point and the Great Wall were also closed pending further study of the tsunami's impact.

The national park service allows visitors to stay on Ko Miang (island 4) and Ko Similan (island 8). The tsunami destroyed all the original bungalows on the islands but new ones were scheduled for completion by November 2005. Ko Miang, where the park headquarters is located, will have bungalows with 24-hour electricity and, like the old ones, some will have air-conditioning, and some will have ocean views. Beachside camping will also be available on Ko Miang (the park rents out roomy tents, large enough to stand in, which have two camping cots). Ko Similan has no bungalows, but has the same large tents for rent, as well as an area for visitors to set up their own tents for B80 per person. Tour groups, such as Jack's Similan (☎ 07/644–3205) have their own smaller tents set up in this area, and rent them out for the same fee charged by the national park. There are also overnight packages, which include tours of the islands, as well as camping and food.

Contact the park or dive operators in Phuket for the latest on the status of the Similans. Note that the islands are normally closed to visitors from mid-May through mid-November. ☎ *076/595045 for campsite reservations, 02/5620760 for bungalow reservations* ⊕ *www. dnp.go.th.*

Mu Ko Surin National Marine Park

60 km (37 mi), 2 hrs by boat from Kuraburi pier

Ko Surin is a remote island paradise practically unknown to anyone other than adventurous scuba divers and Thais. Five islands make up Mu Ko Surin National Park, each featuring sea turtles, varieties of shark, and plentiful coral (some even claim to have spotted the occasional whale shark, the world's largest fish). There are several hiking trails that lead to waterfalls and a sea gypsy village if you get tired of sun and sea.

The tsunami hit the Surin islands quite hard, damaging shallow reefs and destroying all park structures. As of this writing all diving was closed indefinitely, pending evaluation of the reefs. Contact the **National Park Service** (☎ 076/5620760 general inquiries, 02/5620760 for bungalow reservations ⊕ www.dnp.go.th) for the latest information. Note that the park is normally closed during rainy season (June–November).

There were basic but comfortable wooden huts on Koh Surin Nua, and tent camping was allowed at a site that had decent facilities, including toilets and showers. We assume that these services will resume when the park reopens, but you should inquire through the numbers listed above.

Krabi Town

③⑦ *814 km (506 mi) south of Bangkok, 180 km (117 mi) southeast of Phuket, 43 km (27 mi) by boat east of Ko Phi Phi.*

Krabi Town is a pleasant place to visit, but most visitors pause just long enough to cash traveler's checks, arrange onward travel, and catch up on the news at one of the cafés on Uttarakit Road. However, there are several decent restaurants, a Tourism Authority of Thailand office, and a night market for souvenir shopping. Krabi locals are determined to keep Phuket-style development at bay, and so far—despite the opening of an airport 12 km (7 mi) from town—they are succeeding. Not even the tsunami had much effect on Krabi Town, causing minimal damage to infrastructure. If anything it has helped keep Krabi quiet and inexpensive, as many tourists are only slowly returning to the province.

Just 3 km (2 mi) from Krabi Town is **Wat Tham Sua.** Built in 1976 as a monastery and meditation retreat, Wat Tham Sua is both respected by the local population and popular with tourists. Locals come to participate in Buddhist rituals, tourists to climb the 1,277 steps to panoramic views of the cliffs, Krabi Town, Krabi river, and the Panom Benja mountain range. There's also a cave with many chambers, which can be fun to explore, though it's not terribly attractive. A really large tree grows outside the entrance. The wat is between Krabi Town and the airport. ✉ *Tambon Muang Chum, 4 km after Wachiralongkorn Dam.*

> **off the beaten path**
>
> **THAN BOKKHARANI NATIONAL PARK** – Between Krabi and Phang Nga is this forested park, which has several emerald-green ponds surrounded by tropical foliage, including wild gardenia and apocynaceae. The pools are filled with refreshing cool water, fed by a mountain spring 4 km (2½ mi) away. The largest pond is 40 by 30

meters, deep and suitable for swimming. The pools are best visited in the dry season, as they get quite murky when it rains. There's a B200 admission fee. ⊹ *From Krabi: take Highway 4 to Ao Luek, then turn onto Route 4039* ☎ *066/7568–1071.*

Where to Stay & Eat

¢–$$ ✗ **Kotung Restaurant.** Although surrounded by various Western-style cafés, guesthouses, and tour agents, Kotung still stands out with its unassuming classic Thai style and is frequented by Krabi locals. The menu is standard Thai and Chinese, with a selection of fresh seafood, too. Neither the design of the restaurant or the food itself is flashy, but it's genuinely good. The location by the busy riverside makes Kotung an excellent place for people-watching. ⊠ *Kong Ka Rd.* ☎ *075/611522* ▭ *No credit cards.*

¢ ✗ **Chao Fa Pier Street Food Stalls.** Looking for local quality food at a low price? This strip of street-side foodstalls serves everything from simple fried rice to more sophisticated southern delicacies such as *kanom jeen* (rice noodles topped with whatever sauces and vegetables you want). Open from nightfall until midnight, these stalls serve as an excellent opportunity to discover some exotic and enjoyable Thai foods. ⊠ *Chao Fa Pier, Khong Kha Rd.* ▭ *No credit cards.*

$$–$$$$ ▦ **Krabi Maritime Park and Spa Resort.** This resort extends over 25 acres, and features a mangrove forest, a sprawling lagoon, a large swimming pool, and views of Krabi's signature limestone cliffs. The spa has a Jacuzzi that sits upon small tented piers above the lagoon. The large rooms look out over water, forest, and stunning cliffs. ⊠ *1 Tungfa Rd., 81000* ☎ *075/620028–46* 📠 *075/612992* ⊕ *www.maritimeparkandspa.com* ➥ *221 rooms* ⟑ *Restaurant, room service, cable TV, minibars, gym, massage, spa, bar, pool, pond, laundry service, meeting rooms, travel services* ▭ *AE, MC, V.*

¢–$ ▦ **City Hotel.** Rooms in the old wing of this hotel are simple but very clean, with air-conditioning or fans; rooms in the new wing are standard, modern hotel rooms with carpet and air-conditioning. Both buildings are near the night market and the river. ⊠ *15/2–4 Sukon Rd., 81000* ☎ *075/611961 or 075/621280* 📠 *075/621282* ➥ *124 rooms* ⟑ *Cable TV, laundry service, travel services; no a/c in some rooms* ▭ *No credit cards.*

¢–$ ▦ **Thai Hotel.** Miss the boat to Phuket? If you need an inexpensive place to stay overnight, this will do the trick. The location, a block from the pier, couldn't be more convenient. Rooms are cozy and comfortable, if a bit run-down. ⊠ *7 Isara Rd., 81000* ☎ *075/611474 up to 6* 📠 *075/620564* ➥ *150 rooms* ⟑ *Restaurant; no a/c in some rooms* ▭ *MC, V.*

en route | **Shell Cemetery** is a pleasant beach park between Ao Nang and Krabi Town. It has a small information center explaining how snails from tens of millions of years ago were preserved for us to wonder about today. The fossils are probably not that interesting to most people, but the beach here is pleasant for a dip (although sunbathing in skimpy suits would be inappropriate, as many Thai families picnic on the hill above). Also, the view from the hill is quite nice, and if you're cruising on a motorbike, this is a fine place to get some shade in between destinations.

Ao Nang

★ ❸❽ *20 km (12 mi) from Krabi Town.*

Although Ao Nang beach is not much of an attraction, the strip facing it underwent a face-lift in 2002 that transformed it into a pleasant promenade of hotels, shops, and restaurants. During the day, longtail boats depart Ao Nang for the more spectacular beaches and waters of Nang Cape and Hong, Poda, Gai, Lanta, and Phi Phi Islands. Less adventurous types can find nicer sand and better water for swimming on the far eastern end of the beach or at Noppharat Thara Beach National Park to the west. In the evening, storefronts light up the sidewalk and open-air restaurants provide excellent venues to kick back with a beer and watch the crowd go by. For a more romantic atmosphere, head to the half-dozen seafood restaurants atop a pier extending from the bend in Liab Chai Haad road in between Ao Nang and Noppharat Thara beaches.

Noppharat Thara Beach, a 15-minute walk from central Ao Nang is a quieter, more relaxing environment. The renovated walking path was extended here from Ao Nang in 2004, but as of this writing, the development had not yet followed it. The National Park at the western end has shady casuarina trees and a clean, quiet beach.

A narrow river pier delineates the western edge of Noppharat Thara National Park. Here, you can catch boats departing from the pier to Railey, Phi Phi, and Lanta, or simply cross to the other side and enjoy the unspoiled natural beauty of **Laem Son Beach.** Farther north are the beaches of **Klong Muang** and **Tubkaak,** beautiful stretches of sand with amazing views that are occupied by the upmarket resorts situated there.

Both Ao Nang and Noppharat Thara beaches received only minimal damage from the tsunami. Disrepair was quickly mended—the impact from declining tourist arrivals has been more harmful than the effects of the waves.

Where to Stay & Eat

$–$$$ ✕ **Ao Nang Cuisine.** Believe the hype! The sign outside the restaurant brags that its chef, Mrs. Phaichat, is world famous, having worked at several well-known Thai eateries, including Chao Phraya Restaurant in Hollywood, California. The melt-in-your-mouth chicken satay (curry chicken skewers), an otherwise ordinary dish, is prepared superbly here, with a side of spicy peanut sauce. More elaborate Thai dishes are available for tourists who are tired of streetside barbecue seafood. ✉ *245/4 Liab Chai Haad Rd.* ☎ *075/637253 or 075/695399* ▭ *MC, V.*

$–$$$ ✕ **Café 154 Restaurant and Gallery.** This groovy French fusion café is owned by a classy Frenchman, Ton, who has become a Krabi establishment himself. 154's menu is entirely "farang" food, but it's quality farang food. Incredible sandwiches are served on French loaves with real Dijon mustard. Entrées feature lamb and beef imported from Australia. Filet mignon with potato gratin is one of the house specialties, served with a sauce of your selection. Also recommended is the homemade sausage flambeé. The backyard has alfresco candlelight dining with a view of the cliffs. And there's a happy hour from 5 to 8 PM. It's just north of Ao Nang Beach. ✉ *153 Liab Chai Haad Rd., Ao Nang* ☎ *075/637838* ⚓ *Reservations essential* 🖃 *MC, V.*

$$$$ 🏨 **The Cliff.** You can get a good view of the cliff that inspired the hotel's name as soon as you enter the lobby. But then your attention will quickly shift to burned bricks, charred wooden tiles, and natural wooden beams that create an atmosphere reminiscent of ancient Srivijaya Period of Siam. The Cliff's villas are set around a nonchlorine, ozone-treated swimming pool. The rooms, each with outdoor shower, feature glass bay doors on two sides. The suite is on stilts above a small private fish-pond and is particularly popular with honeymooners. ✉ *85/2 Liab Chai Haad Rd., Ao Nang, 81000* ☎ *075/638117* 🖷 *075/638116* ⊕ *www.k-bi.com* ⇆ *20 rooms, 1 suite* ♨ *Restaurant, minibars, cable TVs, pool, room service* 🖃 *AE, DC, MC, V.*

$$$$ 🏨 **Sheraton Krabi Beach Resort.** The Sheraton Krabi is built around an expansive mangrove forest that covers the grounds, but there's a wide, sandy beach on the premises. All of the contemporary and colorful standard rooms overlook the forest, while the six suites have views of the sea. There are many activities to keep guests occupied, including Muay Thai classes taught by a World Champion Thai boxer, Frisbee golf, and swimming with Rara, the baby elephant. The pool, restaurants, and bar are down by the beach, where various water sports are available, and sunbathing and swimming are great. ✉ *155 Klong Muang Beach, Nongtalay, 810000* ☎ *075/628000* 🖷 *075/628028* ⊕ *www.sheraton.com* ⇆ *246 rooms, 6 suites* ♨ *2 restaurants, room service, in-room safes, minibars, cable TV, tennis court, pool, gym, shops, 2 bars, Internet, travel services* 🖃 *AE, DC, MC, V.*

★ **$$$$** 🏨 **The Tubkaak.** The elegant wooden buildings here each resemble a *kor lae,* a traditional Southern Thai fishing boat. Tubkaak Beach is calm and lovely, and the rooms have spectacular views of the Hong Islands. All superior and deluxe rooms are a few steps to the free-form swimming pool, while seaview villas are only steps from the beach. A cozy library and bar has books and games for rainy days and relaxing evenings. The small size of the Tubkaak makes you feel at home and friendly staff make everyone feel like family. ✉ *123 Taab Kaak Beach, Nongtalay, 81000* ☎ *075/628400* 🖷 *075/628499* ⊕ *www.tubkaakresort.com* ⇆ *44 rooms, 2 suites* ♨ *Restaurant, in-room safes, minibars, cable TV, CDs, sauna, massage, spa, boating, fishing, bar, library, laundry service, car rental* 🖃 *AE, MC, V.*

★ **$$–$$$** 🏨 **Ao Nang Inn.** When selecting a room at this inn on the shore of Ao Phra Nang Beach, you can choose between the coconut wing and the betelnut wing. The difference? Well, the rooms in the former are constructed from coconut palms, while those in the latter . . . well, you get the picture. The resort has a wonderfully kooky vibe—you might find headboards decorated with bright paintings of seashells and fish in the coconut wing and a few pieces of furniture might look like they're made from tree branches in the betelnut wing. Even the bar, called the 75 Million Year Pub, is a little odd. The central location is also a big plus. ✉ *119 Liab Chai Haad Rd., Ao Nang, 81000* ☎ *075/637130* 🖷 *075/637134* ⊕ *www.*

phrananginn.com 🖾 *83 rooms* ☖ *2 restaurants, room service, minibars, cable TV, 2 pools, hot tub, massage, spa, snorkeling, boating, library, Internet, laundry service, airport shuttle* 🖃 *AE, DC, MC, V.*

$–$$ 🏨 **Krabi Resort.** Krabi Resort is the only beachfront lodging in Ao Nang town. You can also find the best swimming here and a seaside "park" with plenty of benches positioned for gazing at the sea. That said, the resort is aging a bit, with rows of well-built, but noticeably dated wooden bungalows near the beach featuring day-glow interior paint and clashing bedspreads. The two-story building with rooms overlooking the pool is also well kept, but looks and feels very 1970s. Fortunately, some renovations are underway. Likewise, new junior suites were built in 2004 on the hillside not far from the beach. 🖾 *232 Liab Chai Haad Rd., Ao Nang, 81000* ☎ *075/637030–5, 02/208–9165 in Bangkok* 🖶 *075/637051* ⊕ *www.krabiresort.net* 🖾 *167 rooms, 5 suites* ☖ *Restaurant, minibars, cable TV, pool, tennis court, boating, meeting rooms, nightclub* 🖃 *AE, DC, MC, V.*

$$ 🏨 **Best Western Anyavee Ao Nang and Spa.** The resort is a cluster of four-story buildings in Thai design, including Northern-style peaked roofs. The large swimming pool has a waterfall you can swim through to have a drink at the pool bar. Rooms are contemporary Thai, austere but tastefully trimmed with hardwood. The resort is on a small rise a bit far from the sea, but that means it overlooks the hills and water around (and below) it. 🖾 *31/3 Liab Chai Haad, Ao Nang, 81000* ☎ *075/695051–4* 🖶 *075/695050* ⊕ *www.anyavee.com* 🖾 *71 rooms* ☖ *Restaurant, cable TV, minibars, in-room safes, pool, massage, spa, laundry service, airport shuttle* 🖃 *AE, DC, MC, V.*

$ 🏨 **Srisuksant Resort.** On the eastern end of Noppharat Thara, Srisuksant is a short walk from Ao Nang's shops and directly across from the beach. The beach across from the resort is not ideal for swimming, but longtail boats are available to whisk you away to more suitable beaches, and if you feel like walking west a few miles, you can swim or picnic in the shade by the Noppharat Thara National Park headquarters. The resort has two swimming pools for cooling off if you're too lazy to do any of the above. The clientele here is mostly Thai families, although Westerners are greeted warmly. The bright rooms have tile floors and small decks. Some rooms have partial ocean views. 🖾 *145 Noppharat Thara Beach, 81000* ☎ *075/638002–4* 🖶 *075/695260* ⊕ *www.srisuksantresort.com* 🖾 *66 rooms* ☖ *Restaurant, cable TV, minibars, in-room safes, 2 pools, travel services* 🖃 *MC, V.*

★ ¢–$ 🏨 **The Emerald Bungalow.** If quiet relaxation is your goal, this is your destination. On isolated Laem Son beach, Emerald Bungalow is a family-run resort that provides genuine Thai hospitality. Tall pines, arching coconut trees, flowers, and ferns abound, and many birds, including a few chickens, inhabit the grounds. Budget-conscious travelers can enjoy proximity to the beach from basic wooden huts. Larger, newer air-conditioned villas have individually designed layouts and interior design, but all include some Thai art. The resort is across the river from Noppharat Thara National Park. 🖾 *Noppharat Thara Beach, 81000* ☎ *01/8921072 or 01/9562566* 🖶 *075/631119* ☖ *Restaurant, a/c in some rooms, volleyball, laundry service* 🖃 *No credit cards.*

¢ ⊡ **Jinda Guesthouse 1 & 2.** Inexpensive lodgings are hard to find in Ao Phra Nang, but a short walk from the beach you can find this basic guesthouse. It's not luxurious, but manages to be quite cozy nonetheless and the price is definitely right. Jinda Guesthouse 1 is older, facing the main street. Jinda Guesthouse 2 is new, around the corner, on the small alley, where several other budget accommodations can be found. ⊠ *247/6 Liab Chai Haad Rd., Ao Nang, 81000* ☎ *075/695068 or 075/637524* 🖷 *075/ 695414* 🛏 *17 rooms* ♿ *Restaurant; no a/c in some rooms* ▭ *No credit cards.*

Nightlife

Funky tunes, a view of the beach, and an extremely inviting atmosphere make most people become repeat customers at the aptly named **Bad Habit Bar** (⊠ Noppharat Thara Beach, Liab Chai Haad Rd., Ao Nang ☎ 075/ 637882 or 06/2792712). The bar is midway down Noppharat Thara beach directly across from the beach and next to the Andaman Spa. The bar serves food, thanks to owner Khun Oil, a native Southerner and great cook. Drink prices are reasonable (beer for B50 and cocktails for B100). It's one of the nicest pubs in the area and good times are pretty much guaranteed.

Encore Café (⊠ 245/23 Liab Chai Haad, Nang Beach, Ao Nang ☎ 075/ 637107) has live music five to seven nights a week from prominent local and expat musicians who play rock, reggae, blues, jazz, funk, folk, and fusion Western-Thai tunes. Hidden back behind the main road in Central Ao Nang, Encore Café is one of the only places to hear quality music while knocking back some beers and eating Thai and Western pub grub.

Nang Cape

39 *15 min by longtail boat east of Ao Nang*

Don't strain your neck admiring the sky-scraping cliffs as your longtail boat delivers you to Nang Cape; the isolated beaches on Tonsai, Phra Nang, and East and West of Railay, only accessible by boat, are sandy oases surrounded by vertical sandstone cliffs. The four beaches are connected by walking paths and each have their own attractions. Tonsai Beach, with a pebble strewn shore and shallow, rocky water, caters to budget travelers and rock climbers. West Railay has powdery white sand, shallow but swimmable water, gorgeous sunset views, and many kayaks for hire. East Railay, a mangrove-lined shore unsuitable for beach or water activities, draws rock-climbing enthusiasts, as well as younger travelers looking for late-night drinks and loud music. Phra Nang Beach, one of the nicest beaches in all Krabi, is ideal for swimming, sunbathing, and rock climbing.

Damage from the tsunami was superficial and repairs were made quickly. Like other areas, the impact from reduced tourist arrivals has been more damaging than the waves.

Where to Stay & Eat

★ $$$$ ✕⊡ **Rayavadee Premier Resort.** Scattered across 26 landscaped acres, this magnificent resort is set in coconut groves with white-sand beaches on three sides. The lobby faces East Railay, the pool looks out over

West Railay Bay, and the beach bar and restaurant are the only structures on Phra Nang beach—Rayavadee has the only direct access to this beautiful stretch of sand. Circular pavilions built in traditional Thai style have spacious living rooms with curving staircases that lead up to opulent bedrooms and baths with huge, round tubs. Some of the best rooms have secluded gardens with private hot tubs. Four restaurants assure variety—the beach front Krua Pranang set in a breezy pavilion, serves outstanding Thai food. ⊠ *214 Railay Beach, Ao Nang, 81000* ☎ *075/620740* 🖷 *075/620630* ⊕ *www.rayavadee. com* ⟋ *98 rooms 5 suites ♢ 4 restaurants, room service, in-room safes, kitchenettes, minibars, cable TV, in-room VCRs, pool, massage, spa, boating, fishing, bar, shop, Internet, laundry service, airport shuttle, travel services* ▱ *AE, DC, MC, V.*

$$-$$$$ ⤬🏨 **Railay Bay Resort and Spa.** Great Thai food and a beachside patio and bar from which you can watch the sunset are a few good reasons to visit Railay Bay Resort and Spa. Basic cottages and rooms in a row of modern two-story buildings are suitable reasons to lodge here, also. Get a massage in a room overlooking the beach and pool and you may never want to leave. This resort in the center of West Railay appeals to people who like a natural environment—one that comes with plenty of amenities, such as a minimart, Internet, and air-conditioning. A walking path connects West and East Railay for easy access to Phra Nang beach. ⊠ *145 Moo 2, Railay West Beach, Krabi, 81000* ☎ *075/ 622570-2* 🖷 *075/622573* ⊕ *www.railaybay-resort.com* ⟋ *133 rooms, 10 suites ♢ Restaurant, minibars, in-room safes, pool, massage, spa, Internet, travel services* ▱ *MC, V.*

$$-$$$$ 🏨 **Railei Beach Club.** Each of the 20 privately owned homes here is in-
Fodor'sChoice dividually designed (and named) giving each its own unique character.
  ★ Solly's house, a two-story glass house on the beach, is particularly popular. The houses sleep between two and eight persons and most have large decks and kitchens. Powdery white sand is a short walk away and kayaks are available. Feeling lazy? The staff can go into town and shop for you. Really lazy? A cook can be arranged. Booking ahead is a must. Note that there's no electricity from 6 AM to 6 PM. ⊠ *Box 8, Krabi, 81000* ☎ *075/622582* 🖷 *075/622596* ⊕ *www.raileibeachclub.com* ⟋ *20 houses ♢ Fans, kitchenettes, minibars* ▱ *No credit cards.*

  ¢ 🏨 **Railay Highland Resort.** While admiring the sweeping view of the towering limestone cliffs, take a closer look and you may see teeny people scaling the rockface. Awake early and you can witness the sunrise over the distant bay. The restaurant and bar have amazing views, the rooms are set back in the hillside, spread out among the trees. Basic huts with rattan walls and thatched roofs have mattresses on the floor with mosquito nets. There's no hot water, but electricity runs 24 hours. This is a great spot for rock-climbers or people who want to chill out and don't mind roughing it a bit. ⊠ *Moo 1, Railay East Beach, Krabi, 81000* ☎ *075/621730-2* 🖷 *075/637814* ⟋ *20 bungalows ♢ Restaurant, fans, dive shop, bar, laundry service* ▱ *No credit cards.*

Sports & the Outdoors

ROCK-CLIMBING Climbers discovered the cliffs around Nang Cape in the late 1980s. The mostly vertical cliffs rising out of the sea were, and certainly are, a dream comes true for hardcore climbers. Today, anyone daring enough can learn to scale the face of a rock in one of the most beautiful climbing destinations in the world. Level of difficulty ranges from American standard 5.8 to 5.13c (V to X, according to UIAA). There are 500 to 600 established routes. Notable climbs include the Tonsai beach overhang and Thaiwand Wall, where climbers must use lanterns to pass through a cave and then rappel down from the top. Most climbing organizations are found on East Railay. Cliffs Man, Tex, and King Climbers are a few of the originals. King Climbers provides rescue services, though hopefully you won't need them.

Koh Phi Phi

40 *48 km (30 mi) 90 min by boat southeast of Phuket Town; 42 km (26 mi) 2 hrs by boat southwest of Krabi.*

The Phi Phi Islands consist of six islands, approximately 40 km off the coast of Krabi. **Phi Phi Don**, the largest of the islands, is shaped like a butterfly: The "wings," covered by limestone mountains, are connected by a flat 2-km (1 mi) narrow body featuring two opposing sandy beaches. Phi Phi Don is the only inhabited island.

The tsunami drastically changed the face of the islands, Phi Phi Don in particular. It devastated Loh Dalam Bay and a great deal of Tonsai Bay, too, where much of the "town" was, as well as the docks where tourists would pour off ferries every day. Practically all of the resorts along the narrow body between the two beaches were destroyed. Newer, better constructed shops, bars, and restaurants at Tonsai were strong enough to survive the waves. But only resorts and businesses on Long Beach and the more remote, eastern facing beaches were spared heavy damage. Consequently, these beaches are now getting the attention that they deserve. Visitors, few in number at first, have began to discover the magic of sandy and swimmable Laem Tong beach and peaceful and beautiful Long Beach, which had lived in the shadow of busier Tonsai Beach. It's difficult to predict how soon the island will recover. As of April 2005, repair of salvageable buildings was underway, but reconstruction of destroyed property was on hold pending new zoning regulations.

The popularity of the Phi Phi Islands stems from the outstanding scuba diving. The tsunami had very little effect on the dive sites here. Some say the diving is better than before, as the water seems clearer.

A popular day trip from Phi Phi Don is a visit to nearby **Phi Phi Lae** via longtail or speed boat. The first stop is Viking Cave, a vast cavern of limestone pillars covered with crude drawings. Most boats continue on for an afternoon in Maya Bay, aka "The Beach." Avoid Maya Bay, where snorklers practically outnumber the fish; secluded Loh Samah Bay is smaller but much nicer. If you don't mind huge crowds, however, Maya Bay is a spectacular site.

Alternately, you can take a 45-minute trip by longtail boat to circular **Bamboo Island**, with a superb beach around it. The underwater colors of the fish and the coral are brilliant. The island is uninhabited, but you can spend a night under the stars if you're adventuresome. You can also hike up to a series of viewpoints towards the 314-meter peak on the east side of the island. The trail-head is near Tonsai Bay; ask your hotel for directions.

Where to Stay & Eat

The following properties were either on the side of the island that was not greatly impacted by the tsunami or suffered superficial damage that already had been repaired at this writing.

¢–$$ ✕ **Siam Kitchen and Restaurant.** Wafts of mouth-watering smoke fill the air outside Siam Kitchen and Restaurant (across from Sea Frog Divers, towards the eastern end of the Tonsai town). B120 gets you half a chicken, a baked potato, and a salad at this colorful corner cafe. They serve a variety of other food, too, including Thai and seafood, but the chicken is fabulous. ⊠ *Between Tonsai and Loh Dalam Beaches* ☎ *01/ 7972682* ▭ *No credit cards.*

¢–$$ ✕ **Thai Cuisine.** This restaurant was damaged by the tsunami, although not nearly as badly as others along the main Tonsai road. It may not be open again until late 2005, but once it's up and running, it's definitely worth a visit. Fresh seafood is not hard to come by on Phi Phi, but even so, Thai Cuisine's selection of white shark, barracuda, swordfish, lobster, and crab had people lining up outside to get a table. In addition to finely cooked fish, Thai Cuisine makes great fried rice. Look for the restaurant with all rattan walls and ceiling across from the air-conditioned bakery in the middle of Tonsai "town." ⊠ *Central Tonsai Beach, Koh Phi Phi* ☎ *01/8943205* ▭ *No credit cards.*

¢–$ ✕ **Hippies Restaurant and Bar.** Located on the eastern end of Tonsai beach, Hippies recovered quickly from the tsunami and was serving tasty Thai and international cuisine and cocktails to relief workers and tourists within two months of the tragedy. Middle Eastern food, such as falafel and *motobel* (eggplant puree with olive oil), is prepared excellently. The staff at both the restaurant and seaside bar is very friendly. ⊠ *Tonsai Beach* ☎ *No phone* ▭ *No credit cards.*

$$$$ ✕▥ **Holiday Inn Resort.** The Holiday Inn Resort is on 20 acres of tropical gardens along a private beach, which has gorgeous blue water with a sandy sea floor, where you can swim and snorkel year-round. Most bungalows have identical design with parquet floors, comfortable indoor day beds, and decks with lounge chairs. However, a few rooms are family-style duplexes—those numbered 100–118 are beachfront. The terrace restaurant, serving Thai and international cuisines, has splendid views of the sea, and the cliffside satay bar has one of the only sunset viewpoints on the entire island. Classes in Thai culture, arts, and language are offered throughout the week. Snorkeling equipment is free and there's a reef a short distance from the shore, but the helpful staff can easily arrange fancier fishing and diving expeditions. The resort offers boat service from Phuket. ⊠ *Cape Laemtong, 81000* ☎ *0075/ 621334 or 0075/620798* 🖷 *076/215090 in Phuket* ⊕ *www.holidayinn. com* ↪ *80 bungalows* ᎖ *2 restaurants, café, room service, in-room safes, minibars, cable TV, 2 tennis courts, pool, massage, sauna, library, beach, volleyball, kayaking, snorkeling, windsurfing, boating, dive shop, 3 bars, shops, babysitting, laundry service, travel services* ▭ *AE, MC, V.*

\$\$\$–\$\$\$\$ 🖼 **Pee Pee Island Village.** Coconut palms tower over this cluster of small thatched bungalows on the northern cape. You can find the same amenities in other lodgings on the island, but the atmosphere here is more laid-back. On the other hand, the views are less impressive. The water is not best for swimming as it's quite shallow. However, kayaks are available for rent and there's a large pool. Longtail boats can take you to better beaches or out for snorkeling excursions. ⊠ *Loh Bakao Bay, Cape Laemtong, 81000* ☎ *075/6289000–9* 📠 *075628955* ⊕ *www.ppisland.com* 🛏 *104 rooms* ⚐ *Restaurant, minibars, cable TV, pool, kayaking, snorkeling, boating, tennis court, massage, spa, travel services* ☰ *AE, MC, V.*

\$\$–\$\$\$\$ 🖼 **Phi Phi Viewpoint Resort.** On the western hillside overlooking Loh Dalam bay, Phi Phi Viewpoint Resort was the sole survivor of the tsunami that devastated the resorts on this beautiful beach. After the debris is all cleared away, the views from the rooms will be magnificent once again. Although the hillside huts are stacked pretty tightly next to and on top of each other, the six beachfront huts will give you a little more breathing room and privacy. The outdoor bar and the pool also have outstanding views of the beach and bay. Note that some huts don't have hot water. ⊠ *107 Loh Dalam Bay, 81000* ☎ *075/622351 or 075/618111* 📠 *075/622351 or 075/618112* ⊕ *www.phiphiviewpoint.com* 🛏 *54 rooms, 1 suite* ⚐ *Restaurant, cable TV in some rooms, pool, massage, dive shop, kayaking, fishing, bar, library, shop, Internet, travel services; no a/c in some rooms* ☰ *MC, V.*

\$\$–\$\$\$ 🖼 **Bay View Resort.** This resort on a hill at the far eastern end of Tonsai Bay was unscathed by the tsunami. All bungalows have large decks with great views of both Phi Phi Lae and Tonsai Bay. Some rooms have wooden floors, others have tile floors—the wood-floor rooms feel more traditional and natural, which suits the environment better. Electric cars transfer guests from distant rooms to the reception and restaurant areas. The water here is quite shallow and not great for swimming, but it's the quietest spot along Laem Hin Beach. It's only a short (although sometimes slippery) 15-minute walk along the rocks to gorgeous Long Beach. ⊠ *69 Laem Hin Beach* ☎ *076/289363* 📠 *076/289365* 🛏 *109 bungalows* ⚐ *Restaurant, room service, cable TV, minibars, in-room safes, pool, Internet* ☰ *AE, D, MC, V.*

\$\$–\$\$\$ 🖼 **Phi Phi Erawan Palm Resort.** Erawan Palm is a small, comfortable resort in the middle on Laem Tong beach, next to the sea gypsy village. The spacious cottages all have wooden floors and ceilings with golden curtains and comforters. The beach bar is great for lazy afternoon cocktails and there is a small museum about the sea gypsy community that you can check out when you need a break from the beach. ⊠ *Moo 8, Laem Tong Beach, 81000* ☎ *075/613010 up to 3, ext. 701* 📠 *075/613000* 🛏 *18 cottages* ⚐ *Restaurant, room service, cable TV, pool, massage, dive shop, bar, Internet, travel services* ☰ *MC, V.*

\$–\$\$\$ 🖼 **Phi Phi Villa Resort.** Large, thatch-covered huts in a natural setting give Phi Phi Villa a relaxing island feeling quite different than bustling Tonsai Bay, a short walk away. All bungalows have small patios with wooden handrails, and interiors large enough to fit desks, chairs, wardrobes, and enormous bathrooms. The resort is on a stretch of private beach where boats are prohibited from landing; the absense of longtails that clutter Tonsai's shore makes the beach here more suitable for swimming, although it's still shallow and quite rocky. It's great for travelers who want to stay close to the action without being a part of it. ⊠ *Tonsai Bay, 81000* ☎ *09/8716467* 🖷 *075/623343* ⊕ *www. phiphivilla.com* ⤳ *59 bungalows* ♨ *Restaurant, cable TV in some rooms, some minibars, pool, massage, laundry service; no a/c in some rooms* ▭ *MC, V.*

$-$$ 🏨 **Phi Phi Natural Resort.** Beautiful sunrise views from the deluxe seaside bungalows are this resort's biggest draw. The 20 deluxe rooms are also the most recently renovated (the rest are scheduled for a much needed fix-up some time in 2006), with wooden floors and Thai arts and crafts. The resort is on a hill between the north end of Laem Tong beach and a smaller secluded beach, which is quite private, but less than ideal for swimming. Budget rooms also have good views, as they are high up on the hill. ⊠ *Moo 8, Laem Tong Beach, 81000* ☎ *075/613010* 🖷 *076/ 236355* ⊕ *www.phiphinatural.com* ⤳ *69 rooms* ♨ *Restaurant, room service, cable TV in some rooms, minibars, IDD telephones, in-room safes, pool, massage, kayaking, volleyball, bar, library, babysitting, Internet, travel services* ▭ *MC, V.*

¢-$$ 🏨 **Phi Phi Paradise Pearl Resort.** Phi Phi Paradise is a mixed bag. It's location couldn't be more perfect—on Long Beach, a beautiful, sandy swimming beach, it will give you a look at the beauty of Phi Phi, far from the development of Tonsai Bay. Accommodations, on the other hand, leave a little to be desired (they were looking a bit shabby at this writing), though the resort had started a long-overdue renovation during the post-tsunami tourism lull. Make sure you request a renovated room; note that the cheaper bungalows are farther from the beach and don't have ocean views. Lastly, the staff's attitude ranges from island-induced laziness to indifference, so if you expect to be pampered, go elsewhere. ⊠ *Long Beach, 81000* ☎ *075/622100 or 075/ 618050* ⊕ *www.ppparadise.com* ⤳ *52 rooms* ♨ *Restaurant, some in-room safes, bar, Internet, laundry service, travel services; no a/c in some rooms* ▭ *MC, V.*

$ 🏨 **Chao Koh Phi Phi Lodge.** One of the few remaining budget options on the island, Chao Koh Phi Phi Lodge is a collection of basic but comfortable bungalows near Tonsai Bay. Major renovations had already been scheduled for Spring 2005 even before the tsunami hit—repairs have been completed and a swimming pool and family-style suites have been added. Several simple fan huts survived both the waves and the renovation, so the place still welcomes budget travelers. Evenings, the lodge runs a popular seafood restaurant by the sea, with a nice view of the bay. ⊠ *Tongsai Bay, 81000* ☎ *075/501821* 🖷 *075/236616* ⊕ *www. kohphi-phi.com* ⤳ *44 bungalows* ♨ *Restaurant, minibars, cable TV, hair salon, massage, dive shop, boating, shops, Internet, travel services; no a/c in some rooms* ▭ *MC, V.*

¢-$ 🏨 **Phi Phi Long Beach Hotel.** Phi Phi Long Beach provides extremely basic accommodations on a gorgeous stretch of beach. Rooms aren't much more than concrete squares with fans, mosquito nets, and mattresses. The rates are actually a bit high considering that the rooms themselves are quite primitive, but you're really paying for the soft white sand

and crystal clear water. Note that there's no hot water. ⊠ *33 Long Beach, 81000* ☎ *01/510–6451, 040/537438* ⇌ *80 rooms* ⌂ *Restaurant, bar, volleyball, laundry service, travel services; no a/c* ▤ *No credit cards.*

Nightlife

There's still nightlife to be found in Tonsai Bay town. Before the tsunami it seemed like many people came to Phi Phi for two reasons only: to go to Maya Bay during the day, and to party in Tonsai Bay at night. As a result, a large number of bars were constructed primarily out of concrete, most of which were strong enough to survive the impact from the waves. Tonsai's nightlife will flourish again as visitors return. Along the path running parallel to the sea, there are several popular bars, notably **Apache Bar,** which has an impressive "katoey" (drag cabaret) show. Once you head down the side streets away from the beach there are mazes of bars and clubs competing in stereo wars, filled with young travelers eager to drink and dance the night away. If you like Khao San Road in Bangkok, you will love Tonsai Bay at night. More remote beaches around the island have more subdued nightlife, primarily centered around resort restaurants and bars.

Koh Lanta

❹ *70 km (42 mi) south of Krabi Town; 2 hrs by car from Krabi Airport, 2 hrs by boat from Ao Nang*

Long, uncrowded beaches, crystal clear water, and a laid-back natural environment are Koh Lanta's main attractions. Although "discovered" by international travelers in early 2000, Koh Lanta remains fairly quiet. Early development resulted in the construction of hundreds of budget bungalows and several swanky resorts along the west coast of Lanta Yai (Lanta Noi's coast is less suitable for development), however, as one of the largest islands in Thailand, Lanta was able to absorb the "boom" and therefore remains relatively uncluttered. In addition, Lanta is approximately 70 km (44 mi) south of Krabi Town, far enough outside of established tourist circuits that visitor arrivals have increased more slowly than at other Krabi and Phang Nga beaches and islands. Most smaller resorts are closed during the low season (May though October). However, some do stay open in late October and remain open until mid-May—during these (slightly) off times, the weather is still generally good, and you can find that the rates are much lower and the beaches much less crowded.

The tsunami was a mixed blessing for Koh Lanta. It had a small effect on the buildings along the coast, and most damage was repaired within months of the disaster. However, it had a hugely beneficial effect on the environment, cleansing the beaches and replenishing the shore with clear deep-ocean water. Before the tsunami it was hard to imagine how Koh Lanta could be any more beautiful, but afterwards the water was bluer and more sparkling, the sand whiter and softer. Though the huge decrease in visitor arrivals to the island has caused its share of economic hardship, it shouldn't be long before word of Koh Lanta's renewal spreads and lucky travelers will find their way to its shores.

Sports & the Outdoors

Diving, snorkeling, hiking, and elephant trekking are a few activities available on Koh Lanta and the nearby islands. Diving and snorkeling around Koh Lanta can be arranged through dive and tour operators though most people choose to book through their resort. Popular nearby dive sites are **Koh Ha** and **Koh Rok** off Koh Lanta. If you would like to enjoy Koh Lanta from another view point, elephant trekking is available near Phra Ae (Long) Beach. A boat trip to the famous **Emerald Cave** on **Koh Muk** is a worthwhile experience; it's easiest to inquire at your resort about day trip options.

Klong Dao Beach

Klong Dao Beach is a 2-km-long beach on the northern coast of Lanta Yai. Most resorts along Klong Dao are larger facilities catering to families and couples looking for a quiet environment. The water is shallow but swimmable, and at low tide the firm, exposed sand is ideal for long jogs on the beach.

WHERE TO STAY & EAT

¢ ✕⛺ **Chaba Guesthouse and Picasso Restaurant.** Once you spot the giant mushrooms, you'll know you've found Picasso Restaurant and Chaba Guesthouse. Thai people believe that southerners make the best food, and Picasso Restaurant lives up to this southern reputation. Proprietor and artist Khun Toi creates pastel-color oil paintings incorporating shells and driftwood from Klong Dao beach. Finished products adorn the walls of the restaurant, which itself is a Monet-inspired swirl of impressionist pastels and sculpture. Toi's style of art has even been granted a patent by the Thai government. ⊠ *Klong Dao Beach, Lanta Yai, 81150* ☎ *075/684118 or 09/7387710* ⊕ *www.krabidir.com/ chababungalows* ➭ *16 huts* ⛨ *Restaurant, fans, in-room safes, Internet, bar, car rental, laundry service, travel services; no a/c in some rooms* ☰ *No credit cards.*

¢ ✕⛺ **Time For Lime.** Time for Lime is a large, open-air kitchen right off the beach where you can learn to cook Thai food, using fresh seafood and vegetables. Instruction is provided in selecting the best ingredients and then cooking and presenting your own visual feast. It's fun, easy, and taught in a great environment. Spartan but cozy accommodation is available for those who wish to take multiple classes or just enjoy the smell of Thai cooking. At night, reclining chairs are placed on the recessed sandbar while music plays and cocktails are served. ⊠ *72/2 Klong Dao Beach, Lanta Yai, 81150* ☎ *075/6845990 or 09/ 9675017* ⊕ *www.timeforlime.net* ➭ *9 rooms* ⛨ *Fans, bar* ☰ *No credit cards.*

★ $$$-$$$$ ⛺ **Costa Lanta.** The coolest thing about Costa Lanta is the room design; each room at this trendy boutique resort is a convertible box, so if you're too hot you can open up the "walls" and allow the breeze to blow through your room. The small number of rooms dispersed over a large area allows you to enjoy your open space in relative privacy. The resort is at the northern end of Klong Dao beach—the quiet end of an already quiet beach. Isolation is a blessing here as the resort has almost everything you might need, including a game room and a spa. The water here is swimmable, and snorkeling around Kaw Kwang Cape, while not exceptional, is pleasant and there are fish to be seen. ✉ *212 Klong Dao Beach, Lanta Yai, 81150* ☎ *075/618092* ⊕ *www.costalanta.com* ➘ *22 rooms* ⚘ *Restaurant, IDD phones, minibars, pool, massage, shop, recreation room, bar, lounge, travel services* ⊟ *AE, DC, MC, V.*

\$–\$\$\$ ⌸ **Southern Lanta.** With a fun-slide plunging into a big pool and several two-bedroom villas each with large multibed rooms, Southern Lanta is quite popular with families. Standard rooms are bungalows built closely to each other with slightly run-down exteriors, but comfortable interiors. Seaside rooms are newer and have sofas indoors and deck chairs outdoors for maximum lounging. ✉ *105 Klong Dao Beach, Lanta Yai, 81150* ☎ *075/684174–77* 📠 *075/684174* ⊕ *www.southernlanta.com* ➘ *80 rooms, 10 suites* ⚘ *2 restaurants, minibars, pool, massage, spa, Internet, bar, travel services* ⊟ *MC, V.*

Phra Ae Beach (Long Beach)

Long and wide, Phra Ae Beach (aka Long Beach) is Lanta Yai's main tourist destination. The sand is soft and fine, perfect for both sunbathing and long walks. The water is less shallow than other Lanta beaches, and therefore more suitable for diving in and having a swim. However, kayaks, catamarans, and other water activities, while available, are not as ubiquitous as on other islands. Although most lodging consists of simple budget bungalows, the beachfront does have several three- and four-star resorts. Along the beach and on the main road are many restaurants, bars, Internet cafés, and dive operators.

WHERE TO STAY & EAT
¢–\$ ✕ **Funky Fish Bar and Bungalows–Mr. Wee Pizzeria.** Feeling funky? Dine while you recline on a triangular Thai pillow atop one of dozens of elevated wooden platforms. Mr. Wee serves thin-crust pizzas that should satisfy both American and Italian palates. We enjoyed pizza Raul: mozzarella, tomato, mushroom, and shrimp. They also serve Thai and Italian food as well as ice cream and other desserts. Funky Fish is also a happening bar at night, and they rent super simple bungalows with crushed shell–coral bathroom floors and thatched roofs. ✉ *241 Moo. 3 Phra Ae Beach, Lanta Yai* ☎ *07/2740750* ⊟ *No credit cards.*

\$\$\$–\$\$\$\$ ⌸ **Lanta Sand Resort and Spa.** Large ponds with water lilies and spraying fountains cover the grounds of Lanta Sand Resort and Spa. Aged-brick paths meander from villa to pool to spa, where aromatic candles burn, illuminating Thai silk tapestries. Northern Thai–style villas have marble floors and all but the standard rooms have outdoor garden baths. Honeymooners are greeted with flowers, cake, and champagne. Beachside massage is available for all. ✉ *279 Moo 3, Phra Ae Beach, Lanta Yai, 81150* ☎ *075/684633–5* 📠 *075/684636* ⊕ *www.lantasand. com* ➘ *46 rooms, 2 suites* ⚘ *Restaurant, cable TV, minibars, pool, massage, spa, 2 bars, laundry service, travel services* ⊟ *AE, MC, V.*

\$\$ ⌸ **Lanta Resortel.** If you're staying in a resort on a beautiful, white-sand beach with crystal-clear, blue water you should treat yourself to a room with a view. Fortunately, if you stay at Lanta Resortel you will have such a view, even if you get stuck in a room at the back—each wooden bungalow is positioned so that you can look down a sandy walkway to the beach, so whether laying in bed and looking through the picture window, or lounging on one of two daybeds on the deck, you'll appreciate the tranquility of the Andaman Sea. When it gets too hot, retreat to the air-conditioned bliss of your cottage—which has wooden floors and rattan walls—a perfect blend of island design and modern amenities. ✉ *172 Moo, Phra Ae Beach* ☎ *075/684673* ➟ *47 rooms* ⚒ *Restaurant, bar, massage, laundry service* ☰ *MC, V.*

$ 🏨 **Lanta Long Beach Resort.** The exteriors of the thatched roof wooden huts appear weathered and worn and the restaurant's "common area" is a large, open rectangle of basic wooden tables and chairs. But, in fact, the resort's simplicity is its charm. The rooms are rustic—floors and walls are made of wood the way Thai huts should be, natural, but air-tight, to keep the mosquito's out. Some huts, however, have a few amenities like air-conditioning, large windows, and decks with roll-down wind–rain screens. Years of expansion have resulted in a variety of rooms for the thriftiest backpacker as well as the spendthrifty hippie. ✉ *172 Moo 3, Phra Ae Beach, Lanta Yai, 81150* ☎ *075/684673 or 075/684674* 🖷 *075/ 684198* ⊕ *www.lantalongbeach.com* ➟ *95 rooms* ⚒ *Restaurant, laundry service, travel services; no a/c in some rooms* ☰ *No credit cards.*

¢–$ 🏨 **Best House.** The entry to Best House is an inviting high-ceiling room with many comfortable chairs, white tile floors, and wooden beams, trim, and hand railings. The rooms are spacious and comfortable, the closest thing to "normal" Western hotel rooms on an island of bungalows and upscale spa-resorts. The place isn't on the beach, but it's very close by. At this writing, air-conditioned rooms were supposed to be added by mid-2005. Note that there's no hot water. ✉ *5/1 Moo 3, Phra Ae Beach, Lanta Yai, 81150* ☎ *01/1740241* ➟ *40 rooms* ⚒ *Fans, laundry service, travel services* ☰ *V* ☽ *Closed June–Sept.*

¢ 🏨 **Lanta Long Beach Bungalows.** This throwback resort will appeal to those who are looking for budget rooms or for those who want a Robinson Crusoe/Gilligan's Island vacation. The huts (and they really are huts rather than "bungalows") are simple structures of bamboo and rattan with thatch roofs. Most have squat toilets—only the larger ones that sleep three or four have Western-style toilets. Three huts were built high up on stilts treehouse-style and one of these only has knee-high walls so that you have an unobstructed view of the sea. All huts have mosquito nets and fans to protect you from the bugs and the heat. The beach here is perfect and the resort is worth a look even if you can't handle living like a castaway for a few days. ✉ *120 Moo 3 Long Beach, Saladan, 81150* ☎ *075/684217* ⊕ *www.ko-lanta.com/lantalongbeach* ➟ *20 huts* ⚒ *Restaurant, bar, massage, dive shop, snorkeling, volleyball, travel services; no a/c, no room TVs* ☰ *MC, V.*

¢ 🏨 **Somewhere Else.** If you like your huts to be innovative, check out Somewhere Else. The six octagonal rooms in the front of the clearing are particularly cool. They have fold-down windows, wooden floors, and loose-pebble bathroom floors. This resort is nothing fancy (expect cold water and fans) but it has a great vibe, and you'll enjoy playing Ping-Pong with friendly staff in the common room or just watching the sunset on the chill-out pillows strewn on various wooden platforms. Note that there's no hot water. ✉ *253 Moo 3, Phra Ae Beach, Lanta Yai, 81150* ☎ *01/5360858 or 09/7311312* ➟ *16 rooms* ⚒ *Restaurant, fans, Ping-Pong, laundry service* ☰ *No credit cards* ☽ *Closed June–Sept.*

Klong Nin Beach

Klong Nin beach, approximately 30 minutes south of Long Beach by car or boat, is one of the larger, nicer beaches toward the southern end of Lanta Yai. Klong Nin is less developed and more tranquil than Long Beach. A typical day on Klong Nin could consist of a long walk on the silky soft sand interrupted by occasional dips in the sea, a spectacular sunset, a seaside massage, and a candle-lighted barbecue beneath a canopy of stars. Central Klong Nin, near Otto bar, is the best for swimming, as rocks punctuate the rest of the shoreline. Kayaks are available from some resorts and longtail boat taxis are for hire along the sea. Most resorts here rent motorbikes as well, as the road to the south is much smoother than the road from Long Beach.

WHERE TO
STAY & EAT
$
Fodor'sChoice
★

✕ **Cook Kai.** From the outside, the restaurant appears to be a standard, wooden Thai beach restaurant. Once inside, fairy lights along the ceiling light up your eyes and the food does likewise to your tastebuds. Sizzling "hotpan" dishes of seafood in coconut cream and sweet-and-sour shrimp are succulent. Specials, such as duck curry served in a hollowed-out pineapple, change daily. Everything on their extensive menu tastes amazing. They even share their recipes, offering cooking classes upon request. ⊠ *Moo 6, Klong Nin Beach* ☎ *01/6063015* ▬ *No credit cards.*

$$–$$$ 🏨 **Srilanta.** One of the first upscale resorts in the area to market the "less is more" philosophy, Srilanta remains a cool yet classy island getaway for trendy urbanites. Breezy rooms are primitive but have comfortable lounging areas and are tastefully decorated with flowers. Unfortunately, most rooms have no view and are a short walk down the hill to the beach. The beachside pool, sunbathing lawn, spa, and common areas follow stylish Hindu and Balinese themes. The spa has massage tables on a platform above a large fishpond. Srilanta is reasonably priced for what you get (one of the nicest resorts on one of the nicest beaches), but the service is quite ordinary for such an extraordinary resort. ⊠ *111 Moo 6, Klong Nin Beach, Lanta Yai, 81150* ☎ *075/697288* 🖷 *075/697288* ⊕ *www.srilanta.com* 🛏 *49 rooms, 3 suites* ♻ *2 restaurants, cable TV, in-room safes, pool, massage, spa, DVDs, beach, bar, laundry service, Internet, travel services* ▬ *AE, DC, MC, V.*

$–$$$ 🏨 **Lanta Miami Bungalows.** The Lanta Miami is on the beach, it's affordable, and it's open year-round—you truly need little more. The rooms are spacious, and have big beds and tile floors, though you can probably spend your days on the beach or under a shady palm. ⊠ *13 Moo. 6, Klong Nin Beach, Lanta Yai, 81150* ☎ *075/697081* 🛏 *22 rooms* ♻ *Restaurant, minibars, laundry service, travel services; no a/c, no hot water in some rooms* ▬ *No credit cards.*

¢–$ 🏨 **Lanta Paradise Resort.** It's only a short walk along the beach to the best swimming spot, but the sand gets so hot you'll be glad to have the pool outside your room. Bungalows come in all permutations from fans and cold water only to air-conditioning, hot water, and minibars. Shady twin massage beds and southern Thai–style elevated dining tables with chill-pillows and peaked roofs (both by the beach) help you keep your cool. There's even a hip little hippie beach bar that sells shell necklaces. The resort has plenty of amenities, but management seems to help out of duty rather than courtesy. ⊠ *67 M. 6 Klong Nin Beach,*

Lanta Yai, 81150 ☎ *09/9790237, 01/5357534, or 09/4733279* ⊕ *www. lantaparadise.com* ➪ *35 rooms* ⌂ *Restaurant, minibars, pool, laundry service, Internet, travel services; no TVs, no hot water in some rooms.*

NIGHTLIFE In 2002, some forward-thinking club promoter decided to build a nightclub on relatively isloated Klong Nin beach. Positioned up on the hill beyond the Srilanta resort, **I-Bark Club** has panoramic views of the sea from its deck and is set amongst Lanta's tropical forest. The club is two-tiered with an open-air sala and a "Japanese lounge bar." Chill-out music is played in one area, DJs spin various styles of music in the other.

Southern Lanta Beaches

Southern Lanta beaches consist of several widely dispersed small coves and beaches ending at Klong Chak National Park. Immediately south of Klong Nin the road suddenly becomes well paved (much smoother than the road from Long Beach to Klong Nin), making the southern beaches accessible by road as well as by taxi boat. The nicest of the southern beaches is Bakantiang Beach, a beautiful one to visit on the way to the National Park.

WHERE TO STAY ✕ **Same Same But Different.** This restaurant is tucked away in a shady
& EAT grove near the southern end of Bakantiang Beach. The "dining room"
★ **$** is very Robinson Crusoe, enclosed by a rudimentary roof with a dozen tables on the sand and wood bar. Have your longtail boat drop you off here and pick you up on the northern end of the beach an hour or so later, so you have time for a swim before you eat, and nice walk on the beach when you're done. Same Same serves some southern Thai dishes, typically spicy. We recommend the fried prawns with tamarind sauce topped with fried shallot and chili. Smoothies and ice-cold beer are perfect for combatting the afternoon heat. ⊠ *85 M. 5 Bakantiang Beach, Lanta Yai* ☎ *01/7878670* ▤ *No credit cards.*

★ **$$$$** ▦ **Pimalai Resort and Spa.** Pimalai Resort and Spa is a premier resort encompassing hundreds of acres of beachfront and hillside along southern Bakantiang Beach. Standard rooms are luxurious enough, but exclusive villas have full kitchens, private pools, and drivers to shuttle you to the spa, beach, or other facilities around the sprawling resort. The spa was carefully landscaped with tall palms and sloping trails. The soothing sounds of streams and waterfalls around the spa and classical Thai music in the lobby are just as tranquilizing as the treatments. Thai royalty and celebrities have been guests here. Booking ahead is essential. ⊠ *99 M. 5 Bakantiang Beach, Lanta Yai, 81150* ☎ *075/607999* ▤ *075/ 607988* ⊕ *www.pimalai.com* ➪ *72 rooms, 7 suites, 40 private houses* ⌂ *3 restaurants, room service, cable TV, in-room DVD players, in-room safes, minibars, IDD phones, some kitchenettes, pool, health club, massage, spa, dive shop, library, 3 bars, lounge, beach, meeting rooms, car rental, travel services, airport shuttle* ▤ *AE, DC, MC, V.*

★ **$–$$** ▦ **Narima Resort.** The owners staggered the bungalows when they were built so that almost all could enjoy the awesome view of Koh Ha. If that were not enough, they strung hammocks on each deck and threw in a couple of palm-straw rocking chairs. The rooms have cloth canopy ceilings and rattan walls. It almost doesn't matter that the shore here is rocky rather than sandy. The guests do not seem to mind; many take dive courses with the in-house dive shop, practicing in the pool or the crystal clear sea. Others snorkel or just soak up the view from the large Jacuzzi. Owner–manager Dr. Jotibhan is a doting, pleasant host. ⊠ *98 M. 5 Klong Nin Beach, Lanta Yai, 81150* ☎ *075/607700 or 075/618081* 🖷 *075/607700* ⊕ *www.narima-lanta.com* 🛏 *32 rooms* ⚘ *Restaurant, fans, minibars, pool, massage, laundry service, dive shop, travel services; no a/c in some rooms* ⊟ *MC, V.*

ANDAMAN COAST A TO Z

AIR TRAVEL

Six domestic airlines, ranging from pricy boutique to no frills budget, travel to Phuket and Krabi International Airports daily. Thai Airways, Bangkok Airways, and Phuket Air are among the more sophisticated ones where food and full service are offered on board. Budget airlines, like Nok Air, Orient Thai Air, and Air Asia provide similar service, but food and beverages must be purchased on board for a reasonable price. Each day, more than 20 domestic flights fly from Bangkok to Phuket, whereas only 10 flights go to Krabi. One-way prices from Bangkok to either destination range from B500 to B2,500; flight duration averages about one hour to either destination.

🖪 **Info Air Asia** ☎ 02/5159999 ⊕ www.airasia.com. **Bangkok Airways** ☎ 1771 ⊕ www.bangkokair.com. **Nok Air** ☎ 1318 ⊕ www.nokair.com. **Orient Thai Air** ☎ 02/2673210–58 ⊕ www.orient-thai.com. **Phuket Air** ☎ 02/6798999 ⊕ www.phuketairlines.com. **Thai Airways** ☎ 02/6282000 ⊕ www.thaiairways.com.

AIRPORTS & TRANSFERS

Most travelers head to Phuket International Airport as flights generally cost less and arrive with greater frequency. Phuket International Airport lies on the northern end of the island. A ride to Phuket Town (where you get the ferry to Phi Phi and Krabi) takes about 45 minutes; and to Khao Lak it's about 1½ hours. Krabi International Airport is very close to Krabi Town, only a 20-minute taxi ride away. It's a 45-minute trip to Ao Nang from Krabi's airport, and two hours by taxi or minibus to Koh Lanta.

Both Krabi and Phuket International Airports have taxis waiting outside, but they also have cheaper minivan service to most tourist destinations. Minivans won't leave until they're full, so if you don't want to wait— or if you're headed to somewhere off the beaten path—opt for a taxi.

BOAT & FERRY TRAVEL

Ferry travel is easiest way for travelers to island-hop. The most popular routes start in Phuket, stopover on Koh Phi Phi, and then continue on to Ao Nang and Koh Lanta or vice versa. However, ferry routes are seasonal, so always double-check schedules.

Boats running the Phuket–Koh Phi Phi routes operate year-round. Seatran and Royal Fern Ferry depart from Rasada Pier on Phuket at about 8 AM and 1:30 PM for the two-hour journey to Phi Phi Don. PP Cruiser also takes about two hours to reach Phi Phi Don, but departs from

Makham Pier. One-way prices on any carrier range from B250 to B350 per person.

Royal Fern and Ao Nang Travel & Tour also offer other inter-beach and inter-island connections. Routes are Koh Phi Phi to Koh Lanta, Koh Phi Phi to Krabi, Koh Phi Phi to Ao Nang, and Krabi Town to Koh Lanta. These routes are usually more convenient than land transfer, however they are only in operation from November to May.

Speed boats to the Similan and Surin Islands from Phuket or Khao Lake only operate when the National Parks are open to the public (November–May). Speed boats to Surin National Park depart from Kuraburi Pier in Takuapa district early morning once a day. Speed boats to Similan National Park leave from Thaplamu Pier in Tai Muang district at 8:30 AM.

Fisherman boats from Phuket's Bang Rong Pier take you to Koh Yao Yai and Noi five times daily starting from 8:30 AM for a mere B50 per person. The journey takes 45 minutes to one hour.

Longtail boats from Krabi Town and Ao Nang to Nang Cape serve tourists all year round. Travel via longtail from Ao Nang takes 15 minutes and costs B50 per person.

🚢 **Boat & Ferry Lines** **Ao Nang Travel & Tour Co.** ✉ 183/87 Phang Nga Rd., Muang, Phuket, 83000 ☎076/232040, 076/232041 ⊕www.krabi-tourism.com/aonangtravel. **Royal Fern Co.** ✉ 148/11 Suthat Road, Talad Yai, Muang, Phuket, 83000 ☎ 076/232240, 076/232317, 076/232975 ⊕ www.phuketdir.com/royalfernco/.**Seatran Travel** ✉ 64/423 Anupas-Phuket-Karn Rd, Rassada, Muang, Phuket, 83000 ☎ 076/355410 up to 2, 076/219391 ⊕ www.seatran.co.th.

BUS TRAVEL

Buses from Bangkok to Krabi, Phang Nga and Khao Lak leave from Bangkok's Southern Bus Terminal. VIP and first-class buses leave once every evening around 6 or 7 PM. Reservations are reccommended for VIP and first-class, especially during Thai holidays. Trips to the Andaman Coast take at least 12 hours. If you are pressed for time, flying is a much quicker option, and costs only a little more if booked in advance or if travel is done on off-peak days.

There's also bus service from Phuket to Krabi, Phang Nga, and Khao Lak. First-class buses (B117) leave Phuket every hour for the three-hour journey to Krabi. There is no direct bus from Phuket to Khao Lak, but you can take a bus that is bound for Ranong, Surat Thani, or Kuraburi and ask to get dropped off in Khao Lak.

CAR RENTALS

Krabi Airport has Avis and National rental counters. Budget also has an office in Ao Nang. Prices start from B1,400/day. There is a B300 extra charge to have the car picked up elsewhere in Krabi if you are planning on departing via boat, rather than heading off from the airport.

🚗Agencies **Avis** ✉Krabi Airport ☎075/691941. **National** ✉Krabi Airport ☎075/691939.

CAR TRAVEL

If you are driving from Bangkok, Phang Nga is 788 km (400 mi) and Krabi is 814 km (505 mi) south, as the crow flies. The main road that leads south is Petchakasem Road or Highway 4, which narrows to a one-lane road once you leave the greater Bangkok sprawl. The road is heavily trafficked by long-haul transport trucks and driving without familiarity of Thai driving habits can be unsettling, especially at night.

EMERGENCIES

Tourist police are on call 24/7; call 1699 or 1155 in the Andaman Coast area if you need assistance. Hospitals in Krabi and Phuket should be able to deal competently with most medical emergencies; if you have more serious problems, you should try to get back to Bangkok.

It's a good practice to alert your hotel's staff if you are taking day trips to more remote islands.

🕿 Emergency Numbers **Marine Police** ☎ 076/211883. **Tourist Police** ☎ 1155, 1699, 076/219878 in Phuket, 075/637028 in Krabi.

🕿 Hospitals **Bangkok Phuket Hospital** ✉ 2/1 Hongyok Rd., Phuket Town ☎ 076/254425. **Krabi Hospital** ✉ 325 Uttarakit Rd., Krabi Town ☎ 075/631769, 075/611203. **Phang Nga Hospital** ✉ 436 Petchakasem Rd., Phang Nga Town ☎ 076/412034.

HEALTH

The tsunami made some areas a bit swampier, so the risk of mosquito-borne diseases has increased slightly. Health authorities and resort operators have done a respectable job controlling mosquitoes around the southern resorts, but you'll still need a good supply of repellent. Most accommodations, from luxury resorts to humble bungalows, either have screens on all windows and doors or at least mosquito netting over the beds. Regardless, be vigilant during dusk and dawn, and make sure there are no mosquitoes within your net before you fall asleep! When exploring in the wilderness, off established tourist routes, use mosquito repellent with DEET, as viruses such as dengue fever and malaria still exist in Thailand.

Be careful at the beach, as the sun can be stronger than you think. Wear a hat and bring along plenty of sunscreen. Protective clothing while diving or snorkeling is a good idea, as accidentally brushing against or stepping on coral can be painful. Keep an eye out for dangerous creatures, especially jellyfish and sea urchins. If you are stung, seek medical attention immediately.

MAIL & SHIPPING

The reception desk at your hotel will post your cards and letters, a much easier option than hunting down the nearest post office.

🕿 Post Offices **Krabi** ✉ 190–202 Uttarakit Rd. Krabi Town. **Phang Nga** ✉ 503 Petchakasem Rd. Phang Nga Town.

MONEY MATTERS

Banks and ATM's are easy to locate in big towns like Krabi Town and Ao Nang. All banks will exchange foreign currency. Remember that hotel exchange rates differ significantly from those at banks or currency exchange houses. The more remote the hotel, the less you'll get for your dollar. Most major credit cards are accepted by medium to large tour operators and accommodations. Some will charge a service fee for accepting your card.

TAXIS

Taxi is the most expensive way to travel by land in Southern Thailand, usually only worth the cost if you're traveling with a group that can split the cost. Phuket has "taxi meters" that rarely run their meters (they usually don't even have them). Both Phuket and Krabi airports have reliable limousine service at fixed prices. A taxi ride from Phuket Airport to Phuket town costs B300 and from Krabi Airport to Ao Nang costs B500. In many touristy destinations, un-registered taxi drivers are in every corner touting for customers. Make sure you negotiate a price that you are happy with prior to accepting a ride. A good negotiator can often procure a taxi and driver for an entire day for little more than the price of a rental car. As westerners are often at fault in car accidents regardless of actual fact, a chauffered car can be safer and less stressful than renting a car.

TRAIN TRAVEL

There is no train service to Phuket, Phang Nga or Krabi. The nearest train station for travel to Phang Nga is to the east in Surat Thani and the nearest to Krabi and Phuket is to the south in Trang.

VISITOR INFORMATION

The Tourism Authority of Thailand (TAT) has a central office covering Phang Nga, Krabi, and Phuket at the visitor information center in Phuket Town. Krabi and Phang Nga towns have their own small TAT offices, where you can pick up maps and brochures, as well as information about local excursions. Tour operators and your hotel's tour desk are also good sources of information.

🗂 **Krabi** ✉ Uttarakit Rd. ☎ 075/612740. **Phuket** ✉ Phuket Rd. ☎ 076/211036, 076/212213 or 076/217138.

CAMBODIA

7

Reinhard
Hohler and
Robert Tilley

THE KINGDOM OF CAMBODIA, encircled by Thailand, Laos, Vietnam, and the sea, is a land of striking extremes. Internationally, it's most well known for two contrasting chapters of its long history. The first is the Khmer empire's rule, which bequeathed the ruins of Angkor—ancient temples that attest to the nation's immutable cultural heritage. The second is the country's recent political turmoil and legacy of Khmer Rouge brutality. It wasn't until the 1993 United Nations–sponsored elections that a sense of normality returned to the ravaged land, which decades of war and revolution had reduced to one of the poorest in the world.

The Cambodians are an energetic and friendly people, whose quick smiles belie the inordinate suffering their nation has endured. Though practically destroyed by the regional conflict and homegrown repression of the 1970s, Cambodia has risen from those disasters like a phoenix. The streets of Phnom Penh are abuzz with a youthful vibrancy, and the tourism boomtown of Siem Reap, near the Angkor ruins, is full of construction sites.

More than half of Cambodia was once covered with forest, but the landscape has changed in recent decades thanks to ruthless and mercenary deforestation. The mighty Mae Khong River bisects the country into two halves and irrigates the central arable plain, which, in turn, is a rice granary for Cambodia's 13 million people. The surrounding mountain ranges protect Cambodia's long river valleys, which over the centuries developed into settlement centers.

The three ranges of low mountains—the northern Dang Reak, the exotically named Elephant Mountains in the south, and the country's highest range, the Cardamom, in the southwest—formed natural barriers against invasion. Among these ranges is a depression in the northwest of Cambodia connecting the country with the lowlands in Thailand; by allowing communication between the two countries, this geographic feature played an important part in the history of the Khmer nation. In eastern Cambodia, the land rises to a forested plateau that continues into the Annamite Cordillera, the backbone of neighboring Vietnam.

As the seat of the Khmer empire from the 9th to the 13th century, Cambodia developed a complex society based first on Hinduism and then on Buddhism. After the decline of the Khmers and the ascendancy of the Siamese, Cambodia was colonized by the French, who ruled from the mid-1860s until 1953. Shortly after the end of World War II, during which the Japanese had occupied Cambodia, independence became the rallying cry for all of Indochina. Cambodia became a sovereign power with a monarchy ruled by King Norodom Sihanouk, who abdicated in favor of his father in 1955 and entered the public stage as a mercurial politician.

In the early 1970s, the destabilizing consequences of the Vietnam War sparked a horrible chain of events. The U.S. government secretly bombed Cambodia, arranged a coup to oust the king, and invaded parts of the country in an attempt to rout the Vietcong. Civil war ensued, and in 1975 the Khmer Rouge, led by French-educated Pol Pot, emerged as the victors. A regime of terror followed. Under a program of Mao Tse-tung–inspired reeducation centered on forced agricultural collec-

Numbers in the text correspond to numbers in the margin and on the Cambodia and Phnom Penh maps.

If you have
3 days

You need three days at minimum just to skim the surface of Cambodia's highlights. Spend your first day and night in the lively city of 🗺 **Phnom Penh ❶ – ❻ ▸**. Spend the next two days based in 🗺 **Siem Reap ❶**, from which you can take and a leisurely tour of the magnificent **Angkor Temple Complex ❶**.

7

If you have
4 days

For a four-day tour, follow the three-day tour above, but spend an extra night in 🗺 **Phnom Penh ❶ – ❻ ▸** so you can enjoy some of the nearby day trips the next day. Possibilities include the pagoda-studded hilltop at **Udong ❶** and the island of **Koh Dach ❾**.

If you have
7 days

Start your tour with a visit to 🗺 **Phnom Penh ❶ – ❻ ▸**. The next day, take a morning flight to 🗺 **Siem Reap ❶**. Spend the rest of the day and the following day exploring the **Angkor Temple Complex ❶**. The next day, fly back to Phnom Penh; spend more time exploring the capital city, or head out on a day trip if you have time. Overnight in Phnom Penh. On Day 5, take a bus south to the coastal town of 🗺 **Sihanoukville ❶**. Spend a leisurely Day 6 at the beach. On your last day, head back to Phnom Penh, from where you can fly home.

---

tives, the cities were emptied, and hundreds of thousands of civilians were tortured and executed. Hundreds of thousands more succumbed to starvation and disease. During the four years of Khmer Rouge rule, somewhere between 1 and 2 million Cambodians—almost one third of the population—were killed.

By the end of the revolution in 1979, the country lay in ruins. Vietnam, unified under the Hanoi government, seized its chance and invaded the country, forcing the Khmer Rouge into the region bordering Thailand, where they remained entrenched until United Nations–brokered peace accords were signed in 1991. International mediation allowed the return of Norodom Sihanouk as king and the formation of a coalition government that included Khmer Rouge elements after parliamentary elections in 1993.

In 1997 Second Prime Minister Hun Sen toppled First Prime Minister Norodom Ranariddh, but political pressure forced new elections in 1998. Hun Sen won a plurality and formed a new government, despite charges of election rigging. Pol Pot died in his mountain stronghold in April 1998, and the remaining Khmer Rouge elements lost any influence they still had. Most of the surviving Khmer Rouge leaders are still free, but Hun Sen is reluctant to bring them to justice. There's been some controversial back-and-forth about a human rights tribunal for the surviving Khmer Rouge leaders; in view of rising international pressure, especially from the United States, the case of genocide will likely be settled in a court.

Foreign investment and the development of tourism have been very strong in recent years, but it remains to be seen whether domestic problems can be solved and whether Hun Sen can maintain his hard-line rule.

Exploring Cambodia

Cambodia is Southeast Asia's smallest country—about the size of the American state of Washington. On a map, the country looks like a flat plate, bordered by Thailand to the west and northwest, Laos to the northeast, and Vietnam to the east and southeast. In the south, Cambodia faces the Gulf of Thailand, which gives the country access to the Indian and Pacific oceans and the world beyond. The coastline here is small, largely undeveloped, and isolated by a low mountain range.

Much of the country is a low-lying plain dominated by the region's largest lake, Tonle Sap (Great Lake), and a network of waterways forming the start of the Mae Khong Delta. Its northern border with Thailand is a remarkable escarpment, rising directly from the plains to heights of up to 1,800 feet—a natural defensive border and also the site of many ancient Khmer fortresses.

The Mae Khong River enters Cambodia from Laos and runs 600 km (370 mi) north–south through the country; it splits into four branches at Phnom Penh, forming the Upper and Lower Mae Khong, the Tonle Basak, and the Tonle Sap (which is distinct from the lake of the same name). From June to September, when the Mae Khong River is flooded, the sheer force of water coming downstream pushes the Tonle Sap upstream, causing it to flow backward into Tonle Sap lake. When the lake drains back into the Mae Khong River in October, all the fish are forced into the shrinking body of water that slowly carries them downstream. This seasonal swelling and shrinking of the Great Lake is comparable to a beating heart, pumping life into the Mae Khong River system as it triggers a remarkable fish migration. Not surprisingly, the Mae Khong River basin has the greatest diversity of freshwater fish in the world.

The myriad waterways are also a favorite means of domestic travel. From the central port of Phnom Penh, you can easily travel by boat along the Tonle Sap to reach Siem Reap and the ruins of Angkor. Along the Upper Mae Khong, you can reach the river towns of Kampong Cham, Kratie, and Stung Treng by regular fast ferries, called "bullet" boats; on the Lower Mae Khong and Tonle Basak, you have ready access to the Vietnamese cities of Chau Doc, Can Tho, and Ho Chi Minh City.

Cambodia has a fairly comprehensive domestic bus network, and bus travel is cheap. Within the cities and for shorter journeys, songthaews, motorcycle taxis, and cyclos (pedal-powered trishaws) are the best ways of getting around.

About the Restaurants

As might be expected from a country once ruled by the French, Cambodia has plenty of food to please demanding palates. Phnom Penh may not be Paris or Bangkok, but there are a few restaurants and upscale eateries among the plethora that serve excellent meals. In Siem Reap, some of the best food is served in the restaurants of a few hotels, but

Architecture

Hands-down, Southeast Asia's most magnificent archaeological treasure is the Angkor Temple Complex—hundreds of centuries-old ruins and monuments, many still hidden deep within the jungle. Even leaving aside the architectural splendor of the Angkor temples, Cambodia has a wealth of ancient monasteries to admire, and fascinating ruins to explore. Every quarter in Phnom Penh has a wat, or Buddhist temple, and wherever you travel in the countryside you can find a wat to rival the best the capital has to offer. The most prominent of those in Phnom Pen is Wat Phrah Keo in the Royal Palace compound, with its venerated Emerald Buddha. Phnom Penh also has plenty of colonial architecture, which melds Khmer and French influences to varying degrees; notable buildings include the National Museum and the Hotel Raffles Le Royal.

Cambodia's Cultural Heritage

At the top of the list of Cambodia's cultural gems is the Angkor Temple Complex, but you can find cultural highlights throughout the country. The National Museum in Phnom Penh, for example, houses a priceless collection of pre-Angkorian, Angkorian, and post-Angkorian antiquities. At Phnom Penh's National Theater, presentations of the epic dance drama the *Reamker* are highlights of any visit to Cambodia.

If you want to bring a piece of Cambodian culture home with you, you're in luck: Cambodian artisans abound, practicing traditions handed down through the generations. Look throughout the country for handicrafts in silver, stone, and wood, as well as homespun silks and basketwork.

Natural Beauty

Along the coastline on the Gulf of Thailand lie some of Southeast Asia's most unspoiled beaches and coral islands. The coastal resorts at Sihanoukville, Kampot, and Kep are nice beach destinations. Cambodia's remaining forest reserves in the north and east are lush and shelter rare species of flora and fauna. In a farsighted move to preserve the region, King Norodom Sihanouk decreed the creation of 23 protected areas, national parks (such as Virachey National Park), and wildlife sanctuaries.

---

local eateries are opening all the time to cater to the rising numbers of tourists. In both cities you can encounter French, Italian, Japanese, Indian, and Vietnamese and Thai food. Khmer cuisine is similar to Thai, Chinese, and Vietnamese food; a few restaurants meld the culinary traditions with laudable results.

Rice, fish, and meat soup—all prepared with a liberal use of aromatic herbs, sauces, and spices—are staples throughout the country.

About the Hotels

Both Phnom Penh and Siem Reap have an abundance of hotel rooms, and the range of rates is remarkably wide. Lodgings offering colonial elegance and a refined atmosphere can be had at prices comparable to those of any city in the world, but comfortable budget accommodations are also available in modest guesthouses at a mere fraction of those prices. The rapidly rising number of tourists visiting Angkor Wat has generated a startling hotel construction boom in Siem Reap, with most of the new properties catering to tour groups. In Sihanoukville, guesthouses predominate, but there's also a modern seaside resort.

All hotels expect payment in U.S. dollars. Hotel prices range from $300 and up at the exclusive Raffles properties to $15 for a basic guesthouse room with a private bath and air-conditioning or fan. Within that spread, there are business-class hotels that charge $100–$150, and many hotels with decent rooms complete with cable TV and minibars in the $30–$50 range.

WHAT IT COSTS In U.S. dollars					
	$$$$	**$$$**	**$$**	**$**	**¢**
RESTAURANTS	over $16	$12–$16	$8–$12	$5–$8	under $5
HOTELS	over $150	$100–$150	$50–$100	$25–$50	under $25

Restaurant prices are per person for a main course at dinner. Hotel prices are for a standard double room, excluding tax and service.

Timing

Cambodia's tropical climate consists of two seasons affected by the monsoon winds. The northeastern monsoon blowing toward the coast ushers in the cool, dry season in November, which lasts through February, with temperatures between 65°F (18°C) and 80°F (27°C). December and January are the coolest months. It heats up to around 95°F (35°C) in March and April, when the southwestern monsoon blows inland from the Gulf of Thailand, bringing downpours that last an hour or more most days. This rainy, humid season runs through October, with temperatures ranging from 80°F (27°C) to 95°F (35°C). The climate in Phnom Penh is always very humid—the relative humidity can hit 90%.

In addition to the weather, you should also take into consideration Cambodia's festival-packed calendar when planning your trip. It's important to book well in advance if you plan on visiting during mid-April's New Year celebrations or for the Water Festival in November. Most festivals are scheduled according to the Buddhist lunar calendar and the yearly flood levels of the river waters.

PHNOM PENH & ENVIRONS

Cambodia's capital is also the country's commercial and political hub, a busy city in the midst of rapid change. Over the past few years, the number of international hotels, large restaurants, sidewalk cafés, art galleries, boutiques, Internet cafés, and sophisticated nightclubs has increased dramatically. So has the city traffic: motorbikes and cyclos (trishaw taxis) fight for space with the new automobiles that testify to the rapid growth of the Cambodian middle class. For now, however, cyclos still dominate the street scene, and Phnom Penh is in no danger yet of losing its "city of cyclos" soubriquet.

Phnom Penh is the natural gateway to a slew of the north's accessible towns, far-off Rattanakiri Province in the northeast, and the beach town of Sihanoukville in the south. Seven paved but often potholed highways lead from the capital in all directions. These roads penetrate deep into the countryside, but also lead to day-trip destinations like the ruins of Tonle Bati and Phnom Chisor in the south, and the pagoda-topped hill of Udong and the Mae Khong island of Koh Dach in the north.

Phnom Penh

The capital of Cambodia, Phnom Penh is strategically positioned at the confluence of four branches of the Mae Khong River. The city's origins date to 1372, when a wealthy woman named Penh, who lived at the eastern side of a small hill near Tonle Sap, is said to have found five Buddha statues hidden in a large tree drifting down the river. With the help of her neighbors, she built a wooden sanctuary on top of the hill and invited Buddhist monks to settle on its western slope. In 1434 King Ponhea Yat established his capital on the same spot and constructed a brick pagoda on top of the hill. The capital was later moved twice, first to Lovek and later to Udong. In 1866 during the reign of King Norodom, the capital was moved back to Phnom Penh.

It was approximately during this time that France colonized Cambodia, and the French influence in the city is palpable—the legacy of a 90-year period that saw the construction of many colonial buildings, including the grandiose post office and railway station (both now in urgent need of repair). Phnom Penh's era of modern development took place after independence in 1953, with the addition of tree-lined boulevards, large stretches of gardens, and Independence Monument, built in 1958.

Today Phnom Penh has a population of about 2 million people. But during the Pol Pot regime's forced emigration of people from the cities, Phnom Penh had fewer than 1,000 residents. Buildings and roads deteriorated, and most side streets are still a mess. The main routes are now well paved, however, and the city's wats (temples) sport fresh coats of paint, as do many homes. This is a city on the rebound, and its vibrancy is in part due to the abundance of young people, many of whom were born after those dark years. Its wide streets are filled with motorcycles, which weave about in a complex ballet that only the dancers seem to understand, making it a thrilling achievement merely to cross the street (the best way is to screw up your courage and step straight into the flow, which should part for you as if by magic).

There are several wats and museums worth visiting, and the old city has plenty of attractive colonial buildings scattered about. The wide park that lines the waterfront between the Royal Palace and Wat Phnom—a great place for a sunset stroll—is about as lovely a spot as you'll find anywhere.

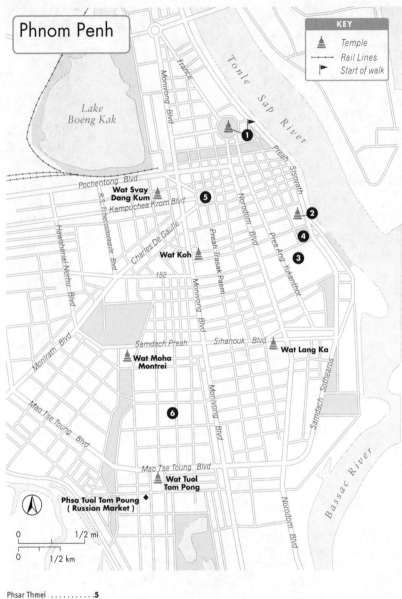

Phnom Penh

KEY

🛕 Temple

━━ Rail Lines

🚩 Start of walk

Lake Boeng Kak

Tonle Sap River

France

Monivong Blvd

Preah Sisowath

🛕🚩 ❶

Pochentong Blvd

Wat Svay Dang Kum 🛕

❺

R.S. Tchecoslovaquie Blvd

Kampuchea Krom Blvd

Norodom Blvd

Prea Ang Yukanthor

🛕 ❷

❹

❸

Hawaharlat Nehru Blvd

Charles De Gaulle

Wat Koh 🛕

Preah Trasak Paem

152

Monivong Blvd

Monirath Blvd

Samdach Preah

Sihanouk Blvd

Wat Lang Ka 🛕

🛕 **Wat Moha Montrei**

Samdach Sothearos

Mao Tse Toung Blvd

❻

Monivong Blvd

Bassac River

Mao Tse Toung Blvd

🛕 **Wat Tuol Tom Pong**

Norodom Blvd

⊕

Phsa Tuol Tom Poung (Russian Market) ◆

| 0 | 1/2 mi |
| 0 | 1/2 km |

Start your tour by taking a taxi to Phnom Penh Hill; after a walk in the surrounding gardens, climb the staircase and head for **Wat Phnom ❶ ▶**, where King Ponhea Yat is venerated. After descending the hill, head east to the Tonle Sap Riverside Restaurant (perhaps stopping for a snack and coffee), and then walk south along Sisowath Quay, which lines the Tonle Sap River. From here you have a fine view of the Chroy Changvar Peninsula—home to Khmer and Cham fisherfolk. The cobbled riverside path leads you to **Wat Unalom ❷**, one of Phnom Penh's largest and oldest pagodas.

After visiting the wat, continue south on Sisowath Quay, past a busy strip of bars and restaurants, including the popular colonial-era Foreign Correspondents Club, and on to a huge lawn in front of the ocher-color **Wayan ❸**, or Royal Palace. On the grounds of the palace is the must-see Wat Phrah Keo. On the northern side of the palace, a side street leads to the traditional-style **Sarak Monty Cheat ❹**, or National Museum, which is worth an hour or two of your time.

Retrace your steps back to the riverbank. Here you find a pavilion, from which you have a fine view of the Royal Palace on one side and the confluence of Phnom Penh's four rivers on the other. At each end of the riverside promenade there are small religious shrines, where vendors sell refreshments and birds in cages—you're expected to release them to help you earn your way through the Buddhist cycle of existence. Follow the riverside road past the Royal Palace, and from there to the modern white concrete Chaktomuk Theater, one of Phnom Penh's best surviving examples of postcolonial architecture. End your tour by strolling a little farther down the road for tea or cocktails at the stately Hotel Cambodiana, from which you can soak in breathtaking views of the Mae Khong River.

TIMING You can visit these sights in half a day, though you may want to allot more time if you want to linger at any one destination.

What to See

Choeung Ek Genocidal Museum (The Killing Fields). In the mid- to late 1970s, thousands of Khmer Rouge prisoners who had been tortured at the infamous Toul Sleng prison were taken to the extermination camp of Choeung Ek, also known as the Killing Fields, for execution. Today the camp is a memorial called the Choeung Ek Genocidal Museum. The site consists of little more than a monumental glass stupa built in 1989 and filled with 8,000 skulls, which were exhumed from mass graves nearby. It's an extremely disturbing sight: many of the skulls, which are grouped according to age and sex, bear the holes and slices from the blows that killed them. The site, which is 15 km (9 mi) southwest of the city center, at the end of a rough and dusty road, can be reached in 30 minutes on a motorbike taxi or by car. Guides are available, and there's a shop selling souvenirs and books. ⊠ *15 km (9 mi) southwest of downtown Phnom Penh* ☎ *No phone* ☜ *$2* ☉ *Daily 7–6.*

❺ **Phsar Thmei** (Central Market). An inescapable sightseeing destination in Phnom Penh is the colonial-era Central Market, built in the late 1930s on land that was once a watery swamp. This wonderfully ornate build-

CAMBODIA'S FESTIVALS

L IKE MANY SOUTHEAST ASIAN NATIONS, Cambodia celebrates a lot of important festivals. Quite a few of them are closely tied to Buddhism, the country's predominant religion.

Bonn Chaul Chhnam: This is also known as the Khmer Traditional New Year, which the government has set on April 13–15. It's a new-moon festival spread over the three days following the winter rice harvest. People celebrate by cleaning and decorating their houses, making offerings at their home altars, and going to Buddhist temples.

Bonn Om Touk: The Water Festival ushers in the fishing season and marks the "miraculous" reversal of the Tonle Sap waters. It's celebrated throughout the country: longboat river races are held, and an illuminated flotilla of naga, or dragon boats, adds to the festive atmosphere.

Chrat Preah Nongkol: The Royal Plough Ceremony, a celebration of the start of the summer planting season, is held in front of the Royal Palace in Phnom Penh in May. The impressive ceremony includes soothsaying rites meant to predict important events like the rice harvest.

Meak Bochea: On the day of the full moon in February, this festival commemorates the Buddha's first sermon to 1,250 of his disciples. In the evening, Buddhists parade three times around their respective pagodas.

King Sihanouk's Birthday: The birthday of King Norodom Sihanouk, born October 31, 1922, in Phnom Penh, is celebrated October 30–November 1; the whole nation joins in to honor him, and a grand fireworks display is held along the riverfront in Phnom Penh.

Phchom Ben (All Souls' Day): In mid-October, the spirits of deceased ancestors are honored according to Khmer tradition. People make special offerings at Buddhist temples to appease these spirits.

Visakha Bochea: This Buddhist festival, on the day of the full moon in May, celebrates the Buddha's birth, enlightenment, and death.

ing with a fine yellow dome combines art deco and Mesopotamian styles. The market's Khmer name, Phsar Thmei, translates as "new" market to distinguish it from Phnom Penh's original market, Phsar Chas, near the Tonle Sap River; it's popularly known as Central Market, however.

You enter the market through one of four great doors that face the directions of the compass. The main entrance, facing east, is lined with souvenir and textile merchants hawking everything from cheap T-shirts and postcards to expensive silks, handicrafts, and silverware. Other stalls sell electronic goods, mobile phones, watches, jewelry, household items, shoes, secondhand clothing, flowers, and just about anything else you can imagine. Money changers mingle with beggars and war veterans with disabilities asking for a few riel. ⊠ *Blvd. 128, Kampuchea Krom, at 76 St.* ☎ *No phone* ☉ *Daily 7–5.*

Phsar Tuol Tom Pong (Russian Market). This popular covered market earned its nickname in the 1980s, when the wives and daughters of Russian diplomats would often cruise the stalls on the lookout for curios and antiques. Today the market has a good selection of Cambodian handicrafts made from gold, silver, bronze, brass, cotton, silk, stone, and wood. Wood carvings and furniture abound, as do "spirit houses, " used for offerings of food, flowers, and incense. Colorful straw mats and hats as well as baskets are in high demand. The market is the city's best source for art objects, including statues of the Buddha and Hindu gods, and you can also buy valuable old Indo-Chinese coins and paper money printed during different times of Cambodia's turbulent modern history. A jumble of stalls concentrated at the market's south side sells CDs, videos, and all kinds of electronic items. ⊠ *Adjacent to Wat Tuol Tom Pong, at 154 and 155 Sts.* ☎ *No phone* ☉ *Daily 7–5.*

④ Sarak Monty Cheat (National Museum). Within this splendid, rust-red, colonial landmark are many archaeological treasures. Exhibits chronicle the various stages of Khmer cultural development, from the pre-Angkor periods of Fu Nan and Zhen La (5th–8th centuries) to the Indravarman period (9th century), classical Angkor period (10th–13th centuries), and post-Angkor period. Among the more than 5,000 artifacts and works of art are 19th-century dance costumes, royal barges, and palanquins. A palm-shaded central courtyard with lotus ponds houses the museum's showpiece: a sandstone statue of the Hindu god Yama, the Leper King, housed in a pavilion. Guides, who are usually waiting just inside the entrance, can add a lot to a visit here. ⊠ *Junction of 178th and 13th Sts., next to Royal Palace* ☎ *No phone* 💲 *$3, camera fee $1* ☉ *Daily 8–5.*

⑥ Sarak Monty Toul Sleng (Toul Sleng Genocide Museum). This museum is a horrific reminder of the cruelty of which humans are capable. Once a neighborhood school, the building was seized in 1975 by Pol Pot's Khmer Rouge and turned into a prison and interrogation center, the dreaded S-21. During the prison's four years of operation, some 17,000 Cambodians were tortured here; many of them died and were dumped into mass graves in back, but most were taken to the infamous "Killing Fields" for execution. Many of the soldiers who did the torturing were children, some as young as 10—many may be walking the streets of Phnom Penh today. The four school buildings that made up S-21 have been left as they were when the Khmer Rouge left in January 1979. The prison kept extensive records and photos of the victims, and many of the documents are on display. Particularly chilling are the representations of torture scenes painted by S-21 survivor Vann Nath. ⊠ *At 113th St. (Boeng Keng Kang) and 350th St.* ☎ *023/300698* 💲 *$2* ⊙ *Daily 8–11 and 2–5.*

📌 **①** **Wat Phnom.** According to legend, a wealthy woman named Penh found five statues of Buddha washed up on the banks of the Mae Khong, and in 1372 she commissioned this sanctuary to house them. Wat Phnom is perched atop the 90-foot knoll for which the city was named: Phnom Penh means "Hill of Penh." Sixty years later, King Ponhea Yat had a huge stupa built here to house his funeral ashes after his death. You approach the temple by a flight of steps flanked by bronze friezes of chariots in battle and heavenly *apsara* dancers. Inside the temple hall, the *vihear,* are some fine wall paintings depicting scenes from the Buddha's lives, and on the north side is a charming Chinese shrine. The bottom of the hill swarms with vendors selling everything from devotional candles and flowers to elephant rides. ⊠ *96th St. at Norodom Blvd.* ☎ *No phone* 💲 *$1* ⊙ *Daily 7–6:30.*

★ **Wat Phrah Keo** (Temple of the Emerald Buddha). Within the ⇨ **Wayan** (Royal Palace) grounds is Phnom Penh's greatest attraction: the Temple of the Emerald Buddha, built in 1892–1902 and renovated in 1962. The temple is often referred to as the Silver Pagoda because of the 5,329 silver tiles—more than 5 tons of pure silver—that make up the floor in the main vihear. At the back of the vihear is the venerated **Preah Keo Morokot** (Emerald Buddha)—some say it's carved from jade, whereas others maintain that it's Baccarat crystal. In front of the altar is a 200-pound solid-gold Buddha studded with 2,086 diamonds. Displayed in a glass case are the golden offerings donated by Queen Kossomak Nearyreath (King Sihanouk's mother) in 1969; gifts received by the royal family over the years are stored in other glass cases. The gallery walls surrounding the temple compound, which serves as the royal graveyard, are covered with murals depicting scenes from the Indian epic, the *Ramayana.* Pride of place is given to a bronze statue of King Norodom on horseback, erected in 1875, and there's a nearby shrine dedicated to the sacred bull Nandi. ⊠ *Sothearos Rd. between 184th and 240th Sts.* ☎ *No phone* 💲 *Included in $3 admission to Royal Palace* ⊙ *Daily 8–11 and 2:30–5.*

② **Wat Unalom.** The 15th-century Wat Unalom is now the center of Cambodian Buddhism. Until 1999 it housed the Institute Buddhique, which originally contained a large religious library destroyed by the Khmer Rouge in the 1970s. Wat Unalom's main vihear, built in 1952 and still intact, has three floors; the top floor holds paintings illustrating the lives of the Buddha. The central feature of the complex is the large stupa, **Chetdai,** which dates to Angkorian times and is said to contain hair from the Buddha's eyebrows. Four niche rooms here hold priceless bronze sculptures of the Buddha. The sanctuary is dedicated to the Angkorian king Jayavarman VII (circa 1120–1215). ⊠ *Riverfront, about 250 yards north of National Museum* ☎ *No phone* 💲 *Free* ⊙ *Daily 7–5.*

❸ **Wayan** (Royal Palace). A walled complex that covers several blocks near the river, the former official residence of King Sihanouk and Queen Monineath Sihanouk is a 1913 reconstruction of the timber palace built in 1866 by King Norodom. The residential areas of the palace are closed to the public, but within the pagoda-style compound are a number of structures worth visiting. These include ⇨ **Wat Phrah Keo;** the Throne Hall, with a tiered roof topped by a 200-foot-tall tower; and a pavilion donated by the Emperor Napoleon III and shipped from France to Cambodia. Guides can be hired at the entrance for $5. ✉ *Sothearos Rd. between 184th and 240th Sts.* ☎ *No phone* 🖅 *$3, camera fee $2, video-camera fee $5* ⊙ *Daily 8–11 and 2:30–5.*

Where to Stay & Eat

French cuisine dominates the restaurant scene, but if you're looking for authentic Khmer fare, cross the Japanese Friendship Bridge over the Tonle Sap River and enter the restaurant district known as Preak Lap. Dozens of restaurants—not only Khmer, but also Chinese and more upscale establishments serving Western food—line this culinary mile.

Phnom Penh has several international-standard hotels, including Raffles's flagship hotel in Southeast Asia. Clean and comfortable guesthouses are not easy to find, but there's a good selection of small hotels charging $50 or less a night.

$–$$ ✕ **Topaz.** The foie gras and other French specialties at this fine riverside restaurant are flown in directly from the homeland. You dine by candlelight, at tables sparkling with the best glass- and silverware. The entrecote steak in burgundy sauce is a local favorite. ✉ *102 Sothearos Rd.* ☎ *023/211054* 🖃 *AE, MC, V.*

¢–$$ ✕ **River House Restaurant.** The River House evokes a French bistro, with sidewalk seating and a daily set menu. It stands on a corner across the street from the northern end of the waterfront park, with half the tables outside, behind a potted hedge, and half beneath the ceiling fans of the open-air dining room. The menu is eclectic, ranging from couscous to coq au vin to homemade pastas. The exquisite "royal Khmer" dishes are based on traditional Thai cuisine; try the river fish cooked in a coconut shell. With a balcony overlooking the street and river, the upstairs evening bar is a great place for a drink or a game of pool. It's a good idea to reserve ahead. ✉ *Sisowath Quay at 110th St.* ☎ *023/212302* 🖃 *AE, MC, V.*

¢–$$ ✕ **Shiva Shakti.** Succulent samosas, vegetable *pakoras* (fritters), spicy lamb masala, chicken korma, and prawn *biryani* (with rice and vegetables) are among the dishes served at this small Indian restaurant popular with expats from India, England, and elsewhere. In the pleasant dining room, a statue of the elephant-headed Hindu god Ganesha stands by the door, and reproductions of Mogul art line the walls. There are also a few tables on the sidewalk. It's just east of Independence Monument. ✉ *70E Sihanouk Blvd.* ☎ *012/813817* 🖃 *AE, MC, V* ⊙ *Closed Mon.*

$ ✕ **Foreign Correspondents Club of Cambodia.** You don't have to be a journalist to join the international crowd at what has been described as Southeast Asia's best press club. People drop in as much for the atmosphere of the French colonial building and its river views as for the food, which

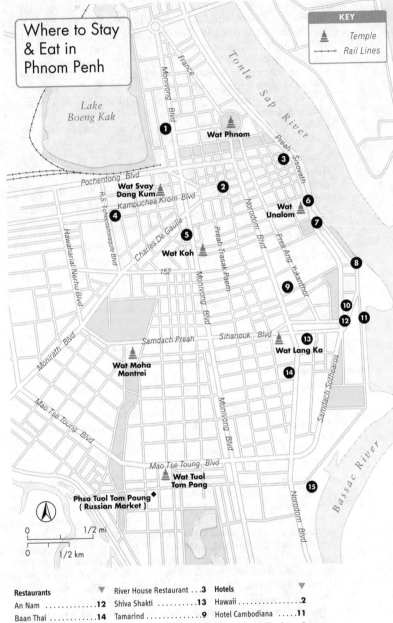

Where to Stay & Eat in Phnom Penh

Lake Boeng Kak

Tonle Sap River

Wat Phnom

Wat Svay Dang Kum

Wat Unalom

Wat Koh

Wat Moha Montrei

Wat Lang Ka

Wat Tuol Tom Pong

Phsa Tuol Tom Poung (Russian Market)

Bassac River

KEY

🔺 Temple
├┼┤ Rail Lines

0 ___ 1/2 mi
0 ___ 1/2 km

Restaurants ▼
An Nam 12
Baan Thai 14
Café California 6
Foreign
Correspondents Club ...7
Ginga 5

River House Restaurant ...3
Shiva Shakti 13
Tamarind 9
Topaz 10

Hotels ▼
Hawaii 2
Hotel Cambodiana 11
Hotel Raffles Le Royal ...1
Juliana 4
Ranak Se Hotel 8
Royal Phnom Penh 15

is as eclectic as the diners. Though the place is not particularly known for its food, you can grab a reliable cheeseburger and the pizza is good. If you find it difficult to leave this pleasant corner of Phnom Penh, you're in luck: there are even rooms for overnight guests. As befits a press club, there's also a business center with access to the Internet. ⊠ *363 Sisowath Quay* ☎ *023/724014* ▭ *AE, MC, V.*

$ ✕ **Ginga.** Phnom Penh's in-crowd packs this smart Japanese restaurant, which has a sushi bar stocked with the freshest appetizers. Servers keep diners well supplied with steaming hot sake and green tea. ⊠ *295–297 Monivong Blvd.* ☎ *023/217323* ▭ *MC, V.*

$ ✕ **Tamarind.** The Mediterranean comes east at this popular three-story bar-restaurant in the heart of the arty Vithei Okhna Chunn Street area. The menu extends from North African couscous specialties to Spanish tapas. The wine list is comprehensive and quite good. ⊠ *31 240th St.* ☎ *012/830139* ▭ *MC.*

¢–$ ✕ **Café California.** Travelers love this laid-back riverside Mexican restaurant, which also organizes tours and is a mine of tourist information. The restaurant is best known for its Baja-style fish tacos and Mexican burgers, but it serves excellent Khmer food as well. ⊠ *317 Sisowath Quay* ☎ *023/982182* ▭ *No credit cards.*

¢ ✕ **An Nam.** Delicious Vietnamese food is served at this air-conditioned restaurant next to the Hong Kong Center. The cuisine is central Vietnamese; try the fresh shrimp spring rolls as a starter. ⊠ *118 Sothearos Rd.* ☎ *023/212460* ▭ *MC, V.*

¢ ✕ **Baan Thai.** Although the garden setting is distinctly Cambodian, complete with an authentic Khmer wooden house, this popular restaurant serves Thai food. Favorite dishes include curries cooked with coconut milk and spicy *tom yam* soups. ⊠ *2 306th St., at Norodom Blvd.* ☎ *023/362991* ▭ *MC, V.*

★ $$$$ ✕▥ **Hotel Raffles Le Royal.** Phnom Penh's best hotel first opened in 1929, was practically destroyed during the Khmer Rouge years, and was meticulously restored by the Raffles group in 1996. A colonial landmark surrounded by gardens, Le Royal has an elegant lobby, a tranquil pool area shaded by massive trees, and various bars and restaurants that are a world apart from this slightly chaotic city—as are the prices. Guest rooms combine art deco furniture with fine Cambodian handicrafts and overlook the pool or gardens—older Landmark rooms are nicer. The Elephant Bar is famous for its cocktails, and the sumptuous Restaurant Le Royal ($$–$$$$) serves Khmer haute cuisine. ⊠ *92 Rukhak Vithei Daun Penh* ☎ *023/981888, 800/637–9477 in U.S., 800/6379–4771 in U.K.* 🖷 *023/981168* ⊕ *www.raffles-hotelleroyal.com* ➘ *208 rooms* △ *3 restaurants, patisserie, in-room safes, minibars, cable TV, pool, health club, spa, bar, lobby lounge, library, shops, laundry service, concierge, business services, meeting rooms, no-smoking rooms* ▭ *AE, MC, V* ⦿❙ *BP, MAP.*

$$–$$$ ✕▥ **Hotel Cambodiana.** Massive and modern, the Cambodiana towers over the Mae Khong riverbank a short walk from the Royal Palace. Spacious guest rooms are short on personality but have large baths and picture windows—be sure to request a river view. Rooms on the fifth-floor Mekong Club, which include such perks as a private lounge and free airport transfers, are worth the extra money. Four restaurants ($$–$$$$)

provide a choice of French (the smart Mekong Brasserie l'Amboise), pan-Asian (Asian Wok), international, and Italian food (by the pool). ✉ *313 Sisowath Quay* ☎ *023/426288* 🖷 *023/426392* 🌐 *www.hotelcambodiana. com* 🖙 *300 rooms* 🛆 *4 restaurants, patisserie, IDD phones, minibars, cable TV, tennis court, pool, exercise equipment, gym, hair salon, sauna, spa, bar, shops, laundry service, concierge, business services, meeting rooms, travel services, no-smoking rooms* ⊟ *AE, MC, V* ❙❍❙ *BP, MAP.*

★ **$$$** 🏨 **Royal Phnom Penh.** This tranquil hotel on the southern end of town has the good fortune to be set amid beautifully tended gardens. Guest rooms, in rows of one-story buildings, have sliding glass doors that overlook the abundant foliage. They are large, bright, and colorful, if not terribly Cambodian. The lobby, with its patisserie, wicker furniture, and live Khmer music, has much more charm. A large, modern restaurant serves a mix of Western and Asian cuisines. ✉ *Samdech Sothearos Blvd., Sankat Tonle Bassac* ☎ *023/982673* 🖷 *023/982661* 🌐 *www. royalphnompenhhotel.com.kh* 🖙 *75 rooms* 🛆 *Restaurants, patisserie, IDD phones, minibars, cable TV, driving range, 2 tennis courts, pool, health club, spa, bar, shops, laundry service, concierge, business services, no-smoking rooms* ⊟ *AE, MC, V* ❙❍❙ *BP.*

$$ 🏨 **Juliana.** A quiet resort hotel near the city center, the Juliana is run with efficiency and courtesy. Although this Thai-owned property was attacked by a mob during the anti-Thai riots in 2003, it emerged reasonably unscathed, and it's business as usual now. Local fabrics and rattan furnish the comfortable rooms, which surround a garden and swimming pool. There are two restaurants, one Thai and the other Japanese. ✉ *152 16th St.* ☎ *023/880530 or 023/880531* 🌐 *www. julianacambodia.com* 🖙 *59 rooms* 🛆 *2 restaurants, IDD phones, minibars, cable TV with movies, pool, gym, hair salon, sauna, shop, laundry service, business services* ⊟ *AE, MC, V.*

$ 🏨 **Hawaii.** Modest but with adequate services, this small, well-run, comfortable hotel is ideal for those who want to stay in the city center but shrink from paying the prices of more upscale lodgings. The Central Market is just a short walk away, and most of the other sights in town are easily accessible from here. The area abounds with restaurants. Rooms are basic but clean. ✉ *130 18th St.* ☎ *023/426747* 🖷 *023/426652* 🖙 *65 rooms* 🛆 *Fans, refrigerators, laundry service* ⊟ *No credit cards.*

$ 🏨 **Ranakse Hotel.** If this place were for sale, it would be advertised as a fixer-upper. The lovely, Khmer-style building dates from the colonial era and has the perfect location, across the street from the Royal Palace. Rooms are timeworn but clean, with small windows, dark-wood furniture, and paintings of Cambodian landscapes. A few rooms have small balconies overlooking the ample grounds, which are shaded by coconut palms and large trees but littered with rubble. A simple, complimentary breakfast is served in the foyer, which is the most pleasant spot in the place. ✉ *Samdach Sothearos* ☎ *023/215701* 🖷 *023/722457* 🖙 *30 rooms* 🛆 *Fans, refrigerators, cable TV, laundry service; no a/c* ⊟ *MC, V* ❙❍❙ *CP.*

Nightlife & the Arts

THE ARTS There are a few small theaters with programs of traditional music and dancing, although Siem Reap has more and better venues. **Chaktomuk**

Theater (⊠ Sisowath Quay ☏ No phone) hosts performances of traditional music and dance. The dates and times of shows are listed in the English-language newspaper *Cambodia Daily*. Very authentic and aesthetically pleasing performances of traditional music and dance are presented Friday evenings at 7 at the **Sovannaphum Art Association** (⊠ 111 360th St. ☏ 012/846020).

NIGHTLIFE Phnom Penh's nightlife rivals that of Bangkok. Most of the dusk-to-dawn nightspots are near the Tonle Sap riverside and along 240th Street. With its American and Australian music, **Freebird** (⊠ 69 240th St. ☏ 012/810569) attracts an expat crowd. **Rubies** (⊠ 13 240th St. ☏ 012/ 823962) is a smart, laid-back wine bar enhanced by sophisticated piped music and an occasional live combo.

Ginger Monkey (⊠ 178th St. ☏ 012/413492) is a popular haunt in a former artist's studio. The music, a good mix of Western and Khmer, bounces off walls, which are hung with interesting art. It's open until 3 AM and sometimes later. **GooChi** (⊠ 50 Sihanouk Blvd. ☏ 023/224666) hosts live music nightly—mostly R&B and Western pop—and has a happy hour from 4 to 8. Dancers make for the disco **Heart of Darkness** (⊠ 26 51st St. ☏ 023/231776).

Shopping

The city has many boutiques selling everything from fake antiques to fine jewelry. Prices are generally set at these boutiques, so you won't be able to bargain. The best of these are on 178th Street.

Bazar (⊠ 28 Sihanouk Blvd. ☏ 012/866178) includes some rare Chinese pieces among its eclectic collection of Asian art and antiques. **Couleurs d'Asie** (⊠ 19 360th St. ☏ 012/902650) has regular exhibitions of Asian art and also many fine examples of local artists' work. **Kravanh House** (⊠ 13E 178th St. ☏ 012/756631) has one of the city's best selections of raw silk and silk products. **Le Lezard Bleu** (⊠ 61 240th St. ☏ 023/986978) has a gallery of local artists' work and a collection of small antiques. **Lotus Pond** (⊠ 57 178th St. ☏ 012/833149) has a good selection of fine Cambodian silks, carvings and statues, spirit houses, and small items of furniture. **Roth Souvenir Shop** (⊠ 8 178th St. ☏ 012/ 603484) is the outlet for curios, handicrafts, and small decorative items. **Sayon Silk Shop** (⊠ 40 178th St. ☏ 023/990219) has an exquisite collection of silks and ready-made items.

The largest market in Phnom Penh is **Phsar Thmei** (⊠ Blvd. 128, Kampuchea Krom, at 76 St.), popularly known as Central Market, an art deco–style structure in the center of the city that sells foodstuffs, household goods, fake antiques, and some silver and gold jewelry. You're expected to bargain—start off by offering half the named price and you'll probably end up paying about 70%. It's busiest in the morning.

The **Phsar Tuol Tom Pong** (Russian Market ⊠ Adjacent to Wat Tuol Tom Pong, at 154 and 155 Sts. ☏ No phone) sells Cambodian handicrafts, wood carvings, baskets, electronics, and much more.

RELIGION IN CAMBODIA

A S IN NEIGHBORING THAILAND, LAOS, AND VIETNAM, the belief in spirits is widespread in Cambodia. Although 90% of Cambodians are Buddhist, many believe in powerful neak ta, or territorial guardian spirits. Spirit shrines are common in Khmer houses as well as on temple grounds. The Khmer Loeu hill tribes, who live in the remote mountain areas of Rattanakiri and Mondulkiri provinces, and some tribes of the Cardamom Mountains are pure animists, believing in spirits living in trees, rocks, and water.

The main layer of Cambodian religion is a mix of Hinduism and Buddhism. These two religions reached the country from India about 2,000 years ago and played a pivotal role in the social and ideological life of the earliest kingdoms. Buddhism flourished in Cambodia in the 12th–13th centuries, when King Jayavarman VII embraced Mahayana Buddhism. By the

15th century, influenced by Buddhist monks from Siam, most Cambodians practiced Theravada Buddhism.

Cambodian religious literature and royal classical dance draw on Hindu models, such as the Reamker, an ancient epic about an Indian prince searching for his abducted wife and fighting an evil king. Brahman priests still play an important role at court rituals.

Cambodia's 500,000 Cham, who migrated here in the 15th century when forced from present-day Vietnam, are Muslim. The country's 60,000 Roman Catholics are mainly ethnic Vietnamese. A small Chinese minority follows Taoism.

Around Phnom Penh

Within easy reach to the south of Phnom Penh are the beaches of Tonle Bati, a small lake with a couple of temples nearby, and the lovely temple at Phnom Chisor. North of Phnom Penh are two easily accessible destinations: the river island of Koh Dach and the pilgrimage center of Udong.

Buses to Tonle Bati, Phnom Chisor, and Udong leave hourly every day. For Tonle Bati and Phnom Chisor take a bus headed to Takeo—there's a Tonle Bati stop, but for Phnom Chisor, you'll have to get out at Prasat Neang Khmau, where you can hire a moto to take you up the hill. Though the bus is dirt cheap, it might be easier to hire a car and driver; you can combine Tonle Bati and Phnom Chisor in one trip.

Tonle Bati
🕐 **7** *33 km (20 mi) south of Phnom Penh.*

On weekends, Phnom Penh city dwellers head for this small lake just a half hour's drive south on Highway 2. It has a beach, with refreshment stalls and souvenir stands, as well as many beggars and children clamoring for attention. You can avoid this by visiting the nearby, but more remote, **Ta Phrom**, a 12th-century temple built around the time of Siem Reap's Angkor Thom and Bayon. The five-chambered laterite temple has several well-preserved Hindu and Buddhist bas-reliefs. Nearby is an attractive, smaller temple, **Yeah Peau**. Both temples are free and open to the public at all times. About 11 km (7 mi) farther south is Phnom Tamao, Cambodia's leading zoo.

Phnom Chisor

8 *55 km (34 mi) south of Phnom Penh.*

A trip to Phnom Chisor is worth the drive just for the view from the top of the hill of the same name. There's a road to the summit, but most visitors prefer the 20-minute walk to the top, where stunning vistas of the Cambodian countryside unfold. At the summit, the 11th-century temple, which is free and open to the public, is a Khmer masterpiece of laterite, brick, and sandstone.

Koh Dach

9 *30 km (19 mi) north of Phnom Penh.*

This Mae Khong River island is home to a handicrafts community of silk weavers, woodcarvers, potters, painters, and jewelry makers. Boats from Phnom Penh's Sisowath Quay ferry visitors to the island—a fascinating trip along a wide stretch of the Mae Khong bordered by fishing villages.

Udong

10 *45 km (28 mi) north of Phnom Penh.*

This small town served as the Khmer capital from the early 1600s until 1866, when King Norodom moved the capital south to Phnom Penh. Today it's an important pilgrimage destination for Cambodians paying homage to their former kings. You can join them on the climb to the pagoda-studded hilltop, site of the revered Vihear Prah Ath Roes assembly hall, which still bears the scars of local conflicts from the Khmer Rouge era.

North of Phnom Pehn

If you're looking to go even farther afield, you can visit the ancient ruins of Kampong Thom or Kampong Cham, see freshwater dolphins at Kratie, or head to the truly remote and largely undeveloped Rattankiri Province. The city of Battambang (Cambodia's second-largest) may be closer to Siem Reap on the map, but Phnom Pehn is the logical jumping point for a visit there. Note that many of these destinations are quite removed from one another or accessed via different routes, and thus can't be combined in one tour.

Kampong Cham

11 *125 km (78 mi) northeast of Phnom Penh.*

Cambodia's third-largest city was also an ancient Khmer center of culture and power on the Mae Khong River, and it has a pre-Angkorian temple, **Wat Nokor**. The temple is free and open to the public at all times.

    ¢   🏨 **Mekong Hotel.** A Japanese enterprise built this riverside hotel but kept to a high-eaved Cambodian style. The boat pier is close by and river-craft skippers tend to blast their horns early to announce their departure, so if you like to sleep late, book a room at the back. Rooms are large and smartly furnished in light woods and fabrics. ⊠ *River Rd.,* ☎ *042/941536* ↗ *18 rooms* ⚹ *Restaurant, refrigerators, cable TV, laundry service, travel services* ▤ *No credit cards.*

Kampong Thom
⑫ *160 km (99 mi) north of Phnom Penh.*

This provincial town, exactly halfway between Phnom Penh and Siem Reap, boasts ruins that are even older than those at Angkor. They are all that remain of the 7th-century Sambor Prei Kuk, the capital of Zhen La, a loose federation of city states. The ruins, which are free and open to the public at all times, are near the Stung Sen River, 35 km (22 mi) northeast of Kampong Thom.

Kratie
⑬ *350 km (217 mi) northeast of Phnom Penh.*

Kratie is famous for the colony of freshwater dolphins that inhabits the Mae Khong River some 15 km (9 mi) north of town. The dolphins are most active in the early morning and late afternoon. Taxis and hired cars from Kratie charge about $10 for the journey to the stretch of river where the dolphins can be observed. Ferries from Phnom Penh take 5 hours and cost about $8; there's also ferry service from Kampong Cham for about $4.

    ¢   🏨 **Santepheap Hotel.** Ask for a room with a river view at this newly built hotel across the road from the boat pier. Rooms are simple, with little decoration, but comfortable enough, and the bathrooms are large, with tubs. ⊠ *River Rd., Kratie* ☎ *072/971537* ↗ *24 rooms* ⚹ *Restaurant, some rooms with a/c, some rooms with TV* ▤ *No credit cards.*

Rattanakiri Province
Ban Lung is 635 km (394 mi) northeast of Phnom Penh.

The government aims to turn the northeastern province of Rattankiri (and nearby Mondulkiri province) into an ecotourism destination. The region is mountainous and covered with dense jungle. Together, Rattankiri and Mondulkiri provinces are home to 12 different Khmer Loeu ethnic-minority groups. Visiting the region evokes a feeling of arriving ⑭ at the end of the world. The provincial capital of Rattanakiri is **Ban Lung;** it's best to fly here from Phnom Penh, rather than attempt the arduous drive. In Ban Lung you can hire a jeep (preferably with a driver-guide) or, if you're very adventurous, a motorcycle, to visit the fascinating destinations an hour or two away: the gem-mining area of **Bo Keo,** some 35 km (22 mi) to the east; mystical **Yeak Laom Lake,** deep in a volcanic crater and sacred to many of the Khmer Loeu hill tribes; and the beautiful **Virachey National Park,** 35 km (22 mi) to the northeast, with its the two-tiered Bu Sra Waterfall.

CAMBODIA'S EARLY HISTORY

THE EARLIEST PREHISTORIC SITE EXCAVATED in Cambodia is the cave of Laang Spean in the northwest. Archaeologists estimate that hunters and gatherers lived in the cave 7,000 years ago. Some 4,000 years ago, this prehistoric people began to settle in permanent villages. The Bronze Age settlement of Samrong Sen, near Kampong Chhnang, indicates that 3,000 years ago, people knew how to cast bronze axes, drums, and gongs for use in religious ceremonies; at the same time, they domesticated cattle, pigs, and water buffaloes. Rice and fish were then, as now, the staple diet. By 500 BC, ironworking had become widespread, rice production increased, and circular village settlements were surrounded by moats and embankments. It was at this stage that Indian traders and missionaries arrived—in a land then called Suvarnabhumi, or Golden Land.

Legend has it that in the first century AD, the Indian Brahman Kaundinya arrived by ship in the Mae Khong Delta, where he met and married a local princess named Soma. The marriage led to the founding of the first kingdom on Cambodian soil. Archaeologists believe that the kingdom's capital was located at Angkor Borei in Takeo Province.

In the 6th century, the inland kingdom of Zhen La emerged. It comprised several small city states in the Mae Khong River basin. A period of centralization followed, during which temples were built, cities enlarged, and land irrigated. Power later shifted to Siem Reap Province, where the history of the Khmer empire started when a king of uncertain descent established the Devaraja line by becoming a "god-king." This royal line continues today.

WHERE TO STAY & EAT
$

✕🏠 **Terres Rouge Lodge.** This handsome property on the edge of Ban Lung's Boeung Kan Siang Lake is the region's best. It's a traditional wooden-built Cambodian country house, decorated in traditional style, with antiques and local artifacts in the spacious rooms. The restaurant is also one of the best of the area. ✉ *Boueung Kan Siang Lake, Ban Lung* ☎ *075/974051* 🛏 *14 rooms* ⚑ *Restaurant, refrigerators, TV, shop, laundry service, travel services* 🚫 *No credit cards.*

Battambang
⑮ *290 km (180 mi) northwest of Phnom Penh.*

Cambodia's second-largest city straddles the Sanker River in the center of the country's rice bowl. Dusty Battambang is bypassed by most visitors to Cambodia, but it's still an interesting city to explore. The French left their mark here with some fine old buildings. Long before the French arrived, Battambang was an important Khmer city, and among its many temples is an 11th-century Angkorian temple, **Wat Ek Phnom.** The temple has some fine stone carvings in excellent condition. It's free and open to the public at all times. Outside the city is the 11th-century hilltop temple **Phnom Banan,** with five impressive towers. It's free and open to the public at all times.

Phsar Nath Market is an exotic place to spend an hour or two souvenir-hunting. The market is known for its gems, but it also sells local market wares—everything from fresh produce to electronics imported from China. Some stalls sell textiles, but most of these are imported. ⊠ *On the River Sangker* ☎ *No phone* ⊘ *Daily 7–5.*

WHERE TO
STAY & EAT
¢

✕☲ **Teo Hotel.** Battambang's best hotel sits on a busy main road, so insist on a room at the rear. Rooms are reminiscent of French provincial auberges, with lots of fussy chintz and incongruous decorations. There are even floor-to-ceiling French windows. The garden restaurant serves Khmer, Thai, and Western dishes. ⊠ *3rd St., Svay Pro Commune* ☎ *012/857048* 🖨 *012/857048* 📞 *81 rooms* ♨ *Restaurant, IDD phones, shop* ⊟ *MC, V.*

PHNOM PENH & ENVIRONS A TO Z

AIR TRAVEL
There are direct flights to Phnom Penh from Bangkok, Hong Kong, Shanghai, Guangzhou (China), Taipei, Hanoi, Ho Chi Minh City, Kuala Lumpur, Singapore, Vientiane, and Pakse (Laos).

Major carriers with service to Phnom Penh are Bangkok Airways, Lao Airlines, Siem Reap Airways, Thai International Airways, and Vietnam Airlines. There are two domestic carriers serving Cambodian cities: President Airlines and Royal Phnom Penh Airways.

Thai International Airways flies twice daily from Bangkok to Phnom Penh, and Bangkok Airways has three flights a day. The trip takes about an hour and costs less than $200 round-trip. Cambodia's President Airlines has charter flights from Bangkok to Phnom Penh; a round-trip flight with one night's accommodation and airport transfers costs less than $200. Vietnam Airlines has daily flights from Ho Chi Minh City to Phnom Penh, and four flights from Hanoi.

President Airlines flies once daily from Phnom Penh to Battambang and four times a week to Rattanakiri. All inquiries are handled by the Phnom Penh office.

🎴 Carriers **Bangkok Airways** ☎ 023/426624 ⊕ www.bangkokair.com. **Lao Airlines** ☎ 023/216563 ⊕ www.laoairlines.com. **President Airlines** ☎ 023/212887 ⊕ www. presidentairlines.com. **Royal Phnom Penh Airways** ☎ 023/216487 ⊕ www.gocambodia. com/airway/background.shtml. **Siem Reap Airways** ☎ 023/720022 ⊕ www. siemreapairways.com. **Thai International Airways** ☎ 023/214359 ⊕ www.thaiairways. com. **Vietnam Airlines** ☎ 023/363396 ⊕ www.vietnamairlines.com.vn.

AIRPORTS & TRANSFERS
Phnom Penh's modern Pochentong Airport is 10 km (6 mi) west of downtown. The international departure tax is $25, and the charge for domestic departures is $5.

A taxi from the airport to downtown Phnom Penh costs $7. Motorcycles are much cheaper ($2), but very uncomfortable, particularly if you're traveling with anything more cumbersome than a small backpack.

BOAT TRAVEL

Boats from Phnom Penh make the six-hour trip on the Mae Khong River to Chong Khneas, near Siem Reap and Angkor. Ferries depart Phnom Penh from the municipal port on Sisowath Quay, at 84th Street, early in the morning. The cost is $20–$30 one-way. Tickets can be purchased at most hotels and travel agencies. Mekong Express has the quickest boats.

There's a daily boat from Battambang to Siem Reap, which takes 3–4 hours on the Tonle Sap lake and costs $15.

Mekong Express ☎ 023/427518 in Phnom Penh, 063/963662 in Siem Reap.

BUS TRAVEL

Buses to outlying cities and towns leave from Phnom Penh's Central Market, at the end of Old Kampuchea Krom Boulevard. Tickets can be purchased at the market or from Phnom Penh's two leading travel agencies, Diethelm Travel and Christinair Tours.

Buses run regularly to Kampong Cham and Kampong Thom, but it's just as easy to take a taxi, which will probably be more comfortable.

There are several buses daily from Phnom Penh to Battambang, generally departing between 6:30 AM and 8 AM and costing around $4. However, it's a long trip (6 to 8 hours), so most people take an express boat.

Christinair Tours ✉ 19–20 371st St., off Maida St., Phnom Penh ☎ 023/884432 ⊕ www.cambodia-exotic-holidays.com. **Diethelm Travel** ✉ 65 240th St., Phnom Penh ☎ 023/219151 ⊕ www.diethelm-travel.com.

CAR TRAVEL

A hired car with a driver costs about $20 a day, but settle on the price before setting off. You can arrange to hire a car with driver through any hotel. This is perhaps the easiest way to visit Tonle Bati, Phnom Chisor, and Kratie.

Kampong Cham and Kampong Thom are both two hours by car, but it's advisable to hire a driver.

EMERGENCIES

For medical emergencies, visit the International SOS Medical Clinic or Tropical & Travelers Medical Clinic.

Hospitals Calmette Hospital ✉ 3 Monivong Blvd., Phnom Penh ☎ 023/426948. **International SOS Medical Clinic** ✉ 161 51st St., Phnom Penh ☎ 023/216911, 015/912100 mobile. **Tropical & Travelers Medical Clinic** ✉ 88 108th St., Phnom Penh ☎ 023/366802, 015/912100 mobile.

HEALTH

Always drink bottled water and avoid uncooked food. Phnom Penh is malaria free, but it's still a good idea to bring mosquito-repellent spray or cream.

INTERNET

Internet cafés are opening all the time in Phnom Penh, so you'll have no problem finding one. Battambang also has several Internet cafés. Rates are about $2 an hour.

MAIL & SHIPPING

🏢 Post Offices **Main Post Office** ✉ 13th St., between 98th and 102nd Sts., Phnom Penh.

MONEY MATTERS

Phnom Penh's Mekong Bank has exchange windows that remain open weekends. Banks in Battambang and other northern centers can change money and traveler's checks.

🏢 Banks **Mekong Bank** ✉ 1 114th St., Phnom Penh ☎ 023/217112. **Cambodia Asia Bank** ✉ 252 Monivong Blvd., Phnom Penh ☎ 023/722105. **Cambodian Commercial Bank** ✉ 26 Monivong Blvd., Phnom Penh ☎ 023/426145.

SAFETY

After years of instability, Cambodia is now no less safe than anywhere else in Southeast Asia. There have been muggings, however, on the streets of Phnom Penh, mostly at night, but these are rare. Still, it's a good idea to keep most of your cash, valuables, and passport in a hotel safe, and avoid walking on side streets after dark. If you do stay out late, return to your hotel in a taxi rather than on a moto or cyclo.

SIGHTSEEING TOURS

Various companies arrange day tours of Phnom Penh and nearby sights; note, however, that guides can be hired right at the Royal Palace and National Museum.

The best of the tour companies are Christinair Tours and Diethelm Travel, which offer half- and full-day tours of Phnom Penh and Mae Khong and Tonle Sap boat trips for $30–$69.

🏢 **Christinair Tours** ✉ 19–20 371st St., off Maida St., Phnom Penh ☎ 023/884432 ⊕ www.cambodia-exotic-holidays.com. **Diethelm Travel** ✉ 65 240th St., Phnom Penh ☎ 023/219151 ⊕ www.diethelm-travel.com.

TAXI, MOTO & CYCLO TRAVEL

The most common form of transportation in Phnom Penh is the moto (motorcycle taxi). They cruise the streets in abundance, as well as gathering outside hotels and restaurants—wherever you walk, you'll attract them. The standard fare for a short trip in a moto is 2,000–4,000 riels, though they often try to get more from foreigners. Less-abundant cyclos (pedal trishaws) charge the same. Cruising taxis are nonexistent, but there are usually a couple parked outside large hotels, and the receptionist at any hotel can call one. Few drivers speak much English.

TRAIN TRAVEL

There's limited train service from Phnom Penh, but it's slow and uncomfortable. Train service connects Phnom Penh to Battambang in the northwest; the journey takes 12 hours and costs $3. You can purchase tickets through Diethelm Travel, Christinair Tours, or another tour company in Phnom Penh.

VISITOR INFORMATION

The best sources of local information are the offices of Diethelm Travel and Christinair Tours. In addition to serving Mexican food, Café California is a good source of tourist information.

For the most part, the people at the information booth in the Phnom Penh airport are in the business of booking hotel rooms, but they may have city maps to give away. There's a city tourism office across from Wat Unalom that produces a brochure, though the map in it is not very helpful. It's open weekdays 8–noon and 2–5:30. Ministry of Tourism can provide brochures.

🍴 **Café California** ✉ 317 Sisowath Quay, Phnom Penh ☎ 023/982182 ⊕ www. cafecaliforniaphnompenh.com. **Christinair Tours** ✉ 19–20 371st St., off Maida St., Phnom Penh ☎ 023/884432 ⊕ www.cambodia-exotic-holidays.com. **Department of Phnom Penh Tourism** ✉ 313 Preah Sisowath Quay, Phnom Penh ☎ 023/913483. **Diethelm Travel** ✉ 65 240th St., Phnom Penh ☎ 023/219151 ⊕ www.diethelm-travel.com. **Ministry of Tourism** ✉ 3 Monivong Blvd., Phnom Penh ☎ 023/216484.

SIEM REAP & ANGKOR TEMPLE COMPLEX

The temples of Angkor constitute one of the world's great ancient sites and Southeast Asia's most impressive archaeological treasure. The massive structures, surrounded by monsoon forest, are comparable to the Maya ruins of Central America; the abundant statues and extensive bas-relief murals are as beautiful as those in the great temples of India, or the art of the ancient Egyptians. The complex is usually overrun with tourists from several continents, who arrive by the busload to gawk, sigh, contribute to a babble of collective admiration, and wander into each other's snapshots.

Siem Reap is a small, provincial town that has won renown because of the nearby Angkor ruins. The town—actually a cluster of rice-farming villages with an older French colonial center—stretches just over a mile along both sides of the Siem Reap River, some 315 km (195 mi) northwest of Phnom Penh. In recent years, it has grown out of all proportion to its original size and importance, thanks to the influx of tourists visiting Angkor. An international airport, about 6½ km (4 mi) outside town, works almost to capacity, with flights landing and taking off throughout the day—passengers are treated to spectacular views of the Angkor site and Angkor Wat from the air.

Siem Reap

🔟 *322 km (200 mi) north of Phnom Penh.*

There's little to see in Siem Reap itself, despite its portentous historical name—"Defeat of Siam" (referring to the 15th-century invasion of the area by the Siamese)—and despite the great boost to its nightlife and bar-and-restaurant scene resulting from the influx of tourists. Construction sites are a common eyesore in this rapidly expanding town, but it does have an old French colonial sector near the river, which has a lively market. Most of the colonial buildings were either destroyed or abandoned during the Khmer Rouge years, but many have been restored and are now attractive hotels and restaurants.

At the end of a day of sightseeing, a relaxing way to pass the evening is to stroll down to the Siem Reap River, which cuts the town in half.

Where to Stay & Eat

Fame has brought the developers to Siem Reap, which is in the grip of a building boom. Luxury hotels are shooting up to cater to an ever more demanding market, and the formerly dreary restaurant scene gets better and better each year.

¢–$ ✕ **The Ivy.** Vegetarians are well catered for at the popular, cheap, and cheerful Ivy, in the Old Market area. You can play a game of pool while waiting for your food—good vegetarian-friendly fare that often incorporates tofu. There's live music most nights. ⊠ *Old Market* ☎ *012/ 800860* ⊟ *No credit cards.*

¢–$ ✕ **The Tell Restaurant.** German dishes, as well as Khmer and Asian specialties, are served at this well-run restaurant. The portions of German pork knuckle and schnitzel are huge, and imported Bavarian wheat beer is an ideal accompaniment. ⊠ *374 Sivatha Rd.* ☎ *063/963289* ⊟ *AE, MC, V.*

¢ ✕ **Chao Praya.** The traditional dance show staged nightly is reason enough to spend an evening at this pleasant buffet-style restaurant. Another draw is the eclectic menu, which even includes Mongolian barbecue. ⊠ *64 Angkor Wat Rd.* ☎ *063/380266* ⊟ *MC, V.*

¢ ✕ **Good Karma.** This friendly, crowded, riverside restaurant is a good place to grab a quick meal on the way to tour the temples. The steaks and pizzas are a good value, and there's a large selection of sandwiches. ⊠ *Pakambor River St.* ☎ *012/835762* ⊟ *No credit cards.*

¢ ✕ **Tonle Sap.** Start your day with a rice-based Khmer breakfast (served from 6:30 AM), such as rice and chicken, at this very traditional restaurant, where dancers entertain in the evening. Japanese sukiyaki is served at the lunch and dinner buffets. ⊠ *117 Airport Rd.* ☎ *063/963388* ⊟ *No credit cards.*

★ $$$$ ✕⬚ **La Résidence d'Angkor.** Packed into a central walled compound, this hotel's guest rooms are stunning and spacious. A subtle mix of hardwoods, white walls and bedspreads, colorful pillows, and Khmer art decorates the elegant Asian-style rooms. Sliding glass doors open onto narrow balconies, and sliding wooden doors enclose a long bathroom/ dressing area with a large round tub at one end. The narrow green-tile pool, gardens, statues, and open-air bar are equally attractive. The restaurant ($$–$$$$), which serves an inventive mix of Asian and Western dishes, is one of the town's best. ⊠ *Vithei Achasvar* ☎ *063/963390* 🖷 *063/963391* ⊕ *www.pansea.com* ↪ *55 rooms* ⚹ *Restaurant, IDD phones, in-room safes, minibars, cable TV, pool, bar, shops, laundry service, concierge, business services* ⊟ *AE, MC, V.*

★ $$$$ ✕⬚ **Raffles Grand Hotel d'Angkor.** Built in 1928, this grande dame was restored and reopened in 1997 after nearly being destroyed by occupying Khmer Rouge guerillas. The Grand now ranks among the region's finest, and most expensive, hotels. It combines French sensibilities and Cambodian art, with Oriental carpets and wicker furniture; rooms are large and elegant, with balconies that overlook the extensive Taj Mahal–inspired gardens and blue-tile pool. The elegant Restaurant Le Grand's steak Rossini is superb, and the wine list is extensive. The Brasserie and the Conservatory are cheaper restaurants, but are also high quality. The nightly cultural show is free. ⊠ *1 Vithei Charles de Gaulle*

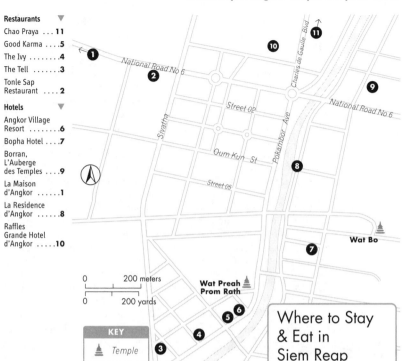

Where to Stay & Eat in Siem Reap

☎ 063/963888 📠 063/963168 ⊕ *www.raffles-grandhoteldangkor.com* 🛏 *150 rooms* ⚴ *3 restaurants, patisserie, room service, IDD phones, in-room safes, minibars, cable TV, pool, health club, spa, bar, lobby lounge, shops, dry cleaning, laundry service, concierge, business services, meeting rooms, no-smoking rooms* ▭ *AE, MC, V* ⍾⍿ *BP, MAP.*

$–$$ ✕🖬 **Bopha Hotel.** Across the street from the Siem Reap River's east bank is this small hotel offering quality Khmer cuisine and comfortable rooms at very competitive prices. The guest rooms have tile floors, wood ceilings, local handicrafts, and mosquito nets. They surround an attractive, open-air restaurant (¢–$) set amid gardens and small pools, where dinner is accompanied by live Cambodian harp music. A delicious and affordable selection—from chicken sautéed with pumpkin to fried fish with ginger and lemongrass—makes this a good dinner option even if you're staying elsewhere. ⊠ *512 Vithei Achasvar* ☎ *063/964928* 📠 *063/964446* ⊕ *www.bopha-angkor.com* 🛏 *23 rooms* ⚴ *Restaurant, minibars, cable TV, laundry service* ▭ *No credit cards.*

★ $$–$$$ 🖬 **Angkor Village Resort.** On a dusty street downtown is this oasis of wooden buildings, gardens, and pools filled with lotus blossoms. It's a warm and welcoming place, from the airy teak lobby to the tasteful rooms. Standard rooms are small, so it's best to pay for superior rooms, which are bigger and brighter and overlook the water and verdure. All rooms have Khmer handicrafts. The open-air restaurant, set in the middle of a pool, serves French and Asian cuisine. The cultural show performed in the hotel's gorgeous theater is a must-see. ⊠ *Sangkat Svay Dong Kum* ☎ *063/963561* 🖷 *063/963363* ⊕ *www.angkorvillage.com* 🛏 *49 rooms* ♨ *Restaurant, in-room safes, minibars, pool, lobby lounge, theater, shop, laundry service, concierge, business services* ▭ *AE, MC, V* ⎮◯⎮ *BP.*

$$ ▦ **La Maison d'Angkor.** This bungalow resort is a low-key alternative to the large luxury hotels springing up in Siem Reap. The 28 spacious bungalows, furnished with local fabrics and woods, are set in a luxuriant garden surrounding a large pool. Although it's on the road to the airport, the resort is very quiet and secluded. It's a five-minute drive from town, and a 10-minute drive from the Angkor temples. ⊠ *71 Hwy. 6* ☎ *063/965045* 🖷 *063/964966* ⊕ *www.lamaisondangkor.com* 🛏 *28 bungalows* ♨ *In-room safes, minibars, cable TV* ▭ *AE, MC, V.*

★ **$** ▦ **Borann, l'Auberge des Temples.** The accommodations are attractive and the rates low at this tranquil small hotel a couple of blocks east of the river. Khmer handicrafts and antiques fill the rooms, which have high ceilings and tile floors. Each one has a large porch or balcony overlooking a nicely planted yard, which holds a small pool and open-air thatched restaurant. Large bathrooms with stone floors have both a shower and the traditional Cambodian bathing option of scooping water out of a giant ceramic urn. ⊠ *1½ blocks east of river, 1 block north of 6th St.* ☎ *063/964740* ⊕ *www.borran.com* 🛏 *20 rooms* ♨ *Restaurant, cable TV, pool, massage, lounge, laundry service* ▭ *No credit cards.*

Around Siem Reap

Siem Reap doesn't have as many side trips as Phnom Penh (probably because the majority of tourists just come to do a hit-and-run on Angkor Wat), but there a few nearby diversions, if you've had your share of the temples.

Tonle Sap

10 km (6 mi) south of Siem Reap.

Covering 2,600 square km (1,000 square mi) in the dry season, Cambodia's vast Tonle Sap is the biggest freshwater lake in Southeast Asia. Its unique annual cycle of flood expansion and retreat dictates Cambodia's rice production and supplies of fish. The cycle is so extreme that during the rainy season, the lake grows to four times its dry-season expanse and depth. Boats make the river journey to the lake from Phnom Penh and Battambang, tying up at Chong Khneas, a floating settlement of fisherfolk 12 km (7½ mi) south of Siem Reap. Two-hour tours of the lake, costing $10, set off from Chong Khneas. The lake has a large bird sanctuary; visits can be booked through **Sam Veasna Center for Wildlife Conservation** (☎ 063/963710 ⊕ www.osmosetonlesap.org). A day tour costs about $80.

Kulen Mountain

50 km (31 mi) north of Siem Reap.

King Jayavarman II established this mountain retreat 50 km (31 mi) northeast of Siem Reap in AD 802, the year regarded as the start of the Angkor

THE ANGKOR CIRCUITS

There are stories of visitors who arrive in Siem Reap with the intention of seeing Angkor Wat, only to leave soon after in dismay after discovering that the "Wat" is just one of many temples in an area covering several square miles.

Forget any idea of strolling casually from temple to temple—even a bicycle tour of the vast site is exhausting. There are two recommended circuits, the shortest 17 km (11 mi) and the longest 26 km (16 mi). If you have just one day, stick to the small circuit, which takes in Bakheng, the south gate of Angkor Thom, Bayon, Baphuon, the Elephant Terrace and the Terrace of the Leper King, and Ta Prohm, and ends with a visit to Angkor Wat itself to catch the sunset. If you have two days, take the longer route—do the shorter circuit on the first day, then tackle Preah Khan, Neak Pean, East Mebon, and Pre Rup (at sunset) on day two.

dynasty. The area is strewn with the ruins of Khmer temples from that time. The mountain was revered as holy, with a hallowed river and a waterfall. Admission to the area costs $20.

Angkor Temple Complex

17 *6 km (4 mi) north of Siem Reap.*

Fodor's Choice

★

The Khmer empire reached the zenith of its power, influence, and creativity from the 9th to the 13th century, when Angkor, the seat of the Khmer kings, was one of the largest capitals in Southeast Asia. Starting in the 15th century, the temples of Angkor's heyday were abandoned and forgotten by the world until their rediscovery in the early 1860s by French naturalist Henri Mouhot. In all there are some 300 monuments reflecting Hindu and Buddhist influence scattered throughout the jungle, but only the largest have been excavated and reconstructed. Most of these lie within a few miles of each other and can be visited in one day, though two or three days will allow you to better appreciate them.

Although the centuries have taken their toll on the temples—some of which still hide their beauty beneath a tangle of undergrowth—they miraculously survived the ravages of the Khmer Rouge years. Many of the monks living in the temples at this time were massacred, however. The Khmer Rouge mined the area, but the mines have been removed, and the temples are now perfectly safe to visit.

Admission to the complex, which opens from 5 AM to 6:30 PM, costs $20 for one day, $40 for three, and $60 for a week. You can get a slight discount if you arrive after 4 PM: if you purchase a ticket for the following day, you'll be allowed into the complex free for the remaining 2½ hours, which is just enough time to do a little exploring and to catch the sunset at Angkor Wat. Most people visit the temples of Bayon and Baphuon, which face east, in the morning—the earlier you arrive, the

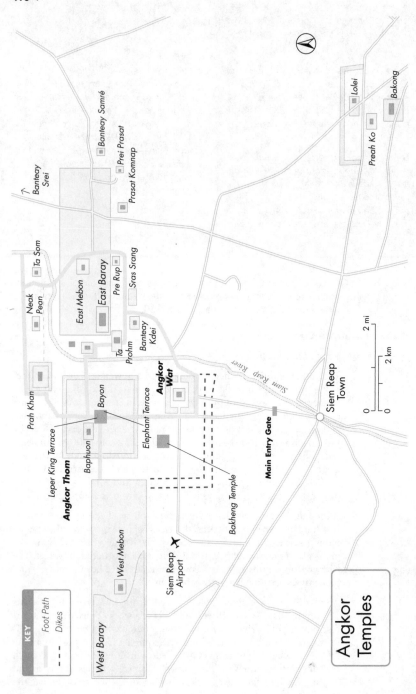

KEY

Foot Path

Dikes

West Baray

West Mebon

Siem Reap Airport ✈

Bakheng Temple

Main Entry Gate

Prah Khan

Angkor Thom

Leper King Terrace

Bayon

Baphuon

Elephant Terrace

Angkor Wat

Neak Pean

Ta Som

East Mebon

East Baray

Ta Prohm

Banteay Kdei

Pre Rup

Sras Srang

Banteay Srei ↑

Prasat Komnap

Prei Prasat

Banteay Samré

Siem Reap River

Siem Reap Town

Lo021

Lolei

Preah Ko

Bakong

0   2 km
0   2 mi

Angkor Temples

better the light and the smaller the crowd—and west-facing Angkor Wat in the late afternoon, though this most famous of the temples can also be a stunning sight at sunrise. The woodland-surrounded Ta Prohm can be visited any time, though it is best photographed when cloudy, whereas the distant Citadel of Women is prettiest in the late-afternoon light. Transport is a necessity, and most independent travelers hire a car and driver ($20–$25 per day) or motorcycle ($6–$8 per day), though bicycles ($3–$4 per day) are available for those who can stand the heat and effort. It's best to hire a guide in Siem Reap, either through your hotel, a tour operator, or at the tourist office next to the Raffles Grand Hotel d'Angkor.

Bakheng

One of the oldest Angkor structures, dating to the 9th century, the hilltop Bakheng temple was built in the center of the first royal city site, dedicated to the Hindu god Shiva, and surrounded by a moat 4 km (2½) mi long. The temple, which resembles a five-tiered pyramid, was constructed from rock hewn from the hill and faced with sandstone. There's a fine view of the Western Baray, one of Angkor's five water reservoirs, from its ancient terrace.

Angkor Thom

Angkor Thom was a city in its own right, the last true Khmer capital, built by King Jayavarman VII in the late 12th century. At the height of Angkor Thom's prosperity in the 12th and 13th centuries, more than 1 million people lived within its walls, and it was the richest city in Southeast Asia. The Siamese destroyed the city in 1432, and it became an insignificant ghost town. The south gate, towering 65 feet and crowned by four characteristic Bodhisattva faces, is so monumental it appears to dominate the entire area.

A defensive wall and moat 12 km (7½ mi) long surrounded the city, which was entered via a bridge lined with massive stone guardians holding a mystical serpent. At its geographic center stands the 12th-century **Bayon,** a large, ornate Buddhist structure that rises into 54 small towers, most of which are topped with huge, strangely smiling faces. On the outer walls of the central sanctuary, and on some of the inner walls, are 1½ km (1 mi) of marvelous bas-relief murals depicting historic sea battles, scenes from daily life, and gods and mythical creatures performing legendary deeds.

Just to the north of the Bayon is the slightly older **Baphuon,** built in the mid-11th century by King Udayadityavarman II (a small settlement was here before Jayavarman VII built up the area in the late 12th century). A fine example of poor planning, the temple was erected on a hill without proper supports, so that when the earth shifted in the 16th century, it collapsed. The French government did a good job of reconstructing the building and correcting its original structural flaws, and it reopened to the public in 2004. Originally the temple was a Shiva sanctuary crowned with a copper-covered cupola. A magnificent reclining Buddha was added to the three-tiered temple pyramid in the 16th century.

CloseUp

UNCOVERING ANGKOR

THE STORY OF THE REDISCOVERY OF ANGKOR is like something from the pages of H. Rider Haggard, the 19th-century English author of King Solomon's Mines and other adventure stories.

Haggard's stories may have been set in Africa, but they evocatively parallel what was happening in Asia at the time he was writing. French colonists and missionaries in Cambodia of the early and mid-19th century heard stories from locals of a lost city deep in the jungle. Most shrugged off the stories as myth, but some adventurers, fired by romantic visions of treasure, hacked their way through the jungle and indeed found ruins, although they could make nothing of these strange piles of stone. It was left to a French botanist, Henri Mouhot, to begin serious investigation of the ruins. Mouhot traveled to Bangkok in 1858 with support from the British Royal Geographic Society. His original intention was to collect samples of the region's unique flora and insects. He ended up going much farther afield than Bangkok—supposedly, a French missionary he met in Battambang told him of the lost city, and he was guided to the site via Tonle Sap in 1861. Mouhot filled many journals with impressions and sketches of the ruins and his notes were published in 1863, bringing the city back onto the world's radar.

Mouhot could only wonder at what type of race created such massive structures—he didn't seem to think that present-day Cambodians could have done it—but subsequent intensive international research soon revealed that Angkor had been the capital of a mighty Khmer empire for more than three centuries, from its founding around AD 880 to the early 13th century, when it fell into decline in the shadow of an even greater power, Siam.

Research also revealed that Angkor was the scene of one of the world's greatest feats of irrigation technology: thousands of experts, workers, and slaves constructed a system of reservoirs and canals to serve a city larger than medieval London or Paris. They built two huge storage basins, the Eastern and Western Barays, each covering about 17 square km (6½ square mi). Today, only the Western Baray has water in it, but both give an indelible impression of the sheer size of the original enterprise.

Elephant Terrace & the Terrace of the Leper King

Built at the end of the 12th century by King Jayavarman VII, the ornamental Elephant Terrace once formed the foundation of the royal audience hall. The gilded wooden palace that once stood here has long since disappeared. Stone-carved elephants and *garuda,* or giant eagles, adorn the 6½-foot-tall wall of the terrace, which abuts an empty field where troops used to parade before the Khmer monarchs.

At the north end of the Elephant Terrace is the Terrace of the Leper King, named after a stone statue found here and identified as the Hindu god Yama. In Hindu mythology, Yama presides as a judge over hell, and the terrace is covered in carved demons.

Ta Prohm

Built in 1186 by the prolific King Jayavarman VII to honor his mother, Ta Prohm is a large Buddhist monastery of five enclosures that has been only partially restored. The eerie temple looks as it more or less did when Western adventurers and explorers rediscovered Angkor in the 19th century; many buildings have been reduced to piles of stone blocks, and giant tropical fig and silk-cotton trees grow on top of the walls. Stone inscriptions reveal that the complex originally had 566 stone dwellings, including 39 major sanctuaries, and was attended by 13 high priests, 2,740 officials, 2,232 assistants, and 615 dancers, who were supported by 3,000 villages. Today you're likely to share it with a couple hundred camera-toting tourists. Still, it's a gorgeous, magical spot, with thick knotted tree roots sprawled over half-tumbled walls, and flocks of parrots squawking in the branches high above.

Angkor Wat

The most impressive and best preserved of the Khmer temples is the one that gave the whole complex its name: Angkor Wat, the beautiful apotheosis of Khmer architecture, and the world's largest religious monument. It was built at the beginning of the 12th century by King Suryavarman II (reigned 1112–52), who dedicated it to the Hindu god Vishnu, making sure that its dimensions were suitably grand for the divine patron. Those dimensions are staggering: the temple compound covers an area of 4,920 feet by 4,265 feet. The surrounding moat is 590 feet wide. A causeway leading to the huge entrance is flanked by balustrades of giant serpents believed to represent cosmic fertility.

The centerpiece of the complex is the giant lotus bud formed by the five familiar beehivelike towers, which alone took 30 years to complete. Three of the towers appear in the white silhouette of Angkor Wat that is the central emblem of the Cambodian national flag, signifying the triple motto of nation, religion, and king.

Like all the other major monuments at Angkor, the 215-foot-high complex represents the Hindu/Buddhist universe. The central shrines symbolize Mt. Meru, the mythical home of the Hindu gods, and the moats represent the seven oceans that surround Mt. Meru. The three-tiered central pyramid itself rises in four concentric enclosures opening to the west, with terraces decorated with images of Hindu deities, many of which have lost their heads to looters. More impressive than the statues, towers, and the sheer size of the temple is the extensive bas-relief work that covers its walls, especially the scenes on its outer front wall depicting epic battles of Hindu mythology, an audience given by the king, and the creation of the world. On top of that, there are nearly 2,000 apsara—celestial female dancers—scattered throughout the temple complex.

Two ornate Buddhist monasteries flank the ancient Hindu temple.

Preah Khan

This former royal retreat was built in 1191 by King Jayavarman VII for his father, but it later became a Buddhist institution with more than 1,000 monks. The moated temple, near the north gate of Angkor Thom, is similar to Ta Prohm, but has only four enclosures. The temple houses a hall decorated with a bas-relief of heavenly apsara dancers, a two-story columnar building to keep the "sacred sword" (an important part of the royal regalia) of the kingdom, and a large lingam, or phallic symbol, representing Shiva.

In the eastern part of the complex is a *baray,* one of the five huge reservoirs built to supply the growing Angkor Thom and irrigate its fields and plantations. The water was channeled from the Tonle Sap lake in an amazing feat of engineering.

Neak Pean

Sitting on an island in the middle of one of Angkor's barays, or water reservoirs, the temple of Neak Pean (meaning "Entwined Serpent") is one of King Jayavarman VII's most unusual creations. King Jayavarman intended to create his own version of the sacred lake Anavatapta in the Himalayas, venerated for its power of healing. From a large square reservoir, gargoyles channel water into four smaller square basin sanctuaries. The temple's central tower is dedicated to the Bodhisattva Avalokitesvara, depicted riding the fabulous horse Balaha along with people escaping a disastrous pestilence and seeking the healing waters of Anavatapta.

East Mebon

The temple of East Mebon was built on a baray island by King Rajendravarman in the 10th century and now sits high and dry in the empty reservoir known as the Eastern Baray. The pyramid-shape temple, dedicated to Shiva, has all the characteristics of the temple mount construction so favored by the Khmer kings: in brick and laterite, with a 10-foot-high platform carrying five imposing towers arranged in a quincunx (one at each corner and one in the center of the ensemble). The sandstone lintels have been superbly carved and preserved, and monolithic elephants stand at the four corners of each enclosure.

Pre Rup

This grander version of the East Mebon temple is thought to have once been the center of the royal city of King Rajendravarman, who ordered its construction in 961. The five upper brick towers are adorned with fine stucco moldings. From the top of the highest platform, there are sweeping views of the palm-studded countryside. If you want to avoid the crowds that gather at Angkor Wat and Bakheng at sunset but you still want a good view, this is the place to come.

Citadel of Women

If you have the time, extend your tour of Angkor to include the Citadel of Women (Banteay Srei), 38 km (24 mi) northeast of Siem Reap. The temple resembles a small fortress and it's dedicated to the Hindu goddess Sri (the Khmer version of this name was Srei, meaning "women"). This small but magnificent 10th-century temple contains fine sculptures of pink sandstone illustrating scenes from the Indian Reamker legend and gods and goddesses of the Hindu pantheon; they're surprisingly well preserved. The temple achieved fame when the former French government minister Andre Malraux was accused of plundering it during reconstruction work in the 1930s. Admission is included in the Angkor ticket, but a hired car will usually charge an extra $5, and a motorbike $2, to drive here.

Roluos Temples

About 12 km (7½ mi) east of Siem Reap on Highway 6 is a group of three temples—**Preah Ko, Bakong,** and **Lolei**—all built in the 9th century, the formative period of the Khmer empire. The capital at that time was called Hariharalaya, when the two gods Shiva and Vishnu were both venerated; the temples were erected in their honor. A large water reservoir was fed from the Tonle Sap lake, via the Roluos River, and Lolei was then on an island. Admission to the site is included in the Angkor ticket.

SIEM REAP & ANGKOR TEMPLE COMPLEX A TO Z

AIR TRAVEL

Bangkok Airways flies direct to Siem Reap from Bangkok. The flight takes about an hour and costs about $250 round-trip.

President Airlines flies to Siem Reap from Bangkok and has attractive package offers—round-trip airfare, two nights at a four-star hotel, and airport transfers for less than $300. You can also fly to Siem Reap from Vientiane and Pakse in Laos on Lao Airlines. Siem Reap Airways also provides service from Ho Chi Minh City.

The road to Siem Reap from Phnom Penh is very rough, so most travelers either fly or take a boat. Siem Reap Airways, Royal Phnom Penh Airways, and President Airlines all have several flights per day between Phnom Penh and Siem Reap. Fares are $60–$70 one-way. Siem Reap Airways charges a bit more, but its planes are much newer.

✈ Carriers **Lao Airlines** ☎ 063/963283 ⊕ www.lao-aviation.com. **President Airlines** ☎ 063/964338 in Siem Reap, 023/212887 in Phnom Penh ⊕ www.presidentairlines. com. **Royal Phnom Penh Airways** ☎ 063/964454 in Siem Reap, 023/216487 in Phnom Penh ⊕ www.gocambodia.com/airway/background.shtml. **Siem Reap Airways** ☎ 063/ 380191 in Siem Reap, 023/720022 in Phnom Penh, 08/823-9288 in Ho Chi Minh City ⊕ www.siemreapairways.com.

AIRPORTS & TRANSFERS

Siem Reap International Airport is 6 km (4 mi) northwest of town. The taxi fare to any hotel in Siem Reap is $5.

BOAT TRAVEL

The road to Phnom Penh is being upgraded, but many tourists prefer the six-hour boat trip on the Mae Khong (the fare is $25). Several high-speed ferries depart Phnom Penh from the municipal port on Sisowath Quay, at 84th Street, early in the morning. A one-way ticket that includes a hotel pickup and a transfer from the landing dock to Siem Reap costs $20–$30 and can be purchased at most hotels and travel agencies. Mekong Express has the quickest boats.

The ferry port is at Chong Khneas, 12 km (7½ mi) south of Siem Reap.
🚢 **Mekong Express** ☎ 063/963662 in Siem Reap, 023/427518 in Phnom Penh.

BUS TRAVEL

Buses from Phnom Penh to Siem Reap take about 7–9 hours via Skun and Kampong Thom on Highway 6. The fare is $4. Regular long-distance bus service links Bangkok and Siem Reap via Sisaphon and Poipet.

Neak Krorhorm Travel in Siem Reap can help you arrange bus trips.
🚌 **Neak Krorhorm Travel** ⊠ Across from Old Market, Siem Reap ☎ 063/964924.

CAR TRAVEL

The road to Siem Reap from Phnom Penh is very rough, so most people fly or take a boat. Once in Siem Reap, you can hire a car and driver through your hotel or guesthouse.

From Siem Reap, Highway 6 heads west out of town to the Angkor temple site and to Thailand, a four-hour drive (Bangkok is an additional eight hours or so away). A lesser-known dirt road runs from Siem Reap to Surin and Sisaket provinces in Thailand.

EMERGENCIES

Siem Reap's Naga International Clinic has 24-hour emergency service.
🏥 Hospital **Naga International Clinic** ⊠ E. River Rd. ☎ 063/964500.

INTERNET

Internet cafés have sprung up everywhere in Siem Reap, keeping pace with the current tourism boom. Prices for Internet use are around $2 an hour.

MONEY MATTERS

Siem Reap has no ATMs with access to foreign bank accounts, although the town's banks will advance money to holders of MasterCard or Visa cards. Siem Reap's leading banks are Cambodia Asia Bank, Cambodian Commercial Bank, and Mekong Bank.
🏦 Banks **Cambodia Asia Bank** ⊠ Sivatha Rd. at Airport Rd. ☎ 063/964741. **Cambodian Commercial Bank** ⊠ 130 Sivatha Rd. ☎ 063/380154. **Mekong Bank** ⊠ 43 Sivatha Rd. ☎ 063/964417.

SAFETY

Siem Reap has much less of a crime problem than Phnom Penh, but it's still unwise to wander its streets alone late at night.

Though once the haunt of Khmer Rouge troops, who buried mines in certain areas, the Angkor temple complex has been scoured by mine-removal teams, and is nowadays quite safe. Nevertheless, here and throughout Cambodia, you should stick to well-traveled paths.

SIGHTSEEING TOURS

A guide can greatly enrich your appreciation of Angkor's temples, which are full of details you might miss on your own. Angkor guides can be hired through your hotel, a tour operator, or at the tourist information stand next to the Raffles Grand Hotel d'Angkor; they charge $20–$30 per day, a true bargain. Guides and drivers expect a few dollars on top of their day rate.

TAXI, MOTO & CYCLO TRAVEL

The number of tourists visiting Siem Reap has grown so fast in recent years that the local cyclos (pedal trishaws) and motos (motorcycle taxis) have hardly been able to cope with demand. They cost about $1–$2 for a trip within town, but be sure to settle on the fare before setting off. Cyclos are fun but slow.

There are no cruising taxis, but hotels can order one.
🚩 **Tuk Tuk Taxi Service** ☎ 063/935018.

VISITOR INFORMATION

The tourist office in Siem Reap (near the Raffles Grand Hotel d'Angkor) does little more than set visitors up with guides, but several free glossy magazines distributed all over town are packed with useful information and ads.
🚩 **Siem Reap Tourism Office** ✉ Pokambor Ave. ☎ 063/964347.

SIHANOUKVILLE & SOUTHERN CAMBODIA

The beaches of Sihanoukville are Cambodia's nearest thing to the coastal resorts and islands of neighboring Thailand. As more and more visitors discover Cambodia's still untouched coastline, Sihanoukville has become the new resort destination, the next big attraction after the temples of Angkor and the bustling, sprawling city of Phnom Penh. Sihanoukville lies some 230 km (143 mi) southwest of Phnom Penh, a four-hour bus ride from the capital or a slightly longer journey by train.

The Road to the Coast

The four-hour bus journey from Phnom Penh to Sihanoukville along Highway 4 is an interesting one, winding through uplands, rice paddies, and orchards. Once you drive past Phnom Penh's Pochentong Airport and the prestigious Cambodia Golf & Country Club, the landscape turns truly rural, dotted with small villages where a major source of income seems to be the sale of firewood and charcoal. After passing through the only sizable town on the route, Kampong Speu, and the entrance to Kirirom National Park, buses stop for refreshment at a roadside restaurant.

The halfway point of the journey lies at the top of the **Pich Nil mountain pass,** guarded by dozens of colorful spirit houses. These spirit houses were built for the legendary deity Yeah Mao, guardian of Sihanoukville

CloseUp

KHMER: A FEW KEY PHRASES

A KNOWLEDGE OF FRENCH will get you far in francophone Cambodia, although English is also spoken in Phnom Penh and tourist resorts. The Cambodian language, Khmer, belongs to the Mon-Khmer family of languages, enriched by Indian Pali and Sanskrit vocabulary.

The following are some useful words and phrases:

Hello: joom reap soo-uh

Thank you: aw-koun

Yes: bah (male speaker), jah (female speaker)

No: odtay

Excuse me: som toe

Where?: ai nah?

How much?: riel bahn dtay?

Never mind: mun ay dtay

Zero: sohn

One: muay

Two: bpee

Three: bay

Four: boun

Five: bpram

Six: bpram muay

Seven: bpram bpee

Eight: bpram bay

Nine: bpram boun

Ten: dop

Eleven: dop muay

Hundred: muay roi

Thousand: muay bpohn

Food: m'hohp

Water: dteuk

Expensive: nah

Morning: bpreuk

Night: youp

Today: t'ngai nih (pronounced tngay nee)

Tomorrow: sa-ik

Yesterday: m'sel mern

Bus: lot me (pronounced lot may)

Ferry: salang

Village: krong

Island: koh

River: tonle

Doctor: bpairt (pronounced bpet)

Hospital: mun dti bpairt (pronounced moonty bpet

Bank: tanee-ageea

Post Office: praisinee

Toilet: bong kuen barah

and the coastal region. Legend has it that Yeah Mao was the wife of a village headman who worked in far-off Koh Kang, an island near today's border with Thailand. On a journey to visit him, Yeah Mao died when the boat transporting her sank in a storm. Her spirit became the guardian of local villagers and fisherfolk.

At the small town of Chamcar Luang, a side road leads to the renowned smuggling port of Sre Ambel. The main highway threads through Ream National Park, with the **Elephant Mountains** as a backdrop. The sprawling Angkor Beer brewery heralds the outskirts of Sihanoukville and the journey's end.

Sihanoukville

🔞 *230 km (143 mi) southwest of Phnom Penh.*

A half a century ago, Cambodia's main port city, Sihanoukville, was a sleepy backwater called Kampong Som. Then, a series of world-shattering events overtook it and gave rise to the busy industrial center and coastal resort now prominent on every tourist map.

The French laid the foundations of Kampong Som back in the mid-1950s, before they lost control of the Mae Khong Delta and its ports following their retreat after the French-Indochina War. The town was renamed Sihanoukville in honor of the then king. A decade later, Sihanoukville received a further boost when it became an important transit post for weapons destined for American forces fighting in the Vietnam War. In the mid-1970s, Sihanoukville itself came under American attack and suffered heavy casualties after Khmer Rouge forces captured the SS *Mayaguez,* a U.S. container ship.

Today Sihanoukville presents a peaceful face to the world as Cambodia's seaside playground. It has six beaches, all different in character and all easily accessible from downtown by motorbike taxi or even a rented bicycle. The closest beach to Sihanoukville is **Victory Beach,** named after the Vietnamese victory over the Khmer Rouge regime in 1979. It's a favorite with backpackers and has plenty of budget accommodation.

Hawaii Beach, where the foundations of Sihanoukville were dug in the early 1950s, almost meets the promise of its name. It has one of Sihanoukville's best seafood restaurants, the Hawaii Sea View Restaurant.

Most locals prefer **Independence Beach,** and on weekends and holidays its long narrow stretch of sand can get crowded. The beach is backed by a neglected little park, where vendors set up food and drink stalls. For something more stylish, make for the Koh Pos Hotel.

The best swimming can be enjoyed at **Sokha Beach,** site of Cambodia's first international-class beach resort, the Sokha Beach Resort.

Underwater enthusiasts favor **Ochheuteal Beach** and neighboring **Serendipity Beach.** This 1-km (½-mi) stretch of sand is bordered at one end by a small fishing community. Well-heeled Cambodians set up holiday homes here before the Khmer Rouge revolution, and fine villas—including a royal residence—line the beach road.

Of the several offshore islands (many of them deserted) accessible by boat, **Koh Rong Samlem** is the most idyllic. Some hotels arrange excursions to the island. You can also head for the busy fishing harbor 5 km (3 mi) northeast of Sihanoukville's main port and hire a boat (expect to pay up to $100 per group per day for the boat).

Where to Stay & Eat

Between the town center and Victory Beach is a small hill, Weather Station Hill, popularly known as Backpackers' Hill because of its cheap guesthouses. The prices are lower here mostly because of the hill's distance from the beaches and the stiff climb necessary to reach the accommodations. Nevertheless, some of the lodgings are quite attractive.

$$–$$$$ ✕ **Hawaii Sea View Restaurant.** You can practically dangle your feet in the surf as you tuck into giant prawns and crabs at this beach restaurant. The sunset alone is reason enough to grab a table, which the staff will set up for you right on the beach. ⊠ *Hawaii Beach* ☎ *012/513008* ⊟ *MC, V.*

¢–$ ✕ **Sea Dragon.** You can start the day in style right on the beach at this friendly restaurant, which serves a genuine Western-style breakfast—eggs, bacon, and steaming coffee—a rarity in Cambodia outside the big hotels. The menu is also rich in Asian dishes. ⊠ *Ochheuteal Beach* ☎ *034/933671* ⊟ *No credit cards.*

$$–$$$ 🏨 **Sokha Beach Resort.** This is the top address in Sihanoukville, a first-class resort hotel with all the facilities required for a fun-filled beach holiday. The resort takes up 6 acres of landscaped gardens that lead directly to the beach. Rooms, with tiled floors and French doors leading to small balconies, are grouped in two wings overlooking the pool and the beach. ⊠ *Sokha Beach* ☎ *034/935999* 🖶 *034/935888* ⊕ *www. sokhahotels.com* 🗗 *188 rooms* ♻ *3 restaurants, room service, IDD phones, cable TV, 2 tennis courts, pool, gym, massage, beach, dive shop, snorkeling, boating, waterskiing, 2 bars, nightclub, shop, laundry service, travel services* ⊟ *AE, MC, V* ❙❀❙ *BP.*

$$ 🏨 **Golden Sand Hotel.** The sleek exterior of this high-rise hotel disguises a quaintly old-fashioned interior. Rooms may be just a bit too dated for some—swagged curtains, colorfully patterned bedspreads, salmon-pink color schemes—but they have an undeniably homey feel to them. ⊠ *Ekareach Rd., Ochheuteal Beach* ☎ *034/933607* 🖶 *034/933609* ⊕ *www.hotelgoldensand.com* 🗗 *108 rooms* ♻ *Restaurant, café, IDD phones, in-room safes, minibars, cable TV, pool, bar, laundry service* ⊟ *V.*

$–$$ 🏨 **Seaside Hotel.** The quaint, evocative name sums up this friendly beach hotel, which wouldn't be out of place on the Mediterranean, despite the Khmer architectural touches. Pastel colors decorate the rooms, and fresh flowers are a nice touch. ⊠ *Beach Rd., Ochheuteal Beach* ☎ *034/933641* 🖶 *034/933640* 🗗 *41 rooms* ♻ *Restaurant, room service, IDD phones, minibars, cable TV* ⊟ *MC, V.*

¢–$ 🏨 **Orchidee Guesthouse.** More of a ranch-style home than a guesthouse, this brick-and-stucco lodging is highly recommended, particularly for families. It's one block, or an easy five-minute walk, from the beach.

For a peaceful stay, book one of the 20 rooms in the main house; otherwise, settle for one of the 12 rooms grouped around the small swimming pool. Rooms are a bit bare, with tile floors and plain walls, but comfortable enough. The small shrub-enclosed patio is pleasant, particularly in the evening. ⊠ *Ochheuteal Beach* ☎ *016/867744* 🖷 *034/933639* ↦ *32 rooms* ⚴ *Restaurant, refrigerators, cable TV, bar, meeting rooms* ▭ *No credit cards.*

¢ 🏨 **Bungalow Village.** Twelve small bungalows set in a lush tropical garden make up this attractive guesthouse high on Weather Station Hill. The owner is proud of his collection of 300 CDs, which provide the nightly entertainment in the smart cocktail bar. ⊠ *Weather Station Hill* ☎ *034/933875* ↦ *12 bungalows* ⚴ *Restaurant, refrigerators, bar* ▭ *No credit cards* ⦿⦾ *BP.*

Sports & the Outdoors

Most hotels and guesthouses arrange boat trips, which include packed lunches, to the many offshore islands. There are two dive centers: **EcoSea Dive** (⊠ Ekareach St. ☎ 012/654104), and Cambodia's first certified PADI dive center, **Scuba Nation Diving Center** (⊠ Weather Station Hill ☎ 012/715785 ⦿ www.divecambodia.com).

Kampot

🔟 *110 km (68 mi) east of Sihanoukville, 150 km (93 mi) south of Phnom Penh.*

This attractive seaside town at the foot of the Elephant Mountain range and straddling the Prek Cha River was once an important colonial port; architectural traces of the French presence can be seen everywhere. It's now the departure point for trips to the seaside resort of Kep and Bokor Hill Station. The coastal road from Sihanoukville to Kampot is rough, but has spectacular views. To get here, take a taxi, or hire a car and driver through your hotel.

Kep, 25 km (16 mi) east of Kampot, has a narrow pebble beach bordered by ruined villas from the Khmer Rouge era. Offshore, **Rabbit Island** is an idyllic spot, and you can hire a boat to take you there for $10.

In the 1920s, the French built **Bokor Hill Station,** 35 km (22 mi) west of Kampot, as a retreat from the heat and humidity of the coast. It's now a collection of ruins, but it's worth visiting for the spectacular sea views from its 3,000-foot heights.

Where to Stay

¢–$ 🏨 **Bokor Mountain Club.** The club has a few rooms to rent in a restored riverfront mansion that has great views of Bokor Mountain. The rooms are basic, but clean and comfortable. It's a good idea to book ahead. ⊠ *Kampot* ☎ *033/932314* 🖷 *033/932277* 🖅 *bokor@fcccambodia. com* ↦ *6 rooms* ⚴ *Restaurant, bar, laundry facilities, travel services.*

¢–$ 🏨 **Champey Inn.** Described in tourist brochures as the only luxury hotel in Kep, the Champey Inn is more of a laid-back resort, with 12 bungalows set in tropical gardens. Rooms are simply but attractively furnished with local dark woods. ⊠ *25 Ave. de la Plage, Phum Thmey* ☎ *012/*

501742 🖙 *12 bungalows* 🍴 *Restaurant, refrigerators, pool* 🖃 *No credit cards.*

SIHANOUKVILLE & SOUTHERN CAMBODIA A TO Z

AIR TRAVEL
Plans are in the works to connect Siem Reap with the airport in Sihanoukville in the future. At this writing, the airport was only serving chartered flights.

BOAT TRAVEL
A daily ferry runs from Sihanoukville to the island of Koh Kong, near the Thai border. The boat departs Sihanoukville's port's passenger terminal at noon, and the trip takes four hours. A ticket costs $15, and you can make it across the Thai border before 5 to catch a bus via Trat to Bangkok.

BUS TRAVEL
Air-conditioned VIP buses from Phnom Penh to Sihanoukville run five times daily (between 6:55 AM and 1:30 PM) and take four hours. Buses depart from Charles de Gaulle Road, at the southwestern corner of the Central Market. The journey takes four hours and costs $3.

Sihanoukville's bus terminal is on Ekareach Street, where moto drivers meet incoming vehicles.

CAR TRAVEL
You can hire a private car and driver through your hotel or guesthouse for the trip to the coast from Phnom Penh. The cost should be around $50.

EMERGENCIES
🏥 Hospital **Sihanouk Public Hospital** ⊠ Ekareach Rd., Sihanoukville ☎ 034/93311.

INTERNET
Internet cafés are common in Sihanoukville. Expect to pay around $2 an hour.

MONEY MATTERS
There are no ATMs in Sihanoukville, but banks can change foreign currency and traveler's checks. The Acleda Bank has Western Union services. Canadia Bank and Mekong Bank can advance money against a MasterCard; Union Commercial Bank can advance cash against a Visa card.
🏦 Banks **Acleda Bank** ⊠ Ekareach St. ☎ 034/320232. **Canadia Bank** ⊠ Ekareach St. at Sopheak-Monkoi St. ☎ 034/933490. **Mekong Bank** ⊠ Ekareach St. ☎ 034/933867. **Union Commercial Bank** ⊠ Ekareach St. ☎ 034/933833.

TRAIN TRAVEL
Limited train service is available from Phnom Penh to Sihanoukville, but the bus is much quicker; the train trip takes 10 hours and costs $2. You can purchase tickets from any travel agency in Phnom Pehn.

VISITOR INFORMATION
The tour counter at your hotel or guesthouse is your best bet for tourist information.

CAMBODIA A TO Z

To research prices, get advice from other travelers, and book travel arrangements, visit www.fodors.com.

AIR TRAVEL
Regular air service connects Phnom Penh with Bangkok and Ho Chi Minh City, and Bangkok with Siem Reap. For more information, *see* the regional A to Z sections in this chapter.

BUS TRAVEL
There's no direct bus service between Bangkok and Phnom Penh, but there's long-distance bus service from Bangkok to Siem Reap, from which local buses complete the journey to Phnom Penh. The round-trip Bangkok–Phnom Penh ticket, obtainable in all Bangkok travel agencies, costs around $20. The journey, over sometimes very rough roads, takes 10–12 hours.

In Siem Reap, bus tickets to Bangkok can be obtained from Neak Krorhorm Travel.
🚌 **Neak Krorhorm Travel** ✉ Across from Old Market, Siem Reap ☎ 063/964924.

BORDER CROSSINGS
From Thailand there are two main overland routes: via Arayanyprathet and Poipet, or, farther south, via the southeastern Thai city of Trat. Both routes are arduous, and the Cambodian roads are not good. Coming from Laos overland, the only way to continue into Cambodia is by boat from the border town of Veun Kham (in Laos) to Stung Treng (in Cambodia), where there's an airport.

One-month tourist visas, which cost $20, are available at the border crossings from Thailand. Note, however, that visas cannot be obtained at the Laos border crossing (get your visa in advance). The border crossings are open daily 7:30–11:30 and 2–5.

BUSINESS HOURS
Business hours are generally weekdays 7:30–11:30 and 2–5. Banks are open weekdays 8–3; some banks may have limited weekend hours for currency exchange. Post offices are open weekdays 7:30–5. Shops and markets are open daily, generally 7–5.

CAR TRAVEL
You can hire a car with driver through most hotels and guesthouses for around $20 a day. You should resist any attempt by private individuals to rent you a vehicle.

CUSTOMS & DUTIES
ON ARRIVAL You are allowed to bring into Cambodia 200 cigarettes, 50 cigars, or ½ pound of tobacco, and 946 ml of liquor. You are not allowed to bring in local currency.

ON DEPARTURE You are not allowed to take out local currency. The export of antiques or religious objects requires a permit—contact your embassy for assistance in obtaining one.

ELECTRICITY

The electrical current is 220 volts AC, 50 Hz.

EMBASSIES

New Zealanders should contact the British embassy.

🏠 Australia **Embassy** ⊠ 2 254th St., Phnom Penh ☎ 023/213466.

🏠 Canada **Embassy** ⊠ 9 245th St., Phnom Penh ☎ 023/426000.

🏠 United Kingdom **Embassy** ⊠ 27–29 75th St., Phnom Penh ☎ 023/427124.

🏠 United States **Embassy** ⊠ 27 270th St., Phnom Penh ☎ 023/216436.

EMERGENCIES

In the case of a lost passport, immediately notify your embassy. In general, if you need assistance, ask your concierge first, if possible. Phnom Penh has adequate hospitals, but if you're really sick, consider flying to Bangkok.

ETIQUETTE & BEHAVIOR

As elsewhere in Southeast Asia, confrontational behavior and displays of anger are considered bad manners, as is too much bare skin at a religious site. The foot is regarded as a base part of the body, so avoid pointing your foot at a person. You should also avoid touching someone on his or her head. Remove your shoes and hat before entering a temple or home. Public displays of affection should be avoided by all couples, gay or straight—Cambodians take this so seriously that even newlyweds are forbidden to kiss at their wedding ceremony. It's polite to ask permission before taking a photo of someone, especially monks. Women should avoid any bodily contact with monks.

HEALTH

Always drink bottled water and avoid uncooked food. There's a threat of malaria in rural areas, including a strain that is resistant to some antimalarials. Consult the Centers for Disease Control's Web site (⊕ www.cdc.gov/travel) before departing, and use insect repellent at all times.

HOLIDAYS

New Year's Day (Jan. 1), Victory Day (Jan. 7), International Women's Day (Mar. 8), Cambodian New Year (Apr. 13–15), Labor Day (May 1), Visak Bochea (Buddha's Birthday; early May), International Children's Day (June 1), Last King's Birthday (late June), Constitution Promulgation Day (Sept. 24), Taing Tok Ceremony (Oct. 20–22), Anniversary of Paris Peace Agreement (Oct. 25), Sihanouk's birthday (Oct. 30–Nov. 1), Independence Day (Nov. 9), Human Rights Day (Dec. 10).

MAIL & SHIPPING

Airmail takes 4–5 days to Europe and 7–10 days to the United States. Letters and parcels are routed through Bangkok, which increases post office reliability considerably.

MONEY MATTERS

COSTS Accommodations run anywhere from $15 for a basic guesthouse to hundreds of dollars for a high-end hotel, with plenty of rooms in between the two extremes. A local beer costs $1 in most restaurants, but an imported beer at a big hotel can be $4.

CURRENCY The monetary unit in Cambodia is the riel, but the U.S. dollar is nearly as widely accepted, and payment in dollars is required by many hotels, airlines, tour operators, and restaurants. In fact, your best bet is to pay bills in dollars, because vendors and hotels often use an inflated rate if you pay in riels.

At this writing, the official exchange rate was approximately 100 riels to the Thai baht, 3,800 riels to one U.S. dollar, 3,200 riels to one Canadian dollar, 3,000 riels to one Australian dollar, and 7,400 riels to one British pound.

CREDIT CARDS Credit cards are accepted only at major hotels and restaurants and at some boutiques. Many banks can give you a cash advance on a Visa or MasterCard.

CURRENCY EXCHANGE & ATMS Because the riel and U.S. dollar operate as almost dual currencies, it's possible to change dollars to riels just about anywhere. There are plenty of banks and money changers in Phnom Penh that will also change other currencies, but they don't give very good rates, so you're better off converting those currencies to dollars before traveling to Cambodia. Banks and businesses usually charge 2% to cash U.S.-dollar traveler's checks. Cambodia lacks ATMs that allow you to access foreign bank accounts, but there are plenty of banks that give cash advances on Visa or MasterCard; shop around, as the commissions on these transactions range from 1% to 5%.

PASSPORTS & VISAS

All visitors must have a valid passport to enter Cambodia. One-month visas are given to tourists from most countries on arrival at the airports in Phnom Penh and Siem Reap; you'll need two passport photos and $20. If you enter by land from Vietnam, you need to get a visa at the consulate in Ho Chi Minh City; allow a few days for processing.

🔼 Cambodian Embassies & Consulates **Cambodian Consulate** ✉ 41 D Phung Khac Khoan, District 1, Ho Chi Minh City, Vietnam ☎ 08/829-2751. **Royal Cambodian Embassy** ✉ 5 Canterbury Crescent, Deakin, ACT 2600, Australia ☎ 02/6273-1259. **Royal Cambodian Embassy** ✉ 4500 16th St. NW, Washington, DC 20001, United States ☎ 202/726-7742.

SAFETY

After years of political instability, Cambodia today is safer than many people realize, but you still need to exercise caution. There have been muggings on the streets of Phnom Penh, mostly at night, but these are rare. Keep most of your cash, valuables, and your passport in a hotel safe, and avoid walking on side streets after dark. If you do stay out late, return to your hotel in a taxi rather than on a moto or cyclo. Siem Reap has much less of a crime problem than the capital, but it's unwise to wander its streets late at night.

Be careful of overly friendly strangers who want to take you someplace, for whatever reason, and be wary of accepting drinks from strangers unless you can keep an eye on them to avoid being drugged and robbed. Avoid confrontations and arguments with locals, particularly in bars.

Land mines laid during the civil war have been removed from all major tourist destinations, such as the temple ruins in Angkor. Mines are a concern, however, if you go too far astray around temples that are off the beaten track (in which case, you should travel with a knowledgeable guide). Mines are also still concentrated in border areas and some mountain forests.

Accidents are common in the chaotic traffic of Cambodia, especially in Phnom Penh, where crossing a street can be a major hazard. Chauffeur-driven cars are the safest way to travel anywhere in the country.

TAXI, MOTO & CYCLO TRAVEL

The most common form of transportation in the cities is the moto (motorcycle taxi); motos cruise streets in abundance and gather outside hotels and restaurants—wherever you walk, you'll attract them. The standard fare is 2,000–4,000 riels for a short trip, though drivers often try to get more from foreigners. Less-abundant pedal trishaws—the romantic cyclos—charge the same.

Cruising taxis are nonexistent, but there are usually a couple parked outside large hotels, and the receptionist at any hotel can call one. Few drivers speak much English.

TELEPHONES

To call Cambodia from overseas, dial the country code, 855, and then the area code, omitting the first "0." The code for Phnom Penh is 023, 063 for Siem Reap. Unfortunately, Cambodia's international lines are usually jammed, which will give you a busy signal. Booking and requesting information through Web sites is consequently the best option. Calling overseas from Cambodia is very expensive (about $7 a minute), and you can't do it from public telephones. If you have to make a call, either go to the main post office or call from your hotel room, but ask how much it costs first. Few public phones work, but there are lots of stands that rent cell phones. For long-distance calls within the country, dial the "0" as part of the area code.

TIPPING

Bellhops and doormen are happy to receive anything from 2,000 riels (50¢) to a dollar. Guides and drivers expect a few dollars on top of their day rate. At tourist hotels, a 10% service charge is added to the bill, but if you consider that most of the staff earns between $1 and $2 per day, you may want to give them something extra.

TOURS & PACKAGES

Though you'll spend much less money making your own arrangements, you can simplify things by booking a full itinerary through an agency, such as Journeys International, in the United States.

🚶 **Journeys International** ✉ 107 April Dr., Ann Arbor, MI 48103 ☎ 734/665-4407 or 800/255-8735 ⊕ www.journeys-intl.com.

VISITOR INFORMATION
The Ministry of Tourism has some information on their Web site www.mot.gov.kh. Tourism Cambodia's site, www.tourismcambodia.com, has similar information, but has more detailed descriptions of top attractions.

LAOS

8

BEST WAY TO BE A DRIFTER
On a boat ride down a spectacular
stretch of the Mae Khong River ⇨*p.460*

MOST AFFORDABLE ROYAL APPOINTMENTS
Hotel Villa Santi, former royal home ⇨*p.456*

BEST UNSOLVED MYSTERY
The massive stone and clay pots
scattered across the Plain of Jars ⇨*p.445*

MOST COMFORTING CAVE DWELLERS
Thousands of Buddha images in Pak Ou ⇨*p.459*

MOST FORGIVABLE FOREIGN INFLUENCE
Vientiane's fantastic French eateries ⇨*p.440*

By Reinhard
Hohler &
Robert Tilley

DESPITE A LIMITED INFRASTRUCTURE, Laos is a wonderful country to visit. The Laotians are some of the friendliest, gentlest people in Southeast Asia—devoutly Buddhist, and traditional in many ways. Not yet inured to countless visiting foreigners, locals volunteer assistance and a genuine welcome. And because this landlocked nation is so sparsely populated—fewer than 6 million people in an area larger than Great Britain—its countryside is dominated by often impenetrable forested mountains. Laos has a rich culture and history, and though it's been a battleground many times in the past, it's a peaceful, stable country today.

Prehistoric remains show that the river valleys and lowland areas of Laos were settled as far back as 40,000 years ago, first by hunters and gatherers and later by more developed communities. The mysterious Plain of Jars—a stretch of land littered with ancient stone and clay jars at least 2,000 years old—indicates the early presence of a sophisticated society skilled in the manufacture of bronze and iron implements and ceramics. Starting in the 3rd century BC, cultural and trading links were forged with Chinese and Indian civilizations.

Between the 4th and 8th centuries, farming communities along the Mae Khong River began to organize themselves into communities called "Muang"—a term still used in both Laos and neighboring Thailand. This network of Muang gave rise in the mid-14th century to the first Lao monarchy, given the fanciful name of Lan Xang, or the "Kingdom of a Million Elephants, " for the large herds of the pachyderms that roamed the land.

At the start of the 18th century, following fighting over the throne, the kingdom was partitioned into three realms: Luang Prabang, Vientiane, and Champasak. In 1828 an invading Siamese army under King Rama III sacked Vientiane, and in 1904 the Lao monarch Sisavang Vong set up court in Luang Prabang. The monarchy was finally dissolved in 1975, when the revolutionary group Pathet Lao, allied with North Vietnam's communist movement during the Vietnam War, seized power after a long guerrilla war.

During the Vietnam War, the U.S. Air Force, in a vain attempt to disrupt the Ho Chi Minh Trail, dropped more tons of bombs on Laos than were dropped on Germany during World War II. Since the end of the Vietnam War, the People's Democratic Party (formerly the Pathet Lao) has ruled the country, first on Marxist-Leninist lines and now on the basis of limited pro-market reforms. Overtures are being made to the outside, particularly to Thailand and China, to assist in developing the country—not an easy task. The Friendship Bridge over the Mae Khong River connects Vientiane with Nong Khai in northeastern Thailand, making Laos more accessible to trade with neighboring countries.

The country is developing slowly. Vientiane, Luang Prabang, and Pakse have new airports; visitors from most countries can now get a visa upon arrival, and those from some ASEAN (Association of Southeast Asian Nations) countries need no visa at all. New hotels are constantly opening. The road from the current capital, Vientiane, to Laos's ancient capital, Luang Prabang, has been paved and upgraded—though it still takes eight hours to make the serpentine, 320-km (198-mi) journey north. The upgraded road running south from Vientiane can now accommodate tour buses going all the way to the Cambodian border. Other border crossings have also opened up, especially along the Vietnamese border.

A low standard of living (the average annual per-capita income is $170, one of the world's lowest) and a rugged landscape that hampers transportation and communication have long made the countryside of Laos a sleepy backwater. But Luang Prabang, boosted by its status as a World Heritage Site, has become a busy and relatively prosperous tourist hub. Vientiane, despite its new hotels and restaurants, remains one of the world's sleepiest capital cities.

Exploring Laos

Boxed in by China, Myanmar (Burma), Thailand, Cambodia, and Vietnam, Laos is geographically divided into three regions, each with its chief city: northern Laos and Luang Prabang, central Laos and Vientiane, southern Laos and Pakse. Luang Prabang is the country's major tourist destination, thanks to its royal palace (now a museum), temples, French colonial architecture, and the villagelike ambience it's managed to retain and refine. Vientiane is a curiosity, more like a small market town than a national capital, but it, too, has some fine temples, colonial buildings (many of them now comfortable hotels and sophisticated restaurants), and a riverside boulevard unmatched elsewhere in Laos.

Few tourists venture to the far south of the country, but Pakse is an interesting town and a convenient base from which to explore ancient Khmer ruins such as the fabulous Wat Phu. Fishing villages line the lower reaches of the Mae Khong River, a water wonderland of 4,000 islands and countless waterfalls and rapids.

About 90% of landlocked Laos is mountainous, so once out of Vientiane, Luang Prabang, and the southern lowlands, you're in true off-the-beaten-track territory. Even the country's main highway, linking Vientiane and Luang Prabang, is a difficult road to travel for much of the way. Most of the mountain terrain is impenetrable jungle, cut by rivers and ravines, and the only practical way of touring the country in anything less than a week is by plane. There's no railroad; car-rental services are still in their infancy; and although a public-transportation network covers the entire country, even the so-called VIP buses are slow and not very comfortable. Fortunately, the national airline, Lao Airlines, runs frequent (and cheap) flights between Vientiane and provincial cities such as Luang Prabang, Savannakhet, and Pakse. Chauffeur-driven cars can be hired for about $50 a day. Motorbikes can be rented in Vientiane and Luang Prabang, but these are recommended only for the adventurous.

Running north–south virtually the entire length of the country, and shaping the way of life of the communities along its banks, the Mae Khong River is a natural highway used by locals and tourists alike. There's also lively traffic on its tributaries: the Nam Ou, Nam Ngum, and Se Don rivers. Because all the main cities and virtually all tourist sights lie on the Mae Khong, boats offer an exotic and practical travel route. "Express" boats, with noisy outboard motors, and more leisurely "slow"

Most visitors confine their visit to Laos to just Vientiane and Luang Prabang. One day is necessary for each city, plus one day should be built into the schedule to cover travel between them. So you can catch some of Laos's highlights in three days, but you'd just be scratching the surface. At least one week is necessary to really get to know the country. Five days is an absolute minimum if you plan to visit the Plain of Jars and perhaps some of the sights around Luang Prabang.

Numbers in the text correspond to numbers in the margin and on the Laos, Vientiane, Side Trips from Vientiane, Northern Laos, Luang Prabang, and Southern Laos maps.

8

If you have
3 days

Spend your first day exploring 🗺 **Vientiane** ❶–❹ ▶, Laos's quiet capital. The next morning, head for 🗺 **Luang Prabang** ❾–⓭, a World Heritage Site. Spend the remainder of your trip admiring the town's ancient temples.

If you have
5 days

Spend the first night and the following day and night in 🗺 **Vientiane** ❶–❹ ▶. The next day, fly to the 🗺 **Plain of Jars** ❼; overnight in Phonesavanh and return the next day to Vientiane, from which you can catch one of the regular flights to 🗺 **Luang Prabang** ❾–⓭. Spend two days in Luang Prabang and the surrounding area, and return to Vientiane on the fifth day.

If you have
7 days

With seven days you can extend the five-day itinerary to include more time in northern Laos, taking in the area around Vientiane, or a trip to **Pakse** ㉕, a jumping-off point for exploring southern Laos.

---

boats ply sections of the river. The most popular water route is between Huay Xai, on the Thai border, and Luang Prabang. It's also possible to travel on cargo boats and barges as far south as Savannakhet, on the crossroads connecting Thailand and Vietnam, and Pakse, the southernmost city of Laos and a gateway to Cambodia.

Whether you travel by boat, bus, or plane, fares are very cheap by Western standards.

Although Laos has opened itself up to international trade and tourism, it's still a secondary destination on most itineraries. Tourism professionals in Thailand and Laos have been energetically pushing a joint cooperation program, making it considerably easier for visitors to Thailand to plan a side trip to Laos. Much of the Thai part of this program is based in Chiang Mai, from which Luang Prabang and Vientiane are easily reached by air in 60–80 minutes. Most travel agents in Chiang Mai can set you up with a tour to Laos for as little as $250 (including airfare). You can also fly to Vientiane and Luang Prabang from Bangkok, or cross the Mae Khong over bridges at Nong Khai and Ubon Ratchathani, in eastern Isan. Ferries link Chang Kong, in northern Thailand, with the Lao river port of Huay Xai.

About the Restaurants

In addition to Lao restaurants, both Vientiane and Luang Prabang have good Vietnamese, Chinese, Thai, and Indian restaurants, as well as bakeries that serve sandwiches made with fresh French-style baguettes. Vientiane and Luang Prabang also have numerous exclusively French restaurants—so Gallic that they stick to French opening hours, almost invariably taking a long afternoon break from 2 until 5 or 6.

About the Hotels

On the whole, hotels in Laos are a good deal. Although no lodgings in the country approach the level of the resorts of Thailand and Malaysia, there are several charming inns in historic buildings, and an abundance of guesthouses that offer real bargains. Because the Lao currency, the kip, suffers from chronic progressive devaluation, all hotel rates are listed in U.S. dollars, as are the menus in their restaurants and bars. Some hotels even charge higher rates for guests who pay their bills in kip.

WHAT IT COSTS In U.S. dollars				
	$$$$	**$$$**	**$$**	**$**	**¢**
RESTAURANTS	over $12	$9–$12	$6–$9	$3–$6	under $3
HOTELS	over $150	$100–$150	$50–$100	$25–$50	under $25

Restaurant prices are per person, for a main course at dinner. Hotel prices are for a standard double room, excluding tax.

Timing

Laos has a tropical climate with two distinct seasons: the dry months from November through April, and the rainy half of the year from May to October. The dry, cooler season is the more comfortable time to tour Laos, but prices come down during the rains—and the countryside is greener and less crowded. During the rainy season, the days can get very hot and sticky, with July and August registering the highest rainfalls. The yearly average temperature is about 82°F (28°C), rising to a maximum of 100°F (38°C). In Vientiane, a minimum temperature of 66°F (19°C) is to be expected in January. In many mountainous areas, however, temperatures drop to 59°F (15°C) in winter; nights in these areas can be chilly, sometimes dropping to the freezing point, so be sure to bring warm clothes.

Another factor to consider when planning a visit to Laos is the country's busy festival calendar. Most *bun* (festivals) are connected with religion and the rice-farming cycle; they're timed according to the Buddhist lunar calendar. Vientiane and Luang Prabang can get very crowded during the most important of these festivals (such as the That Luang Festival in Vientiane in November), so it's advisable to book your hotel room early. Luang Prabang is experiencing a tourism boom, so it's a good idea to reserve lodgings well in advance at any time of year.

VIENTIANE & ENVIRONS

Vientiane is not only the capital of Laos but also the logical gateway to the country, as it's far more accessible to the outside world than Luang

Buddhist Architecture

Laotians are a religious people, and the country's countless Buddhist temples are among its main attractions. Declared a state religion by King Fa Ngum in the mid-14th century, Theravada Buddhism belongs to the southern school of Buddhism, which is also practiced in Sri Lanka, Myanmar, Thailand, and Cambodia. Theravada Buddhist sacred sites are often works of art—collections of statues and structures that celebrate the human desire for perfection. They range from Luang Prabang's most venerable temple, the 16th-century Wat Xieng Thong, to the relatively new (19th-century) Wat Sisaket in Vientiane. Wat Phu's ancient structures in the south date back more than 1,000 years. As interesting as its architecture and statuary may be, a typical *wat* (Buddhist monastery) in Laos is still principally a center of worship and study. The sounds of chanting and chiming bells and the heady scent of incense will accompany you on your temple tour, during which you have a good chance of meeting monks or novices eager to practice their English.

Natural Beauty (and Beautiful Oddities)

Though it may not have the sheer variety of terrain that Thailand has, Laos is indeed a beautiful country. The limestone mountains are riddled with caves—the Pak Ou Caves are filled with statues of Lord Buddha. The river valleys around Luang Prabang hold spectacular waterfalls. The pretty plateau surrounding the southern city of Pakse has volcanic soil, which is put to good use in this agricultural hub. And of course, the Mae Khong River flows along the length of the country. The river and its tributaries provide rafting and swimming opportunities, though simply taking a slow boat between towns is just as interesting.

The most unusual attraction in the country is the Plain of Jars, accessible from Vientiane. The mountain-fringed, windswept plain would be stirring enough without additional decoration, but its intrigue is quadrupled by the presence of 5 to 6 ton stone and clay jars. The origin and purpose of these mysterious vessels are still unknown. If you can make it down to the southern tip of Southern Laos, you can see some freshwater dolphins at Si Phan Don.

Lao Cuisine

It may not be as famous as Thai food, but Lao cuisine is often just as good; the two cuisines are similar, but Lao cooking is usually not as spicy. Chilis are often used as a condiment, but Lao cuisine also makes good use of ginger, lemongrass, coconut, tamarind, crushed peanuts, and fish paste. Because so much of the country is wilderness, there's usually game, such as venison or wild boar, on the menu. Fresh river prawns and fish—including the famous, massive Mae Khong catfish, the world's largest freshwater fish—are also standard fare, along with chicken, vegetables, and sticky rice.

Prabang. The city sits on the Mae Khong River, with Thailand just across the water. A 20-minute ride by taxi or even *tuk-tuk* (three-wheel motorbike) brings you to the Friendship Bridge, which links Laos and Thailand. Crossing the bridge is a mere formality. On the Thai side of the bridge is the riverside frontier town of Nong Khai, which has direct

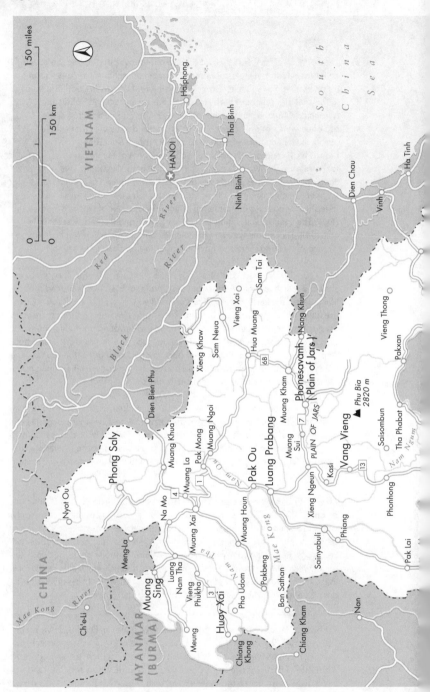

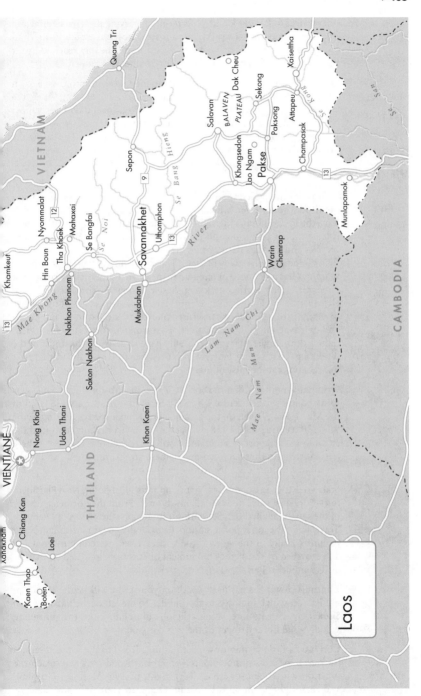

rail services to Bangkok and a bus terminus serving the Thai capital and most cities in eastern Isan. Many tourists choose this route from Thailand into Laos, although Vientiane is easily and cheaply reached by air from Bangkok, Chiang Mai, and most Southeast Asian cities.

Day trips from the small town of Vientiane take you into the heart of Vientiane Province: the popular riverside resort town of Vang Vieng, the still waters of Nam Ngum Lake, and Phu Khao Khouay, Laos's most beautiful nature reserve, 40 km (25 mi) from the capital. You can also fly from Vientiane to Phonesavanh, a jumping-off point for visiting the mysterious Plain of Jars.

Vientiane

Vientiane is the quietest Southeast Asian capital, with a pace as slow as the Mae Khong River, which flows along the edge of town. It doesn't have the kind of imposing sights you find in Bangkok, but neither does it have the air pollution and traffic jams. In fact there are many more bicycles and scooters than cars on the streets of Vientiane, and more trees than buildings lining many of them. The abundance of ugly cement-block buildings in urgent need of paint gives the town a superficially run-down appearance, but scattered among these eyesores are some remnants of elegant colonial French architecture. There are also dozens of temples—ornate, historic Buddhist structures that stand amidst towering palms and extravagantly flowering trees. First-time visitors often find Vientiane a drab, joyless city, but you only have to arrive in the midst of the weeklong That Luang Festival in November to be reminded that first impressions can be misleading.

Originally named Chanthaburi (City of the Moon), Vientiane was founded in the 16th century by King Setthathirat near a wide bend of the Mae Khong River, on the grounds of a Khmer fortress dating to the 9th–13th centuries. In 1828 the Siamese army from Bangkok razed the city. But the old part of Vientiane is still an attractive settlement, where ancient temples that survived the Siamese attack, museums, and parks are all just a short distance from one another.

a good tour

Start your tour in downtown Vientiane at its focal point, **Nam Phu Square ❶ ▶**, near several hotels and guesthouses. From the northeast corner of the square, walk down Setthathirat Road, past the offices of Diethelm Travel and the central police station. Pause at the junction with Lan Xang Avenue to take in the view of the wide avenue stretching to your left and crowned by the victory monument of Pratuxay, modeled on the Arc de Triomphe in Paris.

Continue down Setthathirat Road; on your right will be the Presidential Palace, which is closed to the public. To the left of the palace is **Wat Sisaket ❷**, with its interesting religious museum. Note the intriguing wooden-pile library tower of the wat compound.

Continue a little farther down Setthathirat Road to the art museum of **Ho Phra Keo ❸**. Continue along Setthathirat Road until you reach the junction with Mahosot Road. Turn right, passing Mahosot Hospital, and then right again onto Fa Ngum Quay. To your right stretches Vi-

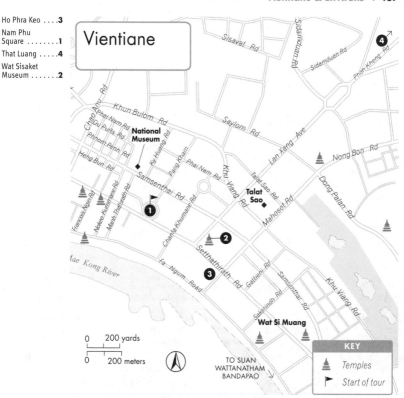

entiane's "Golden Mile, " a raised boulevard at the edge of the Mae Khong River. It's fronted by several restaurants and the historic old Lan Xang Hotel, all of them enticing you to stop for lunch.

After lunch, take a songthaew to **That Luang** ➍, the city's most important monument. Be sure to return to the river bank in the late afternoon to experience one of Vientiane's most spectacular sights—sunset over the Mae Khong.

TIMING You can complete this tour in less than a day, with a few hours in the morning at Nam Phu Square, Wat Sisaket, and Ho Phra Keo, followed by lunch and an afternoon visit to That Luang.

What to See

➌ **Ho Phra Keo.** There's a good reason why Ho Phra Keo, one of the city's oldest and most impressive temples, has a name so similar to the wat in Bangkok's Royal Palace. The original Ho Phra Keo here was built by King Setthathirat in 1565 to house the Emerald Buddha, which he had taken from Chang Mai in present-day Thailand. The king installed the sacred statue first in Luang Prabang and then in Vientiane at Ho Phra Keo, but the Buddha was recaptured by the Siamese army in 1778, and taken to Bangkok. The present temple was restored in 1936, and has become a national museum. On display are Buddha sculptures of

LAOS' FESTIVALS

L AOS HAS MANY FASCINATING FESTIVALS, *quite a few of which are steeped in Buddhism. Be sure to book hotels in advance if you're planning on visiting during festival time, particularly in the big cities.*

Bun Bang Fai: *The Rocket Festival is held in the middle of May. Rockets are fired and prayers are said in the paddy fields to bring rain in time for the planting of the rice seedlings.*

Bun Khao Padab Din: *This is a special rice ceremony held in August (the exact date depends on the harvest schedule). People make offerings at local temples to keep alive the memory of spirits who have no relatives.*

Bun Khao Salak: *This is a similar rice ceremony in September (the exact date depends on the harvest schedule), wherein people visit local temples to make offerings to their ancestors. Boat races are held on the Mae Khong, especially in Luang Prabang and Khammuan Province.*

Bun Ok Pansa: *The day of the full moon in October marks the end of Buddhist Lent and is celebrated with donations to local temples. Candlelight processions are held, and colorful floats are set adrift on the Mae Khong River. The following day, boat races are held in Vientiane, Savannakhet, and Pakse.*

Bun Pimai: *Lao New Year takes place April 13–15. This is a water festival similar to Thailand's celebrated Songkran, when all the important Buddha images get a cleaning with scented water (and the general public gets wet in the bargain). The festivities are particularly lively in Luang Prabang.*

Bun Visakhabucha (Buddha Day): *On the day of the full moon in May, candlelight processions are held in temples to mark the birth, enlightenment, and death of the Buddha.*

That Ing Hang Festival: *This takes place in Savannakhet in December and lasts several days on the grounds of the ancient Wat That Inhang, just outside the city. There are performances of traditional Lao music and dance, sports contests, and a spectacular drumming competition.*

That Luang Festival: *This is a weeklong event in Vientiane in November, which ends with a grand fireworks display. Hundreds of monks gather to accept alms. The festival runs concurrently with an international trade fair showcasing the products of Laos and other countries of the Greater Mae Khong Subregion (GMS).*

Wat Phu Festival: *Also known as Makhabucha Day, this festival is held during the day of the first full moon in February at Wat Phu, near Champasak. A full schedule of events includes elephant races, buffalo fights, cockfights, and traditional Lao music-and-dance performances.*

different styles, some wonderful chiseled images of Khmer deities, and a fine collection of stone inscriptions. The masterpiece of the museum is a 16th-century lacquered door carved with Hindu images. ⊠ *Setthathirat Rd. at Mahosot St.* ☎ *No phone* 💲 *2,000 kip* ⊙ *Daily 8–4.*

▶ ❶ **Nam Phu Square** (Fountain Square). An attractive square with a circular fountain in the middle, this is one of several reminders in the city of French colonial influence—reinforced still further by the presence on the square's perimeter of some very Gallic restaurants.

National Museum. A modern, well-laid-out, two-story building houses interesting geological and historical displays. Exhibits touch on Laos's royal history, its colonial years, and its struggle for liberation. The museum also highlights the country's 50 main ethnic groups and indigenous instruments. ⊠ *Sam Sen Tai Rd.* ☎ *021/212460, 021/212461, or 021/212462* 💲 *5,000 kip* ⊙ *Daily 8–noon and 1–4.*

Suan Wattanatham Bandapao (National Ethnic Cultural Park). The attraction at this park near the river is a model village of miniature Lao houses. Sculptures of Lao heroes dot the grounds, which also include a small zoo in one corner. This is a pleasant place to stroll and admire the sleek lines of the Friendship Bridge, just a short distance downstream. A string of restaurants lines the riverbank here. ⊠ *Km 20 on Tha Deua Rd.* ☎ *No phone* 💲 *5,000 kip* ⊙ *Daily 8–6.*

Talat Sao (Morning Market). To truly immerse yourself in Vientiane, visit this vast indoor bazaar that is, despite its name, actually open all day. The bright, orderly emporium holds everything from handwoven fabrics and wooden Buddha figures to electric rice cookers and tennis shoes. Most of the shops cater to locals, but there's still plenty to interest travelers: handicrafts, intricate gold-and-silver work, jewelry, T-shirts, and bags and suitcases to accommodate all your extra purchases. Many products are imported from abroad. Fruits, confections, and noodle soups are sold at open-door stalls outside, where Vietnamese shoemakers also ply their trade. The market, which is near the main post office, is made up of three Lao-style buildings, each with two floors. The funding of the construction (1989–91) came mainly from the market traders themselves. ⊠ *Lane Xang Ave. at Khoun Boulom St.* ☎ *No phone* ⊙ *Daily 7–6.*

★ ❹ **That Luang.** The city's most sacred monument, this massive, 147-foot-high, gold-painted stupa is also the nation's most important cultural symbol, representing the unity of the Lao people. It was built by King Setthathirat in 1566 (and restored in 1953) to guard a relic of the Buddha's hair and to represent Mount Meru, the holy mountain of Hindu mythology, the center and axis of the world. Surrounding the lotus-shape stupa are 30 pinnacles on the third level and a cloistered square on the ground with stone statues of the Buddha. The complex is flanked by two brilliantly decorated temple halls, the survivors of four temples that originally surrounded the stupa. On the avenue outside the west gate stands a bronze statue of King Setthathirat erected in the 1960s by a pious general. That Luang is the center of a major weeklong festival during November's full moon. It's on the outskirts of town (a 10-minute songthaew ride from the center). ⊠ *North end of That Luang Rd.* ☎ *No phone* 💲 *2,000 kip* ⊙ *Daily 8–4.*

Wat Si Muang. This wat, built in 1956, guards the original city pillar, a revered foundation stone dating to the 16th century. In a small park in front of the monastery stands a rare memorial to Laos's royal past: a large bronze statue of King Sisavang Vong. ⊠ *Lan Xang Ave.* ☎ *No phone* ⊠ *Free* ⊘ *Daily 7–5.*

❷ **Wat Sisaket Museum.** This interesting museum complex is made up of a crumbling temple and monastery compound across the road from Ho Phra Keo. Built in 1818 by King Anu, the temple survived the destruction of the city by the Siamese army in 1828. The monastery stands intact in its original form and is one of the most frequented in the city. Inside the main compound, the courtyard walls have hundreds of little niches and large shelves displaying 6,840 Buddha statues. Although it's in need of more work, the impressive temple hall underwent some restoration in 1938. The paintings that once covered its interior walls have largely been destroyed by the ravages of time, but the intricately carved wooden ceiling and doors are still intact. There's also an intriguing wooden library that stores palm-leaf manuscripts. ⊠ *Setthathirat Rd. at Mahosot St.* ☎ *No phone* ⊠ *2,000 kip* ⊘ *Daily 8–4.*

Xieng Khuan Buddha Park. The bizarre creation of an ecumenical monk who dreamt of a world religion embracing all faiths, this park is "peopled" by enormous Buddhist and Hindu sculptures spread among an attractive landscape of trees, shrubs, and flower gardens. Keep an eye out for the remarkable 165-foot-long sleeping Buddha. The park was laid out by the monk's followers in 1958 on the banks of the Mae Khong, opposite the Thai town of Nong Khai. ⊠ *Km 27–28 on Tha Deua Rd.* ☎ *No phone* ⊠ *5,000 kip* ⊘ *Daily 8–4:30.*

Where to Stay & Eat

$–$$ ✕ **Le Provençal.** A local family that lived in France for many years runs this little bistro behind Nam Phu Square. Chef Daniel's menu is almost exclusively French, although there's a hybrid pizza à la française. Try the beef-based terrine *du maison* to start, then sink your teeth into chicken niçoise, frogs' legs à la lyonnaise, or fillet of fish à la Provençale. Save room for such desserts as crème caramel and chocolate mousse. On fine days, you can sit on the terrace overlooking the square. ⊠ *73/ 1 Pang Kham Rd.* ☎ *021/219685* ⊟ *MC, V* ⊘ *No lunch Sun.*

$–$$ ✕ **L'Opera.** Vientiane's best Italian restaurant serves authentic pastas, pizzas, and fresh salads. From a table at the small front terrace you can watch the action on Nam Phu Square. ⊠ *12 Nam Phu Fountain Sq.* ☎ *021/215099* ⊟ *AE, MC, V.*

★ **$–$$** ✕ **Nam Phu.** A filet mignon as good as any you can find in Paris is one of the specialties at this very French restaurant on central Nam Phu Square. The dish, which comes with a blue-cheese sauce, is one of several unique creations on a menu also distinguished for its seafood and freshwater fish. There's an excellent wine list, with prices for bottles starting at a very reasonable $12. ⊠ *18–20 Nam Phu Fountain Sq.* ☎ *021/216248* ⊟ *AE, MC, V.*

¢–$ ✕ **Khop Chai Deu.** A French colonial structure houses this very popular downtown restaurant. The long menu is crammed with Lao and international dishes, and a daily buffet is also served. Draft beer is on tap. ⊠ *54 Setthathirat Rd.* ☎ *021/223022* ⊟ *MC, V.*

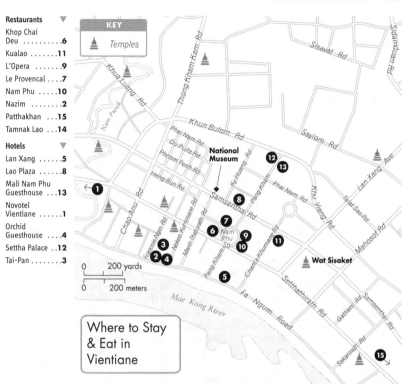

Restaurants ▼

Khop Chai
Deu **6**

Kualao **11**

L'Opera **9**

Le Provencal **7**

Nam Phu **10**

Nazim **2**

Patthakhan . . .**15**

Tamnak Lao . . .**14**

Hotels ▼

Lan Xang **5**

Lao Plaza **8**

Mali Nam Phu
Guesthouse . . .**13**

Novotel
Vientiane **1**

Orchid
Guesthouse **4**

Settha Palace . .**12**

Tai-Pan **3**

Where to Stay & Eat in Vientiane

¢–$ ✕ **Kualao.** In a fading mansion one block southeast of Nam Phu Square, this is Vientiane's best Lao restaurant, despite its rather tacky decor. The food is quite good, and the vast menu ranges from *mok pa fork* (banana-leaf-wrapped steamed fish cooked with eggs, onions, and coconut milk) to *gaeng panaeng* (a thick red curry with chicken, pork, or beef). Servings are small, so most people order several entrées, or set menus with seven to nine dishes, plus dessert and coffee. Photos and English descriptions facilitate ordering. There's Lao folk dancing nightly from 7 to 9. ⊠ *111 Samsenthai Rd.* ☎ *021/215777* ▭ *MC, V.*

¢–$ ✕ **Nazim.** Mr. Nazim has opened Indian restaurants in Luang Prabang, Vang Vieng—and now in Vientiane. His Indian-style curries, served with *papadum* (crunchy lentil bread) and thick rounds of nan, are the real thing. Try for one of the few seats on the small terrace; in the evening, you can watch the sun set over the Mae Khong, which flows just across the road. ⊠ *335 Fa Ngum Quay* ☎ *021/223480* ▭ *V.*

¢–$ ✕ **Patthakhan.** Vientiane's largest Lao restaurant, on the edge of the city, is a new structure built in traditional style. The extensive menu is dominated by Lao dishes, but it also includes Thai, Chinese, and other Asian food. Freshly caught Mae Khong fish is a specialty. ⊠ *Km 4 on Tha Deua Rd.* ☎ *021/312480* ▭ *No credit cards.*

¢–$ ✕ **Tamnak Lao.** Classical Lao dances are performed every evening at this fine outdoor restaurant specializing in the cuisine of Luang Prabang. Many dishes, such as the *pla laab* (minced fish with herbs), are prepared with fish fresh from the Mae Khong River. Note that dinner service doesn't begin until 6. ⊠ *308 That Luang Rd., Ban Phon Xay* 🕾 *021/413562* 🖃 *No credit cards.*

★ $$$$ 🏨 **Settha Palace.** Built by the French at the turn of the 19th century, converted to a hotel in the 1930s, and expropriated by the communist government in the 1970s, this colonial landmark became a hotel again in the late 1990s. Although it has undergone extensive renovation—the marble floors and fixtures are new—the owners have respected the original design. Rooms have high ceilings, hardwood floors, Oriental rugs, and period pieces. Their tall windows open onto lush gardens surrounding a large pool. The lobby, decorated with fine antiques, is adjacent to a small bar and elegant restaurant, La Belle Epoque, which specializes in Lao and French cuisine. ⊠ *6 Pang Kham Rd.* 🕾 *021/217581 or 021/217582* 🖷 *021/217583* ⊕ *www.setthapalace.com* 🛏 *29 rooms* ⌂ *Restaurant, room service, IDD phones, in-room safes, minibars, cable TV, pool, bar, dry cleaning, laundry service, concierge, business services, meeting rooms, no-smoking rooms* 🖃 *AE, MC, V* ⊚| *BP.*

$$$ 🏨 **Lao Plaza.** Something of a local landmark, Vientiane's nearest thing to a high-rise stands six stories tall in the center of town. The sleek exterior is a contrast to the old-fashioned comforts within: rooms furnished with dark woods, shades of powder blue and soft rose, Oriental rugs, and some fussy, homey touches. ⊠ *63 Sam Sen Tai Rd.* 🕾 *021/218800 or 021/218801* 🖷 *021/21808 or 021/21809* ⊕ *www.laoplazahotel. com* 🛏 *142 rooms* ⌂ *4 restaurants, patisserie, room service, IDD phones, in-room safes, minibars, cable TV, golf privileges, pool, gym, massage, sauna, bar, shops, dry cleaning, laundry service, Internet, business services, airport shuttle, car rental, travel services* 🖃 *AE, MC, V.*

$$$ 🏨 **Novotel Vientiane.** Vientiane's Novotel is just a five-minute drive from the airport but is pleasantly located in front of Fa Ngum Park. The modern building, with a sweeping art nouveau facade, has all the usual Novotel comforts and facilities, including a dance club that is popular with locals. Exercise enthusiasts appreciate the tennis court, gym, and swimming pool. ⊠ *Unit 9 Sam Sen Tai Rd.* 🕾 *021/213570* 🖷 *021/213572* ⊕ *www.novotel.com* 🛏 *201 rooms* ⌂ *Restaurant, café, IDD phones, minibars, cable TV, tennis court, pool, massage, gym, bar, dance club, laundry service, business services, travel services* 🖃 *AE, MC, V.*

$$ 🏨 **Tai-Pan.** With a convenient location in the heart of town near the Mae Khong River, and comfort at competitive rates, this hotel is popular with business travelers. Rooms are spacious and have dark parquet floors. The ground floor holds the reception area, restaurant, and lounge, which are separated by potted plants and wooden dividers. Behind the building is a narrow garden and a small pool. ⊠ *2–12 Francois Nginn Rd., Ban Mixay* 🕾 *021/216906 through 021/216909* 🖷 *021/216223* ⊕ *www.travelao.com* 🛏 *44 rooms* ⌂ *Restaurant, cable TV with movies, pool, exercise equipment, sauna, bar, lounge, laundry service, business services, meeting rooms, no-smoking rooms* 🖃 *AE, MC, V.*

$ ⊞ **Lan Xang.** Once a government showpiece, the venerable old Lane-Xang has come down in the world: the furnishings are worn, the ceilings need paint, and the bathrooms show the wear and tear of decades, though they're relatively large and clean. The staff is attentive and friendly, and if you don't mind the dog-eared appearance, it's a good deal, especially when you add in the complimentary breakfast, airport transfers, and nightly folk-dancing show in the Sa Long Xay restaurant. The best rooms overlook the Mae Khong, though they have have two single beds. Back rooms overlook the hotel pool, which has a shady terrace. ⊠ *1 Fa Ngum Quay* ☎ *021/214100 through 021/214107* 🖷 *021/ 214108* ✍ *clxhotel@hotmail.com,* ⟿ *109 rooms* ⌂ *Restaurant, café, in-room safes, cable TV, tennis court, pool, hair salon, bar, shop, laundry service, business services, travel services* ▭ *MC, V* ⦿I *BP.*

¢ ⊞ **Mali Nam Phu Guesthouse.** This spotlessly clean, Vietnamese-run guesthouse is a short walk away from several restaurants and shopping areas. Rooms are comfortable, if small and simply furnished. A central garden-courtyard offers a quiet place to relax after a day of sightseeing. ⊠ *114 Pang Kham Rd.* ☎ *021/215093 or 021/263297* 🖷 *021/263298* ⊕ *www. mali.com* ⟿ *26 rooms* ⌂ *Cable TV* ▭ *No credit cards.*

¢ ⊞ **Orchid Guesthouse.** Vientiane has an abundance of guesthouses, but this is the only one that faces the river. Front rooms and a rooftop deck afford stunning views across the Mae Khong to Thailand. The simple but spacious rooms have shiny tile floors and small desks. The bathrooms are cramped but have hot-water showers. ⊠ *33 Fa Ngum Quay, Ban Mixay* ☎ *021/252825* 🖷 *021/216588* ⟿ *25 rooms* ⌂ *Fans, cable TV, laundry service; no a/c in some rooms* ▭ *No credit cards.*

Nightlife & the Arts

The after-dark scene in Vientiane is very subdued, mostly confined to some of the more expensive hotels and a handful of bars and pubs along the Mae Khong River boulevard. Otherwise, entertainment in Vientiane means a cultural pursuit.

You can enjoy traditional Lao folk music and dancing on a Mae Khong River cruise aboard the **Lan Xang river boat** (☎ 021/212469 ⊕ www. lanexangtravel.com). The three-hour cruise costs $8 and departs from the jetty at the western end of Fa Ngum Quay. The Laos Tradition Show highlights traditional music and dance. It's staged by the Ministry of Information and Culture and takes place nightly at 8:30 at the **National Theater** (⊠ Manthaturat Rd. ☎ 021/242978).

The **Daothong Night Club** (☎ 020/543120), on the Luang Prabang Road at Ban Nakham, has live music nightly. The Lan Xang hotel's **Snack Bar** (⊠ 1 Fa Ngum Quay ☎ 021/214100) is a popular haunt. Vientiane's most popular dance club, **Zeaza Disco** (⊠ Khun Bolom Rd., Ban Haysok ☎ 020/5512858) caters to real night owls. You enter the club through a dragon's mouth.

Shopping

With crafts, jewelry, T-shirts, and more, the **Talat Sao** (Morning Market; ⊠ Lane Xang Ave. at Khoun Boulom St.) market should satisfy all your shopping needs.

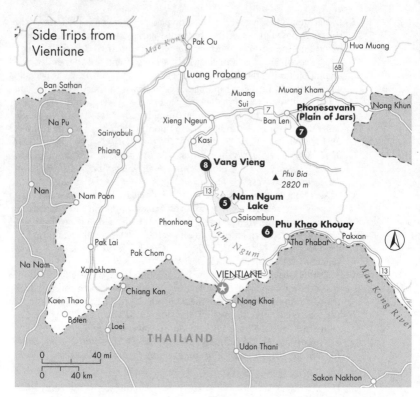

If you're still looking for that something special and you can't find it at Talat Sao, try the **Small and Medium Enterprises Promotion Center** (SMEPC; ⊠Phokheng Rd. ☎021/416736) or the **Lao Handicraft Group** (⊠Ban Thongphanthong ☎021/416267), which sells a wide selection of Lao handicrafts. Lao handwoven silk is world renowned, and you can find fine examples at **Maicome** (⊠Ban Sokpaluang ☎021/312275) and **Phaeng Mai Silk Gallery** (⊠Ban Nongbuathong Tai ☎021/243121). For wood carvings, head to **Humsinh Craft** (⊠Ban Dong Miang ☎021/212329).

Nam Ngum Lake

❺ *90 km (56 mi) north of Vientiane via Phonhong on Hwy. 13.*

Forested mountains surround this island-dotted reservoir lake, accessible by car from Vientiane. Floating restaurants here serve freshly caught lake fish, and there's a large hotel complex, the Dansavanh Nam Ngum Resort.

Where to Stay

$ 🏨 **Dansavanh Nam Ngum Resort.** Among the attractions at this ugly boxlike resort are a water theme park, a casino, and a golf course. The resort organizes treks in the countryside around the lake, and boat trips can be made to some of the islands for about $7 an hour. ⊠ *End of ac-*

cess Rd. ☎ *021/217594* 🖷 *021/252650* ⊕ *www.dansavanh.com* ⇆ *166 rooms* ⚴ *Restaurant, cable TV, golf course, pool, lake, gym, massage, boating, hiking, casino, dance club.*

Phu Khao Khouay

⑥ *40 km (25 mi) northeast of Vientiane on Hwy. 10.*

Phu Khao Khouay, or Buffalo Horn Mountain, lies in a national park—a dramatic area of sheer sandstone cliffs, river gorges, and the Ang Nam reservoir. The park's three rivers empty into the Mae Khong. The banks of the reservoir have several simple restaurants and refreshment stands. The park can be reached on Highway 10 (follow the signs from Ban Napheng).

Plain of Jars

★ ⑦ *390 km (242 mi) northeast of Vientiane, 96 km (60 mi) southeast of Luang Prabang.*

One of the world's major archaeological wonders, the Plain of Jars is also one of the world's most tantalizing mysteries. The broad, mountain-ringed plain northeast of Vientiane is littered with hundreds of ancient stone and clay jars, some estimated to weigh five or six tons. The jars are said to be at least 2,000 years old, but to this day, nobody knows who made them or why. They survived heavy bombing during the Vietnam War, and their sheer size has kept them out of the hands of antiquities hunters.

The jars are scattered over three main areas, but only the Ban Ang site is accessible and worth visiting. Here you can find some 300 jars dotting a windswept plateau about 12 km (7½ mi) from Phonesavanh, capital of Xieng Khuang Province. This is true Hmong territory: you pass Hmong villages on the way from Phonesavanh to Ban Ang and on Highway 7, which leads east to the Vietnamese border at Nong Het. There's much of interest in this remote area along Highway 7, including hot mineral springs at Muang Kham. From Muang Kham, a road leads to Vieng Xay, which has more than 100 limestone caves, some of them used as hideouts by the revolutionary Pathet Lao during the war years.

A hard day's drive along Highway 7 from either Vientiane or Luang Prabang, the vast plain is difficult to reach. Travel operators in both cities, such as Diethelm Travel and Lao Youth Travel, offer these tours by road, but the most comfortable route is by air from Vientiane to the tiny airfield at Phonesavanh. Here, a couple of hotels have basic but adequate accommodations, and a taxi can be hired for around $25 for the 30-km (19-mi) journey to the edge of the plain.

Where to Stay

$ 🏨 **Vansana Plain of Jars.** On a hilltop overlooking Phonesavanh, this is the best hotel in the city. The guest rooms are comfortably furnished and have balconies, minibars, and TVs. ⊠ *Phonthan Rd., Phonesavanh* ☎ *021/413895* 🖷 *021/413171* ⊕ *www.vansanahotel-group.com* ⇆ *36 rooms* ⚴ *Restaurant, minibars, cable TV, shop, laundry service, business center* ⊟ *No credit cards* ¶◯¶ *CP.*

Vang Vieng

★ **❽** *160 km (99 mi) north of Vientiane.*

The town of Vang Vieng was discovered in the mid-1990s by backpackers traveling between Vientiane and Luang Prabang on Highway 13. It's not only a convenient stopover, but also an attractive little town bordered by the Nam Song River and a dramatic range of jagged limestone mountains. During the Vietnam War, the United States maintained an airstrip in the town center; the abandoned tarmac is now part of the bus terminal. Today the town center is jam-packed with bars and backpacker hangouts, but you can escape the noise and the crowds by making for the river, which is lined with modest guesthouses and restaurants. The river is clean and good for swimming and kayaking, and the mountains beyond are riddled with caves. River trips and caving expeditions are organized by every guesthouse and hotel. Note that the treks to the caves can be fairly arduous, and some are only accessible by motorbike.

Where to Stay

¢–$$ ▦ **Bungalow Thavonsouk.** Try for one of the bungalows with a view of the river and the mountains. There's a pleasant and suitably named Sunset Restaurant. ⊠ *Nam Som Bridge* ☎☎ *023/511096* ✍ *thavonsouk@hotmail.com* ➹ *30 bungalows* ♨ *Restaurant, cable TV, refrigerators* ▤ *No credit cards.*

$ ▦ **Nam Song Hotel.** Bamboo and local fabrics decorate the light and airy rooms, many of which overlook the river, at this comfortable hotel. The garden restaurant also has good views of the river and the mountains. ⊠ *Unit 9, Ban Vieng Keo* ☎ *023/511016* ▱ *023/511016* ➹ *16 rooms* ♨ *Room TVs* ▤ *No credit cards* ▯◎▯ *BP.*

VIENTIANE & ENVIRONS A TO Z

AIR TRAVEL

Thai Airways International has daily flights from Bangkok to Vientiane. The national airline, Lao Airlines, has daily flights between Vientiane and Bangkok as well as three flights a week from Chiang Mai. All of these flights last about 80 minutes and cost around $100, plus the departure tax of $10.

Lao Airlines also flies several times a day between Vientiane and Luang Prabang, plus four times weekly from Vientiane to Phonesavanh, a jumping-off point for visiting the Plain of Jars.

🛪 Airlines **Lao Airlines** ☎ 021/212057 in Vientiane, 02/236–9821 in Bangkok ⊕ www. lao-aviation.com. **Thai Airways International** ☎ 021/225271 in Vientiane, 02/280–0060 in Bangkok ⊕ www.thaiair.com.

AIRPORTS & TRANSFERS

Vientiane's Wattay International Airport is about 4 km (2½ mi) from the city center.

You can take a metered taxi from Wattay International Airport into the city for $10; obtain a taxi voucher from the kiosk in the arrivals hall. The ride to the city center takes about 15 minutes. If you don't have much luggage, consider a tuk-tuk, a more exciting and cheaper option at 2,000–4,000 kip. But it's not practical if you're traveling with heavy luggage.

🚩 **Wattay International Airport** ☎ 021/512028 or 021/512165.

BORDER CROSSINGS

Vientiane's border crossing to Thailand is 19 km (12 mi) east of the city at the Friendship Bridge, which spans the Mae Khong River. The taxi fare between the bridge and Vientiane is about $10 or 350 baht (the drivers prefer to be paid in dollars or baht rather than kip). Taxis, songthaews, and some tuk-tuks wait at the Lao side of the bridge to take you to Vientiane. A free shuttle-bus service runs across the bridge. On the Thai side of the bridge, taxis, songthaews, and tuk-tuks can take you into the border town of Nong Khai, 3 km (2 mi) away. The border is open 6 AM–10 PM.

BUS TRAVEL

Although there's city bus service in Vientiane, schedules and routes are confusing for first-time visitors, so it's best to stick to taxis, tuk-tuks, *samlors* (bicycle rickshaws), and songthaews. The city bus station is next to the Morning Market. Comfortable VIP buses depart here for Vang Vieng as well as Pakse and southern Laos. For the overnight journey to Pakse, buses leave Vientiane nightly at 9 PM and arrive in Pakse the next day at 6 AM.

The bus terminal for trips to northern Laos is at Nong Duang Market.

🚩 **City bus station** ☎ 021/216507.

CAR RENTAL

You can rent a car, either with or without a driver, for $25–$50 a day. Car-rental companies are a fairly new enterprise in Laos, but one of the most reliable in Vientiane is Asia Vehicle Rental.

🚩 **Agency** **Asia Vehicle Rental** ✉ Sam Sen Tai Rd. ☎ 021/217493 or 021/223867 🖷 021/217493 ⊕ www.laopdr.com.

EMERGENCIES

The best clinic in the country is Mahosot Hospital International Clinic in Vientiane, though you should go here only if you're unable to obtain assistance through your hotel.

🚩 **Hospital** **Mahosot Hospital International Clinic** ✉ Fa Ngum Quay ☎ 021/214022.

HEALTH

As in all of Southeast Asia, it's advisable to drink bottled water (stay away from ice also) and avoid uncooked foods. Vientiane is malaria-free, but it's still advisable to use mosquito repellent. Drugstores are well stocked with medicine for minor ailments.

MONEY MATTERS

Banks have better exchange rates than money changers. At this writing there was one ATM in the country, at Vientiane's Banque Pour le Commerce Exterieur Lao (BPCE), one block south of Nam Phu Square on Pangkham Road. Major credit cards are accepted in most hotels and many restaurants, but few shops.

SAFETY

The Lao government keeps tight police control over its capital, and crime is low. Nevertheless you should follow the usual precautions for traveling around Southeast Asia: keep only enough cash on you to cover your expected needs, leave valuables in your hotel or guesthouse safe, keep a photocopy of the relevant pages of your passport on you, and avoid arguments or confrontational situations with locals.

TOURS & PACKAGES

Diethelm Travel arranges two- and three-day package tours of Vientiane. Costs range from $238 to $570 and include lodging. The company also has tours to the Plain of Jars, as does Lao Youth Travel.

Diethelm Travel ⊠ Setthathirat Rd. at Nam Phu Fountain Sq. ☎ 021/213833, 021/215920, or 021/215128 🖷 021/216294 or 021/217151 ⊕ www.diethelm-travel.com. **Lao Youth Travel** ⊠ 24 Fa Ngum Quay, Ban Mixay ☎ 021/240939 🖷 021/213037 ⊕ www.laoyouthtravel.com.

TRANSPORTATION AROUND VIENTIANE & ENVIRONS

You can cover Vientiane on foot, but tuk-tuks (three-wheel motorbikes), songthaews (covered pickups with bench seating), samlors (bicycle rickshaws), and "jumbos" (motorcycle taxis) are cheap and easy to flag down. Buses are best avoided, as the routes and schedules can be confusing for first-time visitors. For any of these vehicles, be sure to negotiate the price; you can expect to pay about 1,000 kip for a ride within the city.

Taxis are available but must be reserved, which you can do through your hotel or at the Morning Market. For day trips outside the city, ask your hotel or guesthouse to book a car with a driver.

VISITOR INFORMATION

Diethelm Travel is your best source of information. The National Tourism Authority of the Lao People's Democratic Republic provides some printed materials, but little else.

Diethelm Travel ⊠ Setthathirat Rd. at Nam Phu Fountain Sq. ☎ 021/213833, 021/215920, or 021/215128 🖷 021/216294 or 021/217151 ⊕ www.diethelm-travel.com. **National Tourism Authority of the Lao People's Democratic Republic** ⊠ BP 3556, Ave. Lang Xang ☎ 021/212248.

LUANG PRABANG & NORTHERN LAOS

For all its popularity as a tourist destination, Luang Prabang remains one of the most remote cities in Southeast Asia. Although a highway now runs north to the Chinese border, the hinterland of Luang Prabang is mostly off-the-beaten-track territory, a mountainous region of impenetrable forests and deep river valleys. Despite Luang Prabang's air links to the rest of the country and the outside world, the Mae Khong River is still a preferred travel route. Passenger craft and freight barges ply the river's length as far as China in the north and near the Cambodian border in the south.

Northern Laos

Luang Prabang

390 km (242 mi) north of Vientiane.

Most travelers to Laos don't come to see Vientiane, the present-day capital, but to visit its ancient capital and former royal city: Luang Prabang, a sleepy town of about 68,000 inhabitants that sits high on the banks of a peninsula, where the Nam Khan River flows into the Mae Khong River. Luang Prabang was capital of the kingdom of Lan Xang until the mid-16th century, when King Setthathirat moved the seat to the more secure location of what is now Vientiane. At the end of the 17th century, the Lan Xang kingdom, now virtually a vassal state of Vietnam, was divided into three sections, and Luang Prabang reestablished its own dynasty, which survived threats of conquest and assimilation by Siam, Vietnam, Chin Haw marauders from China, and the colonial French. The city's modest palace (now the city museum) and some princely homes (two of them now hotels) are all that remain of city's days of glory.

Nevertheless this is still Laos's religious and artistic capital, and its combination of impressive natural surroundings, historic architecture, and friendly inhabitants make it one of the region's most pleasant towns. The city's abundance of ancient temples led UNESCO to declare it a World Heritage Site in 1995, and since then it's been bustling with construction and renovation activity.

Some 36 temples are scattered around town, making Luang Prabang a pleasant place to explore on a rented bicycle or on foot. But the charm of Luang Prabang is not exclusively architectural—just as pleasant are the people, who seem to spend as much time on the streets as they do in their homes. Children play on the sidewalks while matrons gossip in the shade, young women in traditional dress zip past on motor scooters, and Buddhist monks in saffron robes stroll by with black umbrellas, which protect their shaven heads from the tropical sun.

Laotians aren't the only people you can see on the streets in Luang Prabang, however. With each passing year, the increase in visitors seems to overwhelm the town during the November–April high season. Despite scores of guesthouses, finding accommodation can be a challenge in the peak season. And when you visit the main attractions, be prepared for crowds of tourists.

a good walk

Start your tour of Luang Prabang at the throbbing heart of the city: the **Tribal Market** ⑨ ▶, at the crossroads of Sisavang Vong Road and Setthathirat Road. You can find it thronged with shoppers hunting through a large variety of goods. From here, head northeast along Sisavang Vong Road, stopping on the left at one of the city's most beautiful temples, **Wat Mai** ⑩. Magnificent wood carvings and golden murals decorate the main pillars and portico entrance to the temple. Continue down Sisavang Vong Road to the compound of the **Royal Palace** ⑪, with its large bronze statue of King Sisavang Vong. The palace, more of a large country house than a royal residence, is now a museum. On leaving the palace grounds by the main entrance, climb the staircase to **Phu Si Hill** ⑫, which watches over the city. The climb is steep and takes about 15 minutes, but you'll be rewarded with an unforgettable view of Luang Prabang and the surrounding countryside.

Back in front of the Royal Palace, follow Sisavang Vong Road toward the confluence of the Mae Khong and Nam Khan rivers, where you can find another fascinating Luang Prabang temple, **Wat Xieng Thong** ⑬. Walk inside the temple to marvel at the classic Lao religious architecture. Leaving the compound on the Mae Khong River side, walk back to the city center along the romantic waterside road, fronted by several French colonial houses and Lao traditional homes. Passing the port area behind the Royal Palace, continue on to the crossroads at Wat Phu Xay; turn right here to return to the Tribal Market. Every evening there's a local night bazaar, stretching from the Tribal Market to the Royal Palace on Sisavang Vong Road.

TIMING   This tour should take about a half day—longer if you climb Phu Si Hill, which has particularly lovely views at sunset. You'll need about two hours to work through the Royal Palace's maze of rooms; note that it's closed weekends. The evening bazaar on Sisavang Vong Road starts around 6.

What to See

⑫ **Phu Si Hill.** Several shrines and temples and a golden stupa crown this forested hill, but the best reason to ascend its 328 steps is to enjoy the

Luang
Prabang

KEY

▲ *Temple*

0   200 yards

0   200 meters

Mae Khong River

Khem Kong Rd

Sakkalin Rd

Kingkitsalath Rd

Nam Khan River

Manthaturath Rd

Sisavangvong Rd

Khunkhampheng Rd

Wat Aham
Wat Visun

Chao Sisophon Rd

Phalanxay Rd

Suvannaphomma Rd

Sukhaseum Rd

Kitsarat Setthathirat Rd

Visunalat Rd

Vat Meun Na Rd

Phetsarath Rd

view from the summit: a panorama of Luang Prabang, the Nam Khan
and Mae Khong rivers, and the surrounding mountains. It's a popular
spot for watching the sunset (just be sure to bring insect repellent), but
the view from atop old Phu Si is splendid at any hour. ⊠ *Rathsavong
Rd.* ☎ *No phone* 💲 *5,000 kip* ⊙ *Daily 6–6.*

★ ⓫ **Royal Palace** (National Museum). In a walled compound at the foot of
Phu Si Hill stands this palace, the former home of the royal Savang family. Built at the beginning of the 20th century, the palace served as the
royal residence until the Pathet Lao took over Laos in 1975 and exiled
Crown Prince Savang Vatthana and his children to a remote region of
the country (their fate has never been established). It still has the feel of
a large family home—a maze of teak-floor rooms surprisingly modest
in scale. The largest of them is the **throne room,** with its gilded furniture, colorful-mosaic-covered walls, and display cases filled with rare
Buddha images, royal regalia, and other priceless artifacts.

The walls of the **king's reception room** are decorated with scenes of traditional Lao life painted in 1930 by the French artist Alex de Fautereau.
The **queen's reception room** contains a collection of royal portraits by
a Russian artist. The room also has cabinets full of presents given to the
royal couple by visiting heads of state; a model moon lander and a piece

CloseUp

RELIGION IN LAOS

THE OVERWHELMING MAJORITY OF Laotians are Buddhists, yet, as in neighboring Thailand, spirit worship is widespread, blending easily with temple traditions and rituals. A common belief holds that supernatural spirits called phi have power over individual and community life.

Laotians believe that each person has 32 khwan, or individual spirits, which must be appeased and kept "bound" to the body. If one of the khwan leaves the body, sickness can result, and then a ceremony must be performed to reattach the errant spirit. In this ritual, which is known as bai-si, white threads are tied to the wrist of the ailing person in order to fasten the spirits. Apart from the khwan, there are countless other spirits inhabiting the home, gardens, orchards, fields, forests, mountains, rivers, and even individual rocks and trees.

Luang Prabang has a team of ancestral guardian spirits, the Pu Nyeu Na Nyeu, who are lodged in a special temple, Wat Aham. In the south, the fierce guardian spirits of Wat Phu are appeased every year with the sacrifice of a buffalo to guarantee an abundance of rain during the rice-growing season.

Despite the common belief in a spirit world, more than 90% of Laotians are officially Theravada Buddhists, a conservative nontheistic form of Buddhism said to be derived directly from the words of the Buddha. Buddhism arrived in Laos in the 3rd century BC by way of Ashoka, an Indian emperor who helped spread the religion. A later form of Buddhism, Mahayana, which arose in the 1st century AD, is also practiced in Laos, particularly in the cities. It differs from Theravada in that followers venerate the bodhisattvas. This northern school of Buddhism spread from India to Nepal, China, Korea, and Japan and is practiced by Vietnamese and Chinese alike in all the bigger towns of Laos. The Chinese in Laos also follow Taoism and Confucianism.

Buddhism in Laos is so interlaced with daily life that you have a good chance of witnessing its practices and rituals firsthand—from the early-morning sight of women giving alms to monks on their rounds through the neighborhood, to the evening routine of monks gathering for their temple recitations. If you visit temples on Buddhist holy days, which coincide with the new moon, you'll likely hear monks chanting texts of the Buddha's teachings.

Christianity is followed by a small minority of mostly French-educated, elite Laotians, although the faith also has adherents among hill-tribe converts in areas that have been visited by foreign missionaries. Missionary activity has been curbed in recent years, however, as the Lao government forbids the dissemination of foreign religious materials.

Islam is practiced by a handful of Arab and Indian businesspeople in Vientiane. There are also some Muslims from Yunnan, China, called Chin Haw, in the northern part of Laos. More recently, a very small number of Cham refugees from Pol Pot's Cambodia (1975–79) took refuge in Vientiane, where they have established a mosque.

of moon rock from U.S. president Richard Nixon share shelf space with an exquisite Sevres tea set presented by French president Charles de Gaulle and fine porcelain tea cups from Chinese leader Mao Tse-tung. Other exhibits in this eclectic collection include friezes removed from local temples, Khmer drums, and elephant tusks with carved images of the Buddha.

The museum's most prized exhibit is the **Pha Bang,** a gold image of the Buddha slightly less than 3 feet tall and weighing more than 100 pounds. Its history goes back to the first century, when it was cast in Sri Lanka; it was brought to Luang Prabang from Cambodia in 1353 as a gift to King Fa Ngum. This event is celebrated as the introduction of Buddhism as an official religion to Laos, and Pha Bang is venerated as the protector of the faith. An ornate temple called Ho Pha Bang, near the entrance to the palace compound, is being restored to house the image.

Tucked away behind the palace is a crumbling wooden garage that houses the royal fleet of aging automobiles. ⊠ *Sisavang Vong Rd. across from Phu Si Hill* ☎ *071/212470* 🎫 *20,000 kip* ☉ *Weekdays 8:30–11 and 1–4.*

▶ ❾ **Tribal Market.** A hive of daily activity, this central covered market is usually packed with shoppers sifting through piles of produce and household goods, including textiles and Chinese-made items. Hill-tribe people often shop here, particularly during cooler weather, when they journey into town to buy winter blankets and clothing. ⊠ *Sisavang Vong Rd. at Setthathirat Rd.* ☉ *Daily 7–5.*

❿ **Wat Mai.** This small but lovely temple next to the Royal Palace compound dates from 1796. Its four-tier roof is characteristic of Luang Prabang's religious architecture, but more impressive are the magnificent wood carvings and gold-leaf murals on the main pillars and portico entrance to the temple. These intricate panels depict the last life of the Buddha, as well as various Asian animals. During the Bun Pimai festival (Lao New Year), the Pha Bang sacred Buddha Image is carried from the Royal Palace compound to Wat Mai for ritual cleansing ceremonies. ⊠ *Sisavang Vong Rd.* ☎ No phone 🎫 *10,000 kip* ☉ *Daily 6–6.*

Wat Visun. The 16th-century Wat Visun and neighboring **Wat Aham** play a central role in Lao New Year celebrations, when ancestral masks, called *phu gneu gna gneu,* are taken from Wat Aham and displayed in public. Wat Visun was built in 1503, during the reign of King Visunalat, who had the temple named after himself. Within the compound is a large and unusual watermelon-shape stupa called **That Makmo** (literally Watermelon Stupa). The 100-foot-high mound is actually a royal tomb, where many small precious Buddha statues were found when Chin Haw marauders destroyed the city in the late 19th century (these statues have since been moved to the Royal Palace). The temple hall was rebuilt in 1898 along the lines of the original wooden structure and now houses an impressive collection of Buddha statues, stone inscriptions, and other Buddhist art. ⊠ *Visunalat Rd.* ☎ No phone 🎫 *10,000 kip* ☉ *Daily 6–6.*

★ ⓭ **Wat Xieng Thong.** Luang Prabang's most important and impressive temple complex is Wat Xieng Thong, a collection of ancient buildings near

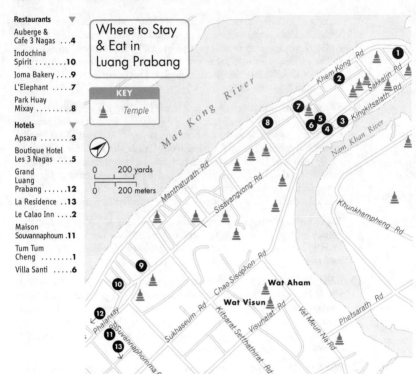

the tip of the peninsula, where the Mae Khong and Khan rivers meet. Constructed in 1559–60, the main temple is one of the few structures to have survived centuries of marauding Vietnamese, Chinese, and Siamese armies, and it's regarded as one of the region's best-preserved examples of Buddhist art and architecture. The intricate golden facades, colorful murals, sparkling glass mosaics, and low, sweeping roofs of the entire ensemble of buildings (which overlap to make complex patterns) all combine to create a feeling of harmony and peace.

The interior of the main temple has decorated wooden columns and a ceiling covered with wheels of dharma, representing the Buddha's teaching. The exterior is just as impressive thanks to mosaics of colored glass that were added at the beginning of 20th century. Several small **chapels** at the sides of the main hall are also covered with mosaics and contain various images of the Buddha. The bronze 16th-century reclining Buddha in one chapel was displayed in the 1931 Paris Exhibition. The mosaic on the back wall of that chapel commemorates the 2,500 anniversary of the Buddha's birth with a depiction of Lao village life. The chapel near the compound's east gate, with a gilded facade, contains the royal family's funeral statuary and urns, including a 40-foot-long wooden boat that was used as a hearse. ✉ *Sisavang Vong Rd.* ☎ *071/212470* 💰 *10,000 kip* 🕒 *Daily 6–6.*

Where to Stay & Eat

New hotels are shooting up in Luang Prabang to accommodate the growing numbers of tourists. Many of the most attractive of them are in converted buildings dating from French colonial days, and two old favorites are former royal properties.

★ $$–$$$$ ✕ **L'Elephant Restaurant Francais.** When you can't face another serving of rice or spicy sauces, it's time to walk down the hill from the Villa Santi to this pleasant corner restaurant. The menu is traditional French, with a bit of Lao influence, especially when it comes to the ingredients. Consider, for example, the *chevreuil au poivre vert* (local venison in a pepper sauce). There's always a three-course set meal and several daily specials, which usually include fish fresh from the Mae Khong. Seating is available in the bright, airy dining room or on the sidewalk, behind a barrier of plants. ⊠ *Ban Wat Nong* ☎ *071/252482* ▤ *MC, V* ☽ *No lunch weekdays.*

$$$ ✕ **Auberge & Cafe 3 Nagas.** Local buffalo meat with green-pepper sauce, and fillet of perch with mushrooms are two delicious specialties served at this stylish French restaurant under the same management as L'Elephant Restaurant Francais. It's opposite the Boutique Hotel Les 3 Nagas. ⊠ *Sakkalin Rd.* ☎ *071/253888* ▤ *MC, V.*

¢–$$ ✕ **Indochina Spirit.** For a hearty meal, head to this circa-1920s former residence of a royal physician, now an eclectic Thai-run restaurant where a selection of Lao specialties costs just $5. Start with an appetizer of Mae Khong seaweed, followed by the "Indochina" steak. Italian pastas and pizza are also on the menu, and delicious pancakes are served for breakfast. ⊠ *52 Ban Wat That* ☎ *071/252372* ▤ *MC, V.*

$ ✕ **Park Huay Mixay.** Venison steak is recommended at this long-established pan-Asian restaurant, a favorite with locals. Start your meal, though, with a more conventional Lao dish, such as *tom yam* soup (with lemongrass, coriander, chilies, and chicken or fish), and end it with a glass of the local *lao-lao* (home-brewed rice whiskey). ⊠ *75/6 Sothikuman Rd., Ban Xieng Muan* ☎ *071/212260 or 020/5511496* ▤ *No credit cards.*

¢ ✕ **Joma Bakery Cafe.** Two Canadians run this cheap and friendly self-service restaurant, where an in-house bakery turns out delicious pastries and French bread. The homemade soups are excellent. ⊠ *Chao Fa Ngum Rd.* ☎ *071/252292* ▤ *No credit cards* ☽ *Closed Sun.*

$$$ ✕▦ **La Residence Phou Vao Hotel.** Its prime position on Kite Hill gives this sumptuous hotel the best views in town. Traditional Lao touches are everywhere and create a sense of exotic luxury in the rosewood-furnished rooms. In the evening, you can relax over cocktails at the Dok Chama Bar and soak in the restful garden surroundings. The restaurant ($$$$) is among Luang Prabang's best, serving authentic Lao food and rich French dishes. ⊠ *Phu Vao Hill* ☎ *071/212194* 🖷 *071/212534* ⊕ *www.pansea.com* ⇨ *34 rooms* ⚐ *Restaurant, room service, in-room safes, minibars, cable TV, shop* ▤ *AE, MC, V.*

$$ ✕▦ **Boutique Hotel Les 3 Nagas.** This turn-of-the-19th-century mansion stands under official UNESCO World Heritage Site protection, thanks in no small measure to the efforts of the French owner to retain its weathered but handsome colonial look. The wooden floors and clay tiles are original, and the large rooms are furnished with dark wood, silks, and

homespun local fabrics (you can also buy these fabrics in the hotel shop, along with Lao teas, coffee, and spices). Some rooms have four-poster beds. The hotel's restaurant is one of the few in Luang Prabang serving exclusively vegetarian Lao dishes. ⊠ *Sakkalin Rd., Ban Wat Nong* ☎ *071/252079* 🖷 *071/252384* ⊕ *www.3nagas.com* 🖘 *15 rooms* ⚘ *Restaurant, IDD phones, refrigerators, cable TV, laundry service, Internet* ▭ *MC, V* ⭐ *BP.*

★ **$$** ✕⬚ **Villa Santi.** This 19th-century royal residence in the heart of town was converted to a boutique hotel in 2001 by a local princess's son-in-law, who also built a resort outside of town. Rosewood furniture, handicrafts, and fine silks decorate the rooms. The lovely garden courtyard doubles as the Elephant Garden Bar, and the Princess Restaurant, which has live folk music at dinner, serves authentic "royal" Lao and Western cuisine. The affiliated resort, 5½ km (3½ mi) from town, re-creates a traditional setting, and has larger rooms with balconies overlooking lily pools, lush gardens, rice paddies, and forested hills. The open-air terrace restaurant serves Lao and international cuisine. ⊠ *Sakkalin Rd.* ☎ *071/252157* 🖷 *071/252158* ⊕ *www.villasantihotel.com* 🖘 *25 rooms in hotel, 52 rooms in resort* ⚘ *Restaurant, room service, in-room safes, minibars, bar, 2 pools, laundry service, concierge, airport shuttle, travel services, no-smoking rooms; no room phones, no room TVs* ▭ *MC, V* ⭐ *BP* ⊠ *Resort: Nadeuay Rd.* ☎ *071/253470* 🖷 *071/253471* ⊕ *www.villasantihotel.com* 🖘 *55 rooms* ⚘ *Restaurant, minibars, cable TV, pool, laundry service, meeting rooms* ▭ *MC, V* ⭐ *BP.*

★ **$–$$** ✕⬚ **Apsara.** With its white facade and balustrades and its riverside location, this French-style *maison* would be at home in southern France. The plush and silk-hung restaurant ($), with a terrace overlooking the Nam Khan River, is worth a visit, even if you're not staying the night (it claims to serve the driest martini in town). The reasonably priced rooms have floor-to-ceiling windows that face east, so you can catch the sunrise over the nearby mountains. Under the same management is a pretty, city-center, three-bedroom house in secluded gardens that's ideal for families ($165–$210). ⊠ *Kingkitsarat Rd.* ☎ *071/212420* 🖷 *071/212420* ⊕ *www.theapsara.com* 🖘 *2 rooms, 1 house* ⚘ *Restaurant, refrigerators, cable TV, bar, laundry service* ▭ *MC, V* ⭐ *BP.*

★ **$** ✕⬚ **Tum Tum Cheng.** Although accommodations here don't rank among this town's best, the restaurant definitely does. The intimate spot serves an inventive menu of Lao food, with such treats as Mae Khong catfish in a sweet ginger sauce and venison with mushrooms. Seating is available inside on cushions or on the garden terrace, but is limited, so reservations are essential in peak season. Rooms are simple but sufficient—they're decorated with local handicrafts, but are short on amenities, and have rather basic bathrooms. The location, a stone's throw from Wat Xieng Thong, is perfect, and the owners, a Lao/Hungarian couple, are charming. ⊠ *50/1 Ban Xieng Thong* ☎ *071/253224* 🖷 *071/253262* 🖘 *10 rooms* ⚘ *Restaurant, bicycles, laundry service; no room phones, no room TVs* ▭ *MC, V.*

$$–$$$ ⬚ **Grand Luang Prabang.** This Thai-owned hotel occupies the former residence of nationalist hero Prince Petsarath (1890–1959), whose villa stands amid the hotel's new (but traditionally designed) buildings. The hotel has an unmatched location on a bend of the Mae Khong River, and though guest rooms are set back a bit, most have river views. Rooms are spacious and have hardwood floors, white marble baths, and sliding glass doors that open onto large balconies. It's 4 km (2½ mi) from Luang Prabang, near the village of Xieng Keo; a shuttle provides regular transportation to town and the airport. In summer a boat ferries guests into town. ⊠ *Ban Xieng Keo, Khet Sangkalok* ☎ *071/253851 through 071/ 253856* 🖷 *071/253027 or 071/253028* ⊕ *www.grandluangprabang.com* ⤳ *78 rooms* ⚒ *Restaurant, in-room safes, minibars, cable TV, pool, bicycles, bar, laundry service, concierge, meeting rooms, airport shuttle, no-smoking rooms* ☰ *AE, MC, V* ⍾ *BP.*

$$ 🏨 **Le Calao Inn.** Fronting the Mae Khong and just down the street from Wat Xieng Thong is this small hotel, which was resurrected from a ruined mansion built by a Portuguese merchant in 1904. Four guest rooms upstairs open onto a colonnaded veranda to views of the river and the hills beyond. The two rooms on the lower floor are larger—with three beds each—and have private terraces, but are a bit dark. The Buasavan Restaurant on the ground floor serves French and Asian fare. Because of the hotel's small size and popularity, it's highly advisable to book ahead November–April. ⊠ *Suvanna Kham Phong Rd.* ☎ *071/212100* 🖷 *071/ 212085* ✉ *calaoinn@laotel.com* ⤳ *6 rooms* ⚒ *Restaurant, laundry service; no room phones, no room TVs* ☰ *V* ⍾ *BP.*

$ 🏨 **Maison Souvannaphoum.** The once-run-down residence of Prince Souvannaphoum, prime minister in the 1960s, has been transformed into one of the top hotels in Luang Prabang. The colonial-style mansion contains the reception area, an open-air restaurant, and a bar; guest rooms occupy a newer building in back. Rooms are large and bright, with small balconies overlooking tropical greenery. Ask for a room at the back, away from the busy street, for more peace and quiet. ⊠ *Chao Fa Ngum Rd.* ☎ *071/212200* 🖷 *071/212577* ⤳ *25 rooms* ⚒ *Restaurant, refrigerators, cable TV, bar, laundry service, travel services* ☰ *MC, V* ⍾ *BP.*

Nightlife & the Arts

Luang Prabang's nightlife is limited. Monday, Wednesday, Friday, and Saturday evenings, the **Royal Ballet Theater Phralak-Phralam** (☎ 071/ 253705) performs at the Royal Palace museum. The program includes a local *bai-si* ceremony, classical dances enacting episodes from the Indian *Ramayana* epos, and outdoor presentations of the music and dances of Lao minorities. In Laos the minorities are grouped and identified according to where they live: the Lao Lum in the valleys, the Lao Theung on plateaus, and the Lao Sung in the mountains.

Locals head to the nightclub **Muong Swa** (⊠ Phu Vao Rd.) for Lao-style folk and rock music. If you need a dancing partner, the waiters will find you one!

Sports & the Outdoors

Many of the tour operators in town offer interesting rafting and kayaking trips, plus cycling expeditions. Several guesthouses and hotels rent bikes for about $1 a day.

Shopping

Luang Prabang has two principal markets where you can find a large selection of handicrafts: the Dala Central Market, on Setthathirat Road,

A HISTORY OF LAN XANG

1353: The Lan Xang kingdom is founded by King Fa Ngum, who marries a Khmer princess and installs the Prabang Buddha statue in present-day Luang Prabang.

1373–1416: King Sam Sen Tai Tai comes to the throne of Lan Xang. Civil warfare follows his death.

1520–48: King Pothisarath reunifies the kingdom and marries a Thai princess.

1548–71: King Setthathirat brings the Emerald Buddha statue from Chiang Mai to Luang Prabang; in 1560 he moves the capital to Vientiane.

1637–94: King Suligna Vongsa reigns in Vientiane. He receives foreign emissaries and traders.

1707: Feuding over the throne leads to the partition of the kingdom into Luang Prabang, Vientiane, and Champasak.

1778: Under the Siamese king Taksin, the Emerald Buddha is returned to Bangkok.

1828: Vientiane is destroyed by the Siamese army under King Rama III.

1893: France takes control of all Lao territory east of the Mae Khong River.

1904–59: King Sisavang Vong reigns in Luang Prabang. In 1953 Laos gains independence just before the French lose the battle of Dien Bien Phu in Vietnam.

1959–75: Under Crown Prince Sisavang Vatthana, a secret war rages in Indochina until the communist Pathet Lao seize power in December 1975, finally dissolving the monarchy.

and the Tribal Market, on Sisavang Vong Road. In the evening, most of Sisavang Vong Road turns into an open bazaar, similar to Thailand's night markets. It's a pleasant place to stroll, bargain with hawkers, and stop for a simple meal and a beer at one of many roadside stalls.

Locally worked silver is cheap and very attractive. You can find a good selection at **Thit Peng** (⊠ 48/2 Ban Wat That ☎ 071/212327).

Tad Saefall Waterfall

⑭ *15 km (9 mi) east of Luang Prabang.*

Accessible only by boat, this spectacular waterfall is best visited in the rainy season, when the rivers are high and their waters thunder over the cascade. The waterfall features multilevel limestone formations divided into three steps with big pools beneath them—don't forget your bathing suit. There are some old waterwheels here and a small, simple resort nearby.

The rainy-season route takes you from Luang Prabang (depart from the jetty on the river side of Wat Xieng Thong) up the Nam Khan River to its confluence with the Huay Sae River. On the way you pass the weaving village of Ban Phanom; the tomb of the French naturalist Henri Mouhot, who died in Luang Prabang in 1861; and the Xieng Lom Resort, with an elephant camp founded by a German benefactor, Markus Peschke. The other route to the waterfall follows Highway 13 south from Luang Prabang for 13 km (8 mi) to the turnoff to the pristine Lao Lum riverside village of Ban Aen. A boat can then be hired at Ban Aen for a short trip upstream to the waterfall. ▦ *8,000 kip.*

Pak Ou Caves

★ ⑮ *25 km (16 mi) up the Mae Khong from Luang Prabang.*

Set in high limestone cliffs above the Mae Khong River, at the point where it meets the Nam Ou River from northern Laos, are two sacred caves filled with thousands of Buddha statues dating from the 16th century. The lower cave, **Tham Thing,** is accessible from the river by a stairway and has enough daylight to allow you to find your way around. The stairway continues to the upper cave, **Tham Phum,** for which you need a flashlight. The admission charge of 10,000 kip includes a flashlight and a guide.

Slow boats make the three-hour journey to the caves from Luang Prabang, many of them stopping at waterside villages for a perusal of the rich variety of local handicrafts, a nip of lao lao, and perhaps a bowl of noodles. If you're in a hurry you can catch a speedboat from Luang Prabang to the caves—a noisy one-hour trip. An alternative route is by bus from the Northern Bus Terminal or taxi to the town of Pak Ou, where boats ferry visitors across the river to the caves. Pak Ou has several passable restaurants.

Tad Khuang Si Waterfall

★ ⑯ *29 km (18 mi) south of Luang Prabang.*

A series of cascades surrounded by lush foliage, Tad Khuang Si is a popular spot with Lao and foreigners alike. Many visitors merely view the falls from the lower pool, where picnic tables and food vendors invite you to linger, but a steep path through the forest leads to pools above the falls that are the perfect spot for a swim. Tour operators and taxi drivers in Luang Prabang offer day trips for $25 that combine Tad Kuang Si with a visit to a Khamu tribal village nearby. The drive, past rice farms and small Lao Lum tribal villages, is half the adventure. The best time to visit the falls is after the rainy season, between November and April. At this writing, a new resort, the Xiang Lom Resort, was in the works—among its offerings will be elephant-back trips to the waterfall. ▦ *15,000 kip.*

Ban Muang Ngoi

⑰ *150 km (93 mi) northeast of Luang Prabang.*

This picturesque river village sits on the eastern side of the Nam Ou River, which descends from Phong Saly Province in the north to meet the Mae Khong River opposite the famous Pak Ou Caves. The village, populated by Lao Lum, is surrounded by unusual limestone peaks. The journey here is an adventure in itself: a songthaew takes you from Luang Prabang's Northern Bus Terminal to a pier at Nong Khiaw, where boats continue on a one-hour trip upstream to the village.

Where to Stay

¢ ⊞ **Ning Ning Guesthouse.** Of the many guesthouses in Ban Muang Ngoi, this is among the best. It has five clean bungalows to rent for $5 a day. ⊠ *Ban Muang Ngoi* ☎ *No phone* ⇆ *5 bungalows* � *Fans; no a/c, no room phones, no room TVs* ▭ *No credit cards* ⦿ *BP.*

Luang Nam Tha

⑱ *319 km (198 mi) north of Luang Prabang.*

The capital of Laos's northernmost province, Luang Nam Tha is the headquarters of the groundbreaking Nam Ha Ecotourism. The program, a model for Southeast Asia, actively encourages the involvement of local communities in the development and management of tourism policies. You can join a two- or three-day trek, organized through the Boat Landing Guesthouse, through the Nam Ha Protected Area, which shelters numerous animals, including elephants, tigers, and bears. Khamu, Akha, and Lanten Yao tribes live in the dense forest.

Where to Stay

$-$$ ⊞ **Boat Landing Guesthouse.** Comfortable accommodations can be found in the timber-and-bamboo bungalows at this ecofriendly guesthouse run by an American. Rooms are furnished in rattan. The guesthouse organizes two- and three-day treks into the Nam Ha Protected Area. ⊠ *Ban Kone* ☎ *086/312398* 🖷 *086/12239* ⊕ *www.theboatlanding.laopdr. com* ⇆ *10 rooms* � *Restaurant, boating, fishing, biking, hiking* ▭ *No credit cards* ⦿ *BP.*

Muang Sing

⑲ *60 km (37 mi) north of Luang Nam Tha.*

In the late 19th century, this mountain-ringed town on the Sing Mountain River was the seat of a Tai Lue prince, Chao Fa Silino; Muang Sing lost its regional prominence, however, when French colonial forces occupied the town and established a garrison here. Muang Sing is known for its daily market, which draws throngs of traditionally robed tribespeople. Shoppers from among the 20 different tribes living in the area, and even traders from China visit the market to buy locally produced goods and handicrafts. The market is open 6 AM–9 AM.

River Journey to Huay Xai

⑳ *297 km (184 mi) up the Mae Khong from Luang Prabang.*

Growing rapidly in popularity is the 300-km (186-mi) Mae Khong River trip between Luang Prabang and Huay Xai, across the river from Chiang Khong in Thailand. It's a highly dramatic journey on what must qualify as one of the world's most spectacular stretches of river. Your boat ploughs through the rushing water and a constantly changing primeval scene of towering cliffs, huge mud flats and sandbanks, rocky islands, and riverbanks smothered in thick jungle, with the occasional patch of cultivated land, mulberry trees, bananas, and tiny garlic fields. There are no roads, just forest paths linking dusty settlements where the boats tie up for refreshment stops.

The only village of note is a halfway station, Pakbeng, which has a few guesthouses and a general store along its one main street. Once you arrive in Huay Xai (which has little of interest in itself), a good way to return to Thailand is to cross the river to Chiang Khong and then take a bus to Chiang Rai, 60 km (37 mi) inland.

There are two main ways to make the journey to Huay Xai from Luang Prabang: either by regular "slow" boat, which holds about 50 passengers, or by speedboat, which seats about four. The regular boat takes 12 hours or more over the course of two days. The night is spent at Pakbeng in very basic lodgings—guesthouses with cold water and limited electricity. The speedboats make the journey between Luang Prabang and Huay Xai in six hours. Speedboats, although thrilling for the first hour, become extremely uncomfortable after the novelty wears off. The seats are hard and uncomfortable, the engine noise is deafening (earplugs are advised), and the wind and spray can be chilling. Bring a warm, waterproof windbreaker, and be sure to get a life jacket and crash helmet with a visor from the boat driver. Another option is to journey to Pakbeng by speedboat, overnight at the village, and continue the following day by either speedboat or regular boat. For the regular boat, the fare is about $15; the speedboat is $35 per person. Only three slow boats make the trip per week.

Much more comfortable than the regular boat and speedboat, but far more expensive, is the *LuangSay* luxury boat, which is specially designed for leisurely river travel. The river cruise includes accommodation in Pakbeng at the very comfortable LuangSay Lodge. The *LuangSay* departs from Luang Prabang every Tuesday and Saturday (and Wednesday November–April), and returns from Huay Xai every Monday and Friday (and Thursday November–April). The cruise costs $200–$260. Contact **LuangSay Cruises** (✉ Sakkarine Rd., Luang Prabang ☎ 071/252553 🖷 071/252304).

Where to Stay

PAKBENG   🏨 **LuangSay Lodge.** This comfortable lodging sits on the riverbank amid
$ lush green hills. ✉ *Pakbeng* ☎ *020/670177, 021/215958 in Luang Prabang, 071/252553 in Vientiane* ⊕ *www.asian-oasis.com* 🛏 *19 rooms* ⚠ *No a/c.*

HUAY XAI   🏨 **Keo Udomphon Hotel.** This old town house is more comfortable than
¢   its outside appearance might lead you to believe. Rooms are furnished in an eclectic mix of styles, but are bright and clean. ✉ *Saikang Rd., Huay Xai* ☎ *084/211504* 🛏 *20 rooms* ⚠ *Restaurant* ▭ *No credit cards.*

Phong Saly

㉑ *425 km (264 mi) north of Luang Prabang.*

If you're looking for off-the-beaten-track "soft" adventure, head for the provincial capital Phong Saly, in the far north of Laos. It's a hill station and market town nearly 5,000 feet above sea level in the country's most spectacular mountain range, Phu Fa. Trekking through this land of forest-covered mountains and rushing rivers may be as close as you'll ever get to the thrill of exploring virgin territory; you can arrange for a guide (a must) through any of the hotels or guesthouses in town. There are about 25 different ethnic groups in the area, and the local **tribal museum** offers a fascinating look into their lives and culture. Among the exhibits is a kaleidoscopic display of tribal costumes. ☎ *No phone* 🎫 *1,000 kip* ☉ *Weekdays 7:30–11:30 and 1:30–4:30.*

The journey to Phong Saly is quite an adventure; a bus from Luang Prabang's Northern Bus Terminal takes you the 115 km (71 mi) to Udom Xay, where you have to hire a car to continue, via the towns of Bun Sin Xay and Bun Nua. From Bun Nua it's an additional 40 km (25 mi) to Phong Saly via a side road that branches off Highway 13. Note that it's possible to catch a flight from Udom Xay or Bun Nua to Vientiane—a good option if the journey back to Luang Prabang seems too daunting.

Where to Stay

PHONG SALY 🏨 **Phu Fa.** Formerly the Chinese consulate, this forbidding building in
¢ an industrial compound is now a government-run hotel. You're unlikely to want to linger in the rooms, but some have stunning views of the surrounding countryside. ⊠ *Phong Saly* ☎ *088/210031* 🛏 *24 rooms* ⚒ *Restaurant; no a/c* ▤ *No credit cards.*

UDOM XAY 🏨 **Linda Guesthouse.** This is a good choice if you're overnighting in Udom
¢ Xay on the way to Phong Saly. All rooms have hot showers, a luxury in this neck of the woods. ⊠ *Udom Xay* ☎ *081/312147* 🛏 *17 rooms (15 with fan, 2 with a/c)* ⚒ *No a/c in some rooms* ▤ *No credit cards.*

LUANG PRABANG & NORTHERN LAOS A TO Z

AIR TRAVEL

The only direct flights to Luang Prabang from neighboring Thailand originate in Chiang Mai, from which Lao Airlines operates a thrice-weekly service. Thai Airways International has three flights a week from Chiang Mai to Luang Prabang. Bangkok Airways flies four times a week from Bangkok to Luang Prabang via Sukhothai.

Lao Airlines has several flights a day between Vientiane and Luang Prabang, plus a daily flight from Vientiane to Huay Xai. Lao Airlines also offers four flights a week from Luang Prabang to Phonesavanh, near the Plain of Jars. Lao Airlines has three flights a week to Vientiane from

Bun Nua and Udom Xay, which are both on the route from Luang Prabang to Phong Saly.

🔲 Carriers **Bangkok Airways** ☎ 071/253253 in Luang Prabang, 02/229-3434 in Bangkok ⊕ www.bangkokair.com. **Lao Airlines** ☎ 071/212172 in Luang Prabang, 021/212057 in Vientiane, 02/236-9821 in Bangkok ⊕ www.lao-aviation.com. **Thai Airways International** ☎ 053/210210 in Chiang Mai ⊕ www.thaiairways.com.

AIRPORTS & TRANSFERS

Luang Prabang International Airport is 4 km (2½ mi) northeast of the city. The taxi ride to the city center costs $5.

🔲 Airports **Luang Prabang International Airport** ☎ 071/212173 or 071/212856.

BIKE TRAVEL

Biking is one of the best ways to visit all of the interesting sights within Luang Prabang. At many guesthouses and hotels you can rent a bicycle for about $1 for 12 hours.

BOAT & FERRY TRAVEL

There are several interesting destinations in northern Laos that are accessible from Luang Prabang by boat, including the Tad Saefall Waterfall, the Pak Ou Caves, and Huay Xai. In Luang Prabang you can find a boat for hire just about anywhere along the entire length of the road bordering the Mae Khong River; the main jetty is on the river side of Wat Xieng Thong.

The slow boats to Huay Xai depart from the river side of Wat Xieng Thong; the speedboats to Huay Xai depart from a pier on the northern outskirts of the city.

Adventurous travelers can board boats in Huay Xai for Xieng Kok in northern Luang Nam Tha Province, or negotiate with barge captains for a passage from Luang Prabang to Vientiane and even farther south. The port office in Huay Xai is the place to find obliging skippers, who demand $10–$20 for a place on deck as far as Luang Prabang, and $50 or more for the longer upstream trip to Chinese ports.

BUS TRAVEL

Luang Prabang's bus service is basically a fleet of songthaews; a short trip within town costs about $1. There are two bus terminals with service out of town: one serving northern Laos and the other Vientiane and the south. Buses from the Northern Bus Terminal can take you part of the way to Ban Muang Ngoi and Phong Saly. You can also catch a bus from this terminal to Luang Nam Tha, where you can change to a bus to Muang Sing.

CAR TRAVEL

Although you can drive from Vientiane to Luang Prabang, it takes seven to eight hours to make the 242-km (150-mi) trip along the meandering, but paved, road up into the mountains.

EMERGENCIES

For medical and police emergencies, use the services of your hotel or guesthouse, which will invariably be able to summon a doctor or of-

LAO: A FEW KEY PHRASES

THE OFFICIAL LANGUAGE IS LAO, *part of the extensive Tai family of languages of Southeast Asia spoken from Vietnam in the east to India in the west. Spoken Lao is very similar to the northern Thai language, as well as local dialects in the Shan States in Myanmar and Sipsongbanna in China. Lao is tonal, meaning a word can have several meanings according to the tone in which it's spoken.*

In tourist hotels, the staff generally speaks some English. You can find a smattering of English speakers in shops and restaurants. A few old-timers know some French.

Here are a few common and useful words:

Hello: *sabai di (pronounced sa-bye dee)*

Thank you: *khop chai deu (pronounced cop chi dew; use khop cheu neu in Northern Laos)*

Yes: *heu (pronounced like deux) or thia*

No: *bo*

Where?: *iu sai (pronounced you sai)?*

How much?: *to dai (pronounced taw dai)?*

Zero: *sun (pronounced soon)*

One: *neung*

Two: *song*

Three: *sam*

Four: *si*

Five: *ha*

Six: *hok*

Seven: *tiet (pronounced tee-yet)*

Eight: *pet*

Nine: *kao*

Ten: *sip*

Hundred: *neung loi*

Thousand: *neung phan*

To have fun: *muan*

To eat: *kin khao (pronounced kin cow)*

To drink: *kin nam*

Water: *nam*

Rice: *khao*

Expensive: *peng*

Bus: *lot me (pronounced lot may)*

House: *ban*

Road: *thanon*

Village: *ban*

Island: *don*

River: *mae nam (pronounced may nam)*

Doctor: *mao (pronounced mow)*

Hospital: *hong mo (pronounced hong maw)*

Post Office: *paisani*

Hotel: *hong hem*

Toilet: *hong nam*

ficial quickly. Otherwise, consult the International Clinic in Luang Prabang.

Hospital **International Clinic** ✉ Ban Thongchaloen, Luang Prabang ☎ 071/252048.

MONEY MATTERS

There are no ATMs in Luang Prabang or northern Laos, so make sure you have enough kip or dollars to cover your visit; you can, however, change money at Luang Prabang's Lan Xiang Bank, on Sisavang Vong Road. Major credit cards are accepted in most hotels and many restaurants, but few shops.

SAFETY

Trekking is increasingly popular in Laos, but beware: there's still unexploded ordnance left over from the Vietnam War in remote areas of northern Laos. Stay on well-traveled trails. Don't photograph anything that may have military significance (airports and military installations).

TOURS & PACKAGES

Diethelm Travel is the major tour operator in Luang Prabang and the most reliable. The company offers "stopovers" of 3–4 days, which cost $321–$781; these include tours of Luang Prabang, plus excursions to outlying villages, waterfalls, and the Pak Ou Caves. Tours to the Plain of Jars are available through Diethelm Travel, as well as Lao Youth Travel.

Diethelm Travel ✉ Sisavang Vong Rd., Luang Prabang ☎ 071/212277 ⊕ www.diethelm-travel.com. **Lao Youth Travel** ✉ 72 Sisavang Vong Rd., Ban Pakham ☎ 071/253340 ⊕ www.laoyouthtravel.com.

TRANSPORTATION AROUND NORTHERN LAOS

You can cover Luang Prabang on foot or by bicycle. The few taxis in town must be booked through your hotel or guesthouse. Tuk-tuks and songthaews make up Luang Prabang's public transport system. They cruise all the streets and are easy to flag down. Plan on paying around $1–$2 for a trip within the city.

Depending on the destination, you can take a car, taxi, bus, or, in some cases, boat, to travel outside of Luang Prabang.

VISITOR INFORMATION

Diethelm Travel has an office in Luang Prabang, as does the less helpful Luang Prabang Tourism Office.

Tourist Information **Diethelm Travel** ✉ Sisavang Vong Rd., Luang Prabang ☎ 071/212277 ⊕ www.diethelm-travel.com. **Luang Prabang Tourism Office** ✉ 72 Sisavang Vong Rd. ☎ 071/212198.

SOUTHERN LAOS

In some ways, Laos is really two countries: the south and north are as different as two sides of a coin. The mountainous north was for centuries virtually isolated from the more accessible south, where lowlands, the broad Mae Khong valley, and high plateaus were easier to traverse and settle. The south does have its mountains, however: no-

tably the Annamite range, called Phu Luang, home of the aboriginal Mon-Khmer ethnic groups who lived here long before Lao farmers and traders arrived from northern Laos and China. The Lao were followed by French colonists, who built the cities of Pakxan, Tha Khek, Savannakhet, and Pakse. Although the French influence is still tangible, the southern Lao cling tenaciously to their old traditions, making the south a fascinating destination.

Pakse is the regional capital and has an international airport with daily flights to Vientiane, as well as Phnom Penh and Siem Reap in neighboring Cambodia. There's also overnight bus service to Pakse from Vientiane, plus good local service in the area.

The Road South of Vientiane

Highway 13 out of Vientiane penetrates as far as the deep south of Laos and the Cambodian border, a distance of 835 km (518 mi). It's paved all the way. The first stop of interest, about 80 km (50 mi) southeast of Vientiane, is the pilgrimage temple complex **Wat Phrabat**, which has a revered footprint in stone said to be that of the Buddha.

㉒ Pakxan, 150 km (93 mi) south of Vientiane, in Bolikhamxay Province, is a former French colonial outpost, a Mae Khong River port, and now the center of the Lao Christian community. Traveling south of Pakxan, Highway 13 crosses the Nam Kading River, for which the protected forested NBCA (National Biodiversity Conservation Area Nam Kading) is named. About 90 km (56 mi) south of Pakxan, Highway 13 meets Highway 8, which leads via Lak Sao to Nam Pho on the Vietnamese border. From here the road leads to the Vietnamese coastal city of Vinh and other areas of north Vietnam.

㉓ Tha Khek, 350 km (217 mi) south of Vientiane, in Khammuan Province, is a bustling Mae Khong River port, with some of its ancient city wall still intact. It's surrounded by stunning countryside and karst (limestone caverns and sinkholes). There are some spectacular limestone caves in the area—notably **Tham Khong Lor.** This cave is more than 6½ km (4 mi) long and is so large that the Nam Hin Bun River runs through it. Opposite Tha Khek is Thailand's provincial capital of Nakhon Phanom. Ferries ply between the two cities, although a bridge has been planned.

Where to Stay

¢ ▦ **Phudoi Hotel.** This is a very basic but reliable lodging choice in Tha Khek. Note that only cold water is available. ✉ *13 Kouvolavong St., Ban Phonsanam, Tha Khek* ☎ *051/212048* 🖷 *051/212216* 🛏 *12 rooms* ⚐ *Fans; no a/c in some rooms* ▭ *No credit cards.*

Savannakhet

㉔ *470 km (290 mi) south of Vientiane.*

A former French colonial provincial center, the pleasant riverside town of Savannakhet is today the urban hub of a vast rice-growing plain. It's distinguished by some fine examples of French colonial architecture. The Thai town of Mukhadan (*see* chapter 5, Isan) lies just across the Mae Khong River and is accessible by ferry; at this writing, there were plans to create a bridge connecting the two towns. When complete, the bridge will be an important link in the projected East-West Economic Corridor connecting the Vietnamese port of Da Nang with Laos, Thailand, Myanmar (Burma), and eventually the Indian Ocean.

One of Savannakhet's curiosities is a **dinosaur museum,** which displays fossils discovered in the area. ✉ *Khantaburi Rd.* ☎ *No phone* 🎟 *1,000 kip* ⊙ *Weekdays 8–11:30 and 1–3:30.*

Pakse

㉕ *205 km (127 mi) south of Savannakhet, 675 km (420 mi) south of Vientiane.*

Pakse is a former French colonial stronghold, linked now by a bridge with neighboring Thailand. It plays a central role in an ambitious regional plan to create an "Emerald Triangle"—a trade and tourism community grouping Laos, Thailand, and Cambodia. The city is also the starting point for tours to the Khmer ruins at Wat Phu, and the Boloven Plateau, which straddles the southern provinces of Saravan, Sekon, Attapeu, and Champasak. The volcanic soil of the plateau makes the vast region ideal for agriculture: it's the source of much of the country's prized coffee, tea, and spices. Despite its beauty and central role in the Lao economy, the plateau has virtually no tourist infrastructure and is very much off-the-beaten-track territory.

Pakse's **Historical Heritage Museum** displays stonework from the famous Wat Phu in Champasak, handicrafts from the Boloven Plateau ethnic groups, and locally made musical instruments. ⊠ *Hwy. 13* ☎ *No phone* 🎫 *3,000 kip* ☉ *Daily 8–11:30 and 1–4.*

Where to Stay & Eat

$ ✕🍴 **Champa Residence Hotel.** Five handsome traditional-style houses make up this comfortable hotel complex near Pakse's evening market and the Historical Heritage Museum. Rooms have terraces overlooking the leafy grounds. ⊠ *Champasak Rd.* ☎ *031/212120* 📠 *031/212765* ✉ *champare@laotel.com* 🛏 *45 rooms* ᐊ *Restaurant, IDD phones, in-room safes, minibars, cable TV, massage, steam room, bar, shop, dry cleaning, laundry service* ☰ *MC, V.*

$ 🍴 **Pakse Hotel.** Fully renovated in 2004, this central hotel now offers international standards of comfort and service. Its rooftop terrace is a pleasant evening retreat, with a fine view of the town and surrounding countryside. ⊠ *Rd. 5, Ban Vat Luang* ☎ *031/212131* 📠 *031/212719* ✉ *info@paksehotel.com* 🛏 *65 rooms* ᐊ *Restaurant, coffee shop, IDD phones, minibars, cable TV, bar, shop, dry cleaning, laundry service, meeting rooms* ☰ *AE, MC, V.*

¢–$ 🍴 **Champasak Palace.** On the banks of the Seddon River on the town outskirts, this former residence of a local prince is impressive but scarcely palatial. It's a vast four-story complex with flanking wings and pagodalike eaves. Rooms are royally large and comfortably furnished, with an antique here and there. ⊠ *Ban Prabaht* ☎ *031/212263 or 031/212779* 📠 *031/212781* ✉ *thouyp@yahoo.com* 🛏 *90 rooms* ᐊ *Restaurant, IDD phones, minibars, cable TV, bar, shop, dry cleaning, laundry service, meeting rooms* ☰ *AE, MC, V.*

Champasak

❷❻ *40 km (25 mi) south of Pakse.*

In the early 18th century, the kingdom of Laos was partitioned into three realms: Luang Prabang, Vientiane, and Champasak. During the 18th and 19th centuries this small village on the west bank of the Mae Khong River was the royal center of a wide area of what is today Thailand and Cambodia. Every February, at the time of the full moon, the village holds a nationally renowned festival that includes elephant racing, cock-fighting, concerts, and lots of drinking and dancing.

★ **Wat Phu** sits impressively on heights above the Mae Khong River, about 6½ km (4 mi) south of Champasak, looking back on a centuries-old history that won it UNESCO recognition as a World Heritage Site. Wat Phu predates Cambodia's Angkor Wat—Wat Phu's hilltop site was chosen by Khmer Hindus in the 6th century AD, probably because of a nearby spring of fresh water. Construction of the wat continued into the 13th century, at which point it finally became a Buddhist temple. Much of the original Hindu sculpture remains unchanged, however, including representations on the temple's lintels of the Hindu gods Vishnu, Shiva, and Kala. The staircase is particularly beautiful, its protective *nagas* (mystical serpents) decorated with plumeria, the national flower of Laos. Many of the temple's treasures, including pre–Angkor era inscriptions, are preserved in an archaeology museum that is part of the complex. ☎ *No phone* ⌨ *30,000 kip* ⊙ *Daily 8–4:30.*

Si Phan Don

★ ⑳ *80 km (50 mi) south of Champasak, 120 km (74 mi) south of Pakse.*

If you've made it as far south as Champasak, then a visit to the Si Phan Don area—celebrated for its 4,000 Mae Khong River islands and freshwater dolphins—is a must. *Don* means island, and two of them in particular are worth visiting: Don Khong and the similarly named Don Khon, both of which are accessible by boat.

Don Khong is the largest island in the area, inhabited by a community of fisherfolk living in small villages amid ancient Buddhist temples.

You can hike to the spectacular Liphi waterfall on the island known as **Don Khon.** A second stunning waterfall, Khon Phapeng, is just east of Don Khon on the mainland. Also on Don Khon are the remains of a former French-built railway (you can also see them on another island, Don Det).

Downstream of Don Khon, at the border between Laos and Cambodia, **freshwater dolphins** frolic in a protected area of the Mae Khong. Boat trips to view the dolphins set off from Veun Kham and Don Khon.

Where to Stay & Eat

$ ✕▥ **Villa Muong Khong Hotel.** At this little residence on the island of Don Khon, you live alongside local Lao fisherfolk. Not surprisingly, Mae Khong fish figures prominently at the hotel's open-air restaurant (¢–$). ⊠ *Don Khong Island* ☎ *031/213011* ⊟ *031/252051* ⌨ *xbtrvlmk@laotel.com* 🛏 *32 bungalows* ⌾ *Restaurant, bar; no room phones* ⊟ *No credit cards.*

SOUTHERN LAOS A TO Z

AIR TRAVEL

There's one Lao Airlines flight a day from Vientiane to Pakse, sometimes routed via Savannakhet.

There's also one Lao Airlines flight between Pakse and Cambodia from Siem Reap. Flights depart every Wednesday, Friday, and Sunday morning. The price of a one-way ticket is $68.
🛈 Carriers **Lao Airlines** ☎ 031/212252 in Pakse.

AIRPORTS & TRANSFERS

A taxi from Pakse International Airport to the Pakse city center costs $5.
🛈 **Pakse International Airport** ☎ 032/212844.

BOAT & FERRY TRAVEL

Ferries crisscross the Mae Khong River along its entire length. The main ferry crossings into neighboring Thailand are at Tha Khek and Savannakhet; the one-way fare is about $1.

A luxurious double-deck houseboat, the *Wat Phu,* operated by Indocruise Ltd., plies the southern length of the Mae Khong between Pakse and Si Phan Don. The cruises, which last three days and two nights, depart from Pakse every Wednesday and Saturday.

🚢 **Indocruise Ltd.** ✉ 23 Ban Anou, Haengboun Rd., Chanthaboury, Vientiane ☎ 021/215958 🖨 021/215958 ⊕ www.asian-oasis.com.

BORDER CROSSINGS

There are border crossings between Laos and Thailand at Tha Khek in Khammuan Province; Savannakhet in Savannakhet Province; and Vang Tao (a land crossing) in Champasak Province. Border crossings are open 8:30–5.

BUS TRAVEL

Efficient local bus service connects all the towns of the south. From Pakse, buses depart from the central bus station (Km 8 on the road east of Pakse) for local destinations such as Savannakhet and Champasak.

Buses from Pakse to Vientiane and the north depart from a terminal at Km 7 on Highway 13 (running north of Pakse).

CAR TRAVEL

Highway 13, the main north–south route, penetrates the deep south as far as the Cambodian border. It's fully paved, but once you get off the highway and onto minor roads, driving conditions get difficult. This is particularly true of the Boloven Plateau region.

EMERGENCIES

Pakse's Provincial Hospital can handle emergencies.

🏥 Hospital **Provincial Hospital** ✉ Ban Pakse, Pakse ☎ 031/212018.

HEALTH

Take the same precautions in the south that you would in other parts of Laos. Pakse and most of the towns in the region are malaria free, but it's still advisable to travel with mosquito repellent. If you plan on traveling to the Boloven Plateau, seek advice from your doctor on necessary inoculations, possibly for malaria, typhoid, hepatitis, tetanus, and Japanese encephalitis. All the towns of the south are well served by drugstores selling the latest medicines from China and the West.

MONEY MATTERS

There are no ATMs in the south, but all banks change money and traveler's checks. Nevertheless, make sure you travel with enough cash (in dollars or kip) to cover your likely expenses. Credit cards are accepted at major hotels and some restaurants, but few shops.

SAFETY

Southern Laos is as safe as the rest of the country, provided certain rules are followed: leave valuables in your hotel safe, keep cash well hidden on your body, always carry a copy of the relevant pages of your passport, and avoid confrontations with locals.

TOURS & PACKAGES

Diethelm Travel runs tours of southern Laos (originating in Pakse) that last between a half day and two days. The half-day tour to the Boloven Plateau, ethnic villages, and a tea-and-coffee plantation costs $44. An overnight excursion by boat to Champasak, Wat Phu, and Don Khong costs $331. Diethelm Travel has an office in Pakse, but it's best to book the tours through the Vientiane office.

🚩 **Diethelm Travel** ✉ Ban Tha Luang, Pakse ☎ 031/251941 ✉ Setthathirat Rd. at Nam Phu Fountain Sq., Vientiane ☎ 021/213833, 021/215920, or 021/215128 🖷 021/216294 or 021/217151 ⊕ www.diethelm-travel.com.

TRANSPORTATION AROUND SOUTHERN LAOS

The easiest way to travel around the area is to hire a car and driver or use the bus system. Taxis must be booked by your hotel, but tuk-tuks and songthaews cruise the streets of every town and are easy to flag down. They rarely demand more than a dollar or two for a short trip in town.

LAOS A TO Z

To research prices, get advice from other travelers, and book travel arrangements, visit www.fodors.com.

AIR TRAVEL

Thai Airways International flies daily from Bangkok to Vientiane and from Chiang Mai to Luang Prabang three times a week. Bangkok Airways flies from Bangkok via Sukhothai to Luang Prabang four times a week. The national carrier, Lao Airlines, has daily flights between Vientiane and Bangkok, as well as three flights a week from Chiang Mai to Luang Prabang and Vientiane. They also have flights from Phnom Penh and Siem Reap to Pakse, where connections can be made to Vientiane. Lao Airlines also offers regular service between some provincial capitals; there are at least three flights a day between Vientiane and Luang Prabang for $60 one-way.

China Yunnan Airlines flies once a week from Kunming to Vientiane. Vietnam Airlines has several flights a week from Hanoi and Ho Chi Minh City to Vientiane.

The international departure tax in Luang Prabang, Vientiane, and Pakse is $10. The domestic airport tax is 5,000 kip.

🚩 Carriers **Bangkok Airways** ☎ 071/253253 in Luang Prabang, 02/229-3434 in Bangkok ⊕ www.bangkokair.com. **China Yunnan Airlines** ☎ 021/252888. **Lao Airlines** ☎ 021/212057 in Vientiane, 02/236-9822 or 02/236-9823 in Bangkok, 053/404033 in Chiang Mai ⊕ www.laoairlines.com. **Thai Airways International** ☎ 021/225271 in Vientiane, 02/280-0060 in Bangkok, 053/210210 in Chiang Mai ⊕ www.thaiairways.com. **Vietnam Airlines** ☎ 021/217562 ⊕ www.vietnamairlines.com.vn.

BIKE TRAVEL

Bikes are a popular option for sightseeing within cities. You can rent bicycles and mountain bikes from many hotels and guesthouses for $1–$5 a day.

BOAT & FERRY TRAVEL

The Mae Khong River is one of the major means of transport in Laos, taking the place of roads in many places. Tourist craft ply the busiest section, between Huay Xai and Luang Prabang. More adventurous travelers can board boats in Huay Xai for Xieng Kok in northern Luang Nam Tha Province, or negotiate with barge captains for a passage from Luang Prabang to Vientiane and even farther south.

Two luxury vessels ply the Mae Khong: the *Wat Phu*, moored at Pakse and run by the Vientiane-based Indocruise Ltd., and the *LuangSay*, which makes a twice-weekly run between Luang Prabang and Huay Xai. **Indocruise Ltd.** ✉ 23 Ban Anou, Haengboun Rd., Chanthaboury, Vientiane ☎ 021/215958 🖷 021/215958 ⊕ www.asian-oasis.com. **LuangSay Cruises** ✉ Sakkarine Rd., Luang Prabang ☎ 071/252553 🖷 071/252304.

BORDER CROSSINGS

In addition to the three international airports in Vientiane, Luang Prabang, and Pakse, there are numerous land and river crossings into Laos. The busiest is the Friendship Bridge, which spans the Mae Khong River 29 km (12 mi) east of Vientiane; it connects to the Thai railhead of Nong Khai.

Other border crossings from Thailand to Laos are: Chiang Khong to Huay Xai, in Bokeo Province (by ferry across the Mae Khong River); Nakhon Phanom to Tha Khek, in Khammuan Province; Mukdahan to Savannakhet, in Savannakhet Province; Chongmek to Vang Tao, in Champasak Province.

You can cross into Laos from Cambodia at Veun Kham, in Champasak Province; and from Boten, in Luang Nam Tha Province, into Mohan, in China's Yunnan Province.

There are two major crossings between Laos and Vietnam. The first is on Highway 9 at Dansavan and the Vietnamese town of Lao Bao, which leads to Hue and Danang. The second crossing is on Highway 8 at Lak Sao and the Vietnamese town of Nam Phao, leading to Vinh.

All of the border crossings are open daily 8:30 AM–5 PM, aside from Friendship Bridge, which is open 6 AM–10 PM.

If you enter the country at any of the Vietnamese border crossings, you need to show visas for all the countries you will be visiting aside from Laos.

BUS TRAVEL

A network of bus services covers almost the entire country. The favorite mode of transportation for most visitors, bus travel is cheap, but slow and not very comfortable. "VIP" buses connect Vientiane, Luang Prabang, and Pakse, and are somewhat more comfortable than regular buses.

BUSINESS HOURS
Business hours are generally weekdays 7–11:30 and 2–5:30. Post offices keep the same schedule. Banks are open weekdays 8:30–3:30.

CAR & MOTORBIKE TRAVEL
Although it's possible to enter Laos by car or motorbike and drive around on your own, it's not recommended, as driving conditions are difficult: 80% of the country's 14,000 km (8,700 mi) of roads are unpaved, and road signs are often indecipherable. Security checkpoints are frequent on highways, a daunting prospect for foreign drivers.

A good alternative is to hire a car and driver within Laos. Not only can hired drivers save you the trouble of trying to decipher Lao road signs and navigate security checkpoints, but they are also generally quite familiar with the area and any sights you may want to see.

CAR RENTAL
Car-rental companies are a recent phenomenon in Laos. One of the most reliable is Asia Vehicle Rental in Vientiane. You can rent a car here with or without a driver for $25–$50 a day.
🚗 Agency **Asia Vehicle Rental** ⊠ Sam Sen Tai Rd. ☎ 021/217493 or 021/223867
🖷 021/217493 ⊕ www.laopdr.com.

CUSTOMS & DUTIES
Tourists are allowed to bring into Laos one quart of spirits and 200 cigarettes, 50 cigars, or ½ lb of tobacco. Bringing in or taking out local currency is prohibited, as is the export of antiques and religious artifacts without a permit.

Note that the dissemination of foreign religious and political materials is forbidden, and you should refrain from bringing such materials into the country.

ELECTRICITY
The electrical current is 220 volts AC, 50Hz. Outside of Vientiane and Luang Prabang, electricity is uncertain, and even in Luang Prabang there are frequent late-afternoon outages in hot weather.

EMBASSIES
British, Canadian, and New Zealand residents should contact their respective embassies in Bangkok for assistance in Laos.
🚩 Australia **Embassy** ⊠ Nehru Rd., Ban Phon Xhay, Vientiane ☎ 021/413600.
🚩 United States **Embassy** ⊠ BP 114, rue Bartholomé, Vientiane ☎ 021/212581 or 021/212582.

EMERGENCIES
In the event of an emergency or health problem, first consult your hotel or guesthouse, which can direct you to the proper authorities or English-speaking doctors and hospitals with suitable facilities. Vientiane has the country's best clinic, the Mahosot Hospital International Clinic. Luang Prabang has the International Clinic, and Pakse has the Provincial Hospital. For serious medical emergencies, get to Thailand as quickly as possible.

🏥 Hospitals International Clinic ✉ Ban Thongchaloen, Luang Prabang ☎ 071/212123. **Mahosot Hospital International Clinic** ✉ Fa Ngoum Quay, Vientiane ☎ 021/214022. **Provincial Hospital** ✉ Ban Pakse, Pakse ☎ 031/212018.

ETIQUETTE & BEHAVIOR
Laotians are generally gentle and polite, and visitors should take their lead from them—avoiding any public display of anger or impolite behavior. Even showing affection in public is frowned upon.

Laotians traditionally greet others by pressing their palms together in a sort of prayer gesture known as a *nop;* it is also acceptable for men to shake hands. If you attempt a nop, remember that it's basically reserved for social greetings; don't greet a hotel or restaurant employee this way. The general greeting is *sabai di* ("good health"), invariably said with a smile.

Avoid touching or embracing a Laotian, and keep in mind that the head has spiritual significance; even patting a child affectionately on the head could be misinterpreted. Feet are considered "unclean, " so when you sit, make sure your feet are not pointing directly at anyone, and never use your foot to point in any situation. Shoes must be removed before you enter a temple or private home, as well as some restaurants and offices.

Shorts and sleeveless tops should not be worn in temple compounds. When visiting a temple, be careful not to touch anything of spiritual significance, such as altars, Buddha images, or spirit houses. Ask permission from any individual before taking a photograph of him or her.

HEALTH
As in all of Southeast Asia, it's advisable to drink bottled water and avoid uncooked food (except for peeled fruit such as bananas). For minor stomach upsets, try bananas and boiled rice. Pharmacies are well stocked and often staffed with assistants who speak some English. Carry mosquito repellent at all times, and sleep under mosquito nets in rural areas. Before venturing into very remote, mountainous regions, it's advisable to be inoculated against malaria, typhoid, hepatitis, tetanus, and Japanese encephalitis. Note that AIDS is widespread in border areas.

HOLIDAYS
New Year's Day (Jan. 1); Army Day (Jan. 24); International Women Day (Mar. 8); Lao New Year (Water Festival, Apr. 13–15); Labor Day (May 1); National Day (Dec. 2).

MONEY MATTERS
COSTS Compared to the West, costs in Laos are very low. You can spend from $20 to $150 for a double room with a private bath; rooms that cost less than $20 tend to share bathrooms and have no air-conditioning. An evening meal in an international restaurant will cost $8–$15, whereas in a local restaurant, the bill will seldom exceed $5. A local beer or a glass of house wine runs $1–$2. The average city taxi trip costs $2–$3.

CREDIT CARDS Credit cards are accepted at the more expensive hotels and restaurants in Vientiane, Luang Prabang, and Pakse. Few shops accept credit cards.

CURRENCY The currency is the kip, which continually drops against the dollar. Hence, dollars are preferred and are always used to pay hotel and airline bills. The Thai baht is accepted in Vientiane, Luang Prabang, and other border towns along the Mae Khong River. Kip cannot be changed back into a hard currency. At this writing, the official exchange rate was 276 kip to the Thai baht, 10,800 kip to one U.S. dollar, 9,000 kip to one Canadian dollar, 8,400 kip to one Australian dollar, and 21,000 kip to one British pound.

Bank notes of 500; 1,000; 2,000; 5,000; 10,000; and 20,000 kip are available.

CURRENCY EXCHANGE & ATMS There are many money changers at the Morning Market in Vientiane and at the Dala Central Market in Luang Prabang, but be aware that banks normally give better exchange rates than money changers. At this writing, there was only one ATM in the country—at Vientiane's Banque Pour le Commerce Exterieur Lao (BPCE), one block south of Nam Phu Square on Pang Kham Road.

Diethelm Travel is the American Express representative in Laos.
⚑ **Diethelm Travel** ✉ Setthathirat Rd. at Nam Phu Fountain Sq. ☎ 021/213833, 021/215920, or 021/215128 📠 021/216294 or 021/217151 ✉ Sisavang Vong Rd., Luang Prabang ☎ 071/212277 ⊕ www.diethelm-travel.com.

PASSPORTS & VISAS

All visitors to Laos (aside from those coming in from some ASEAN countries) need a passport and visa. Some travelers obtain their visas at the embassy in Bangkok, but if you fly to Vientiane or Luang Prabang, you can get a visa on arrival at the airport. Visas cost $30, and must be paid in cash (in U.S. dollars). You need to have a passport photo with you. You can also get a visa at the Friendship Bridge in Nong Khai, in Chiang Khong (near Chiang Rai), and in Khon Kaen in northeastern Thailand, though it can take a few hours to a day. The process takes one to two days in Bangkok, where you can pay a travel agency to do the footwork.

Tourist visas are good for 30 days and can be extended for another 15. Sometimes immigration officials want to see evidence of sufficient funds and an air ticket out of the country. Because the regulations tend to change without warning, it's advisable to check with the Lao embassy in your own country before setting out.
⚑ **Lao Embassies Australia** ✉ 1 Dalman Crescent, O'Malley, ACT 2606 ☎ 026/286-4595. **Thailand** ✉ 1-3 Soi Ramkhamhaeng 39, Bangkok ☎ 02/539-6668. **United States** ✉ Consular Section, 2222 S St. NW, Washington, DC 20008 ☎ 202/667-0076.

SAFETY

Laos is fairly free of crime in tourist areas, though traveling by road puts you at a small risk of encountering highway thieves. Petty crime like pickpocketing is rare, but you should still be careful when visiting crowded fairs and markets. Never leave luggage unattended. Note that the penalties for possession of even small amounts of drugs are very severe.

In the countryside, trekkers should watch out for unexploded ordnance left over from the Vietnam War, especially in Xieng Khuang and Hua Phan provinces and in southern Laos (particularly near the former Ho Chi Minh Trail in Salavan, Attapeu, and Sekong provinces). Don't wander off well-traveled trails. Better yet, trek with a group led by a qualified guide. Be careful not to photograph anything that may have military significance, like airports or military installations.

TELEPHONES & THE INTERNET

To call Laos from overseas, dial the country code, 856, and then the area code, omitting the first 0. The outgoing international code is 00, but IDD phones are rare. If you have to make an international call from Laos, use your hotel's switchboard. This is a good idea even for local calls, as there are few pay phones.

Internet cafés are becoming popular, especially in Vientiane, Luang Prabang, and Pakse. The charge is normally about 200 kip per minute.

TIPPING

At tourist hotels, gratuities are included in the cost of meals and accommodation, but considering that most staff members earn about $1 per day, it's nice to give them something extra. Give bellhops 10,000 kip. Guides expect $10 after a day of sightseeing.

TOURS & PACKAGES

You can make tour arrangements (flights, hotels, guides, and visas) through travel agencies in Bangkok and Chiang Mai. Recommended tour companies with offices in Bangkok are Abercrombie & Kent, Diethelm Travel, and Journeys International. In Chiang Mai, Nam Khong Travel is the leading specialist in package tours to Laos.

🔲 Tour Companies **Abercrombie & Kent** ✉ 1520 Kensington Rd., Suite 212, Oak Brook, IL 60521, United States ☎ 630/954-2944 or 800/323-7308 🖨 630/954-3324 ⊕ www.aandktours.com. **Diethelm Travel** ✉ Kian Gwan II Bldg., 140/1 Wireless Rd., Bangkok, Thailand ☎ 02/255-9150 ⊕ www.diethelm-travel.com. **Journeys International** ✉ 107 April Dr., Ann Arbor, MI 48103, United States ☎ 734/665-4407 or 800/255-8735 ⊕ www.journeys-intl.com. **Nam Khong Travel** ✉ 6 Chaiyaphoom Rd., Chiang Mai, Thailand ☎ 053/874321.

VISITOR INFORMATION

Diethelm Travel, which has offices in Vientiane, Luang Prabang, and Pakse, is your best source of travel information in Laos. Lao Youth Travel in Vientiane is also helpful. The National Tourism Authority of the Lao People's Democratic Republic has offices in Vientiane and all other provinces; they provide some printed materials, but little else. The private Web site ⊕ www.laos-hotels.com can provide information on the major hotels in the country.

🔲 Tourist Information **Diethelm Travel** ✉ Setthathirat Rd. at Nam Phu Fountain Sq. ☎ 021/213833, 021/215920, or 021/215128 🖨 021/216294 or 021/217151 ✉ Sisavang Vong Rd., Luang Prabang ☎ 071/212277 ⊕ www.diethelm-travel.com. **Lao Youth Travel** ✉ 24 Fa Ngum Quay, Ban Mixay, Vientiane ☎ 021/240939 🖨 021/213037

✎ youthtra.laotel.com ✉ 72 Sisavang Vong Rd., Ban Pakham, Luang Prabang
☎ 071/253340 ✉ Ban Sok Amnuay, Unit 6, Pakse ☎ 031/212150 ⊕ www.laoyouthtravel.
com. **National Tourism Authority of the Lao People's Democratic Republic** ✉ BP
3556, Ave. Lang Xang, Vientiane ☎ 021/212248 or 021/250681 ⎙ 021/212769 ⊕ www.
Mae Khongcenter.com.

8

UNDERSTANDING
THAILAND

THAILAND AT A GLANCE

Fast Facts

Name in local language: Prathet Thai (Land of the Free)
Capital: Bangkok
National anthem: Phleng Chat
Type of government: Constitutional monarchy
Administrative divisions: 76 provinces
Independence: 1238 (traditional founding date; never colonized)
Constitution: October 11, 1997 (latest revision)
Legal system: Based on civil law system, with influences of common law
Suffrage: 18 years of age; universal and compulsory
Legislature: Bicameral National Assembly consists of the Senate (200 seats; members elected by popular vote to serve six-year terms) and the House of Representatives (500 seats; members elected by popular vote to serve four-year terms)
Population: 64.9 million
Population density: 127 people per square km (328 people per square mi)
Median age: Female: 31.2 years, male: 29.7 years
Life expectancy: Female: 73.7 years, male: 69.2 years
Infant mortality rate: 21 deaths per 1,000 live births
Literacy: 96%
Language: Thai (official), English (secondary language of the elite), ethnic and regional dialects
Ethnic groups: Thai 75%; Chinese 14%; other 11%
Religion: Buddhism 95%, Muslim 4%, Christianity 1%

Geography & Environment

Land area: 511,770 square km (197,596 square mi); slightly more than twice the size of Wyoming
Coastline: 3,219 km (10,561 mi)
Terrain: Central plain; Khorat Plateau in the east; mountains elsewhere; highest point: Doi Inthanon 2,576 meters (8,451 feet)
Natural resources: Arable land, fish, fluorite, gypsum, lead, lignite, natural gas, rubber, tantalum, timber, tin, tungsten
Natural hazards: Land subsidence in Bangkok area resulting from the depletion of the water table; droughts
Environmental issues: Air pollution from vehicle emissions; water pollution from organic and factory wastes; deforestation; soil erosion; wildlife populations threatened by illegal hunting

Economy

Currency: Baht
Exchange rate: 39.2 baht to the dollar
GDP: $475.7 billion (2003 est.)
Inflation: 2.4%
Unemployment: 2.2%
Work force: 33.4 million; agriculture 49%; services 37%; industry 14%
Debt: $62.5 billion
Economic aid: $131.5 million
Major industries: Agricultural processing, beverages, cement, computers and parts, electric appliances and components, furniture, integrated circuits, light manufacturing, plastics, textiles and garments, tin, tobacco, tourism, tungsten
Agricultural products: Cassava (tapioca), coconuts, corn, rice, rubber, soybeans, sugarcane
Exports: $76 billion

Major export products: Computers, office machine parts, plastic, rubber, seafood, transistors, vehicles (cars and trucks)
Export partners: U.S. 19.6%; Japan 14.5%; Singapore 8.1%; Hong Kong 5.4%; China 5.2%; Malaysia 4.1%
Imports: $65.3 billion

Major import products: Capital goods, consumer goods, fuels, intermediate goods and raw materials
Import partners: Japan 23%; U.S. 9.6%; China 7.6%; Malaysia 5.6%; Singapore 4.5%; Taiwan 4.4%

Political Climate

Despite enduring a harrowing 17 military coups in the 20th century (the last was in 1991), Thailand's political climate has had stability, thanks to the nation's enduring constitutional monarchy. Thailand's electoral process has improved, with allegations of fraud sharply declining in recent years. Thailand boasted the world's highest growth rate for a decade ending 1995 and the economy has played a large role in campaigns, as the bad taste of the 1997–98 Asian economic crisis lingers for many voters. Campaigning on economic growth and development, telecommunications multimillionaire Thaksin Shinawatra and his Thai Rak Thai (TRT) party dominated elections at the beginning of the new millennium.

Did You Know?

• At one time or another, European powers have taken over every country in Southeast Asia, except Thailand.

• The King of Thailand is the world's longest-reigning monarch. Bhumibol Adulyadej took the throne on June 9, 1946, following his older brother's death.

• Hoping to encourage Thais to exercise more, the Ministry of Public Health organized 46,824 people into the world's largest one-day aerobics class. Despite heavy rains, the horde of waving arms and legs kept up the effort for 61 minutes.

• Thailand is home to world's worst monsoon. From September to December 1983, 10,000 people were killed in storms and as many as 100,000 people got sick from diseases in floodwaters. Damage estimates exceeded $400 million.

• The Thai military is trained in the nation's ancient native martial art, a military version of Thai kickboxing.

A BUDDHIST NATION

RELIGION PLAYS A PROFOUND AND HIGH-PROFILE ROLE in day-to-day Thai life. Almost 95% of the population is Buddhist (4% of the population is Muslim, the remaining 1% is shared by Taoism, Confucianism, Hinduism, and Christianity); the country has 400,000 monks and novices, and there are more than 30,000 wats (temples) in villages and forests throughout the land. Buddhism is present on the national flag, denoted by the white bar as one of the foundations of nationhood, alongside the monarchy (blue) and the people (red). Thai monarchs are required to be Buddhist: King Rama IV spent 27 years as a forest monk before ascending the throne in 1851; the current ruler, King Bhumibol, was ordained in 1956. In Bangkok, intricate golden temple rooftops gleam like fairy glitter amid the gray concrete. Images of the Buddha adorn cafés, gas stations, shops, and bars, and many local artists paint according to religious themes. Each morning people rise early to give alms to monks, who are required to beg for food and other essentials.

Thai people are well known for their calm, undemonstrative demeanor and loathing of confrontation, traits that can be attributed to their Buddhist philosophy. Common axioms such as *jai yen* (cool heart) and *mai pen rai* (never mind) are lessons in detachment and the realization that nothing lasts.

Origins

There are two main branches of Buddhism in Asia: Theravada, found today in Thailand, Myanmar, and Sri Lanka; and Mahayana, which spread northward from India to China, Korea, Vietnam, and Japan. The Mahayana movement emerged from Theravada, the original teachings of the Buddha, in the first century. Its main departure was the introduction of *bodhisattvas*, embodiments of enlightened ones who had chosen to stay on earth to help ease suffering. It's a less austere doctrine and therefore more accessible than Theravada, which stresses devotion to study and meditation. Theravada arrived in Thailand via Sri Lanka, and has been the country's official religion since the founding of the nation at Sukhothai in the 13th century. It was written into the Constitution as the state religion of modern Thailand in 1997.

The origins of both forms of Buddhism lie in the life of the Indian prince Siddhartha Gautama (563 BC–483 BC), who gave up his royal privileges to follow an ascetic life. In time, he eschewed both excess materialism and excessive austerity and discovered what he called the Middle Way or Eightfold Path to enlightenment. Gautama taught that there are three aspects to existence: *dukkha* (stress, misery), *anicca* (impermanence), and *anatta* (the absence of self). He maintained that it's the unfulfilled desire for status, self-worth, and material possessions that creates dukkha and that it's pointless to desire such things because anicca dictates that everything is impermanent and cannot be possessed. Therefore, if we can learn to curb desire and cultivate detachment, we will cease to be unhappy.

Gautama devised the Middle Way to achieve this state, based on the triple pillars of wisdom, morality, and concentration. Each pillar covers portions of the Eightfold Path. Within wisdom are the concepts of Right Understanding, where you are able to determine and understand dukkha and its causes, and Right Thought, where you commit to developing a resistance to anger, ill-will, cruel or aggressive thoughts and acts—and to all things that cause dukkha. Within morality are Right Speech (refraining from telling lies, using abusive language, or engaging in idle chatter), Right Action (refraining from harming or killing others, stealing, and engaging in sexual misconduct), and Right Livelihood (earning a living in an honest, peaceful, and righteous way). Within concentration are the facets of Right Effort (using your energy to fuel positive things like discipline, honesty, and kindness, and to work toward abandoning old counterproductive ways), Right Mindfulness (acquiring an acute awareness of one's words, thoughts, and actions), and Right Concentration (total focus on positive things or "pure thoughts, " usually accomplished by extensive meditation).

The ultimate goal of Buddhism is to reach enlightenment or Nirvana, which is basically the cessation of struggle—this happens when you have successfully let go of all desire (and by definition, all suffering). This also signals the end to the cycle of reincarnation, a concept all Buddhists believe in. Guatama's followers believe that he led 500 lives before he ascended to Nirvana, an event that is represented in Thailand by reclining Buddha statues, and is celebrated each May on Visakha Puja Day. However, Guatama is not to be confused with a god. Although he is certainly the most celebrated Buddha, his followers do believe that there were three Buddhas before him. A fifth—Lord Metteya—is predicted to appear in the year AD 4457.

Despite the overwhelming presence of Buddhism, the Thai religious psyche is complicated by the absorption of Hindu deities, superstition, and ancient animist beliefs. The precepts of Buddhism developed within Hinduism, and Thailand retains many Hindu religious elements—the famous Erawan Shrine in Bangkok is a site of homage to Brahma. The Thai epic tale the *Ramakien,* a translation of the Indian *Ramayana,* is a constant source of artistic and spiritual inspiration and is depicted in the classical masked dance theater, *khon.* Brahmin priests still conduct royal rituals, and the early kings of the current Chakri dynasty were believed to be incarnations of Rama, who was himself an incarnation of the Hindu god Vishnu.

Practice & Rituals

Thai children learn Buddhist teachings (Dhamma) in school, and most males will at some time ordain as a *bhikku* (monk). Some only do this for a few days, possibly at the time of a family death, but many join the monkhood for three months at the beginning of the yearly Rains Retreat (a religious retreat, sometimes referred to as Buddhist Lent, when monks are required to remain in their wats for the duration of the rainy season) in July, which is marked by major festivals, such as the Candle Parade, in Nakhon Ratchasima. Joining the monkhood, even for a short time, is such an important event that employers grant time off work for the purpose. Women wanting to devote their lives to Buddhism may become white-robed nuns, known as *mae chi.* However, women are not allowed to be officially ordained, they observe fewer precepts than monks, and rarely oversee public ceremonies. A growing feminist lobby increasingly questions their lower status.

Although Thais don't really visit temples on a regular basis in the way that practicing Christians or Muslims do, wats are the center of community life, particularly up-country, and serve many functions, such as schools, meeting halls, and hospitals (monks are traditional healers, originators of the herbal remedies that now form the basis for New Age spa treatments). The country's most important temples are associated with royalty, revered monks, or religious icons thought to be close to the Buddha. Temples often have the most ornate gilt work and statuary, so they tend to become tourist attractions, which is why you often see more foreigners than Thais at temples.

Alongside spiritual guidance and funeral rites, monks also provide ceremonies in houses and businesses to bring good fortune, and will even bless vehicles to keep drivers safe from accidents. Some Thais say that monks should have no place in politics, yet they are often the community spokesmen on political issues, and politicians are as likely to court respected monks for endorsement as they are to reprimanded them for political interference.

All Buddhists believe in reincarnation (a concept inherited from Hinduism) and the goal of Nirvana, which is the end of the cycle of rebirth. Advancement along the cycle is, in part, achieved through good deeds called *tham boon* (merit making). These deeds result in good karma, something striven for daily to either atone for bad deeds or to build credit for a better future life. Tham boon can be accomplished by small gestures such as placing a candle at a place of worship or wai-ing (bowing) toward a significant shrine or statue. At fairs and markets anyone can make merit by releasing caged birds offered by vendors specifically for the purpose. Larger deeds might involve a lifetime's devotion to monastic life—or a large cash donation to a worthy cause. Families can attain merit by sending their sons to study as a novice monk.

Modern Concerns

Many Thai commentators believe that a rapidly modernizing Thailand is eroding traditional Buddhist values. Greater personal wealth has brought billowing consumerism to the middle classes, while younger generations are progressively more Westernized through education abroad, satellite TV, and the Internet. The concern that, as material rewards begin to overshadow the temporal, Thais may be less inclined toward religion; this is borne out to some extent by a slight decrease in the number of wats, although other factors, such as greater migration to cities, also play a part.

Worries over the health of Buddhism have intensified in the wake of recent scandals involving monks—some have been caught gambling and in relationships with women. One celebrated Bangkok abbot was imprisoned for murder (he later escaped to San Diego), while another was charged with embezzlement. A growth in personality inspired cults has coincided with accusations of materialism and abandonment of the doctrine taught by the Buddha.

However, despite undeniable changes in Thailand's economic and cultural condition, the country is adapting, rather than abandoning, its heritage. Buddhism remains hugely manifest in all aspects and sectors of society and the religion continues as the dominant influence on the unique national psyche.

— Howard Richardson

INTRODUCTION TO THAI ARCHITECTURE

THOUGH REAL ARCHITECTURE BUFFS are few and far between, you'd be hard pressed to find a visitor to Thailand that doesn't spend at least a little time staring in slack-jawed amazement at the country's glittering wats and ornate palaces—and the elegant sculptures of the mythical beasts that protect them. As befitting this spiritual nation, most of the fanfare is saved for religious structures, but you can find plenty to admire in the much simpler lines of the traditional houses of the Central Plains and Northern Thailand.

Wats

Wat is the Thai name for what can range from a simple ordination hall for monks and nuns to a huge sprawling complex comprising libraries, bell towers, and meditation rooms. Usually the focal point for a community, it's not unusual for a wat to also be the grounds for village fetes and festivals. Although most wats you come across symbolize some aspect of Theravada Buddhism, examples of other architectural styles are relatively easy to find: Khmer ruins dot the Isan countryside to the east, while Northern Thailand is littered with Burmese-style temples.

Wats are erected as acts of merit—allowing the donor to improve his karma and perhaps be reborn as a higher being—or in memory of great events. You can tell much about a wat's origin by its name. A wat *luang* (royal wat) for example, was constructed or restored by royals and may have the words *rat, raja,* or *racha* in its name (e.g., Ratburana or Rajapradit). The word *phra* may indicate that a wat contains an image of the Buddha. Wats that contain an important relic of the Buddha have the words *maha* (great) and *that* (relic) in their names. Thailand's nine major wat mahathats are in Chiang Rai, Chai Nat, Sukhothai, Phisanulk, Ayut-thaya, Bangkok, Yasothon, Phetchaburi, and Nakhon Si Thammarat.

Thai wats, especially in the later periods, were seldom planned as entire units, so they often appear disjointed and crowded. To appreciate a wat's beauty you often have to look at its individual buildings.

Perhaps the most recognizable feature of a wat, and certainly a useful landmark when hunting them down, is the towering conelike *chedi*. Originally used to hold relics of the Buddha (hair, bones, or even nails), chedis can now be built by anyone with enough cash—to house their ashes. At the base of the chedi you can find three platforms representing hell, earth, and heaven, while the 33 Buddhist heavens are symbolized at the top of the tallest spire by a number of rings.

The main buildings of a wat are the *bot,* which contains a Buddha image and functions as congregation and ordination hall for the monks, and the *viharn,* which serves a similar function, but will hold the most important Buddha image. Standard bot and viharn roofs will feature three steeply curved levels featuring red, gold, and green tiles; the outer walls range from highly decorated to simply white-washed.

Other noticeable features include the *mondop, prang,* and *ho trai.* Usually square with a pyramid-shape roof, the mondop is reminiscent of Indian temple architecture and serves as a kind of storeroom for holy artifacts, books, and ceremonial objects. The prang is a tall tower similar to the chedi, which came to Thailand by way of the Khmer empire and is used to store images of the Buddha. Easily identifiable by its stilts or raised platform, the ho trai is a library for holy scriptures.

Roofs, which are covered in glazed clay tiles or wooden shakes, generally consist of three overlapping sections, with the lower roof set at gentle slopes, increasing to a topmost roof with a pitch of 60 degrees. Eave brackets in the form of a *naga* (snakes believed to control the irrigation waters of rice fields) with its head at the bottom often support the lower edges of the roofs. Along the eaves of many roofs are a row of small brass bells with clappers attached to thin brass pieces shaped like Bodhi tree leaves.

During the early Ayutthaya period (1350–1767), wat interiors were illuminated by the light passing through vertical slits in the walls (wider, more elaborate windows would have compromised the strength of the walls and, thus, the integrity of the structure). In the Bangkok period (1767–1932), the slits were replaced by proper windows set below wide lintels that supported the upper portions of the brick walls. There are usually five, seven, or nine windows on a side in accordance with the Thai preference for odd numbers. The entrance doors are in the end wall facing the Buddha image; narrower doors may flank the entrance door.

Principal building materials have varied with the ages. Khmer and Lop Buri architects built in stone and laterite; Sukhothai and Lanna builders worked with laterite and brick. Ayutthaya and Bangkok architects opted for brick cemented by mortar and covered with one or more coats of stucco (made of lime, sand, and often, rice husks). In early construction, walls were often several feet thick; when binding materials and construction techniques improved they became thinner.

The mid-13th century saw an enormous wave of men entering the monkhood as the Kingdom of Sukhothai adopted Hinayana Buddhism as its official religion. Consequently there was a need for bigger monasteries. Due to the lack of quality stone and brick available, wood became the building material of choice, marking a shift away from the exclusively stone structures of the Khmer period.

Sculpture

The Thai image of Buddha usually features markedly long ears weighed down by heavy earrings in reference to his royal background, and is caste in bronze and covered in gold leaf by followers. Typically depicted seated or standing, less common images are reclining Buddhas, acknowledging his impending death, and walking Buddhas, which were favored during the Sukhothai period (13th to 15th centuries). Statues from the Lanna period of the 13th to 15th centuries and the present Ratanakosin era feature eyes fashioned from colored gems or enamel, while the Lopburi period of the 10th to 13th centuries favored metal.

A collection of 32 Pali *lakshanas,* descriptions used to identify future incarnations of the Buddha, popularly serve as a kind of blueprint for reproductions. The lakshanas include reference to wedge-shape heels, long fingers and toes of equal length, legs like an antelope, arms long enough that he could touch either knee without bending, skin so smooth that dust wouldn't adhere to it, a body as thick as a banyan tree, long eyelashes like those of a cow, 40 teeth, a hairy white mole between his eyebrows, deep blue eyes, and an *ushnisha* (protuberance) atop his head—either a turban, a topknot, or a bump on his skull.

Palaces

Although King Bhumiphol currently uses Chitlada Palace when in Bangkok, the Chakri dynasty monarchs who preceded him used the showpiece Grand Palace as their official residence. Shots of the palace with its gleaming spires floodlit up at night fill every postcard stand, and it's arguably Bangkok's single most important tourist attraction.

Built in 1782 when King Rama I chose Bangkok as Siam's new capital, the Grand Palace is the only remaining example of early Ratanakosin architecture—Ramas II and III chose not to initiate any large-scale construction projects in the face of economic hardship. A primarily functional collection of buildings, the compound contains the Royal Thai Decorations and Coin Pavilion, the Museum of Fine Art, and the Weapons Museum.

Also worth checking out while in the capital is what is believed to be the world's largest golden teak-wood building. The three-story Vimanmek Palace was moved from Chonburi in the east to Bangkok's Dusit Palace and contains jewelry and gifts given as presents from around the world.

Rama IV led the revival of palace construction in the second half of the 19th century, overseeing the building of several royal getaways. Perhaps the most impressive of these getaways is Phra Nakhon Khiri in the southern town of Phetchaburi. Known locally as Khao Wang, the palace sits atop a mountain with wonderful panoramic views. Sharing its mountain home are various wat, halls, and thousands of macaque monkeys. Klai Kangwon in nearby Hua Hin is still used as a seaside getaway for the royal family and as a base when they visit southern provinces. Built in 1926 by Rama VI, the two-story concrete palace's name translates as Far From Worries and was built in the style of European chateaux.

Houses

Look around many Thai towns and you can see that this is a swiftly modernizing country: whitewashed apartment blocks, everything-under-one-roof shopping malls, and glass-fronted fast-food outlets are tes-taments to a growing economy and general rush to get ahead (as well as to the disappearance of Thailand's forests, which once provided cheap and sturdy building materials). However, peer a little closer and you will find Thailand's heritage staring right back at you.

Traditional Thai houses are usually very simple and essentially boil down to three basic components: stilts, a deck, and a sloping roof. Heavy, annual monsoon rains all over the country necessitate that living quarters be raised on stilts to escape flooding; in the dry season the space under the house is typically used as storage for farming equipment or other machinery. The deck of the house is essentially the living room—it's where you can find families eating, cooking, and just plain relaxing.

As with wats, it's often the roofs of houses that are the most interesting. Lanna-style (Northern Thailand) roofs, usually thatched or tiled, are thought to have evolved from the Thai people's roots in Southern China, where steeply pitched roofs would have been needed to combat heavy snows. Although there's no real chance of a snowball fight in Thailand, the gradient and overhang allows for quick runoff of the rains and welcome shade from the sun.

These basics are fairly uniform throughout the country, with a few small adjustments to accommodate different climates. For example, roofs are steepest in areas with more intense weather patterns, like the Central Plains, and Northern Thai houses have smaller windows to preserve heat better.

BOOKS & MOVIES

Books

History & Culture. Though many books have been written on specific aspects of Thai culture, the list of books detailing Thai history is remarkably short. For decades, former Cornell history professor David K. Wyatt's *Thailand: A Short History* has been one of the only contenders. The book was updated in 2003 to bring readers up to speed on the social and economic changes of the past 20 years. And it's short (384 pages) for such a complex subject.

For a wider historical context (but not as much detail on Thailand), pick up *Exploring Southeast Asia: A Traveller's History of the Region* by Milton Osborne, which offers an accessible summary of the region's history.

The Strange Disappearance of Jim Thompson by Harold Stevens discusses Thailand's most famous resident foreigner as well as other extraordinary men and women who have made Southeast Asia their home.

Sex Slaves, The Trafficking of Women in Asia by Louise Brown takes you through the secret world of the eastern sex trade from the squalor and slums of Burma to the secret lodging houses and luxury hotel rooms of Japan. You can order it through Virago Press (www.virago.co.uk).

For insight into Thai culture and everyday life, read Denis Segaller's *Thai Ways and More Thai Ways* and *Very Thai* by Phil Cornwel-Smith. An excellent account of life in northern Thailand is provided by Gordon Young in *The Hill Tribes of Northern Thailand*.

Thai Food by David Thompson is a mammoth book, but it's probably the best available on the subject. Thompson gives fascinating tidbits on general Thai and kitchen culture, as well as great recipes and detailed explanations of ingredients and regional food characteristics.

Probably the best book on muay thai is *Muay Thai: A Living Legacy* by Kat Prayukvong and Lesley D. Junlakan, which traces the history of the sport and provides drawings and pictures illustrating specific techniques.

Travelogues. University of Pittsburgh professor Faith Adiele went to Thailand for a rest and research trip and stayed on to become a Buddhist nun; she narrates her transformation in the witty *Meeting Faith: The Forest Journals of a Black Buddhist Nun.* Canadian poet Karen Connelly recounts a year's adventures in a small farming community in northern Thailand in *The Dream of a Thousand Lives: A Sojourn in Thailand.* For a humorous account of an expatriate's life in Thailand in the 1950s, read *Mai Pen Rai* by Carol Hollinger. Similarly, the diaries of Henri Mouhot (the French explorer who "discovered" the Angkor ruins), *Travels in Siam, Cambodia, Laos and Annam* are an entertaining read and many of his Cambodia descriptions still hold true today, 140 years later.

Contemporary Literature. *Bangkok 8* by John Burdett got a lot of press for its gritty, hip look at Bangkok through the eyes of a cop searching for his partner's murderer. Pira Sudham portrays life in the northeast of Thailand in *Monsoon Country. Sightseeing* is the debut short-story collection by Rattawut Lapcharoensap, a 25-year-old Thai-American, born in Chicago and raised in Bangkok. Lapcharoensap addresses many of the cliches and peculiarities of Thai culture while tackling larger issues (Thai relationships with foreigners, gambling and drug addictions, the stresses of repatriation). *Spiritland* by Nava Renek picks up where Alex's Garland backpacker tale,

The Beach, left off, depicting the dark side of the backpacker culture through the tale of a young woman who comes to Thailand on a journey of self-discovery only to end up in its underbelly.

Cambodia & Laos. Norman Lewis's *A Dragon Apparent: Travels in Cambodia, Laos, and Vietnam* gives us a glimpse of the region before the Vietnam War, as he narrates his 1952 trip.

Three powerful accounts of the horrors of the Khmer Rouge are *First They Killed My Father: A Daughter of Cambodia Remembers* by Loung Ung, *Music through the Dark: A Tale of Survival in Cambodia* by Bree Lafreniere and Daran Kravanh, and *When Broken Glass Floats: Growing Up Under the Khmer Rouge* by Chanrithy Him.

A Short History of Laos: The Land in Between by Grant Evans is just that, an introduction to the country's history from ancient times to its recovery after the Vietnam War. In *Laos: Culture and Society,* Evans presents a collection of essays on topics ranging from the Lao language to the experiences of Laotian expatriates.

Fodor's updater Karen Coates has reported on Cambodia since 1998. Her experiences have culminated in *Cambodia Now: Life in the Wake of War.*

Movies

The big-budget *The Legend of Suriyothai* (2002) was one of Thailand's biggest box office hits. This epic film spans 57 years and is based on actual events in 16th-century Thailand, at the time when the kingdom of Ayutthaya was threatened by Burmese invasion. Much of the story focuses on the story of Queen Suriyothai, who is legendary for riding an elephant into battle and giving her life to save her husband's. It's worth seeing for the spectacular scenery alone.

The second-highest grossing film in Thailand to date couldn't be more different from a historical epic. *The Iron Ladies*

(Satree Lex) (2000) is a comedy about a volleyball team composed mostly of transsexuals, drag queens, and gay men striving to compete in the 1996 national championship. The film was so popular they made a sequel, *Iron Ladies 2* (2003).

Writer/Director Apichatpong Weerasethakul has been gaining more and more international attention, and his most recent film, *Tropical Malady* (2004) was a hot ticket at the New York Film Festival. The movie languidly follows a budding romance between a soldier and a country boy, with a little Thai folklore about shape-shifting spirits thrown in for good measure.

In foreign films, Thailand has mostly been used as a stand-in for other Southeast Asian countries, most notably as Vietnam in *The Deer Hunter* (1978), *Good Morning Vietnam* (1987), *Casualties of War* (1989) and *Heaven and Earth* (1993); and as Cambodia in *The Killing Fields* (1984) and Angelina Jolie's *Beyond Borders* (2003). Its first notable starring role was in the ninth James Bond movie, *The Man with the Golden Gun* (1974). Bangkok's Rajadamnoen Stadium was used for Bond's kick-boxing tournament and Koh Tapu as the villain's hideaway. The limestone outcroppings of Phang Nga Bay provided a very memorable set.

Other Western movies about Thailand tend toward the "trouble in paradise" theme. The movie version of Alex Garland's novel, *The Beach* (2000), starring Leonardo DiCaprio, has been almost too successful in luring people to the Phi Phi Islands (it was shot on Phi Phi Le). DiCaprio plays an American tourist in Bangkok who goes off to a remote island looking for a secret beach community, which is a real utopia until lust, betrayal, and violence rear their ugly heads. In *Brokedown Palace* (1998) Claire Danes and Kate Beckinsale end up in a Thai prison after trying to smuggle drugs into Hong Kong.

Cambodia's troubles and America's involvement in Southeast Asia are examined in *The Killing Fields* (1984), journalist Sydney Schanberg's tale of the search for his Cambodian aide, Dith Prahn, who was left behind when Phnom Penh fell to the Khmer Rouge in 1975. As a follow-up to this movie, a must-see is Spaulding Gray's *Swimming to Cambodia* (1987). Gray weaves poetry, humor, political discussion, and personal confessions into an entertaining, insightful monologue linked to his small role in *The Killing Fields,* and to U.S. military aggression and the situation in Cambodia.

VOCABULARY

If you want to be polite, add "khrup" (men) or "kah" (women) to the end of your sentence. For the word "I" men should use "phom" and women should use "chan." Note that the "h" is silent when combined with most other consonants (th, ph, kh, etc.). Double vowels indicate long vowel sounds (uu=oo, as in food), except for "aa," which is prounounced "ah."

Basics

Hello/goodbye: Sa-wa-dee-khrup/kah.

How are you?: Sa-bai-dee-rhoo khrup/kah.

I'm fine: Sa-bai dee. (M)/Sa-bai-dee kah. (F)

I'm very well: Dee-mark mark khrup/kah.

I'm so so: Sa-bai sa-bai.

What's your name?: Khun-churr ar-rai khrup/kah?

My name is Joe: Phom-churr Joe khrup.

My name is Alice: Deeshan churr Alice kah.

It's nice to meet you: Yin-dee-tee dy ru jak khun khrup/kah.

Excuse me: Khor tode khrup/kah.

I'm sorry: Phom sia chy khrup (M)/Deeshan sia chy kah (F)

It's okay/It doesn't matter: Mai pen rai.

Yes: Chai khrup/kah

No: Mai chai khrup/kah

Please: Karoona

Thank you: Khop-khun-khrup/kah

You're welcome: Mai pen rai

Numbers

1: nung

2: song

3: sam

4: see

5: hah

6: hok

7: jet

8: paat

9: kao

10: sip

11: sip-et

12:	sip-song
13:	sip-sam
14:	sip-see
15:	sip-hah
16:	sip-hok
17:	sip-jet
18:	sip-paat
19:	sip-kao
20:	yee-sip
21:	yee-sip-et
30:	sam-sip
40:	see-sip
50:	hah-sip
60:	hok-sip
70:	jet-sip
80:	paat-sip
90:	kao-sip
100:	nung-roy
101:	nung-roy-nung
200:	song-roy
1000:	nung-pan

Days and Time

Today: wannee

Tomorrow: proong nee

Yesterday: moo-ah-wannee

Morning: torn-chao

Afternoon: torn bai

Night: torn moot

What time is it? Way-lar ar-rai khrup/kah?

It's 2:00: Way-lar song moang.

It's 4:00: Way-lar see moang.

It's 2:30: Way-lar song moang sarm-sip nartee.

It's 2:45: Way-lar song moang see-sip hah nartee.

Monday: wan-chan

Tuesday: wan-ung-khan

Wednesday: wan-poot

Thursday: wan-pru-roo-hud

Friday: wan-sook

Saturday: wan-sao

Sunday: wan-ar-teet

January: Mok-ka-ra-com

February: Koom-pa-pan

March: Mee-na-com

April: May-sar-yon

May: Pris-sa-pa-com

June: Me-tu-na-yom

July: Ka-rak-ka-da-com

August: Sing-ha-com

September: Kan-ya-yon

October: Tu-la-com

November: Pris-sa-jik-ka-yon

December: Tan-wa-com

Getting Around

How do I get to . . . Phom/chan jai pai.dai yangngai.

. . . the train station? sa-tai-nee rod-fai

. . . the post office? pai-sa-nee

. . . the tourist office? sam-nak-ngan tong-tee-oh

. . . the hospital? rohng-phayar baan

Does this bus go to? Rod-mai-nee pai-nai.chai mai?

Where is . . . Yoo tee-nei

. . . the bathroom? hong nam

. . . the subway? sa-ta-nee rot-fai-tai-din

. . . the bank? ta-na-kahn

. . . the hotel? roang rom

. . . the store? rarn

. . . the market? talaat

Left: sai

Right: kwah

Straight ahead: trong-pai

Is it far? Klai mei khrup/kah?

Useful Phrases

Do you speak English? Khun pood pas-sa ung-grid dai mai?

I don't speak Thai: Phom/chan mai pood pa-sa Thai mai dai.

I don't understand: Phom/chan mai kao chai.

I don't know: Phom/chan mai roo.

I'm American/British. Phom/chan pen American/Ung-grid.

I'm sick. Phom/chan mai sa-bai.

Please call a doctor. Dai-prod re-ak moa mai.

Do you have any rooms? Khun-mee hong-mai?

How much does it cost? Tao rai?

Too expensive: pa-eng goo-pai

It's beautiful: soo-ay.

When? Meuuh-rai?

Where? Tee-nei khrup/kah?

Help! Choo-ay doo-ay!

Stop! Yoot!

MENU GUIDE

The first term you should file away is "aroi," which means delicious. You'll no doubt use that one again and again whether you're dining at foodstalls or upscale restaurants. When someone asks "Aroi mai?" that's your cue to practice your Thai—most likely your answer will be a resounding "dai" (yes).

Another useful word is "ow," which simply means "I would like." However, the most important phrase to remember may be "Gin phet dai mai?" or "Do you eat spicy food?" Answer this one wrong and you might have a five-alarm fire in your mouth. You can answer with a basic "dai" (yes), "mai dai" (no), or "dai nit noi" (a little). Most restaurants will tone down dishes for foreigners, but if you're visiting a foodstall or if you're nervous, you can ask your server "Phet mai?" (Is it spicy?) or specify that you would like your food "mai phet" (not spicy), "phet nit noi" (a little spicy), or if you have very resilient tastebuds, "phet phet" (very spicy). Don't be surprised if the latter request is met with some giggles—and if all Thai eyes are on you when you take your first bite. Remember, water won't put out the fire; you'll need to eat something sweet.

Basic Terms

ahan chao: breakfast
ahan klang wan: lunch
ahan yen: dinner
gin tee nee: eat here
glub baan: take away
Khor bin krup (ka): The check, please.
Khor eek noi krup (ka): More, please.
Khor eek an krup (ka): Another please.
Khor toh song tee krup (ka): A table for two, please.
kin jeh: vegetarian
phet: spicy
Phet mai?: Is it spicy?
mai phet: not spicy
phet nit noi: a little spicy
phet phet: very spicy
neung: steamed
phad king: fried with ginger
phad phed: fried hot and spicy
phat: stir-fried
ping: grilled (use *phao* instead when referring to seafood)
thord: deep-fried
tom: boiled

Utensils

chorn: spoon

jarn: plate

kaew: glass

meed: knife

phar ched park: napkin

sorm: fork

tuaey: cup

tha-geab: chopsticks

Basic Ingredients

galanga: a cousin of ginger used to flavor soups, stews, and curries; it has a sharp lemony taste

kew theow: noodles

kha-nom jeeb: Chinese dumplings

khai: egg

khao: rice

khao dtom mud: steamed sticky rice in banana leaves

khao kaeng: rice with curry sauce

khao niao: sticky rice

khao phad: fried rice

khao suay: white rice

king: ginger

kratiam: garlic

nam pla: a fish sauce, used instead of salt in many dishes

nam prik: various chili dips that accompany many meals, often made with garlic, chili, shrimp paste, and seasoned with fish sauce, lime, and palm sugar

nam tan: sugar

ta krai: lemongrass

satay: satay sauce has a peanut base and other ingredients are co-conut milk, chili, and curry base

yam: spicy salad

Beverages

Thai iced tea (*cha yen*) is Thai black tea mixed with cinnamon, vanilla, star anise, and food coloring. It's usually served cold, but you might see a hot version being enjoyed at the end of a meal. It's very sweet. Don't buy these from foodstalls that are working off a block of ice—there's a good chance that the ice isn't purified.

ga-fare-yen: iced coffee

ka-fare gub noom: coffee with milk

lao wit-gee: whiskey

nam charr: tea

nam plao: plain water

nam soda: sparkling water

nam takrai: a sweet drink brewed from lemongrass

waat gaa: vodka

yin: gin

Appetizers

bor bia thord: spring rolls

mee krob: pan-fried rice noodles

miang kham: a traditional snack of dried shrimp, dried coconut, peanuts, pineapple, chili pepper, and sweet tamarind sauce rolled together in a green leaf

pak: vegetables

som tam: spicy raw papaya salad

soob nor mai: bamboo shoot salad

Meat & Seafood

gai: chicken (you'll also see this written as *kai,* but the word should be pronounced with more of a "g" sound)

gai khapraew: spicy chicken with basil

gai phat met mamuang himmaphan: chicken fried with cashew nuts

gai yang: roasted chicken

jook: rice porridge

kaeng: curry

kaeng keow wan gai: green curry with chicken and Thai eggplant

kaeng massaman: mild curry with coconut milk and peanut

kaeng phed: red curry with coconut milk

kaeng som: hot and sour curry (no coconut milk)

kung: prawns

larb: minced meat with chilies and lime juice

massaman: mild curry made with peanuts

moo: pork

moo daeng: red pork

naw mai thalay: sea asparagus in oyster sauce

nua: beef

pad Thai: pan-fried rice noodles with chicken, shrimp, eggs, peanuts, and bean sprouts

ped: roast duck

pla: fish

pla muek: squid

pu: crab

tom kha gai: soup made with coconut cream, chicken, lemongrass, and chilies

tom yam kung: shrimp and lemongrass soup with mushrooms

yam nua: spicy beef salad

yam pla: raw fish seasoned with lime juice, chili, lemongrass, mint, and fish sauce

Fruit

gluay: banana
ma kharm: tamarind
ma la gore: papaya
ma muag: mango
ma praw: coconut
mung kood: mangosteen
som: orange
tub tim: pomegranate

Desserts

gluay bing: grilled bananas
kha nom krog: coconut pudding
khao chae: a chilled rice dish, soaked in herb-infused water
khao laam: rice-based dessert
nam doc mai: mango with sticky rice

INDEX